1000
HEALTHY
EATING
RECIPES

1000
HEALTHY
EATING
RECIPES

EDITED BY LINDA DOESER

OCTOPUS BOOKS

Notes
Standard spoon measurements are used in all recipes.

1 tablespoon = one 15 ml spoon
1 teaspoon = one 5 ml spoon
All spoon measures are level.

All eggs are size 3 (standard), unless otherwise stated.

For all recipes, quantities are given in both metric and imperial measures. Follow either set but not a mixture of both, as they are not interchangeable.

First published 1989 by Octopus Books Limited
a division of the Octopus Publishing Group
Michelin House
81 Fulham Road
London SW3 6RB

© 1989 Octopus Books Limited

ISBN 0 7064 3832 9

Printed in Austria

CONTENTS

INTRODUCTION

WHAT IS HEALTHY EATING?

Healthy eating is all about eating the right kind of food – wholesome, natural food which is delicious and good for you.

Our diet should provide us with all the vital nutrients that we need to grow and to stay healthy: proteins, fats, carbohydrates and a number of different vitamins and minerals. Carbohydrates and fats are the body's main sources of energy, while the role of proteins, minerals and vitamins is in body building and maintenance. The chart below shows the particular function of the nutrients and what foods they are found in.

We, in the West, are fortunate in that we have a wide range of nutritious foods available and serious deficiencies are rare. But our plentiful diet can bring its own problems. Recent research has shown that most of us would benefit from making certain alterations to our present diet, by eating LESS FAT – LESS SALT – LESS SUGAR and MORE FIBRE.

The diet controversy has focused on a discussion paper prepared by the National Advisory Committee on Nutrition Education – the NACNE report. *Diet 2000*, a layman's interpretation of the NACNE report, recommends the following dietary changes:

● The number of calories (a unit for measuring the potential energy content of any food, as well as the energy consumed in a particular activity) taken in should be appropriate for maintaining optimal body weight for height and sex, with adequate exercise.

Nutrient Chart

Nutrient	Use to the body	Found in
Proteins	Used for maintenance and repair of body tissue, healthy skin, hair, blood and muscles.	Meat, poultry, fish, eggs, cheese, milk, yogurt, nuts, beans and wheatgerm.
Fats	Concentrated source of energy; required for the absorption of fat-soluble vitamins.	Butter, margarine, cream, oily fish, vegetable oils, egg yolk, nuts, fatty meats and cheese.
Carbohydrates	Provide energy.	Sugars, treacle, molasses, honey, fruit and vegetables, dried fruit, bread, flour, cereals and pulses.
Vitamin A	Protects lining of the respiratory tract, throat and bronchial tubes, eyes and skin. Helps resistance to infection, and gives healthy skin, hair and nails.	Liver, butter, margarine, parsley, carrots, spinach, watercress, salad vegetables, apricots, milk, eggs, cheese, oily fish, heart and kidney.

Nutrient	Use to the body	Found in
Vitamin B Complex	Essential for the utilization of carbohydrates. Helps give sound nerves, healthy eyes and hair and resistance to fatigue.	Yeast, yeast extract, molasses, whole grains, wholemeal bread, brown rice, yogurt, soya beans, peanuts, pork, fish, kidney and liver.
Vitamin C	Maintains the strength of blood vessels and increases resistance to infection. Needed for healthy healing of wounds and for absorption of iron.	Rose-hips, citrus fruits, blackcurrants, salads, green vegetables, green peppers and potatoes.
Vitamin D	Forms strong bones and teeth; aids absorption of calcium.	Butter, margarine, milk, cream, egg yolk, fish liver oil and cod's roe.
Vitamin E	Helps normal growth and development.	Vegetable and nut oils, wheatgerm, whole grains, wholemeal bread, eggs.
Vitamin K	Essential for normal clotting of the blood.	Green vegetables such as curly kale, green cabbage and spinach.
Calcium	Aids proper development and maintenance of bones and teeth. Promotes normal clotting of blood and functioning of muscles.	Milk, cheese, eggs, green vegetables, wholemeal bread and potatoes.
Phosphorus	Together with calcium, forms the hard structure of bones and teeth. Involved in reproduction and transfer of hereditary traits.	Fish, meat, molasses, eggs, green vegetables, cheese, milk, nuts, oranges and dried apricots.
Iron and copper	Helps build healthy blood cells and resistance to fatigue.	Meat, eggs, molasses, green vegetables, dried apricots, whole grains and pulses.
Magnesium	Essential for correct nerve functioning and the formation of bones and teeth. Helps functioning of glands.	Cereals and vegetables.
Sodium	Maintains the salt concentration of the blood and controls nerve conductors.	Cereals, butter, eggs, milk and cheese.
Potassium	Develops muscle cells and blood corpuscles.	Most common foods, especially vegetables.
Zinc	Essential for health of skin and sexual functions. Required for growth and wound healing.	Wheat, bran, kelp, shellfish and animal protein.

Being obese (more than 20 per cent above ideal body weight) is associated with middle-age diabetes, heart disease, painful arthritis, hiatus hernia and high blood pressure.

● Fat intake should be, on average, 30 per cent of total calories. The average person should aim to cut his or her total fat intake by nearly a quarter. Saturated fat intake should be on average 10 per cent of total calories.

Strokes, heart attacks, breast cancer, diabetes, gallstones and acne are some of the diseases associated with a high saturated fat intake.

● Average sucrose intake should be reduced to 20 kg per head per year (the average person should halve his or her consumption).

Sugar is bad for teeth: it sticks between them, encouraging the formation of plaque which results in dental decay. Eating a lot of sugary food usually leads to weight problems.

● Average salt intake should fall by 3 g per head per day – representing a 25 per cent cut.

A high salt intake is thought by some scientists to increase blood pressure and high blood pressure is known to cause strokes and heart attacks.

● Fibre intake should increase on average to 30 g per head per day.

Fibre, or roughage, as it used to be called, is a form of carbohydrate found only in plants. Lack of fibre causes constipation and intestinal disorders of later life; piles, diverticular disease, even colon cancer are probably all related to the deficiency of dietary fibre in our meals.

Other recommendations are:
Alcohol – average maximum intake should be four per cent of total calories.
Protein – no change. On average we are getting about twice as much as we need, which is either used by the body or stored as fat.

GETTING THE BALANCE RIGHT

It is difficult to know what different foods contain, particularly when it comes to manufactured foods where all the contents may not be immediately obvious. Most pre-packed manufactured foods have a list of ingredients printed in order of weight on the pack, so by studying this it is possible to get a rough idea of the proportion of each ingredient a product contains. This won't necessarily indicate the nutritional value of products, so a number of companies and manufacturers have started to provide detailed nutrition information on packets and labels. See the label illustration below for an example.

PETITS POIS

INGREDIENTS:
PEAS, WATER, SUGAR, SALT.

NUTRITION

Drained peas

A SERVING = 1/3 OF THE CAN

AVERAGE COMPOSITION	PER 85g (3oz) serving	PER 100g (3 1/2 oz)
Energy	190 kJ/45 kcal	223 kJ/53 kcal
Fat	0.3g	0.3g
Protein	3.4g	4g
Carbohydrate	7.7g	9g
Fibre	2.5g	3g
Added Salt	0.6g	0.7g
Added Sugars	1.4g	1.6g
MINERALS/ VITAMINS	% RECOMMENDED DAILY AMOUNT	
Vitamin C	23%	8mg

THIS CAN CONTAINS 3 SERVINGS

INFORMATION

This table, taken from the nutrition information label on a can of peas, gives details of all the major nutrients in 100 g of the food and also in a typical serving. Added salt and added sugars indicate the amount of salt and sugar added to the product during manufacture.

But what do you do when it comes to homemade food? Doesn't following healthy eating guidelines commit you to endless weighing and analysis of ingredients? The charts that have been provided on the following pages contain enough basic information for you to plan a healthy diet. However, once you become acquainted with the nutritional value of the few basic foodstuffs and make the simple dietary adjustments outlined in this introduction, you will find healthy eating becomes second nature.

THE FACTS ON FAT

Most of us can readily name the sources of fat in our diets – the fat on our Sunday joints, the fat used to fry with, the butter we spread on our toast in the morning. These are all highly visible sources, but what about the invisible fat in foods?

Foods such as sausages, pastries, cakes and biscuits, milk, eggs and cheese also contribute to a daily intake of fat that medical experts agree is far too high. This can not only lead to the health risks associated with unwanted extra weight mentioned above but to an increased risk of heart disease. Although many factors contribute to this – including smoking, stress and high blood pressure – eating too much fat is one we can easily do something about.

We shouldn't attempt to cut out fat completely though – fat is necessary to the body: it keeps us warm, provides padding, keeps the skin and arteries supple, is a store of energy, balances out hormones and is even essential for proper brain function. Perhaps what is more important is to be aware of the kind of fat we eat.

Saturated fats are usually solid at room temperature and have good keeping quality, e.g. butter, lard, hard margarine and meat fat, although there are some exceptions – palm and coconut oils being the most not-

able. Hydrogenized fats start life as unsaturated fats but change through a manufacturing process called hydrogenation to become a type of saturated fat. They are often used in manufactured goods. They are also used in margarine manufacture to make vegetable oil remain solid when it is at room temperature.

Milk fat is saturated, and the butter, cheese and cream products produced from it also contain saturated fat. Dairy foods supply about a third of all the fat we eat and about 40 per cent of all the saturated fat in the British diet.

Eating too much fat does lead to obesity and the incidence of heart disease in obese people is twice as high. Too much saturated fat also raises the level of triglycerides (types of fat) and cholesterol in the bloodstream. Cholesterol is a fat essential for health and is a normal component of the body tissues, especially the brain, nervous system, liver and blood. It acts as a lubricant for the arteries and is needed to make adrenal and sex hormones, as well as Vitamin D and bile, which helps in the digestion of fats. However, the fatty deposit or atheroma that 'furs up' arteries, causing a narrowing that can lead to heart attacks, is high in cholesterol and some triglycerides, which is why eating a diet high in saturated fat is seen as a risk factor for coronary heart disease.

Most cholesterol in the blood is manufactured by the liver. Although many foods we eat contain cholesterol as well, this is usually an insignificant part of the total. Nevertheless, people who have had a heart problem, or who have heart disease in the family, are often advised to watch the amount of cholesterol they eat.

Polyunsaturated fats or oils are liquid at room temperature and are found mainly in vegetable foods, especially in nuts and seeds, although oily fish is also a source of unsaturated fat. They contain essential fatty

MILK LABELLING

Cartoned milk has nutrition information printed on the carton that tells you how much fat is contained inside. Bottled milk has different coloured tops which correspond to different fat values and methods of treating milk.

Silver: pasteurized, full-fat milk (3.8% fat).

Gold: pasteurized, full-fat Channel Islands milk (4.8% fat).

Red: pasteurized, homogenized (all the fat is mixed in to the milk, rather than rising to the top) full-fat milk (3.8% fat).

Red and silver striped: pasteurized semi-skimmed milk (1.5-1.8% fat).

Blue and silver checked: pasteurized, skimmed milk containing almost no fat (less than 0.1% fat).

Blue and silver striped: labelled 'Channel Islands', pasteurized, full-fat Kosher milk for Passover (4.8% fat).

Purple top, silver stripe: pasteurized, full-fat (3.8% fat) Kedassia milk (Kosher for Orthodox Jews).

Clamped blue metal top: sterilized, full-fat milk (3.8% fat).

Clamped pink metal top: UHT, full-fat milk (3.8% fat).

acids – essential because they are necessary for the brain and nerves to grow and develop properly and for their maintenance. Polyunsaturated fats also help to keep our blood less sticky and less likely to deposit atheroma in our arteries. They also make the blood less likely to clot. However, polyunsaturated oil is high in calories and we don't need a lot – the equivalent of two tablespoons a day is ample.

Monounsaturated fats are those found in avocados, cashew nuts, olives and olive oil,

peanuts and peanut butter. Until recently, these were thought to have a neutral effect on the blood, now they are believed to behave rather like polyunsaturates.

How to cut down on fat

● Use a margarine spread high in polyunsaturates rather than butter or hard margarine.

● In cooking, use an oil high in polyunsaturates like corn or sunflower oil rather than a hard fat like margarine or butter.

● Avoid high-fat cheese like cream cheese, Stilton, Cheddar and other hard yellow cheese, Danish Blue and Lymeswold. Medium-fat cheeses include Edam, Camembert, Feta, Tendale and Shape cheese, Curd cheese, Ricotta and Brie. Low-fat cheeses include cottage cheese, low-fat *fromage frais* and Quark. Choose low-fat yogurt in preference to Greek yogurt or the set varieties made from whole milk.

● Choose fish and poultry rather than red meat (remove the skin before eating). If you do eat red meat, buy lean cuts without too much marbling and trim off the fat before cooking.

● Try not to eat meat products like sausages and pies very often.

● Grill or bake food rather than frying it. But if you must fry food, always drain thoroughly on kitchen paper before serving. In general, use as little extra fat as possible when cooking.

● If you are cooking a casserole in advance, skim off the layer of fat which forms on top as it cools.

● Consider changing to semi-skimmed or skimmed milk as this is a good way of cutting down on fat in your diet. Low-fat milks contain all the protein minerals and important water-soluble vitamins that are found in full-fat milk.

● Keep cream for special occasions and try using low-fat yogurt instead. Cut down on pastries and sponge cakes, too.

SALT

Salt is important in our diet. It helps control the fluid balance in our bodies and it is also needed to ensure that our muscles and nerves are working properly and to maintain normal blood pressure. As with sugar and fat, however, most of us tend to consume more salt than we need.

Salt added to food during cooking and at the table makes up one-third of our daily intake. The rest comes from foods like smoked haddock, kipper and bacon, canned and made-up products, bread and cereals.

Although it helps to keep an eye on the amount of obviously salty foods you eat, look at the labels of manufactured foods as salt is often present in foods that do not taste salty. The best way to reduce your salt intake – and, incidentally, your taste for salted food – is to cut down on the amount you use at home. This is important when preparing food for young children, as the salt habit tends to develop early. Never add salt to babies' food; their kidneys are not mature enough to deal with it. Remove the salt pot from the table and try using alternative flavourings instead (see chart). Cutting down doesn't mean that your food need taste bland. On the contrary, if you experiment with different herbs and spices and other flavourings to take the place of salt, you'll find your food tastes better than ever.

SUGAR

Most of us think of sugar as the white or brown varieties that we buy in the shops. But these are only part of a whole family of sugars which includes syrups, honey, treacle, molasses, raw cane sugar, dextrose, glucose, fructose and maltose. Some of these sugars are also found naturally in foods. Fruit juices and dried fruits, in particular, contain quite a large amount of

Alternative Flavourings to Salt

Food	Alternative Flavourings
Beef	Mustard made from powder, grated horseradish, tomato, white wine, beer.
Lamb	Rosemary, oregano, basil, redcurrant jelly, mint, cumin.
Pork	Apple, sage, thyme, cider, coriander, lime, ginger, orange.
Chicken	Lemon juice, tarragon, marjoram, garlic, white wine, ginger, paprika.
Fish	Tarragon, dill, fennel, lemon juice, bay leaf, white wine, parsley.
Green vegetables	Black pepper, lemon juice, mint, toasted flaked almonds.
Mashed potatoes	Nutmeg, yogurt, egg yolk, paprika, black pepper, parsley.
Salad vegetables	Garlic, oregano, basil, black pepper, yogurt, lemon juice.
Rice	Coriander, saffron, onion, red or green peppers.
Cooked pasta	Garlic, nutmeg, basil, black pepper.

fructose, but in general these sugars make up a relatively small proportion of the total sugars we eat.

Although there are many types of sugar, no one sugar (except molasses) has any nutritional advantage over another. Apart from energy, none has nutrients of any significance and they all contain about the same number of calories. So base your choice on taste, rather than the belief that one is any healthier than the other.

How to cut down on sugar

Identify the main sources of sugars in your diet. Plan to cut down on the first, especially if they are snacks.

Cut down on the number of sweets and biscuits you eat. Try some fresh fruit instead.

Watch your consumption of soft and fizzy drinks. If you choose fruit juice, dilute it with mineral water as it is naturally quite high in sugar.

Stop adding sugar to tea and coffee or make a start by putting in less.

Keep an eye on the contents of breakfast cereals. Choose ones with little or no added sugar.

Baby foods and drinks do not need sugar added, whether you buy or make them. Try not to encourage a sweet tooth.

Make use of the sweetness of dried fruit in your cooking – in teabreads, cakes and desserts.

In cooking, use fructose (available at chemists and large supermarkets) rather than sucrose. It has the same calorie value as sucrose, but is much sweeter, so you can halve the amount of sugar you use and cut down on calories at the same time.

FIBRE

Fibre refers to the indigestible parts of vegetable products. It forms the cell walls of cereals, vegetables and plants. Another name for fibre – roughage – dates from a time when the best food was held to be that which was 100 per cent digestible. Since for a long time fibre was thought to be valueless, it was also considered to be of no importance

High Fibre Foods

Food	Single Servings
8+ grams of fibre	
Wholemeal bread★	125 g/4½ oz
Baked beans	140 g/5 oz
Peas, frozen	75 g/2¾ oz
Dried apricots	30 g/1 oz
6-8 grams of fibre	
Granary bread★	125 g/4½ oz
Bran bread★	125 g/4½ oz
Breakfast bran	30 g/1 oz
Wholewheat muesli	50 g/1¾ oz
Wheat bran	14 g/½ oz
Processed peas	85 g/3 oz
Spinach	100 g/3½ oz
Raspberries	100 g/3½ oz
Blackberries	100 g/3½ oz
4-6 grams of fibre	
Wheatgerm bread★	125 g/4½ oz
Bran Flakes	30 g/1 oz
Bran Crunch cereal	30 g/1 oz
Wholewheat cereal	36 g/1¼ oz
Red kidney beans	65 g/2¼ oz
Sweetcorn	75 g/2¾ oz
Spring greens	150 g/5¼ oz
Banana	150 g/5¼ oz
Prunes	30 g/1 oz
Almonds, shelled	30 g/1 oz
Wholewheat pasta	100 g/3½ oz
2-4 grams of fibre	
White bread★	125 g/4½ oz
Porridge oats	50 g/1¾ oz
Swiss-style breakfast cereal	50 g/1¾ oz
Butter beans	65 g/2¼ oz
Lentils, boiled	100 g/3½ oz
Runner beans	75 g/2¾ oz
Carrots	100 g/3½ oz
Brussels sprouts	75 g/2¾ oz
Apples	125 g/4½ oz
Pears	150 g/5¼ oz
Orange	170 g/6 oz
Potatoes	150 g/5¼ oz
Brazil nuts, skinned	50 g/1¾ oz
Brown rice	125 g/4½ oz

★125 g/4½ oz bread = 4-5 slices or one average daily serving.
Weights for vegetables, rice and pasta are boiled weights.

in diet. More recently, it has been shown that fibre plays an important part in digestion in preventing chronic constipation. It is also believed to prevent stomach complaints and even cancer of the colon.

Fibre has two functions: it absorbs a lot of liquid and thus increases the contents of the stomach so that it is transported and excreted more quickly. It also absorbs harmful and decaying substances which either form in the stomach or are ingested with food. Best of all for the functioning of the stomach is fibre such as cereal, wholemeal products and oat flakes. Some fibre, such as that from fruit and vegetables, can even lower the cholesterol level of the blood. Foods high in fibre also give a feeling of fullness even though they are often relatively low in calories.

The food industry has not been slow to latch on to the latest developments. Modern refined flours contain very little fibre, i.e. bran, and the bran that has been removed is sold back to us, attractively packaged, through health food shops at high prices. And we always have to pay more for coarse-ground or wholemeal flour than for white super-fine flour with its low nutritional value.

The chart on page 12 gives a list of high-fibre foods. Your diet should include at least 25-30 g/1 oz of fibre a day, about twice as much as most people currently eat. But sprinkling bran over everything is not the answer and can be bad for you. What you need to do is to make a few simple modifications to your diet and include a mixture of the foods listed on the chart. Here are some ideas to help.

Increasing fibre intake
● Choose wholemeal bread and try using wholemeal flour more in your cooking.
● Choose wholegrain breakfast cereals or bran or oats.
● Eat plenty of fresh fruit and vegetables and eat the skins where possible (scrub them well first).
● Use more pulses in your cooking, e.g. peas, beans, sweetcorn and lentils, as well as wholewheat pasta and rice.
● Use more dried fruits in your recipes, and try adding them to your breakfast cereal.

PROTEIN

Protein is the basic building block of the human organism. It is responsible for building and maintaining tissue fabrics like muscles and organs for instance. Since the body continually uses up protein, we need to replenish it constantly by what we eat. This is not difficult since proteins are found in both animal and vegetable products. The protein we take in our food is broken down by digestion into its separate elements, the amino acids.

There are over 20 amino acids, eight of which the body is incapable of producing itself, known as essential amino acids. Of course we need not worry about whether we are eating the essential amino acids; we do this automatically through our mixed diet. In the industrialised countries there is no deficiency due to shortage of protein, as there is in developing countries. Any deficiency arises from the lack of specific vitamins and minerals.

There are standard values covering protein requirements. Adults need around 0.8g protein per kilogram bodyweight every day. Children, pregnant mothers and old people require more. Of our total daily food intake 10 or 20 per cent at the most should consist of protein. As a rule of thumb, this protein should be made up of animal and vegetable proteins in equal proportions. Many dieticians recommend that we eat only one-third animal and two-thirds vegetable protein. On no account should one live entirely on meat or fish, milk products or eggs, but we should include cereal products and pulses. Even vegetables contain small amounts of essential amino acids. But it is not only the protein content that we must consider but the value of that protein as well.

Protein value

The closer the composition of the protein in food to that in the human body, the better is its nutritional value. Protein that contains all eight essential amino acids in exactly the ratio the body requires to build up body protein is known as 'high value protein'. Animal protein from meat, fish, milk products and eggs is extremely high in value for its composition is the same as body protein. Vegetable protein, on the other hand, is generally of lower value since it contains a lower proportion of essential amino acids and is often very unlike human protein.

Essential amino acids may be low in some forms of protein but present in greater quantities in other proteins. If these are eaten together, they complement each other, so by combining vegetable protein with other sources of protein you get high value protein. An example will illustrate this: milk is a high value food and so is cereal, so by combining a milk product like cheese with wheat you get an even higher protein value. The same is true of a breakfast muesli of yogurt and wheat flakes, or a slice of wholemeal bread topped with cheese.

You will see from the table below that meat or fish are not essential to healthy eating, although the body generally finds it easier to make body protein out of animal protein. By properly combining various

	Milk Milk prod.	Eggs	Bread Cereals	Maize	Potatoes	Pulses	Nuts Seeds
Milk Milk prod.			■	■	■	■	■
Eggs					■	■	
Bread Cereals	■					■	■
Maize	■					■	
Potatoes	■	■					
Pulses	■	■	■	■			■
Nuts Seeds	■		■			■	

The shaded areas in the vertical and horizontal columns show suitable combinations to replace meat.

vegetable proteins your body will get all the essential amino acids it needs. Vegetarian meals usually have the advantage of being lower in fat and cheaper too. Some further examples are beans on toast, or brown rice with nuts and vegetables.

CARBOHYDRATES

If you follow the NACNE guidelines on the proportion of fat and protein in your diet, then it follows that 50 to 60 per cent of total calorie requirement should be composed of carbohydrates.

Carbohydrate is the main constituent of most vegetable foodstuffs. It can be divided into three groups: first the least soluble, starches, which are the most difficult to digest; secondly, soluble sugar which passes quickly in the bloodstream, and thirdly, cellulose (fibre), which is insoluble and indigestible.

Starchy products such as in cereals (rice, wheat, barley, oats, rye) and in starchy root crops (potatoes, yams and cassava) are essential for a healthy diet. Starches are gradually broken down by the body into sugar and it is the slowness of the process which gives the welcome feeling of being full. Digestion begins with the saliva in the mouth. When we eat the easily soluble sugars we get an immediate full feeling, but one that does not last since the body has nothing more to do. In addition, carbohydrates use up the body's vitamin B1. Wholemeal bread is rich in this vitamin, so in this case digestion brings no vitamin loss.

It is quite different with pure sugar. It is simply a source of calories which supplies no vitamins but, in fact, robs the body of them. A shortage of vitamin B_1 also has the effect of making the body store any carbohydrate it does not use as fat. So a lot of sugar in your diet not only does you no good, it can do actual harm.

VITAMINS AND MINERALS

Vitamins, minerals and trace elements (so called because the body needs only tiny amounts of them) are essential to the human body. It cannot make its own vitamins, although it can store fat-soluble vitamins, A, D, E and K, so that we do not need to eat these every day.

The water-soluble vitamins, the various types of vitamin B and the familiar vitamin C, cannot be stored, and if they are not taken regularly in food, signs of deficiency soon appear. Many vitamins, such as vitamin A, are contained in vegetable foodstuffs but only in rudimentary form. The body changes these rudimentary forms into pure vitamin A. It is not only insufficient vitamins that can be harmful but also too high a vitamin intake. Too much vitamin A, for example, changes bone structure. A surplus of vitamins is impossible with a normal mixed diet and a vitamin deficiency is also quite rare if one eats a mixture of wholemeal and milk products and vegetables.

With a good, mixed diet there will be no need for vitamin supplements. We get far too little of the B vitamins which are found in the outer layer of grain and silver skin on rice. These are the parts which are removed to make refined flour and polished white rice, so it is important to eat grain and rice in their natural form fairly often. Foods which contain fat-soluble vitamins should always be eaten in conjunction with a little animal or vegetable fat so that the body can absorb the vitamins. Raw carrots should be served with a few drops of oil or with yogurt.

Minerals and trace elements are basically one and the same thing for the two terms refer to the amounts the body needs.

The daily requirements of minerals is measured in milligrams (mg) or grams, while trace elements are measured in micrograms and milligrams. Minerals and trace elements are like vitamins in that the body cannot manufacture them but needs them for metabolism (magnesium, zinc), to build and maintain bones and teeth (calcium and phosphorus; fluoride prevents decay) for the blood (iron) or to control water retention (e.g. potash, sodium, chlorine).

Our bodies usually get plenty of all these vital nutrients. The main exceptions are iron, fluoride and iodine where specific groups of people suffer deficiency. Women, for example, often suffer from iron deficiency through the blood loss in menstruation or childbirth. In areas where the drinking water contains too little fluoride, caries are common. In certain areas of Europe many people suffer thyroid abnormalities (goitres) because they eat few foods that contain iodine (e.g. sea fish) and because air and water have a low iodine content.

HEALTHY COOKING: FRUIT AND VEGETABLES

Choosing the right ingredients and trying to avoid using too much salt, sugar or fat in the preparation of recipes are important aspects of a healthy, well-balanced diet, but cooking methods are important too – particularly when it comes to preparing fruit and vegetables. These foods are not only useful sources of fibre and generally low in fat but they also provide valuable vitamins and minerals – particularly vitamin C. The right cooking methods can help to preserve the maximum of these nutrients. Here's how.
● Serve plenty of raw fruit and vegetables. This way they retain most of their vitamin content. Include freshly grated vegetables in salads and don't just stick to leafy salads, which contain fewer minerals and are less nutritious.
● Scrub or scrape vegetables rather than peeling them, as most of the vitamins are found just under the skin (always wash them

well first – and seek out suppliers of organically grown produce).
● Use the minimum of water for boiling and don't overcook. Better still, steam or microwave instead.
● Never use bicarbonate of soda when cooking vegetables as this destroys vitamins B and C.
● Use some of the cooking water as a nutritious stock for sauces and soups.
● Don't keep fruit and vegetables warm for too long before eating.
● Use plenty of garnishes of watercress, cress and parsley on your food. Not only do they make the food look more appetizing, they are also rich sources of vitamin C and iron.

HEALTHY COOKING: THE RIGHT EQUIPMENT

If you want to go in for healthy and nutritious cooking you need the right equipment. This will not only save time and trouble, but also give you the best possible results, preserving all the goodness, flavour and aroma of your food.

The basic rule is only to use saucepans and frying pans which allow you to cook with very little fat or liquid. You can get good quality pans in copper, stainless steel or cast iron, each of which is an excellent conductor of heat and will cook evenly while saving energy. Non-stick surfaces will often eliminate the need for fat in cooking.

When buying pans have a careful look at the lid. It should be tight enough to prevent most of the steam escaping during cooking. The best ones are those with an elongated rim which fits down inside the pan. With a lid like this you can cook with little or no liquid. The effect of the heat is to bring moisture out of the food which evaporates and then condenses forming a layer of water between the edge of the lid and the rim of the pan, making the seal on the lid even more efficient. The condensed water also drips back into the pan making extra water unnecessary. So foods cook in their own juices and all their goodness and flavour are preserved.

Any pan needs a firm handle which will remain cold or become only slightly warm. Plastic handles are impractical for they mean that you can't use the pan in the oven.

Steaming

In Chinese cooking, which is recognized as one of the healthiest in the world, foods are often cooked in the steam produced by a liquid. This method ensures maximum retention of flavour and nutritive food value. Professional chefs in the West have also adopted this method which is excellent for delicate foodstuffs, such as fish or young vegetables.

There are three methods of steaming. The first is a quick method of cooking meat, fish or vegetables by suspending them over the direct steam produced from boiling water below. This is the most popular method of steaming used today and has a number of advantages over other cooking methods: the food is kept stationary so that it cooks gently with little possibility for breaking up; the steam dissolves far less of the colour, flavour and goodness of the food than other methods; and if you use proper stock, court bouillon or any other aromatic infusion instead of boiling water, then you both add flavour and nutrients to the steamed food as well as end up with the base for a delicious sauce.

The second method of steaming is the traditional prolonged way of cooking sealed sweet and savoury puddings in a basin over or in boiling liquid where the food steams in its own juice and the boiling liquid or steam does not come into contact with the actual food. This is much the same as placing the sealed pudding in the oven, except that steaming guarantees an exact temperature and evenly spread heat.

The third method of steaming is the oriental classic method of steaming rice, where the rice is washed well and immersed in water. For the best results, make sure that the level of water is no higher than 2.5 cm/ 1 inch above the top of the rice. Bring the water to the boil, then reduce the heat to the lowest possible setting, cover with a tight-fitting lid and allow the rice to steam for 15 to 20 minutes.

There are four golden rules to remember when steaming.
1. Make sure that the steamer is covered with a tight-fitting lid to prevent the steam and any nutrients from escaping, although some leaking is inevitable.
2. You must ensure that the liquid level in the saucepan does not touch the base of the steamer above, otherwise the food will not be steaming but boiling, and you will end up with a stodgy mush.
3. The liquid below must not boil dry, or you will find that your once delicious stock will now be forever welded to the saucepan. It is a good idea to have extra simmering stock or water ready to one side for topping-up when necessary. You must check the liquid level regularly, ideally every 10 to 15 minutes.
4. Finally, the heat of the steam is so intense that even when you turn the cooker off, the food will continue to cook unless you remove it from the steamer immediately.

Steaming equipment

There are many different shapes and sizes of steamer available, but all of them follow the same basic principles.

There are three essential parts to a steaming set. The first is the bottom compartment which contains the boiling liquid: this is usually either a saucepan or wok. On top of this goes the steaming compartment, or steamer, which contains the food to be cooked: this is simply a container with holes or perforations in its base that allows the steam to circulate through. Often more than one steaming compartment can be stacked on the base. Finally a lid is needed to seal the whole system as completely as possible.

The best variety is the large purpose-built steamer which will usually have two, three or more layers comprising the top compartment so that meat and vegetables can be separately steamed at the same time. This type of steamer is available in the form of a work-top appliance. A thermostatically controlled element is located beneath the base compartment to heat the water or liquid. The steaming compartments provide plenty of space for steaming at least two layers of food and a neat-fitting domed lid ensures the maximum amount of steam stays in the containers as well as providing plenty of height for accommodating basins or large poultry.

The wok is a perfect implement for use in steaming, as you can simply put the food on a wire rack over boiling water inside and then cover with a tall dome-like lid and leave to steam.

Perhaps the most common, cheap and easy to use steamers are first the simple aluminium steamer with graduated ridges on its base rim, and second the expanding steel basket, which is made of overlapping steel plates set on short legs. Both of these will fit a whole range of different-sized saucepans.

Improvising

For the conventional method, balance a colander or sieve inside a saucepan and cover with foil or wet towels as a lid; or use a deep roasting tin two-thirds full of water with a wire rack just above the water. Place the food on the rack and then cover with a large dome of foil or greaseproof paper that is tightly sealed at the edges. This method of steaming is the one to use when cooking long fish or other large items of food.

For the covered 'pudding basin' method, place a small wire rack or inverted heatproof plate in a large saucepan to stop the basin touching the bottom. Put the covered basin inside and then half fill the saucepan with boiling water. Simply add a tight lid to the saucepan and steam away. Make sure that the pan is big enough to allow the steam to circulate around the top of the basin.

Finally, if just steaming food in its own juices, you could use two suitable plates, one inverted on top of the other, with the food sandwiched in between, and simply place on top of a saucepan. The bottom plate acts as a lid to prevent the water from boiling away, and the top plate seals in the steam produced by heating the food.

HEALTHY EATING: THE MICROWAVE COOKER

Fish and vegetables cook particularly well in a microwave cooker: they are cooked in minutes so that nutrients and flavour are retained. In the case of vegetables, no or very little water need be added and vitamins that might be lost by traditional cooking methods are not leached away.

Many of the recipes in this book can be cooked in a microwave oven, but bread and pastry are best cooked in a conventional oven, and batter dishes like soufflés and pancakes need conventional cooking to become crisp and firm. In general, foods cook in a microwave oven in between a quarter and a third of their conventional cooking time, but this varies according to the density, quantity and temperature of the food when it goes into the oven. Check the cooking process regularly and remember to allow for standing times. Consult your handbook for specialist techniques.

Quick home-made stock

Wholesome soups and sauces are best made from home-made stock, which is also the base of many recipes. Recipes for stocks cooked in the conventional manner are given in the Soups Chapter, but vegetable, fish and chicken stocks can also be made quickly and easily in the microwave in minutes rather than the usual hours.

To make vegetable stock: use 450 g/1 lb fresh vegetables, including carrots, swedes, turnips, onions and celery, trimmed and diced, and place in a 3 litre/6 pint bowl. Add a few bay leaves, peppercorns and 1 tablespoon chopped fresh parsley and cover with water. Bring to the boil on HIGH, then cook on LOW for 20 minutes. Strain and cool.

To make fish stock: place 1 kg/2 lb of fish bones, heads and trimmings in a 3 litre/6 pint bowl. Add a bay leaf and bouquet garni, and season with pepper. Bring to the boil on HIGH then cook, uncovered, on LOW for 10 minutes. Strain and cool.

To make chicken stock: place a chicken carcass and giblets (excluding the liver) in a 3 litre/6 pint bowl. Add a bay leaf and bouquet garni, and season with pepper. Bring to the boil on HIGH then cook, uncovered, on MEDIUM for 30 to 40 minutes. Strain and cool, then skim off any fat which has risen to the surface.

HEALTHY EATING WITHOUT ADDITIVES

For many years now there has been growing unease over the possible excessive use of food additives. More and more people are reading food labels and selecting those foods with the shortest list of added chemicals. Foods that are high in food additives tend to be the 'convenience' or snack type and by avoiding such foods you reduce the number of additives you consume. Foods cooked at home from natural ingredients are likely to contain far fewer additives than those bought canned, chilled or frozen. When selecting ingredients for home use, read the label of the food before buying it and always opt for the product with the least number of added chemicals. They can be found in the simplest of raw ingredients, like flour.

What are food additives?

If asked for examples of food additives, most people will usually mention preservatives, colourings and artificial flavourings; a few will recognize the terms anti-oxidants, emulsifiers and flavour enhancers. But what exactly are all these chemicals and why are they added to our food?

Preservatives and anti-oxidants extend a food's 'shelf-life' – they enable foods to be distributed to supermarkets, stored at home and eaten weeks, or even months after preparation.

Nitrates and nitrites inhibit the growth of micro-organisms which may render food unpalatable or poisonous or both.

Stabilizers ensure that the texture of foods, especially sauces, is not altered during distribution and storage, and that they remain attractive.

Emulsifiers help prevent sauces and other processed foods from separating.

Colourings and flavourings are not essential but they are used to add appeal to foods. Without colours and flavours some of today's convenience foods would simply not be produced. The colour of food often affects the way we perceive flavour. Experiments show that if a raspberry-flavoured food is coloured yellow, the majority of people will think they are eating a lemon-flavoured food.

Synthetic versus natural additives

Most people believe that chemicals added to food – whether they preserve, colour or flavour the food – are chemicals that have been manufactured in the laboratory, but often this is not the case. Some additives originate in the laboratory, but others are extracted from plants.

Carotene, a yellow colouring agent, can be produced in the laboratory or extracted from foods such as carrots and dark green vegetables. Lecithin is an emulsifier found in many food, notably eggs. (We rely upon the emulsifying qualities when combining oil and egg yolk in the making of mayonnaise.) Lecithin is extracted from foods such as seaweed and used in commercially prepared foods. The label will show 'lecithin' in the ingredients panel, and, strictly speaking, it is an additive.

However, the fact that an additive is produced from a natural food substance is no guarantee that it is healthy. Nucleotides are an essential part of the nucleus of every living cell, the basis of the genetic material which is handed on from generation to generation in all living things. These nucleotides are extracted from organisms such as yeasts and used as flavourings. Being a natural substance it could be regarded as safe. There is, however, a theory that vast quantities of nucleotides, absorbed over a period of many years, may be the cause of uric acid kidney stones, gout and some cases of arthritis.

It is reassuring to know that the body can deal with small quantities of practically any chemical without harm and it is worth remembering that practically any substance can be dangerous to our health if we eat enough of it. Nutmeg, if used too freely, can cause hallucinations. Inadequately cooked red kidney beans contain an alkaloid which, in very large doses, can poison you.

But we go on eating reasonable amounts of salt, nutmeg and kidney beans without giving their contents a thought. And mostly they do us nothing but good. So, whether something is good or bad for us depends largely on how much of it we eat. What may be fine in small doses may be anything but fine in larger amounts.

Quantity and control

No one is able to tell us for certain the number of food additives we consume nor the quantity, but it is thought that, on average, a person will consume anything from 3 to 7 kg (7½ to 15 lb) each year. This figure varies considerably, depending on a person's diet: a teenager who consumes large quantities of prepackaged snack foods and fizzy drinks will consume far more additives than a person who eats mainly simple, home-prepared dishes.

There is growing evidence that some accepted food additives may have adverse effects on some people. Just over 300 food additives are regulated and monitored by government agencies, yet this is only about one tenth of the 3,500 food additives used by the food industry. This means that there could be as many as 3,000 different chemicals being added to our food and drink which are not being fully tested. Flavourings, starches and enzymes are the least regulated of all groups of additives.

Some groups of additives have to be declared by their generic name and either their specific name or a number allocated by the EEC – (their E numbers). So, tartrazine can appear either as 'Colouring – tartrazine' or 'Colouring – E102'. There are additives which do not, as yet, have E numbers, but some of these simply have a number without the E prefix. These are numbers which are not recognized by the EEC but which have been allocated by the UK authorities. Those additives that are controlled by the Government are subjected to extensive tests before they are allocated serial numbers. Obviously, it is not ethical to test food additives on humans so the main tests to assess safety are carried out on animals.

Insecticides and sprays

There are also additives that are *not* listed on food packets. Most fruit, vegetables and cereals are sprayed with chemicals to prevent insects and micro-organisms causing rot and diseases, and with fertilizers to increase vegetable yields. Strictly speaking these are additives that are cause for concern but you won't find them labelled in your greengrocer's shop. The best precaution you can take against the effect of insecticides and sprays is to scrub fruit and vegetables thoroughly in water before you use them. It is important to do this whether or not you are going to peel the skins. Alternatively you can buy organically grown fruit, vegetables and cereals from wholefood shops and some supermarkets.

Some butchers stock meat from animals that have not been fed growth hormones and antibiotics and that have been reared naturally.

Read the label

The following table gives a selection of the additives and serial numbers listed in the Ministry of Agriculture, Foods and Fisheries' leaflet *Look at the Label*. These are among the additives most commonly found in our daily diet. We also list some of the foods in which they are used, as well as the functions they perform.

Colours

E101 Riboflavin (Lactoflavin, Vitamin B_2)
A naturally occurring ingredient used to add yellow colour and Vitamin B_2 to processed cheese.

E102 Tartrazine
A synthetic yellow dye used in many packet convenience foods.

E104 Quinoline yellow
A synthetic dye which is used as a food colouring in products such as Scotch eggs and smoked haddock.

107 Yellow 2G
A synthetic dye without an EEC prefix yet, used as a food colour.

E110 Sunset yellow FCF
(Orange Yellow S)
A synthetic dye used in sweets, orange squash, apricot jam and lemon curd.

E122 Carmoisine (Azorubine)
A synthetic dye used to add red colour to packet soups, packet breadcrumbs, packet cheesecake mixes and packet jellies.

E123 Amaranth
Another red dye used in packet cake and trifle mixes.

E124 Ponceau 4R (Cochineal Red A)
A synthetic red dye used in canned cherry, redcurrant and raspberry fillings.

E127 Erythrosine BS
A synthetic dye used in sausages and cooked meat products.

E132 Indigo carmine (Indigotine)
A synthetic blue dye used in sweets and biscuits.

E140 Chlorophyll
A naturally occurring green colour found in nettles and grass and used in fats, oils and fruits that are preserved in liquid.

Preservatives

E200 Sorbic acid
A naturally occurring substance which can also be manufactured synthetically, it is used in sweets, soft drinks, packet cake toppings and sweet sauces.

E201 Sodium sorbate
A naturally occurring preservative used in frozen pizzas.

E202 Potassium sorbate
A manufactured antifungal preservative used in margarine, salad dressing and cakes.

E210 Benzoic acid
Naturally occurring but also manufactured, it is used to preserve jam, pickles, beer and salad dressing, and is found in marinated herring.

E211 Sodium benzoate
Made from benzoic acid, this is used to preserve fruit pies, barbecue sauce, and packet cheesecake mixes.

E214 Ethyl 4-hydroxybenzoate
Made from benzoic acid, this is used to preserve jams, fruit sauces and crystallized fruits.

E216 Propyl 4-hydroxybenzoate
Produced from benzoic acid, this is used as a preservative in prepacked cooked beetroot, fruit purées and pickles.

E218 Methyl 4-hydroxybenzoate
A synthetic preservative used in snack meals and concentrated soups.

E220 Sulphur dioxide
Occurring naturally but manufactured for use in products such as packet soups, blackcurrant jam, canned cauliflower and sausage meat.

E223 Sodium metabisulphite
A synthetic preservative used in packet mashed potato and orange squash.

E230 Biphenyl (Diphenyl)
A synthetic antifungal agent used on the skins of oranges and lemons.

E231 2 Hydroxybiphenyl (Orthophenyl-phenol)
A synthetic preservative used on the the skins of oranges, lemons and limes.

E250 Sodium nitrite
A sodium derivative used in cured meat, smoked frankfurters and pressed meat.

E251 Sodium nitrate
A natural substance used to preserve bacon, ham, cheese and frozen pizzas.

E252 Potassium nitrate
Artificially manufactured for use as a curing salt in meats and sausages.

E262 Sodium hydrogen diacetate
A synthetic preservative used in shaped crisps.

E270 Lactic acid
A natural substance used in margarines and bottled cheese spreads.

Anti-oxidants
E300 L-Ascorbic acid (Vitamin C)
A naturally occurring vitamin, added to fresh, cut fruits to inhibit browning.

E301 Sodium L-ascorbic acid
A synthetic salt prepared from ascorbic acid and used as an anti-oxidant and colour preservative in sausages, Scotch eggs and frankfurters.

E302 Calcium L-ascorbate
A synthetic anti-oxidant used in Scotch eggs.

E304 6-0-Palmitoyl-L-ascorbic acid (Ascorbyl palmitate)
A synthetic anti-oxidant and colour preservative used in chicken stock cubes.

E306 Extracts of natural origin rich in tocopherols (Vitamin E)
Used in packet dessert toppings to add vitamin E and as an anti-oxidant.

E307 Synthetic *alpha*-tocopherol
Synthetic vitamin E used in sausages.

E308 Synthetic *gamma*-tocopherol
Origin and function as above.

E309 Synthetic *delta*-tocopherol
Origin and function as above.

E310 Propyl gallate
A synthetically prepared anti-oxidant, which is used in some breakfast cereals, as well as instant potato and snack foods.

E311 Octyl gallate
A synthetically prepared anti-oxidant, which is not used in foods intended for babies or young children.

E312 Dodecyl gallate
Another synthetically prepared anti-oxidant.

E320 Butylated hydroxyanisole (BHA)
A synthetically prepared anti-oxidant used in biscuits, sweets, beef stock cubes and savoury rice.

E321 Butylated hydroxytolene (BHT)
A synthetically prepared anti-oxidant used in packet cake mixes, crisps, gravy granules and breakfast cereals.

Emulsifiers, Stabilizers and Others

E322 Lecithins
Naturally occurring emulsifiers used in dessert packet mixes, margarines and chocolate biscuits.

E325 Sodium lactate
Derived from lactic acids, this is used to prevent loss of moisture in confectionery and cheese.

E330 Citric acid
Naturally occurring in citrus fruits but also prepared commercially, it is used in canned vegetables, frozen potatoes, jams, jellies and ice cream. It acts as a flavouring agent as well as preventing discoloration in fresh fruit.

E331 Sodium dihydrogen citrate (*mono*-Sodium citrate, *tri*Sodium citrate)
Sodium salts prepared from citric acid, which can be used to stimulate the action of other anti-oxidants. Used in ice cream and sweets.

E332 Potassium dihydrogen citrate (*mono*Potassium citrate, *di*Potassium citrate, *tri*Potassium citrate)
Potassium salts which are prepared from citric acid and used as emulsifiers and anti-oxidants in some crisps and dessert mixes.

E333 *Mono, di* and *tri* Calcium citrate
Calcium salts prepared from citric acid and used as emulsifiers in fizzy drinks and cheeses.

E334 L-(+)-Tartaric acid
Grapes are the natural source of tartaric acid. It is manufactured for use in jams, jellies and marmalades as an anti-oxidant.

E336 *Mono*Potassium L-(+)-tartrate (Cream of tartar)
Produced from tartaric acid, it is commonly used as a raising agent in baking, but also as an emulsifier. Used in lemon meringue packet mixes.

E337 Potassium sodium L-(+)-tartrate
Prepared from tartaric acid and used to stimulate the action of anti-oxidants in meat and cheese products.

385 Calcium disodium ethylenediamine-NNN'N' tetra-acetate (Calcium disodium EDTA)
A synthetically prepared chemical used to stabilize the ingredients in salad dressings.

E400 Alginic acid
A naturally occurring substance found in some seaweeds and used as a gelling agent in instant desserts.

E401 Sodium alginate
Prepared from alginic acid, this is used as an emulsifier in barbecue sauce mixes, packet cheesecake mixes and canned fruit fillings.

E405 Propane-1,2-diol alginate
Another additive manufactured from alginic acid and used in prepared mint sauce and salad dressings.

E406 Agar
A natural substance derived from some seaweeds. It is used as a thickening agent in ice cream and meat glazes.

E407 Carrageenan
A naturally occuring substance found in some seaweeds and used as an emulsifier and a gelling agent in milk shake mixes, jelly mixes and salad dressings.

E410 Locust bean gum (Carob gum)
Derived from the Carob tree and used to stabilize the ingredients in canned fruit pie fillings and salad cream.

E412 Guar gum
A natural gum used in brown sauce, piccalilli, sauce tartare and milk shakes.

E415 Xanthan gum
A stabilizer found in salad dressings, horseradish sauce and sweet pickle.

E416 Karaya gum
A natural gum used as a thickener in savoury sauces.

E420 Sorbitol, sorbitol syrup
A naturally occurring sugar alcohol that is also manufactured. It is used as a sweetening agent and found in chocolates, pastries and prepacked cakes.

E421 Mannitol
A naturally occurring sugar prepared from some seaweeds. It is used as a sweetener and anti-caking agent.

E422 Glycerol
A naturally occurring sweetener used in cake icing and confectionery.

430 Polyoxyethylene (8) stearate
A manufactured emulsifier used in breads and cakes.

434 Polyoxyethylene (20) sorbitan monopalmitate
Prepared from sorbitol and used for its stabilizing and emulsifying properties.

E440(a) Pectin
A water-soluble carbohydrate, naturally occurring in ripe fruits. Used as a gelling agent in jams and marmalade.

E440(b) Amidated pectin
Produced from pectin and used in jams and jellies.

442 Ammonium phosphatides
A synthetic emulsifier used in products containing cocoa and chocolate.

E460 Microcrystalline cellulose, *Alpha*-cellulose (powdered cellulose)
A naturally occurring substance obtained by chemical preparation and used to add bulk and texture to foods. Found in low-calorie biscuits and cakes, and simulated fruit for pie fillings and so on.

E461 Methylcellulose
Derived from wood pulp by chemical treatment and used as an emulsifier and stabilizer and to add bulk to foods. Found in potato waffles.

E466 Carboxymethylcellulose, sodium salt (CMC)
Made by chemical preparation of cellulose and used to improve the texture and stabilize the moisture of foods. Found in frozen mousses and meringues.

551 Silicon dioxide (Silica)
The main component of sand, it is intensely processed and used as an anti-caking agent and thickener. It is most commonly found in crisps.

621 Sodium hydrogen L-glutamate (monoSodium glutamate)
One source of this is sugar beet pulp. It acts as a flavour enhancer by stimulating the secretion of saliva. It is widely used in Chinese foods, but is also found in sausages, pork pies and chilli sauce.

925 Chlorine
Prepared synthetically and used to bleach flour.

LOSING WEIGHT

There's no doubt that being much fatter than you should be makes it more likely that you'll get one or more of several weight-associated diseases. The disorders which are associated with overweight are well known – middle-age diabetes, coronary heart disease, painful arthritis, hiatus hernia and high blood pressure. Being too fat, on its own, doesn't always cause these disorders, but it can make it easier for things that do cause these conditions to be effective.

The foolproof, sure-to-succeed way to lose weight is to calculate the amount of energy you now eat each day and to make sure you eat less than that. In other words you count calories. It doesn't matter whether the calories are in protein, fat, sugar, starch or alcohol. A calorie is a calorie. Eating large amounts of foods like grapefruits, pineapples or bran doesn't make you lose weight faster – only regular exercise can do that.

On average, women need about 2,100 calories a day to stay the same weight. Some need as few as 1,500. The average for men is about 2,800 calories with a range of 2,200 to 3,500, depending on individual body chemistry. Most women will lose weight successfully by eating about 1,200 a day. Men and children need about 1,500 calories.

A-Z OF WHOLEFOODS AND VEGETARIAN FOODS

Grains

Barley A grain that is principally used in brewing and the making of baby foods. In Europe the grain is mainly eaten as pearl barley or pot barley. Pot barley is the whole grain minus the outer husk.

Barley flakes Produced by rolling the whole grain into fat flakes for quicker cooking.

Barley flour A fine sweet flour that adds a distinctive taste to breads and biscuits.

Bran The tough outer coating of the whole wheat grain which is removed during processing. It is valuable for its fibre but also contains B vitamins and phosphorus.

Buckwheat The whole grain; also called saracen corn.

Buckwheat flour A heavy, strong and savoury flour made from buckwheat. Many recipes call for it to be mixed with other flours, such as rice or wheat, to lighten it.

Buckwheat, roasted The crushed and hulled seeds of the plant buckwheat that have been roasted to give a nutty flavour.

Cornmeal Also called maize meal and polenta, available as fine and coarse meal.

Couscous A cereal processed from semolina. Used principally in the North African dish bearing the same name.

Flour, wheatmeal A flour which has most but not all of the wheatgerm and bran removed.

Flour, white, unbleached A flour with all of the wheatgerm and bran removed. The flour has not however been chemically treated.

Flour, wholewheat A flour made from the whole grain, available stoneground or roller-milled.

Millet Probably the first cereal grain to be used for domestic purposes. Available in many varieties from foxtail to prosso.

Millet flakes Produced by rolling the whole grain. Use in cereals or instead of rice flakes.

Oats The whole grain, rarely used as such for cooking because of its long cooking time.

Oat flakes, rolled Produced by rolling the softened whole oat grain.

Oatmeal Produced by rolling and grinding the softened whole oat grain. Often available in three grades: fine, coarse and medium. It is generally used for making porridge or muesli but can be added to bread, cakes and biscuits.

Rice, basmati A narrow long-grain white rice with a fine flavour. A favourite in Indian cuisine.

Rice, brown A whole long- or short-grain rice which has only the indigestible husks removed.

Rice flakes, brown Brown rice flaked by processing for quick cooking.

Rice flakes, white White rice powder flaked to make a quick-cooking product.

Rice flour Usually made from white flour, including some bran. Popular for use as a thickening agent and for making cakes and biscuits.

Rice, wild Not really a rice at all but looking very much like one. It is an expensive grain, that needs a long cooking time, but has a superior nutty flavour.

Rye The whole grain or groats. Used in bread-making especially in Eastern Europe.

Rye flakes Produced by rolling the whole grain. Used in making muesli and other breakfast cereals.

Rye flour Available dark or light. Dark rye flour is made from the whole grain, light rye flour uses partially husked rye grains.

Semolina A product of the starchy part of the wheat grain. Available as medium or coarse meal.

Wheat The whole grain or berry. There are many kinds but they can be generally divided into soft and hard varieties. Hard is used for bread and pasta making, soft for cake and biscuit making.

Wheat, bulghur A cooked, par-boiled wheat that needs little extra cooking.

Wheat, cracked Produced by cracking the whole grain by pressure machines. This process ensures the grain cooks faster.

Wheat flakes Produced by rolling the whole grain to a flat shape. This process also ensures speedier cooking.

Wheatgerm A valuable constituent of the whole grain wheat that is removed during some processing, it is particularly rich in the B complex vitamins and vitamin E. It is usually available in three forms: as natural wheatgerm; stabilized wheatgerm; or wheatgerm oil.

Nuts and seeds

Almonds Only the sweet variety can be eaten since bitter almonds contain poisonous prussic acid. The kernels are used in making cakes, biscuits, desserts and savoury dishes.

Brazil nuts Also known as the para or cream nut, the Brazil nut has a tough, angular shell and a brown-skinned creamy-white kernel.

Cashew nuts, shelled Generally found only this way since the shell contains an acrid fluid which blisters the skin.

Chestnuts The large brown nut of the Castenea tree. There are over 100 sweet varieties to choose from.

Coconut in shell The fruit of the coconut palm. Consisting of the outer fibrous husk, white flesh and coconut milk.

Coconut, creamed The coconut flesh is cooked and processed into blocks for use as a flavouring.

Coconut, desiccated The dried and grated kernel of the coconut.

Coconut flakes Dried coconut rolled or shredded into flakes.

Coconut, long-thread Dried kernel processed into long threads for a decoration.

Hazelnuts Members of the same corylus family of trees including filberts and cob nuts. Hazelnuts have a brown-skinned round kernel.

Linseeds Seeds of the flax plant. Principally used now for their oil.

Peanuts Also called groundnuts. Two kernels grow in each nut, which has a soft, cardboard-like shell. The kernels have a pinkish skin.

Pecans Smooth, oblong, thin-shelled nuts, native to southern U.S.A. Pecan nuts resemble walnuts and the kernels are separated into halves for mainly dessert use.

Pistachio nuts A nut about the size of a small olive whose shell is cracked for easy separation from the kernel. The small kernel is bright green.

Pine nuts The seeds of the stone pine. Only available in Britain shelled.

Pumpkin seeds Olive green seeds from the pumpkin.

Sesame seeds Seeds from the sesame plant rich in vitamins and minerals. Toasted and ground to a paste, they are used to make tahini.

Sunflower seeds. Delicious seeds rich in B complex vitamins, protein, vitamin E and many minerals. Useful as a snack item or to add to salads.

Walnuts The fruit of the walnut tree. Like most nuts, the walnut has a green smooth outer husk which is removed prior to selling, revealing the characteristic wrinkled and gnarled inner shell.

Dried fruits

Apples, dried Usually peeled, cored and cut into rings, apples when dried still retain all their vitamin C. Many undergo a sulphur treatment to keep the flesh white.

Apricots, dried Plump sun-dried apricots are often preferable to the fresh original since they contain all the goodness of the fresh fruit in a sweetened concentrated form. Particularly valuable to vegetarians for their protein content.

Bananas, dried Fully ripe, high sugar bananas dry superbly well if split lengthwise and dried in the sun. Drying heightens the flavour making it a delicious chewy sweetmeat as well as tasty addition for cakes, cereals and fruit salads.

Currants These are the dried fruit of the tiny, purple Corinth grape, smallest of all the dried fruits. They have a tart flavour and hardish, crisp skin. Also rich in iron and potassium.

Dates, dried Sold dried singly or pressed in blocks, dates dry beautifully due to their high sugar content. Use in making cakes, biscuits, pastries and puddings or as a sweetmeat.

Figs, dried Thin-skinned fresh figs do not travel well but this presents little problem if they are sun-dried first, resulting in sugar deposits on the skin surface – a sure sign of good quality. Eat raw, re-constitute for use or simply chop to use in baking.

Fruits, candied Not just dried but soaked in syrup over time, then dried. Candied fruits are often used with dried fruit mixtures in baking and dessert making. The vast selection available includes crystallized and candied oranges, pineapple, peaches, pears, nectarines, cherries, citrus fruit peel and kumquats.

Fruit mixtures, dried Manufacturers and retailers also offer a good range of mixed dried fruit selections that are worth considering if baking, making a fruit salad or breakfast cereal or muesli mixture.

A basic popular dried fruit mixture will generally include raisins, sultanas, currants and chopped mixed peel. This is a good basic mixture for use in making rich fruit cakes, biscuits and other baked items.

A dried fruit salad mixture will almost invariably contain dried apricots, peaches, prunes, apples, pears and possibly figs. As a general guideline, the more expensive the mix the more exotic will be the ingredients.

Ginger, crystallized This is not a dried fruit but another sweetmeat that is often used with dried fruit mixtures. Here root ginger is peeled then soaked in a sugar syrup. It is then dried and finished with a sugar coating. Use as a decoration, flavouring ingredient or item for a dried fruit salad.

Peaches, dried Halved and dried either naturally by the sun or artificially, dried peaches contain an astonishing amount of iron.

Pears, dried Pears are not peeled before drying and so have a characteristic wrinkled outer skin. Many varieties are now becoming available, some being preserved in syrup before drying.

Prunes Prunes are made from plums with a high sugar content, which can be dried without removing the stone. They have only one half as much sugar as dates, figs or raisins so are valuable dried fruit for the slimmer.

Raisins The most popular of all dried fruits, raisins are dried in the sun or artificially by heat. They are a popular ingredient of dried fruit mixtures for salads and for cake making.

Raisins, muscatel Large, sun-dried plump raisins dried from muscat grapes, more robust than sultanas and chewier than currants. Add to muesli, cakes, biscuits, pastries, stuffings, rice mixtures, puddings and salads.

Sultanas The dried fruit of the white, seedless sultana grape. Large and sweeter than raisins and currants, they are prized for their dessert and baking use.

Dried beans

Aduki beans Very small red beans with a sweet nutty taste. Usually soaked and boiled for use or pounded into a fine paste and made into cakes. Aduki beans make a delicious addition to soups, stews, salads and rice dishes.

Beansprouts Commercially grown for sale, these are usually the sprouts of the mung bean although almost any bean can be sprouted. Use in salads, sandwiches and stir-fry dishes.

Black beans Shiny black beans that are cooked whole for soups, stews and savoury dishes but mainly used for sprouting.

Black-eye beans White, rounded beans, distinguished by a black mark like an eye on one side. They are used in soups, salads, rice dishes and casseroles. In Africa the dried seeds are ground to make a coffee substitute. The tender immature pods can also be eaten as a vegetable and the developing sprouts are eaten like spinach.

Black fermented Chinese beans These wrinkled looking black beans are usually soya beans preserved in salt. They are very popular in Chinese meat and vegetable dishes.

Broad beans Very large, flat, brown beans that are also known as haba, horse or Windsor beans. They are good in vegetable casseroles and hot-pots.

Butter or lima beans Also known as sieva beans, curry beans or pole beans. Lima beans tend to be smaller than the large flat butter bean and have a sweeter taste. Very popular in Britain as an accompanying vegetable.

Cannellini beans Creamy-white kidney beans very popular in Italy. They have a light almost fluffy texture when cooked.

Flageolet beans Pale green beans, long and thin in shape. They are good cooked and puréed, as in pease pudding.

Ful medame beans Small, brown, dull-looking beans with thick skins and an earthy taste. Delicious in soups and stews.

Haricot beans The most popular bean of all and used in Boston baked beans. Also known as white haricots and navy beans.

Lablab beans Also called the hyacinth bean. This is a black bean that must be shelled before cooking. Occasionally it is also called the Egyptian bean since it is very popular in the Middle East.

Large white beans These are large, white, flat beans of the haricot variety. Looking rather like a pale version of broad beans they make a delicious ingredient for stews and casseroles.

Mung beans Also known as the green gram, golden gram, black gram or Oregon pea, these are the most popular of the sprouting beans. Ranging in colour from green through yellow to golden and black, it is the olive green variety that is generally used for sprouting and cooking.

Pinto beans A variety of haricot bean with a mottled brown or speckled appearance that changes colour to pink when cooked.

Quick-dried green beans These are fresh green beans that have been freeze-dried quickly for preservation. This method ensures a good colour to the beans and quick rehydration for use. They make a good store-cupboard standby for a vegetable at short notice.

Red kidney beans Plump, red and shiny, these are the beans used in the classic chilli con carne. Also delicious in salads.

Rice beans These small capsule-like dark red-brown beans are so called because of their rice-like taste and shape. Native to China and South East Asia, they are rarely exported to Britain.

Rose cocoa or borlotti beans Longish, pink beans with dark flecks that have a noticeable sweet taste. They are delicious cooked with apple in both savoury and sweet mixtures.

Soya beans Nutritiously the most superior of all the beans since they contain complete protein, iron and many vitamins. There are two main types, the edible vegetable bean and commercial field bean which is used to make oil and flour.

Urd beans Also known as the black gram bean, these are found in several different forms but mainly as a cream and black bean smaller than the mung bean.

Dried peas

Blue peas These are whole green peas that have a dark blue-green appearance. They have a very floury texture when cooked.

Chick peas Corn-coloured peas also known as garbanzo peas, Bengal grams or Egyptian peas. They can also be white, brown, red or black. They have a distinctive earthy flavour and are used in couscous and hummus.

Garden peas, quick-dried Garden peas that have been freeze-dried quickly for preservation. This method retains colour and flavour yet enables fast rehydration.

Pigeon peas Not a pea really but a bean, also called the gunga pea or toor dal. They are called peas because of their round pea-like shape. Creamy-white and brown they are native to India and the Caribbean.

Split chick peas These are chick peas that have been skinned and then split so that they cook more quickly.

Split green peas Very much like split yellow peas except in colour. They are a favourite pea to cook and purée.

Split yellow peas Also called split yellow dhal peas, these are usually cooked to make a vegetable purée.

Whole green peas These have a dried pale green wrinkled skin. They are used as a vegetable, in stews and savoury dishes.

Lentils

Lentils are leguminous seeds that vary in colour from white to green, orange, pink and brown. They are a valuable ingredient in vegetarian-style eating for their protein value which exceeds most pulses, save the soya bean. The two main types are Chinese and Indian lentils. Chinese lentils are invariably white to green and Indian lentils vary in shade from pink to brown.

Brown lentils Whole small greeny brown lentils also known as Indian lentils. After a short soaking time they cook to a purée.

Continental green lentils Whole green lentils, about half the size of a pea. Rich in protein, they are tasty in casseroles, stews, vegetable type rissoles and patties, as well as thick, healthy soups. Soak, if liked, before cooking.

Split orange or red lentils The most popular lentil, also called the Egyptian lentil. This lentil does not require soaking prior to cooking.

Seasonings, flavourings and thickenings

Agar flakes These are a quick-dissolving popular form of agar.

Agar powder A product of several sea vegetables valuable for its jelling properties. Used by vegetarians as a replacement for animal gelatine. Use 2 tablespoons agar powder to set 600 ml/1 pint liquid.

Brewer's yeast A by-product of the brewing process, it has outstanding nutritional value. It is rich in proteins and the B vitamins. Use in cereals, crunchy toppings, soups, gravies and casseroles.

Gomashio (sesame salt) This Japanese product is sometimes difficult to locate but a good version can be made by grinding 4 parts roasted sesame seeds with 1 portion salt. Use as a replacement for salt.

Miso A fermented soya bean flavouring or seasoning in spoonable form. Ranging in colour from light brown to almost black, the lighter versions contain less salt.

Salt, sea (crystal salt) This is obtained by evaporating sea salt in enclosed areas. It is often prized for its high iodine content.

Salt substitute Low-sodium salt intended for those who wish to cut down on a high intake for medical reasons.

Salt, table Usually salt produced by pumping water into underground salt mines then vacuum drying the resulting brine. Additives like starch, phosphate or lime and potassium may have been added.

Tahini A speciality of the Middle East made from sesame seeds ground to a paste. It can be mixed with lentil purée and oil to make a delicious dip.

Tamari A naturally fermented sauce from the soya bean not unlike but not the same as soya sauce. Gluten-free, this by-product of making miso is invaluable for special wheat-free diets.

Vegetable concentrates Rather like stock cubes but in a spoonable form. They can be used like yeast extract to make delicious drinks, stocks and a tasty spread.

Vegetable stock cubes Cubes of concentrated vegetables, yeast and flavourings that offer a quick and easy way of making stock.

Yeast extract The soluble residue that is produced when fresh brewer's yeast is mixed with salt then evaporated under pressure. Rich in vitamin B, many vegetarian yeast extracts also contain vegetable protein and iron. They make delicious drinks, stocks and spreads but many have a high salt content so should be taken in moderation.

Sweeteners

Carob powder A flavouring from the pulp of the carob or locust bean that has a flavour similar to chocolate. When substituting carob for cocoa powder use only half as much.

Corn syrup or glucose syrup made by heating water and cornstarch with acid.

Honey, clear Nectar from the flowers of plants and trees produced by bees. The composition and flavour depends upon the flowers, the weather, the season and other variations of nature. It can replace sugar in most recipes but only use three-quarters of the amount of sugar specified and also reduce the liquid slightly.

Honey, creamed or set. Honey that has a proportion of beeswax in it.

Malt extract A syrup that is less sweet than sugar. Used to make a malt loaf, cakes and a flavoursome malt drink.

Molasses Also known as blackstrap molasses, is a by-product or end-product of the sugar refining industry. It is rich in vitamins, iron, copper, phosphorus and potassium. Used in milk shakes or as a substitute for honey in all cake, milk and bread recipes.

Sugar, Demerara A raw brown sugar that has been only partially refined by cleaning.

Sugar, Muscovado A dark brown, moist distinctively flavoured sugar that has been only partially refined.

Sugar, soft dark brown A partially refined sugar with cane molasses added (but check, it can simply be white sugar dyed).

Sugar, soft light brown Another version of the above but lighter in colour.

Dairy produce and alternatives

Cheese, cottage A low fat curd cheese made from skimmed milk.

Cheese, Feta A Greek sheep or goat's milk cheese curdled naturally without the use of animal rennet.

Cheese, Gouda A Dutch cheese similar to Edam that is made without animal rennet.

Cheese, Ricotta A low-fat soft cheese made from whey suitable for vegetarians.

Cheese, vegetarian Hard cheese specially made without any animal rennet.

Milk, soya A good vegetarian substitute for dairy or cow's milk.

Suet, vegetable A vegetarian suet made from palm nut oil.

Tofu A fermented soya bean curd with a soft, delicate texture and pale colour. It is slightly thicker than cottage cheese and can be used instead of in many recipes.

Yogurt Milk which has been soured with a special culture.

Useful Food Values

	Quantity	Fat (g)	Sodium (mg)	Calories
All Bran	50 g/2 oz	3	830	135
Apple	125 g/4½ oz	0	3	50
Avocado pear	100 g/4 oz	22	5	220
Bacon	25 g/1 oz	9	400	90
Baked beans	150 g/5 oz	1	720	110
Banana	125 g/4½ oz	0	1	90
Beef, lean, roast	50 g/2 oz	2	30	90
Beer	300 ml/½ pint	0	40	90
Biscuits:				
digestive (1 biscuit)	15 g/½ oz	3	65	70
shortbread (1 biscuit)	25 g/1 oz	7	65	70
Bread:				
white (1 medium slice)	40 g/1½ oz	1	180	95
wholemeal (1 medium slice)	40 g/1½ oz	1	220	85
Butter	15g/½oz	12	110	110
Cabbage, boiled	50 g/2 oz	0	4	10
Carrots, boiled	50 g/2 oz	0	20	10
Cauliflower, boiled	50 g/2 oz	0	4	10
Cheese:				
Cheddar	50 g/2 oz	16	300	200
Cottage	50 g/2 oz	2½	250	55
Cream	50 g/2 oz	23	180	130
Edam	50 g/2 oz	11	490	150
Stilton	50 g/2 oz	20	575	230
Chicken, roast	50 g/2 oz	17	40	90
Chocolate, milk	50 g/2 oz	15	60	270

	Quantity	Fat (g)	Sodium (mg)	Calories
Cod	100 g/4 oz	0	80	95
Corned beef	50 g/2 oz	6	480	110
Cornflakes	25 g/1 oz	0	230	75
Cream:				
double	2 tablespoons	14	8	130
single	2 tablespoons	6	12	60
Egg, boiled	60 g/2¼ oz	3	80	100
Gammon, lean, boiled	50 g/2 oz	6	550	80
Gin	1 measure	0	0	55
Grapefruit	100 g/4 oz	0	1	20
Herring, grilled	100 g/4 oz	13	170	200
Honey	1 tablespoon	0	2	45
Ice cream	100 g/4 oz	8	80	160
Jam	1 tablespoon	0	3	40
Kidney, lamb's	50 g/2 oz	1	110	45
Kipper	50 g/2 oz	5	500	100
Lamb, lean, roast	50 g/2 oz	5	30	80
Liver, grilled	50 g/2 oz	6	80	130
Liver pâté	50 g/2 oz	13	430	160
Macaroni, boiled	100 g/4 oz	0	8	110
Margarine	15 g/½ oz	12	100	100
Milk:				
whole	300 ml/½ pint	11	140	190
skimmed	300 ml/½ pint	1	140	100
Oatmeal, raw	4 tablespoons	2	4	80

	Quantity	Fat (g)	Sodium (mg)	Calories
Olives	25 g/1 oz	3	560	25
Orange	100 g/4 oz	0	3	35
Orange juice	150 ml/¼ pint	0	4	50
Parsnip, boiled	100 g/4 oz	0	5	60
Peach	100 g/4 oz	0	5	35
Peanuts, salted	25 g/1 oz	12	110	140
Peas, boiled	50 g/2 oz	0	3	25
Pork, lean, roast	50 g/2 oz	4	40	95
Potato, boiled	175 g/6 oz	0	10	150
Prawns, cooked	75 g/3 oz	1	1,200	90
Prunes, soaked	40 g/1½ oz	0	5	30
Rice, boiled	50 g/2 oz	0	1	60
Sausage, grilled	40 g/1½ oz	10	430	120
Sugar, refined white	15 g/½ oz	0	0	60
Sardines, canned in tomato sauce	50 g/2 oz	6	350	90
Yogurt:				
low-fat natural	150 ml/¼ pint	1	110	70
low-fat fruit	150 ml/¼ pint	1	90	140

Note: This chart offers a guide to the fat, sodium (salt) and calorie contents of certain foods. This information will give you some guidance if you are trying to adapt your diet to include a lower intake of fat or salt, or if you are trying to cut down on calories.

SOUPS

BROWN BONE STOCK

METRIC/IMPERIAL
1.75 kg/4 lb marrow bones (e.g. beef, veal)
pieces of raw meat (except lamb)
1 onion
1 turnip
1 carrot
1 celery stalk
mushroom trimmings
polyunsaturated vegetable oil
6 parsley stalks
2 bay leaves
pinch of thyme
10 black peppercorns
300-600 ml/½-1 pint red or white wine

You can use any raw meat bones, except for raw lamb bones as they have a strong flavour which could well spoil your intended dish. Cooked lamb bones, however, work perfectly well. Mix the bones for mixed stock, or keep separate for single flavour stocks.

Ask the butcher to break up the bones. Brown them well in the oven. Peel the vegetables, reserving the parings, and chop finely. Heat a little oil in a large stock pot and fry the vegetables until brown. Add the bones and all the remaining ingredients, including the peelings. Pour on enough water to cover the bones (about 2.75 litres/5 pints). Bring to the boil and simmer very gently for 4 hours, skimming off any scum from the surface. Check the liquid level frequently and add more boiling water if necessary. Strain the stock through a cloth or fine sieve, allowing it to drip. If a stronger stock is required, boil rapidly.
MAKES 2.25 to 2.75 litres/4 to 5 pints

Variations
White bone stock: Follow the recipe for brown bone stock, but do not brown the bones and vegetables prior to using. White stocks are used for cream sauces and white stews.
Chicken stock: Follow the recipe for brown and white bone stock and use the giblets (except for the liver) as well as the carcass of a chicken.

VEGETABLE STOCK

METRIC/IMPERIAL
2 tablespoons polyunsaturated vegetable oil
450 g/1 lb onions, peeled and sliced
450 g/1 lb carrots, scraped and sliced
1 head celery, trimmed, with the leaves, roughly chopped
1.75 litres/3 pints water
1 bouquet garni
6 white peppercorns
½ teaspoon salt

Heat the oil in a large pan, add the vegetables and fry gently until softened, stirring frequently. Do not allow the vegetables to become browned or this will spoil the colour of the finished stock.

Stir in the water, then add the remaining ingredients and bring slowly to the boil. Lower the heat, skim off any scum with a slotted spoon, then half-cover with a lid. Simmer for 1 to 2 hours. It may be necessary to top up the water during the cooking time if the liquid reduces more than a little in the pan.

Tip the contents of the pan into a sieve or fine colander lined with muslin wrung out in hot water. Press firmly to extract as much stock as possible.

Leave the stock until completely cold. Cover and store in the refrigerator for up to 5 days, or in the freezer for up to 3 months. Bring to the boil before using as required.
MAKES 1.5 litres/2½ pints

FRESH TOMATO SOUP

METRIC/IMPERIAL
1 tablespoon polyunsaturated vegetable oil
1 large onion, peeled and finely chopped
2 cloves garlic, peeled and crushed
450 g/1 lb ripe tomatoes, skinned and chopped
300 ml/½ pint vegetable stock
2 basil sprigs, chopped
salt
freshly ground black pepper

Heat the oil in a large saucepan and fry the onion and garlic gently. Add the tomatoes to the onion with the vegetable stock, basil, salt and pepper to taste. Simmer for 10 minutes and, if wished, serve sprinkled with chopped parsley.
SERVES 4

VEGETABLE AND PASTA SOUP

METRIC/IMPERIAL
225 g/8 oz carrots, scraped and diced
225 g/8 oz courgettes, sliced
2 large celery stalks, chopped
1 large onion, peeled and finely chopped
100 g/4 oz cabbage, shredded
600 ml/1 pint chicken stock
300 ml/½ pint tomato juice
1 clove garlic, peeled and crushed
100 g/4 oz small pasta shapes
salt
freshly ground black pepper
1 tablespoon chopped parsley, to garnish

Place all the vegetables in a saucepan with the stock, tomato juice and garlic.

Bring to the boil, then reduce the heat and skim off the scum that rises to the surface. Add the pasta and season with salt and pepper. Cover and simmer for 15 to 20 minutes until all the vegetables and the pasta are tender.

Garnish with parsley and serve piping hot in warmed individual soup bowls.
SERVES 4

MUSHROOM SOUP

METRIC/IMPERIAL
350 g/12 oz dark mushrooms, trimmed and finely chopped
1 onion, peeled and sliced
300 ml/½ pint vegetable stock
25 g/1 oz polyunsaturated margarine
25 g/1 oz plain wholemeal flour
600 ml/1 pint skimmed milk
6 tablespoons medium sherry
salt
freshly ground black pepper
6 tablespoons plain low-fat yogurt
Garnish:
50 g/2 oz button mushrooms, trimmed and thinly sliced
1 tablespoon chopped parsley

Put the mushrooms and onion in a pan with the stock and bring to the boil, then cover the pan and simmer for 20 minutes.

Sieve the mushroom mixture, or purée in a blender or food processor. Set aside.

Melt the margarine in the saucepan, stir in the flour and cook for 1 minute. Pour on the milk slowly, stirring all the time. Bring to the boil, stirring, then simmer for 3 minutes. Stir in the mushroom purée and sherry, and season to taste with salt and pepper. Bring to the boil again, stir in the yogurt and heat through without boiling.

Ladle the soup into individual bowls. Float the sliced mushrooms on top and sprinkle with the parsley.
SERVES 4

VEGETABLE BORTSCH

METRIC/IMPERIAL
1 tablespoon polyunsaturated vegetable oil
1 onion, peeled and sliced
1.75 litres/3 pints water
500 g/1¼ lb beetroot, peeled and roughly chopped
1 large carrot, scraped and chopped
2 celery stalks, trimmed and chopped
salt
freshly ground black pepper
225 g/8 oz cabbage, trimmed and shredded
2 cloves garlic, peeled and chopped
2 tablespoons tomato purée
1 tablespoon lemon juice
1 tablespoon chopped parsley
150 ml/¼ pint plain low-fat yogurt

Heat the oil in a large pan, add the onion and fry until softened, about 5 minutes. Add the water, beetroot, carrot, celery, and salt and pepper to taste. Bring to the boil, cover and simmer over a low heat for 30 minutes. Add the cabbage, garlic and tomato purée, and simmer for 20 minutes.

Add the lemon juice and parsley, blending well. Adjust the seasoning. Pour into individual serving bowls and swirl the yogurt over the top. Serve immediately.
SERVES 8

HOT PEPPERY SOUP

METRIC/IMPERIAL
2 cakes bean curd
2 tablespoons polyunsaturated vegetable oil
2 red or green chillies, deseeded and chopped
100 g/4 oz chicken breast, minced
1 tablespoon cornflour
8 crisp lettuce leaves
900 ml/1½ pints chicken stock
2 tablespoons soy sauce
2 spring onions, chopped
100 g/4 oz frozen peeled prawns, thawed
1 tablespoon cider vinegar
freshly ground black pepper

Cut each bean curd cake into 10 pieces. Heat the oil in a wok or frying pan, add the chillies and fry briskly for about 30 seconds to extract all the oil and flavour; discard the chillies. Add the bean curd to the pan and fry for 3 to 4 minutes until golden brown. Drain and set aside.

Mix the chicken and cornflour together. Tear each lettuce leaf into 3 or 4 pieces.

Heat the stock in a large pan. Add the chicken and cornflour mixture and stir until evenly mixed. Add the lettuce, soy sauce, spring onions, prawns and cider vinegar. Bring to the boil, then add pepper to taste. Cook for 2 minutes. Add the bean curd and serve hot.
SERVES 4 to 6

SPINACH SOUP

METRIC/IMPERIAL
450 g/1 lb fresh spinach or 225 g/8 oz packet frozen, chopped spinach, thawed
40 g/1½ oz polyunsaturated margarine
1 onion, peeled and chopped
25 g/1 oz plain flour
600 ml/1 pint stock (chicken or vegetable)
150 ml/¼ pint skimmed milk
grated rind of ½ lemon
2 teaspoons lemon juice
½ teaspoon grated nutmeg
¼ teaspoon grated root ginger
salt
freshly ground black pepper
150 ml/¼ pint plain low-fat yogurt
croûtons, to garnish

If using fresh spinach, wash it and place it in a saucepan with only the water that clings to it. Cover the pan and cook gently for about 10 minutes until tender. Drain the spinach, squeezing out all the water with a wooden spoon, then chop it finely.

Melt the margarine in a saucepan and fry the onion gently for 5 minutes without browning. Stir in the flour, then add the stock and the milk. Bring to the boil, stirring all the time until the sauce thickens. Stir in the chopped spinach with the lemon rind and juice, nutmeg, ginger, and salt and pepper to taste. Simmer for 5 minutes.

For a smoother and greener soup, purée the mixture in a blender or rub through a sieve. Return the soup to the pan. Stir in most of the yogurt and reheat without boiling. Serve hot, garnished with a swirl of yogurt and croûtons.
SERVES 6

ITALIAN BEAN SOUP

METRIC/IMPERIAL
225 g/8 oz dried white beans (e.g. haricot beans, butter beans, etc)
600 ml/1 pint water
1 large onion, peeled and chopped
1 clove garlic, peeled and crushed
1 celery stalk, sliced
1 large carrot, peeled and sliced
4 tomatoes, skinned and chopped
finely grated rind and juice of ½ lemon
1 bay leaf
salt
freshly ground black pepper
2 tablespoons chopped parsley, to garnish

Put the beans in a large bowl, cover with the water, then leave to soak overnight. Alternatively, pour over boiling water and soak for several hours. Drain the beans, reserving the water. Make up to 1.2 litres/2 pints with stock or more water.

Place the beans and liquid in a large pan, then add all the remaining ingredients, except the parsley. Bring to the boil, then lower the heat, cover and simmer for 1 to 1½ hours until the beans are tender, adding more water if necessary. Discard the bay leaf.

Transfer about half the beans and some of the liquid into an electric blender. Work to a smooth purée.

Return the purée to the soup and bring to the boil, stirring constantly. Taste and adjust the seasoning, and add more liquid if the soup is too thick. Sprinkle with parsley and serve hot.
SERVES 4 to 6

ADUKI BEAN SOUP

METRIC/IMPERIAL
100 g/4 oz aduki beans
2 tablespoons polyunsaturated vegetable oil
1 onion, peeled and chopped
1 celery stalk, chopped
1 carrot, scraped and chopped
1 clove garlic, peeled and crushed
2 tomatoes, skinned and chopped
1 tablespoon tomato purée
1 bay leaf
1 teaspoon chopped thyme
900 ml/1½ pints stock or water
salt
freshly ground black pepper
1 tablespoon chopped parsley, to garnish

Soak the beans in cold water to cover for 3 hours; drain well.

Heat the oil in a large pan, add the onion, celery and carrot and cook until softened. Add the remaining ingredients, with salt and pepper to taste. Bring to the boil and simmer for 1 hour.

Pour into a warmed soup tureen and sprinkle with the parsley to serve.
SERVES 4

Note: Aduki beans are a small type of red kidney bean. If unobtainable, use kidney beans instead.

LENTIL SOUP

METRIC/IMPERIAL
2 tablespoons polyunsaturated vegetable oil
1 onion, peeled and chopped
1 carrot, scraped and chopped
1 celery stalk, chopped
1 clove garlic, peeled and crushed
100 g/4 oz red lentils
600 ml/1 pint stock or water
salt
freshly ground black pepper
1 tablespoon chopped parsley, to garnish

Heat the oil in a large pan, add the onion, carrot and celery and fry until softened. Add the remaining ingredients, with salt and pepper to taste. Bring to the boil, then cover and simmer for 45 minutes, stirring occasionally. Adjust the seasoning, if necessary.

Pour into a warmed tureen and sprinkle with the parsley to serve.
SERVES 4

BEETROOT AND ORANGE SOUP

METRIC/IMPERIAL
450 g/1 lb raw beetroot, peeled and diced
1 large onion, peeled and chopped
finely grated rind and juice of 3 oranges
1 bay leaf
1.2 litres/2 pints stock
salt
freshly ground black pepper
150 ml/¼ pint plain low-fat yogurt
1 orange, sliced, to garnish

Put the beetroot in a pan with the onion, orange rind and juice, bay leaf, stock, and salt and pepper to taste.

Bring to the boil, then lower the heat, cover and simmer for 1 hour until the beetroot is tender.

Work the soup to a purée through a sieve, or in an electric blender. Return to the rinsed-out pan, then bring to the boil, stirring occasionally.

Taste and adjust the seasoning. Stir in the yogurt and serve hot or chilled, garnished with orange slices.
SERVES 4 to 6

SPICED VEGETABLE SOUP

METRIC/IMPERIAL
1 litre/1¾ pints beef stock
1 litre/1¾ pints water
1 × 250 ml/8 fl oz can tomato juice
2 tablespoons finely chopped onion
1¼ teaspoons crushed thyme leaves
1 clove garlic, peeled and crushed
1 teaspoon salt
225 g/8 oz chuck steak, cut into 1cm/½inch cubes
½ teaspoon whole black peppercorns
4 whole cloves
225 g/8 oz potatoes, peeled and cut into 1cm/½inch cubes
100 g/4 oz marrow or courgettes, peeled and cut into 1cm/½inch cubes
275 g/10 oz cabbage, coarsely sliced
100 g/4 oz carrots, scraped and sliced
100 g/4 oz celery, sliced
2 corn-on-the-cobs, cut into 2.5 cm/1inch lengths
chopped parsley, to garnish

Place the beef stock, water, tomato juice, onion, thyme, garlic, salt and meat in a pan. Add the black peppercorns and cloves, tied in muslin. Bring to the boil, cover and simmer for 40 minutes.

Add the potatoes and marrow or courgettes. Cover and simmer for 10 minutes. Add the cabbage, carrots, celery and corn. Cover and simmer for about 10 minutes or until the meat and vegetables are tender. Serve the soup sprinkled with chopped parsley.

SERVES 6 to 8

LENTIL SOUP WITH COCONUT

METRIC/IMPERIAL
1 tablespoon polyunsaturated vegetable oil
1 onion, peeled and chopped
1-2 cloves garlic, peeled and chopped
1½ teaspoons cumin seeds or ground cumin
4 cardamoms or ¼ teaspoon ground cardamom
1 carrot, scraped and chopped
1 teaspoon ground turmeric
175 g/6 oz red lentils, rinsed thoroughly
1.5 litres/2½ pints chicken stock
2 bay leaves
1 teaspoon ground coriander
salt
freshly ground black pepper
25 g/1 oz creamed coconut, cut into small pieces
1 tablespoon tomato purée

Heat the oil in a large, deep saucepan, add the onion and garlic and cook for 20 minutes. If using whole spices, crush the cumin seeds and cardamoms together, using the back of a spoon in a cup or a pestle and mortar. Discard the cardamom husks. Add the crushed or ground cumin and cardamom to the onion and garlic with the carrot and turmeric, and cook for 2 minutes.

Add the lentils (discarding any discoloured ones), stock, bay leaves and coriander. Bring to the boil slowly, then add salt and pepper. Cover and simmer for 45 to 60 minutes until the lentils are soft. Add the creamed coconut and stir until melted. Stir in the tomato purée. Remove the bay leaves and purée the soup in a blender. Return the soup to the rinsed pan and reheat gently. Taste and adjust the seasoning and serve very hot.

SERVES 4

MINESTRONE

METRIC/IMPERIAL
1 onion, peeled and sliced
1 clove garlic, peeled and crushed
1 carrot, peeled and diced
1 turnip, peeled and diced
1 leek, trimmed and sliced
1 celery stalk, sliced
225 g/8 oz tomatoes, skinned and roughly chopped
50 g/2 oz broken pasta or long-grain rice
1.2 litres/2 pints stock
salt
freshly ground black pepper
¼ small cabbage, shredded
100 g/4 oz runner beans, sliced
grated Parmesan cheese, to serve

Put the onion, garlic, carrot, turnip, leek, celery, tomatoes and pasta or rice in a large pan. Stir in the stock and add salt and pepper to taste.

Bring to the boil, then lower the heat, cover and simmer for 30 minutes or until the vegetables are tender.

Add the cabbage and beans and cook for a further 5 to 10 minutes until tender. Taste and adjust the seasoning, then serve hot with Parmesan cheese handed separately.

SERVES 6

GREEN PEA AND LETTUCE SOUP

METRIC/IMPERIAL
50 g/2 oz polyunsaturated margarine
450 g/1 lb shelled fresh or frozen peas
2 lettuce hearts, chopped
1.2 litres/2 pints ham stock or water
1 teaspoon salt
1 teaspoon dried basil
1 teaspoon grated nutmeg
2 bay leaves
Garnish:
120 ml/4 fl oz single cream
2 tablespoons chopped parsley

Melt the margarine in a large saucepan over a low heat. Add the peas (straight from the freezer, if using frozen). Add the chopped lettuce, cover the saucepan and sweat for 10 minutes. Add the stock or water, salt, basil, nutmeg and bay leaves and bring to the boil. Reduce the heat and simmer for 40 minutes. Allow the soup to cool slightly, then remove the bay leaves and transfer the soup to a blender or food processor and purée for about 1 minute. Adjust the seasoning if necessary.

Reheat the soup and serve piping hot, garnished with a swirl of cream and a sprinkling of parsley.
SERVES 8

GREEK VEGETABLE SOUP

METRIC/IMPERIAL
450 ml/¾ pint beef stock
100 g/4 oz mixed vegetables, peeled and chopped
1 egg yolk
300 ml/½ pint plain low-fat yogurt
salt
freshly ground black pepper
1 tablespoon chopped mint leaves
finely grated rind of 1 lemon

Put the stock in a pan and bring to the boil. Add the vegetables, then lower the heat, cover and simmer for 10 minutes or until just tender.

Meanwhile, put the egg yolk in a bowl and whisk in the yogurt. Stir in 6 tablespoons of the hot liquid and mix well.

Add to the soup in the pan, stirring constantly, then heat through gently without boiling. Season with salt and pepper to taste.

Pour into 4 individual serving bowls, garnish with chopped mint and lemon rind and serve hot.
SERVES 4

SLIMMER'S WATERCRESS SOUP

METRIC/IMPERIAL
2 bunches watercress, trimmed
1 tablespoon polyunsaturated vegetable oil
1 small onion, peeled and finely chopped
600 ml/1 pint chicken stock
2 egg yolks
150 ml/¼ pint plain low-fat yogurt
salt
freshly ground white pepper

Remove 16 leaves from the watercress and reserve for the garnish. Chop the remaining watercress and stems.

Heat the oil in a pan, add the onion and fry gently until soft and golden. Add the watercress and the stock and bring to the boil. Lower the heat, cover and simmer for 20 minutes.

Rub the soup through a sieve, or work to a purée in an electric blender. Put the egg yolks into a bowl and whisk in the yogurt. Stir in 4 tablespoons of the purée and mix well.

Pour the remaining purée into the rinsed-out pan. Add the yogurt mixture, stirring constantly, then heat through gently without boiling. Add salt and pepper to taste.

Pour into 4 individual bowls and garnish with the reserved watercress leaves. This soup may also be served chilled.
SERVES 4

CARROT AND GINGER SOUP

METRIC/IMPERIAL
350 g/12 oz carrots, scraped and sliced
600 ml/1 pint vegetable stock
1 piece fresh root ginger, peeled
25 g/1 oz polyunsaturated margarine
2 medium onions, peeled and sliced
1 teaspoon ground ginger
1 teaspoon grated orange rind
2 tablespoons orange juice
salt
freshly ground black pepper
Garnish:
4 tablespoons plain low-fat yogurt
4 small parsley sprigs

Put the carrots, stock and root ginger into a pan. Bring to the boil and simmer for 15 minutes. Discard the ginger and remove and reserve 1 tablespoon of the carrot slices.

Melt the margarine in a saucepan, add the onions and fry gently for 3 minutes. Stir in the ground ginger and cook for 1 minute. Stir in the orange rind and juice and add the carrots and stock. Cover the pan, bring to the boil and simmer for 10 minutes.

Purée the soup in a blender or food processor, or rub through a sieve. Return the purée to the pan and season to taste with salt and pepper.

To make the carrot garnish, thinly slice the reserved carrot slices and stamp out shapes with little aspic cutters.

Reheat the soup and pour it into a heated tureen or individual bowls. Swirl in the yogurt and garnish with the carrot shapes and parsley sprigs.
SERVES 4

PURE VEGETABLE SOUP

METRIC/IMPERIAL
4 dried Chinese mushrooms
25 g/1 oz transparent noodles
½ bunch watercress
900 ml/1½ pints stock
2 courgettes, diced
1 small turnip, peeled and diced
50 g/2 oz spinach, chopped
2 carrots, peeled and diced
1 teaspoon salt
1 tablespoon soy sauce
2 spring onions, chopped

Soak the mushrooms in warm water for 15 minutes. Squeeze dry and discard the hard stalks, then slice the mushroom caps.

Soak the noodles in hot water for 10 minutes; drain. Remove the stalks from the watercress and divide the leaves.

Bring the stock to the boil. Add the courgettes, turnip, watercress, spinach and carrots. Simmer for 20 minutes.

Add the remaining ingredients and cook for 5 minutes. Serve hot.
SERVES 4

TRADITIONAL BORTSCH

METRIC/IMPERIAL
2 tablespoons polyunsaturated vegetable oil
2 onions, peeled and finely chopped
3 raw beetroot, peeled and roughly chopped
175 g/6 oz cabbage, finely shredded
750 ml/1¼ pints beef stock
2 tablespoons vinegar
¼ teaspoon salt
freshly ground black pepper
4 tablespoons plain low-fat yogurt, to serve

Heat the oil in a large pan, add the onions and fry gently until soft and golden. Add the remaining ingredients, except yogurt, and bring to the boil. Lower the heat, cover and simmer, for 1 hour.

Rub the soup through a sieve, or work to a purée in an electric blender. Pour the purée into the rinsed-out pan and reheat gently, adding a little stock or water if the soup is too thick.

Pour into 4 individual bowls, swirl 1 tablespoon of yogurt in the centre of each bowl and serve hot. If wished, garnish with freshly chopped parsley.
SERVES 4

PURÉE OF CELERY SOUP

METRIC/IMPERIAL
50 g/2 oz polyunsaturated margarine
450 g/1 lb celery, cut into 1 cm/½ inch pieces
225 g/8 oz potatoes, peeled and cut into 2.5 cm/1 inch cubes
1.2 litres/2 pints chicken stock or water
1 bouquet garni
salt
freshly ground black pepper
120 ml/4 fl oz skimmed milk
chopped parsley, to garnish

Heat the margarine in a large pan and toss the prepared vegetables in this. Add the stock or water, bouquet garni, salt and pepper. Simmer for 30 minutes.

Remove the herbs and sieve the mixture, or purée in a blender or food processor. Return the soup to the pan with the milk and reheat. Garnish with the parsley before serving.
SERVES 4 to 6

PEPPER AND TOMATO SOUP

METRIC/IMPERIAL
2 teaspoons polyunsaturated vegetable oil
1 medium onion, peeled and finely chopped
2 medium green peppers, cored, deseeded and chopped
1 clove garlic, peeled and crushed
450 g/1 lb tomatoes, skinned and chopped
1 tablespoon tomato purée
750 ml/1¼ pints vegetable stock
1 teaspoon dried basil
salt
freshly ground black pepper
Garnish:
2 tablespoons plain low-fat yogurt
fresh basil leaves

Heat the oil in a pan and sauté the onion until soft. Add the pepper and cook for 2 minutes. Stir in the garlic, tomatoes, tomato purée, stock, basil, salt and pepper.

Bring to the boil, cover and simmer for 30 minutes. Allow to cool slightly. Place in a blender or food processor and work to a purée.

Before serving, reheat and adjust the seasoning. Pour into warmed bowls and garnish with yogurt and fresh basil leaves.
SERVES 4

GARDENER'S BROTH

METRIC/IMPERIAL
25 g/1 oz polyunsaturated margarine
1 rasher lean bacon, derinded and diced
2-3 small onions, peeled and sliced
2-3 small carrots, scraped and sliced
small piece of turnip
1 litre/1¾ pints stock or water
2 tomatoes, skinned and sliced
2-3 runner beans, topped and tailed
few young cabbage leaves
salt
freshly ground black pepper
pinch of mixed dried herbs
25 g/1 oz wholemeal macaroni
Garnish:
grated cheese
1 tablespoon finely chopped parsley

Melt the margarine in a saucepan, add the bacon and onions and cook until soft. Add the carrots and turnip and cook for a further 5 minutes. Pour in the stock or water and bring to the boil. Add the remaining vegetables, salt, pepper and herbs, then cover and simmer for 45 minutes.

Add the macaroni and simmer for a further 15 minutes. Serve piping hot, sprinkled with grated cheese and chopped fresh parsley.
SERVES 4

LENTIL AND CELERY SOUP

METRIC/IMPERIAL
2 tablespoons polyunsaturated vegetable oil
1 onion, peeled and chopped
3 celery stalks, chopped
1 clove garlic, peeled and crushed
175 g/6 oz red lentils
1 litre/1¾ pints water
bouquet garni
salt
freshly ground black pepper

Heat the oil in a large pan, add the onion and fry until softened. Add the remaining ingredients, with salt and pepper to taste. Bring to the boil, cover and simmer for 30 to 35 minutes, stirring occasionally.

Check the seasoning and remove the bouquet garni. Pour into a warmed soup tureen to serve. If liked, sieve yogurt into each bowl.
SERVES 4

CARROT AND TURNIP SOUP

METRIC/IMPERIAL
15 g/½ oz polyunsaturated margarine
225 g/8 oz carrots, scraped and sliced
225 g/8 oz turnips, peeled and sliced
1 litre/1¾ pints chicken stock
salt
freshly ground black pepper
2 teaspoons ground coriander
1 teaspoon ground cumin
1 tablespoon finely chopped coriander leaves
coriander leaves, to garnish (optional)

Heat the margarine in a saucepan, add the carrots and turnips and cook gently for about 6 minutes, stirring occasionally. Heat the stock in a separate saucepan and pour it over the vegetables. Bring to the boil, add salt and pepper, and simmer for 30 minutes, covered.

Put through a coarse food mill or blender and return to the clean pan. Reheat, adding more salt and pepper as needed. Add the spices and the chopped coriander leaves, mix well, and stand for 5 minutes before serving. If wished, garnish each bowl with coriander leaves.
SERVES 4

FRENCH ONION SOUP

METRIC/IMPERIAL
1-2 tablespoons polyunsaturated vegetable oil
500 g/1¼ lb onions, peeled and thinly sliced
1 tablespoon plain flour
1.2 litres/2 pints vegetable stock
1 bouquet garni
salt
freshly ground black pepper
4-5 slices French bread, 1 cm/½ inch thick
25 g/1 oz Gruyère cheese, grated

Heat the oil in a large saucepan, add the onions and fry gently, stirring occasionally, for 10 to 15 minutes or until golden. Stir in the flour, then gradually add the stock, stirring constantly. Add the bouquet garni and salt and pepper to taste. Cover and simmer for about 30 minutes.

Toast the slices of French bread lightly on both sides. Ladle the soup into individual flameproof bowls and place a piece of toast on each one. Sprinkle with the cheese and place under a hot grill until golden brown and bubbling.
SERVES 4

SHREDDED PORK AND NOODLES IN SOUP

METRIC/IMPERIAL
3-4 dried Chinese mushrooms (optional)
225 g/8 oz lean pork, shredded
1 tablespoon soy sauce
1 tablespoon dry sherry
350 g/12 oz egg noodles
900 ml/1½ pints stock
4 spring onions, chopped
100 g/4 oz canned bamboo shoots, drained and shredded
few Chinese cabbage leaves, shredded

Soak the mushrooms in warm water for 15 minutes (if using). Squeeze dry, discard the hard stalks, then slice the mushroom caps.

Put the pork in a bowl, add the soy sauce and sherry and leave to marinate for 10 to 15 minutes.

Cook the noodles in boiling salted water for about 5 minutes, or until cooked; drain.

Bring the stock to the boil, add the mushrooms (if using), pork, marinade, spring onions and bamboo shoots. Simmer for 2 to 3 minutes, then add the noodles and cabbage. Cook for 2 minutes. Serve hot.

SERVES 4 to 6

CHESTNUT SOUP

METRIC/IMPERIAL
450 g/1 lb chestnuts
1 large onion, peeled and chopped
2 celery stalks, chopped
1.2 litres/2 pints turkey or chicken stock
1 bay leaf
salt
freshly ground black pepper

Make a small cut through the skins of the chestnuts, then place on a baking sheet and bake on the top shelf of a moderately hot oven (200°C/400°F, Gas Mark 6) until the skins crack. Alternatively, put the chestnuts in a pan, cover with water and bring to the boil. Peel off both layers of skin while the chestnuts are still hot.

Put the peeled chestnuts in a pan, add the remaining ingredients and bring to the boil. Lower the heat, cover and simmer for 45 minutes until the chestnuts and celery are tender. Discard the bay leaf.

Transfer the soup to an electric blender, reserving a few whole chestnuts for the garnish.

Blend to a smooth purée, then return to the rinsed-out pan. Reheat gently, then taste and adjust the seasoning. Stir in a little milk if the soup is too thick. Serve hot, garnished with the reserved chestnuts.

SERVES 6

HAM AND MUSHROOM SOUP

METRIC/IMPERIAL
25 g/1 oz skimmed milk powder
300 ml/½ pint water
25 g/1 oz polyunsaturated margarine
25 g/1 oz plain flour
300 ml/½ pint chicken stock
100 g/4 oz mushrooms, thinly sliced
100 g/4 oz cooked ham, diced
salt
freshly ground black pepper

Stir the skimmed milk powder into the water until dissolved.

Place the milk, margarine, flour and stock in a saucepan and whisk continuously over moderate heat until the sauce thickens.

Add the mushrooms and ham, season to taste and simmer for a further 4 to 5 minutes.

SERVES 4

VELVET CHICKEN AND MUSHROOM SOUP

METRIC/IMPERIAL
175 g/6 oz chicken breast
1 egg white
2 teaspoons cornflour
900 ml/1½ pints chicken stock
50 g/2 oz button mushrooms, sliced
75 g/3 oz canned bamboo shoots, drained and shredded
1 teaspoon finely chopped root ginger
2 spring onions, chopped
½ teaspoon salt
1 tablespoon soy sauce

Cut the chicken into matchstick pieces. Put the egg white and cornflour in a bowl and mix well. Add the chicken and toss until evenly coated.

Bring the stock to the boil, add the chicken and remaining ingredients and simmer for 3 minutes. Serve hot.

SERVES 4 to 6

SOUP WITH BEEF BALLS

METRIC/IMPERIAL
4-5 dried Chinese mushrooms
350 g/12 oz lean minced beef
1 onion, peeled and finely chopped
salt
1 tablespoon cornflour
1 small egg
900 ml/1½ pints beef stock
1 bunch watercress, stalks removed
3 spring onions, finely chopped
1 tablespoon soy sauce

Soak the mushrooms in warm water for 15 minutes. Squeeze dry and discard the hard stalks, then slice the mushroom caps.

Mix the beef, onion, salt to taste, cornflour and egg together and shape the mixture into small balls. Drop the meat balls into iced water for 15 minutes; drain thoroughly.

Heat the stock in a large pan. Add the meat balls and cook for 10 minutes. Add the mushrooms, watercress, spring onions and soy sauce and cook for 2 minutes. Serve hot.
SERVES 4 to 6

GOULASH DUMPLING SOUP

METRIC/IMPERIAL
2 tablespoons polyunsaturated vegetable oil
50 g/2 oz lean bacon, derinded and chopped
1 large onion, peeled and chopped
1 clove garlic, peeled and crushed
2 celery stalks, sliced
2 carrots, peeled and sliced
50 g/2 oz mushrooms, sliced
1 small green pepper, cored, deseeded and sliced
1 tablespoon paprika
1 tablespoon plain flour
1.5 litres/2½ pints stock (beef, chicken or vegetable)
1 tablespoon tomato purée
Dumplings:
100 g/4 oz self-raising flour
50 g/2 oz shredded vegetarian suet
2 tablespoons chopped parsley and thyme
salt
freshly ground black pepper
4 tablespoons water

Heat the oil in a large saucepan and sauté the bacon, onion, garlic, celery, carrots, mushrooms

and green pepper for 10 minutes until lightly browned. Stir in the paprika and flour and cook for 1 minute. Add the stock and tomato purée and bring to the boil. Cover and simmer for 45 minutes until the vegetables are tender.

To make the dumplings: mix the flour, suet, herbs, and salt and pepper to taste in a bowl. Add the water to make a soft dough. Divide into 8 or 12 pieces and shape into balls. Add the dumplings to the soup, cover and simmer for 15 to 20 minutes until they have risen and plumped up. Serve hot, allowing 2 parsley dumplings for each serving.
SERVES 4 to 6

EGG FLOWER SOUP

METRIC/IMPERIAL
4-5 wooden ears (Chinese black fungi)
(optional)
2 tablespoons soy sauce
2 teaspoons cornflour
175 g/6 oz pork fillet, shredded
900 ml/1½ pints stock
1 teaspoon salt
2 eggs
2 spring onions, chopped
1 tablespoon chopped coriander

Soak the wooden ears in warm water (if using) for 20 minutes. Rinse and drain well, then chop roughly.

Blend the soy sauce and cornflour together. Add the pork and toss until evenly coated. Bring the stock to the boil, add the salt, pork and wooden ears (if using) and cook for 5 minutes.

Beat the eggs until frothy and pour into the boiling stock, stirring constantly. Remove from the heat, add the spring onions and coriander and serve immediately.
SERVES 4 to 6

Note: Wooden ears, also known as cloud ears or tree ears, are dried black fungi which should be soaked in warm water before use. When fully soaked, they became gelatinous and crinkly, and have a crunchy texture.

PORK SPARE RIBS SOUP

METRIC/IMPERIAL
450 g/1 lb lean pork spare ribs
1 tablespoon polyunsaturated vegetable oil
2 teaspoons shredded root ginger
1 clove garlic, peeled and sliced
2 spring onions, chopped
900 ml/1½ pints beef stock
1 teaspoon salt
2 tomatoes, skinned and diced
225 g/8 oz bean-sprouts

Cut the spare ribs into 2.5 cm/1 inch pieces.
Heat the oil in a pan, add the spare ribs and fry for 5 minutes until golden brown. Add the ginger, garlic and spring onions and cook for 2 minutes. Add the stock and bring to the boil. Cover and simmer for 1 hour or until the meat is tender.
Add the remaining ingredients and cook for 1 minute. Serve hot.
SERVES 4 to 6

MUSSEL CHOWDER

METRIC/IMPERIAL
1 green pepper, cored, deseeded and chopped
1 small onion, peeled and chopped
350 g/12 oz potatoes, peeled and chopped
1 litre/1¾ pints fish or chicken stock
1 × 439 g/15½ oz can shelled mussels, drained
salt
freshly ground black pepper
4 tablespoons dried skimmed milk powder
finely chopped parsley, to garnish

Place the pepper, onion, potatoes and stock in a large saucepan and bring to the boil. Reduce the heat, skim off the scum that rises to the surface, then cover and simmer for 20 minutes.
Add the mussels and season to taste with salt and pepper, then simmer for a further 5 minutes. Cool slightly. Stir in the milk powder and serve garnished with the chopped parsley,
SERVES 4

Variation
To make this chowder with fresh mussels, buy about 1.5 kg/3 lb mussels in their shells. Scrub them, pulling off the beards and discarding any that are open. Cook quickly in about 200 ml/⅓ pint stock for 5 to 6 minutes. Drain and discard any shells that have not opened.

FISH CHOWDER

METRIC/IMPERIAL
750 g/1½ lb cod or haddock fillets
1.75 litres/3 pints water
freshly ground black pepper
1 onion, peeled and sliced
2 potatoes, peeled and sliced
3 tomatoes, skinned and sliced
2 teaspoons yeast extract
1 teaspoon chopped thyme
2 teaspoons chopped parsley
2 teaspoons tomato purée
salt
2 teaspoons Worcestershire sauce
juice of 1 lemon

Put the fish in a pan with the water and a pinch of pepper. Bring to the boil, then lower the heat and poach gently for 15 minutes or until the fish is tender. Drain off the water and reserve. Cut the fish into 2.5 cm/1 inch cubes, discarding the skin and any bones.
Put the fish and the reserved water in the rinsed-out pan with the remaining ingredients, except the Worcestershire sauce and lemon juice. Bring to the boil, then lower the heat, cover and simmer for 45 minutes.
Stir in the Worcestershire sauce and lemon juice, then serve very hot with wholewheat bread or crackers.
SERVES 4

SWEETCORN AND PRAWN SOUP

METRIC/IMPERIAL
2 teaspoons finely chopped root ginger
1 tablespoon dry sherry
225 g/8 oz frozen peeled prawns, thawed
900 ml/1½ pints chicken stock
1 × 326 g/11½ oz can sweetcorn
salt
50 g/2 oz lean ham, diced
1 tablespoon snipped chives

Mix the ginger, sherry and prawns together Bring the stock to the boil, then stir in the prawn mixture. Drain the sweetcorn and add to the pan with salt to taste. Cook for 2 minutes, stirring occasionally.
Sprinkle with the ham and chives and serve immediately.
SERVES 4 to 6

CLAM AND ABALONE SOUP WITH CHINESE MUSHROOMS

METRIC/IMPERIAL
8-10 dried Chinese mushrooms
1.2 litres/2 pints stock
50 g/2 oz abalone, thinly sliced
100 g/4 oz chicken breast, thinly sliced
1 × 2.5 cm/1 inch piece of root ginger, diced
1-2 tablespoons dry sherry
1 tablespoon soy sauce
1 × 225 g/8 oz can clams, drained
chopped spring onion, to garnish

Soak the mushrooms in warm water for 15 minutes. Squeeze dry and discard the hard stalks, then cut the mushroom caps into quarters.

Bring the stock to the boil and add the abalone, chicken and ginger. Simmer for 2 minutes, add the remaining ingredients and cook for a further 2 minutes.

Sprinkle with the spring onion and serve.
SERVES 4 to 6

PRAWN AND CUCUMBER SOUP

METRIC/IMPERIAL
1 cucumber, peeled and diced
1 × 411 g/14½ oz can chicken consommé
150 ml/¼ pint tomato juice
150 ml/¼ pint plain low-fat yogurt
150 ml/¼ pint single cream
100 g/4 oz peeled, cooked prawns, roughly chopped
2 drops Tabasco
1 tablespoon chopped mint
1 clove garlic, peeled and crushed
salt
freshly ground white pepper
Garnish:
mint sprigs
cucumber slices

Place the cucumber in an electric blender and work until smooth. Transfer to a bowl and add the remaining ingredients, seasoning well with salt and pepper. Mix thoroughly and chill for several hours before serving. Garnish with mint and cucumber slices.
SERVES 4 to 6

HEARTY FISH SOUP

METRIC/IMPERIAL
350 g/12 oz potatoes, scrubbed and sliced
300 ml/½ pint skimmed milk
300 ml/½ pint water
salt
freshly ground black pepper
350 g/12 oz whiting fillets, skinned and cut into 2 cm/¾ inch cubes
4 tablespoons peas
4 tablespoons sweetcorn
2 tablespoons tomato purée
lemon juice

Place the potatoes, milk, water, and salt and pepper in a saucepan and simmer gently for 10 minutes. Add the fish with the peas and sweetcorn. Simmer, covered, for a further 10 to 15 minutes. Just before serving, stir in the tomato purée and lemon juice to taste and serve hot.
SERVES 4

GREEN GARDEN SOUP

METRIC/IMPERIAL
4 celery stalks, chopped
2 leeks, washed and shredded
1 bunch watercress stalks, trimmed
3 courgettes, thinly sliced
600 ml/1 pint chicken stock
salt
freshly ground black pepper
1 clove garlic, peeled and crushed
small bunch of parsley
150 ml/¼ pint plain low-fat yogurt
snipped chives, to garnish

Put the celery, leeks, watercress and courgettes into a saucepan together with the chicken stock, salt and pepper to taste, garlic and parsley. Simmer gently until the vegetables are just tender – about 15 minutes.

Purée in a blender or food processor until smooth. Cool, then stir in half the yogurt. Chill in the refrigerator.

Serve in soup bowls with a little of the remaining yogurt swirled on top of each portion. Garnish with chives.
SERVES 4

SWEDISH TOMATO CREAM

METRIC/IMPERIAL
40 g/1½ oz polyunsaturated margarine
2 onions, peeled and chopped
1 clove garlic, peeled and crushed
1 × 400 g/14 oz can tomatoes
250 ml/8 fl oz chicken stock
1 tablespoon fresh dill or 1 teaspoon dried dill
salt
freshly ground black pepper
3 tablespoons reduced-calorie mayonnaise
few watercress leaves, to garnish

Melt the margarine in a saucepan, add the onion and cook gently for 5 minutes. Stir in the garlic, tomatoes with their juice, stock, dill, and salt and pepper to taste. Bring to the boil and simmer for 10 minutes.

Allow to cool a little, then purée in a blender or food processor until smooth. Mix in the mayonnaise thoroughly, pour into a bowl and leave to cool completely. Cover and chill in the refrigerator. Serve in chilled soup cups, garnished with watercress leaves.
SERVES 4 to 6

CHILLED PEA SOUP

METRIC/IMPERIAL
350 g/12 oz shelled peas (about 750 g/1½ lb fresh peas in the pod)
1 onion, peeled and chopped
1 large mint sprig
finely grated rind and juice of ½ lemon
900 ml/1½ pints chicken stock
salt
freshly ground black pepper
150 ml/¼ pint plain low-fat yogurt or milk
1 tablespoon chopped mint, to garnish

Put the fresh peas in a pan with the onion, mint, lemon rind and juice, chicken stock, and salt and pepper to taste.

Bring to the boil, then lower the heat, cover and simmer for 30 minutes until the peas are soft. Work the soup to a purée through a sieve or in an electric blender. Leave to cool.

Stir in the yogurt or milk, then taste and adjust the seasoning. Cover and chill in the refrigerator for several hours before serving. Sprinkle with chopped mint and serve in chilled soup cups.
SERVES 4 to 6

YOGURT AND MINT SOUP

METRIC/IMPERIAL
300 g/10 oz plain low-fat yogurt
150 ml/¼ pint tomato juice
175 ml/6 fl oz skimmed milk
1 clove garlic, peeled and crushed
1 tablespoon chopped mint
½ cucumber, peeled and finely diced
salt
freshly ground white pepper
mint sprigs, to garnish

Place the yogurt and tomato juice in a bowl and mix together thoroughly. Stir in the milk, garlic, chopped mint, cucumber, and salt and pepper to taste. Transfer to a soup tureen and chill for 2 hours. Garnish with mint to serve.
SERVES 4

GAZPACHO

METRIC/IMPERIAL
700 g/1½ lb tomatoes, skinned, deseeded and chopped
1 × 10 cm/4 inch piece of cucumber, chopped
1 onion, peeled and sliced
½ green pepper, cored, deseeded and chopped
2 cloves garlic, peeled
1 tablespoon vegetable oil
3 tablespoons lemon juice
1 teaspoon chopped thyme
2 tablespoons chopped parsley
salt
freshly ground black pepper
iced water
Garnish:
ice cubes
½ green pepper, deseeded and finely diced
1 × 10 cm/4 inch piece of cucumber, finely chopped
4 celery stalks, trimmed and finely chopped
finely chopped parsley

Put the tomatoes, cucumber, onion, green pepper, garlic, oil, lemon juice, thyme, parsley, and salt and pepper into a blender and work to a purée.

Add enough iced water to make the soup of the desired consistency. The quantity will vary according to the juiciness of the tomatoes, and your preference for a really thick or thin soup.

Chill thoroughly. Float an ice cube in each serving and hand the garnishes in separate bowls.
SERVES 4

CHILLED WATERCRESS VICHYSSOISE

METRIC/IMPERIAL
15 g/½ oz polyunsaturated margarine
1 large onion, peeled and chopped
225 g/8 oz leeks, trimmed and sliced
350 g/12 oz potatoes, peeled and diced
1 litre/1¾ pints vegetable stock
grated rind of ½ lemon
salt
freshly ground black pepper
2 bunches watercress, trimmed
150 ml/¼ pint skimmed milk

Melt the margarine in a large saucepan and cook the onion and leeks gently for 5 minutes, stirring constantly. Add the potatoes to the pan and pour in the stock with the lemon rind, and salt and pepper. Cover the pan and bring to the boil. Simmer for 30 minutes until the vegetables are tender. Reserve a few sprigs of watercress and coarsely chop the rest. Add the chopped watercress to the pan and simmer for 2 minutes.
Liquidize to a smooth purée. Stir in the milk, then taste and adjust the seasoning. Chill well before serving. Garnish with the reserved cress.
SERVES 6

ICED AVOCADO SOUP

METRIC/IMPERIAL
2 ripe avocados, halved and stoned
2 teaspoons lemon juice
1 celery stalk, very finely chopped
1 tablespoon tomato purée
450 ml/¾ pint plain low-fat yogurt
1-2 drops of Tabasco
salt
freshly ground black pepper
300 ml/½ pint vegetable stock
snipped chives, to garnish

Do not prepare this soup more than an hour before you intend to serve it.
Spoon the avocado flesh into a bowl, add the lemon juice and beat to a smooth paste. Beat in the celery, tomato purée, yogurt, Tabasco, and salt and pepper. Add sufficient vegetable stock to obtain a thick but liquid soup, then adjust the seasoning. Chill in the refrigerator, resting the bowl on a bed of ice to hasten the chilling process. Serve garnished with chives.
SERVES 4

CUCUMBER, LEMON AND MINT SOUP

METRIC/IMPERIAL
1 tablespoon polyunsaturated vegetable oil
1 small onion, peeled and finely chopped
½ cucumber, peeled and cut into 5 mm/¼ inch cubes
450 ml/¾ pint plain low-fat yogurt
300 ml/½ pint chicken stock
finely grated rind and juice of 1 lemon
2 tablespoons chopped mint
salt
freshly ground black pepper
mint sprigs, to garnish

Heat the oil in a pan, add the onion and fry gently for 3 minutes. Add the cucumber and fry for a further 5 minutes. Transfer to a bowl and leave to cool.
Stir in the yogurt and stock, then the lemon rind and juice, mint and salt and pepper to taste.
Chill in the refrigerator for 1 hour. Pour into 4 individual chilled bowls, garnish with mint sprigs and serve chilled.
SERVES 4

SUMMER TOMATO SOUP

METRIC/IMPERIAL
600 ml/1 pint tomato juice
600 ml/1 pint plain low-fat yogurt
finely grated rind and juice of 1 lemon
½ cucumber, peeled and cut into 5 mm/¼ inch cubes
salt
freshly ground black pepper
Garnish:
4 lemon slices
2 teaspoons snipped chives

Put the tomato juice in a bowl, add the yogurt and mix well. Stir in the lemon rind and juice, then the cucumber, and salt and pepper to taste.
Chill in the refrigerator for 1 hour. Pour into 4 individual bowls. Garnish with lemon slices and chives. Serve chilled.
SERVES 4

47

APPETIZERS

GUACAMOLE

METRIC/IMPERIAL
2 large very ripe avocados
juice of 1 lemon
4 tomatoes, skinned, deseeded and chopped
1 small onion, peeled and grated
1 clove garlic, peeled and crushed
¼ teaspoon Tabasco
salt
freshly ground black pepper
1 small lettuce (optional)

Cut the avocado pears in half and remove the stones. Scoop out the avocado flesh into a bowl and immediately pour over the lemon juice to prevent discoloration.

Mash the avocados well, then add the remaining ingredients, except the lettuce, and beat well until smooth. Alternatively, put all the ingredients in a blender and work to a smooth purée.

Transfer to a serving bowl or individual plates, lined with lettuce leaves. Serve the Guacamole immediately with toasted bread or crudités.
SERVES 6

CUCUMBER MOUSSE

METRIC/IMPERIAL
1 large cucumber, peeled and finely diced
225 g/8 oz curd cheese
150 ml/¼ pint plain low-fat yogurt
pinch of ground mace
15 g/½ oz powdered gelatine
3 tablespoons water
salt
freshly ground black pepper
2 teaspoons snipped chives

Place the cucumber, curd cheese, yogurt and mace in a blender.

Sprinkle the gelatine over the water in a small heatproof bowl and leave for a few minutes until spongy. Place the bowl in a saucepan of hot water and stir over a very gentle heat until the gelatine

has dissolved. Add to the mixture in the blender. Process the mixture until smooth, then season to taste and stir in the chives. Turn the mixture into a 600 ml/1 pint soufflé dish or 4 individual ramekins; cover and chill in the refrigerator overnight. Serve chilled.
SERVES 4

AVOCADO AND TOMATO APPETIZER

METRIC/IMPERIAL
1 large ripe avocado
grated rind and juice of ½ lemon
100 g/4 oz low-fat soft cheese
1 tablespoon grated onion
1 clove garlic, peeled and crushed
1 teaspoon chopped tarragon
few drops of Tabasco
salt
freshly ground black pepper
4 large tomatoes
fresh parsley, to garnish
1 tablespoon lumpfish roe (optional)

Cut the avocado pear in half and remove the stone. Scoop out the avocado flesh into a mixing bowl and immediately pour over the lemon rind and juice to prevent discoloration. Mash the avocado roughly with a fork, until fairly smooth. Stir in the cheese, onion, garlic and tarragon. Add the Tabasco sauce, and salt and pepper to taste. Either use the avocado filling at once, or place in a dish, cover immediately and chill until required. It will keep for several hours in the refrigerator without browning.

Cut the tops off the tomatoes and scoop out the seeds from the centre. Turn the tomatoes upside down for a minute to drain off the juice. Place the tomatoes on a serving dish or on individual dishes. Pile the avocado mixture into the tomatoes. Garnish with parsley, or, for a special occasion, sprinkle the lumpfish roe on to the tops. Serve at once.
SERVES 4

AVOCADO WITH 'CAVIAR'

METRIC/IMPERIAL
3 ripe avocados
4 tablespoons French dressing
3 tablespoons lumpfish roe

Cut the avocado pears in half and remove the stones. Peel each half and lay, cut side down, on a board. Slice across thinly, then lift on to a serving plate and press firmly to separate the slices.

Add 1 tablespoon of the dressing to the roe and mix well. Spoon the remaining dressing over the avocados to coat completely, then spoon the lumpfish roe down the centre of each pear. Serve immediately.
SERVES 6

AVOCADO WITH GREEN HERB DRESSING

METRIC/IMPERIAL
2 ripe avocados
100 g/4 oz frozen peeled prawns, thawed
4 tablespoons green herb dressing (see page 337)
chopped dill, to garnish

Halve the pears and remove the stones. Scoop out the flesh and cut into neat pieces. Place in a bowl with the prawns and dressing.

Mix together carefully and spoon into individual serving dishes. Sprinkle with chopped dill and serve with wholemeal bread and butter.
SERVES 4

PALM HEART AND AVOCADO VINAIGRETTE

METRIC/IMPERIAL
few curly endive leaves
1 × 425 g/15 oz can palm hearts, drained
1 ripe avocado
3 tablespoons French dressing
2 tablespoons sesame seeds, toasted

Tear the endive into pieces and arrange on 6 individual serving dishes. Cut the palm hearts into quarters lengthwise. Cut the avocado pear in half, remove the stone and slice the flesh lengthwise. Arrange the palm hearts and avocado slices on the endive, pour over the dressing and sprinkle with the sesame seeds.
SERVES 6

MINTED GRAPEFRUIT

METRIC/IMPERIAL
2 large grapefruit
2 oranges
1 tablespoon lemon juice
250 ml/8 fl oz low-calorie lemonade
2 tablespoons finely chopped mint
4 mint sprigs, to garnish

Halve the grapefruit, using a zigzag cut. Remove the flesh from the halves. Peel and segment the oranges, remove the membranes and cut the segments into pieces. Mix with the grapefruit and return to the grapefruit shells.

Mix together the lemon juice, lemonade and chopped mint. Pour into an ice tray and freeze until mushy. Pile on top of the grapefruit and decorate with a sprig of mint. Serve immediately.
SERVES 4

BUTTER BEAN RAMEKINS

METRIC/IMPERIAL
100 g/4 oz dried butter beans, soaked in cold water overnight
25 g/1 oz polyunsaturated margarine
225 g/8 oz leeks, trimmed, washed and finely chopped
2 cloves garlic, peeled and crushed
1 bunch watercress, rinsed and roughly chopped
3 egg whites
salt
freshly ground black pepper
generous pinch of mace
6 tablespoons double cream
6 tablespoons low-fat yogurt
watercress sprigs, to garnish

Grease 4 ramekins with a little oil.

Drain the butter beans and place in a large pan with fresh water. Bring to the boil and cook for 40 minutes. Drain and dry on kitchen paper.

Melt the margarine in a pan and fry the leek and garlic until cooked but not brown. Place the beans, leek mixture and watercress in a food processor and blend until smooth. Add the egg white and continue to blend until absolutely smooth. Season with salt, pepper and mace. With the machine running, pour in the cream and yogurt. Do not process for more than 20 seconds.

Spoon the mixture into the prepared ramekins. Cover each with foil or cling film and place in a steamer. Cover with a tight-fitting lid and steam

the ramekins over boiling water for 35 minutes.
To serve, turn the mousses out on to 4 individual serving plates and garnish with small sprigs of watercress.
SERVES 4

GLOBE ARTICHOKES WITH RUSSIAN SALAD

METRIC/IMPERIAL
100 g/4 oz lean ham, diced
100 g/4 oz cooked peas
100 g/4 oz cooked carrots, diced
100 g/4 oz cooked green beans, diced
100 g/4 oz cooked beetroot, diced
100 g/4 oz cooked potatoes, diced
50 g/2 oz reduced-calorie mayonnaise
salt
freshly ground black pepper
4 globe artichokes, cooked

Stir the ham and vegetables into the mayonnaise and mix well. Add salt and pepper to taste and mix again.
Remove the chokes from the artichokes and push back the leaves to make room for the stuffing. If necessary, remove a few of the inner leaves. Spoon the Russian salad into the centre of the artichokes.
SERVES 4

WATERCRESS WITH ORANGE AND NUTS

METRIC/IMPERIAL
1 bunch watercress, rinsed and trimmed
1 large orange, peeled and segmented,
membrane removed and flesh chopped
2 tablespoons chopped hazelnuts
Dressing:
120 ml/4 fl oz plain low-fat yogurt
½ clove garlic, peeled and crushed with salt
2 teaspoons chopped parsley
freshly ground black pepper

Put the watercress, orange and hazelnuts into a large serving bowl.
To make the dressing, beat the yogurt with the garlic, parsley and pepper to taste. Pour over the watercress mixture and toss well. Leave the salad to stand for about 30 minutes before serving, to allow the flavours to develop.
SERVES 4

HERB PÂTÉ

METRIC/IMPERIAL
450 g/1 lb pig's liver, coarsely minced
100 g/4 oz lean bacon, derinded and coarsely minced
2 cloves garlic, peeled and crushed
1 egg, beaten
3 tablespoons beef stock
1 teaspoon chopped parsley
1 teaspoon chopped thyme
1 teaspoon snipped chives
salt
freshly ground black pepper

Put all the ingredients in a bowl and mix well. Press the mixture into a small casserole, then cover with a lid or foil. Stand the casserole in a roasting tin and pour in enough water to come 2.5 cm/1 inch up the sides of the pan.
Bake in a preheated moderate oven (180°C/350°F, Gas Mark 4) for 1½ hours. Leave to cool, then cover the pâté with clean foil, put a heavy weight on top, and leave in the refrigerator for 24 hours. Serve with toast or salad.
SERVES 4

SPINACH AND RICOTTA TRIANGLES

METRIC/IMPERIAL
750 g/1½ lb spinach, washed and trimmed, or 350 g/12 oz frozen spinach
350 g/12 oz Ricotta cheese
150 ml/¼ pint plain low-fat yogurt
2 tablespoons snipped chives
½ teaspoon grated nutmeg
salt
freshly ground black pepper
350 g/12 oz filo pastry
50 ml/2 fl oz polyunsaturated vegetable oil
watercress sprigs, to garnish

Cook the spinach in a very little boiling salted water for about 7 minutes, until just tender. If using frozen spinach, cook it according to the packet instructions. Drain thoroughly, chop finely and leave to cool.
Combine the Ricotta with the yogurt, chives and the nutmeg. Season with salt and pepper. Add the spinach and mix well.
Preheat the oven to moderate (180°C/350°F, Gas Mark 4). Place the filo pastry on a damp board and cut into 10 cm/4 inch squares, cutting through

all the sheets at once. Cover with a damp cloth to keep the pastry moist.

Take one square of pastry and brush with oil. Place 1 teaspoon of the spinach and cheese mixture in the middle of the square and fold over diagonally to make a triangular parcel. Continue with the pastry squares and spinach mixture until you have made about 80 triangles.

Arrange on lightly oiled baking sheets (about 10 triangles on each) and brush with oil. Bake in the oven for 12 minutes, until nicely browned. Cool on a wire tray before serving garnished with watercress.

MAKES 80

BUTTER BEAN VINAIGRETTE

METRIC/IMPERIAL
225 g/8 oz butter beans, soaked in cold water overnight
salt
4 tablespoons vinaigrette dressing
4 spring onions, chopped
1 clove garlic, peeled and crushed
1 tablespoon chopped parsley, to garnish

Drain the beans, place in a pan and cover with cold water. Bring to the boil and simmer gently for 1 to 1¼ hours, adding a little salt towards the end of cooking; drain.

Mix with the dressing while the beans are still warm. Add the onions and garlic and mix well. Transfer to a serving dish and leave until cold. Sprinkle with the parsley to serve.

SERVES 4

SPINACH RAMEKINS

METRIC/IMPERIAL
25 g/1 oz polyunsaturated margarine
1 small onion, peeled and chopped
4 tablespoons spinach purée
50 g/2 oz Edam cheese, grated
4 eggs, beaten
pinch of grated nutmeg
salt
freshly ground black pepper
300 ml/½ pint skimmed milk
50 g/2 oz fresh wholemeal breadcrumbs

Lightly grease 4 ramekin dishes and preheat the oven to moderate (180°C/350°F, Gas Mark 4).

Melt the margarine in a pan and gently fry the onion until soft, then place in a bowl with the spinach, cheese and eggs. Season with nutmeg and salt and pepper.

Heat the milk until almost boiling and beat into the mixture with the breadcrumbs. Pour into the ramekin dishes. Stand the ramekins in a roasting tin half-filled with water. Cook in the oven for 30 to 35 minutes or until the mixture is risen and firm to the touch. Serve hot.

SERVES 4

TOMATOES STUFFED WITH HERB-ANCHOVY RICE

METRIC/IMPERIAL
4 large, ripe tomatoes
salt
225 g/8 oz cooked, brown rice, well rinsed
2 tablespoons finely chopped parsley
25 g/1 oz chopped fresh basil or 2 tablespoons dried basil chopped with an extra 2 tablespoons parsley
4 tablespoons olive oil
8 flat, canned anchovy fillets, drained and chopped
4 cloves garlic, peeled and crushed
freshly ground black pepper
sugar
parsley sprigs, to garnish

Cut a slice from the top of each tomato and set the slices aside. Scoop out the pulp with a sharp-edged spoon, leaving a shell about 1 cm/½ inch thick, and place the pulp in a sieve set over a bowl. Sprinkle inside the shells with salt and stand upside down on paper towels to drain. Rub the pulp through the sieve.

Place the rice, parsley, basil, oil, anchovies, garlic and 120 ml/4 fl oz of the tomato pulp in a bowl and mix lightly together. Season to taste with salt and pepper and a dash of sugar.

Stand the tomato shells upright in an oiled, shallow baking dish just large enough to hold them (prop them up with crumpled aluminium foil if necessary). Spoon the rice mixture into each shell and cover the tops with the reserved slices. Bake the tomatoes in a preheated moderately hot oven (190°C/375°F, Gas Mark 5) for 10 to 15 minutes, until the tomato shells are slightly softened. Serve hot or cold, garnished with sprigs of parsley.

SERVES 4

AUBERGINE PÂTÉ

METRIC/IMPERIAL
2 large aubergines
1 clove garlic, peeled and crushed
2 teaspoons lemon juice
2 tablespoons olive oil
salt
freshly ground black pepper
2 tablespoons chopped parsley
Garnish:
chopped parsley
lemon wedges

Prick the aubergines all over with a fork, cut in half and place, cut side down, on a greased baking sheet. Bake in a preheated moderately hot oven (190°C/375°F, Gas Mark 5) for 30 to 40 minutes until softened.

Peel, then blend the aubergines in an electric blender with the garlic and lemon juice, adding the oil a teaspoon at a time. Alternatively, chop the flesh finely and rub through a sieve, then add the garlic, lemon juice and oil in a steady stream, beating until smooth.

Season with salt and pepper to taste, stir in the parsley and spoon into ramekin dishes. Chill until required.

Garnish with parsley and lemon wedges. Serve with wholemeal toast.
SERVES 4

STUFFED TOMATO SALAD

METRIC/IMPERIAL
4 large or 6 medium tomatoes
1 dessert apple
finely grated rind of 1 orange
juice of ½ orange
225 g/8 oz cottage cheese
2 tablespoons sultanas
2 tablespoons chopped walnuts
1 tablespoon snipped chives or finely chopped spring onions
salt
freshly ground black pepper
1 small lettuce

Cut the tops off the tomatoes and set aside. Scoop out the centres of the tomatoes, then turn them upside down and leave to drain.

Meanwhile, chop the apple and discard the core. Put the apple in a bowl, sprinkle with the orange rind and juice, then add the remaining ingredients, except the lettuce. Fold gently to mix.

Divide the mixture equally between the tomato cups. Arrange the lettuce leaves on individual serving plates. Place a tomato on each plate and top with the reserved lids. Serve cold.
SERVES 4 to 6

HUMMUS

METRIC/IMPERIAL
225 g/8 oz chick peas, soaked in cold water overnight and drained
1 onion, peeled and roughly chopped
1 bay leaf
juice of 1 lemon
2 cloves garlic, peeled and crushed
2 tablespoons polyunsaturated vegetable oil
300 ml/½ pint plain low-fat yogurt
½ teaspoon ground cumin seed
salt
Garnish:
chopped parsley
black olives

Put the chick peas into a pan and cover with fresh water. Add the onion and bay leaf, then bring to the boil. Lower the heat, cover and cook for 1 to 1½ hours, or until the chick peas are tender. Drain thoroughly, then remove the bay leaf.

Purée the peas and onion and mix in the lemon juice, garlic, oil, yogurt and cumin to make a fairly soft consistency. Season with salt.

Chill the hummus thoroughly, then garnish with parsley and black olives and serve with warm wholemeal pitta bread.
SERVES 8 to 10

LEBANESE PARSLEY DIP

METRIC/IMPERIAL
150 ml/¼ pint tahini
2-3 cloves garlic, peeled and crushed
150 ml/¼ pint lemon juice
4 tablespoons water
pinch of salt
40 g/1½ oz chopped parsley

Beat the tahini in a bowl until smooth. Add the garlic with the lemon juice, water and salt. It should be the consistency of fairly thick cream; if necessary, thin with a little more water. Stir in the parsley and serve with pitta bread or crudités.
SERVES 4 to 6

TOMATO SORBET

METRIC/IMPERIAL
50 g/2 oz fructose
300 ml/½ pint water
300 ml/½ pint tomato juice
juice of ½ lemon
1 teaspoon Worcestershire sauce
6 drops of Tabasco
1 teaspoon soy sauce
salt
freshly ground black pepper
2 egg whites
To serve:
6 large ripe tomatoes
fresh coriander leaves
Melba toast

Put the fructose and water in a heavy-based sauce-pan and heat gently until dissolved. Increase the heat and cook rapidly until the temperature registers 110-112°C/230-234°F on a sugar thermo-meter, or a little of the syrup forms a fine, thin thread when falling from a teaspoon on to a dish. Set aside and allow to cool.

Stir in the tomato juice, lemon juice, Worces-tershire, Tabasco and soy sauces. Add salt and pepper to taste. Pour into a freezer container and, stirring occasionally, freeze for about 1½ hours until mushy.

Beat the egg whites until they form soft peaks and fold into the tomato mixture. Cover, seal and freeze.

To serve, allow the sorbet to defrost for about 45 minutes at room temperature. Halve the toma-toes with zigzag cuts, and scoop out the flesh and pips. Fill with scoops of the sorbet and garnish with sprigs of coriander. Serve with Melba toast.
MAKES 12

ASPARAGUS VINAIGRETTE

METRIC/IMPERIAL
450 g/1 lb asparagus
salt
4 tablespoons lemon vinaigrette dressing
1 hard-boiled egg
1 tablespoon chopped parsley

Cut the asparagus stalks all the same length, tie in bundles and place upright in a deep pan of boiling salted water. Make a lid with foil and dome it over the tips so that the heads cook in the steam. Small asparagus will take 15 minutes to cook; large stems up to 30 minutes. Drain very carefully, then arrange on a serving dish and leave to cool.

Spoon the dressing over the asparagus. Chop the egg white finely and sprinkle over the aspara-gus. Sieve the egg yolk over the top and sprinkle with the parsley.
SERVES 4

JERUSALEM COCOTTES

METRIC/IMPERIAL
450 g/1 lb Jerusalem artichokes, scrubbed
salt
150 ml/¼ pint plain low-fat yogurt
freshly ground white pepper
4 eggs
chopped parsley, to garnish

Preheat the oven to moderate (180°C/350°F, Gas Mark 4).

Cook the artichokes in boiling salted water for about 20 minutes or until tender. Peel off the skins and mash the artichokes well. Stir in the yogurt and season with salt and pepper. Alternatively, work the ingredients to a smooth purée in a blender.

Spread the mixture into 4 individual ovenproof dishes or a large baking dish. Make 4 hollows for the eggs and crack an egg into each hollow.

Bake in the oven for 10 to 15 minutes or until the eggs are just set. Garnish with chopped parsley and serve hot.
SERVES 4

VEGETABLES À LA GRECQUE

METRIC/IMPERIAL
100 g/4 oz cauliflower florets, trimmed
100 g/4 oz broccoli, trimmed
100 g/4 oz carrots, peeled and cut into matchstick strips
100 g/4 oz runner beans, trimmed and sliced
2 tablespoons lemon juice
1 teaspoon ground coriander
1 teaspoon dried rosemary
salt
freshly ground black pepper
6 tablespoons lemon vinaigrette dressing

Place the vegetables in a large saucepan and cover with cold water. Add the lemon juice, coriander and rosemary and season with salt and pepper. Bring to the boil, then reduce the heat, cover and simmer for 10 to 15 minutes, until the vegetables are just cooked but firm.

Remove from the heat and allow the vegetables to cool in the cooking liquid.

Drain well and divide the vegetables between 4 individual salad plates. Pour over the lemon vinaigrette dressing and chill in the refrigerator for 2 to 3 hours before serving.

SERVES 4

and simmer until all the ingredients are soft and most of the liquid from the tomatoes has evaporated.

Beat the eggs and milk in a small pan and scramble lightly. Turn the vegetables on to a heated dish, spread the eggs on top and fork a little of the vegetable mixture into the edges of the egg. Sprinkle with chopped parsley and serve surrounded with small triangles of wholemeal toast spread with garlic-flavoured butter.

SERVES 4

PEPERONATA

METRIC/IMPERIAL
2 large red peppers
2 large green peppers
4 tablespoons olive oil
1 onion, peeled and sliced
2 cloves garlic, peeled and crushed
4 tomatoes, skinned, deseeded and shredded
salt
freshly ground black pepper

Halve the peppers, discard the cores and seeds, and slice thinly. Heat the oil in a pan, add the onion and fry for 5 minutes, until softened. Add the garlic and peppers, cover and cook gently for 10 to 15 minutes, stirring occasionally.

Add the tomatoes, and salt and pepper to taste. Cook for a further 10 minutes, stirring occasionally. Leave to cool. Serve in individual dishes.

SERVES 6

PIPÉRADE

METRIC/IMPERIAL
1 tablespoon polyunsaturated vegetable oil
100 g/4 oz onion, peeled and sliced
100 g/4 oz red or green peppers, cored, deseeded and sliced
2 cloves garlic, peeled and crushed
3 large tomatoes, skinned, deseeded and chopped
salt
freshly ground black pepper
4 eggs
2 tablespoons skimmed milk
chopped parsley, to garnish

Heat the oil and gently fry the onion until almost soft. Add the peppers and, after 5 minutes, the garlic and tomatoes. Season with salt and pepper

GREEK-STYLE LEEKS

METRIC/IMPERIAL
300 ml/½ pint water
finely grated rind and juice of 1 lemon
2 shallots, peeled and thinly sliced
4 sprigs parsley
1 small celery stalk, trimmed, with leaves
1 sprig fennel or a few fennel seeds
1 sprig thyme
6 peppercorns
3 coriander seeds
salt
450 g/1 lb small leeks, trimmed and washed

Put all the ingredients, except the leeks, into a large pan. Bring to the boil, then lower the heat, cover and simmer for 10 minutes.

Add the leeks to the pan, cover and simmer gently for 10 to 15 minutes until tender but not broken up.

Transfer the leeks to a serving dish. Boil the cooking liquid until reduced by half. Strain, if preferred, then pour over the leeks and leave to cool. Serve cold.

SERVES 4

LEEKS VINAIGRETTE

METRIC/IMPERIAL
8 thin leeks
salt
1 hard-boiled egg, finely chopped
1 tablespoon chopped parsley
4 tablespoons French dressing
100 g/4 oz lean bacon, derinded

Trim the leeks, if necessary, to about 15 cm/ 6 inches; split lengthways as far as necessary to clean thoroughly.

Cook in boiling salted water for 6 to 8 minutes,

until just tender. Drain well, arrange on individual serving dishes and leave to cool.

Add the egg and parsley to the dressing and spoon over the leeks. Grill the bacon until crisp, then crumble and sprinkle over the leeks.

SERVES 4

LEEKS WITH CURRY DRESSING

METRIC/IMPERIAL
8 medium leeks
Dressing:
1 teaspoon curry powder
1 teaspoon made mustard
1 teaspoon brown sugar
2 teaspoons grated onion
2 tablespoons white wine vinegar
8 tablespoons sunflower oil
salt
freshly ground black pepper

Cut the leeks to a suitable length to fit the plates; split lengthways as far as necessary to clean thoroughly.

Cook them in boiling salted water for 6 to 8 minutes or until just tender, then drain. Cool slightly and arrange on 4 serving plates.

Place all the ingredients for the dressing in a screw-topped jar and shake well. Pour over the leeks and chill before serving.

SERVES 4

CONTINENTAL COURGETTES

METRIC/IMPERIAL
4 small courgettes (about 350 g/12 oz), washed and trimmed
salt
grated rind and juice of ½ lemon
1 hard-boiled egg, chopped
2 tablespoons cottage cheese
2 tablespoons coarsely chopped mint
25 g/1 oz shelled walnuts, chopped
pinch of paprika
freshly ground black pepper
Garnish:
lettuce leaves
lemon twists or mint leaves

Cook the whole courgettes in boiling, salted water for 5 minutes, then drain well. Cut in half

lengthways and, using a teaspoon, scoop out a channel in the centre. Finely chop the scooped-out flesh and set aside in a bowl.

Put the lemon rind and juice into a bowl, and add the courgette shells. Leave them to marinate in the mixture until quite cold.

Stir the chopped egg into the chopped courgette flesh with the cottage cheese, mint, walnuts, paprika, salt and pepper and a little of the marinade to moisten.

Arrange 2 courgette shells on a bed of lettuce on each serving plate. Pile the egg mixture into the centre of the courgettes, then garnish each serving with a lemon twist or mint leaf. Serve with thinly sliced wholemeal bread.

SERVES 4

MUSHROOMS IN GARLIC SAUCE

METRIC/IMPERIAL
475 ml/16 fl oz skimmed milk
50 g/2 oz onion, peeled and chopped
½ teaspoon marjoram
½ teaspoon dried basil
salt
freshly ground black pepper
2 tablespoons wholemeal flour
225 g/8 oz button mushrooms, wiped and trimmed
300 ml/½ pint vegetable stock
4-5 cloves garlic, peeled and crushed
100 g/4 oz Mozzarella cheese, cubed
chopped parsley, to garnish

Preheat the oven to moderately hot (200°C/400°F, Gas Mark 6).

Heat 350 ml/12 fl oz of the milk, preferably in a double saucepan, with the onion, herbs and seasoning. Stir the remainder of the milk into the flour, then add a little of the hot milk. Whisk this mixture into the hot milk in the saucepan and stir continuously until the mixture thickens and the flour is cooked.

Simmer the mushrooms for 2 minutes in the vegetable stock. Drain the mushrooms and place in an ovenproof dish. Reserve the stock to make soup. Add the garlic to the sauce and pour over the mushrooms and sprinkle with the cheese.

Bake in the oven for 10 minutes. Finish under the grill until the top is an appetizing golden brown colour.

Sprinkle with parsley before serving.

SERVES 4

MARINATED MUSHROOMS

METRIC/IMPERIAL

450 g/1 lb button mushrooms, trimmed and sliced

Marinade:

1 tablespoon cider vinegar
1 tablespoon polyunsaturated vegetable oil
1 tablespoon lemon juice
few drops of Worcestershire sauce
2 tablespoons tomato purée
2 tablespoons cold water
1 tablespoon chopped fresh mixed herbs (thyme, oregano, basil, tarragon), or 1½ teaspoons dried mixed herbs
1 small onion, peeled and grated
1 clove garlic, peeled and crushed

Put all the ingredients for the marinade into a large screw-topped jar and shake well. Add the mushrooms, pushing them down if necessary. Shake the jar once again so the mushrooms are coated with the marinade. If you do not have a large screw-topped jar, use any covered container.

Stand the jar in a cool place and leave for 24 hours, shaking occasionally so that the mushrooms soften. They will reduce in bulk considerably during this time and also produce quite an amount of liquid. Serve them chilled with fresh wholemeal rolls.
SERVES 4

CHILLED MUSHROOMS IN WINE SAUCE

METRIC/IMPERIAL

2 tablespoons polyunsaturated vegetable oil
1 large onion, peeled and sliced
1 large carrot, peeled and sliced
1 celery stalk, sliced
1 large clove garlic, peeled and crushed
150 ml/¼ pint dry white wine
3 tomatoes, skinned, quartered and deseeded
3 tablespoons chopped parsley
1 tablespoon thyme leaves
1 bay leaf
salt
freshly ground black pepper
450 g/1 lb button mushrooms, wiped and trimmed

Heat the oil in a large pan. Add the onion, carrot and celery and fry gently for 3 minutes, stirring

occasionally. Add the crushed garlic and fry for a further 1 minute.

Stir in the white wine, tomatoes, 1 tablespoon parsley, the thyme, bay leaf, and salt and pepper to taste. Bring to the boil, then lower the heat and add the mushrooms. Simmer for 10 minutes. Leave to cool, then pour into a serving dish and chill in the refrigerator. Sprinkle with the remaining parsley and serve chilled.
SERVES 4

MELON, TOMATO AND GRAPE VINAIGRETTE

METRIC/IMPERIAL

2 small Ogen melons
4 tomatoes, skinned, quartered and deseeded
175 g/6 oz black grapes, halved and deseeded
4 tablespoons mint and honey dressing (see page 338)
1 tablespoon sesame seeds, roasted
4 mint sprigs, to garnish

Cut the melons in half and discard the seeds. Scoop the flesh into balls, using a melon baller, or cut into cubes; reserve the shells. Place the melon in a bowl with the tomatoes and grapes. Pour over the dressing.

Toss well, then spoon the mixture into the melon shells. Sprinkle with the sesame seeds and garnish with the mint to serve
SERVES 4

MELON AND MINT SORBET

METRIC/IMPERIAL

600 ml/1 pint water
1 tablespoon lemon juice
2 teaspoons powdered gelatine, soaked in 2 tablespoons cold water
2 mint sprigs, chopped
50 g/2 oz fructose
1 Honeydew melon
1 teaspoon peppermint essence
2 egg whites

Put the water and lemon juice in a heavy-based pan. Bring to the boil and allow to cool. Add the soaked gelatine and stir until dissolved. Mix in the mint and fructose. Scoop the flesh from the melon, remove the pips and purée the flesh in a blender. Alternatively, rub through a sieve Stir

56

into the gelatine mixture with the peppermint essence. Pour the mixture into a freezer container and freeze for about 1½ hours or until mushy, stirring occasionally.

Beat the egg whites until they form soft peaks. Fold into the mixture and freeze. Beat the mixture twice at hourly intervals. Cover, seal and freeze.
SERVES 4 to 6

MINTED MELON AND STRAWBERRY COCKTAIL

METRIC/IMPERIAL
1 small, ripe Honeydew or Cantaloupe melon
100 g/4 oz strawberries, hulled and sliced
5 cm/2 inch piece cucumber, sliced and quartered
finely grated rind and juice of 1 large orange
2 tablespoons chopped mint
15 g/½ oz split blanched pistachio nuts or toasted almonds
½ small lettuce, shredded
mint sprigs, to garnish

Cut the melon into quarters, then remove the seeds and skin. Cut the flesh into 1 cm/½ inch cubes or scoop into balls. Place in a bowl with the strawberries and cucumber.

Mix the orange rind and juice with the mint and nuts, then pour on to the salad. Fold gently to mix.

Divide the lettuce equally between 4 to 6 individual serving dishes or glasses. Spoon the salad on top, pouring over any orange juice from the bowl. Serve chilled, garnished with sprigs of mint.
SERVES 4 to 6

MELON AND ORANGE COCKTAIL

METRIC/IMPERIAL
1 small, ripe Honeydew melon or 2 small Ogen melons
2 large oranges
5 cm/2 inch piece cucumber, sliced and quartered
25 g/1 oz toasted almonds or hazelnuts
2 heads chicory, leaves separated
mint sprigs, to garnish

Cut the melon into quarters and remove the seeds. Using a round vegetable baller, scoop out the flesh into balls, or cut into small cubes with a knife. Place the melon in a mixing bowl.

Cut the peel and pith from the oranges and cut the flesh into segments between the membrane; discard any pips. Add the orange segments to the melon with any juice left from the oranges. Add the cucumber and almonds or hazelnuts, and toss lightly. Chill in the refrigerator until required.

Divide the chicory between 4 to 6 individual serving dishes or glasses. Spoon in the melon cocktail, pouring over the juice. Serve chilled, garnished with sprigs of fresh mint.
SERVES 4 to 6

PINEAPPLE AND PARSLEY ICE CREAM

METRIC/IMPERIAL
750 g/1½ lb fresh pineapple
1 tablespoon fructose
300 ml/½ pint plain low-fat yogurt
1 tablespoon chopped parsley
2 egg whites

Remove the skin and core from the pineapple. Finely chop one-third of the flesh and set aside. Purée the remaining pineapple in a blender with the fructose and yogurt. Pour the purée into a freezer container and freeze for about 1½ hours until mushy.

Beat in the chopped pineapple and the parsley. Beat the egg whites until they form stiff peaks and fold into the pineapple mixture. Cover, seal and freeze.
SERVES 6

PEARS WITH CURD CHEESE

METRIC/IMPERIAL
50 g/2 oz Stilton cheese
150 ml/¼ pint plain low-fat yogurt
100 g/4 oz curd cheese
salt
freshly ground black pepper
2 ripe dessert pears
Garnish:
shredded lettuce leaves
1 tablespoon snipped chives

Mash the Stilton cheese in a bowl, mix with 1 tablespoon of the yogurt and set aside.

Place the curd cheese in a bowl and beat in the remaining yogurt, and salt and pepper to taste. Peel, halve and core the pears. Place a spoonful of the Stilton filling in each cavity. Arrange the lettuce on a serving dish and place the pears, cut side down, on top. Spoon over the yogurt and curd cheese mixture and sprinkle with the chives. Serve chilled.

SERVES 4

Dry-fry the sesame seeds for about 1 minute until they are lightly browned, shaking the pan frequently.

Pound the dried thyme and sesame seeds together in a mortar, then tip them on to a piece of greaseproof paper. Lay the cheese on the paper, turning it over so that it is coated all over with the pounded herbs. Chill before serving.

SERVES 4

PEACHES VINAIGRETTE

METRIC/IMPERIAL
4 peaches, skinned, stoned and sliced
Dressing:
good pinch of mustard powder or ¼ teaspoon French mustard
1 tablespoon wine vinegar
salt
freshly ground black pepper
3 tablespoons polyunsaturated vegetable oil
1 tablespoon chopped fresh herbs (e.g. mint, parsley, chives, chervil, thyme, tarragon, marjoram or basil, or a mixture of these)

To make the dressing, mix the mustard and vinegar in a bowl and season with salt and pepper. Add the oil, a little at a time until well blended, then stir in the herbs.

Arrange the sliced peaches in a serving dish and pour over the dressing.

SERVES 4

YOGURT CHEESE WITH DRIED HERBS

METRIC/IMPERIAL
600 ml/1 pint plain low-fat yogurt
salt
freshly ground black pepper
2 teaspoons olive oil
1 teaspoon sesame seeds
1 teaspoon dried thyme

Line a colander or strainer with muslin and stand it over a bowl. Tip the yogurt into the muslin and tie it up with string, to form a bag. Lift it out of the colander. Tie the strings to a tap over a sink and leave to drain overnight.

The next day, tip the drained curds into a bowl and beat until smooth, adding a little salt and pepper to taste and the olive oil. Form the yogurt cheese into a flat round shape.

YOGURT AND COTTAGE CHEESE DIP

METRIC/IMPERIAL
150 ml/¼ pint plain low-fat yogurt
225 g/8 oz cottage cheese
1 tablespoon grated onion
6 pickled gherkins, very finely chopped
3 celery stalks
3 carrots
½ cucumber
1 tablespoon sea salt
600 ml/1 pint iced water

Put the yogurt, cottage cheese, onion and gherkins in a bowl and stir well to mix. Chill in the refrigerator for 1 hour.

Meanwhile, cut each celery stalk into 4 lengths. Peel the carrots and split each one lengthwise into quarters. Cut the cucumber in half, then cut each half lengthwise into 4 pieces. Put the celery, carrots and cucumber in a bowl, sprinkle with the salt, then pour on the iced water. Chill in the refrigerator for 1 hour.

Put the yogurt dip in a serving bowl and stand the bowl on a large plate. Drain the vegetables and arrange on the plate around the dip.

SERVES 4 to 6

YOGURT DIP WITH FRESH HERBS

METRIC/IMPERIAL
600 ml/1 pint plain low-fat yogurt
salt
freshly ground black pepper
¼ clove garlic, peeled and crushed
½ tablespoon chopped tarragon
½ tablespoon chopped dill
½ tablespoon chopped chervil or parsley

Line a colander or strainer with muslin and stand it over a bowl. Tip the yogurt into the muslin and tie it up with string so that it forms a bag. Lift it out of the colander and leave it to drain overnight, tying the string to a tap over a sink.

The next day, tip the drained curds from the bag into a bowl. Beat until smooth, adding a little salt and pepper. Add the garlic and stir it in with most of the chopped herbs, reserving some to scatter over the top.

Pile the mixture into a small dish, level off with a palette knife, and sprinkle the remaining herbs on top. Chill for 1 to 2 hours before serving.
SERVES 4

PRAWN PÂTÉ

METRIC/IMPERIAL
275 g/10 oz peeled prawns
salt
freshly ground black pepper
pinch of ground mace
pinch of cayenne
½ teaspoon anchovy essence
50 g/2 oz polyunsaturated margarine
4 dill or parsley sprigs, to garnish

Blend 225 g/8 oz of the prawns with the remaining ingredients until smooth. Transfer to a small saucepan, check the seasoning and stir in the remaining prawns. Bring just to the boil. Pour into 4 individual cocottes or 1 large china dish. Smooth the top and place in the refrigerator to chill. Garnish with dill or parsley and serve with hot toast.
SERVES 4

CHICKEN LIVER AND MUSHROOM PÂTÉ

METRIC/IMPERIAL
50 g/2 oz polyunsaturated margarine
2 rashers bacon, derinded and chopped
1 onion, peeled and chopped
1 clove garlic, peeled and crushed
100 g/4 oz mushrooms, wiped and sliced
225 g/8 oz chicken livers, cleaned and roughly chopped
fresh thyme sprigs or pinch of dried thyme
1 bay leaf
1-2 tablespoons brandy
3 tablespoons green peppercorns (optional)
salt
50 g/2 oz polyunsaturated margarine
thyme sprigs (optional garnish)

Melt the margarine in a frying pan and add the bacon, onion, garlic, mushrooms, livers and herbs. Fry for 10 minutes, stirring occasionally, until cooked. Spoon into a blender or food processor with the pan juices and the brandy, discarding the bay leaf, and blend until smooth. Stir in 2 tablespoons of the green peppercorns (if using) and add salt to taste. Spoon into a small serving dish (about 450 ml/¾ pint) and smooth the top.

Clarify the margarine by heating it until it foams, then straining through muslin. Sprinkle the remaining green peppercorns over the surface of the pâté and pour over the melted clarified margarine. Extra small sprigs of fresh thyme may be arranged on top before pouring over the clarified margarine, if liked. Chill in the refrigerator until set. Serve with toast or Melba toast.
SERVES 4

CHICKEN LIVER AND TOMATO PÂTÉ

METRIC/IMPERIAL
225 g/8 oz chicken livers, cleaned and trimmed
175 ml/6 fl oz tomato juice
1 garlic clove, peeled and crushed
1-2 teaspoons Worcestershire sauce
2 teaspoons chopped fresh basil
2 teaspoons medium sherry
salt
freshly ground black pepper
Garnish:
lettuce leaves
lemon slices

Place all the ingredients in a non-stick frying pan. Simmer over a low heat for 5 to 8 minutes, until the chicken livers are cooked but still pink inside.

Place the chicken livers and a little of the cooking liquid in a blender and process until smooth. Spoon the mixture into 4 individual ramekins and smooth the surface of each. Chill in the refrigerator for about 4 hours until firm. Serve chilled, garnished with lettuce leaves and lemon slices.
SERVES 4

Variations
1. Add 2 teaspoons chopped dill pickles or capers.
2. Replace the basil with 2 teaspoons ground mace and the Worcestershire sauce with 4 crushed juniper berries.

PRAWNS AND SCALLOPS IN GARLIC

METRIC/IMPERIAL
25 g/1 oz polyunsaturated margarine
2 tablespoons polyunsaturated vegetable oil
2 cloves garlic, peeled and crushed
225 g/8 oz peeled prawns
8 shelled scallops, halved
2 tablespoons chopped parsley
juice of ½ lemon

Heat the margarine and oil in a frying pan, add the garlic and fry for 2 minutes. Add the prawns and scallops and cook quickly for 2 minutes, or until the scallops are just tender.
Stir in the parsley and lemon juice and serve immediately.
SERVES 4 to 6

PRAWN AND GRAPEFRUIT COCKTAIL

METRIC/IMPERIAL
2 large grapefruit
350 g/12 oz peeled prawns
strips of pared lime rind, to garnish

Peel the grapefruit, carefully removing all the white pith. Cut between the membranes to remove the segments, then cut each segment in half crossways and place in a bowl.
Add the prawns to the grapefruit and stir lightly to mix. Spoon into individual glass dishes and chill for 1 to 2 hours. Serve chilled, garnished with strips of lime rind.
SERVES 4

PRAWN, APPLE AND CELERY COCKTAIL

METRIC/IMPERIAL
1 lettuce, shredded
salt
2 celery stalks, finely chopped
1 dessert apple, peeled, cored and chopped
225 g/8 oz peeled prawns
juice of 1 lemon
freshly ground black pepper
pinch of paprika, to garnish

Divide the lettuce equally between 4 glasses and sprinkle lightly with salt. Put the remaining ingredients in a bowl and mix well.
Divide the mixture equally between the glasses, sprinkle with paprika and serve chilled.
SERVES 4

HOT CRAB AND AVOCADO SOUFFLÉS

METRIC/IMPERIAL
15 g/½ oz polyunsaturated margarine
1 tablespoon plain flour
150 ml/¼ pint skimmed milk
salt
freshly ground black pepper
½ teaspoon finely grated lemon rind
3 eggs, separated
225 g/8 oz white crabmeat
1 avocado, halved, stone removed, peeled and chopped

Grease 4 individual ramekin dishes.
Melt the margarine and stir in the flour; cook for 30 seconds. Gradually add the skimmed milk and bring to the boil, stirring, until the sauce has thickened. Add the salt and pepper to taste and the lemon rind, and beat in the egg yolks.
Beat the egg whites until stiff but not dry. Mix the crabmeat into the sauce mixture and then lightly fold in the avocado and the egg whites.
Divide the mixture among the prepared dishes. Bake in an oven preheated to 190°C/375°F, Gas Mark 5, for 25 minutes or until well risen and golden. Serve immediately.
SERVES 4

FISH ROE STUFFED EGGS

METRIC/IMPERIAL
8 hard-boiled eggs, shelled
150 ml/¼ pint plain low-fat yogurt
juice of 1 lemon
100 g/4 oz lumpfish roe
salt
freshly ground black pepper
lettuce, to serve

Cut the eggs in half lengthwise, then remove the yolks. Put the yolks in a bowl with the yogurt and lemon juice and mash well together. Work in the fish roe, then add salt and pepper to taste.
Pile the mixture into the egg whites and serve on a bed of lettuce.
SERVES 4

PASTA SHELL SALAD

METRIC/IMPERIAL
225 g/8 oz pasta shells
salt
150 ml/¼ pint French dressing with ½ teaspoon
marjoram added
1 tablespoon anchovy essence
1 teaspoon tomato purée
225 g/8 oz white fish, cooked and flaked (cod,
haddock, coley or whiting)
1 × 200 g/7 oz can tuna fish, drained and flaked
100 g/4 oz peeled prawns
freshly ground black pepper
1 lettuce, washed and drained
Garnish:
unpeeled prawns
lemon slices
1 tablespoon chopped parsley and marjoram

Cook the pasta in a large pan of boiling salted
water for 10 to 15 minutes until just tender. Place
the drained pasta in a bowl. Mix the French dressing with the anchovy essence and tomato purée
and pour half of this over the pasta. Toss well and
leave until cold. Add the white fish, tuna fish and
prawns to the pasta. Pour over the remaining
dressing and toss lightly. Season to taste wih pepper. Leave to marinate for at least 30 minutes in a
cold place.
　Line individual dishes with lettuce leaves and
pile the pasta and fish salad in the centre. Garnish
with unpeeled prawns, lemon slices and herbs.
SERVES 4

TOMATO MACKEREL PÂTÉ

METRIC/IMPERIAL
1 × 90 g/3½ oz can tuna in brine, drained
1 × 125 g/4½ oz can mackerel in tomato sauce
100 g/4 oz low-fat soft cheese
2 tablespoons plain low-fat yogurt
2 teaspoons lemon juice
2 spring onions, finely chopped
salt
freshly ground black pepper
Garnish:
lemon slices
shredded lettuce
cucumber slices

Place the drained tuna and mackerel with the
tomato sauce in a bowl and mash well together.

Blend in the soft cheese, yogurt and lemon juice.
Stir in the onions, salt and pepper to taste. Place
on 4 serving plates. Before serving, garnish with
lemon slices, shredded lettuce and cucumber.
SERVES 4

TUNA FISH PÂTÉ

METRIC/IMPERIAL
2 × 200 g/7 oz cans tuna fish in brine, drained
and cut into small pieces
40 g/1½ oz polyunsaturated margarine
1 tablespoon lemon juice
1 tablespoon grated lemon rind
25 g/1 oz wholemeal breadcrumbs
salt
freshly ground black pepper
Garnish:
lemon wedges
parsley sprig

Place the tuna in a blender with the margarine and
blend until smooth. Turn into a bowl and stir in
the lemon, rind and breadcrumbs. Mix well,
adding plenty of salt and pepper. Spoon into a
serving dish and garnish with lemon wedges and a
sprig of parsley. Serve with toast.
SERVES 4

SMOKED COD'S ROE MOUSSE

METRIC/IMPERIAL
175 g/6 oz smoked cod's roe, skinned
50 g/2 oz cottage cheese
finely grated rind of ½ lemon
salt
freshly ground black pepper
2 tablespoons olive oil
2 hard-boiled eggs, shelled
1 tablespoon coarsely chopped parsley

Put the cod's roe into a blender or food processor
with the cottage cheese, lemon rind, salt and pepper to taste and the olive oil; blend until smooth.
　Separate the yolks from the whites of the hard-
boiled eggs; add the yolks to the cod's roe mixture
and blend until smooth. Chop the egg whites
finely; stir into the cod's roe mixture, along with
the parsley. Cover and chill for 1 to 2 hours.
　Serve on small plates in neat scoops, accompanied by fingers of warm wholewheat toast.
SERVES 4

SALMON ROULADE

METRIC/IMPERIAL
1 × 200 g/7 oz can salmon
4 eggs, separated
1 tablespoon tomato purée
salt
freshly ground black pepper
2 tablespoons grated Parmesan cheese
Filling:
300 ml/½ pint skimmed milk
1 small onion, peeled and quartered
2 parsley stalks, finely chopped
1 bay leaf
strip of lemon rind
25 g/1 oz polyunsaturated margarine
25 g/1 oz plain flour
4 hard-boiled eggs, chopped
2 tablespoons chopped dill
2 teaspoons lemon juice
salt
freshly ground black pepper
Garnish:
slices of cucumber and lemon
dill or parsley sprigs

Transfer the salmon and juices from the can to a mixing bowl. Remove the black skin and any bones. Mash the salmon to a purée with a fork. Beat in the egg yolks, tomato purée, salt and pepper. Whisk the egg whites until stiff and fold them into the mixture.

Line a Swiss roll tin or shallow baking sheet, about 33 × 23 cm/13 × 9 inches, with greaseproof paper to come above the sides of the tin, and brush with oil. Pour the roulade mixture into the prepared tin and level the surface. Bake near the top of a preheated moderately hot oven (200°C/400°F, Gas Mark 6) for 10 to 15 minutes until the roulade is well risen, firm and golden.

To prepare the filling, pour the milk into a small saucepan and add the onion, parsley, bay leaf and lemon rind. Bring to the boil, remove from the heat and leave to infuse for at least 10 minutes, then strain into a jug. Melt the margarine in a saucepan, stir in the flour and then the flavoured milk over a low heat. Bring to the boil, stirring until the sauce thickens, and simmer for 2 minutes. Stir in the chopped eggs, dill, lemon juice and salt and pepper to taste.

Just before removing the roulade from the oven, sprinkle a large sheet of greaseproof paper with the Parmesan cheese. Turn the roulade on to the paper, remove the tin and peel off the lining paper. Reheat the filling and spread the mixture over the roulade, leaving a 2.5 cm/1 inch margin all the way round. Roll up the roulade like a Swiss roll by gently lifting the paper so that it falls over into a roll. Lift it on to a serving dish.

Serve immediately or cover and keep warm in the oven for a short time, if necessary. Garnish with cucumber and lemon slices and sprigs of parsley or dill, and serve cut into slices.
SERVES 6 to 8

BLACK EYE FISH HORS D'OEUVRE

METRIC/IMPERIAL
100 g/4 oz black eye peas
600 ml/1 pint water
225 g/8 oz white fish fillets (cod, haddock, etc),
cooked, skinned and flaked
1 × 100 g/4 oz can tuna fish, drained and flaked
100 g/4 oz peeled prawns
1 small onion, peeled and grated
150 ml/¼ pint vinaigrette dressing
finely grated rind and juice of ½ lemon
dash of Tabasco
2 teaspoons tomato purée
2 tablespoons chopped parsley
salt
freshly ground black pepper
Garnish:
few unpeeled prawns
parsley sprigs

Put the peas in a large bowl, cover with the water, then leave to soak overnight. Alternatively, pour over boiling water and soak for several hours.

Transfer the peas and water to a pan and bring to the boil. Lower the heat, cover and simmer for 1 to 1½ hours until the peas are tender, adding more water if necessary.

Drain the peas and place in a bowl. Add the flaked fish and prawns and fold lightly to mix. Mix together the remaining ingredients, then fold into the pea and fish mixture. Leave to marinate for at least 1 hour.

Turn into a serving dish, garnish with the prawns and parsley, and serve cold.
SERVES 6

EGG SCRAMBLE WITH SMOKED FISH

METRIC/IMPERIAL
4 eggs
salt
freshly ground black pepper
2 tablespoons plain low-fat yogurt
1 tablespoon snipped chives
225 g/8 oz thinly sliced smoked halibut or
smoked salmon
2 tablespoons polyunsaturated margarine
4 teaspoons black lumpfish roe

Beat the eggs with salt and pepper to taste, the yogurt and snipped chives.

Arrange the smoked fish on 4 individual plates, leaving a small space in the centre of each one.

Heat the margarine gently in a pan until melted; add the beaten egg mixture and cook over a low heat until the egg forms soft creamy flakes. Spoon into the centre of each plate of smoked fish and top with a little black lumpfish roe.

Serve immediately, before the lumpfish roe has had a chance to discolour the scrambled egg.
SERVES 4

CEVICHE OF SCALLOPS

METRIC/IMPERIAL
12 large scallops, with 6 flat shells
250 ml/8 fl oz fresh lime or lemon juice or
a mixture of the two
1½ tablespoons finely chopped shallot
1½ tablespoons finely chopped parsley
1½ tablespoons olive oil

Start a day in advance. Clean the scallops, wash them and pat dry. Cut away the orange part and slice the white part into 1 cm/½ inch slices. Put them in a bowl and pour the lime or lemon juice over them; chill for 24 hours. Just before serving, pour off the fruit juice and discard. Stir in the shallot, parsley and oil. Serve on the scallop shells.
SERVES 4

PRAWN, SPINACH AND MUSHROOM SALAD

METRIC/IMPERIAL
225 g/8 oz tender spinach, washed
225 g/8 oz button mushrooms
225 g/8 oz cooked, peeled prawns
3 tablespoons sunflower seed oil
3 tablespoons lemon juice
freshly ground black pepper

Pick the leaves off the washed spinach, discarding the stalks and pile loosely in a bowl. Wipe the mushrooms, trim the stalks level with the caps, and cut in halves or quarters, according to size. Scatter over the spinach. Lay the prawns over the mushrooms. Pour over the oil and lemon juice and toss well, sprinkling with freshly ground black pepper. Salt is not necessary.
SERVES 4

SMOKED HADDOCK ROULADE

METRIC/IMPERIAL
4 eggs, separated
salt
pinch of cayenne pepper
pinch of grated nutmeg
Filling:
175 g/6 oz fresh smoked haddock
175 g/6 oz cottage cheese, sieved
2 tablespoons freshly snipped chives
grated rind of ½ lemon
1 tablespoon freshly grated Parmesan cheese

Place the egg yolks, salt, cayenne and nutmeg in a bowl and mix well. Whisk the egg whites until stiff, then carefully fold them into the yolk mixture. Spread evenly in a lined and greased 30 × 20 cm/12 × 8 inch Swiss roll tin. Bake in a preheated moderately hot oven (200°C/400°F, Gas Mark 6) for 10 to 15 minutes until well risen and brown.

Meanwhile, make the filling. Poach the haddock in water for 8 to 10 minutes, drain well and remove the skin and bones. Flake the fish and add the cottage cheese, chives and lemon rind. Heat together in a saucepan, stirring for 2 to 3 minutes.

Turn the roulade on to a piece of waxed paper sprinkled with the Parmesan cheese. Carefully peel off the lining paper, spread with the filling and roll up like a Swiss roll. Serve immediately.
SERVES 4

FISH

FISH PIE

METRIC/IMPERIAL
450 g/1 lb potatoes, peeled, boiled and drained,
then mashed with 25 g/1 oz polyunsaturated
margarine, salt and pepper and enough
skimmed milk to make a creamy spreading
consistency
Filling:
500 g/1¼ lb thick white fish fillets
300 ml/½ pint skimmed milk
1 thick slice onion
good pinch each dried rosemary and thyme
1 small bay leaf
4 peppercorns
salt
40 g/1½ oz polyunsaturated margarine
25 g/1 oz plain unbleached white flour
50 g/2 oz cheese, grated
225 g/8 oz tomatoes, skinned and chopped, or
50 g/2 oz peeled prawns
2 hard-boiled eggs, sliced
2 tablespoons chopped parsley (optional)
freshly ground black pepper

Rinse the fish under cold water, cut each fillet into
2 or 3 pieces and put into a saucepan. Add the
milk, onion, herbs, peppercorns and a little salt.
Bring slowly to simmering point, then cover and
cook very gently for 12 to 15 minutes. Strain off
the liquid and reserve for the cheese sauce.

Melt 25 g/1 oz margarine in a clean saucepan,
stir in the flour and cook gently for 1 to 2 minutes.
Gradually stir in the reserved cooking liquid.
When smoothly blended, stir until boiling, then
simmer gently for several minutes.

Meanwhile, remove any skin or bones from the
pieces of fish and flake the flesh roughly. Discard
the onion, bay leaf and peppercorns. Stir into the
sauce half the cheese, all the tomatoes or prawns,
hard-boiled eggs, parsley (if using), flaked fish
and salt and pepper to taste. Mix gently over a low
heat until thoroughly heated through. Pour the
mixture into a flameproof pie dish, spread the prepared potato topping over the top to cover it completely, and mark the surface with a fork. Sprinkle

with the remaining cheese, dot with flakes of the
remaining margarine and grill gently for a few
minutes until the surface is gold and crisp.
SERVES 4

FISH FILLETS PROVENÇAL

METRIC/IMPERIAL
750 g/1½ lb white fish fillets (e.g. haddock,
whiting, cod or coley), skinned
2 tablespoons unbleached white flour, seasoned
with salt, pepper and dried mixed herbs
4 tablespoons olive oil
1 large onion, peeled, halved and thinly sliced
1-2 cloves garlic, peeled and crushed
450 g/1 lb tomatoes, skinned, deseeded and
chopped, or 1 × 400 g/14 oz can tomatoes,
drained and chopped
2 tablespoons black or green olives (optional)
1 teaspoon caster sugar
salt
freshly ground black pepper
1 tablespoon snipped chives or chervil

Cut the fish into roughly 2.5 cm/1 inch cubes.
Coat the fish in the seasoned flour, shaking off any
surplus flour. Heat 1 tablespoon of the oil in a frying pan and sauté the onion very gently for 6 to 8
minutes, until soft and golden. Add the garlic and
sauté for another minute, then add the tomatoes,
olives (if using), sugar, and salt and pepper to
taste. Stir for several minutes until the tomatoes
begin to soften (if using fresh), then cover the pan
and remove from the heat.

Meanwhile, heat the remaining oil in a large
frying pan and, when sizzling hot, put in the
pieces of fish and fry them over a moderate heat
for about 10 minutes, turning frequently, until
cooked through and lightly browned. Drain the
fish on kitchen paper then transfer to a serving
dish, spoon the vegetables over and sprinkle with
chives or chervil.
SERVES 4 to 6

BAKED FISH WITH HERBS AND MUSSEL SAUCE

METRIC/IMPERIAL
1.5-1.75 kg/3-4 lb fish
lemon juice
salt
50 g/2 oz polyunsaturated margarine, melted
100 g/4 oz soft wholemeal breadcrumbs
1 sprig marjoram, chopped, or pinch dried marjoram
2 tablespoons chopped parsley
salt
freshly ground black pepper
cayenne pepper
2 rashers bacon, derinded and cut in half
Mussel sauce:
25 g/1 oz polyunsaturated margarine
4 teaspoons flour
120 ml/4 fl oz fish stock
120 m/4 fl oz single cream
12 cooked mussels
salt
white pepper

Clean the fish, leaving the head and tail intact. Rub with lemon juice and sprinkle the body cavity with salt. Heat the margarine in a frying pan and lightly brown the crumbs. Add the herbs, salt, pepper and cayenne to taste, and mix together. Stuff the fish loosely with the mixture and close the cavity with skewers and string.

Line a baking dish with aluminium foil by using a double thickness and allowing it to overlap at both ends. This will make it easy to lift out the cooked fish without breaking it. Grease the foil, place the fish on it and arrange the bacon on top. Bake, uncovered, in a preheated moderately hot oven (200°C/400°F, Gas Mark 6) for 30 to 40 minutes or until the fish flakes easily when tested with a fork.

While the fish is cooking, make the sauce. Melt the margarine in a small saucepan. Blend in the flour with a whisk and add the fish stock. Lightly whisk over a gentle heat until thickened. Add the cream gradually until a shiny, smooth sauce results. Add the mussels and heat through (do not allow to boil). Taste and adjust the seasoning.

Using the foil as handles, transfer the fish to a heated platter and pour over the mussel sauce.
SERVES 4 to 6

BOUILLABAISSE

METRIC/IMPERIAL
1 tablespoon polyunsaturated vegetable oil
1 large onion, peeled and sliced
1 clove garlic, peeled and crushed
2 × 400 g/14 oz cans tomatoes
300 ml/½ pint fish stock
2 tablespoons chopped parsley
1 bouquet garni
salt
freshly ground black pepper
450 g/1 lb monkfish, diced
750 g/1½ lb red fish, skinned and filleted
350 g/12 oz coley fillets, skinned and diced
4 × 175 g/6 oz plaice fillets, skinned and cut into strips
chopped parsley, to garnish

Heat the oil in a large pan and cook the onion and garlic gently for 5 minutes. Add the tomatoes and their juice, the stock, parsley, bouquet garni, salt and pepper to taste. Bring to the boil, then simmer for 10 minutes. Add the monkfish and red fish and cook for 5 minutes. Stir in the coley and cook for a further 5 minutes. Finally, add the plaice and simmer for 5 to 10 minutes or until all the fish is cooked.

Remove the bouquet garni and adjust the seasoning. Pour into a tureen and sprinkle with chopped parsley. Serve with thick slices of warm wholemeal bread.
SERVES 8

FISH PULAO

METRIC/IMPERIAL
1 tablespoon ground coriander
2 teaspoons ground cumin
½ teaspoon ground turmeric
½ teaspoon fenugreek
pinch of ground ginger
2 tablespoons polyunsaturated vegetable oil
750 g/1½-1¾ lb filleted white fish, cut into 5 cm/2 inch pieces
2 large onions, peeled and finely chopped
450 g/1 lb brown rice, washed and soaked for 1 hour in cold water
2 tablespoons desiccated coconut
2 tablespoons lemon juice

Mix the coriander, cumin, turmeric, fenugreek and ginger together. Heat 1 tablespoon of the oil in a large frying pan and fry the spice mixture for about 1 minute, then place the fish in the pan. Pour in just enough water to cover the fish. Simmer until the fish is cooked, then remove it carefully with a fish slice and keep warm. Reserve the liquid.

Meanwhile, fry the onions in the remaining oil until brown. Drain the rice and add it to the onions. Mix well, then add the reserved fish liquid, the coconut and lemon juice. Simmer gently until the rice is cooked, adding extra water during cooking when necessary (but make sure that, when the rice is tender, the liquid has been absorbed).

To serve, place the rice in a warm serving dish, and arrange the fish pieces on top.
SERVES 4 to 6

FISH YUCATAN STYLE

METRIC/IMPERIAL
4 large fish fillets
4 cloves garlic, peeled and crushed
1 teaspoon dried oregano
½ teaspoon ground cumin
salt
freshly ground pepper
4 tablespoons orange juice
120 ml/4 fl oz olive oil
2 tomatoes, skinned and chopped
1 onion, peeled and thinly sliced
½ small hot chilli, deseeded and chopped
chopped parsley or coriander, to garnish

Wipe over the fish fillets; skin and cut into serving-sized pieces. Arrange on a large plate or glass dish. Combine the garlic, oregano, cumin, salt and pepper to taste, and the orange juice, and pour over the fish pieces. Allow to marinate for 30 minutes.

Choose a flameproof baking dish just big enough to hold the fillets comfortably. Coat the bottom of the dish with half the oil. Arrange the fillets in the dish and pour over the marinade. Combine the tomatoes with the sliced onion and chopped chilli and spoon over the fish. Sprinkle with the remaining olive oil. Cover the dish with aluminium foil and simmer over a gentle heat for 20 minutes. Sprinkle the fish with chopped parsley or coriander and serve.
SERVES 4 to 6

HOT CHILLI FISH CURRY

METRIC/IMPERIAL
15 g/½ oz polyunsaturated margarine
1 tablespoon curry powder
1 teaspoon chilli powder
2 onions, peeled and chopped
1 clove garlic, peeled and crushed
600 ml/1 pint chicken stock
2 tablespoons tomato purée
3 tablespoons lemon juice
450 g/1 lb cooked white fish fillets, diced, or
225 g/8 oz peeled prawns
salt

Melt the margarine in a saucepan, add the curry and chilli powders and cook over a low heat for 1 minute. Add the onions and garlic and fry for 3 minutes. Stir in the stock, tomato purée and lemon juice. Cover and simmer for 1 hour. The sauce should be quite thick.

Stir in the fish and cook for a further 10 minutes; if using prawns, cook for 5 minutes only. Taste and add salt if required. Serve with rice.
SERVES 4

GEFILTE FISH

METRIC/IMPERIAL
1 slice of fresh white bread
water to soak
1 tablespoon polyunsaturated vegetable oil
1 large onion, peeled and finely chopped
1 carrot, peeled and grated
1 kg/2 lb mixed white fish fillets
2 tablespoons chopped parsley
salt
freshly ground black pepper
2 eggs
capers
300 ml/½ pint fish stock
Garnish:
flat-leaf parsley
lemon wedges

Soak the bread in the water for 15 minutes. Meanwhile, heat the oil in a saucepan and fry the onion and carrot for 3 minutes. Mince together the fish, onion, carrot and parsley. Season well with salt and pepper.

Squeeze the water out of the bread, and add the bread and eggs to the fish mixture. Mix well to incorporate all the ingredients thoroughly. Use your hands to form the mixture into balls the size of plums. Top each one with a caper.

Place the fish balls in a steamer, cover with a tight-fitting lid and steam over the fish stock for 30 minutes. Check the liquid level frequently and add more boiling stock if necessary.

Transfer the balls to a serving plate. Boil the stock to reduce until syrupy. Taste and adjust the seasoning, if necessary. Pour over the fish balls. Cool and place in the refrigerator to chill before serving. Garnish with sprigs of flat-leaf parsley and lemon wedges.
SERVES 4

GRILLED FISH AU FROMAGE

METRIC/IMPERIAL
4 × 150-175 g/5-6 oz steaks or portions of white
fish, skinned if necessary
salt
freshly ground black pepper
25 g/1 oz polyunsaturated margarine
1 teaspoon dried rosemary
100 g/4 oz finely grated Cheddar cheese, or a
mixture of Gruyère and Parmesan
1 tablespoon (scant) French mustard
2-3 tablespoons plain low-fat yogurt
2 firm tomatoes, sliced
watercress sprigs, to garnish

Wipe the fish with damp kitchen paper towels and season generously with salt and pepper. Preheat the grill and melt the margarine with half the rosemary in a shallow flameproof dish, large enough to hold the fish in a single layer. Turn the fish in the melted margarine, then grill under a moderate heat for about 4 to 5 minutes (under a low heat for 7 to 8 minutes, if the fish is still frozen).

Meanwhile, put the cheese, mustard and remaining rosemary into a basin and beat in enough yogurt to make a soft mixture. Turn the fish carefully, spread them evenly with the cheese mixture and continue grilling, very gently, for 5 to 6 minutes. When the surface is golden, but not overbrowned, arrange 2 slices of tomato on each portion and grill for a further minute.

Serve from the dish, garnished at the last moment with sprigs of watercress.
SERVES 4

HUNGARIAN FISH

METRIC/IMPERIAL
1.25 kg/2½ lb firm white fish fillets, skinned
salt
freshly ground black pepper
juice of ½ lemon
25 g/1 oz polyunsaturated margarine
2 onions, peeled and sliced
1 clove garlic, peeled and crushed
6 tomatoes, skinned, deseeded and sliced
1 tablespoon chopped herbs (e.g. dill, parsley,
fennel)
2 teaspoons paprika
150 ml/¼ pint soured cream
Garnish:
paprika
sprigs of fresh herbs

Season the fish with salt, pepper and lemon juice. Cut into bite-sized pieces and lay in a suitable bowl.

Heat the margarine and fry the onions and garlic until cooked but not brown. Stir in the tomatoes and herbs and season well with salt and pepper. Spoon over the fish. Mix the paprika with the soured cream and gently stir into the fish mixture. Cover the bowl with foil or greaseproof paper and tie down with string. Place in a steamer or covered saucepan half-filled with boiling water and steam for 20 minutes.

Transfer to a warmed serving dish. Sprinkle with paprika and sprigs of fresh herbs.
SERVES 4

SEAFOOD COCKTAIL SALAD

METRIC/IMPERIAL
4 scallops, dark beards removed
100 g/4 oz white fish
100 g/4 oz peeled prawns
shredded lettuce leaves
8 tomatoes, skinned and quartered
Sauce:
120 ml/4 fl oz reduced-calorie mayonnaise
1 dessertspoon tomato purée
1 teaspoon chopped basil
salt
freshly ground black pepper

Place the scallops and white fish in a saucepan. Poach in the minimum of water for about 4 to 5 minutes until tender. Drain and cool.

Flake the fish using a fork. Cut the scallops into small pieces. Add the prawns to the fish mixture. Mix the mayonnaise, tomato purée, basil, salt and pepper together, then stir into the fish.

Place the shredded lettuce on a serving dish and surround with the tomato quarters. Spoon the fish mixture into the centre of the dish.

SERVES 4

MARINATED SEAFOOD WITH ORANGES

METRIC/IMPERIAL
450 g/1 lb white fish fillets
225 g/8 oz scallops, dark beards removed
4 tablespoons polyunsaturated vegetable oil
1 small green pepper, cored and deseeded
2 large oranges, thinly peeled (reserve rind)
2 spring onions, trimmed and finely chopped
4 tablespoons vinaigrette
chopped parsley
Marinade:
5 tablespoons olive oil
5 tablespoons orange juice
1 tablespoon lime or lemon juice
1 tablespoon red wine vinegar
1½ teaspoons salt
freshly ground black pepper
2 cloves garlic, peeled and crushed
1 teaspoon grated root ginger
pinch of cayenne

Skin the fish fillets, cut them into strips about 10 × 3 cm/5 × 1¼ inches and remove any bones. Dry the fish and scallops with kitchen paper towels.

Heat the vegetable oil in a frying pan until it gives off a slight haze and lightly brown the fish strips, about 2 minutes each side. Using a slotted fish slice, remove the fish to a shallow serving dish. Add the scallops to the pan and cook on one side for 10 seconds, turn over and cook the other side for 10 seconds. Remove and add to the fish.

Cut the pepper and reserved orange rind into thin strips and sprinkle over the seafood with the chopped spring onions. Mix together all the marinade ingredients and pour over. Cover the dish with cling film and refrigerate overnight.

Next day, remove all white pith from the oranges and cut them into thick slices, removing any pips. Drizzle vinaigrette over the slices and chill, covered, for 1 hour. Arrange the orange slices round the marinated seafood, then sprinkle the seafood with chopped parsley. Serve chilled.

SERVES 4

SESAME FISH STEAKS

METRIC/IMPERIAL
3 large fish steaks or fillets
salt
25 g/1 oz polyunsaturated margarine
100 g/4 oz soft breadcrumbs
pinch of freshly ground pepper
4 tablespoons toasted sesame seeds
½ teaspoon fresh thyme, crumbled
1 teaspoon salt

Dry the fish with kitchen paper towels and place in a buttered baking dish. Sprinkle the steaks or fillets with a pinch of salt and dot each with 2 teaspoons of the margarine. Combine the remaining ingredients and sprinkle the breadcrumb mixture thickly over the steaks.

Bake, uncovered, in a preheated moderate oven (180°C/350°F, Gas Mark 4) for 15 to 20 minutes or until the fish flakes easily when tested with a fork. Serve with hot bread and green salad.

SERVES 6

SPICED FISH CASSEROLE

METRIC/IMPERIAL
3 large tomatoes, skinned and sliced
2 celery stalks, finely chopped
1 clove garlic, peeled and crushed
50 g/2 oz mushrooms, wiped and sliced
salt
freshly ground black pepper
pinch of grated nutmeg
1 teaspoon chopped parsley
1 teaspoon chopped basil
1 bay leaf
1 onion, peeled and sliced
1 carrot, peeled and sliced
750 g/1½ lb cod fillets
3 tablespoons wine vinegar
150 ml/¼ pint water

Arrange half the tomato slices in a baking dish and cover with the celery, garlic and mushrooms. Season well with salt and pepper, then sprinkle with the nutmeg and parsley. Add the basil and the bay leaf and top with the onion and carrot.

Arrange the fish on top of this mixture, then cover with the remaining tomato slices. Pour on the vinegar and water. Cover and bake in a preheated moderate oven (180°C/350°F, Gas Mark 4) for 40 minutes. Serve hot.

SERVES 4

SEAFOOD BROCHETTES

METRIC/IMPERIAL
450 g/1 lb cod fillet, skinned and cut into
2.5 cm/1 inch cubes
12 large prawns, unpeeled
1 small green pepper, cored, deseeded and cut
into 2 cm/¾ inch pieces
4 firm tomatoes, quartered
8 button mushrooms, wiped and trimmed
8 bay leaves
2 tablespoons fresh lime juice
3 teaspoons finely chopped fresh tarragon or
1 teaspoon dried tarragon

Preheat the grill to moderate.

Thread the cod on to 4 greased kebab skewers
with the prawns, green pepper, tomatoes, mushrooms and bay leaves. Sprinkle the brochettes
with a little lime juice and the tarragon.

Cook under the grill for 10 minutes, turning
frequently and basting with the remaining lime
juice, until the cod is cooked through and flakes
easily when pierced with a sharp knife.

Transfer the brochettes to a heated serving dish
and serve with brown rice and a green salad.
SERVES 4

MEDITERRANEAN FISH STEW

METRIC/IMPERIAL
3 tablespoons olive oil
2 onions, peeled and sliced
2 cloves garlic, peeled and crushed
4 large tomatoes, skinned and chopped
150 ml/¼ pint water
150 ml/¼ pint white wine
1 bay leaf
1 teaspoon salt
½ teaspoon pepper
750 g/1½ lb cod fillet, skinned and boned
600 ml/1 pint mussels
175 g/6 oz peeled prawns
1 tablespoon chopped parsley

Heat the oil in a pan, add the onions and fry until
softened. Add the garlic, tomatoes, half the
water, the wine, bay leaf, salt and pepper. Simmer
for 15 minutes.

Cut the cod into 5 cm/2 inch squares, add to the
pan and simmer for 15 minutes.

Scrub the mussels thoroughly, pulling off the
beard. Discard any which are open and do not

close when tapped. Put them into a heavy pan
with the remaining water, cover and cook over a
high heat for 5 minutes until they have opened;
discard any that do not.

Discard the top shell from each mussel. Add the
mussels with their liquid and the prawns to the
stew. Cook for a further 3 minutes. Turn into a
warmed serving dish and sprinkle with the
parsley. Serve with crusty wholemeal bread.
SERVES 4 to 6

STEAMED COD ON RED PEPPER SAUCE

METRIC/IMPERIAL
juice of 1 lemon
1 tablespoon olive oil
1 shallot, finely chopped
2 parsley sprigs
salt
freshly ground black pepper
4 × 200-225 g/7-8 oz cod steaks
2 red peppers
150 ml/¼ pint fish stock

Mix the lemon juice, oil, shallot and parsley sprigs
in a shallow dish. Season well with salt and pepper. Add the cod steaks, cover with the marinade
and leave for up to 2 hours, turning occasionally.

Scorch the red peppers on the gas or electric
ring until the skin is black all over. Peel away the
burnt skin and rinse under clean water. Deseed
and roughly chop one pepper and half of the
second pepper, then cut the remaining half into
thin strips and reserve for the garnish.

Place the fish stock and chopped peppers in a
saucepan and bring to the boil. Lay a piece of wet
greaseproof paper in a steamer compartment and
arrange the cod steaks on top. Cover with a tight-
fitting lid. Steam over the stock for 8 minutes. Remove the cooked fish and keep warm. Blend the
peppers and stock in a blender until smooth. Taste
and adjust the seasoning, if necessary.

Arrange the red pepper sauce on 4 individual
warmed plates. Top with the fish, sprinkle with
thin strips of red pepper, and serve at once.
SERVES 4

NORWEGIAN BRAISED FISH

METRIC/IMPERIAL

4 medium potatoes, peeled and thinly sliced
salt
25 g/1 oz onion, peeled and chopped
1 green pepper, cored, deseeded and cut into strips
4 tomatoes, skinned and sliced
4 × 175 g/6 oz cod steaks
2 tablespoons tomato purée
freshly ground black pepper

Place the potato slices in a saucepan of salted water. Bring to the boil, cover and simmer for about 10 minutes. Drain the potatoes, reserving the cooking water, and arrange them on the base of a casserole dish. Sprinkle over the chopped onion. Add the pepper and tomato slices to the dish. Place the cod steaks on top.

Mix the tomato purée and about 300 ml/½ pint potato cooking water together and pour over the fish; it should come about halfway up the casserole dish. Add salt and pepper.

Cover and cook in a preheated moderately hot oven (200°C/400°F, Gas Mark 6) for about 30 minutes until the fish is tender.

SERVES 4

PORTUGUESE FISH

METRIC/IMPERIAL

4 × 100 g/4 oz pieces white fish (e.g. cod, coley, halibut)
Sauce:
8 tomatoes, skinned and chopped
1 onion, peeled and finely chopped
½ clove garlic, peeled and crushed
1 bay leaf
salt
freshly ground black pepper
1 tablespoon tomato juice
1 tablespoon wine vinegar

To make the sauce, put all the sauce ingredients in a heavy-based saucepan and simmer for 1 hour, uncovered. If the liquid reduces too quickly, add a little more tomato juice.

Meanwhile, place the fish in a wide shallow pan, and poach it in the minimum of water for about 15 minutes until tender. Arrange the fish on a serving dish and spoon the sauce over.

SERVES 4

FISH IN A PACKET

METRIC/IMPERIAL

450 g/1 lb cod fillets
2 tablespoons polyunsaturated vegetable oil
2 tablespoons lemon juice
salt
freshly ground black pepper
2 tomatoes, sliced
4 fennel sprigs

Cut the fish into 4 pieces. Cut out 4 × 30 cm/12 inch squares of foil and brush them liberally with oil. Place one piece of fish on each square of foil, then sprinkle with the remaining oil, the lemon juice and salt and pepper to taste. Place 2 tomato slices on each piece of fish, then top each with a fennel sprig.

Fold the foil around each fish to form a parcel, then place the parcels on a baking sheet. Bake in a preheated moderate oven (180°C/350°F, Gas Mark 4) for 30 minutes.

Unwrap each parcel carefully, lift the fish out on to warmed serving plates, pour over the cooking juices and serve hot.

SERVES 4

FISH NIÇOISE

METRIC/IMPERIAL

4 × 225 g/8 oz cod fillets, skinned
salt
freshly ground black pepper
150 ml/¼ pint dry white wine
150 ml/¼ pint water
slice of onion
bouquet garni
1 clove garlic, peeled and crushed
25 g/1 oz polyunsaturated margarine
25 g/1 oz plain unbleached white flour
150 ml/¼ pint skimmed milk
2 large tomatoes, skinned, deseeded and diced
1 pepper, cored, deseeded and finely chopped
Garnish:
12 black olives, stoned
parsley sprigs

Preheat the oven to 180°C/350°F, Gas Mark 4. Rinse and dry the cod, lay it in an ovenproof dish, and add salt and pepper. Pour over the wine and water, adding the onion, bouquet garni and garlic. Cover with oiled greaseproof paper and poach in the oven for 20 minutes. Drain and reserve the liquid; keep the fish hot.

Melt the margarine, stir in the flour and cook for 1 minute. Remove from the heat and gradually stir in 300 ml/½ pint of the fish liquid and the milk. Return to the heat and bring to the boil, stirring, until thickened. Simmer for 2 to 3 minutes; taste and adjust the seasoning. Add the tomato and pepper and reheat to boiling. Pour over the fish. Garnish with olives and parsley.
SERVES 4

COLOURFUL FISH KEBABS

METRIC/IMPERIAL
1 small green pepper, cored, deseeded and
roughly chopped
450 g/1 lb cod, cut into small cubes
4 firm tomatoes, quartered
12 grapes, deseeded
8 button mushrooms, wiped and trimmed
8 bay leaves
lemon juice
2 teaspoons chopped fresh tarragon or
1 teaspoon dried tarragon

Place the chopped peppers in a saucepan and simmer in the minimum of water for 10 minutes, then drain.
Thread the fish cubes on to skewers with the tomato quarters, grapes, mushrooms, pieces of pepper and bay leaves.
Sprinkle the kebabs with lemon juice and tarragon. Place under a preheated moderate grill for about 10 minutes until the fish is cooked, turning frequently and sprinkling with more lemon juice, if necessary.
SERVES 4

COD AND PINEAPPLE KEBABS

METRIC/IMPERIAL
1 × 425 g/15 oz can pineapple chunks
120 ml/4 fl oz light soy sauce
4 tablespoons dry sherry
1 tablespoon grated fresh root ginger
1 teaspoon dry mustard
1 clove garlic, peeled and crushed
1 kg/2 lb cod, cut into 2.5 cm/1 inch cubes
1 green pepper, cored, deseeded and cut into
2.5 cm/1 inch squares

Drain the pineapple, reserving 4 tablespoons of the liquid. Mix the reserved liquid with the soy sauce, sherry, ginger, mustard and garlic in a shallow dish. Add the fish cubes and turn to coat. Cover and leave to marinate for at least an hour.
Drain the fish cubes, reserving the marinade. Thread the fish cubes, pineapple and green pepper on to skewers. Cook under a preheated grill (or over charcoal) 10 to 13 cm/4 to 5 inches from the source of heat, for 8 to 10 minutes, or until the fish flakes easily when tested with a fork. Turn and baste with the marinade during cooking. Serve hot with rice.
SERVES 6

BRAISED FISH WITH BLACK BEAN SAUCE

METRIC/IMPERIAL
3 tablespoons black beans
2 tablespoons polyunsaturated vegetable oil
2 spring onions, chopped
1 × 2.5 cm/1 inch piece root ginger, peeled and
finely chopped
1 small red pepper, cored, deseeded and diced
2 celery stalks, chopped
2 tablespoons soy sauce
2 tablespoons dry sherry
4 cod or haddock cutlets, each weighing
150 g/5 oz
shredded spring onion, to garnish

Soak the black beans in warm water for 10 minutes, then drain.
Heat the oil in a wok or deep frying pan, add the spring onions, ginger, red pepper and celery and stir-fry for 1 minute. Stir in the soy sauce and sherry. Place the fish on top of the vegetables and simmer for 5 to 10 minutes until almost tender, depending on the thickness of the fish. Spoon over the black beans and cook for 2 minutes.
Arrange the fish on a warmed serving dish and spoon the sauce over. Serve hot, garnished with spring onion.
SERVES 4

COD AND BEAN PIE

METRIC/IMPERIAL
175 g/6 oz haricot beans, soaked overnight in cold water
2 medium onions, peeled and chopped
1 kg/2 lb cod or other white fish fillets, skinned and cut into small pieces
4 rashers lean bacon, derinded and cut into strips
salt
freshly ground black pepper
pinch of dried thyme
pinch of dried marjoram
600 ml/1 pint skimmed milk or milk and fish stock, mixed
450 g/1 lb potatoes, peeled and very thinly sliced

Drain the haricot beans, cover with fresh cold water and bring to the boil. Simmer for 1½ hours or until tender, then drain.

Put the onions into a greased casserole and cover with the fish and strips of bacon. Season to taste and add the herbs. Add a layer of cooked beans and pour in the milk or milk and stock. Top with the potatoes which should overlap and be arranged to form an attractive crust. Bake in a preheated moderate oven (180°C/350°F, Gas Mark 4) for about 40 minutes or until the potatoes are cooked and golden brown.
SERVES 6

COD AND BACON KEBABS

METRIC/IMPERIAL
450 g/1 lb cod fillet, skinned and cut into 5 cm/2 inch squares
salt
freshly ground black pepper
2 tablespoons lemon juice
4 tablespoons corn oil
1 teaspoon chopped parsley
1 teaspoon chopped marjoram (optional)
1 clove garlic, peeled and crushed
4 lean bacon rashers
1 green pepper, cored and deseeded
4 small tomatoes

Place the fish in a shallow dish and sprinkle liberally with salt and pepper. Mix together the lemon juice, oil, parsley, marjoram and garlic and pour over the fish. Cover and leave to marinate in a cool place for about 4 hours.

Cut the bacon rashers and green pepper into 5 cm/2 inch squares. Drain the fish, reserving the marinade. Thread alternate pieces of fish, bacon and green pepper on to kebab skewers. Press the pieces together firmly and place a whole tomato on the end of each skewer.

Place on a grill rack and baste with the marinade. Cook under a preheated moderate grill for 8 to 10 minutes until the fish is tender and the green pepper softened. Turn the skewers and brush with the oil mixture frequently during cooking.

Serve the kebabs hot, with a crisp green salad and brown rice or wholemeal bread.
SERVES 4

CHILLED FISH CURRY

METRIC/IMPERIAL
350 g/12 oz thick cod fillet
350 g/12 oz salmon fillet
150 ml/¼ pint fish stock
150 ml/¼ pint dry white wine
3 spring onions, trimmed and finely chopped
1 tablespoon olive oil
1 tablespoon curry powder
1 tablespoon mango chutney
150 ml/¼ pint plain low-fat yogurt
salt
freshly ground black pepper
1 medium ripe mango, peeled, deseeded and chopped
Garnish:
lime wedges
mint sprigs

Put the cod and salmon fillet into a deep pan; add the fish stock and white wine. Cover and poach gently for 10 minutes.

Lift the fish out carefully with a slotted spoon. Skin and flake it coarsely while it is still warm; reserve the cooking liquid.

Sauté the spring onions gently in the oil for 1 minute. Add the curry powder and cook for a further minute. Stir in 150 ml/¼ pint of the fish cooking liquid and bring to the boil, then cool.

Mix the cooled curry sauce with the chutney, yogurt, and salt and pepper to taste; stir in the fish carefully, together with the mango. Cover the prepared fish curry and chill in the refrigerator for at least 4 hours.

Spoon on to a shallow serving dish and garnish with wedges of lime and sprigs of fresh mint. Serve with cooked brown rice, mixed with a light oil and vinegar dressing, and chilled.
SERVES 4

COD IN TOMATO SAUCE

METRIC/IMPERIAL
4 cod steaks, fresh or frozen
Tomato sauce:
4 tablespoons olive oil
450 g/1 lb tomatoes, skinned and chopped
1 clove garlic, peeled and crushed
1 tablespoon chopped parsley
4 tablespoons dry white wine
salt
freshly ground black pepper

First make the tomato sauce. Heat the oil in a pan, add the tomatoes, garlic, parsley, wine, and salt and pepper to taste. Simmer for 7 to 10 minutes, stirring occasionally.

Pour half the sauce into a shallow casserole dish, lay the fish on top and cover with the remaining sauce. Cover and cook in a preheated moderately hot oven (190°C/375°F, Gas Mark 5) for 20 to 25 minutes until cooked. Turn on to a warmed dish and serve immediately.
SERVES 4

SMOKED COD JUMBLE

METRIC/IMPERIAL
225 g/8 oz wholemeal macaroni
25 g/1 oz polyunsaturated margarine
3 tablespoons skimmed milk
350 g/12 oz smoked cod or haddock fillets, skinned and cut into 2.5 cm/1 inch cubes
4 tomatoes, skinned and chopped
6 spring onions, trimmed and chopped
salt
freshly ground black pepper

Cook the macaroni for 10 to 15 minutes in plenty of boiling, slightly salted water. Drain well.

Melt the margarine in a saucepan. Add the milk and fish, then cover and cook very gently for 10 minutes, or until the fish is tender. Remove the lid, add the cooked macaroni, tomatoes and spring onions. Season with salt and pepper. Stir the mixture lightly to avoid breaking up the fish, and reheat well.
SERVES 4

HADDOCK IN TOMATO SAUCE

METRIC/IMPERIAL
450 g/1 lb haddock fillets
1 teaspoon salt
½ teaspoon freshly ground black pepper
Tomato sauce:
1 tablespoon polyunsaturated vegetable oil
1 onion, peeled and finely chopped
1 green pepper, cored, deseeded and finely chopped
2 celery stalks, finely chopped
1 clove garlic, peeled and crushed
1 teaspoon chilli powder
1 bay leaf
1 tablespoon Worcestershire sauce
1 × 450 g/1 lb can tomatoes

Cut the fish into 4 pieces, then place in a lightly oiled shallow baking dish. Sprinkle with the salt and pepper, then chill for 30 minutes.

Meanwhile, heat the oil in a pan. Add the onion, green pepper, celery and garlic and fry gently for 5 minutes, stirring occasionally. Add the remaining ingredients and continue cooking gently for 10 minutes, stirring well.

Work the mixture through a sieve, taste and adjust the seasoning, then pour over the fish. Bake in a preheated moderate oven (180°C/350°F, Gas Mark 4) for 45 minutes or until the fish is cooked.
SERVES 4

SUMMER FISH SALAD

METRIC/IMPERIAL
450 g/1 lb haddock or cod fillets
1 onion, peeled
450 ml/¾ pint water
1 teaspoon salt
4 tablespoons reduced-calorie mayonnaise
1 teaspoon chopped parsley
1 teaspoon grated onion
1 teaspoon Worcestershire sauce
¼ teaspoon freshly ground black pepper
2 celery stalks, finely chopped
1 dessert apple, peeled, cored and diced
½ cucumber, peeled and diced
Garnish:
1 lettuce, shredded
1 hard-boiled egg, shelled and finely chopped

Put the fish in a pan with the onion, water and salt. Bring to the boil, then lower the heat and poach gently for 25 minutes or until the fish is tender. Drain off the water, then flake the fish into a serving bowl, discarding the skin and any bones. Leave the fish to cool.

Mix together the mayonnaise, parsley, onion, Worcestershire sauce and pepper. Add the celery, apple, cucumber and mayonnaise mixture to the fish and fold gently to mix.

Arrange a border of shredded lettuce around the edge of the bowl and sprinkle the chopped egg in the middle.

SERVES 4

CURRIED HADDOCK CRUMBLE

METRIC/IMPERIAL
500 g/1¼ lb haddock or other white fish
300 ml/½ pint skimmed milk
25 g/1 oz polyunsaturated margarine
1 small onion, peeled and chopped
2 teaspoons mild curry powder
25 g/1 oz plain wholemeal flour
25 g/1 oz sultanas
4 tablespoons cooked sweetcorn
1 tablespoon mango chutney
salt
freshly ground black pepper
Topping:
40 g/1½ oz porridge oats
50 g/2 oz plain wholemeal flour
1 tablespoon chopped parsley
50 g/2 oz polyunsaturated margarine

Place the fish and milk in a shallow pan and poach for 10 to 15 minutes. Drain the liquid and reserve. Remove any skin and bones, then flake the fish. Preheat the oven to 180°C/350°F, Gas Mark 4. Melt the margarine in a pan and sauté the onion for 3 minutes. Add the curry powder and cook for 1 minute, then stir in the flour and cook for a further minute.

Remove from the heat and gradually blend in the reserved milk. Heat, stirring, until the sauce thickens. Add the sultanas, sweetcorn, chutney and a little salt and pepper. Put the flaked fish in a greased 1.2 litre/2 pint ovenproof dish and pour over the sauce.

To make the topping, place the oats, flour, parsley and margarine in a bowl. Using a fork, mix the margarine into the dry ingredients. Season to taste and spoon the mixture over the fish. Cook in the oven for 40 minutes.

SERVES 4

HADDOCK CHARLOTTE

METRIC/IMPERIAL
450 g/1 lb haddock
175 g/6 oz canned sweetcorn, drained
1 large onion, peeled and chopped
50 g/2 oz button mushrooms, sliced
1 tablespoon chopped parsley
300 ml/½ pint fish stock or water
salt
freshly ground black pepper
25 g/1 oz polyunsaturated margarine
4 slices wholemeal bread

Cut the haddock into small pieces and arrange in a casserole or soufflé dish. Stir in the sweetcorn, onion, mushrooms, parsley, stock or water, and salt and pepper to taste.

Spread a little margarine on to the bread slices, cut into quarters and arrange on top of the fish mixture. Place in a preheated moderately hot oven (190°C/375°F, Gas Mark 5) and bake for 40 to 45 minutes or until the fish is cooked and the bread topping browned. Serve immediately.

SERVES 4

STUFFED HADDOCK

METRIC/IMPERIAL
2 haddock fillets, about 350 g/12 oz each
2 slices wholemeal bread, crumbled
3 tablespoons finely chopped parsley
¼ teaspoon finely grated lemon rind
½ teaspoon thyme
½ teaspoon salt
freshly ground white pepper
25 g/1 oz polyunsaturated margarine, melted
skimmed milk
2 large tomatoes, sliced

Place one haddock fillet, skin side down, in a greased shallow heatproof dish.

Make a stuffing by combining the breadcrumbs with 1 tablespoon of the parsley, the lemon rind, thyme, salt and pepper, and binding loosely with 15 g/½ oz of the margarine and a little milk. Cover the fish with the stuffing and put the second fillet, skin side up, on top. Arrange a line of tomato slices along the centre and sprinkle with the remaining parsley. Coat with the remaining margarine and bake, uncovered, in a preheated moderate oven (180°C/350°F, Gas Mark 4) for 40 minutes.

SERVES 4

SMOKED HADDOCK AND CHEESE BAKE

METRIC/IMPERIAL
450 g/1 lb smoked haddock fillets
25 g/1 oz grated Parmesan cheese
salt
freshly ground white pepper
150 ml/¼ pint plain low-fat yogurt
300 ml/½ pint skimmed milk
2 eggs, beaten
1 tablespoon chopped parsley

Put the fish in a pan with just enough water to cover. Bring to the boil, then lower the heat and poach gently for 15 minutes or until the fish is tender. Drain off the water, then place the fish in a baking dish.

Sprinkle the cheese and salt and pepper to taste over the fish. Put the remaining ingredients in a bowl, mix well, then pour over the fish.

Stand the dish in a roasting tin and pour in enough water to come 2.5 cm/1 inch up the sides of the pan. Bake in a preheated moderate oven (180°C/350°F, Gas Mark 4) for 40 minutes.
SERVES 4

SMOKED HADDOCK AND YOGURT MOUSSE

METRIC/IMPERIAL
225 g/8 oz smoked haddock fillets
300 ml/½ pint plain low-fat yogurt
2 hard-boiled eggs, shelled
finely grated rind of ½ lemon
2 teaspoons lemon juice
2 teaspoons powdered gelatine
2 tablespoons water
salt
freshly ground white pepper
paprika, to garnish

Poach the haddock in water to cover for 10 minutes. Drain well, then remove the skin and any bones and flake the flesh finely into a bowl. Add the yogurt and mix gently together. Chop 1 egg finely and add to the fish mixture with the lemon rind.

Put the lemon juice, gelatine and water in a small cup. Stand the cup in a pan of hot water and stir well until the gelatine becomes syrupy. Remove from the heat and cool for 2 minutes.

Stir the gelatine into the fish mixture, add salt and pepper to taste, then divide the mixture equally between 4 individual ramekins. Chill in the refrigerator for 1 hour.

Slice the remaining egg and use to decorate each ramekin, then sprinkle with paprika to garnish.
SERVES 4

SMOKED HADDOCK FLAN

METRIC/IMPERIAL
wholemeal pastry made with 175 g/6 oz flour
(see page 334)
225 g/8 oz smoked haddock fillets
150 ml/¼ pint water
juice of 1 lemon
25 g/1 oz polyunsaturated margarine
1 small onion, peeled and chopped
50 g/2 oz button mushrooms, wiped and sliced
2 eggs, beaten
3 tablespoons single cream
100 g/4 oz cottage cheese
1 tablespoon chopped parsley
salt
freshly ground white pepper
25 g/1 oz grated Parmesan cheese
Garnish:
parsley sprig
tomato slices

Roll out the pastry dough on a lightly floured surface and use to line a 20 cm/8 inch flan ring placed on a baking sheet. Prick the base lightly with a fork, cover with foil or greaseproof paper, then weigh down with baking beans or rice. Bake blind in a preheated moderately hot oven (200°C/400°F, Gas Mark 6) for 15 minutes, then remove the beans or rice and the foil or paper.

Meanwhile, put the fish in a pan with the water and half the lemon juice and poach gently for 15 minutes until the fish is tender. Drain off the water, then flake the fish into a bowl, discarding the skin and any bones.

Melt the margarine in a pan, add the onion and mushrooms and fry gently for 3 minutes, stirring occasionally. Add to the fish, and mix well, then spread the mixture in the flan case.

Put the eggs, cream, cottage cheese, parsley, remaining lemon juice and salt and pepper to taste in a bowl. Beat well and pour over the fish. Sprinkle with the Parmesan cheese.

Bake in a preheated moderately hot oven (190°C/375°F, Gas Mark 5) for 40 minutes. Garnish with the parsley sprig and tomato slices, and serve hot.
SERVES 4

SMOKED HADDOCK KEDGEREE

METRIC/IMPERIAL
350 g/12 oz smoked haddock
75 g/3 oz long-grain rice
salt
225 g/8 oz peas
1 tablespoon chopped onion
2 hard-boiled eggs, shelled and chopped
1 teaspoon curry paste
salt
freshly ground black pepper
chopped parsley, to garnish

Place the haddock in a saucepan. Poach in the minimum of water for about 12 minutes until tender, then drain and flake into small pieces.

Meanwhile, cook the rice in boiling salted water for about 12 minutes, then drain. Cook the peas and chopped onion in boiling salted water for about 6 minutes, then drain.

Mix the fish, rice, peas, onion, chopped hard-boiled eggs and curry paste together, and add salt and pepper to taste. Serve garnished with chopped fresh parsley.
SERVES 4

SEAFOOD SALAD WITH DILL

METRIC/IMPERIAL
450 g/1 lb smoked haddock fillets
600 ml/1 pint water
1 bay leaf
1 small onion, peeled and sliced
1 small carrot, peeled and sliced
4 black peppercorns
225 g/8 oz peeled prawns
120 ml/4 fl oz polyunsaturated vegetable oil
3 tablespoons wine vinegar
freshly ground black pepper
1 lettuce
1 bunch watercress, trimmed
1 tablespoon chopped parsley
2 tablespoons chopped dill

Put the fish in a pan with the water, bay leaf, onion, carrot and peppercorns. Bring to the boil, then lower the heat and poach gently for 15 minutes or until the fish is tender. Drain off the water, then flake the fish into a bowl, discarding the skin and any bones.

Add the prawns to the haddock. Mix together

the oil, vinegar and black pepper and pour over the fish. Chill in the refrigerator for 2 hours.

Arrange a bed of lettuce leaves in a serving bowl, then arrange the watercress on top. Drain the fish, place in the centre of the bowl and sprinkle generously with parsley and dill.
SERVES 4

SMOKED HADDOCK PANCAKES

METRIC/IMPERIAL
polyunsaturated vegetable oil for frying
wholemeal pancake batter made with 100 g/4 oz
   wholemeal flour (see page 292)
Filling:
450 g/1 lb smoked haddock fillets
300 ml/½ pint skimmed milk
40 g/1½ oz polyunsaturated margarine
40 g/1½ oz wholemeal flour
2 hard-boiled eggs, shelled and chopped
salt
freshly ground black pepper
25 g/1 oz polyunsaturated margarine, melted
25 g/1 oz grated Parmesan cheese

Brush a 20 cm/8 inch non-stick frying pan with a little oil. Pour in enough batter to cover the bottom and tilt the pan to coat it evenly. Cook until the underside is brown, then turn over and cook for 10 seconds.

Transfer to a plate and keep warm. Continue cooking pancakes until all the batter is used up.

Place the haddock in a pan, add the milk, cover and bring to the boil. Simmer for 5 minutes. Leave the fish to cool slightly in the pan, then lift out with a fish slice. Remove the skin and flake, discarding any bones. Strain the liquid and make up to 300 ml/½ pint with extra milk if necessary; keep on one side.

Melt the margarine in a pan, remove from the heat and stir in the flour. Pour in the reserved liquid and stir until blended. Return to the heat and bring to the boil, stirring, until thickened. Add the eggs, fish, and salt and pepper to taste.

Place a spoonful of filling on each pancake, roll up and place in an oiled shallow ovenproof dish. Brush with the melted margarine and sprinkle with the Parmesan cheese. Cook in a preheated moderately hot oven (190°C/375°F, Gas Mark 5) for 15 minutes until crisp. Serve immediately.
SERVES 4 to 6

POACHED HADDOCK AND EGGS

METRIC/IMPERIAL
450 g/1 lb smoked haddock fillets, cut into
4 pieces
600 ml/1 pint water
4 eggs
freshly ground black pepper
25 g/1 oz polyunsaturated margarine

Put the fish in a frying pan and cover with the water. Bring slowly to the boil, then simmer for about 10 minutes or until the fish is tender but not breaking up. Transfer with a slotted spoon to warmed serving plates and keep hot.

Bring the cooking liquid to the boil. Using a spoon, stir the water very quickly to create a 'whirlpool'. Crack one egg into a cup, then slide it carefully into the water. Repeat with the remaining eggs. Simmer for 3 minutes until each egg is firmly set.

Meanwhile, sprinkle the fish with pepper to taste and put a little margarine on each piece. Keep the dishes hot.

Remove the eggs from the pan with a slotted spoon and place one on each piece of fish. Serve immediately.
SERVES 4

PINEAPPLE HALIBUT

METRIC/IMPERIAL
4 × 100 g/4 oz halibut steaks
250 ml/8 fl oz unsweetened pineapple juice
2 teaspoons cornflour
1 tablespoon water
salt
freshly ground black pepper

Put the halibut steaks in a wide shallow pan and add the pineapple juice. Simmer for about 15 minutes until the fish is tender. Place the fish on a heated serving dish and keep warm.

Blend the cornflour with the water and add to the pineapple juice. Cook for 3 minutes. Add a little more pineapple juice if the sauce is too thick, and season with salt and pepper to taste.

Pour the pineapple sauce over the halibut or serve separately.
SERVES 4

HALIBUT WITH TARRAGON

METRIC/IMPERIAL
4 × 175 g/6 oz halibut or cod steaks
grated rind and juice of 2-3 lemons
few tarragon sprigs
salt
freshly ground black pepper

Place the halibut in a large shallow dish. Sprinkle over the lemon rind and juice, tarragon leaves, salt and pepper. Turn the fish to coat with the lemon and herb mixture. Cover and leave to marinate for about 3 hours.

Place each piece of fish on a sheet of foil large enough to enclose it. Spoon over a little of the marinade and wrap up the fish. Cook in a pre-heated moderately hot oven (200°C/400°F, Gas Mark 6) for about 15 to 20 minutes, depending on the thickness of the halibut. Unwrap and serve on a heated dish.
SERVES 4

STUFFED FILLETS OF PLAICE

METRIC/IMPERIAL
4 plaice fillets, cut in half and skinned
2 tablespoons olive oil
1 tablespoon white wine vinegar
10 small basil leaves
salt
freshly ground black pepper
350 g/12 oz courgettes, finely sliced
450 g/1 lb ripe tomatoes, skinned, deseeded and
finely sliced
600 ml/1 pint court bouillon
juice of 2 lemons
basil sprigs, to garnish

Lay the fillets flat in a shallow dish with the oil and vinegar. Roughly chop two of the basil leaves and sprinkle over the fish. Season well with salt and pepper and marinate for up to 2 hours.

Meanwhile, place the courgettes in a colander and sprinkle with salt. Leave for 30 minutes. Rinse well under running cold water to remove all the salt and pat dry with absorbent kitchen paper. Mix together a quarter of the tomato and courgette slices in a bowl and season well.

Remove the fillets from the marinade and gently pat dry. Place 1 teaspoon of the tomato and courgette mixture and 1 basil leaf at one end of each fillet. Season well. Roll up tightly and place side by side in a steamer compartment. Bring the court bouillon to the boil. Cover the plaice with a tight-fitting lid and steam over the court bouillon for 6 to 8 minutes.

Heat the remaining courgette and tomato slices in a saucepan but do not allow them to stew. Check and adjust the seasoning. Divide the mixture between 4 individual plates. Arrange the stuffed plaice on top, and spoon on a little lemon juice. Garnish with basil sprigs.
SERVES 4

STEAMED SWEET AND SOUR FISH

METRIC/IMPERIAL
1 large whole plaice, cleaned
salt
1 × 5 cm/2 inch piece root ginger, peeled and shredded
3 spring onions, sliced
Sauce:
150 ml/¼ pint fish or chicken stock
1 tablespoon soy sauce
1 tablespoon sugar
1 tablespoon wine vinegar
1 tablespoon dry sherry
1 tablespoon tomato purée
1 teaspoon chilli sauce
pinch of salt
1 tablespoon cornflour
Garnish:
coriander leaves
tomato flowers

Score the fish by making 3 diagonal cuts on each side. Rub the fish with salt and sprinkle with the ginger and spring onions. Put on an ovenproof plate and place in a steamer. Steam for 12 to 15 minutes until tender.

Meanwhile, make the sauce. Mix all the ingredients, except the cornflour, together in a small saucepan, bring to the boil and cook for 1 minute. Blend the cornflour with 2 tablespoons water and stir into the sauce. Cook, stirring, until thickened.

Carefully lift the plaice on to a warmed serving dish. Spoon over the sauce and serve at once, garnished with coriander and tomato flowers.
SERVES 4

SWEDISH BAKED FISH

METRIC/IMPERIAL
4 halibut fillets
1 onion, peeled and sliced
4 tablespoons chopped parsley
450 ml/¾ pint tomato juice
salt
freshly ground black pepper

Put the fish in a greased baking dish. Arrange the onion slices on top and sprinkle with half the parsley. Pour on the tomato juice, season well with salt and pepper, then cover with a large sheet of aluminium foil.

Bake in a preheated moderately hot oven (200°C/400°F, Gas Mark 6) for 30 minutes or until the fish is cooked. Sprinkle with the remaining parsley and serve hot.
SERVES 4

CHINESE PLAICE

METRIC/IMPERIAL
8 medium plaice fillets
3 tablespoons apple juice
1 tablespoon soy sauce
Stuffing:
75 g/3 oz fresh wholemeal breadcrumbs
1-2 cloves garlic, peeled and crushed
1 small onion, peeled and grated
50 g/2 oz ground almonds
½ tablespoon ground ginger
3 tablespoons apple juice
1 tablespoon soy sauce
freshly ground black pepper
Garnish:
chervil leaves
diamonds of red pepper

Heat the oven to 180°C/350°F, Gas Mark 4. In a bowl, blend together the stuffing ingredients.

Remove any dark skin from the plaice and lay all the fillets, flesh side down, on a board. Divide the stuffing between them and roll up. Secure with cocktail sticks.

Place them in a shallow, greased ovenproof dish, packing close together. Mix together the apple juice and soy sauce and pour over the plaice. Cover the dish with foil and cook in the oven for 30 minutes.

Serve hot, garnished with chervil leaves and red pepper diamonds.
SERVES 4

PAPER-WRAPPED FISH

METRIC/IMPERIAL
4 plaice or sole fillets, each weighing 100 g/4 oz
pinch of salt
2 tablespoons dry sherry
1 tablespoon polyunsaturated vegetable oil
2 tablespoons shredded spring onion
2 tablespoons shredded root ginger
polyunsaturated vegetable oil for deep-frying
Garnish:
spring onion flowers (made by shredding
trimmed spring onions almost completely and
immersing in iced water)

Cut the fish fillets into 2.5 cm/1 inch squares.
Sprinkle with salt and toss in the sherry.
Cut out 15 cm/6 inch squares of greaseproof
paper and brush with the oil. Place a piece of fish
on each square of paper and arrange some spring
onion and ginger on top. Fold into envelopes,
tucking in the flaps to secure.
Heat the oil in a wok or deep-fryer to 180°C/
350°F. Deep-fry the wrapped fish for 3 minutes.
Drain on kitchen paper and arrange on a warmed
serving dish. Garnish with spring onion flowers
and serve immediately. Each person unwraps his
own parcel.
SERVES 4

SOLE FLORENTINE

METRIC/IMPERIAL
4 small lemon or Dover sole
3 tablespoons lemon juice
50 g/2 oz polyunsaturated margarine
100 g/4 oz cottage cheese
150 ml/¼ pint skimmed milk
750 g/1½ lb spinach, cooked, drained and
chopped
salt
freshly ground black pepper
lemon slices, to garnish

Preheat the grill to moderate.
Sprinkle the sole with a tablespoon of the lemon
juice and dot with half the margarine. Place on the
grill rack and grill for about 15 minutes, turning
frequently and brushing with the remaining
lemon juice and margarine, until the fish is cooked
and flakes easily when pierced with a sharp knife.
Purée the cheese and milk together in a blender
until smooth. Place the spinach in a saucepan with
the cheese mixture and heat gently, stirring con-

stantly. Do not allow to boil or the mixture will
curdle. Season to taste with salt and plenty of
freshly ground black pepper.
Spoon the spinach mixture on to a large heated
serving dish and arrange the grilled sole on top.
Garnish with lemon slices and serve immediately.
SERVES 4

SOLE VERONICA

METRIC/IMPERIAL
4 × 100 g/4 oz sole fillets
250 ml/8 fl oz white grape juice
salt
freshly ground black pepper
40 white grapes, deseeded

Put the sole in a wide shallow pan and pour over
the grape juice. Season with salt and pepper. Simmer for about 15 minutes until the fish is tender.
Add the grapes and cook for a further 5
minutes.
Place the fish on a heated serving dish and pour
the sauce and grapes over.
SERVES 4

SOLE FILLETS WITH SOY AND GINGER

METRIC/IMPERIAL
500-750 g/1¼-1½ lb sole fillets, skinned
2 egg whites
1 teaspoon cornflour
½ teaspoon Maldon or sea salt
3 tablespoons peanut or grapeseed oil
1 × 5 cm/2 inch piece fresh root ginger, peeled
and grated
1 large clove garlic, peeled and very finely
chopped
3 tablespoons soy sauce
1 tablespoon dry sherry
3 tablespoons fish stock
3 spring onions, cut into matchstick strips

Cut the sole into long thin strips. Beat the egg
whites, cornflour and salt until frothy, then pour
over the fish, mixing well. Chill for 20 minutes.
Heat the oil in a wok or large frying pan. When
nearly smoking, add the fish and stir-fry over a
fairly high heat for 2 minutes. Remove from the
pan with a slotted spoon, then discard all but 1
tablespoon of the oil.
Add the ginger and chopped garlic and stir-fry

for 1 minute, then pour in the soy sauce, sherry and fish stock. Bring to the boil quickly, then bubble for 2 minutes.

Return the fish to the pan and heat through for 1 minute, stirring constantly. Pile on to a warmed serving dish, sprinkle with the spring onion strips and serve at once, with boiled wild rice or baby corn-cobs.

SERVES 6

SPINACH AND FISH TERRINE

METRIC/IMPERIAL
8-10 well-shaped young spinach leaves
4 small sole fillets, skinned
1 tablespoon chopped parsley
finely grated rind of ½ lemon
salt
freshly ground black pepper
150 ml/¼ pint dry white wine
1 × 200 g/7 oz can tuna in brine, drained
450 g/1 lb spinach, cooked and thoroughly drained
150 ml/¼ pint plain low-fat yogurt
225 g/8 oz cooked, peeled prawns
3 teaspoons powdered gelatine
3 tablespoons dry vermouth
Garnish:
thin lemon wedges
feathery fennel sprigs

Grease and line an 18 × 7.5 cm/7 × 3 inch loaf tin or terrine with non-stick silicone or greased waxed paper.

Remove any tough stem from each spinach leaf; blanch in boiling water for about 30 seconds and then immediately refresh in cold water. Drain thoroughly and spread out flat.

Line the prepared loaf tin or terrine with some of the spinach leaves; reserve 2 for covering the top of the mixture.

Spread out the fillets of sole, skin-side uppermost; sprinkle with parsley, lemon rind, and salt and pepper to taste. Roll up neatly like Swiss rolls and secure each one with a wooden cocktail stick. Place the rolled fillets in a small frying pan; add the wine and salt and pepper to taste, and poach, covered, for 5 minutes. Remove the cooked fillets and reserve the cooking liquid.

Put the tuna, cooked spinach, yogurt, half the prawns and the fish cooking liquid into a blender or food processor; blend until smooth and add salt and pepper to taste.

Put the gelatine and vermouth into a small bowl and set aside for 1 minute. Stand in a pan of hot water and stir until the gelatine has dissolved, about 2 minutes. Stir into the tuna and spinach mixture, together with the remaining prawns. Spread half the tuna and spinach mixture into the prepared loaf tin or terrine; lay the cooked sole fillets on this, and then cover with the remaining tuna and spinach mixture. Cover and chill for 3 to 4 hours. Unmould carefully.

Cut in fairly thin slices and arrange 2 slices on each plate. Garnish with the lemon wedges and fennel sprigs.

SERVES 4

MEXICAN-STYLE FISH

METRIC/IMPERIAL
450 g/1 lb sole fillets, skinned
1 small onion, peeled and thinly sliced
1 tablespoon crushed coriander seeds
juice of 4 limes
finely grated rind of 2 limes
3 tablespoons olive oil
3 tablespoons dry white wine
salt
freshly ground black pepper
2 cloves garlic, peeled and crushed
Garnish:
1 green pepper, cored, deseeded and cut in thin strips
12 cooked unpeeled prawns

Cut the sole fillets in long thin strips; put them into a shallow dish with the onion rings and coriander seeds.

Mix the lime juice with the lime rind, olive oil, white wine, salt and pepper to taste, and the garlic; spoon evenly over the sole strips. Cover the fish and chill for at least 6 hours, until the fish turns opaque and looks 'cooked'. Turn the fish strips once or twice during this time.

Lift the marinated fish strips on to a serving dish and spoon over a little of the liquid. Garnish with the green pepper and the prawns.

SERVES 4

CIDER-SOUSED MACKEREL

METRIC/IMPERIAL
4 small mackerel
salt
freshly ground black pepper
1 onion, peeled and thinly sliced
1 tablespoon lemon juice
1 dessert apple, peeled, cored and sliced
6 peppercorns
1 teaspoon fennel seeds
2 bay leaves
300 ml/½ pint dry cider

Remove the heads, fins and guts from the mackerel. Clean the fish and remove the backbones without removing the tails. Season with salt and pepper, then roll up each fish towards the tail.

Place the rolled mackerel in a shallow ovenproof dish, with the tails pointing upwards. Scatter the onion slices over and around the fish. Add the lemon juice to the apple and put the slices in the dish, with the peppercorns, fennel and bay leaves. Pour over the cider.

Cover and bake in a preheated moderate oven (180°C/350°F, Gas Mark 4) for 30 to 40 minutes until the fish is tender. Serve cold.
SERVES 2

MONK'S MACKEREL

METRIC/IMPERIAL
4 medium mackerel, cleaned
2 onions, peeled and chopped
2 bay leaves
4 tablespoons lemon juice
2 teaspoons dried mixed herbs
12 black olives, stoned
salt
freshly ground black pepper
Garnish:
watercress sprigs
lemon wedges

Place the mackerel in a non-stick baking dish and cover with the onions, bay leaves, lemon juice, herbs and stoned olives. Season with salt and pepper. Cover with foil and bake in a preheated moderate oven (180°C/350°F, Gas Mark 4) for 30 to 40 minutes or until the fish is cooked. Serve hot, garnished with the watercress sprigs and lemon wedges.
SERVES 4

MACKEREL FISH CAKES

METRIC/IMPERIAL
350 g/12 oz cooked or canned mackerel
350 g/12 oz cooked potatoes
1 tablespoon curry powder
salt
freshly ground black pepper
polyunsaturated vegetable oil

If using canned mackerel, drain well. Mash the fish and potatoes together using a fork and potato masher. Mix in the curry powder and salt and pepper to taste.

Cover the grill rack with foil and brush or spray with oil.

Shape the mixture into 12 fish cakes and place under a hot grill. Cook for about 5 minutes on each side until browned.
SERVES 4

SCANDINAVIAN MACKEREL

METRIC/IMPERIAL
3 tablespoons cider vinegar
300 ml/½ pint water
1 onion, peeled and sliced
1 bay leaf
1 parsley sprig
1 thyme sprig
6 peppercorns
½ teaspoon salt
4 mackerel, cleaned
Sauce:
150 ml/¼ pint plain low-fat yogurt
1 tablespoon French mustard
1 teaspoon Muscovado sugar
1 tablespoon cider vinegar
1 tablespoon chopped fennel

Put the vinegar, water, onion, herbs, peppercorns and salt in a pan. Bring to the boil and simmer for 20 minutes.

Place the mackerel in a shallow ovenproof dish and pour over the infused liquid. Cover and cook in a preheated moderate oven (180°C/350°F, Gas Mark 4) for 20 to 25 minutes. Transfer the fish to a warmed serving dish and keep hot.

Put all the sauce ingredients in a small bowl and place over a pan of simmering water. Stir until blended and heated through. Pour the sauce over the fish and serve immediately.
SERVES 4

MACKEREL IN A BAG

METRIC/IMPERIAL
12 slices of lemon
4 small mackerel, cleaned
2 teaspoons chopped fresh sage or 1 teaspoon
dried sage
salt
freshly ground black pepper
olive oil

Place 3 slices of lemon on each mackerel and sprinkle with the sage. Season with salt and pepper. Lightly oil 4 pieces of greaseproof paper cut large enough to enclose the fish. Place the mackerel on the oiled paper and fold over to form a parcel, tucking in the ends to seal.

Bake in a preheated moderately hot oven (190°C/375°F, Gas Mark 5) for about 20 minutes or until the fish is tender. Serve the mackerel in the paper parcels.
SERVES 4

MACKEREL WITH CAPER DRESSING

METRIC/IMPERIAL
6 tablespoons polyunsaturated vegetable oil
1 large clove garlic, peeled and crushed
juice of 1 large lemon
75 g/3 oz capers, rinsed and lightly crushed
salt
freshly ground black pepper
4 fresh mackerel, cleaned and heads removed
2 tablespoons snipped chives or parsley

Mix together the oil, garlic, lemon juice, capers, and salt and pepper to taste in a bowl; cover and set aside to allow the flavours to blend. Before cooking, slash the fish 3 times diagonally on each side, sprinkle with a little salt and pepper and arrange side by side on the grill rack. Spoon the dressing over the fish.

Cook under a preheated, moderately hot grill for about 5 minutes each side, turning once and basting with the dressing from time to time. If necessary, increase the heat towards the end to brown and crisp the skin. Lift out the fish with a slotted fish slice on to a serving plate. Add the chives or parsley to the pan juices and spoon over the mackerel.

Serve the mackerel hot, with a mixed green salad and plain boiled potatoes.
SERVES 4

FRIED MACKEREL WITH TAMARIND SAUCE

METRIC/IMPERIAL
4 medium mackerel
2 tablespoons polyunsaturated vegetable oil
15 g/½ oz tamarind pulp
3 cloves garlic, peeled and finely chopped
2 tablespoons grated root ginger
3 tablespoons water
1 teaspoon sugar
Garnish:
few spring onions, chopped
1 cucumber, peeled and cut into 1 cm/½ inch
slices

Clean the fish, but do not remove the skin. Wrap the fish together in well-greased aluminium foil, then bake in a preheated cool oven (150°C/300°F, Gas Mark 2) for 45 minutes until tender. Unwrap the fish, then leave until cool and dry.

Heat the oil in a deep frying pan, add the fish and fry gently until golden brown. Remove from the pan carefully and drain, reserving the pan for the sauce. Transfer the fish to a warmed serving dish and keep hot.

To make the sauce, first make some tamarind water: soak the tamarind pulp in 150 ml/¼ pint water for 5 to 10 minutes. Squeeze, strain and reserve the water.

Add the garlic to the pan in which the fish was fried and fry over high heat until light brown. Add the ginger and fry for 1 minute. Stir in the water, sugar and 3 tablespoons of tamarind water. Heat through, then pour over the fish. Sprinkle with the spring onions. Serve hot, with the cucumber as a side dish.
SERVES 4

SPICED HERRINGS

METRIC/IMPERIAL
4 herrings
2 onions, peeled and chopped
2 tablespoons whole pickling spice
salt
freshly ground black pepper
450 ml/¾ pint dry cider

Split the herrings down the back, open out and clean thoroughly. Reserve the roes. Wash the herrings well and dry them on kitchen paper towels. Mash the roes with a fork and mix with one quarter of the chopped onion. Stuff the fish with this mixture and arrange them, head to tail, in a baking dish.

Sprinkle the remaining onion, the pickling spice, and salt and pepper to taste, over the fish. Pour on the cider. Cover and bake in a preheated moderate oven (160°C/325°F, Gas Mark 3) for 1¼ hours. Leave the fish to cool in the cooking liquid, then chill in the refrigerator overnight. Serve cold with salad.

SERVES 4

SOUSED HERRINGS

METRIC/IMPERIAL
150 ml/¼ pint white wine vinegar
150 ml/¼ pint white wine
150 ml/¼ pint water
1 tablespoon pickling spice
8 peppercorns
1 bay leaf
1 onion, peeled and thinly sliced
1 teaspoon salt
1 tablespoon Muscovado sugar
6 boned herrings

Put all the ingredients, except the fish, into a pan. Bring to the boil then leave to cool.

Place the herrings in a shallow ovenproof dish and pour over the liquid. Cover and cook in a preheated moderate oven (160°C/325°F, Gas Mark 3) for 1 hour. Allow to cool, then chill in the refrigerator overnight.

Serve with salad and crusty wholemeal bread.

SERVES 6

MARINATED KIPPERS

METRIC/IMPERIAL
8 kipper fillets, fresh or frozen and thawed
1 onion, peeled and very thinly sliced
8 black peppercorns
2 bay leaves
8 tablespoons polyunsaturated vegetable oil
2 tablespoons cider vinegar

Skin the kipper fillets and place in a shallow earthenware or china dish with the onion, peppercorns and bay leaves. Spoon over the oil and vinegar, then cover and leave to marinate for 24 hours, turning once or twice.

Serve chilled with wholemeal bread and butter.

SERVES 4

KIPPER SOUFFLÉ

METRIC/IMPERIAL
350 g/12 oz kippers
25 g/1 oz polyunsaturated margarine
25 g/1 oz plain unbleached white flour
300 ml/½ pint skimmed milk
salt
freshly ground black pepper
2 eggs, separated

Place the kippers in a wide saucepan. Cook in the minimum of water for about 10 minutes until soft. Alternatively, place in a deep jug and cover with boiling water. Leave for 5 to 10 minutes, then drain.

Mash the kippers. Melt the margarine in a saucepan and stir in the flour. Cook for 2 minutes, stirring. Remove from the heat. Gradually add the milk, stirring well after each addition.

Return to the heat and mix in the mashed kipper. Add salt, if necessary, and plenty of pepper.

Remove from the heat and stir the egg yolks into the mixture. Whisk the egg whites until they will form stiff peaks and fold in. Turn into a lightly buttered soufflé dish and bake in a preheated moderately hot oven (200°C/400°F, Gas Mark 6) for 20 minutes if you like a runny centre or 25 minutes for a drier soufflé.

SERVES 4

TUNA-STUFFED GLOBE ARTICHOKES

METRIC/IMPERIAL
4 globe artichokes
salt
100 g/4 oz long-grain rice
1 × 350 g/12 oz can tuna fish
4 tablespoons tomato purée
2 teaspoons chopped fresh basil or 1 teaspoon dried basil
2 teaspoons chopped fresh oregano or 1 teaspoon dried oregano
salt
freshly ground black pepper

Cut off the artichoke stalks. Plunge the heads into boiling salted water. Simmer for about 20 minutes or until the bottom leaves pull away easily. Drain and leave until cold.

Remove the hairy chokes from the centre of the artichokes.

Meanwhile, cook the rice in boiling salted water for about 12 minutes. Drain well, fluff up with a fork and leave until cold.

Thoroughly drain the oil from the tuna fish and flake it using a fork. Add to the rice together with the tomato purée, herbs and salt and pepper to taste. Fill each globe artichoke with the tuna and rice mixture. Serve with a tomato salad.

SERVES 4

TUNA HERB PANCAKES WITH TOMATO SAUCE

METRIC/IMPERIAL
polyunsaturated vegetable oil for frying
wholemeal pancake batter made with 100 g/4 oz wholemeal flour (see page 292)
Sauce and filling:
1 tablespoon polyunsaturated vegetable oil
1 large onion, peeled and finely chopped
1 green pepper, cored, deseeded and chopped
1 tablespoon bran
2 × 400 g/14 oz cans chopped tomatoes
1 teaspoon dried mixed herbs
½ teaspoon brown sugar
salt
freshly ground black pepper
1 × 200 g/7 oz can tuna in brine, drained
1 × 439 g/15½ oz can borlotti beans (or other pulse), drained

Lightly oil an 18 cm/7 inch non-stick frying pan and place over a moderate heat. Add a little batter to cover the base of the pan and cook until the mixture has set. Turn or toss and cook the other side. Place the pancake on a wire cooling rack and then use the remaining batter to make a further 7 pancakes. Stack together on the cooling rack, interleaved with greaseproof paper.

Preheat the oven to 180°C/350°F, Gas Mark 4. To make the sauce and filling, heat the oil in a pan and sauté the onion for 5 minutes. Add the pepper and cook for 2 minutes. Stir in the bran and cook for 1 minute. Stir in the tomatoes with their juice, the herbs, sugar and salt and pepper to taste. Bring to the boil, cover and simmer for 10 to 15 minutes.

Place the tuna and beans in a bowl and add half the sauce. Mix well and adjust the seasoning. Divide the mixture between the pancakes and roll up. Arrange in a greased, shallow ovenproof dish. Pour the remaining sauce over the pancakes, cover with foil and heat through in the oven for 25 to 30 minutes.

SERVES 4

PITTA BREAD WITH TUNA AND SWEETCORN

METRIC/IMPERIAL
½ wholemeal pitta bread
50 g/2 oz tuna fish, drained and flaked
25 g/1 oz sweetcorn
1 tablespoon tomato purée
2-3 cucumber slices, chopped into small pieces

Slit the wholemeal pitta in half across the width, and open with a sharp knife to form a pocket. This can be done more easily if the pitta is slightly warmed first. Mix together the tuna, sweetcorn, tomato purée and cucumber and spoon into the pitta bread to serve.

SERVES 1

TUNA FISH MOUSSE

METRIC/IMPERIAL
300 ml/½ pint skimmed milk
1 small onion, peeled and quartered
2 parsley stalks
1 bay leaf
strip of lemon rind
25 g/1 oz polyunsaturated margarine
25 g/1 oz plain unbleached white flour
1 × 200 g/7 oz can tuna fish
150 ml/¼ pint reduced-calorie mayonnaise
150 ml/¼ pint plain low-fat yogurt
grated rind and juice of ½ small lemon
chopped basil
1 tablespoon tomato purée
2 teaspoons anchovy essence
salt
freshly ground black pepper
1 egg, separated
15 g/½ oz powdered gelatine
2 tablespoons water
Garnish:
cucumber slices
100 g/4 oz prawns (optional)

To make the sauce, pour the milk into a small saucepan, and add the onion, parsley, bay leaf and lemon rind. Bring to the boil, remove from the heat and leave to infuse for at least 10 minutes, then strain. Melt the margarine in a saucepan, stir in the flour and then the flavoured milk over a low heat. Bring to the boil, stirring until the sauce is thickened and smooth. Simmer for 2 minutes.

Spoon the tuna fish into a mixing bowl, with the juices from the can, and mash well with a fork.

84

Beat in the sauce, then the mayonnaise and the yogurt. Stir in the lemon rind and juice, basil, tomato purée, anchovy essence, and salt and pepper to taste. Beat in the egg yolk.

Dissolve the gelatine in the water and stir into the mixture. Whisk the egg white until stiff and fold in. Turn into a 900 ml/1½ pint ring or fish mould, or soufflé dish, and chill in the refrigerator until set.

To serve, dip the mould in hot water for a few seconds, then unmould on to a serving plate. Garnish with cucumber and prawns (if using).
SERVES 6 to 8

PITTA BREAD WITH SALADE NIÇOISE

METRIC/IMPERIAL
1 wholemeal pitta bread
1 teaspoon polyunsaturated margarine
25 g/1 oz French beans, cooked and chopped
50 g/2 oz tuna fish, drained and chopped
25 g/1 oz red pepper, chopped
25 g/1 oz green pepper, chopped
4 black olives, stoned
salt
freshly ground black pepper

Slit the pitta bread down one side and spread the inside with the margarine. Mix the remaining ingredients together with salt and pepper to taste and spoon into the bread. Serve immediately.
SERVES 1 to 2

GRILLED SARDINES WITH OREGANO

METRIC/IMPERIAL
1.5 kg/3 lb large sardines, thawed if frozen
Maldon or sea salt
freshly ground black and white pepper
100 ml/3½ fl oz olive oil
3-4 tablespoons lemon juice
1 tablespoon dried oregano
1 clove garlic, peeled and crushed
Garnish:
lemon wedges
thinly sliced brown bread and butter

Rinse the sardines under a cold tap and pat dry. Cover a grill rack with foil and arrange the sardines on top. Heat the grill.

Put a good pinch of salt and a generous grinding of black and white peppers into a bowl. Whisk in the olive oil, then the lemon juice, then add dried oregano and garlic. Brush each fish with a little of the oil mixture, then cook under a hot grill for 3 to 4 minutes.

Turn the fish over and brush with the remaining mixture, then cook for a further 3 to 4 minutes until crisp. Serve at once with lemon wedges and thinly sliced brown bread and butter.
SERVES 4 to 6

STEAMED SPICED FISH

METRIC/IMPERIAL
1 × 1.5 kg/3¼-3½ lb whole bass, bream or grey mullet, cleaned but head and tail left on
1 tablespoon Maldon or sea salt
freshly ground black pepper
1 tablespoon cumin seeds, lightly crushed
1 × 5 cm/2 inch piece fresh root ginger, peeled and finely chopped
2 tablespoons lemon juice
2 tablespoons olive oil
2-3 cloves garlic, peeled and finely chopped
1 tablespoon coriander seeds, crushed
celery leaves, to garnish

Rinse the fish in cold water, then rub all over with the salt and lots of black pepper. Leave to stand at room temperature for 30 minutes, to draw out excess moisture and firm up the flesh.

Put the grill rack into a roasting tin, and pour in boiling water to a depth of 2.5 cm/1 inch. Set over a low heat so the liquid is gently simmering.

Transfer the fish to a heatproof serving plate, discarding any liquid which may have collected around it. Sprinkle on the cumin seeds and ginger, then put the plate on the rack. Cover the whole roasting tin with foil, pressing it around the edges to form as close a seal as possible, then cook for 15 to 25 minutes until the fish flakes easily. Test it with the point of a sharp knife near the gills so as not to spoil the appearance of the fish. Take off the heat, remove the foil, and sprinkle over the lemon juice.

Quickly heat the oil in a small frying pan, add the garlic and coriander seeds and stir-fry over a high heat for about 1 minute, until the aroma of the spices is quite powerful. Pour the sizzling oil over the fish and serve at once, garnished with celery leaves.
SERVES 6

JAPANESE STEAMED WHOLE FISH

METRIC/IMPERIAL
2 dried shiitake mushrooms, soaked in tepid
water for 20 minutes
450 g/1 lb sea bass or perch, scaled and cleaned
2 slices root ginger, peeled and finely shredded
2 spring onions, finely shredded
50 g/2 oz cooked ham, finely shredded
50 g/2 oz bamboo shoots, finely shredded
3 tablespoons dry sherry
3 tablespoons soy sauce
1 teaspoon salt

Dry the mushrooms and discard the stalks.
Slash both sides of the fish diagonally, as deep
as the bone, at intervals of about 1 cm/½ inch. Dry
the fish thoroughly with paper towels, then place
it on a plate.
Arrange the ginger root, spring onions, ham,
mushrooms and bamboo shoots on top of the
fish. Mix the sherry, soy sauce and salt in a jug and
pour it all over the fish. Steam vigorously for 15
minutes and serve.
SERVES 4

CHINESE-STYLE BASS

METRIC/IMPERIAL
1.5 kg/3-3½ lb sea bass, cleaned
1 teaspoon sea salt
1 teaspoon sugar
½ tablespoon sesame oil
½ tablespoon soy sauce
8 thin slices root ginger
2 large cloves garlic, peeled and thinly sliced
4 spring onions, sliced lengthwise
2 tablespoons dry vermouth
2 tablespoons sunflower seed oil
1 tablespoon sesame oil
1 tablespoon soy sauce

Rub the fish inside and out with the salt, sugar,
sesame oil and soy sauce. Lay a large piece of foil
on a table and scatter half the sliced ginger, garlic
and spring onions over it. Lay the fish on them
and scatter the remainder on top of it. Wrap the
foil round the fish so that it is totally enclosed, and
lay on the rack of a fish kettle. Bring about 1.5 cm/
¾ inch water to the boil in the kettle, then lower
the rack into it and cover. Boil steadily for 30
minutes, until the fish is cooked.
Mix the remaining ingredients in a small bowl.

When the fish is ready, unwrap it and slide on to a
platter. Strain the juices into the sauce and discard
the garlic, ginger and spring onions. Remove the
top skin from the fish, give the sauce a final whisk,
and pour it over.
SERVES 4

ORANGE AND PAPRIKA FISH

METRIC/IMPERIAL
4 × 175 g/6 oz pieces of skate or cod
250 ml/8 fl oz unsweetened orange juice
1 teaspoon paprika
salt
freshly ground black pepper

Place the fish in a shallow dish. Mix the orange
juice with the paprika and salt and pepper and
pour over the fish. Leave to marinate for 2 hours.
Drain the fish and place under a preheated hot
grill for about 15 minutes, turning frequently and
adding more paprika and orange juice marinade to
prevent drying.
SERVES 4

FIVE-WILLOWS FISH

METRIC/IMPERIAL
1 small cucumber
2 carrots, peeled
1 × 2.5 cm/1 inch piece root ginger, peeled and
sliced
3 spring onions, chopped
2 cloves garlic, peeled and 1 crushed and 1 sliced
120 ml/4 fl oz vinegar
1 grey mullet, carp or bass, cleaned
4 tablespoons polyunsaturated vegetable oil
1 tablespoon hoisin sauce
2 tablespoons sugar
1 tablespoon sesame seed oil

Cut the cucumber in half lengthways and discard
the soft centre. Slice the cucumber flesh and carrots into 5 cm/2 inch matchstick pieces.
Put the cucumber, carrots, ginger, spring
onions, crushed garlic and vinegar in a bowl and
mix well. Leave to marinate for 30 minutes.
Score the fish by making 3 diagonal cuts on
both sides. Heat the oil in a wok or deep frying
pan, add the sliced garlic and fry for 1 minute. Add
the fish and fry for 1 minute on each side until
golden brown.

Add the vegetables and marinade, stir in the hoisin sauce and sugar and cook for 2 minutes; sprinkle with the sesame seed oil.

Transfer the fish to a warmed serving dish and spoon over the vegetables and sauce. If liked, garnish with a cucumber fan and carrot flower.

SERVES 4 to 6

POACHED FISH WITH GARLIC-HERB DRESSING

METRIC/IMPERIAL
4 whole fish, each weighing about 225 g/8 oz, or 4 large fillets (e.g. red mullet, bream, snapper or whiting)
2 kg/4 lb mussels, beards removed and scrubbed
fresh basil, to garnish
Dressing:
150 ml/¼ pint olive oil
1 clove garlic, peeled and crushed
1 tomato, skinned, deseeded and chopped
1 teaspoon finely chopped fennel
½ teaspoon finely chopped rosemary
1 tablespoon finely chopped basil
pinch of paprika
pinch of ground coriander
salt
freshly ground black pepper
Court bouillon:
350 ml/12 fl oz dry white wine
1 tablespoon wine vinegar
450 ml/¾ pint water
pinch of salt
freshly ground black pepper
bouquet garni
sprig each rosemary, basil and fennel
2 orange slices
2 lemon slices

Make the dressing 2 or 3 days in advance. Mix all the ingredients together, seasoning to taste with salt and pepper. Cover and leave in a cool place (not the refrigerator) until needed.

Put all the ingredients for the court bouillon into a shallow pan big enough to hold the fish in one layer. Bring to the boil, partially cover and simmer very gently for 1 hour. Add the fish and mussels (discarding any that do not close tightly when tapped), cover and poach (the water should not bubble) for 5 minutes or until the mussels open (discard any that do not open). Remove the mussels and keep warm; continue cooking the fish, if necessary, just until the flesh turns white and flakes at the touch of a fork.

Lift the fish out carefully with a slotted fish slice and arrange on a large, heated oval platter. Arrange the mussels in their shells round the platter, garnish with fresh basil and pour the dressing over the fish. Serve immediately.

SERVES 4

GREY MULLET WITH PIQUANT TOMATO SAUCE

METRIC/IMPERIAL
1 kg/2 lb grey mullet, cleaned and thoroughly scaled
salt
freshly ground black pepper
2 tablespoons white wine vinegar
2 tablespoons polyunsaturated vegetable oil
parsley sprigs
Tomato sauce:
1 tablespoon olive oil
2 shallots, peeled and finely chopped
1 large yellow pepper, cored, deseeded and roughly chopped
1 × 400 g/14 oz can chopped tomatoes
1 teaspoon capers, rinsed
300 ml/½ pint fish stock
salt
freshly ground black pepper

Rinse the fish under cold water and remove any remaining blood from the backbone. Season well with salt and pepper. Place the fish in a shallow dish with the vinegar, oil and parsley. Marinate for 3 hours or overnight if possible, turning occasionally.

Meanwhile, make the sauce: heat the oil in a saucepan and fry the shallot and pepper until cooked but not brown. Stir in the tomatoes, capers and stock. Season well with salt and pepper. Bring to the boil.

Discard the marinade, place the fish in a steamer and cover with a tight-fitting lid. Steam over the sauce for 20 minutes. Check the liquid level frequently and add boiling water if necessary.

Remove the fish from the steamer, peel away the skin and keep warm. Purée the sauce in a blender or food processor until smooth.

To serve, flood a warmed serving dish with half the sauce. Lay the fish gently on top and spoon on the remaining sauce. If liked, garnish with bunches of herbs and strips of tomato.

SERVES 4

BOURRIDE

METRIC/IMPERIAL
450 g/1 lb fish trimmings (heads, bones,
skin, etc)
2 leeks, washed and chopped
1 large onion, peeled and chopped
2-3 cloves garlic, peeled and halved
1 × 7.5 cm/3 inch piece lemon peel or Seville
orange peel
1 bay leaf
1 thyme sprig
3-4 parsley sprigs
1 tablespoon wine vinegar
1 litre/1¾ pints cold water
olive oil for frying
450 g/1 lb potatoes, peeled and finely sliced
1.5 kg/3 lb whole fish fillets (monkfish, brill or
John Dory), thickly sliced
sea salt
freshly ground black pepper
6 slices white bread, crusts removed
4-5 tablespoons finely chopped fresh parsley,
to garnish
Aïoli:
4-8 cloves garlic, peeled
2 egg yolks
about 300 ml/½ pint olive oil
white pepper
1-3 teaspoons lemon juice

Rinse the fish trimmings under running water, removing any traces of blood. Put in a large pan
with 1 leek, the onion, 1 clove garlic, the peel,
herbs and vinegar. Add the water and simmer
gently for 20 to 25 minutes.

Meanwhile, make the aïoli: mash the garlic
cloves with a good pinch of salt, then beat in the
egg yolks. Add a few drops of oil, whisking constantly, then a few more, still whisking, until the
mixture is thick enough to absorb the oil in a thin,
steady stream. This will take longer than when
making ordinary mayonnaise, as the garlic 'thins'
the eggs. When all the oil is added you should
finish with a very thick, yellow mayonnaise. Season with white pepper and lemon juice to taste,
then transfer to a small heavy-based pan and reserve.

Strain the cooked stock and discard the seasonings. Heat 1 tablespoon olive oil in a large pan, add
the remaining leek and 1 clove garlic, and fry
gently for 2 to 3 minutes; then arrange the finely
sliced potatoes in a layer on top, covering the base
of the pan.

Lay the fish fillets on top of the potatoes, season

lightly with salt and black pepper, then pour the
strained stock over. Simmer gently for 10 to 20
minutes until the fish is just cooked and flakes
easily – check after 10 minutes.

While the fish is simmering, pour enough oil
into a large frying pan to cover the bottom. Rub
both sides of the bread with the remaining clove
of garlic, then fry, two at a time, until golden on
both sides. Drain thoroughly on paper towels, cut
into croûtons and put in a bowl.

Place the fish in the centre of a warmed dish and
arrange the potatoes around it. Cover and keep
warm.

Reduce the liquid left in the pan by fast boiling
until you have a scant 450 ml/¾ pint. Check the
seasoning, then pour through a sieve on to the
aïoli, stirring. Put over a low heat and stir for 1 to 2
minutes until the sauce thickens slightly, then
pour over the fish and potatoes. Garnish and serve
with the croûtons.

SERVES 6 to 8

SOUSED MULLET

METRIC/IMPERIAL
4 small mullet, cleaned and thoroughly scaled
1 onion, peeled and sliced
2 bay leaves
1 clove
4 allspice berries or peppercorns
1 teaspoon salt
120 ml/4 fl oz vinegar
water, to cover

Remove the fish heads, cut off the fillets and remove any bones. Place slices of onion on the
centre of each fillet and roll up, skin side out, from
head to tail and fix with a cocktail stick.

Place the rolled fish in a heavy flameproof casserole or pot with the bay leaves, clove, allspice or
peppercorns and salt. Pour over the vinegar and
just cover with water. Cover and cook over a low
heat for 1 to 1½ hours or until the fish flakes easily
when tested with a fork.

Transfer the fish to a deep serving dish so that
the fish can be covered with liquid. Strain over
sufficient cooking liquid to cover the fish. Cool,
then chill in the refrigerator, where the liquor will
set into a soft jelly.

SERVES 4

FISH AND TOMATO BAKE

METRIC/IMPERIAL
225 g/8 oz coley
100 g/4 oz cod
4 scallops, dark beards removed
100 g/4 oz Cheddar or Gruyère cheese, grated
2 eggs
2 tablespoons dried skimmed milk powder
2 tablespoons water
salt
freshly ground black pepper
4 tomatoes, sliced
parsley sprigs, to garnish

Place the white fish and scallops in a wide saucepan. Poach in water for about 4 to 5 minutes until tender, then drain and reserve the liquid.

Cut the scallops into quarters and the rest of the fish into chunks. Place in an ovenproof dish. Add most of the cheese, reserving some for the topping.

Beat the eggs and skimmed milk powder with the water. Add about 300 ml/½ pint of the fish cooking liquid and salt and pepper to taste, then pour it over the fish and cheese.

Arrange the sliced tomatoes on top of the dish. Sprinkle with the remaining cheese and bake in a preheated moderately hot oven (190°C/375°F, Gas Mark 5) for about 20 minutes until the egg mixture has set. Garnish with parsley before serving.
SERVES 4

MONKFISH AND WILD MUSHROOM KEBABS

METRIC/IMPERIAL
1 kg/2 lb monkfish, skinned and boned and cut into 32 bite-sized cubes
6 chanterelle mushrooms, rinsed
salt
freshly ground black pepper
juice of 1 lemon
1 tablespoon white wine vinegar
1 tablespoon olive oil
3 teaspoons green peppercorns, well rinsed
300 ml/½ pint fish stock
50 g/2 oz polyunsaturated margarine
chervil sprigs, to garnish

Thread 2 cubes of fish on to each of 4 wooden skewers followed by a mushroom half, then continue the pattern until you have 8 cubes of fish and 3 pieces of mushroom on each skewer. Season

well with salt and black pepper. Mix the lemon juice, vinegar, oil and 1 teaspoon of the green peppercorns in a shallow dish. Lay the skewers in the marinade and marinate for 3 hours, turning them occasionally.

Prepare a steamer by laying a flat sheet of foil over the base. Arrange the kebabs on top. Bring the marinade to the boil in a saucepan with the fish stock and the remaining 2 teaspoons green peppercorns. Cover with a tight-fitting lid and steam the kebabs gently over the marinade and stock mixture for 15 minutes. Check the liquid level frequently and add more boiling stock or water if necessary.

Arrange the kebabs on warmed individual plates and keep hot. Reduce the stock by boiling rapidly until rich and syrupy. Over the heat, whisk in the margarine, bit by bit, until the sauce is creamy and smooth. Spoon over the fish and garnish with sprigs of chervil. Serve at once.
SERVES 4

SOUTH ASIAN CURRY

METRIC/IMPERIAL
15 g/½ oz polyunsaturated margarine
1 tablespoon mild curry powder
¼ teaspoon turmeric
¼ teaspoon Mexican chilli powder
¼ teaspoon crushed coriander seeds
¼ teaspoon cumin
1 kg/2 lb monkfish or any other firm white fish, boned and thickly sliced
1 tablespoon olive oil
4 cloves garlic, peeled and crushed
2 chillies, deseeded and finely chopped
2 onions, peeled and finely chopped
1 × 400 g/14 oz can chopped tomatoes
1 teaspoon caster sugar
salt
freshly ground black pepper
coriander or parsley sprigs, to garnish

Heat the margarine in a pan and fry the curry powder, turmeric, Mexican chilli powder, coriander and cumin for 3 minutes without burning. Stir in the fish and coat with the spices. Leave to one side for up to 2 hours.

Heat the oil in a pan and fry the garlic, chilli and onion until cooked but not brown. Stir in the tomatoes and sugar. Season well with salt and pepper. Stir in the fish and spices. Pour the mixture into a suitable bowl. Cover with a piece of foil or greaseproof paper and tie down with string. Place in a steamer or covered saucepan half-filled with boiling water and steam for 15 minutes. Taste and adjust the seasoning.

Serve on a bed of rice, garnished with coriander or parsley sprigs.
SERVES 4

DEVILLED FISH

METRIC/IMPERIAL
4 × 100 g/4 oz pieces coley or cod
120 ml/4 fl oz lemon juice
2 teaspoons Worcestershire sauce
1 teaspoon French mustard
1 teaspoon light brown sugar
salt
freshly ground black pepper

Place the fish in a casserole dish. Mix together the remaining ingredients, adding salt and pepper to taste, and pour them over the fish.

Cover and cook in a preheated moderately hot oven (190°C/375°F, Gas Mark 5) for about 20 minutes or until the fish is tender.
SERVES 4

CONGER EEL WITH SWEETCORN DRESSING

METRIC/IMPERIAL
1 corn on the cob
300 ml/½ pint fish stock
4 round cutlets of conger eel, skinned
salt
freshly ground black pepper
1 tablespoon snipped chives
1 tablespoon white wine vinegar
1 tablespoon olive oil
1 tablespoon lemon juice
mixed salad leaves (e.g. iceberg, curly endive and radicchio)
Garnish:
4 rashers lean bacon, derinded, cooked and finely chopped
1 tablespoon snipped chives

Remove the kernels from the sweetcorn and place both parts in a saucepan with the stock. Bring to the boil. Place the eel cutlets in a steamer, season with salt and pepper and sprinkle with the chives. Steam over the stock for 15 to 20 minutes. Remove, cover with damp greaseproof paper and allow to cool.

Remove the sweetcorn cob from the stock and discard. Stir in the vinegar. Taste and adjust the seasoning if necessary. Purée in a blender or food processor and sieve into a clean pan. Boil to reduce until syrupy. Allow the sauce to cool.

To serve, mix the oil and lemon together and season to taste. Toss the lettuce leaves lightly in the dressing. Arrange on 4 plates. Add the eel cutlets and spoon the sweetcorn sauce over the top. Sprinkle with chopped bacon and chives.
SERVES 4

SOFT ROES ON TOAST

METRIC/IMPERIAL
450 g/1 lb soft roes, washed
salt
2 tablespoons mushroom ketchup
1 tablespoon Worcestershire sauce
½ teaspoon anchovy essence
freshly ground black pepper
4 slices wholemeal bread
juice of 1 lemon
pinch of cayenne pepper

Poach the roes in salted water to cover for 15 minutes, then drain very thoroughly.

Mix together the mushroom ketchup, Worcestershire sauce and anchovy essence. Add salt and pepper to taste, then add the roes and mix well.

Toast the bread lightly on both sides. Pile the roes on the toast and grill under medium heat for 3 minutes. Arrange on individual plates, then sprinkle with the lemon juice and cayenne pepper.
SERVES 4

SALMON BAKE

METRIC/IMPERIAL
350 g/12 oz cooked or canned salmon
2 eggs
350 ml/12 fl oz skimmed milk
50 g/2 oz Cheddar cheese, grated
salt
freshly ground black pepper

Flake the salmon with a fork, discarding the bones, and place in a casserole dish.

Beat together the eggs and milk, then stir in the cheese, salt and pepper. Pour over the salmon and bake in a preheated moderate oven (180°C/350°F, Gas Mark 4) for about 20 minutes or until set.
SERVES 4

POACHED SALMON STEAKS WITH YOGURT SAUCE

METRIC/IMPERIAL
6 salmon steaks, about 175-225 g/6-8 oz each
1 onion, peeled and finely sliced
1 celery stalk, finely sliced
1 bay leaf
2 parsley sprigs
1 × 5 cm/2 inch piece orange peel
12 white peppercorns, lightly crushed
300-450 ml/½-¾ pint dry white wine
Sauce:
¾ teaspoon cornflour
300 ml/½ pint plain low-fat yogurt
finely ground sea salt
½ teaspoon coriander seeds, ground
pinch of ground cinnamon
½ teaspoon dried dill
2-3 tablespoons fresh orange juice
freshly ground black pepper
1 teaspoon arrowroot (optional)
fresh herbs, to garnish

Rinse any blood off the salmon steaks, and pat dry with kitchen paper.

To make a court bouillon, put the onion, celery, bay leaf, parsley, orange peel and peppercorns in a large pan. Make the wine up to 1.2 litres/2 pints with water and pour into the pan. Simmer for 30 minutes then set aside to cool.

While the stock is cooling, stabilize the yogurt. Mix the cornflour with enough cold water to make a smooth paste. Whisk the yogurt until quite smooth, then beat in the cornflour mixture and a pinch of salt. Stir well, and bring to the boil, stirring slowly and constantly, always in the same direction. When just boiling, turn the heat as low as possible and simmer, uncovered (a lid would generate condensation, which would destroy the stabilization), for 10 minutes until the yogurt is thick and creamy. Take off the heat until ready to complete the sauce.

Arrange the fish steaks in a single layer in a large pan. Strain over the cooled stock, bring to the boil over a moderate heat, then simmer very gently for 5 to 6 minutes until the salmon is opaque and firm, taking care that it doesn't overcook. Transfer the steaks to a plate, cover and keep warm by standing over a pan of simmering water.

Strain the bouillon again into a clean pan and boil hard to reduce to about 150 ml/¼ pint. Add the ground coriander, cinnamon, dill, 2 tablespoons orange juice and black pepper, then reduce the heat and stir in the yogurt. Let the sauce simmer until slightly thickened, then taste, adding more salt if necessary. If it seems a little thin (this will depend to a certain extent on the type of yogurt used), mix the arrowroot with a teaspoon of water and stir a little into the sauce. Continue to stir for a few minutes more, adding the remaining arrowroot paste if the sauce is still not thickening; it should be fairly light but not liquid, about the consistency of double cream. Add the rest of the orange juice.

Pour the sauce over or around the steaks and serve immediately.
SERVES 6

SMOKED SALMON QUICHE

METRIC/IMPERIAL
50 g/2 oz plain white flour
50 g/2 oz wholemeal flour
pinch of salt
pinch of cayenne pepper
50 g/2 oz polyunsaturated margarine
ice-cold water
Filling:
3 eggs
150 ml/¼ pint skimmed milk
100 g/4 oz cottage cheese, sieved
2 tablespoons snipped chives
salt
freshly ground black pepper
½ teaspoon grated lemon rind
150 g/5 oz smoked salmon

Place the flours in a bowl and add the salt and cayenne. Rub the margarine into the flour until the mixture resembles fine breadcrumbs. Stir in 2 teaspoons of water at a time, until the dough is firm. Lightly knead the dough on a floured board, roll out and use to line 4 individual tins 7.5 cm/3 inches in diameter. Chill for 20 minutes.

Beat the eggs, milk and cottage cheese together. Add the chives, seasoning and lemon rind. Roughly chop the smoked salmon and arrange in the bottom of the pastry cases. Spoon over the egg and cheese mixture.

Bake in a preheated moderately hot oven (200°C/400°F, Gas Mark 6) for 20 to 25 minutes until set and golden brown. Serve hot or cold.
SERVES 4

SALMON IN RED WINE

METRIC/IMPERIAL
6 salmon steaks, about 2.5 cm/1 inch thick
100-150 g/4-5 oz polyunsaturated margarine
6 shallots, finely chopped
small bunch fresh parsley, finely chopped
1 clove garlic, peeled and finely chopped
6 black peppercorns, crushed
Maldon or sea salt
300 ml/½ pint red wine
parsley sprig, to garnish

Rinse the salmon quickly in cold water, then pat dry with kitchen paper.

Melt 50 g/2 oz of the margarine in a large flameproof dish into which the salmon will fit snugly. Add the shallots and sweat for 2 minutes, then put in the steaks and brown for 1 minute on each side over a high heat.

Sprinkle over the remaining ingredients, cover with greased paper and cook in the oven preheated to 190°C/375°F, Gas Mark 5, for 10 to 15 minutes until the steaks are just done.

Pour off the cooking juices into a small saucepan. Meanwhile, keep the salmon warm. Cut the rest of the margarine into small pieces and whisk into the pan, one piece at a time, constantly beating until each piece is absorbed. Stop when the sauce is smooth and glossy. Pour immediately over the salmon, garnish and serve.
SERVES 6

MIDSUMMER FANTASIE

METRIC/IMPERIAL
225 g/8 oz cucumber
100 g/4 oz sliced smoked salmon
8 white asparagus stalks, peeled
20 small green asparagus stalks, peeled
salt
freshly ground black pepper
juice of 1 lemon
1 tablespoon Dijon mustard
1 tablespoon granulated sugar
6 tablespoons olive oil
2 tablespoons Quark
1 tablespoon chopped dill
dill sprigs, to garnish

Cut the cucumber and salmon into julienne strips. Season the asparagus with salt and pepper and lemon juice. Steam the asparagus over boiling water for 3 minutes.

Meanwhile, make the dressing: place the mustard, sugar, oil, Quark, dill and seasoning to taste in a screw-topped jar. Shake thoroughly, then taste and adjust the seasoning if necessary.

Arrange the cooked asparagus on 4 individual plates, and sprinkle on the cucumber and salmon. Garnish with sprigs of dill and serve with mustard dressing.
SERVES 4

BAKED TROUT

METRIC/IMPERIAL
2 tablespoons polyunsaturated vegetable oil
2 cloves garlic, peeled and crushed
2 onions, peeled and finely chopped
100 g/4 oz mushrooms, chopped
2 tablespoons capers
2 tablespoons wholemeal flour
25 g/1 oz ground almonds
4 × 225 g/8 oz trout, cleaned, washed and dried
2 tablespoons chopped parsley
pinch of chopped marjoram
1 teaspoon salt
½ teaspoon freshly ground black pepper
150 ml/¼ pint chicken stock
Garnish:
parsley sprigs
toasted flaked almonds

Heat the oil in a large, shallow flameproof casserole or heavy-based pan. Add the garlic and onions and fry gently for 5 minutes until the onions are soft and golden, stirring occasionally. Stir in the mushrooms, capers, flour and ground almonds and fry gently for a further 3 minutes.

Put the trout on top of the onion mixture, then sprinkle with the parsley, marjoram, salt and pepper. Pour on the stock.

Bake in a preheated moderately hot oven (200°C/400°F, Gas Mark 6) for 25 minutes, basting twice. Garnish with sprigs of parsley and sprinkle with toasted almonds. Serve with green beans and boiled new potatoes.
SERVES 4

TROUT IN FOIL

METRIC/IMPERIAL
1 carrot, peeled and finely chopped
few celery leaves, finely chopped
1 dessertspoon chopped parsley
1 clove garlic, peeled and finely chopped
15 g/½ oz butter
4 small trout, cleaned
salt
freshly ground black pepper

Mix the carrot, celery leaves, parsley and garlic together. Melt the butter in a pan and fry the mixture quickly for about 10 minutes until soft.

Place each trout on a piece of foil large enough to cover the fish completely, and season with salt and pepper. Divide the carrot mixture into 4 and spoon a portion over each fish.

Wrap the fish in foil, tucking the ends in firmly. Bake in a preheated moderately hot oven (190°C/375°F, Gas Mark 5) for about 20 minutes until tender. Serve the trout in the foil parcels.
SERVES 4

TROUT WITH SALTED CABBAGE

METRIC/IMPERIAL
2 tablespoons polyunsaturated vegetable oil
1 onion, peeled and chopped
1 × 5 cm/2 inch piece root ginger, peeled and finely shredded
4 trout, cleaned
150 ml/¼ pint chicken stock
25 g/1 oz pickled cabbage, chopped
25 g/1 oz canned bamboo shoots, drained and sliced
1 tablespoon soy sauce
2 teaspoons dry sherry
Garnish:
lemon twists
coriander leaves

Heat the oil in a wok or deep frying pan, add the onion and ginger and cook for 1 minute. Add the trout and fry for 1 minute on each side, until browned.

Stir in the stock, then add the cabbage, bamboo shoots, soy sauce and sherry. Cook for 10 minutes, basting the fish occasionally.

Transfer to a warmed serving dish and garnish with lemon twists and coriander.
SERVES 4

TROUT WITH HAZELNUTS

METRIC/IMPERIAL
4 × 175 g/6 oz trout, cleaned, heads and tails left on, fins removed
salt
freshly ground black pepper
flour for coating
good pinch of ground nutmeg
1 tablespoon polyunsaturated vegetable oil
75 g/3 oz polyunsaturated margarine
75 g/3 oz hazelnuts
4 tablespoons dry wholemeal breadcrumbs
2 tablespoons snipped chives or chopped parsley
1 lemon, quartered, to garnish

Wash the trout, pat them dry with kitchen paper towels and season them inside and out with salt and pepper. (If using frozen trout, allow time to thaw.) Just before cooking, roll the trout in the flour and nutmeg, coating them evenly. Heat the oil and 50 g/2 oz margarine in a large, heavy frying pan and, when the margarine ceases to foam, put in the trout and cook gently for 12 to 15 minutes, turning carefully halfway through cooking.

Meanwhile, spread the hazelnuts in the grill pan and toast them gently for a few minutes until the skins burst. Rub the nuts in a rough cloth to remove the skins, then chop them coarsely.

When the fish are cooked through and golden, lift them out carefully; arrange them side by side on a hot serving dish and keep hot. Add the remaining margarine to the fat remaining in the frying pan (if it has overbrowned, wipe out the pan and start again, using 50 g/2 oz margarine). When the margarine is hot, add the nuts and enough breadcrumbs to absorb all the fat. Fry fairly briskly, stirring, until golden brown and crisp. Stir in the chives or parsley with a little salt and pepper, and scatter immediately over the trout. Arrange the trout on individual, warmed serving plates and garnish with lemon wedges. Serve with a crisp green salad and new potatoes.
SERVES 4

TROUT WITH HERBS

METRIC/IMPERIAL
4 tablespoons wholemeal flour
½ teaspoon salt
¼ teaspoon pepper
4 trout, cleaned
3 tablespoons polyunsaturated vegetable oil
Sauce:
25 g/1 oz polyunsaturated margarine
juice of ½ lemon
1 tablespoon chopped mixed herbs (parsley, chives and thyme)
salt
freshly ground black pepper

Mix together the flour, salt and pepper and use to coat the trout. Heat the oil in a heavy frying pan, add the fish and fry for 5 to 6 minutes on each side until golden brown. Place on a warmed serving dish and keep hot.

Wipe the frying pan with kitchen paper. Add the margarine and cook until golden. Quickly add the lemon juice, herbs, and salt and pepper to taste. Pour over the trout and serve immediately.

SERVES 4

TROUT IN YOGURT SAUCE

METRIC/IMPERIAL
150 ml/¼ pint wine vinegar
150 ml/¼ pint water
1 small onion, peeled and sliced
1 bay leaf
1 parsley sprig
1 thyme sprig
salt
freshly ground white pepper
4 × 225 g/8 oz trout, cleaned, washed and dried
Sauce:
150 ml/¼ pint plain low-fat yogurt
3 tablespoons grated horseradish
juice of ½ lemon
1 tablespoon tarragon vinegar
1 teaspoon snipped chives
pinch of cayenne pepper

Put the vinegar, water, onion, bay leaf, parsley and thyme in a small pan with salt and pepper to taste. Bring to the boil, then lower the heat and simmer for 30 minutes.

Put the trout in a separate pan, then strain the vinegar liquid over the trout. Simmer very gently for 20 minutes, then drain well and place on a warmed serving dish. Keep hot.

To make the sauce, put all the ingredients in a heatproof bowl and stand over a pan of gently simmering water. Stir until the sauce is thick and creamy, then pour over the fish and serve immediately. Alternatively, this dish can be served cold.

SERVES 4

CANTONESE WHOLE FISH

METRIC/IMPERIAL
4 dried Chinese mushrooms
1 × 1-1.25 kg/2-2½ lb fish (trout, mullet, bass), cleaned
1 × 5 cm/2 inch piece root ginger
2 spring onions
50 g/2 oz cooked ham
50 g/2 oz canned bamboo shoots, drained
Marinade:
2 spring onions, chopped
1 clove garlic, peeled and sliced
3 tablespoons soy sauce
2 tablespoons dry sherry
2 tablespoons chicken stock
2 teaspoons cornflour

Soak the mushrooms in warm water for 15 minutes. Squeeze dry, discard the hard stalks, then slice the mushroom caps.

Score the flesh of the fish by making 3 diagonal cuts on each side. Place in a shallow dish. Mix all the marinade ingredients together and spoon over the fish. Leave to marinate for 30 minutes.

Finely shred the ginger, spring onions, ham and bamboo shoots and mix together with the mushrooms.

Place the fish on a heatproof plate. Pour over the marinade and place in a steamer. Sprinkle with the mushroom mixture and steam vigorously for 15 to 20 minutes, until tender. Transfer to a serving platter and serve immediately.

SERVES 4 to 6

STEAMED SALMON TROUT

METRIC/IMPERIAL
1.25 kg/2½ lb salmon trout, cleaned
225 g/8 oz smoked lean back bacon, derinded and cut into strips
100 g/4 oz mushrooms, roughly chopped
salt
freshly ground black pepper
juice of 2 lemons
2 tablespoons olive oil
5 tablespoons white wine
1 large Cos lettuce, separated into leaves and washed
600 ml/1 pint court bouillon (see page 87)
sprigs of fresh herbs, to garnish (e.g. dill, fennel, chives, parsley)
Hollandaise sauce (optional):
225 g/8 oz polyunsaturated margarine
2 egg yolks
2 tablespoons lemon juice

Wash the trout under running water. Check that there is no blood along the inside of the backbone, and if there is remove all of it to prevent a bitter tasting end result. Mix the bacon and mushrooms together, season well, and use to stuff the fish.

Lay the fish in a shallow dish containing lemon juice, olive oil and white wine. Turning once or twice, marinate for 2 to 3 hours.

Steam the lettuce leaves for 30 seconds to 1 minute, plunging them immediately afterwards into a bowl of iced water. Lay enough leaves, side by side and overlapping slightly, to completely blanket the whole fish. Lift the salmon trout from the marinade and wrap in the lettuce leaves, seasoning well as you go.

Bring the remaining marinade to the boil with the court bouillon. Place the lettuce parcel in a steamer above the pan. Cover well and steam for 20 minutes.

If you are making the hollandaise sauce, melt the margarine in a saucepan until it bubbles. Blend the egg yolks with the lemon juice in a blender or food processor, and season well with salt and pepper. Gradually pour in the margarine in a thin stream. When all of the margarine has been incorporated, turn off the machine immediately. Pour the sauce into a bowl and place it on top of a pan of hot water to warm through.

Lay the fish parcel on a warmed serving dish sprinkled with sprigs of fresh herbs and serve the sauce separately.
SERVES 4

SALMON TROUT IN ASPIC

METRIC/IMPERIAL
1 × 1.5 kg/3 lb salmon trout, cleaned
salt
freshly ground black pepper
polyunsaturated vegetable oil
600 ml/1 pint aspic jelly
2 tablespoons chopped herbs such as tarragon and dill
300 ml/½ pint reduced-calorie mayonnaise
Garnish:
tarragon, fennel or dill sprig
3 medium tomatoes, halved, scooped out and filled with cooked peas (optional)
3 hard-boiled eggs, halved, yolks sieved and creamed with reduced-calorie mayonnaise, then piled back into whites
½ cucumber, thinly sliced

Wash the trout under running water and remove any blood along the inside of the backbone. Wipe with kitchen paper towels and sprinkle the cavity with salt and pepper.

Lay the fish on a large piece of well-oiled aluminium foil and twist the foil edges together to form a loose but watertight parcel. Place the parcel on a baking sheet and bake in the centre of a preheated moderate oven (180°C/350°F, Gas Mark 4) for 45 minutes. Meanwhile, make up the aspic jelly and leave to cool.

When the fish is cooked, remove the parcel from the oven and leave, unopened, to allow it to cool a little. While the fish is still warm, open the parcel and skin the fish. To do this, cut the skin around the head and across the tail and peel it away from the flesh. Roll the fish over and repeat on the other side. Carefully transfer the fish to a flat serving dish. When the aspic is on the point of setting (if necessary, stir it over crushed ice until it coats the back of a metal spoon), spoon a thin film of jelly over the fish and leave to set.

Garnish the fish with a spray of herbs, coat with a second layer of aspic and leave to set again. Chill the remaining aspic until set. Chop the set aspic into small pieces and arrange the pieces along either side of the fish. Set the filled tomatoes (if using) and eggs alternately in the chopped aspic and border the dish with overlapping slices of cucumber. Stir the freshly chopped herbs into the mayonnaise and serve separately.
SERVES 6

SQUID SALAD WITH CITRUS HERB DRESSING

METRIC/IMPERIAL
675 g/1½ lb prepared squid
16 small green asparagus tips
75 g/3 oz mangetout, topped and tailed
juice of 1 lemon
salt
freshly ground black pepper
small head of radicchio, separated into leaves
and washed
Dressing:
4 tablespoons olive oil
3 tablespoons lemon vinegar
50 g/2 oz Quark
1 tablespoon finely chopped herbs (e.g. dill,
chervil, parsley)
dill and chervil sprigs, to garnish (optional)

Slice the squid into thin rings. Lay a piece of wet greaseproof paper in a steamer, then arrange the asparagus, mangetout and squid on top. Sprinkle over the lemon juice and season well with salt and pepper. Cover and steam over boiling water for 3 minutes.

Meanwhile, mix all the dressing ingredients in a screw-topped jar. Season well with salt and pepper. Arrange the radicchio leaves on a serving dish. Toss the warm food in the dressing and pile on to the radicchio leaves. Garnish with sprigs of dill and chervil, if liked.
SERVES 4

PRAWN RISOTTO

METRIC/IMPERIAL
4 tablespoons polyunsaturated vegetable oil
1 onion, peeled and chopped
225 g/8 oz brown rice, well washed
600 ml/1 pint water
salt
freshly ground black pepper
1 red pepper, cored, deseeded and chopped
1 clove garlic, peeled and crushed
50 g/2 oz flaked almonds
350 g/12 oz cooked, peeled prawns
1 tablespoon chopped parsley

Heat half the oil in a pan, add the onion and fry until softened. Add the rice and cook for 2 minutes, stirring. Add the water and 1 teaspoon salt and bring to the boil. Simmer for 40 to 45 minutes, adding more water if necessary.

Heat the remaining oil in a pan, add the pepper and fry for 3 minutes. Add the garlic, almonds and prawns. Fry for a further 2 minutes, until the almonds are browned and the prawns heated through.

Stir into the cooked rice, add pepper to taste and more salt if necessary. Transfer to a warmed dish and sprinkle with the parsley.
SERVES 4

SWEDISH PICKLED SHRIMP

METRIC/IMPERIAL
450 g/1 lb cooked, peeled shrimps
6 black peppercorns, crushed
½ teaspoon chopped thyme
1 bay leaf
150 ml/¼ pint tarragon vinegar
1 lettuce
dill leaves, to garnish

The shrimps may be fresh, or thawed frozen ones which have been well drained. Put the shrimps in a bowl and sprinkle with the crushed peppercorns and the thyme. Put the bay leaf on top and pour on the tarragon vinegar. Chill in the refrigerator for 2 hours.

Arrange a bed of lettuce leaves in 4 individual serving bowls. Drain the shrimps and arrange a mound of them on each bed of lettuce. Sprinkle with dill leaves. Serve with thinly sliced brown bread or crispbread.
SERVES 4

COLD CURRIED PRAWNS

METRIC/IMPERIAL
450 g/1 lb cooked, peeled prawns
Sauce:
4 tablespoons sunflower oil
4 teaspoons curry paste
8 tablespoons wine vinegar
pinch of salt

Put the prawns in a shallow dish.

Mix the sunflower oil, curry paste and wine vinegar together. Add a pinch of salt, unless the prawns are already salty.

Pour the sauce over the prawns and leave to marinate for 1 hour in a cool place, turning frequently. Serve the prawns in the sauce.
SERVES 4

HOT PRAWN CURRY

METRIC/IMPERIAL
25 g/1 oz polyunsaturated margarine
1 small onion, peeled and chopped
1 teaspoon curry powder
2 teaspoons flour
150 ml/¼ pint plain low-fat yogurt
1 small dessert apple, cored and chopped
225 g/8 oz cooked, peeled prawns
2 tomatoes, skinned, deseeded and chopped
salt
freshly ground black pepper
lemon wedges, to garnish

Melt the margarine in a pan, add the onion and fry gently for 3 minutes until soft and golden, stirring occasionally. Stir in the curry powder and flour and cook for 2 minutes.
Remove from the heat and stir in the yogurt, apple and prawns. Return to the heat and cook gently for 5 minutes.
Add the tomatoes to the pan and continue cooking for 3 minutes. Add salt and pepper to taste. Garnish with lemon wedges and serve hot, with brown rice.
SERVES 2

SHELLFISH RAGOÛT

METRIC/IMPERIAL
12 scampi or Mediterranean prawns
300 ml/½ pint strong fish stock
12 baby new carrots
8 radishes, topped and tailed
75 g/3 oz mangetout, topped and tailed
4 prepared large scallops, fresh if possible, or 8 Queen scallops
350 g/12 oz mussels, scrubbed and beards removed
225 g/8 oz fresh clams, scrubbed
juice of 1 lemon
2 dill sprigs
salt
freshly ground black pepper
½ bunch watercress
75 g/3 oz Quark
Garnish:
dill sprigs
watercress sprigs

If the scampi or prawns are raw, steam for 5 minutes over the fish stock, and leave to cool slightly. Remove the shells from the scampi,

roughly chop and add the shells to the fish stock (leave the scampi to one side). Simmer for 10 minutes, then discard the shells.
Otherwise, place the carrots, radishes and the mangetout in a steamer compartment, cover with a tight-fitting lid and steam over the fish stock for 3 minutes. Meanwhile cut the scampi and scallops in half, taking care to leave the coral whole. Place all the shellfish in the steamer with the vegetables. Sprinkle with lemon juice and dill sprigs. Season well with salt and pepper. Steam for 3 to 5 minutes. Remove, set aside and keep warm.
Reduce the stock by half by boiling rapidly. Add the watercress and Quark, then purée the sauce in a blender or food processor. Taste and adjust seasoning, if necessary.
Pour the sauce into a warmed serving dish, pile the shellfish in the centre, and garnish with dill and watercress. Serve immediately.
SERVES 4

QUICK-FRIED SQUID WITH CRAB AND TOMATO SAUCE

METRIC/IMPERIAL
450 g/1 lb cleaned squid, fresh or frozen and thawed
1 tablespoon polyunsaturated vegetable oil
1 × 5 cm/2 inch piece root ginger, finely chopped
3 spring onions, finely chopped
1 × 175 g/6 oz can crabmeat
1 × 65 g/2½ oz can tomato purée
1 teaspoon sugar
1 tablespoon light soy sauce
4 tablespoons chicken stock
1 tablespoon dry sherry
2 teaspoons cornflour
chopped spring onion, to garnish

Cut the squid into 2.5 cm/1 inch pieces
Heat the oil in a wok or deep frying pan, add the ginger and spring onions and stir-fry for 1 minute. Add the squid and cook for 2 minutes. Add the remaining ingredients, except the cornflour, and mix well. Cook for 2 minutes, stirring.
Blend the cornflour to a smooth paste with 1 tablespoon water. Stir into the pan and cook, stirring, until thickened. Spoon into a warmed serving dish, garnish with spring onion and serve immediately.
SERVES 4

QUICK-FRIED PRAWNS

METRIC/IMPERIAL
100 g/4 oz fresh asparagus, cut into 2.5 cm/
1 inch pieces (optional)
4 tablespoons dry sherry
1 egg white
pinch of salt
450 g/1 lb peeled prawns, fresh or frozen and
thawed
1 tablespoon polyunsaturated vegetable oil
1 teaspoon finely chopped root ginger
2 spring onions, chopped

Cook the asparagus in boiling salted water for 5 minutes (if using); drain thoroughly.

Mix 2 tablespoons of the sherry with the egg white and salt. Add the prawns and toss until evenly coated; drain.

Heat the oil in a wok or frying pan, add the ginger and half of the spring onions and fry for 2 minutes. Add the prawns and cook for 5 minutes, or until they become pink. Add the asparagus (if using) and remaining sherry and cook for 1 minute.

Transfer to a warmed serving dish and sprinkle with the remaining spring onion. Serve immediately.
SERVES 4 to 6

PRAWN AND SPINACH PILAU

METRIC/IMPERIAL
450 g/1 lb cooked, unpeeled prawns
1 × 5 cm/2 inch piece lemon peel
3 parsley sprigs
1 thyme sprig
1 bay leaf
6 white peppercorns, lightly crushed
1.2 litres/2 pints water
750 g/1½ lb fresh spinach, or 400 g/14 oz frozen
leaf spinach, thawed
350 g/12 oz long-grain rice
4 tablespoons olive oil
2 large onions, peeled and finely chopped
1 clove garlic, peeled and crushed
freshly grated nutmeg
Maldon or sea salt
freshly ground white pepper

Peel the prawns and put the heads and shells into a large pan with the lemon peel, herbs and peppercorns. Add the cold water and bring to the boil,

then simmer for 20 minutes. Strain and reserve the stock.

Wash the fresh spinach, then chop off and discard the tough stalks. Shred finely. Thawed frozen spinach only needs to be squeezed to extract moisture, then chopped.

Measure and note the volume of rice, rinse in boiling water and soak in fresh boiled water for 5 minutes.

Heat the oil in a large saucepan, add the onions and cook gently for about 5 minutes, until starting to soften. Add the garlic and spinach and stir-fry for 2 to 3 minutes.

Drain the rice and add to the pan, stirring until it gleams with a light coating of oil, then grate over a generous amount of nutmeg. Measure out the same volume of prawn stock as the rice and pour over the rice. Season well, bring quickly to the boil, bubble for 10 seconds, then reduce the heat. Add the prawns, cover and cook for 15 to 20 minutes until the liquid is absorbed.

Turn off the heat, stir the contents of the pan, then cover and leave for 5 minutes to 'fluff' the rice. Serve immediately.
SERVES 6

PRAWNS IN HERB SAUCE

METRIC/IMPERIAL
12 uncooked Mediterranean or Dublin Bay
prawns
1 leek, trimmed and washed
2 carrots, peeled
½ celeriac, peeled
½ bunch parsley
1 tablespoon polyunsaturated margarine
1 onion, peeled and quartered
120 ml/4 fl oz dry white wine
2 white peppercorns
1 bay leaf
½ bunch dill
120 ml/4 fl oz single cream
1 teaspoon lemon juice
salt
freshly ground white pepper
dill sprigs, to garnish

Rinse and peel the prawns, then remove the black thread-like intestine.

Coarsely chop the leek, carrots and celeriac. Wash the parsley, strip off the leaves. Keep 3 stalks for the stock.

Melt the margarine in a saucepan and fry the prawn shells and vegetables until the shells are red in colour. Add the wine and stir well to mix. Add the parsley stalks, peppercorns and bay leaf.

Simmer for 30 minutes, then strain. Bring the stock back to the boil in a clean pan. Add the prawns and simmer for about 8 minutes.

Wash the dill and finely chop with the parsley leaves. Lift the prawns out of the stock and keep hot on 4 warmed plates.

Boil to reduce the stock by half. Gradually add the cream and continue boiling until creamy and sauce-like, stirring continuously. Stir in the herbs and lemon juice and season to taste with salt and pepper. Pour over the prawns. Serve garnished with sprigs of dill.

SERVES 4

MINIATURE PRAWN KEBABS

METRIC/IMPERIAL
450 g/1 lb cooked, unpeeled prawns
4 tablespoons olive oil
1 tablespoon lemon juice
1 teaspoon soy sauce
1 × 2.5 cm/1 inch piece fresh root ginger, peeled and grated
¼ teaspoon cumin seeds, lightly ground
freshly ground sea salt
freshly ground black pepper
3 spring onions, green tops only, shredded diagonally
1 small bunch fresh parsley, finely chopped
6 lemon wedges, to garnish

Peel the prawns (keep the heads and shells to make soup or stock) and put into a deep dish.

Mix together the olive oil, lemon juice, soy sauce, ginger and cumin, then pour over the prawns. Stir to coat, cover and then leave to marinate for at least 1 hour (preferably unchilled as the flavours should be allowed to develop). Turn them once or twice during this time.

About 20 minutes before serving, put 12 bamboo skewers into water to soak. Sprinkle the prawns with a little salt and pepper, then thread them on to the soaked bamboo skewers – about 5 per skewer. Cook under a hot grill for 4 to 5 minutes, turning the skewers halfway through and basting with a little of the marinade.

Make a bed of the shredded onion tops and chopped parsley on 6 small plates, and arrange the skewers on top. Serve with the lemon wedges.

SERVES 6

PLAICE WITH PRAWNS AND ASPARAGUS

METRIC/IMPERIAL
4 plaice fillets
salt
freshly ground black pepper
1 × 350 g/12 oz can asparagus spears, drained
15 g/½ oz polyunsaturated margarine
100 g/4 oz peeled prawns
few drops of lemon juice
150 ml/¼ pint half dry white wine and half water, mixed
4 white peppercorns
2 bay leaves
25 g/1 oz dry skimmed milk powder
1 tablespoon cornflour
Garnish:
1 tablespoon chopped parsley
lemon twists

Skin the fish and season well with salt and pepper to taste. Divide the asparagus into 4 portions and roll a portion in each fish fillet. Secure each roll with a wooden cocktail stick. Lightly grease an ovenproof dish with the margarine and arrange the fish rolls in it. Scatter the prawns over the top. Sprinkle with lemon juice, wine mixture, peppercorns and bay leaves; cover and cook in a preheated moderate oven (180°C/350°F, Gas Mark 4) for 30 to 40 minutes. Lift out the fish rolls and prawns, remove the cocktail sticks, and set aside on a serving dish. Keep warm.

Strain the fish liquid and stir in the skimmed milk powder. Mix the cornflour with a little of the liquid in a bowl, then stir in the rest. Pour into a saucepan and bring to the boil, stirring continuously until thickened. Taste and adjust the seasoning if necessary. Pour the sauce over the fish rolls, sprinkle with chopped parsley and garnish with twists of lemon.

Serve at once with a crisp green salad and new potatoes or tiny carrots and mangetout.

SERVES 4

MARINATED MUSHROOMS WITH PRAWNS

METRIC/IMPERIAL
2 shallots or spring onions, trimmed and sliced
1 clove garlic, peeled and crushed
finely grated rind and juice of 1 lemon
5 tablespoons polyunsaturated vegetable oil
2 tablespoons thyme leaves
2 tablespoons chopped parsley
salt
freshly ground black pepper
225 g/8 oz mushrooms, wiped and sliced
100 g/4 oz peeled prawns
pinch of paprika
Garnish:
4 lemon slices
4 unpeeled prawns

Put the shallots or spring onions in a bowl with the garlic, the lemon rind and juice, oil, herbs and salt and pepper to taste. Beat well to mix.

Add the mushrooms and toss in the dressing until thoroughly coated. Cover and leave to marinate for 2 hours.

Divide the mushrooms between 4 serving plates. Top with the prawns and sprinkle with paprika. Garnish each plate with a lemon slice and a prawn.
SERVES 4

COQUILLES ST JACQUES

METRIC/IMPERIAL
350 g/12 oz scallops, dark beards removed
1 dessertspoon wine vinegar
350 g/12 oz potatoes, peeled
2 tablespoons dried skimmed milk powder
15 g/½ oz butter
1 dessertspoon plain white unbleached flour
25 g/1 oz Gruyère cheese, grated

Gently poach the scallops in enough water to cover and the vinegar for 4 to 5 minutes until tender. Drain and reserve the poaching liquid.

Meanwhile, place the potatoes in a saucepan of salted water, bring to the boil and simmer for about 20 minutes until tender. Strain and reserve the cooking water. Mash the potatoes with a little of the cooking water and ½ tablespoon of the skimmed milk powder.

Melt the butter in a saucepan and stir in the flour. Cook for 2 minutes, stirring. Mix the

remaining skimmed milk powder with the scallop poaching liquid and make up to about 300 ml/ ½ pint with the potato cooking water. Gradually add enough of this liquid to make a fairly thick sauce.

Put the drained scallops on their shells or in individual flameproof dishes. Put the potato into a piping bag fitted with a vegetable nozzle and pipe round the edge of the shells or dishes.

Pour on the sauce and sprinkle the cheese over. Place under a preheated hot grill until the cheese has melted and lightly browned.
SERVES 4

MUSSELS WITH MIXED VEGETABLES

METRIC/IMPERIAL
2 kg/4½ lb mussels, scrubbed
25 g/1 oz polyunsaturated margarine
2 shallots, peeled and very finely chopped
3 cloves garlic, peeled and crushed
bulb of fennel, very finely chopped
150 ml/¼ pint white wine
1 tablespoon fennel leaves
1 tablespoon chopped parsley
½ tablespoon snipped chives
1 carrot, cut into julienne strips
1 leek, trimmed, washed and cut into julienne strips
1 parsnip, peeled and cut into julienne strips
salt
freshly ground black pepper
50 g/2 oz Quark
fennel leaves, to garnish

Discard any open mussels or those that do not shut when firmly tapped. Melt the margarine in the base of a large saucepan. Gently fry the shallot, garlic and fennel until cooked but not brown. Add the wine and simmer for 5 minutes. Put the mussels in the pan, and sprinkle with the herbs and vegetable strips. Season with salt and pepper. Cover with a tight-fitting lid. Cook the mussels for 3 to 5 minutes, shaking the pan from time to time, but without lifting the lid.

Discard any unopened mussels. Transfer the mussels and vegetable strips to a warmed serving dish and keep hot. Blend the fennel and garlic mixture in a blender, adding the Quark. Taste and adjust the seasoning, if necessary. Pour the sauce over the mussels and garnish with fennel leaves.
SERVES 4

SCALLOP BROCHETTES

METRIC/IMPERIAL
16 large scallops, dark beards removed
juice of 2 limes
2 teaspoons chopped tarragon
salt
freshly ground black pepper
6 tablespoons olive oil
1 mango, peeled, stoned and diced
300 ml/½ pint white wine
4 tarragon sprigs
2 bay leaves
150 ml/¼ pint water
Garnish:
tarragon sprigs
mango slices (optional)
lime slices (optional)

Cut the white flesh of the scallops into quarters. Keep the pink coral whole. Marinate in the lime juice and tarragon, seasoned well with salt and pepper, for up to 2 hours.

Skewer 8 scallop quarters and 2 corals on each of 8 wooden kebab sticks, retaining the marinade for the dressing. Make a dressing by mixing the oil, marinade and mango in a screw-topped jar. Shake well and season to taste.

Put the wine, sprigs of tarragon, bay leaves and water into a saucepan. Place the kebabs in a steamer above the pan, cover with a tight-fitting lid and cook for 3 minutes.

Arrange 2 kebabs on each of 4 plates, spoon on plenty of lime and mango dressing. Garnish with sprigs of tarragon and slices of mango and lime, if wished, and serve immediately.
SERVES 4

SCALLOPS PROVENÇAL

METRIC/IMPERIAL
12 large scallops, dark beards removed
Maldon or sea salt
freshly ground black pepper
3-4 tablespoons lemon juice
100-150 g/4-5 oz polyunsaturated margarine
1 tablespoon olive oil
6 tablespoons home-made dried breadcrumbs
2-3 cloves garlic, peeled and finely chopped
4 tablespoons finely chopped parsley
lemon wedges, to serve (optional)

Separate the coral from the white flesh. Cut each scallop in half to give 2 flat discs. Scrub and thoroughly dry the deep curved shells if you have been able to get them.

Put the discs into a shallow bowl, sprinkle them lightly with salt and black pepper, then pour over the lemon juice.

Melt 50 g/2 oz margarine in a large frying pan, add the oil, then the breadcrumbs and gently fry for 2 to 3 minutes until lightly crisp. Add another 25 g/1 oz margarine if necessary – the breadcrumbs shouldn't burn but neither should they become too greasy. When they are golden and crisp, tip the breadcrumbs into a bowl and reserve.

Wipe the pan clean with paper towels and return to the heat. Melt the remaining 50 g/2 oz margarine and when just starting to bubble, add the scallop discs and fry for 1 to 2 minutes. Stir in the finely chopped garlic and parsley, then add the corals and continue cooking for another minute. Mix in the breadcrumbs, then quickly divide between the shells or small serving dishes and serve immediately with lemon wedges, if wished.
SERVES 4 to 6

SAILORS' MUSSELS

METRIC/IMPERIAL
48 mussels, scrubbed
6 shallots, peeled and chopped
300 ml/½ pint dry cider
2 teaspoons flour
15 g/½ oz polyunsaturated margarine
2 tablespoons chopped parsley
salt
freshly ground black pepper

Wash the mussels and scrub them very thoroughly. Discard any which are open. Put them in a heavy pan with the shallots and cider. Cover and cook over high heat for 5 minutes until all the mussels have opened; discard any which are still closed.

Lift out the mussels and discard the top shell from each one. Divide them equally between 4 individual soup bowls and keep hot.

Work the flour and margarine together to form a ball. Drop the ball into the cooking liquid and simmer until the sauce has thickened slightly, stirring constantly. Stir in the parsley, then add salt and pepper to taste. Pour the sauce over the mussels and serve immediately.
SERVES 4

PEPPERED SCALLOPS

METRIC/IMPERIAL
2 tablespoons sesame oil
juice of 1 lemon
15 g/½ oz fresh root ginger, peeled and grated
1 large clove garlic, peeled and crushed
salt
freshly ground black pepper
16 large scallops, dark beards removed
300 ml/½ pint fish stock
1 red pepper, cored, deseeded and finely
chopped
1 green pepper, cored, deseeded and finely
chopped
1 yellow pepper, cored, deseeded and finely
chopped
1 tablespoon sesame seeds, to garnish
Dressing:
3 tablespoons sesame oil
1 tablespoon lemon juice
1 shallot, finely chopped
1 tablespoon soy sauce
100 g/4 oz polyunsaturated margarine

Mix together the oil, lemon juice, ginger and garlic, and season well with salt and pepper. Remove the pink coral whole from the scallop shells. Cut the white flesh in two. Marinate in the oil and lemon mixture for up to 2 hours.

Meanwhile, make the dressing. Place all the ingredients in a screw-topped jar and shake well. Taste and adjust the seasoning, if necessary.

Put the stock and any remaining marinade in the base of a steamer. Arrange the mixed peppers in the steaming compartment with the scallops on top. Cover with a tight-fitting lid and cook for 3 minutes. Remove the scallops, toss in the dressing and keep warm. Add the peppers to the stock. Boil to reduce until syrupy. Reduce the heat and whisk in the margarine, bit by bit, until you have a creamy sauce. Check the seasoning.

Flood 4 individual plates with the mixed pepper sauce. Arrange the scallops on top and sprinkle with sesame seeds.
SERVES 4

CRAB AND COTTAGE CHEESE MOUSSE

METRIC/IMPERIAL
15 g/½ oz powdered gelatine
150 ml/¼ pint water
450 g/1 lb cottage cheese, sieved
salt
freshly ground black pepper
225 g/8 oz crabmeat
3 tablespoons single cream
2 teaspoons lemon juice
watercress sprigs, to garnish

Put the gelatine and water in a small cup. Stand the cup in a pan of hot water and stir until the gelatine has dissolved.

Put the cottage cheese in a bowl, add salt and pepper to taste, then stir in the crabmeat, cream and lemon juice. Mix very thoroughly, then stir in the gelatine. Spoon the mixture into a serving bowl, then chill in the refrigerator for 2 hours. Garnish the mousse with watercress sprigs.
SERVES 4

CRAB CREOLE

METRIC/IMPERIAL
1 teaspoon polyunsaturated margarine
1 small onion, peeled and thinly sliced
1 red pepper, cored, deseeded and finely
chopped
1 clove garlic, peeled and crushed
1 teaspoon soft light brown sugar
1 tablespoon tomato chutney
salt
freshly ground black pepper
Tabasco or chilli sauce
1 × 400 g/14 oz can chopped tomatoes
450 g/1 lb frozen crabmeat, thawed and flaked

Melt the margarine in a non-stick frying pan, add the onion and red pepper and cook for about 6 minutes, stirring occasionally, until soft. Add the garlic, sugar, tomato chutney, salt and pepper and Tabasco or chilli sauce to taste. Stir well and cook for a further 1 to 2 minutes.

Add the tomatoes with their juice and simmer gently for 25 minutes, until reduced and thickened. Gently stir the crabmeat into the creole sauce. Cover and simmer gently for a further 5 to 7 minutes. Pile on to a heated serving dish and serve immediately.
SERVES 4

BAKED CRAB

METRIC/IMPERIAL
2 tablespoons polyunsaturated vegetable oil
1 onion, peeled and finely chopped
1 clove garlic, peeled and crushed
2 green peppers, cored, deseeded and finely chopped
2 tomatoes, skinned, deseeded and chopped
2 tablespoons chopped parsley
450 g/1 lb crabmeat
salt
freshly ground white pepper
2 eggs, lightly beaten
2 tablespoons wholemeal breadcrumbs

Heat the oil in a pan, add the onion and fry gently for 5 minutes until soft and golden, stirring occasionally. Add the garlic, green peppers, tomatoes and parsley and continue cooking gently for 15 minutes, stirring occasionally.

Add the crabmeat to the pan with salt and pepper to taste. Then add the eggs and cook until just set, stirring constantly.

Spread the crab mixture in a greased shallow baking dish and sprinkle the breadcrumbs on top. Bake in a preheated moderately hot oven (190°C/375°F, Gas Mark 5) for 10 minutes or until the crumbs are crisp and brown. Serve hot.
SERVES 4

QUICK-FRIED CRAB IN AROMATIC OIL

METRIC/IMPERIAL
1 large freshly cooked crab or 2 × 175 g/6 oz cans crabmeat
2 tablespoons polyunsaturated vegetable oil
1 clove garlic, peeled and crushed
1 × 5 cm/2 inch piece root ginger, finely chopped
4 spring onions, chopped
1 leek, washed and thinly sliced
salt
1 egg, beaten
150 ml/¼ pint fish or chicken stock
2 tablespoons dry sherry
2 teaspoons cornflour, blended with 1 tablespoon water
2 teaspoons sesame seed oil
lemon wedges, to garnish

Break off the legs and crack the claws of the fresh crab. Place each crab on its back and firmly pull

the body away from the shell. Remove and discard the grey stomach sac and the grey feathered gills. Remove all the meat and cut into pieces.

Heat the oil in a wok or frying pan, add the garlic, ginger and spring onions and stir-fry for 1 minute. Add the crabmeat and stir-fry for 5 minutes. Add the leek and salt to taste.

Lower the heat and pour in the egg in a thin stream. Add the stock and sherry and cook for 1 minute. Add the cornflour mixture and sesame oil; cook, stirring, until thickened.

Turn on to a warmed serving dish and serve immediately, garnished with lemon wedges.
SERVES 4 to 6

ONION AND GINGER CRAB WITH EGG

METRIC/IMPERIAL
2 large or 3 small freshly cooked crabs
salt
4-5 slices root ginger, shredded
2 tablespoons soy sauce
1 tablespoon chilli sauce
2 tablespoons dry sherry
150 ml/¼ pint clear stock
4 tablespoons polyunsaturated vegetable oil
2 onions, peeled and thinly sliced
4 cloves garlic, peeled and crushed
3-4 spring onions, cut into 2.5 cm/1 inch pieces
1 egg, beaten

Separate the claws from each crab and crack them open. Place each crab on its back and firmly pull the body, with the legs attached, away from the shell. Remove and discard the grey stomach sac and the grey feathered gills. Cut the body part into 4 pieces, and sprinkle with the salt and ginger. Combine the soy sauce, chilli sauce, sherry and stock together. Heat the oil in a large pan over high heat. Add the onions and garlic. Stir-fry for 30 seconds. Add all the crab pieces, including the body shells, and the spring onions. Stir-fry for 3 to 4 minutes, until cooked through. Pour the soy sauce mixture over the crab pieces and bring to the boil, stirring constantly. Pour the egg into the pan in a thin stream and stir-fry for 30 seconds.

Turn the mixture on to a warmed serving dish. Eat by scraping the crabmeat out of the main shells and claws.
SERVES 4 to 6

SHELLFISH IN RICH HERB SAUCE

METRIC/IMPERIAL

1 × 450 g/1 lb lobster, lightly boiled
3 tablespoons olive oil
1 onion, peeled and finely chopped
1 red pepper, cored, deseeded, and thinly sliced
1 green pepper, cored, deseeded, and thinly sliced
2 cloves garlic, peeled and chopped
2 teaspoons paprika
2 baby squid, cleaned and cut into rings (optional)
4 tomatoes, skinned and chopped
12 blanched almonds, crushed
3 pinches of powdered saffron
1 bay leaf
200 ml/⅓ pint dry white wine
3 tablespoons brandy
juice of 1 lemon
200 ml/⅓ pint water
salt
freshly ground black pepper
12 prawns, unpeeled
8 mussels, scrubbed and bearded
8 clams or cockles, scrubbed
chopped parsley, to garnish

Slit the lobster in half lengthwise. Discard the head and stomach sac and the dark intestinal vein which runs along the inside of the body. Twist off the large claws and crack them. Put on one side with the rest of the shellfish.

Heat the oil in a large flameproof casserole. Add the onion, peppers, garlic, paprika and squid (if using). Cook gently for 10 to 15 minutes. Add the tomatoes, almonds, saffron and bay leaf, then stir in the wine, brandy, lemon juice and water. Stir well and allow to bubble for 1 to 2 minutes over a high heat. Season to taste with salt and pepper. Add all the shellfish to the pan, cover and cook over a low heat for about 15 minutes. Discard any mussels or clams or cockles that have not opened. Correct the seasoning and sprinkle with parsley before serving.

SERVES 4

FRESH LOBSTER SALAD

METRIC/IMPERIAL

2 × 450 g/1 lb live female lobsters
25 g/1 oz polyunsaturated margarine
500 g/1¼ lb carrots, peeled and grated
2 shallots, peeled and finely chopped
300 ml/½ pint vegetable stock
2-3 dill sprigs
2-3 thyme sprigs
1 tablespoon snipped chives
salt
freshly ground black pepper
1 tablespoon red wine vinegar
3 tablespoons olive oil
juice of 1 lemon
1 head of chicory, separated into leaves and washed
1 small curly endive, separated into leaves and washed
1 lettuce heart, separated into leaves and washed
2 avocados

Bring a large saucepan of water to the boil then let it go cold; this removes the oxygen from the water and effectively anaesthetizes the lobsters before they are steamed.

Bring a second large saucepan of water to the boil. Place the live lobsters in the cool water for 3 minutes, then put them straight into a steamer and steam over the boiling water for 15 minutes. Remove the lobsters and leave them to cool down

Melt the margarine in a pan, and gently fry the carrots and shallots until soft but not brown. Add the stock and herbs, and season well. Simmer for 10 to 15 minutes. Blend the sauce in a blender, and add the vinegar.

When the lobsters are slightly cooler, remove the tails and cut through the shell underneath with scissors. Carefully open out the shells and remove the tail meat in one piece. Remove and carefully crack the claws; lift out the meat and discard the cartilage. Cut the tail meat into thin medallions and cut the claws in half.

Mix together the oil and 2 tablespoons of the lemon juice. Season well with salt and pepper Toss the chicory, endive and lettuce leaves in the dressing. Peel, stone and slice the avocados and brush with a little lemon juice. Pour the carrot coulis on to 4 individual plates. Arrange the leaves, lobster and avocado on each plate. Serve at once, or cover and chill in the refrigerator.

SERVES 4

MUSSEL ANTIPASTO

METRIC/IMPERIAL
1 kg/2 lb mussels, scrubbed
120 ml/4 fl oz dry white wine or water
40 g/1½ oz fresh wholemeal breadcrumbs
2 cloves garlic, peeled and chopped
2 tablespoons finely chopped parsley
freshly ground black pepper
3 tablespoons olive oil

Discard any mussels that do not close when firmly tapped. Boil the wine or water in a large, heavy saucepan. Add the mussels, cover and cook over a high heat for 5 to 6 minutes, shaking the pan frequently, until the mussel shells have opened (discard any that have not opened). Remove from the heat.

Detach and discard the top shells, leaving each mussel in its lower shell. Arrange, side by side, in a large, shallow gratin dish or 4 individual gratin dishes. Mix together the breadcrumbs, garlic, parsley and pepper and spoon over the mussels. Sprinkle the oil evenly over the top. Cook in a preheated hot oven (230°C/450°F, Gas Mark 8) for 3 to 4 minutes or until the crumbs are just tinged brown. Take care not to overcook the mussels.
SERVES 4

VERMICELLI WITH TOMATO AND MUSSEL SAUCE

METRIC/IMPERIAL
1 kg/2 lb mussels, scrubbed and steamed open
2 tablespoons polyunsaturated vegetable oil
1 onion, peeled and finely chopped
2 cloves garlic, peeled and sliced
750 g/1½ lb tomatoes, skinned and chopped
350 g/12 oz vermicelli
salt
freshly ground black pepper
2 tablespoons chopped parsley, to garnish

Reserve a few of the mussels in their shells for garnish (discard any that have not opened). Remove the remaining mussels from their shells and discard the shells. Heat 1½ tablespoons of the oil in a large saucepan and fry the onion gently until soft and golden. Stir in the garlic, then the tomatoes. Simmer gently for about 30 minutes or until the tomatoes have reduced to a pulp.
Cook the pasta in boiling salted water for about

10 minutes or until tender. Drain, place in a heated serving dish containing the remaining oil and toss until lightly coated.

Season the sauce with salt and pepper to taste, add the shelled mussels and heat through for a few minutes, stirring well. Pile the sauce over the pasta, garnish with parsley and the reserved mussels in shells and serve immediately.
SERVES 4

LOBSTER WITH BASIL SAUCE AND MANGOES

METRIC/IMPERIAL
1.2 litres/2 pints court bouillon (see page 87)
2 uncooked lobster tails
2 large, ripe mangoes
Sauce:
1 tablespoon wine vinegar
4 tablespoons olive oil
1 small clove garlic, peeled
20 basil leaves
salt
freshly ground black pepper

Bring the court bouillon to the boil in a large saucepan. Add the lobster tails and simmer for 6 to 8 minutes or until the shells turn red. Remove the lobster tails from the pan and, when cool enough to handle, remove the shells and cut the flesh into slices, 1 cm/½ inch thick.

Meanwhile, make the sauce. Place the vinegar, oil, garlic and basil leaves in a blender or food processor and process until smooth. Season to taste.

With a sharp knife, make a slit lengthwise around the mangoes and peel off the skin. Cut the flesh into very thin slices.

Assemble the ingredients on 4 large, individual plates. First make a circle of mango slices on each plate, leaving a space in the centre. Heap lobster in the space and spoon the sauce over.
SERVES 4

PASTA & RICE

SPAGHETTI WITH TOMATO AND RED PEPPER SAUCE

METRIC/IMPERIAL
1 tablespoon polyunsaturated vegetable oil
1 clove garlic, peeled and crushed
1 onion, peeled and sliced
450 g/1 lb minced lean beef
1 × 400 g/14 oz can tomatoes
1 red pepper, cored, deseeded and sliced
1 tablespoon chopped parsley
salt
freshly ground black pepper
350 g/12 oz wholemeal spaghetti

Heat the oil in a saucepan and brown the garlic, onion and beef. Add the tomatoes, red pepper and parsley. Cook for 5 minutes, then add sufficient hot water to make a sauce. Season with salt and pepper. Simmer the sauce until thickened slightly, stirring occasionally.

Cook the spaghetti for 10 to 15 minutes in boiling water. Drain well and add the sauce.
SERVES 4

SPAGHETTI WITH ALMOND CHEESE

METRIC/IMPERIAL
350 g/12 oz wholemeal spaghetti
salt
1 tablespoon chopped parsley
freshly ground black pepper
25 g/1 oz browned flaked almonds, to garnish
Sauce:
25 g/1 oz grated Parmesan cheese
100 g/4 oz ground almonds
100 g/4 oz cottage cheese
pinch of grated nutmeg
pinch of grated cinnamon
3 tablespoons plain low-fat yogurt

Cook the spaghetti for 10 to 15 minutes in boiling salted water. Drain, saving 150 ml/¼ pint of the

water for the sauce, and mix the spaghetti with the parsley and pepper to taste. Put the spaghetti in a large heated dish and keep hot.

Mix together all the sauce ingredients and the reserved cooking water and season well with salt and pepper. Spoon over the spaghetti and garnish with the almonds.
SERVES 4

MACARONI CRUNCH

METRIC/IMPERIAL
1 tablespoon polyunsaturated vegetable oil
2 onions, peeled and chopped
225 g/8 oz wholemeal macaroni
1 × 400 g/14 oz can tomatoes
225 g/8 oz Cheddar cheese, grated
2 tablespoons Bran Flakes

Heat the oil in a frying pan and fry the onions for 10 minutes. In a deep casserole dish, arrange layers of onion, uncooked macaroni and tomatoes, together with all but 2 tablespoons of the cheese. Mix the Bran Flakes with the remaining cheese for the topping and bake in a preheated moderate oven (160°C/325°F, Gas Mark 3) for 1 hour.
SERVES 4

WHOLEMEAL MACARONI CARBONARA

METRIC/IMPERIAL
350-450 g/12 oz-1 lb wholemeal macaroni
15 g/½ oz polyunsaturated margarine
175 g/6 oz cooked lean ham, cut into short thin strips
salt
freshly ground black pepper
2 tablespoons skimmed milk
3 eggs
about 50 g/2 oz grated Parmesan cheese

Cook the macaroni in boiling water for 10 to 15 minutes or until tender.

Meanwhile, melt the margarine in a large pan, add the ham and fry gently until it is fairly crisp. Add a little salt, depending upon how salty the ham is, and plenty of pepper. In a bowl beat the milk with the eggs.

Drain the macaroni and stir into the ham. Turn off the heat and add the beaten egg mixture, stirring constantly. The eggs will cook and thicken slightly from the warmth of the pasta. Serve at once on hot plates and sprinkle with Parmesan cheese. A fresh tomato salad with herb vinaigrette would make an interesting and colourful accompaniment.
SERVES 6

NOODLES TOSSED WITH MEAT AND VEGETABLES

METRIC/IMPERIAL
2 carrots, peeled
3 celery stalks
½ cucumber
2 green chillies, deseeded
1 clove garlic, peeled
2 tablespoons polyunsaturated vegetable oil
350 g/12 oz minced lean pork
4 spring onions, sliced
1 small green pepper, cored, deseeded and sliced
1 tablespoon soy sauce
2 tablespoons sweet red bean paste
1 tablespoon dry sherry
350 g/12 oz noodles, cooked

Cut the carrots, celery and cucumber into matchstick lengths. Slice the chillies and garlic thinly.

Heat the oil in a wok or deep frying pan, add the chillies and garlic and fry quickly for about 30 seconds. Add the pork and cook for 2 minutes. Increase the heat, add the vegetables and cook for 1 minute. Stir in the soy sauce, bean paste, sherry and noodles. Stir well to mix and heat through.

Pile on to a warmed serving dish and serve immediately.
SERVES 4 to 6

NOODLES WITH COTTAGE CHEESE

METRIC/IMPERIAL
175 g/6 oz wholemeal noodles
salt
freshly ground black pepper
150 g/5 oz cottage cheese
25 g/1 oz grated Parmesan cheese
25 g/1 oz polyunsaturated margarine
2 tablespoons chopped parsley
1 small onion, peeled and chopped
2 eggs, beaten

Cook the noodles in boiling, slightly salted water until soft (approximately 15 minutes). Strain and add the remaining ingredients, mixing well. Place the mixture in a lightly greased casserole and bake in a preheated moderately hot oven (190°C/375°F, Gas Mark 5) for 20 minutes.
SERVES 4

MIXED SEAFOOD STICK NOODLES

METRIC/IMPERIAL
4 dried Chinese mushrooms
450 g/1 lb rice stick noodles
salt
2 tablespoons polyunsaturated vegetable oil
4 spring onions, chopped
2 cloves garlic, peeled and sliced
1 × 2.5 cm/1 inch piece root ginger, finely chopped
50 g/2 oz frozen peeled prawns, thawed
100 g/4 oz fresh or frozen squid, sliced
1 × 225 g/8 oz can clams, drained
2 tablespoons dry sherry
1 tablespoon soy sauce

Soak the mushrooms in warm water for 15 minutes. Squeeze well, discard the stalks, then slice the mushroom caps.

Cook the rice stick noodles in boiling salted water for 7 to 8 minutes until just tender. Drain and rinse in cold water. Keep on one side.

Heat the oil in a wok or deep frying pan, add the spring onions, garlic and ginger and stir-fry for 30 seconds. Stir in the mushrooms, prawns and squid, then cook for 2 minutes. Stir in the remaining ingredients, then carefully stir in the noodles and heat through. Pile the mixture into a warmed serving dish and serve immediately.
SERVES 4 to 6

DAN-DAN NOODLES

METRIC/IMPERIAL
450 g/1 lb noodles
salt
2 tablespoons sesame seed paste
6 spring onions, chopped
2 cloves garlic, peeled and crushed
1 × 2.5 cm/1 inch piece root ginger, peeled and
finely chopped
1 tablespoon soy sauce
2 teaspoons red wine vinegar
900 ml/1½ pints beef or chicken stock
2 teaspoons hot pepper oil (optional)

Cook the noodles in boiling salted water according to packet instructions, until just tender. Drain and keep hot.

Blend the sesame seed paste with 4 tablespoons water and place in a pan, together with the remaining ingredients, except the stock and pepper oil. Cook over moderate heat, stirring frequently, for about 5 minutes.

Meanwhile, bring the stock to the boil and simmer for 2 minutes.

Divide the noodles and hot sauce between 4 individual soup bowls. Spoon over the hot stock and top with the hot pepper oil (if using).
SERVES 4

HERBED CHICKEN PASTA

METRIC/IMPERIAL
100 g/4 oz shell pasta or macaroni
1 teaspoon chopped fresh oregano or ½ teaspoon
dried oregano
1 teaspoon chopped fresh rosemary or
½ teaspoon dried rosemary
350 g/12 oz cooked chicken meat
100 g/4 oz mushrooms, chopped
1 tablespoon olive oil
1 teaspoon ground coriander
salt
freshly ground black pepper

Put the pasta into boiling salted water with the herbs and cook for about 10 minutes until tender but still firm.

Cut the chicken meat into bite-sized pieces. Add the chicken and mushrooms to the pasta and cook for a further 10 minutes. Drain if necessary.

Add the olive oil and coriander. Add salt and pepper just before serving. Serve hot or cold.
SERVES 2

MIXED PASTA SALAD

METRIC/IMPERIAL
25 g/1 oz blanched almonds
100 g/4 oz mixed coloured pasta shells or twists
100 g/4 oz peas, fresh or frozen
3 tablespoons polyunsaturated vegetable oil
3 celery stalks, chopped
1 small bunch spring onions, chopped
6 black olives, stoned and chopped
1 tablespoon wine vinegar
salt
freshly ground black pepper
watercress sprigs, to garnish

To toast the almonds, dry-fry for about 1 minute until lightly browned, shaking the pan.

Cook the pasta and fresh peas in boiling salted water with 1 tablespoon of the oil for about 10 minutes, or until tender. If using frozen peas, add them halfway through the cooking time.

Drain well and run cold water through the pasta pieces to keep them separate. Leave to cool.

Put the celery into a bowl with the pasta and peas. Add the spring onions, olives and almonds.

Mix the remaining oil with the vinegar and season with salt and pepper. Pour over the pasta salad and toss all the ingredients together. Transfer to a serving dish and garnish with watercress sprigs. This salad is very suitable for picnics and packed lunches, when it should be transported in a lidded container.
SERVES 4

PASTA WITH RATATOUILLE SAUCE

METRIC/IMPERIAL
1 large onion, peeled and chopped
1 clove garlic, peeled and crushed
450 g/1 lb courgettes, sliced
1 large aubergine, diced
1 green pepper, cored, deseeded and diced
450 g/1 lb tomatoes, skinned and chopped
1 tablespoon chopped oregano or basil
salt
freshly ground black pepper
450 g/1 lb pasta (spaghetti, noodles, etc)
1 tablespoon chopped parsley
grated Parmesan cheese, to serve

Put all the ingredients in a large pan, except the pasta, parsley and Parmesan cheese. Cover and cook gently for 30 minutes until the vegetables are tender and the juices have thickened slightly, stirring occasionally.

Meanwhile, cook the pasta in a large pan containing plenty of boiling salted water until just tender. Drain and pile into a warmed dish.

Taste and adjust the seasoning of the sauce, then pour over the pasta. Sprinkle with the parsley and grated Parmesan cheese. Serve hot.

SERVES 4 to 6

TAGLIATELLE ALLA BOLOGNESE

METRIC/IMPERIAL
2 tablespoons olive oil
2 rashers lean bacon, derinded and coarsely chopped
1 onion, peeled and chopped
1 celery stalk, sliced
100 g/4 oz mushrooms, chopped
100 g/4 oz minced lean beef
50 g/2 oz chicken livers, cleaned and chopped
2 tablespoons tomato purée
120 ml/4 fl oz red wine
250 ml/8 fl oz beef stock
1 tablespoon chopped basil
1 tablespoon oregano
1 teaspoon sugar
pinch of nutmeg
salt
freshly ground black pepper
225 g/8 oz tagliatelle
small knob of butter
100 g/4 oz grated Parmesan cheese

Heat the oil in a large saucepan and gently fry the bacon, onion, celery and mushrooms until soft. Add the meat and chicken livers and continue cooking, stirring frequently, until all the meat is brown. Stir in the tomato purée, then the wine and stock. Add the basil, oregano, sugar, nutmeg and salt and pepper to taste. Bring to the boil, stirring, then cover the pan and simmer the sauce for 45 minutes.

Fifteen minutes before the sauce is ready, start to cook the tagliatelle in plenty of boiling salted water. It will take about 10 minutes, and should be tender but still firm. Drain well, season with salt and pepper to taste and fork through a knob of butter. Arrange in a heated serving dish. Taste the sauce and adjust the seasoning if necessary, then spoon it over the tagliatelle. Serve with a bowl of grated Parmesan cheese handed separately.

SERVES 2

PESTO WITH NOODLES

METRIC/IMPERIAL
50 g/2 oz fresh basil
2 cloves garlic, peeled
25 g/1 oz pine nuts
salt
25 g/1 oz freshly grated Parmesan cheese
2 tablespoons olive oil
450 g/1 lb white tagliatelle or other noodles

Put the basil into a mortar and pound for 2 minutes. Add the garlic, pine nuts and salt to taste and pound until smooth. Stir in the Parmesan cheese and pound until the mixture is quite smooth.

When the pesto is quite thick, gradually add the olive oil, drop by drop, so that the finished sauce is the consistency of creamed butter.

Cook the pasta in boiling salted water for about 10 minutes or until tender but still firm to the bite. Drain and return to the pan. Stir in the pesto sauce and heat through. Pile the mixture into a warmed serving dish and serve at once.

SERVES 4

CREAMY NOODLES WITH FRESH HERBS

METRIC/IMPERIAL
450 g/1 lb wholemeal tagliatelle
2 cloves garlic, peeled and crushed
50 g/2 oz polyunsaturated margarine
120 ml/4 fl oz single cream
2 tablespoons chopped parsley
2 tablespoons snipped chives
1 tablespoon chopped basil
1 tablespoon chopped oregano or marjoram
salt
freshly ground black pepper
freshly grated Parmesan or Cheddar cheese, to serve

Cook the pasta in plenty of boiling salted water until tender but still firm to the bite, about 15 to 20 minutes. Drain thoroughly and toss with the crushed garlic and margarine.

Heat the cream just to boiling point, and add the chopped herbs. Season to taste with salt and plenty of pepper. Pour over the pasta and toss gently but thoroughly until mixed. Serve at once in heated bowls, and pass freshly grated cheese at the table.

SERVES 4

TAGLIATELLE WITH FRESH TOMATO AND BASIL SAUCE

METRIC/IMPERIAL
225 g/8 oz wholemeal tagliatelle
salt
Sauce:
1 tablespoon polyunsaturated vegetable oil
1 onion, peeled and thinly sliced
1 clove garlic, peeled and crushed
450–750 g/1–1½ lb tomatoes, skinned and cut into wedges
1 tablespoon chopped basil (or mint and parsley)
freshly ground black pepper

Cook the tagliatelle in a large pan of boiling salted water for 15 to 20 minutes until it is just tender.

Meanwhile, make the sauce: heat the oil in a non-stick saucepan and fry the onion and garlic for 5 minutes until lightly browned. Add the tomatoes and cook, stirring occasionally, for a further 5 minutes, to make a thick sauce with pieces of whole tomato.

Drain the pasta and place in a serving dish. Pour over the tomato sauce and serve.

SERVES 4

PERSIAN NOODLES

METRIC/IMPERIAL
1 large aubergine, fairly thickly sliced
salt
600 ml/1 pint chicken stock
100 g/4 oz tagliatelle or spaghetti
1 teaspoon mace
4 courgettes, sliced
freshly ground black pepper

Place the aubergine slices in a colander, sprinkle with salt and leave for 30 minutes. Rinse and dry the aubergine and chop into bite-sized pieces.

Bring the stock to the boil in a saucepan. Add the noodles, and after a few minutes add the aubergine, mace, courgettes and pepper to taste. Continue cooking for about 15 minutes or until the noodles and vegetables are just cooked. Taste and adjust the seasoning.

SERVES 2

TAGLIATELLE WITH SALMON

METRIC/IMPERIAL
350 g/12 oz wholemeal tagliatelle
1 × 200 g/7 oz can salmon
1 tablespoon polyunsaturated vegetable oil
1 medium onion, peeled and chopped
100 g/4 oz mushrooms, wiped and sliced
salt
freshly ground black pepper
2 tablespoons tomato purée

Cook the tagliatelle in a large pan of boiling water for 15 to 20 minutes or until tender.

Meanwhile, drain the salmon, remove the skin and bones and set aside. Heat the oil in a saucepan and cook the onion until tender, then add the mushrooms and cook until soft. Season to taste.

When the tagliatelle is cooked, drain well and return to the pan. Flake the salmon and add with the onion and mushrooms. Add the tomato purée and mix all the ingredients together over a low heat. Adjust the seasoning and serve immediately.

SERVES 4

TAGLIATELLE WITH GAMMON AND MUSHROOMS

METRIC/IMPERIAL
350 g/12 oz lean gammon, cubed and soaked for 15 minutes
1 tablespoon olive oil
1 onion, peeled and finely sliced
1 clove garlic, peeled and crushed
175 g/6 oz mushrooms, wiped and sliced
1 × 400 g/14 oz can chopped tomatoes
1 tablespoon chopped basil
1 tablespoon chopped parsley
1 tablespoon tomato purée
salt
freshly ground black pepper
225 g/8 oz tagliatelle
15 g/½ oz butter
50 g/2 oz Parmesan cheese, grated
basil sprigs, to garnish (optional)

Drain the gammon and dry on absorbent kitchen paper. Heat the oil in a pan and gently fry the onion and garlic until cooked but not brown. Stir in the gammon and mushrooms. Continue to fry for 3 minutes. Mix in the tomatoes, basil, parsley and tomato purée. Season well with salt and pepper to taste, and pour into a pudding basin. Cover with foil or cling film. Bring a large pan of salted water to the boil. Place the pudding basin in a steamer and cover with a tight-fitting lid. Steam over the water for 25 minutes. Check the liquid level frequently and add more boiling water if necessary.

Fifteen minutes before serving, place the tagliatelle in the boiling water, cover and continue to steam the food above for 12 minutes.

Drain the pasta and pile on to a warmed serving dish, dot with butter and season with salt and pepper. Remove the foil from the bowl and spoon the gammon and sauce over the pasta. Sprinkle with Parmesan, garnish with basil, if liked, and serve immediately.
SERVES 4

LINGUINE WITH COURGETTE-ANCHOVY SAUCE

METRIC/IMPERIAL
450 g/1 lb linguine or other flat noodles
150 g/5 oz polyunsaturated margarine
3 tablespoons olive oil
6 firm young courgettes, thinly sliced
6 flat anchovy fillets, finely chopped
3 large, ripe tomatoes, skinned, deseeded and chopped
salt
freshly ground black pepper
2 tablespoons finely chopped parsley
50 g/2 oz freshly grated Parmesan cheese

Cook the linguine in plenty of boiling salted water until tender but still firm, about 8 to 9 minutes.

Meanwhile, heat 75 g/3 oz margarine and the oil in a large, heavy frying pan and add the courgettes. Stir over medium heat until barely tender, about 3 minutes. Add the anchovies and tomatoes and cook a further few minutes until the tomatoes are softened. Taste and season with salt and pepper – be careful with the salt, as the anchovies are very salty and it probably will not be necessary to add any extra.

Drain the linguine and place in a heated serving bowl. Add the remaining margarine, cut into small pieces, the parsley and grated cheese and toss to combine. Pour the sauce over and toss lightly again. Serve at once on heated plates.
SERVES 6

SPAGHETTINI WITH TOMATOES AND BASIL

METRIC/IMPERIAL
450 g/1 lb spaghettini or vermicelli
Sauce:
4 large, ripe tomatoes
2 cloves garlic, peeled and crushed
3 tablespoons chopped parsley
15 g/½ oz chopped basil
4 tablespoons olive oil
salt
freshly ground black pepper

Peel, seed and coarsely chop the tomatoes. Place with the garlic, parsley, basil and oil in a blender or food processor and blend to a purée. Heat gently in a saucepan to boiling point, then taste and season well.

Meanwhile, cook the pasta in plenty of boiling salted water for about 8 to 10 minutes, until tender but still firm. Drain well and toss at once with the fresh tomato sauce. Serve with crusty bread.
SERVES 4 to 6

FETTUCINE WITH COURGETTES AND MUSHROOMS

METRIC/IMPERIAL
1 tablespoon polyunsaturated vegetable oil
1 medium onion, peeled and sliced
1 clove garlic, peeled and chopped
450 g/1 lb courgettes, trimmed and grated
225 g/8 oz button mushrooms, sliced
450 g/1 lb fettucine
85 ml/3 fl oz skimmed milk
100 g/4 oz curd cheese
½ teaspoon grated nutmeg
salt
freshly ground black pepper

Heat the oil in a heavy frying pan and gently cook the onion and garlic until soft. Add the courgettes and the mushrooms, mixing well together. Cook the vegetables gently, stirring occasionally, for about 10 minutes.

Cook the fettucine in boiling salted water. Boil for about 7 minutes, until tender but still firm, then drain. Whisk the skimmed milk into the curd cheese, then add to the courgette and mushroom mixture with the nutmeg. Season with salt and pepper. Mix with the fettucine and serve at once.
SERVES 6

RAVIOLI NAPOLETANA

METRIC/IMPERIAL
Ravioli paste:
225 g/8 oz plain flour, sifted
50 g/2 oz semolina
pinch of salt
1½ tablespoons olive oil
2 eggs, beaten
3-4 tablespoons water or skimmed milk
Filling:
225 g/8 oz chopped frozen spinach
50 g/2 oz Ricotta or cream cheese
salt
freshly ground black pepper
pinch of grated nutmeg
Napoletana sauce:
15 g/½ oz butter
1 large onion, peeled and sliced
1 clove garlic, peeled and crushed
50 ml/2 fl oz red wine
1 × 400 g/14 oz can chopped tomatoes
1 tablespoon tomato purée
1 bay leaf
¼ teaspoon sugar
150 ml/¼ pint meat or vegetable stock
2 teaspoons chopped fresh basil
basil sprigs, to garnish

Place the flour, semolina and salt in a bowl. Make a well in the centre and put in the oil, eggs and half of the water or milk. Mix well, gradually incorporating the dry ingredients. Add more liquid when necessary. Work the paste into a smooth and firm dough. Knead well, cover with a cloth, and leave to rest for 30 minutes.

Meanwhile, make the filling. Place the spinach in a pan over high heat to evaporate all of the water. Dry on absorbent kitchen paper. Place in a bowl with the cheese. Mix well and season with salt, pepper and nutmeg. Leave to one side.

Dust the work surface with flour, cut the ravioli dough in half and roll each half until paper thin. Brush one thin sheet of paste with water and place a generous teaspoon of filling at regular intervals on the paste. Place the other sheet of paste on top of the fillings with floured hands; press the top piece down around each mound of filling. Stamp each one out with a fluted cutter or cut squares with a pastry wheel. Leave the shapes to dry for 2 hours. Place in a large pan of boiling salted water and cook for 5 minutes. Drain the ravioli and rinse under cold water.

To make the sauce, melt the butter in a pan and fry the onion and garlic until cooked but not brown. Stir in the remaining ingredients and season well with salt and pepper.

Place the ravioli and tomato sauce in a pudding basin. Cover with foil or cling film and place in a steamer. Cover with a tight-fitting lid and steam over boiling water for 15 minutes.

Pile on to a warmed serving dish and garnish with sprigs of fresh basil. Serve immediately.
MAKES 16

CANNELLONI

METRIC/IMPERIAL
25 g/1 oz polyunsaturated margarine
25 g/1 oz plain unbleached white flour
150 ml/¼ pint skimmed milk
salt
freshly ground black pepper
2 tablespoons chopped parsley
pinch of oregano
pinch of marjoram
1 egg yolk
1 tablespoon polyunsaturated vegetable oil
225 g/8 oz boneless chicken, finely chopped
75 g/3 oz cooked ham, finely diced
1 onion, peeled and finely chopped
2 cloves garlic, peeled and crushed
1 green pepper, cored, deseeded and finely chopped
1 celery stalk, finely chopped
12-16 cannelloni (allow 3-4 per person)
1 × 400 g/14 oz can chopped tomatoes
1 teaspoon sugar
150 ml/¼ pint chicken stock
25 g/1 oz Parmesan cheese

Melt the margarine in a pan, stir in the flour and cook for 2 minutes. Add the milk and bring to the boil, stirring constantly. Season with salt and pepper, stir in the herbs and simmer for 3 minutes. Remove from the heat and stir in the egg yolk. Cover and keep to one side.

Heat the oil in a pan and fry the chicken, ham, onion, garlic, green pepper and celery for 6 minutes, stirring occasionally. Season well with salt and pepper. Leave to cool, then stir in the herb sauce.

Place the cannelloni in a large pan of boiling salted water and cook for 5 minutes. Lift out and dip them into a bowl of ice-cold water. Dry on absorbent kitchen paper. Place the filling in a forcing bag with a large plain nozzle (or use the handle of a spoon). Pipe (or spoon) into the cannelloni tubes and then place them in a suitable bowl.

Mix the tomatoes, sugar and stock together and pour over the cannelloni. Cover with foil or greaseproof paper and tie down with string. Place in a steamer or covered saucepan half-filled with boiling water and steam for 40 minutes. Check the liquid level frequently and add more boiling water if necessary.

Just before serving heat the grill. Remove the foil or paper and sprinkle the surface with Parmesan. Grill until the top is golden brown and serve immediately.

SERVES 4

COURGETTE AND TOMATO LASAGNE

METRIC/IMPERIAL
175 g/6 oz wholemeal or white lasagne
2.4 litres/4 pints water
1 teaspoon salt
1 teaspoon polyunsaturated vegetable oil
175 g/6 oz cottage cheese
50 g/2 oz Cheddar cheese, grated
Sauce:
1 tablespoon polyunsaturated vegetable oil
1 onion, peeled and sliced
1 green pepper, cored, deseeded and chopped
1-2 cloves garlic, peeled and crushed
450 g/1 lb courgettes, finely chopped
1 tablespoon tomato purée
1 × 400 g/14 oz can tomatoes
½ teaspoon dried basil
½ teaspoon dried oregano
¼ teaspoon sugar
salt
freshly ground black pepper
Topping:
150 ml/¼ pint plain low-fat yogurt
2 eggs
25 g/1 oz Parmesan cheese, grated
salt
freshly ground black pepper
basil leaves, to garnish

To make the sauce, heat the oil in a large pan and sauté the onion and pepper for 5 minutes. Add the garlic and courgettes and cook for a further 5 minutes. Stir in the tomato purée and canned tomatoes with their juice. Add the herbs, sugar and salt and pepper. Bring to the boil, cover and simmer for 20 minutes. Preheat the oven to 190°C/375°F, Gas Mark 5.

Meanwhile, place the lasagne in a large pan with the water, salt and oil. Bring to the boil then simmer for 10 to 15 minutes or until the lasagne is just tender. Drain, rinse with cold water and lay pieces separately on a clean teatowel to dry.

Mix together the cottage and Cheddar cheeses. In a greased, 1.8 litre/3 pint ovenproof dish, layer the sauce, lasagne and cheeses, finishing with a thin layer of sauce.

For the topping, beat together the yogurt, eggs and Parmesan cheese. Season to taste and pour over the lasagne. Cook in the oven for 30 minutes until golden and bubbling. Serve immediately, garnished with basil leaves.

SERVES 4

WHOLEMEAL LASAGNE

METRIC/IMPERIAL
225 g/8 oz wholemeal lasagne
few drops of polyunsaturated vegetable oil
600 ml/1 pint fresh tomato sauce (see page 341)
225 g/8 oz Ricotta, curd or sieved cottage cheese
50 g/2 oz Parmesan cheese
Sauce:
25 g/1 oz polyunsaturated margarine
2 tablespoons plain wholemeal flour
150 ml/¼ pint hot skimmed milk
salt
freshly ground black pepper
pinch of grated nutmeg

Cook the lasagne in boiling water, to which a few drops of oil have been added, for 10 to 20 minutes or until just tender. Drain on a clean teatowel.

Preheat the oven to moderate (180°C/350°F, Gas Mark 4).

Spread one-quarter of the fresh tomato sauce over the bottom of a greased deep ovenproof dish. Cover with one-third of the lasagne, then one-third of the soft cheese. Sprinkle with 1 teaspoon of the Parmesan cheese. Repeat the layers twice, then spoon over the remaining sauce.

To make the white sauce, melt the margarine in a pan, stir in the flour and cook for 2 minutes. Gradually stir in the milk and simmer until thickened. Season with salt, pepper and nutmeg then pour over the lasagne.

Sprinkle over the remaining Parmesan cheese. Cook in the oven for 30 to 35 minutes until lightly browned and hot.

SERVES 6

VEGETABLE LASAGNE

METRIC/IMPERIAL
100 g/4 oz green lasagne
1 teaspoon polyunsaturated vegetable oil
450 g/1 lb spinach, trimmed, or 225 g/8 oz
chopped frozen spinach
225 g/8 oz cottage cheese
100 g/4 oz chopped walnuts
2 tablespoons grated Parmesan cheese
450 ml/¾ pint thick tomato sauce (see page 340)
Sauce:
50 g/2 oz polyunsaturated margarine
50 g/2 oz plain wholemeal flour
600 ml/1 pint skimmed milk
100 g/4 oz Cheddar cheese, grated
salt
freshly ground black pepper

Grease a shallow rectangular or square ovenproof dish and preheat the oven to moderately hot (200°C/400°F, Gas Mark 6).

Place the lasagne in a large saucepan of boiling salted water with the oil added to separate the pasta, and cook for about 12 minutes. Drain and drape the pasta pieces around a mixing bowl to prevent them sticking together.

Cook the spinach with a minimum of boiling salted water until completely softened. Drain and finely chop. If using frozen spinach, cook according to the instructions on the packet and drain thoroughly. Combine the spinach, cottage cheese and walnuts together to make a thick paste.

To make the cheese sauce, melt the margarine in a saucepan, add the flour and cook for 1 minute. Remove from the heat and gradually add the milk. Bring to the boil, stirring until thickened, then add the cheese and salt and pepper to taste.

Line the ovenproof dish with half the lasagne. Layer the thick tomato sauce, the cheese sauce, spinach mixture and remaining lasagne. Sprinkle the top with Parmesan cheese and bake in the oven for 30 minutes. Serve immediately.
SERVES 4 to 6

ANGEL HAIR PASTA

METRIC/IMPERIAL
450 g/1 lb strong unbleached white flour,
warmed in the oven
2 large eggs
1½ tablespoons olive oil
100 ml/4 fl oz water

Place all the ingredients in a food processor and process for 1 minute. Cover the dough with cling film and leave to rest for 1 hour at room temperature. Divide the dough into 10 equal pieces. Flour a work surface and roll the dough until paper thin; you should be able to see right through the dough.

Dust the sheets with flour and lay on a wire rack to dry for 1 hour. To cut into angel hair, spread out the sheets of pasta and cut into very thin strips. Coil up about 20 at a time, very loosely, and put to one side. Cover with cling film until needed.
MAKES 450 g/1 lb

VEGETABLE PILAFF

METRIC/IMPERIAL
Pilaff:
1 tablespoon polyunsaturated vegetable oil
1 onion, peeled and chopped
225 g/8 oz long-grain rice
600 ml/1 pint vegetable stock
1 cinnamon stick or pinch of ground cinnamon
1 bay leaf
salt
freshly ground black pepper
Vegetables:
2 tablespoons polyunsaturated vegetable oil
1 onion, peeled and sliced
1 clove garlic, peeled and crushed
450 g/1 lb courgettes, trimmed and sliced
1 green pepper, cored, deseeded and diced
100 g/4 oz button mushrooms, wiped and
trimmed
450 g/1 lb tomatoes, skinned and roughly
chopped
1 tablespoon chopped fresh herbs (oregano,
marjoram, basil and parsley) or 1 teaspoon dried
mixed herbs

To make the pilaff, heat the oil in a saucepan and fry the onion for 5 minutes. Add the rice and cook, stirring, for 1 minute. Pour in the vegetable stock and add the remaining ingredients. Bring to the boil, stirring occasionally. Cover the pan and simmer gently for 15 to 20 minutes until the rice is cooked and all the stock has been absorbed. Meanwhile, prepare the vegetables. Heat the oil in a saucepan and fry the onion, garlic and courgettes for about 5 minutes, stirring occasionally until the vegetables are lightly browned. Add the pepper and mushrooms and fry for 2 minutes. Add the tomatoes with the herbs, salt and pepper. Cook for 10 to 15 minutes, stirring occasionally until the tomatoes are reduced to a pulp and the courgettes are just tender.

Transfer the pilaff to a warm serving dish and pour over the vegetables. Serve hot.

SERVES 4

STEAMED PAELLA

METRIC/IMPERIAL
2 tablespoons olive oil
3 boneless chicken or rabbit pieces, cut into bite-sized cubes
100 g/4 oz small spicy salami sausage, cut into cubes
1 onion, peeled and sliced
1 clove garlic, peeled and crushed
1 green pepper, cored, deseeded and cut into strips
175 g/6 oz long-grain rice, well washed
chicken or fish stock
225 g/8 oz firm white fish, skinned and cubed
2 canned red pimientos, cut into strips
salt
freshly ground black pepper
12 prawns with shells, washed
12 mussels, scrubbed and beards removed
75 g/3 oz frozen or cooked fresh peas
lemon or lime wedges, to garnish

Heat the oil in a heavy-based pan, fry the chicken or rabbit pieces to brown on all sides. Remove and put to one side. Fry the salami, onion, garlic, pepper and rice in the saucepan for 5 minutes to colour slightly and allow the rice to turn white.

Pour in enough stock to bring the liquid level 2.5 cm/1 inch above the top of the rice. Return the chicken to the pan and stir in the fish and pimientos. Season well with salt and pepper. Cover with a tight-fitting lid and cook for 15 minutes without lifting the lid. Add all of the remaining ingredients and continue to cook, covered, for 15 minutes.

Pile the paella on to a warmed serving dish and garnish with lemon or lime wedges.

SERVES 4

CLASSIC RISOTTO

METRIC/IMPERIAL
50 g/2 oz polyunsaturated margarine
1 large onion, peeled and finely chopped
1 red pepper, cored, deseeded and finely diced
2 cloves garlic, peeled and crushed
450 g/1 lb cooked chicken or beef, diced
225 g/8 oz long-grain rice, well washed
salt
freshly ground black pepper
pinch of saffron
chicken or beef stock
100 g/4 oz peas, fresh or frozen
50 g/2 oz Parmesan cheese

Melt the margarine in a large pan. Fry the onion, pepper and garlic until cooked but not brown. Stir in the chicken or beef and rice and fry until the rice turns white. Season very well with salt, pepper and saffron. Pour on enough stock to bring the liquid level about 2.5 cm/1 inch above the top of the rice. Bring to the boil. Cover with a tight-fitting lid and cook over the lowest heat for 15 minutes, without lifting the lid. Stir in the peas, cover and continue to cook for 5 minutes.

Stir in the Parmesan. Check the seasoning, adjust if necessary, and serve immediately.

SERVES 4

HERBED RICE SALAD

METRIC/IMPERIAL
100 g/4 oz long-grain brown rice, well washed
salt
freshly ground black pepper
2 tablespoons polyunsaturated vegetable oil
2 teaspoons white wine vinegar
squeeze of lemon juice
2 tablespoons chopped parsley
2 tablespoons snipped chives
1 tablespoon chopped dill
1 tablespoon chopped tarragon

Cook the rice in a saucepan of boiling salted water for 35 to 40 minutes or until tender, then drain well. While the rice is still hot, season with salt and black pepper to taste and add the oil, vinegar and lemon juice.

When the rice has cooled, stir in the chopped herbs and serve.

SERVES 4

PRAWN AND HAM JAMBALAYA

METRIC/IMPERIAL
50 g/2 oz polyunsaturated margarine
1 green pepper, cored, deseeded and chopped
1 red pepper, cored, deseeded and chopped
4 celery stalks, sliced
1 large onion, peeled and finely sliced
2 cloves garlic, peeled and crushed
100 g/4 oz long-grain rice
3 tablespoons chopped parsley
1 × 400 g/14 oz can chopped tomatoes
6 drops of Tabasco
salt
freshly ground black pepper
450 g/1 lb peeled, cooked prawns
450 g/1 lb cooked lean ham, roughly chopped
100 g/4 oz peas, fresh or frozen
Garnish:
lemon twists
flat-leaf parsley sprigs

Melt the margarine in a large pan and fry the peppers, celery, onion, garlic and rice, until the onion is cooked and the rice has turned white. Stir in the parsley, tomatoes and Tabasco. Season very well with salt and pepper.

Add enough water to bring the liquid level about 2.5 cm/1 inch above the top of the rice. Cover with a tight-fitting lid and cook, without lifting the lid, for 15 minutes. Add the prawns, ham and peas. Cover and continue to cook for 5 minutes.

Pile on to a warmed serving plate, garnish with lemon twists and parsley, and serve at once.
SERVES 4

BOKARI PILAFF

METRIC/IMPERIAL
450 g/1 lb chicken livers, washed and sinew removed
salt
freshly ground black pepper
1 tablespoon olive oil
1 large onion, peeled and sliced
1 small leek, trimmed, washed and finely chopped
225 g/8 oz long-grain rice
½ teaspoon turmeric
1 × 200 g/7 oz can tomatoes
2 tablespoons chopped parsley
300 ml/½ pint chicken stock

100 g/4 oz mushrooms, wiped and sliced
100 g/4 oz frozen peas
Garnish:
sliced tomatoes
flat-leaf parsley sprigs

Season the chicken livers with salt and pepper. Heat the oil in a pan and fry the onion and leek until cooked but not brown. Stir in the rice, and fry until the rice turns white.

Mix the turmeric, tomatoes and parsley and add to the rice mixture. Pour on enough boiling stock to bring the liquid level 2.5 cm/1 inch above the top of the rice. Cover the pan with a tight-fitting lid and cook, without lifting the lid, for 15 minutes. Add the mushrooms, peas and seasoned livers; cover and continue to cook for 5 to 8 minutes. Season with salt and pepper to taste.

Transfer the rice mixture to a heated serving dish and garnish with tomato slices and sprigs of parsley. Serve at once.
SERVES 4

CURRIED RICE

METRIC/IMPERIAL
100 g/4 oz polyunsaturated margarine
3 onions, peeled and finely sliced
2 teaspoons turmeric
4 teaspoons curry powder
1 kg/2 lb long-grain rice
1.6 litres/2¾ pints chicken stock
12 peppercorns
4 whole cloves
8 cardamom pods, bruised
1 stick cinnamon
4 teaspoons salt
Garnish:
cashew nuts
225 g/8 oz cooked peas

Heat the margarine in a large heavy saucepan or flameproof casserole. Sauté half the onions until golden brown, then add the turmeric and curry powder and stir well for a minute. Add the rice and fry for a few minutes, stirring, until golden in colour. Add boiling stock, peppercorns, spices, salt and remaining onions. Stir well, cover and cook over a gentle heat for about 20 minutes.

Turn off the heat and keep covered until ready to serve. A few minutes before serving, uncover the pan to allow the steam to escape. Fluff up with a fork and garnish with nuts and peas.
SERVES 12

CHINESE STEAMED RICE WITH CHICKEN

METRIC/IMPERIAL
4 chicken breasts
salt
freshly ground black pepper
2 tablespoons soy sauce
1 tablespoon sherry or rice wine
2 teaspoons oyster sauce
15 g/½ oz fresh root ginger, peeled and grated
2 cloves garlic, peeled and crushed
225 g/8 oz long-grain rice, well washed
100 g/4 oz canned sliced bamboo shoots
2 celery stalks, roughly chopped
½ small cabbage, shredded
spring onion tassels, to garnish

Season the breasts with salt and pepper. Mix together the soy sauce, sherry or rice wine, oyster sauce, root ginger and garlic and pour over the chicken. Leave to marinate for up to 2 hours.

Place the rice in a large saucepan, and add enough water to bring the liquid level about 2.5 cm/1 inch above the top of the rice. Bring to the boil. Add the chicken and marinade. Reduce the heat to as low as possible, cover with a tight-fitting lid and cook, without lifting the lid, for 20 minutes. Add the prepared vegetables. Cover again and continue to cook for 5 minutes.

Pile the food on to a warmed serving dish and serve piping hot, garnished with spring onions.
SERVES 4

HERB RISOTTO

METRIC/IMPERIAL
1 tablespoon polyunsaturated vegetable oil
1 shallot, peeled and chopped
225 g/8 oz brown rice, well washed
about 750 ml/1¼ pints hot vegetable stock
pinch of saffron
1 bay leaf, crushed
12 sage leaves, finely chopped
12 thyme sprigs, finely chopped
12 tarragon leaves, finely chopped
12 marjoram leaves, finely chopped
salt
freshly ground black pepper

Heat the oil in a heavy saucepan and cook the shallot until soft. Add the rice to the pan and stir around until coated with oil, then pour on 400 ml/14 fl oz of the stock. Cover the pan and

simmer gently until almost all the liquid is absorbed.

Add the saffron, bay leaf and fresh herbs to 175 ml/6 fl oz of the stock and pour it over the rice. Cover again, and cook gently until the stock is absorbed. If the rice is tender, season with salt and pepper and serve; otherwise add the remaining stock and continue to simmer until cooked.
SERVES 4

GREEK RICE RING

METRIC/IMPERIAL
3 tablespoons polyunsaturated vegetable oil
1 onion, peeled and sliced
1 clove garlic, peeled and crushed
225 g/8 oz brown rice, well washed
750 ml/1¼ pints water
salt
1 green pepper, cored, deseeded and chopped
50 g/2 oz dried apricots, soaked and sliced
50 g/2 oz dried prunes, soaked, stoned and sliced
75 g/3 oz walnuts, roughly chopped
50 g/2 oz black olives, halved and stoned
freshly ground black pepper

Heat the oil in a large pan and sauté the onion and garlic until soft. Stir in the rice and cook, stirring, for 1 minute. Add the water and salt. Bring to the boil, cover and simmer for 20 minutes. Stir in the green pepper, apricots and prunes. Continue to simmer, covered, for about 20 minutes or until the rice is cooked and the liquid absorbed. Stir in the walnuts, olives and salt and pepper to taste.

Turn the mixture into a greased 900 ml/1½ pint ring mould and cook in a preheated moderate oven (180°C/350°F, Gas Mark 4) for 30 minutes. Turn out and serve hot or cold. Fill the centre with courgettes provençal or a crisp green salad.
SERVES 4

SPICY RICE MUSHROOMS

METRIC/IMPERIAL
1 tablespoon polyunsaturated vegetable oil
4 large flat mushrooms, wiped and stalks finely chopped
2 shallots, peeled and finely chopped
1 clove garlic, peeled and crushed
1 chilli, deseeded and finely chopped
7 g/¼ oz fresh root ginger, peeled and grated
1 teaspoon hot curry powder
¼ teaspoon ground cumin
50 g/2 oz long-grain rice, well washed
tomato juice
salt
freshly ground black pepper
chopped parsley, to garnish

Heat the oil in a pan and fry the chopped mushroom stalks, shallots, garlic, chilli, ginger, spices and rice until the shallots are cooked and the rice has turned white.

Pour on enough tomato juice to bring the liquid level 2.5 cm/1 inch above the top of the rice. Season well with salt and pepper, cover with a tight-fitting lid and cook for 15 minutes without lifting the lid.

Pile the rice on to the mushrooms and place in a steamer. Cover with a tight-fitting lid and steam over boiling water for 5 minutes.

Sprinkle with parsley and serve at once.
SERVES 4

SPICED LAMB AND BEAN RISOTTO

METRIC/IMPERIAL
450 g/1 lb shoulder of lamb
1 onion, peeled and chopped
1 clove garlic, peeled and crushed
300 ml/½ pint chicken stock
100 g/4 oz brown rice, well washed
2 carrots, peeled and diced
100 g/4 oz peas
2 × 225 g/8 oz cans curried baked beans with sultanas
4 tablespoons chopped parsley or mint
salt
freshly ground black pepper

Cut the meat into small pieces, removing any excess fat. Place in a large saucepan with the onion and garlic and heat gently until the fat begins to run. Increase the temperature slightly and cook, stirring all the time, until the meat colours and the onion becomes soft but not brown.

Add the stock and rice and simmer gently for 30 minutes, adding more stock if the rice looks as though it is going to burn. Add the carrots, peas, curried beans and parsley or mint. Stir well and cook for a further 10 minutes or until the meat is tender and the rice cooked. Adjust seasoning to taste and serve.
SERVES 4

SCAMPI RISOTTO

METRIC/IMPERIAL
450 g/1 lb scampi
1.2 litres/2 pints water
1 fish head or small, whole fish
1 celery stalk, sliced
1 small onion, peeled and sliced
1 small carrot, peeled and sliced
1 bay leaf
salt
freshly ground black pepper
65 g/2½ oz polyunsaturated margarine
2 tablespoons olive oil
1 clove garlic, peeled and crushed
175 g/6 oz round-grain rice
good pinch each ground cinnamon, nutmeg and cloves
1 tablespoon finely chopped parsley
3 tablespoons freshly grated Parmesan cheese

If the scampi are still in their shells, peel, devein and place the shells and heads in a large saucepan with the water, fish head or whole fish, celery, onion, carrot, bay leaf, and salt and pepper to taste. Bring to the boil, simmer for 30 minutes, then strain into a measuring jug.

Heat 50 g/2 oz margarine and the oil in a wide, heavy saucepan or deep frying pan. Sauté the garlic over medium heat for 1 to 2 minutes, then add the rice and stir until golden. Add 250 ml/8 fl oz of the reserved fish stock, cover the pan and simmer for 10 minutes, or until the liquid is absorbed. Add another 600 ml/1 pint of the fish stock and simmer, covered, for a further 10 minutes. Add the raw scampi and continue cooking, covered, for 5 to 6 minutes longer or until the scampi are pink and the stock has been absorbed.

Gently stir in the spices, remaining margarine, freshly chopped parsley and Parmesan cheese. Taste and adjust the seasoning, and serve at once on heated plates.
SERVES 4

PILAU RICE

METRIC/IMPERIAL
225 g/8 oz Basmati or long-grain rice, soaked
for 20 minutes
1 green pepper
1 red chilli
1 tablespoon polyunsaturated vegetable oil
1 small onion, peeled and finely chopped
2 cloves garlic, peeled and crushed
½ teaspoon ground cumin
¼ teaspoon turmeric
¼ teaspoon ground coriander
salt
freshly ground black pepper
chicken stock or boiling water
coriander leaves, to garnish

Drain the rice and rinse thoroughly; leave to
drain, shaking occasionally. Deseed and finely
chop the pepper and chilli. Heat the oil in a frying
pan. Fry the onion, garlic, pepper and chilli until
cooked but not brown.
Stir in the rice and spices. Fry until the rice turns
white. Season well with salt and pepper and pour
on enough chicken stock or water to bring the
liquid 2.5 cm/1 inch above the top of the rice.
Cover with a tight-fitting lid and cook for 15 to 20
minutes without lifting the lid.
Fluff up the rice mixture with a fork. Taste and
adjust the seasoning, if necessary. Serve hot, garnished with coriander leaves.
SERVES 4

ALMOND AND HERB RICE RING

METRIC/IMPERIAL
225 g/8 oz long-grain or medium-grain rice
600 ml/1 pint water
salt
4 tablespoons chopped fresh mixed herbs
(e.g. chives, oregano, thyme, basil and parsley)
or 2 tablespoons dried mixed herbs
50 g/2 oz split almonds

Preheat the oven to moderate (180°C/350°F, Gas
Mark 4).
Cook the rice in the boiling salted water for 10
minutes. Add the chopped herbs and cook for 5
minutes or until the rice is just tender. Drain
thoroughly.
Place the almonds on a baking sheet in the preheated oven for about 5 minutes, until golden.

Lightly grease a 900 ml/1½ pint ring mould.
Then place the split almonds in the base of the
ring. Spoon the rice into the mould, pressing it
down firmly with the back of the spoon. Cover
and bake in the oven for 20 minutes until heated
through.
Cover the mould with a serving plate, invert
and remove the mould. Serve at once.
SERVES 4 to 6

RICE BALLS IN TOMATO SAUCE

METRIC/IMPERIAL
225 g/8 oz brown rice, well washed
1 egg, lightly beaten
1 tablespoon wholemeal flour
100 g/4 oz Mozzarella cheese, cubed
1 tablespoon finely chopped parsley, to garnish
Sauce:
25 g/1 oz polyunsaturated margarine
1 large onion, peeled and finely chopped
500 g/1¼ lb tomatoes, skinned, deseeded and
chopped or 1 × 400 g/14 oz can tomatoes,
drained and chopped
1 teaspoon dried basil
½ teaspoon dried thyme
salt
freshly ground black pepper
300 ml/½ pint light stock

To make the sauce, melt the margarine in a saucepan. Add the onion and fry for 5 minutes or until
soft. Add the tomatoes, basil, thyme, salt and
pepper and cook for a further 3 minutes. Stir in the
stock. Bring to the boil, then simmer, covered,
for 15 minutes.
Meanwhile, cook the rice in boiling salted
water for 30 minutes or until tender. Drain well
and allow to cool. Mix the rice with the egg and
flour. Take a large spoonful of the rice mixture,
roll into a ball and insert a cube of cheese. Completely enclose the cube of cheese. Continue
making the rice balls until all the rice mixture and
cheese have been used.
Add the rice balls to the sauce and simmer for a
further 10 minutes.
To serve, turn the rice balls and the sauce into a
warmed serving dish and sprinkle with the
parsley.
SERVES 4

LOTUS LEAF RICE

METRIC/IMPERIAL
8 lotus leaves or 24 vine leaves
1 tablespoon polyunsaturated vegetable oil
1 clove garlic, peeled and crushed
3 spring onions, chopped
100 g/4 oz button mushrooms, wiped and sliced
50 g/2 oz cooked lean ham, diced
100 g/4 oz cooked chicken, diced
few green peas
50 g/2 oz canned bamboo shoots, drained and chopped
175 g/6 oz long-grain rice, cooked
2 tablespoons soy sauce
2 tablespoons dry sherry

Soak the leaves in warm water for 30 minutes. Drain thoroughly.

Heat the oil in a wok or deep frying pan, add the garlic and spring onions and stir-fry for 1 minute. Add the remaining ingredients, except the lotus leaves, and cook for 2 minutes.

Cut each lotus leaf into 2 or 3 pieces and divide the mixture between them, spooning into the centre. (Alternatively, use one vine leaf for each parcel.) Fold the leaf, enclosing the filling, to form a parcel and secure with string or raffia. Place in a steamer and steam vigorously for 15 to 20 minutes.

Pile on to a warmed serving dish and serve immediately. Each diner opens his own parcels.
SERVES 4 to 6

OVEN-COOKED PILAFF

METRIC/IMPERIAL
350 g/12 oz boneless raw chicken, finely diced
600 ml/1 pint chicken stock
25 g/1 oz polyunsaturated margarine
25 g/1 oz flaked almonds
1 tablespoon pine nuts (optional)
225 g/8 oz brown rice, well washed
½ teaspoon ground ginger
¼ teaspoon ground cinnamon
salt
freshly ground black pepper
2 bay leaves

Place the diced chicken in a saucepan and pour over the chicken stock. Bring to the boil, reduce the heat, cover and simmer for 5 minutes.

Heat the margarine in a clean saucepan and use to fry the flaked almonds and pine nuts, then the rice, stirring until the rice is transparent. Sprinkle in the ground ginger and cinnamon and stir for 1 minute. Add the strained stock from cooking the chicken and bring to the boil. Remove from the heat and stir in the diced chicken. Season with salt and pepper and pour the mixture into a greased shallow casserole. Lay the bay leaves on top. Cover and cook in a preheated moderately hot oven (190°C/375°F, Gas Mark 5) for 35 minutes, or until all the liquid has been absorbed.
SERVES 4

CHICKEN RISOTTO

METRIC/IMPERIAL
100 g/4 oz long-grain rice
500 ml/18 fl oz chicken stock
350 g/12 oz cooked chicken meat, cut into bite-sized pieces
1 dessertspoon chopped fresh tarragon or
1 teaspoon dried tarragon
salt
freshly ground black pepper

Put the rice in a saucepan and cover with the stock, reserving a little. Cover the pan and cook briskly, adding more stock if necessary.

Remove the rice from the heat when nearly cooked, after about 12 minutes. Stir in the chicken and tarragon. Add more stock if the mixture is too dry and return to the heat for about 5 minutes until the chicken is hot. Add salt and pepper to taste. All the stock should be absorbed; if not, drain. Serve immediately.
SERVES 4

Variation
This dish is also very good cold. Make as above and then leave to cool thoroughly. Mix in 1 tablespoon tarragon vinegar and 1 tablespoon olive oil.

VEGETABLE AND BEAN BIRYANI

METRIC/IMPERIAL

1 medium aubergine, cubed
salt
freshly ground black pepper
4 tablespoons polyunsaturated vegetable oil
¾ teaspoon poppy seeds
1 teaspoon mustard seeds
pinch of cayenne pepper
¼ teaspoon turmeric
¾ teaspoon garam masala
¼ teaspoon ground coriander
1 red pepper, cored, deseeded and sliced
75 g/3 oz cooked butter beans or haricot beans
2 tomatoes, skinned, deseeded and chopped
225 g/8 oz brown rice, cooked with a little saffron
toasted pine nuts
raisins
coriander sprig, to garnish

Place the aubergine cubes in a colander, sprinkle with salt and leave for 30 minutes. Rinse the cubes and dry.

Heat the oil in a large pan. Add the poppy and mustard seeds and cook for 2 minutes, stirring.

Add the cayenne pepper, turmeric, garam masala, coriander, aubergine, red pepper, beans, tomatoes, and salt and pepper. Cover and cook for about 10 minutes.

Layer the rice and vegetable mixture in an ovenproof dish. Cover and cook in a preheated moderate oven (180°C/350°F, Gas Mark 4) for 30 minutes. Sprinkle with toasted pine nuts and raisins. Garnish with a coriander sprig and seve hot.
SERVES 4

BROWN RICE WITH NUTS AND SPICES

METRIC/IMPERIAL

25 g/1 oz polyunsaturated margarine
25 g/1 oz flaked almonds
25 g/1 oz cashew nuts
1 onion, peeled and thinly sliced
2 carrots, coarsely grated
175 g/6 oz brown rice, well washed
2 cloves garlic, peeled and thinly sliced
1 teaspoon ground cumin
1 teaspoon ground coriander
1 teaspoon turmeric
½ teaspoon ground cinnamon

¼ teaspoon ground cloves
salt
freshly ground black pepper
3 tablespoons raisins
1 eating apple, peeled, cored and chopped
300 ml/½ pint consommé, diluted to make 600 ml/1 pint
150 ml/¼ pint dry white wine
100 g/4 oz frozen peas

Melt the margarine in a large saucepan and fry the nuts for 1 to 2 minutes until brown. Add the onion carrots, rice, garlic, spices and seasoning and fry for 2 minutes. Stir in the raisins, chopped apple, consommé and wine, and simmer for 30 to 35 minutes. Add the peas and cook for 1 minute, then sprinkle with the toasted nuts.
SERVES 4

VEGAN RICE WITH DRIED FRUITS

METRIC/IMPERIAL

4 tablespoons polyunsaturated vegetable oil
1 tablespoon chopped onion
75 g/3 oz dried apricots or nectarines, soaked overnight and chopped
75 g/3 oz dried prunes, soaked overnight and chopped
50 g/2 oz sultanas
25 g/1 oz raisins
150 ml/¼ pint apple or orange juice
2 large bananas, peeled and sliced
75 g/3 oz walnut pieces
25 g/1 oz pine nuts
1 tablespoon clear honey
225 g/8 oz brown rice, well washed
450 ml/¾ pint water
salt
freshly ground black pepper
1 red dessert apple, cored and chopped

Heat the oil in a large pan. Add the onion and cook for 3 minutes. Add the apricots or nectarines, prunes, sultanas, raisins and apple or orange juice, blending well. Cook for 5 minutes, stirring occasionally.

Add the bananas, walnuts, pine nuts, honey, rice, water, and salt and pepper to taste. Bring to the boil, reduce the heat, cover and simmer until the rice is tender, about 25 to 30 minutes.

Stir in the apple and cook gently to reheat. Spoon into a warmed serving dish.
SERVES 4

SALADS

CAULIFLOWER AND WATERCRESS SALAD

METRIC/IMPERIAL
1 small cauliflower, broken into florets
salt
1 bunch watercress, trimmed
4 spring onions, chopped
5 tablespoons French dressing
1 tablespoon sesame seeds, roasted

Cook the cauliflower in boiling salted water for 3 minutes; drain and cool. Add the watercress, spring onions and dressing and toss thoroughly. Transfer to a salad bowl and sprinkle with the sesame seeds. Serve immediately.
SERVES 6

BROCCOLI AND ALMOND SALAD

METRIC/IMPERIAL
350 g/12 oz broccoli
salt
50 g/2 oz split almonds, toasted
1 small red pepper, cored, deseeded and thinly sliced
4 tablespoons vinaigrette dressing

Break the broccoli into florets and blanch in boiling salted water for 4 minutes. Drain and cool.
Place in a salad bowl with the almonds and red pepper. Pour over the vinaigrette dressing and toss thoroughly.
SERVES 4 to 6

AVOCADO, GRAPEFRUIT AND SESAME SALAD

METRIC/IMPERIAL
2 tablespoons sesame seeds
2 large avocados, peeled, stoned and sliced
juice of 1 lemon
2 grapefruit, peeled and segmented
1 tablespoon chopped mint
lettuce leaves

Toss the sesame seeds in a dry frying pan until they begin to colour. Set aside.
Toss the avocado slices in the lemon juice to prevent discoloration. Mix in the grapefruit and chopped mint leaves.
Place a few lettuce leaves on 4 serving plates and pile the avocado mixture on top. Sprinkle over the sesame seeds and serve.
SERVES 4

AUBERGINE AND TOMATO SALAD

METRIC/IMPERIAL
2 aubergines
salt
4 tablespoons olive oil
1 onion, peeled and chopped
2 cloves garlic, peeled and finely chopped
4 tomatoes, skinned, deseeded and chopped
2 tablespoons chopped parsley
1 tablespoon lemon juice
freshly ground black pepper
lettuce leaves

Cut the aubergines into 1 cm/½ inch cubes. Place in a colander, sprinkle with salt and leave for 30 minutes. Rinse and dry with kitchen paper.
Heat the oil in a frying pan, add the onion and aubergine and fry for 10 to 15 minutes, stirring occasionally, until golden. Add the garlic and tomatoes and fry for 2 to 3 minutes.
Leave to cool, then mix with the parsley, lemon juice, and pepper to taste. Arrange the lettuce leaves in a serving dish and spoon the salad into the centre.
SERVES 4 to 6

BEETROOT AND YOGURT SALAD

METRIC/IMPERIAL
350 g/12 oz cooked beetroot
2 dill cucumbers
2 tablespoons wine vinegar
4 tablespoons plain low-fat yogurt
salt
freshly ground black pepper
1 tablespoon chopped dill or fennel

Cut the beetroot and dill cucumbers into 1 cm/½ inch dice and place in a mixing bowl.

Mix together the vinegar, yogurt, and salt and pepper to taste. Pour over the beetroot and cucumber and mix thoroughly. Turn into a shallow serving dish and sprinkle with the chopped dill or fennel to serve.
SERVES 4

BEETROOT AND ORANGE SALAD

METRIC/IMPERIAL
450 g/1 lb raw beetroot, peeled
2 oranges
4 tablespoons lemon vinaigrette dressing
1 tablespoon chopped parsley

Grate the beetroot finely and place in a salad bowl. Finely grate the orange rind and mix with the dressing. Peel the pith from the oranges, break into segments, discarding the membrane, and chop roughly. Mix the orange pieces with the grated beetroot.

Place in a serving bowl, pour over the dressing and toss thoroughly. Sprinkle with the chopped parsley to serve.
SERVES 4 to 6

GAZPACHO RING

METRIC/IMPERIAL
1 × 400 g/14 oz can tomatoes
2 cloves garlic, peeled and chopped
150 ml/¼ pint water
1 bouquet garni
½-1 teaspoon sugar
salt
freshly ground black pepper
1 tablespoon powdered gelatine, soaked in
4 tablespoons cold water

6 tablespoons French dressing
4 tomatoes, skinned, deseeded and diced
¼ cucumber, diced
½ green pepper, cored, deseeded and diced
½ onion, peeled and finely chopped
watercress sprigs, to garnish

Place the tomatoes, with their juice, in a pan with the garlic, water and bouquet garni. Add sugar, salt and pepper to taste. Bring slowly to the boil, then simmer for 5 minutes. Discard the bouquet garni.

Place the mixture in an electric blender or food processor. Add the soaked gelatine and blend on maximum speed for 30 seconds. Leave to cool.

Add 4 tablespoons of the French dressing and half the salad ingredients and stir well. Turn into a 750 ml/1¼ pint non-stick ring mould and chill in the refrigerator for about 3 hours, or until set.

Mix the remaining salad ingredients with the remaining French dressing. Turn out the tomato ring on to a serving plate and arrange the salad in the centre. Garnish with watercress sprigs.
SERVES 6

BEAN-SPROUT SALAD

METRIC/IMPERIAL
225 g/8 oz fresh or canned bean-sprouts, drained
1 canned pimiento, drained and chopped
1 pickled cucumber, diced
1 tablespoon finely snipped chives
Dressing:
2 tablespoons olive oil
1 tablespoon wine vinegar
½ teaspoon made mustard
2 teaspoons soy sauce

Put the bean-sprouts into a salad bowl with the pimiento, pickled cucumber and chives.

Mix together all the ingredients for the dressing and pour over the salad. Toss to coat thoroughly and chill for about 30 minutes before serving.
SERVES 4

GOLDEN SALAD

METRIC/IMPERIAL
lettuce leaves, washed
450 g/1 lb Jerusalem artichokes, cooked and sliced
wine vinegar
pinch of ground mace
4 hard-boiled eggs
6 tablespoons lemon vinaigrette dressing

Line a salad bowl with lettuce leaves. Arrange the sliced artichokes on top of the lettuce. Sprinkle with a little vinegar to keep them white. Add the mace.
Sieve the egg yolks and chop the whites, then scatter over the lettuce and artichokes. Serve with lemon vinaigrette dressing.
SERVES 4

CAULIFLOWER WITH EGG

METRIC/IMPERIAL
1 small cauliflower, broken into florets
salt
3 hard-boiled eggs, chopped
150 ml/¼ pint Roquefort dressing
1 tablespoon snipped chives

Blanch the cauliflower in boiling salted water for 2 to 3 minutes; drain and leave to cool completely.
Place in a bowl, add the eggs and dressing and toss thoroughly. Transfer to a serving dish and sprinkle with the chives.
SERVES 6

CHICORY AND CUCUMBER MOULD

METRIC/IMPERIAL
1 or 2 heads chicory
225 g/8 oz curd cheese
1 cucumber, peeled and sliced
1 bunch spring onions, trimmed and finely chopped
15 g/½ oz powdered gelatine
75 ml/3 fl oz water

Separate the chicory leaves. Put the curd cheese, cucumber and onions in a blender.
Sprinkle the gelatine over the water in a teacup, stand the cup in a bowl of hot water and stir until dissolved. Add the dissolved gelatine to the mix-

ture in the blender and liquidize until smooth. Pour into a deep 18 cm/7 inch cake tin with a spring clip.
Put the chicory leaves round the inside edge of the tin in an upright position so that they form a circle enclosing the curd cheese mixture. Place in the refrigerator or a cool place and leave to set for about 3 hours. Carefully release the spring clip and lift off the tin.
SERVES 4

CHICORY AND ORANGE SALAD

METRIC/IMPERIAL
3 heads chicory
3 oranges
1 tablespoon chopped parsley
4 tablespoons honey and lemon dressing (see page 337)

Cut the chicory diagonally across into 1 cm/½ inch slices and place in a salad bowl.
Remove the peel and pith from the oranges and break into segments, holding the fruit over the salad bowl so that any juice is included. Add the parsley and dressing and toss thoroughly.
SERVES 4

CHICORY AND FRUIT SALAD

METRIC/IMPERIAL
5 heads chicory, trimmed and thinly sliced into rings
2 celery hearts, trimmed and thinly sliced into rings
4 oranges, peeled and segmented
225 g/8 oz seedless white grapes
225 g/8 oz black grapes, halved and deseeded
2 bunches watercress, trimmed
100 g/4 oz button mushrooms, wiped and thinly sliced
Dressing:
4 tablespoons polyunsaturated vegetable oil
1 tablespoon orange juice
2 teaspoons lemon juice
2 spring onions, trimmed and thinly sliced
salt
freshly ground black pepper

Toss together all the chicory, celery, oranges, grapes, watercress and mushrooms.

Mix together all the ingredients for the dressing, with salt and pepper to taste.

About 1 hour before serving, pour the dressing on to the salad and toss to mix well.

SERVES 6 to 8

CELERY, APPLE AND WATERCRESS SALAD

METRIC/IMPERIAL
3 red-skinned dessert apples, quartered and cored
6 tablespoons lemon vinaigrette dressing
1 small head celery, thinly sliced
1 bunch watercress, divided into sprigs
25 g/1 oz walnut pieces

Slice the apples into a small bowl, pour over the dressing and toss well. Add the celery, watercress and walnuts. Mix well, then transfer to a salad bowl to serve.

SERVES 6 to 8

CELERY, APPLE AND SESAME SALAD

METRIC/IMPERIAL
1 head celery, thinly sliced
4 red-skinned dessert apples, cored and thinly sliced
4 tablespoons vinaigrette dressing
1 tablespoon sesame seeds

Place the celery and apples in a salad bowl. Pour in the dressing and toss well.

Dry fry the sesame seeds, shaking the pan frequently, until golden. Mix them into the salad just before serving.

SERVES 6

CELERY JULIENNE

METRIC/IMPERIAL
4 celery stalks
½ cucumber
salt
½ bulb of fennel
6 tablespoons green herb dressing (see page 337)

Cut the celery and cucumber into julienne strips 3.5 cm/1½ inches long. Place the cucumber in a colander, sprinkle with salt and leave to drain for 30 minutes to remove the excess moisture.

Trim the stalk, base and tough outer leaves from the fennel. Cut in half, then shred finely.

Dry the cucumber on kitchen paper and place in a bowl with the fennel and celery. Pour over the dressing and toss well. Transfer to a serving dish.

SERVES 4

CAPONATA

METRIC/IMPERIAL
1 large aubergine
salt
freshly ground black pepper
2 celery stalks, diced
3 tablespoons olive oil
1 onion, chopped
1 × 225 g/8 oz can tomatoes, drained and chopped
1½ teaspoons tomato purée
40 g/1½ oz green olives, stoned
1 tablespoon wine vinegar
1½ teaspoons soft brown sugar
1 tablespoon capers
few lettuce leaves

Cut the aubergine into 1 cm/½ inch cubes. Place in a colander, sprinkle with salt and leave for 30 minutes. Rinse and dry with kitchen paper.

Blanch the diced celery in boiling water for 5 minutes; drain.

Heat 2 tablespoons of the oil in a heavy-based pan, add the aubergines and fry for 10 to 15 minutes, stirring frequently, until beginning to turn golden. Remove from the pan.

Add the remaining oil to the pan and fry the onion gently for 5 minutes, until softened. Add the tomatoes, tomato purée, olives, celery, and salt and pepper to taste. Cover and simmer for 5 minutes.

Add the vinegar, sugar, capers and aubergine; cover and simmer for 5 minutes. Leave to cool. Serve on individual dishes lined with the lettuce leaves.

SERVES 4 to 5

125

CALIFORNIAN COLESLAW

METRIC/IMPERIAL
1 dessert apple, cored
4 tablespoons honey and lemon dressing (see
page 337)
2 oranges
100 g/4 oz each white and black grapes, halved
and deseeded
225 g/8 oz white cabbage, finely shredded
2 tablespoons snipped chives
2 tablespoons toasted sunflower seeds

Slice the apple thinly into the dressing and toss
until thoroughly coated.
Remove the peel and pith from the oranges,
break into segments and add to the bowl.
Add the remaining ingredients and toss well.
Transfer to a salad bowl.
SERVES 6 to 8

CAESAR SALAD

METRIC/IMPERIAL
2 cloves garlic, peeled and crushed
6 tablespoons olive oil
3 slices bread
2 tablespoons lemon juice
1 teaspoon Worcestershire sauce
salt
freshly ground black pepper
1 large Cos lettuce
2 eggs, boiled for 1 minute
4 tablespoons grated Parmesan cheese

Place the garlic in the olive oil and leave to soak for
3 to 4 hours. Strain the oil.
Cut the bread into 5 mm/¼ inch cubes and fry
in 4 tablespoons of the garlic-flavoured oil until
golden. Drain on kitchen paper
Place the remaining oil in a small bowl with the
lemon juice, Worcestershire sauce, and salt and
pepper to taste, and mix well.
Tear the lettuce into pieces and place in a salad
bowl. Pour over the prepared dressing and toss
well. Break the eggs over the lettuce, scraping out
the partly set egg white, and mix thoroughly to
combine the egg with the dressing.
Add the cheese and croûtons and give a final
toss just before serving.
SERVES 6

CURRIED MUSHROOM SALAD

METRIC/IMPERIAL
450 g/1 lb button mushrooms, wiped and
trimmed
½ cucumber, peeled
225 g/8 oz cooked lean ham
300 ml/½ pint plain low-fat yogurt
2 teaspoons curry paste
4 teaspoons lemon juice
salt
freshly ground black pepper

Cut the larger mushrooms into quarters. Dice the
cucumber and cut the ham into bite-sized pieces.
Stir the mushrooms, ham and cucumber together in a bowl. Mix the yogurt, curry paste and
lemon juice together. Chill both mixtures for 1
hour.
Combine the mushroom and yogurt mixtures
together, adding salt and pepper to taste. Chill for
a further hour before serving.
SERVES 4

EGG AND CUCUMBER SALAD

METRIC/IMPERIAL
1 bunch watercress, trimmed
1 cucumber, peeled and sliced
4 hard-boiled eggs, finely chopped
1 bunch spring onions, chopped
Dressing:
300 ml/½ pint plain low-fat yogurt
1 tablespoon lemon juice
1 teaspoon mustard powder
salt
freshly ground black pepper

Arrange the watercress in a serving dish and cover
with the cucumber slices. Mix the chopped eggs
and spring onions together and spoon into the
centre.
To make the dressing, mix all the ingredients
together. Pour over the salad and serve.
SERVES 4

ENDIVE AND AVOCADO SALAD

METRIC/IMPERIAL
½ head curly endive
1 bunch watercress
2 avocados, halved and stoned
6 tablespoons French dressing

Tear the endive into pieces and separate the water cress into sprigs; place in a salad bowl.

Peel the avocados and slice into a bowl. Pour over the dressing and toss until completely coated. Add to the endive and watercress and toss thoroughly.
SERVES 6

FENNEL SALAD

METRIC/IMPERIAL
2 dessert apples, Cox's Orange Pippins
      preferably
lemon juice
2 fennel bulbs, trimmed
4 celery stalks, trimmed
salt
freshly ground black pepper
chopped spring onion, to garnish
6 tablespoons lemon vinaigrette dressing

Core the apples, cut into slices and dip in lemon juice to prevent discoloration. Place in a serving dish.

Slice the fennel and celery and mix with the apple, adding salt and pepper to taste. Garnish with chopped spring onion and serve with lemon vinaigrette dressing.
SERVES 4

FRENCH BEAN, TOMATO AND PEPPER SALAD

METRIC/IMPERIAL
225 g/8 oz French beans, trimmed
pinch of salt
1 large red pepper, cored, deseeded and chopped
4 large tomatoes, skinned and quartered
1 tablespoon chopped basil or oregano
6 tablespoons lemon vinaigrette dressing

Cook the beans in boiling salted water for about 12 minutes, until just tender. Drain and cut the beans in half.

Blanch the red pepper in boiling water for 1 minute, then drain. Place the beans in a salad bowl with the pepper and tomatoes. Carefully mix together and sprinkle over the basil or oregano. Pour over the lemon vinaigrette and chill in the refrigerator before serving.
SERVES 4

PINEAPPLE MADRAS

METRIC/IMPERIAL
2 small pineapples
1 large, ripe avocado, peeled and stoned
100 g/4 oz low-fat curd cheese (e.g. Quark)
½-1 teaspoon dried curry powder
50 g/2 oz seedless grapes, cut in half
Garnish:
4 orange slices
4 maraschino cherries

Cut the pineapples in half lengthways, retaining some of the leaves on each of the halves. Remove the flesh, reserving the juice. Measure the juice and make up to 25 ml/1 fl oz with canned pineapple or orange juice if necessary. Chop the flesh finely, discarding the core. Reserve the skins.

Place the avocado flesh in a food processor or liquidizer with the cheese, curry powder and pineapple juice. Process until a thick purée has been formed. Place in a basin and fold in the pineapple and grapes.

Pile this mixture into the pineapple skins and decorate with orange slices, threaded through cocktail sticks, topped with maraschino cherries.

Serve on a bed of lettuce and watercress with a grilled poppadum to accompany the salad.
SERVES 4

ITALIAN SALAD

METRIC/IMPERIAL
½ head curly endive, separated into leaves
1 head chicory, sliced into rings
1 bulb fennel, sliced into rings
1 small head radicchio, separated into leaves
8 radishes, sliced if large
4 tablespoons vinaigrette dressing
salt
freshly ground black pepper

Put all the ingredients in a salad bowl, toss well, then taste and adjust the seasoning. Serve cold.
SERVES 4

HOT POTATO SALAD

METRIC/IMPERIAL
750 g/1½ lb new waxy potatoes, scrubbed
2 tablespoons finely chopped onion
3 tablespoons polyunsaturated vegetable oil
1 tablespoon white wine vinegar
salt
freshly ground black pepper
4 tablespoons snipped chives

Cook the potatoes in their skins in boiling salted water for about 20 minutes until tender. Drain well and cut into thick slices. Stir in the chopped onion. Pour over the oil and vinegar, and mix gently, trying not to break the potatoes. Season with salt and pepper and stir in 3 tablespoons of the chives.

Turn the salad into a serving dish and scatter the remaining chives over the top.
SERVES 4

JELLIED TOMATO RING

METRIC/IMPERIAL
4 tomatoes, skinned and sliced
600 ml/1 pint tomato juice
1 teaspoon Worcestershire sauce
salt
freshly ground black pepper
15 g/½ oz powdered gelatine
1 bunch watercress

Arrange the tomato slices in the bottom of a 19 cm/7½ inch ring mould.

Heat the tomato juice and stir in the Worcestershire sauce, salt and pepper. Sprinkle in the gelatine and heat gently, stirring until the gelatine has dissolved.

Pour into the ring and place in the refrigerator or a cool place and leave to set for about 3 hours. Turn out carefully and fill the centre with sprigs of watercress.
SERVES 4

CHINESE CABBAGE AND ORANGE SALAD

METRIC/IMPERIAL
1 small Chinese cabbage, shredded
1 bunch watercress, trimmed
4 oranges, segmented
5 tablespoons mint and honey dressing
(see page 338)

Put the cabbage, watercress and orange segments in a salad bowl. Pour in the dressing and toss well.
SERVES 6

CHINESE CABBAGE AND CUCUMBER SALAD

METRIC/IMPERIAL
2.5 cm/1 inch piece root ginger, peeled and finely chopped
4 tablespoons French dressing
1 Chinese cabbage
½ cucumber
100 g/4 oz bean-shoots
6 spring onions, chopped
1 tablespoon chopped parsley, to garnish

Mix the ginger with the dressing and leave for 30 minutes. Shred the Chinese cabbage and cut the cucumber into julienne strips. Place all the ingredients in a bowl and toss thoroughly to combine with the dressing. Transfer to a serving dish and sprinkle with the parsley.
SERVES 6

COLESLAW WITH YOGURT DRESSING

METRIC/IMPERIAL
½ medium white cabbage, finely shredded
2 celery stalks, chopped
2 dessert apples, cored and chopped
1 small onion, peeled and finely chopped
50 g/2 oz sultanas
50 g/2 oz walnuts, chopped
2 tablespoons chopped parsley
120 ml/4 fl oz yogurt dressing (see page 339)

Mix together the cabbage, celery, apples, onion, sultanas, walnuts and parsley in a salad bowl. Add the yogurt dressing and toss thoroughly before serving.
SERVES 6

COS LETTUCE WITH YOGURT DRESSING

METRIC/IMPERIAL
1 Cos lettuce, trimmed, leaves torn
3-4 tablespoons plain low-fat yogurt
1 clove garlic, peeled and crushed
1 teaspoon tomato purée
salt
freshly ground black pepper

Put the lettuce leaves into a salad bowl.
To make the dressing, mix the yogurt with the garlic, tomato purée, and salt and pepper to taste, until smooth.
Pour the dressing over the lettuce and toss thoroughly to coat. Serve at once.
SERVES 4

CRUNCHY SALAD

METRIC/IMPERIAL
225 g/8 oz green pepper, cored, deseeded and chopped
225 g/8 oz fennel, finely chopped
225 g/8 oz celery, roughly chopped
1 cucumber, peeled and diced
100 g/4 oz spring onions, chopped
1-2 teaspoons chopped tarragon
6 tablespoons lemon vinaigrette dressing

Blanch the green pepper in boiling water for 1 minute; drain.
Mix the pepper, fennel, celery, cucumber and spring onions together in a salad bowl and sprinkle with the tarragon. Serve with lemon vinaigrette dressing.
SERVES 4

LAMB'S LETTUCE SALAD

METRIC/IMPERIAL
225 g/8 oz lamb's lettuce, washed
1 head radicchio
1 head chicory
½ bulb fennel
few dandelion leaves, halved (optional)
2 tablespoons chopped parsley
50 g/2 oz walnuts
6 tablespoons French dressing

Remove the roots from the lamb's lettuce and place the leaves in a salad bowl. Tear the radicchio into manageable pieces and slice the chicory into 1 cm/½ inch pieces. Slice the fennel very thinly.
Place the lamb's lettuce, radicchio, chicory and fennel in the salad bowl with the dandelion leaves (if using), parsley, walnuts and French dressing, and toss thoroughly.
SERVES 6 to 8

APPLE AND CELERIAC SALAD

METRIC/IMPERIAL
750 g/1½ lb celeriac
3 tablespoons plain low-fat yogurt
2 tablespoons reduced-calorie mayonnaise
1 tablespoon finely chopped chervil or borage
1 tablespoon finely chopped parsley
2 crisp red dessert apples, cored and thinly sliced into rings
100 g/4 oz cashew nuts, finely chopped

Put the celeriac into a saucepan and cover with water. Bring to the boil, lower the heat and cook for 15 minutes. Drain thoroughly, allow to cool, then peel and cube.
Mix together the yogurt, mayonnaise, chervil or borage and parsley. Add the apple slices to the yogurt mixture with the celeriac. Stir to coat and transfer to a salad bowl. Sprinkle the nuts over and serve.
SERVES 6

BABY ONIONS WITH CAPERS

METRIC/IMPERIAL
450 g/1 lb pickling onions
3 tomatoes, skinned and chopped
1 tablespoon capers
2 teaspoons tomato purée
½ teaspoon soft brown sugar
2 teaspoons wine vinegar
2 tablespoons olive oil
2 tablespoons chopped parsley

Plunge the onions into boiling water and boil for 1 to 2 minutes. Drain, cool slightly, then remove the skins.
Return to the pan with the tomatoes, capers, tomato purée, sugar, vinegar and oil. Cover and simmer for 5 minutes, then stir in the parsley. Transfer to a serving dish and chill before serving.
SERVES 4

CUCUMBER WITH MINT

METRIC/IMPERIAL
1 cucumber, thinly sliced
salt
1 bunch mint, finely chopped
8 tablespoons yogurt dressing (see page 339)

Place the cucumber in a colander, sprinkle with salt and leave to drain for 30 minutes.

Dry the cucumber on kitchen paper and place in a shallow serving dish. Add the mint and yogurt dressing and mix well.
SERVES 4 to 6

CUCUMBER AND TOMATO RAITA

METRIC/IMPERIAL
1 small or ½ large cucumber, sliced
½ teaspoon salt
4 tomatoes, thinly sliced
300 ml/½ pint plain low-fat yogurt
2 tablespoons chopped mint
freshly ground white pepper

Put the cucumber in a colander, sprinkle with the salt and leave to drain for 30 minutes.

Dry the cucumber with kitchen paper and place in a serving dish with the tomatoes. Mix the yogurt with the chopped mint and pepper to taste, then pour over the salad. Serve chilled.
SERVES 4

CUCUMBER MOULD

METRIC/IMPERIAL
15 g/½ oz powdered gelatine
250 ml/8 fl oz lemon juice
250 ml/8 fl oz hot water
1 cucumber, peeled and sliced
225 g/8 oz white grapes, deseeded

Sprinkle the gelatine on to the lemon juice and allow to soften. Add to the hot water and stir until the gelatine has dissolved.

Arrange about half the cucumber slices in a 19 cm/7½ inch mould with the grapes. Pour over the lemon jelly mixture. Arrange the remaining cucumber slices on top of the mould. Place in the refrigerator or a cool place and leave to set for about 3 hours. Turn out and serve.
SERVES 4

TOMATO RING SALAD

METRIC/IMPERIAL
750 g/1½ lb tomatoes, roughly chopped
1 onion, peeled and chopped
150 ml/¼ pint stock or water
finely grated rind and juice of 1 orange or lemon
1 small bunch herbs (basil, oregano, parsley, mint, as available)
1 bay leaf
1 clove garlic, peeled and crushed
salt
freshly ground black pepper
15 g/½ oz powdered gelatine
2 tablespoons water
1 teaspoon Worcestershire sauce
Garnish:
1 bunch watercress, or 1 box mustard and cress
4 hard-boiled eggs, shelled and cut into wedges
cucumber slices

Put the tomatoes and onion in a pan. Pour in the stock or water then add the orange or lemon rind and juice, herbs, garlic, and salt and pepper to taste.

Bring to the boil, then lower the heat, cover and simmer for 20 minutes until the tomatoes are reduced to a pulp. Rub through a sieve to make a purée.

Sprinkle the gelatine over the water in a small cup. Stand the cup in a pan of hot water and stir until the gelatine has dissolved. Stir the gelatine into the purée, then add the Worcestershire sauce and salt and pepper to taste.

Pour into a 600 to 900 ml/1 to 1½ pint ring mould, then chill in the refrigerator until set. Unmould just before serving and garnish with the cress, egg slices and cucumber.
SERVES 4

MANGETOUT SALAD

METRIC/IMPERIAL
225 g/8 oz mangetout peas
1 tablespoon sesame seeds
1 red pepper, cored, deseeded and finely sliced
4 tablespoons French dressing

Top and tail the mangetout and, if large, cut in half diagonally. Dry fry the sesame seeds over gentle heat, shaking the pan, until golden.

Place all the ingredients in a bowl and toss thoroughly. Turn into a shallow serving dish.
SERVES 4

LEEKS À LA GRECQUE

METRIC/IMPERIAL
300 ml/½ pint water (or 150 ml/¼ pint dry
white wine and 150 ml/¼ pint water)
finely grated rind and juice of 1 lemon
2 shallots, peeled and thinly sliced
4 parsley sprigs
1 small celery stalk, with leaves
1 fennel sprig or few fennel seeds
1 thyme sprig
6 peppercorns
3 coriander seeds
salt
450 g/1 lb leeks, trimmed and cleaned

Put all the ingredients in a large pan, except the
leeks. Bring to the boil, then lower the heat, cover
and simmer for 10 minutes.

Add the leeks to the pan, cover and simmer
gently for 10 to 15 minutes until tender but not
broken up.

Transfer the leeks to a serving dish. Boil the
cooking liquid until reduced by half. Strain if preferred, then pour over the leeks and leave to cool.
Serve cold.
SERVES 4

MELON, TOMATO AND KIWI VINAIGRETTE

METRIC/IMPERIAL
2 Ogen or Charentais melons
4 tomatoes, skinned
3 kiwi fruit, peeled and sliced
1 tablespoon chopped mixed herbs (e.g. chives,
mint, parsley)
4 tablespoons honey and lemon dressing
(see page 337)
2 tablespoons pumpkin seeds (optional)

Cut the melons in half and discard the seeds.
Scoop the flesh into balls, using a melon baller, or
cut into cubes; reserve the shells. Cut each tomato
into 8 wedges and discard the seeds.

Place the melon in a bowl with the tomatoes,
kiwi fruit and herbs. Pour over the dressing and
toss well.

Spoon the mixture into the melon shells and
sprinkle with pumpkin seeds, if using.
SERVES 4

MIXED VEGETABLE SALAD

METRIC/IMPERIAL
4 medium waxy potatoes, peeled, cooked and
diced
1 large celery stalk, finely chopped
2 carrots, scrubbed and grated
1 small onion, peeled and finely chopped
½ small white cabbage, cored and shredded
2 tablespoons chopped pickled gherkins
8 black olives, stoned and chopped
3 tablespoons vinaigrette dressing
2 tablespoons chopped parsley, to garnish

Put all the prepared ingredients in a salad bowl,
pour over the vinaigrette dressing and toss well.
Sprinkle with chopped parsley before serving.
SERVES 6

MUSHROOM AND BEAN-SHOOT SALAD

METRIC/IMPERIAL
350 g/12 oz button mushrooms, wiped and
quartered
6 tablespoons vinaigrette dressing
225 g/8 oz bean-shoots
1 red pepper, cored, deseeded and finely sliced

Place the mushrooms in a salad bowl, add the
dressing and toss well. Leave to marinate for 1
hour, stirring occasionally. Add the bean-shoots
and pepper. Toss thoroughly before serving.
SERVES 6

ONION AND CHILLI SALAD

METRIC/IMPERIAL
5 tablespoons cider vinegar
3 tablespoons water
1 green chilli, deseeded and chopped
salt
freshly ground black pepper
2 Spanish onions, peeled and thinly sliced

Mix together the vinegar, water, chilli, and salt
and pepper to taste.

Place the onions in a shallow serving dish and
pour over the dressing. Leave to stand for 1 hour,
stirring occasionally.
SERVES 6

MUSHROOM SALAD WITH HERBS

METRIC/IMPERIAL

225 g/8 oz very fresh button mushrooms, stalks removed, caps thinly sliced
salt
freshly ground black pepper
2 tablespoons finely chopped onion
1 clove garlic, peeled and crushed
3 tablespoons polyunsaturated vegetable oil
1½ tablespoons lemon juice
2 tablespoons chopped chervil
2 tablespoons snipped chives

Put the mushroom caps into a serving bowl and season with salt and pepper. Stir in the onion and garlic. Stir in the oil, lemon juice and chopped herbs. Serve soon after making, or the mushrooms will dry up and need yet more oil.
SERVES 4

ORANGE AND DANDELION SALAD

METRIC/IMPERIAL

450 g/1 lb young dandelion leaves, washed
2 oranges, peeled, sliced and quartered
1 bunch watercress, trimmed
50 g/2 oz spring onions, chopped
Dressing:
75 ml/3 fl oz olive oil
2 tablespoons orange juice
½ teaspoon clear honey
1 clove garlic, peeled and crushed
1 tablespoon chopped parsley
salt
freshly ground black pepper

Shred the dandelion leaves and pile into a serving dish. Arrange the orange slices and watercress on top. Scatter over the chopped spring onions.
Put all the dressing ingredients in a screw-topped jar, adding salt and pepper to taste. Shake well to blend before using.
Serve the salad with the dressing.
SERVES 4

ORANGE AND WATERCRESS SALAD

METRIC/IMPERIAL

1 large bunch watercress, trimmed
3 oranges, peel and pith removed and thinly sliced into rounds
1 onion, peeled and thinly sliced into rings
1 small green pepper, cored, deseeded and thinly sliced into rings
6 tablespoons vinaigrette dressing
black olives, to garnish

Put the watercress in a salad bowl. Arrange the orange slices on top with the onion and pepper rings. Pour on the vinaigrette dressing and garnish with the olives.
SERVES 4

TOMATO AND FENNEL SALAD

METRIC/IMPERIAL

2 bunches spring onions, thinly sliced
½ small bulb fennel, trimmed and thinly sliced horizontally
350 g/12 oz tomatoes, skinned and chopped
25 g/1 oz parsley, coarsely chopped
5 tablespoons coarsely chopped mint
2 tablespoons polyunsaturated vegetable oil
1 tablespoon lemon juice

Put the spring onions into a salad bowl with the sliced fennel and chopped tomatoes. Mix in the chopped parsley and mint. Pour over the oil and lemon juice and mix again until all the ingredients are thoroughly coated.
SERVES 4

TOMATO AND LEEK SALAD

METRIC/IMPERIAL

450 g/1 lb tomatoes, sliced
100 g/4 oz leeks, washed and thinly sliced
4 tablespoons honey and lemon dressing (see page 337)
1 tablespoon chopped parsley

Arrange the tomatoes and leeks in layers in a shallow serving dish, finishing with leeks. Pour over the dressing evenly and sprinkle with the parsley.
SERVES 4

TRADITIONAL COLESLAW SALAD

METRIC/IMPERIAL

350 g/12 oz white cabbage, trimmed and finely
shredded
225 g/8 oz carrots, scraped and grated
1 dessert apple, cored and chopped
25 g/1 oz sultanas
25 g/1 oz unsalted peanuts
Dressing:
1 tablespoon plain wholemeal flour
2 teaspoons French mustard
salt
freshly ground black pepper
150 ml/¼ pint wine vinegar
15 g/½ oz polyunsaturated margarine
1 egg
a little skimmed milk

To make the dressing, put the flour and mustard
into a pan. Season with salt and pepper and mix in
a little vinegar to make a smooth paste, then
gradually stir in the remainder. Place the pan over
a low heat and, stirring all the time, bring the mixture to the boil. Simmer for 5 minutes. Remove
the pan from the heat and stir in the margarine.

Beat the egg in a bowl, then gradually beat in
the vinegar mixture. Return to the pan and cook
until it thickens. Leave to cool, then dilute with
sufficient milk to make the required consistency.
Taste and adjust the seasoning.

Mix the cabbage, carrots, apple, sultanas and
peanuts together in a salad bowl, then stir in
enough dressing to moisten the ingredients.
SERVES 6

WATERCRESS AND TOFU SALAD

METRIC/IMPERIAL

1 × 300 g/10 oz cake of tofu
2 tablespoons sesame seeds, roasted
4 tablespoons soy sauce dressing (see page 337)
2 bunches watercress, trimmed

Cut the tofu into 1 cm/½ inch cubes. Place in a
bowl with the sesame seeds, pour over the dressing and toss carefully. Divide the watercress into
sprigs, add to the tofu and mix gently. Transfer to
a salad bowl.
SERVES 4 to 6

WATERCRESS, BEAN-SPROUT AND GRAPEFRUIT SALAD

METRIC/IMPERIAL

1 bunch watercress, trimmed and washed
225 g/8 oz bean-sprouts, washed and drained
1 small grapefruit, peeled and segmented with
the segments cut in half
2 teaspoons snipped chives
Dressing:
½ teaspoon made mustard
2 teaspoons soy sauce
½ teaspoon sugar
¼ teaspoon ground ginger
freshly ground black pepper
1 tablespoon white wine vinegar
3 tablespoons polyunsaturated vegetable oil

In a bowl, mix the watercress, bean-sprouts,
grapefruit segments and chives.

Place all the dressing ingredients in a screw-
topped jar and shake well. Pour over the salad just
before serving and toss well.
SERVES 4

WARM POTATO SALAD WITH THYME

METRIC/IMPERIAL

750 g/1½ lb new potatoes, washed and scrubbed
salt
freshly ground black pepper
grated rind and juice of 1 lemon
½ teaspoon light brown sugar
3 spring onions, trimmed and minced
3 tablespoons olive oil
1 tablespoon chopped thyme
1 clove garlic, peeled and crushed

Cook the new potatoes in boiling salted water
until just tender – about 8 to 10 minutes.

Meanwhile, put the lemon rind and juice,
brown sugar, spring onions, olive oil, thyme and
garlic into a shallow pan, and heat through until
the mixture is just bubbling. Season to taste.

Drain the cooked new potatoes thoroughly and
toss immediately in the prepared dressing. Leave
to stand for 4 to 5 minutes to give the potatoes the
chance to absorb the flavour of the dressing, and
then serve while still warm.
SERVES 4

WINTER SALAD

METRIC/IMPERIAL
1 tablespoon sesame seeds
1 carrot, scraped and finely grated
75 g/3 oz mushrooms, wiped and finely sliced
50 g/2 oz cooked beetroot, peeled and cubed
¼ small onion, peeled and finely chopped
1 large parsley sprig, finely chopped
¼ bunch watercress, chopped
1-2 tablespoons balsamic vinegar (available from speciality delicatessens)

Toss the sesame seeds in a thick frying pan over a moderate heat until a light golden colour. Cool on absorbent kitchen paper. Then mix in a salad bowl with all the other ingredients and serve.
SERVES 4

TOSSED GREEN SALAD

METRIC/IMPERIAL
½ lettuce, trimmed and separated into leaves
¼ bunch curly endive, trimmed
½ bunch watercress, trimmed
¼ cucumber, sliced
1 green pepper, cored, deseeded and sliced
few spring onions, trimmed
120 ml/4 fl oz French dressing

Put all the prepared vegetables into a deep salad bowl. Pour over the dressing and toss well.
SERVES 4

SWEDISH POTATO SALAD

METRIC/IMPERIAL
750 g/1½ lb small new potatoes
salt
2 tablespoons French dressing
100 g/4 oz cooked beetroot, diced
1 pickled dill cucumber, diced
5 tablespoons yogurt dressing (see page 339)
1 tablespoon chopped dill

Scrub the potatoes clean but leave the skins on. Cook in boiling salted water until tender. Drain and mix with the dressing while still warm.

When cool, add the beetroot, cucumber and yogurt dressing. Mix well, then transfer to a salad bowl. Sprinkle with the dill to serve.
SERVES 6

SPINACH AND ONION SALAD

METRIC/IMPERIAL
750 g/1½ lb spinach, washed and trimmed
2 tablespoons olive oil
1 large onion, peeled and chopped
2 cloves garlic, peeled and crushed
salt
freshly ground black pepper
150 ml/¼ pint low-fat cream
grated nutmeg

Cook the spinach in a large pan, with just the water clinging to the leaves after washing, about 5 minutes. Drain thoroughly and chop.

Heat the oil in a pan, add the onion and fry until softened. Add the garlic, spinach, and salt and pepper to taste, and heat through.

Season the cream to taste with nutmeg and pepper. Pour over the spinach and mix well. Leave to cool, then transfer to a salad bowl.
SERVES 4

SPRING GREEN SALAD

METRIC/IMPERIAL
225 g/8 oz spring greens
4 tablespoons olive oil
2 teaspoons soy sauce
1 tablespoon lemon juice
2 cloves garlic, peeled and crushed
salt
freshly ground black pepper
3 celery stalks
½ × 200 g/7 oz can sweetcorn, drained
2 tablespoons chopped parsley

Shred the spring greens finely and place in a mixing bowl. Mix together the oil, soy sauce, lemon juice, garlic, and salt and pepper to taste and pour over the greens. Mix thoroughly and leave to marinate for 1 hour.

Slice the celery and add to the salad with the sweetcorn and parsley. Mix thoroughly, then transfer to a serving dish.
SERVES 6

SWEETCORN AND PEPPER SALAD

METRIC/IMPERIAL
1 × 300 g/11 oz can sweetcorn kernels, drained
½ green pepper, deseeded and chopped
½ red pepper, deseeded and chopped
1 Spanish onion, peeled and cut into rings
4 tablespoons French dressing
2 tablespoons chopped fresh parsley
1 bunch watercress, trimmed

Mix the sweetcorn with the green and red peppers. Reserve the larger onion rings for garnish and mix the rest into the sweetcorn mixture.

Put the dressing into a screw-topped jar with the parsley and shake well, then pour over the salad ingredients.

Arrange the watercress around the outside of a salad bowl. Spoon the sweetcorn mixture into the centre and garnish with the large onion rings.
SERVES 4

TOMATO AND AVOCADO SALAD

METRIC/IMPERIAL
Dressing:
4 tablespoons polyunsaturated vegetable oil
2 tablespoons vinegar
1 teaspoon dry mustard
2 teaspoons chopped marjoram
salt
freshly ground black pepper
Salad:
4 tomatoes, quartered and deseeded
1 avocado, peeled, stoned and diced
100 g/4 oz fresh dates, stoned
1 × 200 g/7 oz can red kidney beans, drained and rinsed
100 g/4 oz Mozzarella cheese, diced
few lettuce leaves

Put all the dressing ingredients in a screw-topped jar and shake well.

Put the tomatoes into a bowl. Add the diced avocado to the tomatoes with the dates. Mix in the beans and Mozzarella. Pour the dressing over the salad and toss all the ingredients together.

Line a dish with lettuce leaves, then turn the salad into the centre and chill before serving.
SERVES 4

TOMATO AND BASIL SALAD

METRIC/IMPERIAL
450 g/1 lb Marmand tomatoes
salt
freshly ground black pepper
3 tablespoons olive oil
2 tablespoons chopped basil

Slice the tomatoes thinly and lay them in a shallow serving dish, sprinkling each layer with salt and pepper. Pour over the oil and sprinkle with basil.
SERVES 4

Note: Marmand tomatoes are the large round variety, often called Mediterranean tomatoes. The basil and the olive oil greatly enhance the flavour of the tomatoes in this delicious salad.

SPICY TOMATO SALAD

METRIC/IMPERIAL
4 large, ripe tomatoes
3 spring onions, including some green tops,
finely chopped
1 tablespoon lime juice
¾ teaspoon grated fresh ginger
salt
freshly ground black pepper

Cut the tomatoes crosswise into thin slices and arrange in overlapping circles on a small platter. Sprinkle with the remaining ingredients, adding salt and pepper to taste. Serve at once.
SERVES 4

RED CABBAGE AND APPLE SALAD

METRIC/IMPERIAL
350 g/12 oz red cabbage
1 small leek, well washed
6 tablespoons vinaigrette dressing
3 dessert apples

Finely shred the cabbage, and thinly slice the leek. Place in a salad bowl, add the dressing and toss thoroughly. Leave to marinate for 1 hour, tossing occasionally.

Core the apples and slice thinly. Add to the bowl and toss again just before serving.
SERVES 8

RED CABBAGE AND CARROT SALAD

METRIC/IMPERIAL
450 g/1 lb red cabbage, trimmed and shredded
225 g/8 oz carrots, scraped and grated
50 g/2 oz raisins
2 large oranges, rinds grated, flesh segmented
2 tablespoons reduced-calorie mayonnaise
2 tablespoons plain low-fat yogurt

Put the cabbage into a bowl with the carrots and raisins, and add the orange segments.

Mix the mayonnaise and yogurt together and stir in the orange rind. Just before serving, mix the dressing into the salad and toss well.
SERVES 4

SPINACH AND MUSHROOM SALAD

METRIC/IMPERIAL
225 g/8 oz button mushrooms, wiped and sliced
4 tablespoons French dressing
225 g/8 oz young spinach leaves
4 spring onions, chopped

Put the mushrooms in a bowl, add 3 tablespoons of the dressing and toss well. Leave to marinate for 1 hour, stirring occasionally.

Wash and thoroughly dry the spinach. Remove the thick centre stalks and tear the spinach leaves into a salad bowl. Add the mushrooms, onions and remaining dressing. Toss well.
SERVES 4

CRISPY ORANGE SALAD

METRIC/IMPERIAL
4 oranges, peeled, pith removed and segmented
1 × 425 g/15 oz can red kidney beans, drained
225 g/8 oz bean-sprouts, sorted
4 celery stalks, chopped
2 tablespoons French dressing
1 tablespoon chopped parsley
salt
freshly ground black pepper

Mix the orange with the beans, bean-sprouts and celery in a bowl. Mix the French dressing with the parsley and salt and pepper to taste, blending well. Pour over the salad and toss gently.
SERVES 4 to 6

POTATO AND COURGETTE SALAD

METRIC/IMPERIAL
450 g/1 lb new potatoes, scrubbed
salt
225 g/8 oz courgettes, sliced
4 tablespoons polyunsaturated vegetable oil
finely grated rind and juice of 1 small orange
1 tablespoon wine vinegar
1 tablespoon chopped parsley
1 tablespoon snipped chives or finely chopped spring onions
freshly ground black pepper
Garnish:
50 g/2 oz bacon, crisply grilled and crumbled
chopped parsley
snipped chives

Cook the potatoes in boiling salted water until they are just tender but not broken up. Remove from the water and leave to drain. Add the courgettes to the boiling water, simmer for about 3 minutes until just tender, then drain.

Put the oil in a bowl with the orange rind and juice, vinegar, parsley and chives or spring onions. Add salt and pepper to taste and beat well.

Cut the larger potatoes into halves or quarters and leave the small ones whole. Put the potatoes and courgettes in a salad bowl, pour on the orange dressing and toss lightly to mix. The potatoes will absorb the flavour better if they are still warm.

Sprinkle the crumbled bacon, parsley and chives over the salad just before serving for extra flavour and crunchiness. Serve cold.
SERVES 4

POTATO AND RADISH VINAIGRETTE

METRIC/IMPERIAL
450 g/1 lb small new potatoes
salt
4 tablespoons French dressing
4 spring onions, sliced
1 bunch radishes, thinly sliced

Scrub the potatoes clean but leave the skins on Cook in boiling salted water until tender. Drain well and mix with the dressing while still warm. Leave to cool.

Add the spring onions and radishes, mix well and transfer to a salad bowl to serve.
SERVES 4

RADICCHIO SALAD

METRIC/IMPERIAL
½ head curly endive
1 head radicchio
1 large head chicory
25 g/1 oz pine nuts
Dressing:
4 tablespoons olive oil
1 tablespoon lime juice
½ teaspoon clear honey
1 clove garlic, peeled and crushed
1 teaspoon chopped parsley
salt
freshly ground black pepper

Separate the endive and radicchio into leaves, rinse and dry well, then tear into pieces and place in a bowl. Cut the chicory diagonally across into 1 cm/½ inch slices and add to the bowl.

Put all the dressing ingredients in a screw-topped jar, adding salt and pepper to taste. Shake well to blend. Pour the dressing over the salad and toss well.

Transfer to a salad bowl and sprinkle with the pine nuts to serve.
SERVES 4 to 6

LENTIL SALAD

METRIC/IMPERIAL
225 g/8 oz green lentils
salt
6 tablespoons soy sauce dressing (see page 337)
4 tomatoes, skinned and chopped
1 small onion, peeled and chopped
100 g/4 oz bean-sprouts
2 celery stalks, sliced
1 tablespoon chopped summer savory
freshly ground black pepper

Cover the lentils with boiling water and leave to soak for 20 minutes. Drain, place in a pan and cover with cold water. Bring to the boil, add a little salt, then cover and simmer for 20 minutes, until softened. Drain well and place in a bowl. Pour over the dressing and mix well while still warm. Leave to cool.

Add the remaining ingredients, seasoning with salt and pepper to taste, toss thoroughly and transfer to a serving dish.
SERVES 6 to 8

LENTIL AND TOMATO SALAD

METRIC/IMPERIAL
225 g/8 oz brown lentils, soaked for 1 hour
salt
6 tablespoons tomato and garlic dressing (see page 336)
4 spring onions, chopped
4 tomatoes, skinned and chopped
2 celery stalks, sliced
1 tablespoon chopped parsley
freshly ground black pepper

Drain the lentils, place in a pan and cover with cold water. Add a little salt and simmer gently for 30 to 40 minutes until softened. Drain well and mix with the tomato and garlic dressing while still warm. Leave to cool.

Add the remaining ingredients, seasoning with salt and pepper to taste. Mix together thoroughly. Transfer to a salad bowl to serve.
SERVES 6

RATATOUILLE SALAD

METRIC/IMPERIAL
6 tablespoons olive oil
1 small aubergine, sliced
225 g/8 oz courgettes, sliced
1 green pepper, cored, deseeded and sliced
2 cloves garlic, peeled and crushed
salt
freshly ground black pepper
4 tomatoes, skinned and sliced

Heat half the oil in a frying pan, add the aubergine and fry on both sides until light golden brown, adding more oil if necessary. Place in a salad bowl.

Add the remaining oil to the pan and fry the courgettes and pepper for 8 to 10 minutes, stirring occasionally, until softened. Add the garlic, and salt and pepper to taste, and fry for 2 minutes. Add to the aubergines with the tomatoes and toss thoroughly. Cool before serving.
SERVES 4 to 6

MEXICAN BEAN SALAD

METRIC/IMPERIAL
225 g/8 oz red kidney beans
900 ml/1½ pints water
1 small cauliflower, divided into florets
1 small green pepper, cored, deseeded and cut
into strips
2 celery stalks, sliced
1 tablespoon grated onion
2 tablespoons chopped parsley
few drops of Tabasco
150 ml/¼ pint vinaigrette dressing

Put the beans in a bowl, pour on the water and
leave to soak overnight. Alternatively, pour on
boiling water and leave for at least 2 hours.
Transfer the beans and soaking water to a pan
and bring to the boil. Boil for 15 minutes, then
lower the heat and simmer for about 1½ hours
until the beans are tender. Drain and leave to cool.
Put the beans in a bowl, then add the vegetables
and parsley and stir well.
Add Tabasco to taste to the vinaigrette dressing
– it should be quite hot. Mix well, then pour over
the salad. Leave to marinate for a few hours until
the flavour of the dressing penetrates the salad
ingredients. Serve cold.
SERVES 4

KIDNEY BEAN AND CHILLI SALAD

METRIC/IMPERIAL
175 g/6 oz red kidney beans, soaked overnight
salt
6 tablespoons chilli dressing (see page 338)
100 g/4 oz frozen sweetcorn, cooked, or
1 × 200 g/7 oz can, drained
1 red pepper, cored, deseeded and chopped
2 tablespoons chopped parsley

Drain the kidney beans, place in a pan and cover
with cold water. Bring to the boil and boil for 15
minutes. Lower the heat, cover and simmer for 1
to 1½ hours, until tender, adding a little salt
towards the end of cooking.
Drain the beans thoroughly and place in a bowl.
Pour over the dressing and mix well while still
warm. Leave to cool.
Add the sweetcorn and red pepper and toss
thoroughly. Transfer to a serving dish and
sprinkle with the chopped parsley to serve.
SERVES 4 to 6

BLACK EYE BEAN AND MUSHROOM SALAD

METRIC/IMPERIAL
175 g/6 oz black eye beans, soaked overnight
salt
100 g/4 oz button mushrooms, wiped and sliced
4 tablespoons French dressing
1 small red pepper, cored, deseeded and sliced
2 tablespoons chopped parsley
lettuce leaves

Drain the beans, place in a pan and cover with cold
water. Bring to the boil, cover and simmer for 40
to 45 minutes until tender, adding a little salt
towards the end of cooking.
Drain thoroughly and place in a bowl with the
mushrooms. Pour over the dressing and toss well
while still warm. Leave to cool.
Add the red pepper and chopped parsley, and
toss thoroughly. Line a salad bowl with lettuce
leaves and spoon the mixture into the centre.
SERVES 6

MIXED BEAN SALAD

METRIC/IMPERIAL
100 g/4 oz butter beans
100 g/4 oz red kidney beans
100 g/4 oz haricot beans
salt
100 g/4 oz French beans, cut into 2.5 cm/1 inch
lengths
6 spring onions, chopped
4 tablespoons French dressing
2 tablespoons chopped parsley

Soak the beans separately overnight. Drain and
place in separate pans. Cover with cold water,
bring to the boil and boil steadily for 15 minutes.
Lower the heat, cover and simmer for 1 to 1½
hours, adding a little salt towards the end of cooking; drain.
Cook the French beans in boiling salted water
for 7 to 8 minutes; drain. Place all the beans in a
bowl and mix in the onions and dressing while
still warm. Leave to cool.
Stir in the chopped parsley and transfer to a
salad bowl to serve.
SERVES 6 to 8

MIDDLE-EASTERN SALAD

METRIC/IMPERIAL
175 g/6 oz chick peas
600 ml/1 pint water
1 large clove garlic, peeled and crushed
juice of 1 lemon
4 tablespoons tahini or sesame seeds
150 ml/¼ pint plain low-fat yogurt
salt
freshly ground white pepper
Garnish:
1 small lettuce
2 tomatoes, sliced
12 black olives
2 tablespoons chopped parsley

Put the chick peas in a large bowl, cover with the water, then leave to soak overnight. Alternatively, pour over boiling water and soak for several hours.

Transfer the chick peas and water to a pan and bring to the boil. Lower the heat, cover and simmer for 1 to 1½ hours until they are soft, adding more water if necessary.

Drain the chick peas, then mash them to a purée. Stir in the garlic, lemon juice, tahini or sesame seeds, yogurt and salt and pepper to taste. Beat to a smooth, creamy paste, adding a little water if too thick. Alternatively, work all the ingredients to a smooth purée in an electric blender or food processor, adding a little more water, as necessary, to blend.

To serve, arrange the lettuce leaves on individual serving plates, then divide the purée equally between them, piling it up in the centre. Garnish with tomato slices, black olives and chopped parsley. Serve cold.
SERVES 4

CHICK PEA SALAD

METRIC/IMPERIAL
225 g/8 oz chick peas, soaked overnight
salt
4 tablespoons ginger dressing (see page 337)
1 small onion, peeled and finely chopped
1 red pepper, cored, deseeded and diced
2 tablespoons chopped parsley

Drain the chick peas, place in a pan and cover with cold water. Bring to the boil and simmer for 1 to 1½ hours or until softened, adding a little salt towards the end of cooking.

Drain thoroughly and place in a bowl. Pour over the dressing and toss well while still warm. Leave to cool.

Add the onion, red pepper and freshly chopped parsley. Toss thoroughly and transfer to a salad bowl to serve.
SERVES 6

BROAD BEAN SALAD

METRIC/IMPERIAL
450 g/1 lb shelled broad beans
salt
juice of ½ lemon
1 teaspoon polyunsaturated vegetable oil
3 tablespoons plain low-fat yogurt
4 tablespoons reduced-calorie mayonnaise
1 tablespoon chopped mixed herbs (parsley, thyme and chives)

Cook the beans in boiling salted water for 10 minutes, then drain and place in a bowl. Mix with the lemon juice and oil and leave to cool.

Mix together the yogurt, mayonnaise and most of the herbs. Pour over the beans and mix well. Transfer to a salad bowl and sprinkle with the remaining herbs before serving.
SERVES 4 to 6

BUTTER BEAN AND CAULIFLOWER SALAD

METRIC/IMPERIAL
100 g/4 oz butter beans, soaked overnight
salt
1 small cauliflower, broken into florets
100 g/4 oz button mushrooms, wiped and sliced
6 tablespoons green herb dressing (see page 337)

Drain the beans, place in a pan and cover with cold water. Bring to the boil and simmer for 1 hour or until softened, adding a little salt towards the end of cooking. Drain and leave to cool.

Cook the cauliflower in boiling salted water for 3 minutes. Drain and leave to cool.

Place the beans, cauliflower and mushrooms in a salad bowl. Add the dressing and toss well. Serve immediately.
SERVES 6 to 8

SALADE DE FLAGEOLETS

METRIC/IMPERIAL
225 g/8 oz flageolet beans, soaked overnight
salt
6 tablespoons garlic dressing (see page 337)
50 g/2 oz salami, cut into 5 mm/¼ inch squares
4 spring onions, sliced

Drain the beans, place in a pan and cover with cold water. Bring to the boil, cover and simmer for 1¼ to 1½ hours, until tender, adding a little salt towards the end of cooking. Drain thoroughly and place in a bowl. Pour over the dressing and mix well while still warm. Leave to cool.
Add the salami and spring onions to the beans. Toss well to serve.
SERVES 4 to 6

THREE BEAN SALAD

METRIC/IMPERIAL
225 g/8 oz cooked chick peas
225 g/8 oz cooked red kidney beans
225 g/8 oz cooked green beans
2 teaspoons chopped fresh mixed herbs or
1 teaspoon dried mixed herbs
6 tablespoons lemon vinaigrette dressing
chopped spring onion, to garnish

Mix the chick peas and red kidney beans together in a salad bowl. Cut the green beans into short pieces and add to the bean mixture.
Sprinkle with the mixed herbs and fold in the lemon vinaigrette dressing. Transfer to a salad bowl and garnish with spring onion.
SERVES 4

WHITE BEAN SALAD

METRIC/IMPERIAL
225 g/8 oz dried white beans (haricot, butter and black-eye beans), soaked overnight in cold water
600 ml/1 pint water
1 onion, peeled and chopped
1 bay leaf
2 hard-boiled eggs, cut into wedges
8 black olives
Dressing:
3 tablespoons polyunsaturated vegetable oil
grated rind and juice of 1 small lemon
1 tablespoon capers
2 gherkins, sliced
2 tablespoons chopped fresh parsley
salt
freshly ground black pepper

Drain the beans and place in a saucepan with 600 ml/1 pint water. Add the onion and bay leaf, cover and bring to the boil. Simmer for 45 minutes to 1 hour until the beans are tender, adding salt towards the end of cooking. Drain and leave to cool thoroughly.
To make the dressing, mix together the ingredients in a screw-topped jar, adding salt and pepper to taste, and shake well. Pour half the dressing over the beans and leave to marinate for at least 30 minutes.
Turn the beans into a serving dish and arrange the eggs and olives on the top. Add the remaining dressing and serve.
SERVES 4

CHICKEN SALAD VÉRONIQUE

METRIC/IMPERIAL
1 × 1.5 kg/3 lb chicken, with giblets
300 ml/½ pint water
1 small onion, peeled and chopped
finely grated rind and juice of ½ lemon
1 slice fresh root ginger, peeled and chopped
few thyme or parsley sprigs
1 bay leaf
salt
freshly ground white pepper
150 ml/¼ pint plain low-fat yogurt
1 head curly endive, separated into leaves
100 g/4 oz green grapes, halved and deseeded
50 g/2 oz flaked almonds

Put the chicken in a large pan with the giblets and the water. Add the onion, lemon rind and juice, ginger, herbs, and salt and pepper to taste. Bring to the boil, then lower the heat, cover and simmer for 45 minutes or until tender.
Remove the chicken from the cooking liquid, discard the skin and bones and cut the chicken flesh into neat pieces.
Boil the cooking liquid rapidly until reduced to 150 ml/¼ pint. Strain, leave to cool, then skim off the fat. Stir into the yogurt, add salt and pepper to taste and mix well.
Arrange the endive on a serving dish. Top with the chicken and grapes. Pour over the yogurt sauce and scatter the flaked almonds over the top. Serve cold.
SERVES 4 to 6

ORIENTAL SALAD

METRIC/IMPERIAL
450 g/1 lb cottage cheese
3 tablespoons whipping cream, lightly whipped
225 g/8 oz cooked chicken, diced
1 orange, peeled, divided into segments and
skinned
25 g/1 oz stem ginger, finely chopped
1 small lettuce
1 bunch watercress, trimmed
12 black grapes, halved and deseeded,
to garnish

Put the cottage cheese, cream and chicken in a
bowl and fold gently to mix. Stir in the orange
segments and ginger.
Arrange a bed of lettuce and watercress on individual plates. Spoon the cheese mixture on the
centre of each plate. Garnish with the grapes
before serving.
SERVES 4 to 6

MUSHROOM AND BACON SALAD

METRIC/IMPERIAL
450 g/1 lb button mushrooms
120 ml/4 fl oz garlic dressing (see page 337)
100 g/4 oz smoked streaky bacon rashers,
derinded
3 tablespoons chopped parsley

Trim the mushroom stalks level with the caps.
Wipe the mushrooms with a damp cloth, place in
a bowl with the dressing and toss well. Leave to
stand for several hours, stirring occasionally, or
overnight if possible.
Grill the bacon until crisp, then crumble. Add
to the marinated mushrooms with the parsley.
Toss thoroughly and transfer to a serving dish.
SERVES 4 to 6

BLACK BEAN AND BACON SALAD

METRIC/IMPERIAL
175 g/6 oz black beans, soaked overnight
salt
6 tablespoons garlic dressing (see page 337)
75 g/3 oz thick-cut streaky bacon, cut into strips
1 red pepper, cored, deseeded and sliced
3 celery stalks, sliced

Drain the beans, place in a pan and cover with cold
water. Bring to the boil and boil for 15 minutes.
Cover and simmer for 1½ to 2 hours, until tender,
adding a little salt towards the end of cooking.
Drain the beans thoroughly and place in a bowl.
Pour over the dressing and toss while still warm.
Grill the bacon until crisp, then crumble. Stir
into the beans and leave to cool.
Stir in the red pepper and celery and transfer to a
salad bowl.
SERVES 6 to 8

BEEF AND ORANGE SALAD

METRIC/IMPERIAL
450 g/1 lb lean beef (boned sirloin or topside,
rump or fillet steak)
finely grated rind and juice of 1 large orange
1 tablespoon wine vinegar
1 bay leaf
salt
freshly ground black pepper
200 ml/⅓ pint water or stock
100 g/4 oz mushrooms, wiped and sliced
1 lettuce
1 large carrot, peeled and grated
50 g/2 oz bean-sprouts

Put the beef in a pan with the orange rind and
juice, vinegar, bay leaf and salt and pepper to
taste. Pour on the water or stock and bring to the
boil.
Lower the heat, cover and simmer for 5
minutes for rare beef, 10 minutes for well done
beef. Add the mushrooms and simmer for a
further 2 minutes.
Remove the beef and mushrooms from the pan
and leave to cool. Boil the cooking liquid until reduced to 150 ml/¼ pint. Leave to cool, then taste
and adjust the seasoning.
Cut the beef into strips, then place in a bowl
with the mushrooms. Pour over the reduced
cooking liquid and leave to marinate for at least
1 hour, turning occasionally.
Arrange the lettuce leaves on a serving dish.
Pile the beef mixture in the centre, then strain over
the marinade. Mix together the carrot and bean-
sprouts and arrange around the beef. Serve cold.
SERVES 4

NEAPOLITAN SALAD

METRIC/IMPERIAL
100 g/4 oz shell pasta
1 × 200 g/7 oz can tuna fish in oil
4 tomatoes, skinned
1 medium onion, peeled and chopped
1 teaspoon chopped oregano, to garnish
150 ml/¼ pint lemon yogurt dressing (see page 337)

Simmer the pasta in boiling salted water for about 10 minutes until just cooked but still firm. Drain and cool.

Drain the oil from the tuna and separate the fish into bite-sized pieces. Cut the tomatoes into quarters.

Mix the cold pasta shells, tuna, tomatoes and onion together in a salad bowl and sprinkle with the oregano. Pour over the lemon yogurt dressing and serve.
SERVES 4

TOMATO AND ANCHOVY SALAD

METRIC/IMPERIAL
4 hard-boiled eggs
1 tablespoon capers
2 tablespoons chopped gherkins
6 tomatoes, skinned and halved
Dressing:
4 tablespoons French dressing
2 tablespoons tomato ketchup
2 tablespoons chopped mixed herbs
Garnish:
1 × 50 g/2 oz can anchovy fillets, drained
watercress or parsley sprigs

Slice the hard-boiled eggs and arrange them in 4 individual shallow dishes. Sprinkle with the capers and gherkins. Place 3 tomato halves, cut side down, on each dish.

Place the dressing ingredients in a small bowl and mix together thoroughly. Spoon over the tomatoes to cover completely.

Split the anchovies lengthways into 2, or 3 if very thick, and arrange in a cross on top of each tomato. Garnish each dish with sprigs of fresh parsley or watercress before serving.
SERVES 4

SEAFOOD AND ASPARAGUS

METRIC/IMPERIAL
225 g/8 oz cod
8 fresh asparagus stalks, or 1 × 225 g/8 oz can asparagus spears, drained
lettuce leaves
100 g/4 oz cooked, peeled prawns
1 × 100 g/4 oz can mussels, drained
chopped dill
plain low-fat yogurt (optional)
salt
freshly ground black pepper

Poach the cod in the minimum of water for 10 to 15 minutes. Drain, cool and flake with a fork.

Meanwhile, cook the fresh asparagus (if using). Line a salad bowl with lettuce leaves and arrange the prawns, mussels and asparagus around the edge.

Place the cod in the centre and sprinkle with dill. If liked, serve with plain low-fat yogurt with a little dill, salt and pepper stirred in.
SERVES 4

PASTA AND FISH SALAD

METRIC/IMPERIAL
225 g/8 oz spinach pasta
salt
100 g/4 oz cooked, shelled mussels
100 g/4 oz cooked, peeled prawns
1 × 50 g/2 oz can anchovy fillets, drained
50 g/2 oz button mushrooms, wiped and sliced
2 tomatoes, cut into wedges
150 ml/¼ pint vinaigrette dressing
Garnish:
2 tablespoons chopped parsley
2 tablespoons grated Parmesan cheese

Cook the pasta in plenty of boiling salted water for 10 to 15 minutes until tender but still firm. Drain in a colander and rinse under cold running water. Drain thoroughly.

Put the cooked pasta in a bowl, then add the seafood, mushrooms and tomatoes. Pour on the dressing and mix gently. Sprinkle with parsley and Parmesan just before serving.
SERVES 4

NORWEGIAN MACKEREL SALAD

METRIC/IMPERIAL
4 × 75 g/3 oz mackerel fillets
100 g/4 oz boiled potatoes, peeled and sliced
lettuce leaves
4 tomatoes, sliced
Mustard sauce:
4 tablespoons reduced-calorie mayonnaise
4 teaspoons French or English made mustard
salt
freshly ground black pepper

Place the mackerel under a preheated hot grill and cook for about 15 minutes, turning occasionally. Leave to cool, then remove the skin with a sharp knife. Divide the flesh into pieces and arrange on 4 serving plates.

Place the potato slices on one side of each plate. On the other side, place the lettuce leaves and tomato slices.

Mix together the mayonnaise, mustard, and salt and pepper to taste. Serve the mustard sauce separately in a sauceboat or pour a little over each mackerel fillet
SERVES 4

GREEK SALAD

METRIC/IMPERIAL
1 Cos lettuce, washed
½ cucumber, peeled
4 tomatoes, skinned
8 spring onions, trimmed
1 × 50 g/2 oz can anchovy fillets
1 tablespoon chopped fresh basil or 1 teaspoon dried basil
225 g/8 oz Feta cheese
6 tablespoons lemon vinaigrette dressing

Shred the lettuce and arrange on a large platter or shallow serving dish

Cut the cucumber into 2.5 cm/1 inch lengths and arrange on top of the lettuce.

Slice the tomatoes thinly and arrange round the edge of the platter.

Chop the spring onions. Drain the oil from the anchovies and cut them into small pieces. Sprinkle the spring onions, anchovies and basil over the salad.

Cut the Feta cheese into small dice and pile on top of the salad. Pour over the dressing and serve.
SERVES 4

DANISH HERRING SALAD

METRIC/IMPERIAL
225 g/8 oz beetroot, cooked, peeled and diced
2 dessert apples, cored and thinly sliced
1 onion, peeled and thinly sliced
finely grated rind and juice of ½ lemon
150 ml/¼ pint plain low-fat yogurt
salt
freshly ground white pepper
4 pickled herrings or rollmops
parsley sprigs, to garnish

Put the beetroot, apples and onion in a bowl. Stir the lemon rind and juice into the yogurt, then add salt and pepper to taste.

Add the yogurt to the beetroot mixture and stir well until the salad is pale pink in colour. Spoon into a shallow serving dish, arrange the herrings or rollmops on top, then garnish with parsley sprigs. Serve cold.
SERVES 4

CHRISTMAS SALAD

METRIC/IMPERIAL
175 g/6 oz red or white cabbage, washed and shredded
2 large carrots, peeled and grated
2 dessert apples, cored and chopped
2 celery stalks, chopped
100 g/4 oz dates, stoned and chopped
50 g/2 oz sultanas
100 g/4 oz shelled nuts (Brazils, walnuts, almonds, hazelnuts), chopped if large
2 tangerines or oranges, peel and pith removed and divided into segments
100 g/4 oz Stilton cheese, diced
150 ml/¼ pint salad dressing (yogurt, fruit juice or vinaigrette)
salt
freshly ground black pepper

Place all the ingredients in a salad bowl, and toss well to mix. Taste and adjust the seasoning and serve very cold.

If not to be used immediately, store in an air-tight container in the refrigerator. The salad will keep fresh for several days.
SERVES 4

CHEESE AND BREAD SALAD

METRIC/IMPERIAL
150 ml/¼ pint vinaigrette dressing
2 slices or crusts wholemeal bread, diced
100 g/4 oz Cheddar or Edam cheese, diced
100 g/4 oz Mozzarella cheese, diced
4 tomatoes, sliced
10 cm/4 inch piece cucumber, sliced
1 × 50 g/2 oz can anchovy fillets, drained
8 olives, halved and stoned
1 lettuce

Pour the dressing into a bowl. Add the bread and toss to coat thoroughly. Add all the remaining ingredients, except the lettuce, and fold together gently to mix.

Line a serving dish or bowl with lettuce leaves, then pile the salad in the centre. Pour over any remaining dressing. Serve cold.
SERVES 4

ENDIVE AND GRUYÈRE SALAD

METRIC/IMPERIAL
1 head curly endive
75 g/3 oz Gruyère cheese, diced
25 g/1 oz hazelnuts, chopped and browned
75 g/3 oz smoked ham, diced
4 tablespoons French dressing
1 tablespoon chopped parsley

Tear the endive into pieces and place in a bowl with the cheese, nuts and ham. Pour over the dressing and toss thoroughly. Transfer to a salad bowl and sprinkle with the parsley.
SERVES 6 to 8

SPINACH AND ROQUEFORT SALAD

METRIC/IMPERIAL
225 g/8 oz young spinach leaves
50 g/2 oz walnuts, roughly chopped
250 ml/8 fl oz Roquefort dressing

Trim the stalks from the spinach, wash and dry the leaves thoroughly, then tear into pieces. Place in a salad bowl with the walnuts and pour over the dressing. Toss thoroughly before serving.
SERVES 6

MUSHROOM AND BLUE CHEESE SALAD

METRIC/IMPERIAL
350 g/12 oz firm white button mushrooms, wiped and very thinly sliced
1 tablespoon snipped chives
100 g/4 oz Dolcelatte cheese
3 tablespoons plain low-fat yogurt
1 teaspoon pesto sauce
salt
freshly ground black pepper
1 tablespoon grated Parmesan cheese

Put the mushrooms into a bowl with the chives

Put the Dolcelatte cheese into a blender or food processor with the yogurt, pesto sauce, and salt and pepper to taste; blend until smooth. Stir the dressing into the mushrooms, taking care not to spoil their shape.

Sprinkle the Parmesan cheese over the salad
SERVES 4

TOMATO AND MOZZARELLA SALAD WITH BASIL

METRIC/IMPERIAL
450 g/1 lb tomatoes, skinned and thinly sliced
225 g/8 oz Mozzarella cheese, thinly sliced
salt
freshly ground black pepper
3-4 teaspoons balsamic vinegar (available from speciality delicatessens)
1½ tablespoons chopped basil

Lay the sliced tomatoes on one half of a flat serving dish and the cheese on the other half. Season the tomatoes with salt and black pepper, the Mozzarella with pepper only. Pour over the vinegar and scatter the chopped basil over all. Allow the salad to stand for a little time before serving.
SERVES 4

MIXED RICE SALAD

METRIC/IMPERIAL
175 g/6 oz brown rice, well rinsed
2 teaspoons polyunsaturated vegetable oil
50 g/2 oz aduki or mung beans, soaked
overnight
3 spring onions, finely sliced
1 red pepper, cored, deseeded and cut into short
strips
40 g/1½ oz salted peanuts
40 g/1½ oz raisins
salt
freshly ground black pepper
2 mint sprigs, finely chopped
150 ml/¼ pint lemon vinaigrette dressing

Cook the rice in boiling salted water with 1 teaspoon oil for 30 to 40 minutes or until tender.
Drain and rinse. Drain the aduki or mung beans,
place in a pan and cover with cold water. Add the
remaining oil, bring to the boil and cook for 30 to
40 minutes, then drain.
  Place the rice and beans in a bowl and add the
spring onions, pepper, peanuts, raisins, salt and
pepper to taste, mint and dressing. Mix well.
SERVES 4

RICE AND PINEAPPLE SALAD

METRIC/IMPERIAL
225 g/8 oz brown rice, well rinsed
12 whole cardamom seeds
salt
1 × 200 g/7 oz can pineapple rings, drained and
roughly chopped
½ cucumber, diced
50 g/2 oz hazelnuts, roasted
Dressing:
grated rind and juice of 1 orange
3 tablespoons polyunsaturated vegetable oil
2 teaspoons curry paste

Cook the rice with the cardamom seeds in boiling
salted water for 40 minutes or until the rice is just
tender. Drain the rice and run cold water through
the grains to remove any excess starch.
  Mix the chopped pineapple into the rice with
the cucumber and hazelnuts.
  Put all the dressing ingredients in a screw-
topped jar and shake well. Stir the dressing
through the rice salad so that it is evenly coated.
SERVES 4

BROWN RICE SALAD WITH CASHEW NUTS

METRIC/IMPERIAL
225 g/8 oz brown rice, well rinsed
salt
3 spring onions, finely chopped
1 red pepper, cored, deseeded and roughly
chopped
50 g/2 oz raisins
50 g/2 oz cashew nuts, roasted and chopped
2 tablespoons chopped parsley
6 tablespoons soy sauce dressing (see page 337)

Cook the rice in boiling salted water for about 40
minutes until tender. Rinse, drain well and cool.
  Place in a bowl and add the remaining ingredients. Toss thoroughly before serving.
SERVES 6

BROWN RICE SALAD WITH SWEETCORN

METRIC/IMPERIAL
100 g/4 oz brown rice, well rinsed
salt
100 g/4 oz shelled peas or sliced beans
100 g/4 oz sweetcorn kernels
150 ml/¼ pint vinaigrette dressing
1 red pepper, cored, deseeded and diced
50 g/2 oz salted peanuts
1 small onion, peeled and grated
freshly ground black pepper

Cook the rice in boiling salted water for 30
minutes or until tender. Add the peas or beans and
corn and simmer for a further few minutes until
just tender. Drain thoroughly.
  Transfer to a bowl and add half of the dressing
while the rice and vegetables are still hot. Toss
well to mix, then leave to cool.
  Add the remaining ingredients and dressing
and mix well. Taste and adjust the seasoning just
before serving. Serve cold.
SERVES 4

TABBOULEH

METRIC/IMPERIAL
100 g/4 oz fine bulgar (cracked wheat)
4 spring onions, trimmed and finely chopped
4 tablespoons finely chopped parsley
2 tablespoons finely chopped mint
2-3 tablespoons olive oil
juice of ½ lemon
salt
freshly ground black pepper
Garnish:
black olives
diced red peppers

Cover the bulgar with plenty of cold water and leave to expand for about 30 minutes. Drain the bulgar first in a sieve, then squeeze out in a piece of muslin to remove as much moisture as possible.

Mix the bulgar with the spring onions, parsley, mint, olive oil and lemon juice and season with salt and pepper.

Pile the tabbouleh into mounds on small serving plates. Garnish with black olives and red pepper, and serve with hot wholemeal pitta bread.
SERVES 4

TURKISH BARLEY SALAD

METRIC/IMPERIAL
200 g/7 oz barley
1 small cucumber, peeled, deseeded and chopped
2 large ripe tomatoes, skinned, deseeded and chopped
½ bunch radishes, trimmed and thinly sliced
15 g/½ oz chopped parsley
2 tablespoons chopped mint
4 spring onions, shredded into matchstick lengths
salt
freshly ground black pepper
lettuce leaves, to serve
Dressing:
3 tablespoons lemon juice
½ teaspoon salt
120 ml/4 fl oz olive oil

Cover the barley with cold water and bring to the boil. Remove from the heat, cover, and stand for 1 hour. Drain, cover again with salted cold water, bring to the boil and simmer for 1 to 1½ hours.

Meanwhile, make the dressing: put the lemon juice and salt into a bowl and gradually whisk in

the oil. Drain the barley, and toss gently with the dressing. Toss the barley with the chilled vegetables and herbs and season with salt and pepper to taste. Serve on lettuce leaves.
SERVES 6

BROWN RICE, PRAWN AND NUT SALAD

METRIC/IMPERIAL
75 g/3 oz brown rice
salt
freshly ground black pepper
50 g/2 oz peeled, cooked prawns
2 spring onions, finely chopped
25 g/1 oz green pepper, deseeded and thinly sliced
25 g/1 oz red pepper, deseeded and thinly sliced
2 tablespoons lemon vinaigrette
15 g/½ oz cashew nuts
15 g/½ oz flaked almonds, toasted
2 tablespoons chopped parsley

Cook the rice in boiling salted water for 30 to 35 minutes until 'al dente'. Drain and cool.

Place the rice in a bowl and season. Add the prawns, spring onions and peppers. Pour over the dressing and stir in the nuts and parsley. Mix well.
SERVES 2

TUSCAN BEAN AND NUT SALAD

METRIC/IMPERIAL
225 g/8 oz brown rice, cooked
1 green pepper, cored, deseeded and sliced
1 yellow pepper, cored, deseeded and sliced
4 tomatoes, cut into quarters
100 g/4 oz cooked flageolet or cannellini beans
50 g/2 oz hazelnuts, coarsely chopped
10 stuffed green olives, sliced
2 spring onions, trimmed and chopped
¼ cucumber, cut into thin julienne strips
100 ml/4 fl oz French dressing

Place the rice, peppers, tomatoes, beans, hazelnuts, olives, spring onions and cucumber in a bowl.

Pour over the dressing and toss to mix. Spoon into a serving bowl and chill lightly; or spoon into an oiled ring mould and turn out on to a plate. Serve with wedges of wholewheat bread.
SERVES 4

MUSHROOM BEAN SALAD

METRIC/IMPERIAL
350 g/12 oz cooked flageolet beans
450 g/1 lb small button mushrooms, wiped and trimmed
½ red pepper, cored, deseeded and finely chopped
4 spring onions, trimmed and chopped
Dressing:
175 ml/6 fl oz plain low-fat yogurt
5 tablespoons reduced-calorie mayonnaise
2 tablespoons snipped chives
salt
freshly ground black pepper
spring onion tassels, to garnish

Mix the flageolet beans with the mushrooms, red pepper and spring onions in a serving bowl.
To make the dressing, mix the yogurt with the mayonnaise, half of the chives, and salt and pepper to taste, blending well. Drizzle the dressing over the salad and chill until required. Serve the salad sprinkled with the remaining chives, then garnish with the spring onions.
SERVES 4

MIXED RED AND GREEN SALAD

METRIC/IMPERIAL
1 round lettuce, inner leaves only
25 g/1 oz tender spinach, cut in thinnest possible strips
1 small head radicchio, when available, cut in squares
25 g/1 oz mâche (corn salad, lambs' lettuce), trimmed
Dressing:
1 tablespoon white wine vinegar
½ tablespoon lemon juice
3 tablespoons sunflower seed oil
sea salt
freshly ground black pepper

Lay the lettuce leaves in a salad bowl and scatter the strips of spinach over them. Lay the red squares of radicchio over the spinach, and the individual leaves of mâche (corn salad) over all. Mix the dressing in a small bowl. Before serving, mix the dressing again, pour over the salad, and toss lightly.
SERVES 4

GRILLED PEPPER SALAD

METRIC/IMPERIAL
6 medium peppers, preferably red, yellow and green, or just red and green
2 tablespoons olive oil
sea salt
freshly ground black pepper

Preheat the grill, lay the peppers on the grill pan and cook as close to the heat as possible. Turn them over as the skin blisters, until they are evenly charred and blackened all over. Remove from the heat and leave to cool.
Later, scrape away the skin with a small knife, and cut away the stalk and inner membrane, washing away the seeds under cold running water. Cut the flesh into petal shapes and lay on a flat dish. Sprinkle with olive oil, sea salt and black pepper. Serve as an hors d'oeuvre with stuffed tomatoes.
SERVES 4

PASTA SALAD WITH APPLE, AVOCADO AND CELERY

METRIC/IMPERIAL
225 g/8 oz pasta shapes (e.g. bows, rings, wheels, shells, twists or bows)
1 avocado, peeled, stoned and sliced
1 red dessert apple, cored and sliced
2 teaspoons lemon juice
3 celery stalks, scrubbed and chopped
4 tablespoons French dressing
salt
freshly ground black pepper

Cook the pasta in a pan of boiling salted water until tender or 'al dente', according to the packet instructions. Drain and refresh under cold water.
Mix the avocado and apple slices with the lemon juice to prevent browning. Place the cooked pasta, avocado and apple, celery, dressing, and salt and pepper to taste in a serving bowl. Toss gently to mix before serving.
SERVES 4

EGGS & CHEESE

SPICED SCRAMBLED EGGS

METRIC/IMPERIAL
8 eggs
4 tomatoes, skinned and chopped
1 teaspoon salt
50 g/2 oz polyunsaturated margarine
1 medium onion, peeled and sliced
2 green chillies, deseeded and chopped
1 teaspoon turmeric
1 teaspoon ground coriander

Put the eggs, tomatoes and salt in a bowl and beat well. Melt the margarine in a pan, add the onion and fry gently until soft. Add the chillies and spices and fry for 2 minutes, stirring constantly. Add the beaten egg mixture and stir with a wooden spoon until the eggs are scrambled. Serve hot on toast for breakfast, or as a light supper.
SERVES 4

POACHED EGGS ON WHOLEMEAL TOAST

METRIC/IMPERIAL
300 ml/½ pint water
pinch of salt
4 eggs
4 slices wholemeal bread
25 g/1 oz polyunsaturated margarine
1 teaspoon yeast extract

Put the water and salt in a small pan and bring to the boil. Crack one egg into a cup. Using a spoon, stir the water very quickly to create a 'whirlpool'. Slide the egg into the water, then simmer for 3 minutes until the egg is firmly set.

Toast one slice of bread lightly on both sides, then spread with margarine and a little yeast extract. Remove the egg from the pan with a slotted spoon and place on top of the toast. Serve immediately. Repeat this method with the remaining eggs and bread.
SERVES 4

ITALIAN EGGS

METRIC/IMPERIAL
25 g/1 oz parsley sprigs
1 teaspoon fresh marjoram or pinch of dried marjoram
1 clove garlic, peeled and crushed
6 black olives, stoned
1 shallot, peeled
2 anchovy fillets
freshly ground black pepper
120 ml/4 fl oz olive oil
salt
6 hard-boiled eggs, shelled and sliced
Garnish:
tomato wedges
chopped parsley

Blend the parsley, marjoram, garlic, olives, shallot, anchovy fillets and pepper in a blender or food processor until smooth, then add the oil. Adjust the seasoning.

Arrange the eggs on a serving dish and pour the sauce over them. Garnish with tomato wedges and sprinkle with chopped parsley.
SERVES 4

FARMHOUSE SCRAMBLE

METRIC/IMPERIAL
100 g/4 oz lean bacon rashers, derinded and chopped
3 eggs
salt
freshly ground white pepper
175 g/6 oz cottage cheese
4 slices wholemeal bread
25 g/1 oz polyunsaturated margarine
watercress sprigs, to garnish

Put the bacon in a small pan and fry gently until the fat runs, stirring frequently. Fry for a further 4 minutes, then remove from the pan with a slotted spoon and keep hot.

Crack the eggs into a bowl. Add salt and pepper

to taste, then whisk with a fork until lightly mixed.

Pour into the pan and cook gently until the eggs begin to coagulate but are not fully set, stirring and lifting constantly. Stir in the cottage cheese thoroughly and continue cooking until the mixture is just firm.

Meanwhile, toast the bread lightly on both sides, then spread with the margarine. Arrange on warmed, individual serving plates. Stir the bacon into the egg mixture, then pile on to the toast and garnish with watercress. Serve immediately.
SERVES 4

FLORENTINE EGGS

METRIC/IMPERIAL
750 g/1½ lb fresh leaf spinach, trimmed
salt
50 g/2 oz polyunsaturated margarine
50 g/2 oz plain unbleached white flour
600 ml/1 pint skimmed milk
50 g/2 oz mature Cheddar cheese, grated
freshly ground black pepper
4 eggs

Put the spinach leaves into a large pan with a minimum of water. Season with salt and cook, uncovered, for 10 to 15 minutes until completely softened. Drain well and chop.

Melt the margarine in a saucepan. Stir in the flour, then gradually blend in the milk to make a smooth consistency. Bring to the boil over a medium heat, stirring constantly, and cook for 3 to 4 minutes. Mix in half the cheese and season with salt and pepper to taste.

Lower the eggs into boiling water and boil for just 3 minutes so they are still soft in the centre. Immediately plunge the eggs into cold water.

Stir a quarter of the sauce into the spinach and divide the mixture between 4 individual dishes. Carefully peel the shells off the eggs and place 1 egg in the centre of each dish. Spoon over the rest of the sauce. Sprinkle the tops with the remaining cheese and put under the grill for about 10 minutes. Serve at once.
SERVES 4

SPICY EGG CURRY

METRIC/IMPERIAL
8 hard-boiled eggs
2 cloves garlic, peeled and crushed
1 large onion, peeled and finely chopped
1 tablespoon polyunsaturated vegetable oil
1 teaspoon ground coriander
1 teaspoon ground cumin
½ teaspoon chilli powder (or to taste)
2 tablespoons sesame seeds
½ teaspoon salt
250 ml/8 fl oz plain low-fat yogurt
2 tablespoons lemon juice

Shell the eggs. Cook the garlic and onion in oil until soft. Add the remaining ingredients, except the yogurt and lemon juice, and cook for 1 minute, stirring. Blend in the yogurt and juice and cook for 5 minutes. Cut the eggs in half lengthwise, add to the sauce, and heat through. Serve with boiled rice.
SERVES 4

EGGS FLAMENCO

METRIC/IMPERIAL
2 tablespoons olive oil
1 onion, peeled and chopped
2 red peppers, cored, deseeded and cut into strips
175 g/6 oz piece smoked streaky bacon, derinded and cut into strips
2 potatoes, boiled and diced
100 g/4 oz shelled fresh or frozen peas
4 tomatoes, skinned and chopped
1 tablespoon chopped parsley
salt
freshly ground black pepper
4 eggs

Heat the oil in a pan, add the onion, peppers and bacon and fry for 5 to 6 minutes. Add the potatoes and cook until lightly browned. Add the peas, tomatoes, parsley, and salt and pepper to taste. Cook gently for 10 minutes, adding a little water, if necessary, to prevent the mixture sticking.

Turn the vegetable mixture into a greased shallow ovenproof dish. Make 4 hollows in the mixture and break an egg into each one. Cook in a preheated moderate oven (180°C/350°F, Gas Mark 4) for 15 minutes until the egg whites are just set. Serve immediately.
SERVES 4

EGGS FU-YUNG

METRIC/IMPERIAL
3 dried Chinese mushrooms
2 tablespoons polyunsaturated vegetable oil
3 spring onions
1 × 2.5 cm/1 inch piece root ginger, peeled
1 clove garlic, peeled and crushed
25 g/1 oz canned bamboo shoots, drained and
diced
6 canned water chestnuts, drained and chopped
(optional)
25 g/1 oz frozen peeled prawns, thawed
1 × 175 g/6 oz can crabmeat, drained
1 tablespoon dry sherry
salt
6 eggs, beaten
Garnish:
radish flower, made by making V cuts in the
top of a trimmed radish
cucumber twist

Soak the dried mushrooms in warm water for 15 minutes. Squeeze dry and discard the hard stalks, then chop the mushroom caps. Chop the spring onions and ginger finely.

Heat the oil in a wok or deep frying pan, add the spring onions, ginger and garlic and stir-fry for 1 minute. Add the mushrooms, bamboo shoots and water chestnuts (if using) and cook for 30 seconds. Stir in the prawns, crabmeat and sherry and season with salt. Lower the heat and pour in the beaten eggs, then scramble until the mixture is just set, stirring constantly.

Pile on to a warmed serving dish and serve immediately, garnished with the radish flower and cucumber twist.

SERVES 4 to 6

EGGS MILTON

METRIC/IMPERIAL
50 g/2 oz polyunsaturated margarine
225 g/8 oz tomatoes, skinned and sliced
2 slices white bread, crusts removed, and cut
into triangles for croûtes
2 spring onions, trimmed and chopped
100 g/4 oz button mushrooms, wiped and sliced
½ green pepper, cored, deseeded and diced
4 eggs
4 tablespoons skimmed milk
salt
freshly ground black pepper
1 teaspoon dried thyme

Heat one third of the margarine in a frying pan and sauté the tomato slices for a few minutes. Place in the base of an ovenproof serving dish and keep warm.

Wipe out the pan and melt a further third of the margarine in it. Fry the bread triangles on both sides and drain well. Put them aside. Gently sauté the spring onions, mushrooms and green pepper until soft. Take off the heat.

In a basin, beat together the eggs and milk. Add salt and pepper to taste, and the thyme. Melt the remaining margarine in a saucepan and cook the eggs gently, stirring from time to time, until they become creamy and thickened. Stir the cooked vegetables into the eggs and spoon this mixture over the tomatoes. Arrange the croûtes down each side of the dish and serve immediately.

SERVES 4

EGGS EN COCOTTE WITH MUSHROOMS

METRIC/IMPERIAL
salt
freshly ground black pepper
pinch of paprika
25 g/1 oz polyunsaturated margarine
50 g/2 oz mushrooms, wiped and chopped
4 eggs
150 ml/¼ pint single cream
chopped parsley, to garnish

Lightly grease 4 cocotte or ramekin dishes, or a shallow ovenproof dish, and sprinkle with salt, pepper and paprika. Melt the margarine in a saucepan and sauté the mushrooms until softened. Divide the mushrooms between the dishes or put into the large dish.

Break an egg into each dish, if using individual ones, and place the dishes or dish in a roasting tin half-filled with water. Bake in the centre of a pre-heated moderate oven (180°C/350°F, Gas Mark 4) for about 10 minutes until the whites are barely set, and the yolks still soft.

Meanwhile, heat the cream in a saucepan, but do not let it boil. Remove the dishes or dish from the oven and spoon the cream over each egg. Garnish with chopped parsley. Serve with hot toast.

The eggs will continue cooking after the dish has been removed from the oven, so be careful not to overcook them.

SERVES 4

EGGS BENEDICT

METRIC/IMPERIAL
40 g/1½ oz polyunsaturated margarine
40 g/1½ oz plain unbleached white flour
450 ml/¾ pint skimmed milk
salt
freshly ground black pepper
450 g/1 lb flaked, cooked cod
1 clove garlic, peeled and crushed
1 tablespoon chopped parsley
2 tablespoons polyunsaturated vegetable oil
2 slices wholemeal bread, crusts removed and
cut into triangles for croûtes
4 eggs
finely chopped parsley, to garnish

Melt the margarine in a pan, stir in the flour and cook for 2 minutes. Gradually stir in the milk over a low heat. Bring to the boil, stirring continuously. Add salt and pepper to taste. Put 5 tablespoons of the sauce in a bowl with the flaked fish and stir in the crushed garlic and parsley. Heat the oil and fry the triangles of bread. Drain them well on kitchen paper towels.

Poach the eggs until just set and dry them on kitchen paper towels. Gently reheat the fish mixture and the remaining sauce in 2 separate saucepans. Spoon the fish mixture over the base of a serving dish. Top with the poached eggs and pour over the remaining sauce. Garnish with the croûtes and chopped parsley. Serve immediately.
SERVES 4

EGG MOUSSE

METRIC/IMPERIAL
4 hard-boiled eggs
1 teaspoon Worcestershire sauce
dash of Tabasco
pinch of paprika
salt
freshly ground white pepper
2 teaspoons powdered gelatine
2 tablespoons water
150 ml/¼ pint plain low-fat yogurt
225 g/8 oz peeled prawns

Cut the eggs in half lengthwise, then remove the yolks and work them through a sieve into a bowl. Add the Worcestershire sauce, Tabasco, paprika and salt and pepper to taste. Mix well. Chop the egg whites finely. Place the gelatine and water in a cup over a pan of hot water and stir until dis-

solved. Whisk the yogurt into the egg yolk mixture with the gelatine, then fold in the chopped egg whites. Pour the mixture into a 15 cm/6 inch straight-sided serving dish, then chill in the refrigerator for 2 hours.

Pile the prawns in the centre of the mousse just before serving. Serve with a crisp green salad.
SERVES 4

BAKED TOMATO EGGS

METRIC/IMPERIAL
4 large tomatoes
100 g/4 oz cooked ham, finely chopped
1 teaspoon chopped parsley
salt
freshly ground black pepper
4 eggs

Cut the tops off the tomatoes, then scoop out the pulp and seeds. Work the pulp through a sieve to remove the seeds. Put in a bowl with the ham, parsley and salt and pepper to taste. Stir well.

Divide the mixture equally between the tomatoes, pressing it down well. Stand the tomatoes in a baking dish and crack one egg into each tomato. Sprinkle lightly with salt and pepper.

Bake in a preheated moderately hot oven (190°C/375°F, Gas Mark 5) for 15 minutes until the eggs are set. Serve immediately.
SERVES 4

BAKED EGG WITH MIXED VEGETABLES

METRIC/IMPERIAL
1 tablespoon cooked mixed vegetables
1 egg
salt
freshly ground black pepper
1 tablespoon whipping cream

Put the cooked vegetables into a small cocotte dish. Break in the egg and sprinkle with seasoning. Pour the whipping cream on to the egg. Bake in a preheated moderate oven (180°C/350°F, Gas Mark 4) for 7 minutes. Serve at once.
SERVES 1

BROCCOLI PANCAKES

METRIC/IMPERIAL

polyunsaturated vegetable oil for frying
wholemeal pancake batter made with 100g/4oz
wholemeal flour (see page 292)

Filling:

450 g/1 lb broccoli spears
salt
25 g/1 oz polyunsaturated margarine
25 g/1 oz plain unbleached white flour
300 ml/½ pint skimmed milk
100 g/4 oz Gruyère or Cheddar cheese, grated
freshly ground black pepper
1 × 50 g/2 oz can anchovy fillets, drained

Heat a little oil in a 20 cm/8 inch frying pan. When
the oil is hot, quickly pour in enough batter to
coat the bottom of the pan, tilting the pan to
spread the batter evenly. Cook until the top of the
batter is set and the underside is golden brown.
Turn with a palette knife or toss the pancake over
and cook the other side.

Slide on to a warm plate, cover and keep warm
by standing the plate over a pan of hot water.
Continue making pancakes in this way until all
the batter is used up, making 8 pancakes in all.

To make the filling, cook the broccoli in boiling
salted water for 5 to 10 minutes until just tender,
then drain thoroughly and keep warm.

Meanwhile, melt the margarine in a pan. Add
the flour and cook for 1 to 2 minutes, stirring constantly. Remove from the heat and gradually stir
in the milk, beating well after each addition. Return to the heat and simmer until the sauce is thick
and smooth, stirring constantly. Stir in the
Gruyère or Cheddar cheese, reserving a little for
the topping, then add pepper to taste.

Divide the broccoli and anchovies equally between the pancakes, then roll up and place in a
baking dish. Pour over the sauce and sprinkle
with the reserved cheese.

Bake in a preheated moderately hot oven
(200°C/400°F, Gas Mark 6) for 10 to 15 minutes
until heated through. Serve hot.

Alternatively, leave the pancakes until cold
before filling, then cover and bake in a preheated
moderately hot oven for 15 minutes. Remove the
lid and bake for a further 10 to 15 minutes until hot
and bubbling. Serve hot.

SERVES 4

OVEN POTATO OMELETTE

METRIC/IMPERIAL

25 g/1 oz polyunsaturated margarine
2 large cooked potatoes, sliced
2 canned red peppers, cut into small pieces
6-8 eggs
2 tablespoons skimmed milk
salt
freshly ground black pepper
1 tablespoon snipped chives
1 tablespoon chopped parsley
1 teaspoon grated lemon rind

Put the margarine into a 20 to 23 cm/8 to 9 inch
round ovenproof dish and heat towards the top of
a preheated hot oven (220°C/425°F, Gas Mark 7)
until melted. Add the potatoes and peppers and
heat for another few minutes.

Beat the eggs with the remaining ingredients,
and pour over the potato and pepper mixture. Return to the oven, just above the centre, and bake
for 10 to 15 minutes or until set to personal taste.
SERVES 4

SPANISH VEGETABLE OMELETTE

METRIC/IMPERIAL

2 tablespoons polyunsaturated vegetable oil
4 large boiled potatoes, chopped or sliced
2 onions, peeled and chopped
2 peppers, 1 green and 1 red, cored, deseeded
and chopped or cut into strips
2 courgettes, cut into julienne strips
2 small aubergines, finely chopped
2-3 cloves garlic, peeled and crushed
350 g/12 oz tomatoes, finely chopped
3 eggs
salt

Heat the oil in a large non-stick pan, add the
potatoes and fry, over a low heat, turning frequently, for about 5 minutes.

Add the onions, peppers, courgettes and aubergines and fry, over a low heat, for about 8 to 10
minutes. Just before the vegetables are cooked,
add the garlic and finely chopped tomatoes.

Beat the eggs with a little salt. Pour the mixture
evenly over the vegetables and cook, over a low
heat, until the egg has just set. Turn the omelette
out on to a large plate and serve cut into wedges.
SERVES 4

SPINACH OMELETTE

METRIC/IMPERIAL
40 g/1½ oz polyunsaturated margarine
225 g/8 oz spinach, finely chopped
1 tablespoon plain low-fat yogurt
grated nutmeg
salt
freshly ground black pepper
4 eggs

Melt 25 g/1 oz of the margarine in a pan. Add the spinach and cook over a gentle heat for 4 to 5 minutes, stirring occasionally. Remove from the heat and stir in the yogurt. Season with nutmeg, salt and pepper to taste and keep hot.

Beat the eggs in a bowl, with salt and pepper to taste. Melt the remaining margarine in a 25 cm/10 inch omelette pan. When the margarine is foaming, pour in the eggs. When the omelette begins to set, lift the cooked edge to allow the unset egg to run on to the pan.

Place the filling in the centre of the omelette, cook for 1 minute then fold in half. Slide on to a warmed plate and serve immediately.
SERVES 2

TUNA AND PEPPER OMELETTES

METRIC/IMPERIAL
1 green pepper, cored, deseeded and sliced
1 × 200 g/7 oz can tuna fish, drained and flaked
100 g/4 oz cooked peas
2 tomatoes, skinned and chopped
salt
freshly ground black pepper
Omelette mixture:
8 eggs
2 tablespoons water
salt
freshly ground black pepper
25 g/1 oz polyunsaturated margarine
Garnish:
tomato slices
chopped parsley

Cook the green pepper in boiling water for 2 to 3 minutes, then drain. Place in a saucepan and add the remaining ingredients, with salt and pepper to taste. Heat the mixture through gently while making the omelettes.

Beat the eggs with the water and salt and pepper to taste. Melt a quarter of the margarine in an omelette pan and pour in a quarter of the egg mixture. Cook over a moderate heat, moving the cooked mixture towards the centre with a palette knife. When the omelette is just cooked, place a quarter of the filling on one side and fold over. Transfer to a warmed serving plate and keep warm while making three more omelettes with the remaining ingredients. Garnish with tomato slices and parsley. Serve immediately.
SERVES 4

SPINACH PANCAKE LAYER

METRIC/IMPERIAL
polyunsaturated vegetable oil for frying
wholemeal pancake batter made with 100 g/4 oz
wholemeal flour (see page 292)
Filling:
750 g/1½ lb spinach
salt
225 g/8 oz cottage cheese
1 egg, beaten
freshly ground black pepper
grated nutmeg
Topping:
50 g/2 oz Cheddar cheese, grated

Heat a little oil in a 15 cm/6 inch omelette pan. Pour in 1 tablespoon of the batter and tilt the pan to coat the bottom evenly. Cook until the underside is brown, then turn over and cook for a further 10 seconds. Turn on to a warmed plate. Repeat with the remaining batter, making 12 pancakes. As they are cooked, stack the pancakes on a plate, interleaving them with sheets of greaseproof paper; keep warm.

Cook the spinach in a large pan with just the water clinging to the leaves after washing and a pinch of salt for 5 minutes; drain thoroughly. Chop finely and put in a bowl. Add the cottage cheese, egg, and salt, pepper and nutmeg to taste; mix thoroughly.

Place a pancake on a heatproof plate, spread with some of the filling and cover with another pancake. Continue layering in this way, finishing with a pancake. Sprinkle with the cheese and cook in a preheated moderately hot oven (190°C/375°F, Gas Mark 5) for 30 to 40 minutes. Serve immediately, as a main dish.
SERVES 4

BEAN AND CHEESE PANCAKES

METRIC/IMPERIAL
1 teaspoon dried dill
wholemeal pancake batter made with 100g/4oz wholemeal flour (see page 292)
oil for frying
Filling:
225 g/8 oz cottage cheese
salt
freshly ground black pepper
2 × 225 g/8 oz cans curried beans with sultanas
Topping:
150 ml/¼ pint soured cream (optional)
snipped chives

Add the dill to the pancake batter. Lightly oil a small frying pan. Add a spoonful of batter to the pan, tilt the pan to coat evenly, then cook lightly over a medium heat until golden on the underside. Turn the pancake and brown on the other side. Transfer the pancake to a plate and continue making pancakes until all the batter has been used.

For the filling, mix the cottage cheese with the salt, pepper and curried beans. Divide the filling between the pancakes and roll up each one. Arrange on a greased ovenproof serving dish, cover with foil and cook in a moderately hot oven (190°C/375°F, Gas Mark 5) for about 8 minutes.

Meanwhile, heat the soured cream over a low heat (if using), spoon over the heated pancakes and serve sprinkled with chives.

SERVES 4 to 6

BEANS AND EGGS AU GRATIN

METRIC/IMPERIAL
450 g/1 lb shelled broad beans, fresh or frozen
salt
2-3 hard-boiled eggs, sliced
40 g/1½ oz polyunsaturated margarine
40 g/1½ oz plain wholemeal flour
450 ml/¾ pint skimmed milk
cayenne pepper
Topping:
25 g/1 oz fresh wholemeal breadcrumbs
50 g/2 oz mature Cheddar cheese, grated

First preheat the oven to hot (220°C/425°F, Gas Mark 7).

Cook the beans in boiling salted water until just soft, then drain. Layer the beans and eggs in an ovenproof dish, starting and ending with a layer of beans.

Melt the margarine in a pan and stir in the flour, then gradually blend in the milk. Bring to the boil, stirring constantly, and cook for 3 to 4 minutes. Season with salt and cayenne pepper and pour over the beans.

For the topping, sprinkle the breadcrumbs and cheese over the sauce. Bake in the oven for 15 minutes or until the topping is browned and crisp.

SERVES 6

PEPPER QUICHE

METRIC/IMPERIAL
Cheese pastry:
175 g/6 oz wholemeal flour
½ teaspoon dry mustard
pinch of salt
pinch of cayenne pepper
75 g/3 oz polyunsaturated margarine
75 g/3 oz Cheddar cheese, grated
2-3 tablespoons water
Filling:
2 tablespoons polyunsaturated vegetable oil
1 onion, peeled and chopped
1 clove garlic, peeled and crushed
1 green pepper, cored, deseeded and sliced
1 red pepper, cored, deseeded and sliced
2 eggs
150 ml/¼ pint skimmed milk
50 g/2 oz wholemeal breadcrumbs
salt
freshly ground black pepper

Place the flour, mustard, salt and cayenne pepper in a mixing bowl. Rub in the margarine until the mixture resembles breadcrumbs. Stir in the cheese, add the water and mix to a firm dough. Turn on to a floured surface and knead lightly until smooth. Roll out thinly and use to line a 23cm/9inch flan ring placed on a baking sheet. Chill for 15 minutes.

Meanwhile, heat the oil in a pan, add the onion and fry until softened. Add the garlic and peppers and cook for 10 minutes. Mix the eggs and milk together, then stir in the pepper mixture, breadcrumbs, and salt and pepper to taste.

Pour into the flan case and bake in a preheated moderately hot oven (190°C/375°F, Gas Mark 5) for 35 to 40 minutes until golden. Serve hot or cold, with salad.

SERVES 4

QUICHE LORRAINE

METRIC/IMPERIAL

wholemeal pastry made with 175 g/6 oz flour
(see page 334)
4 rashers streaky bacon
75 g/3 oz Gruyère cheese, sliced
2 eggs
1 teaspoon flour
pinch of grated nutmeg
½ teaspoon salt
pinch of cayenne pepper
120 ml/4 fl oz single cream
120 ml/4 fl oz skimmed milk
watercress, to garnish

Roll out the pastry on a lightly floured board and use to line a 20 cm/8 inch flan tin.

Remove the rind from the bacon and grill until crisp. Cut into 1 cm/½ inch squares, and cut the cheese the same size. Place in layers in the pastry case. Beat the eggs with the flour, nutmeg, salt, cayenne, cream and milk until just combined (over-beating causes bubbles on top). Strain over the bacon and cheese and bake in a preheated moderately hot oven (200°C/400°F, Gas Mark 6) for 10 minutes. Reduce the heat to moderate (180°C/350°F, Gas Mark 4) and bake for a further 20 minutes, or until a knife inserted in the centre comes out clean. Serve the quiche warm, garnished with watercress.
SERVES 4 to 6

PRAWN QUICHES

METRIC/IMPERIAL

wholemeal pastry made with 225 g/8 oz flour
(see page 334)
25 g/1 oz polyunsaturated margarine
1 small onion, peeled and chopped
2 eggs, beaten
100 g/4 oz cottage cheese, sieved
2 tablespoons single cream
2 teaspoons chopped parsley
salt
freshly ground white pepper
100 g/4 oz peeled prawns
chopped parsley, to garnish

Roll out the pastry dough on a lightly floured surface and use to line 4 individual quiche dishes. Prick the bases lightly with a fork, cover with kitchen foil or greaseproof paper, then weigh down with baking beans or rice.

Bake in a preheated moderately hot oven (200°C/400°F, Gas Mark 6) for 10 minutes, then remove the beans or rice and the foil or paper. Meanwhile, melt the margarine in a pan, add the onion and fry gently for 3 minutes, stirring occasionally.

Put the eggs, cottage cheese, cream, parsley and salt and pepper to taste in a bowl and beat well to mix. Stir in the onion and prawns. Divide the mixture equally between the flan cases and bake in a preheated moderate oven (180°C/350°F, Gas Mark 4) for 20 minutes. Garnish with parsley and serve hot.
SERVES 4

TOMATO QUICHE

METRIC/IMPERIAL

1 × 20 cm/8 inch wholemeal cheese pastry case
(see opposite)
Filling:
350 g/12 oz tomatoes, skinned and thinly sliced
1 small onion, peeled and chopped
1 teaspoon chopped basil
1 teaspoon chopped parsley
1 teaspoon thyme
2 tablespoons boiling water
salt
freshly ground black pepper
1 egg
250 ml/8 fl oz skimmed milk
Garnish:
tomato slices
parsley

Heat the oven to moderately hot (190°C/375°F, Gas Mark 5).

To make the filling, put the tomatoes, onion, basil, parsley, thyme and water in a saucepan and season with salt and pepper. Simmer for 5 to 6 minutes or until the vegetables are soft, then cool.

Beat together the egg and milk, then add to the tomato mixture. Pour into the flan case and bake in the oven for 35 to 40 minutes until the filling is set and golden. Garnish with the tomato and parsley.
SERVES 4

155

COURGETTE QUICHE

METRIC/IMPERIAL

wholemeal pastry made with 175 g/6 oz flour
(see page 334)
2 tablespoons polyunsaturated vegetable oil
2 onions, peeled and sliced
450 g/1 lb courgettes, sliced
salt
freshly ground black pepper
2 eggs, beaten with 150 ml/¼ pint milk
2 tablespoons grated Parmesan cheese

Roll out the pastry dough on a lightly floured surface and use to line a 20 cm/8 inch flan dish or flan ring, placed on a baking sheet. Prick the base lightly with a fork, cover with foil, then weigh down with baking beans or rice.

Bake in a preheated moderately hot oven (200°C/400°F, Gas Mark 6) for 15 minutes. Remove the beans or rice and the foil, return the flan case to the oven and bake for a further 5 minutes.

Meanwhile, make the filling: heat the oil in a frying pan. Add the onions and courgettes and fry gently for about 10 minutes until lightly browned, stirring occasionally.

Remove the onions and courgettes from the pan with a slotted spoon, then place in the flan case. Add salt and pepper to taste to the egg and milk mixture, then pour into the flan case. Sprinkle with the Parmesan cheese.

Bake in a preheated moderately hot oven (190°C/375°F, Gas Mark 5) for 25 to 30 minutes until the filling is set and lightly browned on top. Serve hot or cold.
SERVES 4 to 6

BREAKFAST OMELETTE

METRIC/IMPERIAL

2 eggs
salt
freshly ground black pepper
100 g/4 oz cottage cheese
1 tablespoon polyunsaturated vegetable oil

Break the eggs into a bowl. Add the salt and pepper to taste and whisk until light and frothy. Stir in half of the cottage cheese and mix well.

Heat the oil in a small omelette pan and pour in the egg mixture. Cook over moderate heat, drawing the edge of the omelette into the centre with a knife, as it becomes firm.

When the omelette is lightly set, spread the re-
maining cottage cheese over the top and continue to cook gently for 1 minute. Fold the omelette in half and transfer to a hot serving plate. Serve immediately, with wholewheat toast and a glass of orange juice, if liked.
SERVES 1

CHEESE AND ONION OAT FLAN

METRIC/IMPERIAL

Oat pastry:
100 g/4 oz wholemeal flour
100 g/4 oz medium oatmeal
pinch of salt
100 g/4 oz polyunsaturated margarine
2-3 tablespoons water
Filling:
2 tablespoons polyunsaturated vegetable oil
2 onions, peeled and chopped
2 eggs
150 ml/¼ pint skimmed milk
225 g/8 oz Cheddar cheese, grated
salt
freshly ground black pepper

Place the flour, oatmeal and salt in a mixing bowl and rub in the margarine until the mixture resembles breadcrumbs. Add the water and mix to a firm dough. Turn on to a floured surface and knead lightly until smooth. Roll out and use to line a 20 cm/8 inch flan dish. Chill for 15 minutes.

Meanwhile, make the filling. Heat the oil in a pan, add the onions and fry gently until transparent. Mix the eggs and milk together, then stir in the cheese, onions, and salt and pepper to taste.

Pour into the flan case and bake in a preheated moderately hot oven (190°C/375°F, Gas Mark 5) for 35 to 40 minutes. Serve hot or cold, with salad.
SERVES 4

CHEESE SOUFFLÉ

METRIC/IMPERIAL

15 g/½ oz polyunsaturated margarine
25 g/1 oz plain unbleached white flour
300 ml/½ pint skimmed milk
2 egg yolks
75 g/3 oz Cheddar cheese, grated
salt
freshly ground black pepper
grated nutmeg
4 egg whites

Grease a 1.2 litre/2 pint soufflé dish and preheat the oven to moderately hot (190°C/375°F, Gas Mark 5).

Melt the margarine in a saucepan, stir in the flour and cook for 1 minute. Remove from the heat and gradually blend in the milk. Cook, stirring, until the sauce thickens. Simmer, stirring, for 2 minutes, then remove from the heat and cool slightly. Beat in the egg yolks and cheese and season with salt, pepper and nutmeg.

Whisk the egg whites until stiff and fold into the cheese mixture quickly. Turn into the soufflé dish and cook on a baking sheet in the centre of the oven for 30 to 35 minutes until well risen and golden brown. Serve immediately.
SERVES 3

COTTAGE PEARS

METRIC/IMPERIAL
4 ripe dessert pears
juice of ½ lemon
225 g/8 oz cottage cheese
25 g/1 oz walnuts, chopped
salt
freshly ground black pepper
2 celery stalks, cut into 2.5 cm/1 inch slices
1 carrot, peeled and coarsely grated
1 bunch watercress, stems removed and leaves roughly chopped

Cut the pears in half lengthwise but do not peel them. Remove the cores, then brush the pears immediately with the lemon juice to prevent discoloration.

Put the cottage cheese and walnuts in a bowl, stir well, then add salt and pepper to taste. Fill the pears with the cheese mixture.

Mix together the celery, carrot and watercress, then arrange on individual plates. Place the pear halves on top. Serve immediately.
SERVES 4 to 8

CHEESE THINS

METRIC/IMPERIAL
100 g/4 oz rolled oats
½ teaspoon mustard powder
¼ teaspoon cayenne pepper
50 g/2 oz polyunsaturated margarine
75 g/3 oz Cheddar cheese, grated
¼ teaspoon bicarbonate of soda
2 tablespoons boiling water

Mix together the rolled oats, mustard and cayenne. Rub in the margarine, then stir in the grated cheese. Dissolve the soda in the boiling water and pour over the dry ingredients. Mix to a stiff consistency, adding a little extra water if necessary.

Turn out on to a floured board and knead lightly. Roll out the mixture until it is about 5 mm/¼ inch thick. Cut into rounds using a 7 cm/2½-3 inch biscuit cutter.

Transfer the rounds to a greased baking sheet and bake in a preheated moderately hot oven (190°C/375°F, Gas Mark 5) for about 10 minutes or until golden. Transfer to a wire rack to cool.
MAKES about 20

VENETIAN FLAN

METRIC/IMPERIAL
wholemeal pastry made with 100 g/4 oz flour
(see page 334)
50 g/2 oz Gruyère cheese
75 g/3 oz Cheddar cheese
1 onion, peeled
1 tablespoon olive oil
225 g/8 oz Italian salami, cut into cubes
100 g/4 oz lean ham, cut into strips
3 eggs
300 ml/½ pint skimmed milk
salt
freshly ground black pepper
grated nutmeg

Roll out the pastry on a floured board and use to line a 20 cm/8 inch flan tin. Grate the Gruyère and set aside. Grate the Cheddar and set aside. (Keep the cheeses separate.) Slice the onion. Heat the oil in a frying pan and add the onion. Cook gently until soft. Stir in the salami and cook for 5 minutes. Put the onion and salami into the pastry case and sprinkle with half the Gruyère and half the Cheddar. Arrange the ham strips over the top of the cheeses.

In a bowl, beat together the eggs, milk and remaining cheese, and add salt, pepper and nutmeg to taste. Pour over the cheese and ham. Bake in a moderately hot oven (200°C/400°F, Gas Mark 6) and bake for a further 20 minutes or until the custard is set and lightly golden.
SERVES 6

WHOLEWHEAT CHEESE BISCUITS

METRIC/IMPERIAL
100 g/4 oz wholemeal flour
½ teaspoon sea salt
1 teaspoon mustard powder
25 g/1 oz polyunsaturated margarine
225 g/8 oz Cheddar cheese, finely grated
2 tablespoons cold water

Put the flour, salt and mustard in a bowl and mix well. Rub in the margarine, then stir in the cheese. Add the water and mix to a firm dough.
Turn out on to a lightly floured surface and knead lightly. Roll out to 5 mm/¼ inch thickness, then cut out 30 rounds with a 5 cm/2 inch biscuit cutter.
Place the rounds on greased baking sheets and prick each one 3 times with a fork. Bake in a preheated hot oven (230°C/450°F, Gas Mark 8) for 6 minutes. Transfer to a wire rack to cool.
MAKES 30

WHOLEMEAL PIZZA

METRIC/IMPERIAL
Dough:
225 g/8 oz wholemeal flour
½ teaspoon salt
7 g/¼ oz fresh yeast
150 ml/¼ pint warm water
1 tablespoon olive oil
Topping:
1 tablespoon olive oil
1 large onion, peeled and sliced
450 g/1 lb tomatoes, skinned and chopped
1 tablespoon chopped marjoram
salt
freshly ground black pepper
2 tablespoons tomato purée
225 g/8 oz Mozzarella or Bel Paese cheese, thinly sliced
1 × 49 g/1¾ oz can anchovy fillets, halved lengthwise
8 black olives, halved and stoned

Mix the flour and salt together in a bowl. Cream the yeast with a little of the water and leave until frothy. Add to the flour with the remaining water and the oil and mix to a soft dough.
Turn on to a floured surface and knead for 10 minutes until smooth and elastic. Place in a clean bowl, cover with a damp cloth and leave to rise in a warm place for about 1½ hours, until the dough is doubled in size.
Meanwhile, heat the oil in a pan, add the onion and fry until softened. Add the tomatoes, marjoram, and salt and pepper to taste and cook for 5 minutes.
Turn the dough on to a floured surface and knead for a few minutes. Divide in half and roll each piece out to a 20 cm/8 inch circle. Place on greased baking sheets and spread with the tomato purée. Spoon over the tomato mixture and cover with the cheese. Top with the anchovies and olives.
Bake in a preheated moderately hot oven (200°C/400°F, Gas Mark 6) for 15 to 20 minutes. Serve immediately.
SERVES 4

COTTAGE CHEESE MOUSSE

METRIC/IMPERIAL
450 g/1 lb cottage cheese, sieved
150 ml/¼ pint plain low-fat yogurt
squeeze of lemon juice
1 tablespoon tomato purée
salt
freshly ground black pepper
100 g/4 oz peeled shrimps
Garnish:
½ teaspoon paprika
1 teaspoon snipped chives

Put the cottage cheese and yogurt in a bowl and mix together, using a fork. Add the lemon juice and tomato purée and season well with salt and pepper. Stir well.
Divide the mixture equally between 4 individual ramekins, pressing down well. Top each ramekin with shrimps, then chill in the refrigerator for 1 hour.
Sprinkle the tops with paprika and snipped chives before serving.
SERVES 4

SPINACH AND CHEESE FLAN

METRIC/IMPERIAL

Wholemeal pastry:
175 g/6 oz wholemeal flour
pinch of salt
75 g/3 oz polyunsaturated margarine
2-3 tablespoons water
Filling:
450 g/1 lb spinach, washed and trimmed
salt
freshly ground black pepper
225 g/8 oz cottage cheese
2 eggs
50 g/2 oz Parmesan cheese
150 ml/¼ pint skimmed milk
grated nutmeg

Place the flour and salt in a mixing bowl and rub in the margarine until the mixture resembles breadcrumbs. Add the water and mix to a firm dough, then turn on to a floured surface and knead lightly until smooth. Roll out thinly and use to line a 20 cm/8 inch flan ring placed on a baking sheet. Chill for 15 minutes.

Meanwhile, prepare the filling. Put the spinach in a large pan with just the water clinging to the leaves after washing. Cook gently for 5 minutes, turning twice. Drain thoroughly and chop finely. Place in a bowl with the remaining ingredients, seasoning to taste. Mix thoroughly.

Pour into the flan case, smooth the top and bake in a preheated moderately hot oven (190°C/375°F, Gas Mark 5) for 35 to 40 minutes.
SERVES 4

QUICK PIZZA GRILL

METRIC/IMPERIAL
1 wholemeal roll
polyunsaturated margarine
25 g/1 oz lean ham, chopped
1 tomato, sliced
1 tablespoon chopped onion (optional)
25 g/1 oz Cheddar cheese, sliced

Split the wholemeal roll in two and spread each half with a little margarine. Divide the ham, tomato and onion (if using) between the two halves, and cover each half with slices of cheese. Cook under a fairly hot grill for 5 to 10 minutes, or until the cheese is lightly browned.
SERVES 1

OVEN-BAKED TOMATO TOASTS

METRIC/IMPERIAL
5 eggs
3 tablespoons skimmed milk
few drops of Worcestershire sauce
salt
freshly ground black pepper
50 g/2 oz Bran Flakes breakfast cereal, crushed
4 slices wholemeal bread
4 small tomatoes, sliced
polyunsaturated vegetable oil for frying

Beat 1 egg with the milk, Worcestershire sauce, salt and pepper. Place the crushed Bran Flakes on a plate. Remove the crusts from the bread and cut each slice in half.

Dip the bread into the egg mixture and then into the crumbs, coating evenly. Place the bread in an ovenproof serving dish and arrange the tomato slices on top.

Bake in a moderately hot oven (190°C/375°F, Gas Mark 5) for 15 minutes. While the bread is baking, fry the remaining 4 eggs in a little oil. Top each slice of bread with a fried egg and serve immediately while hot.
SERVES 4

MUSHROOM AND CHEESE SAVOURY

METRIC/IMPERIAL
100 g/4 oz mushrooms, wiped and trimmed
600 ml/1 pint skimmed milk
100 g/4 oz Cheddar cheese, grated
3 eggs, beaten
4 large tomatoes, skinned and sliced
salt
freshly ground black pepper
1 bay leaf

If any of the mushrooms are large, slice them. Beat the milk, cheese and eggs together.

Place the mushrooms and tomatoes in an ovenproof dish and pour over the egg and milk mixture. Add salt, pepper and the bay leaf. Place in a roasting tin of hot water and bake in a preheated moderately hot oven (190°C/375°F, Gas Mark 5) for about 25 minutes until the custard sets.
SERVES 4

MIXED CHEESE WITH HERBS

METRIC/IMPERIAL
175 g/6 oz curd cheese
25 g/1 oz Gruyère cheese, grated
25 g/1 oz Parmesan cheese, grated
pinch of mustard powder
salt
freshly ground black pepper
pinch of cayenne pepper
4–6 tablespoons chopped burnet or chervil

Mash the soft cheese until smooth, then beat in the two grated hard cheeses. Add a pinch of mustard and season with salt and black pepper. Stir in a pinch of cayenne pepper, then chill for 2 hours until firm.

Form the cheese into balls and roll each one in the chopped herb. Lay them on a small flat plate and serve with warm water biscuits.
SERVES 4

FRUIT AND CHEESE KEBABS

METRIC/IMPERIAL
225 g/8 oz Cheddar cheese, cubed
4 tomatoes, cut into quarters
4 slices wholemeal bread, spread with polyunsaturated margarine and cut into squares
2 rashers streaky bacon, derinded and cut into quarters
1 banana, peeled and sliced
1 dessert apple, unpeeled, cored and cubed
polyunsaturated margarine, melted

Place cubes of cheese, quarters of tomato, squares of wholemeal bread, bacon and fruit alternately on to skewers. Brush the kebabs all over with the melted margarine.

Cook under a preheated hot grill for approximately 3 minutes, turning once, until the bacon is cooked. Serve the kebabs on a bed of brown rice.
SERVES 4

COTTAGE CHEESE GRIDDLE CAKES

METRIC/IMPERIAL
25 g/1 oz polyunsaturated margarine, melted
100 g/4 oz cottage cheese
2 eggs, beaten
50 g/2 oz wholemeal self-raising flour
1 tablespoon skimmed milk

Put the margarine and cottage cheese in a bowl and mix well. Beat in the eggs, then stir in the flour and milk and beat to a smooth thick batter.

Grease a griddle or heavy-based frying pan very lightly with fat, then heat until very hot. Drop tablespoonfuls of the batter on to the hot surface. Cook for 1 minute until just set, then turn over and cook for a further 1 minute. Turn over again and continue cooking until the griddle cakes are set and golden in colour.

Transfer to a wire rack and cover with a clean cloth to keep hot while cooking the remaining batter. Serve hot with honey or a savoury spread.
MAKES 10 to 12

COTTAGE CHEESE COCOTTES

METRIC/IMPERIAL
2 eggs
1 large slice wholemeal bread, crusts removed
3 tablespoons hot skimmed milk
100 g/4 oz peeled prawns or shrimps
225 g/8 oz cottage cheese
1 teaspoon made mustard
salt
freshly ground black pepper
1 small green pepper, cored, deseeded and sliced into rings
parsley sprigs, to garnish

Break the eggs into a bowl and whisk with a fork until frothy. Place the bread in an electric blender and grind coarsely. Fold the breadcrumbs, milk, prawns or shrimps and cottage cheese into the beaten eggs. Stir in the mustard and season with salt and pepper to taste.

Grease 4 individual ovenproof ramekin dishes and divide the mixture evenly between them. Top each one with a green pepper ring.

Stand the dishes in a roasting tin containing about 2.5 cm/1 inch water and bake in a preheated moderately hot oven (190°C/375°F, Gas Mark 5) for 35 minutes. Serve hot, garnished with parsley and accompanied by peas and baked tomatoes.
SERVES 4

COTTAGE CHEESE DIP

METRIC/IMPERIAL
450 g/1 lb cottage cheese
1 teaspoon caraway seeds
½ green pepper, cored, deseeded and finely
chopped
2 tablespoons finely chopped watercress
½ teaspoon salt
freshly ground black pepper
1 clove garlic, peeled and crushed (optional)
½ teaspoon paprika, to garnish

If a smoother dip is preferred, sieve the cottage cheese or work in a blender.

Blend together the cottage cheese, caraway seeds, green pepper, watercress, salt, pepper and garlic (if using). Pile the dip into a serving bowl and sprinkle with paprika. Serve with crisp sticks of carrot, celery and cucumber, cauliflower florets or bread sticks.
SERVES 10 to 12

CHEESE AND MUSHROOM FONDUE

METRIC/IMPERIAL
½ clove garlic, peeled
150 ml/¼ pint dry cider
1 teaspoon lemon juice
400 g/14 oz Gouda cheese, grated
1 tablespoon cornflour
1½ tablespoons sherry
freshly ground white pepper
pinch of grated nutmeg
100 g/4 oz button mushrooms, trimmed and
chopped

Rub the inside of a flameproof earthenware casserole with the cut garlic, then chop a little of it and put into the casserole. Pour in the cider and lemon juice. Heat slowly until the cider is nearly boiling.

Gradually add the grated cheese, a little at a time, stirring constantly with a fork, until all the cheese has melted. When the mixture is boiling, blend the cornflour with the sherry until smooth, and stir into the fondue. Season with pepper and nutmeg, add the mushrooms and mix well.

Serve the fondue in the earthenware casserole with a bowl of French bread cubes. The cubed bread is speared with a long fork and dipped into the fondue.
SERVES 6 to 8

COTTAGE BAKE

METRIC/IMPERIAL
1 tablespoon polyunsaturated vegetable oil
1 small onion, peeled and finely chopped
100 g/4 oz mushrooms, wiped and sliced
225 g/8 oz cottage cheese
2 eggs
50 g/2 oz cooked lean ham, chopped
2 tablespoons chopped mixed fresh herbs
salt
freshly ground black pepper
chopped parsley, to garnish

Heat the oil in a pan, add the onion and fry gently until soft and golden. Add the mushrooms and fry for a further 3 minutes.

Meanwhile, put the cottage cheese and eggs in a bowl and beat together with a fork. Stir in the ham, then the cooked onion and mushrooms. Add the herbs and salt and pepper to taste.

Spoon the mixture into a lightly oiled baking dish, then bake in a preheated moderately hot oven (200°C/400°F, Gas Mark 6) for 20 minutes. Sprinkle with chopped parsley and serve hot.
SERVES 4

CHEESE POTS

METRIC/IMPERIAL
1 celery stalk, diced
1 large ripe dessert pear, peeled, cored and diced
1 large dessert apple, peeled, cored and diced
½-1 teaspoon snipped chives
½-1 tablespoon lemon juice
225 g/8 oz Lancashire or crumbly Cheddar
cheese
Garnish:
1 tablespoon chopped parsley
paprika

Toss the celery, pear and apple dice with the chives and lemon juice.

Divide the mixture between 4 individual flameproof or ovenproof dishes. You should use flameproof dishes if heating under the grill. Crumble the cheese over the fruit and celery. Place under a preheated grill for 5 to 6 minutes or until golden brown on top or towards the top of a preheated hot oven (220°C/425°F, Gas Mark 7) for 10 minutes.

Garnish with the parsley and a sprinkling of paprika.
SERVES 4

CHEESE AND HERB MOUSSE

METRIC/IMPERIAL

350 g/12 oz cottage cheese, sieved
½ cucumber, peeled and diced
1 tablespoon chopped parsley
1 tablespoon snipped chives
1 tablespoon chopped thyme
salt
freshly ground black pepper
15 g/½ oz gelatine, soaked in 3 tablespoons cold water
150 ml/¼ pint reduced-calorie mayonnaise
watercress, to garnish

Put the cottage cheese in a bowl with the cucumber, herbs, and salt and pepper to taste; mix well.

Place the soaked gelatine in a bowl over a pan of simmering water and stir until dissolved. Cool slightly, then stir into the cheese mixture with the mayonnaise. Turn into a greased 750 ml/1¼ pint ring mould and leave to set in the refrigerator.

Turn out on to a serving dish and garnish with watercress to serve.

SERVES 6

CHEESE DIP WITH CRUDITÉS

METRIC/IMPERIAL

175 g/6 oz low-fat soft cheese
75 g/3 oz blue Stilton cheese, crumbled
2 teaspoons snipped chives
4 tablespoons plain low-fat yogurt
2 teaspoons finely grated onion
freshly ground white pepper
Crudités:
carrots
celery
cauliflower
cucumber
radishes
peppers

Mix together the soft cheese and Stilton in a bowl. Stir in the chives (reserving ½ teaspoon), yogurt and onion and mix well. Season with pepper. Put in a serving bowl, sprinkle with the reserved chives and chill.

The crudités can be prepared in advance and kept in cold water in the refrigerator. Before serving, drain well and dry on kitchen paper. Arrange on a platter with the dip in the centre.

Carrots: cut into thick sticks.
Celery: cut into thick sticks; or make curls by cutting 10 cm/4 inch pieces of celery then making slits in one end not quite to the centre. Leave in cold water for 2 hours or until the ends curl.
Cauliflower: cut into small florets with a short stalk for holding.
Cucumber: cut into thick sticks or slices 5 mm/¼ inch thick.
Radishes: to make 'roses', cut a deep cross on the top of each radish and place in iced water for 2 hours or until they open out. To make 'fans', make several cuts along the length of the radish, not quite right through. Soak them in iced water until they open out.
Peppers: cut into thick strips.
SERVES 4

CAULIFLOWER CHEESE TIMBALE

METRIC/IMPERIAL

450 g/1 lb cauliflower, chopped, with leaves and stalks finely chopped
1 large onion, peeled and chopped
300 ml/½ pint water
salt
4 eggs, lightly beaten
50 g/2 oz fresh wholemeal breadcrumbs
100 g/4 oz Cheddar cheese, grated
pinch of grated nutmeg
freshly ground white pepper
300 ml/½ pint skimmed milk

Put the cauliflower and onion in a large pan with the water and salt. Bring to the boil, then lower the heat, cover and simmer for about 10 minutes until the cauliflower is just tender, then drain thoroughly.

Put the eggs in a bowl with the breadcrumbs, cheese, nutmeg and salt and pepper to taste. Mix well. Heat the milk, but do not allow to boil, then stir into the egg mixture.

Put the cauliflower in a 1.5 litre/2½ pint baking dish or greased ring mould. Pour over the egg custard to cover the cauliflower. Stand the dish or mould in a roasting pan, half-filled with hot water. Bake in a preheated moderate oven (180°C/350°F, Gas Mark 4) for 45 minutes or until the custard is set and a skewer comes out clean when inserted in the centre. Alternatively, cover the dish or mould and steam over boiling water for about 1 hour until set.

Serve straight from the dish, or leave to stand

for a few minutes, then turn out of the mould on to a warmed serving platter. Serve hot with a mushroom or tomato sauce.

The timbale can also be served cold, in which case it should be left to cool in the mould before turning out on to a serving platter.
SERVES 4

RICOTTA WITH HERBS, CELERY AND WATER BISCUITS

METRIC/IMPERIAL
2 tablespoons chopped herbs (chives, dill, parsley, etc)
175 g/6 oz ricotta or low-fat curd cheese
sea salt
freshly ground black pepper
1 head celery, inner stalks only
water biscuits

Stir a quarter of the chopped herbs into the ricotta, adding a little salt and freshly ground black pepper. Form the ricotta into a round and flatten the top. Sprinkle the remaining herbs over the disc, and press into a ramekin to shape it. Turn out on to a flat dish and serve, with the celery and water biscuits.
SERVES 4

CHEESE AND NOODLE HOT POT

METRIC/IMPERIAL
225 g/8 oz ribbon noodles
50 g/2 oz polyunsaturated margarine
1 onion, peeled and chopped
25 g/1 oz plain unbleached white flour
300 ml/½ pint skimmed milk
2 tablespoons tomato purée
50 g/2 oz hazelnuts, roughly chopped
225 g/8 oz cottage cheese
salt
freshly ground black pepper
50 g/2 oz low-fat cheese, grated
To garnish:
1 tomato, sliced
parsley sprigs

Cook the noodles in a pan of boiling salted water until tender, according to the packet instructions, then drain well.

Meanwhile, melt half the margarine in a pan. Add the onion and fry until golden, about 10 minutes.

Place the remaining margarine, flour and milk in a pan and heat, whisking constantly, until the sauce thickens. Stir in the noodles, onion, tomato purée, hazelnuts, cottage cheese, and salt and pepper to taste, blending well. Spoon into a 1.2 litre/2 pint greased ovenproof dish and sprinkle with the grated cheese.

Cook in a preheated moderately hot oven (190°C/375°F, Gas Mark 5) until golden.
SERVES 4

SAVOURY CHEESECAKE

METRIC/IMPERIAL
Base:
50 g/2 oz polyunsaturated margarine
100 g/4 oz wholewheat crackers, crushed
Topping:
225 g/8 oz curd cheese
3 eggs, separated
175 g/6 oz Mozzarella cheese, grated
150 ml/¼ pint plain low-fat yogurt
1 teaspoon chopped mixed herbs
100 g/4 oz raisins
1 red pepper, cored, deseeded and chopped
50 g/2 oz mushrooms, wiped and chopped
salt
freshly ground black pepper
red pepper rings, to garnish

To make the base, melt the margarine in a pan. Add the cracker crumbs and mix to coat. Press the crumb mixture into a greased 20 cm/8 inch loose-bottomed cake tin.

To make the topping, beat the curd cheese with the egg yolks. Add the Mozzarella cheese, yogurt, herbs, raisins, chopped pepper, mushrooms, and salt and pepper to taste, blending well.

Whisk the egg whites until they stand in stiff peaks and fold into the cheesecake mixture with a metal spoon. Spoon over the cracker base and level the surface. Bake in a preheated moderate oven (160°C/325°F, Gas Mark 3) for 40 to 45 minutes until golden and firm to the touch. Leave to cool in the tin for 10 minutes, then loosen the edges with a knife and remove from the tin. Serve warm or cold, garnished with red pepper rings.
SERVES 6 to 8

VEGETABLES

NEST OF BABY VEGETABLES

METRIC/IMPERIAL
12 baby carrots, washed
12 baby turnips, washed
50 g/2 oz mangetout, topped and tailed
100 g/4 oz French beans, topped and tailed
8 button onions, peeled
8 radishes, washed
50 g/2 oz polyunsaturated margarine
4 tablespoons white wine
4 strips lemon peel
4 teaspoons chopped fresh herbs (e.g. chervil, chives, mint)
salt
freshly ground black pepper

Fold 8 sheets of greaseproof paper in half, and cut a semi-circle of 15 cm/6 inch radius through each so that, when opened out, you have 8 × 30 cm/ 12 inch rounds of paper. Place the circles together in pairs so that you have 4 double-thick circles.

Divide all of the ingredients between the 4 circles, arranging the food on one half of each circle only, and season well with salt and pepper. Fold the free half over to make a parcel rather like an apple turnover. Fold the edges of the layers of paper over twice together, twisting and pressing hard to make an air-tight seal.

Lay the parcels inside a steamer. Cover with a tight-fitting lid and steam over boiling water for 8 to 10 minutes. Serve at once.
SERVES 4

FRENCH-STYLE BEANS AND CARROTS

METRIC/IMPERIAL
25 g/1 oz polyunsaturated margarine
1 onion, peeled and chopped
8 lettuce leaves, shredded
225 g/8 oz carrots, peeled and cut into matchsticks
225 g/8 oz green beans
salt
freshly ground black pepper
2 tablespoons water
chopped mixed herbs, to garnish

Melt the margarine in a pan and sauté the onion for 2 minutes. Add the lettuce and carrots and cook for 2 minutes, then add the beans, salt and pepper and continue cooking for 5 minutes with the lid on the pan.

Stir in the water, cover and cook for 15 minutes. Transfer to a warm serving dish and garnish with the herbs (if using).
SERVES 4

RATATOUILLE

METRIC/IMPERIAL
4 courgettes, sliced
4 tomatoes, skinned and quartered
2 medium aubergines, sliced
2 onions, peeled and sliced
2 large red peppers, cored, deseeded and sliced
2 bay leaves
300 ml/½ pint tomato juice
salt
freshly ground black pepper

Place all the vegetables in a saucepan with the bay leaves, tomato juice, salt and pepper. Bring to the boil and skim. Cover and simmer for about 20 minutes or until all the vegetables are tender.

If there is still too much tomato juice, reduce by boiling briskly for a few minutes.
SERVES 4

MIXED VEGETABLE CURRY

METRIC/IMPERIAL
2 tablespoons polyunsaturated vegetable oil
225 g/8 oz onions, peeled and sliced
1 clove garlic, peeled and crushed
1 cooking apple, peeled, cored and chopped
2.5 cm/1 inch piece fresh root ginger, peeled and grated
1 tablespoon mustard seeds
1 teaspoon ground turmeric
1 teaspoon ground coriander
1 teaspoon ground cumin
½ teaspoon ground fenugreek
¼ teaspoon chilli powder
450 ml/¾ pint stock
finely grated rind and juice of ½ lemon
salt
freshly ground black pepper
225 g/8 oz potatoes, peeled and diced
225 g/8 oz carrots, peeled and sliced
225 g/8 oz tomatoes, skinned and roughly chopped
225 g/8 oz cauliflower florets
225 g/8 oz runner beans, sliced
50 g/2 oz sultanas
50 g/2 oz shelled Brazil nuts
Garnish:
1 tablespoon grated fresh coconut
flaked almonds

Heat the oil in a large pan. Add the onions, garlic, apple and ginger and fry gently for 5 minutes, stirring occasionally. Stir in the spices and fry gently for a further 3 minutes, stirring constantly.

Add the stock and bring to the boil, stirring constantly until the sauce thickens slightly. Add the lemon rind and juice, and salt and pepper to taste, then lower the heat and simmer for 2 minutes.

Add the potatoes, carrots and tomatoes. Cover the pan and simmer for 10 minutes.

Add the cauliflower, beans, sultanas and nuts. Cover and simmer for a further 10 minutes or until the vegetables are just tender but still crisp and not broken up.

Taste and adjust the seasoning. Sprinkle with the coconut and almonds, and serve hot. Alternatively, serve cold as a salad.
SERVES 4

QUICK VEGETABLE CURRY

METRIC/IMPERIAL
4 tablespoons polyunsaturated vegetable oil
2 onions, peeled and sliced
2 teaspoons ground coriander
2 teaspoons turmeric
1 teaspoon curry powder
2 teaspoons chopped root ginger
2 cloves garlic, peeled and crushed
4 carrots, peeled and sliced
350 g/12 oz courgettes, sliced
300 ml/½ pint stock
salt
freshly ground black pepper
1 small cauliflower
50 g/2 oz cashew nuts, roasted
150 ml/¼ pint plain low-fat yogurt

Heat the oil in a large pan, add the onions and fry until softened. Add the spices and garlic and cook for a further 1 minute. Add the carrots and courgettes and fry for 2 to 3 minutes, stirring. Add the stock and salt and pepper to taste.

Cover and simmer for 10 minutes. Break the cauliflower into florets and cook for a further 10 minutes. Stir in the nuts and yogurt and heat through gently.
SERVES 4 to 6

VEGETABLE KEBABS

METRIC/IMPERIAL
1 medium onion, peeled and quartered
4 courgettes, thickly sliced
4 tomatoes, skinned and quartered
8 button mushrooms, wiped and thickly sliced
1 medium eating apple, cored and cut into eighths
8 bay leaves
apple juice, to baste
salt
freshly ground black pepper

Boil the onion quarters for about 5 minutes until tender but still firm. Boil the courgette slices for 1 to 2 minutes to soften.

Thread the onion, tomatoes, mushrooms, courgettes, apple and bay leaves on to 4 skewers and place under a preheated hot grill. Turn frequently, basting with seasoned apple juice, for 10 to 15 minutes until cooked.
SERVES 4

VEGETABLE HOT POT

METRIC/IMPERIAL
4 carrots, peeled and sliced
4 parsnips, peeled and sliced
2 large courgettes, sliced
2 turnips, peeled and sliced
2 red or green peppers, cored, deseeded and
    coarsely chopped
2 onions, peeled and sliced
2 large tomatoes, skinned, deseeded and
    chopped
600 ml/1 pint chicken stock
salt
freshly ground black pepper
1 bay leaf
1 tablespoon chopped parsley
1 teaspoon chopped thyme
1 teaspoon chopped marjoram
dash of Worcestershire sauce

Place all the ingredients in a flameproof casserole.
Bring to the boil, skim off the scum, then cover
and cook gently for about 25 minutes, until all the
vegetables are tender. Serve immediately.
SERVES 6

VEGETABLE MORNAY

METRIC/IMPERIAL
15 g/½ oz polyunsaturated margarine
15 g/½ oz plain flour
300 ml/½ pint skimmed milk
100 g/4 oz cheese, grated
salt
freshly ground black pepper
450 g/1 lb mixed cooked vegetables
(e.g. carrots, peas, parsnips, cauliflower,
    celery), prepared and diced

Melt the margarine in a saucepan and add the
flour. Cook for 2 minutes, stirring.
Gradually add enough milk to make a fairly
thick sauce. Stir in the cheese, and salt and pepper
to taste. When the cheese begins to melt, add the
cooked vegetables and cook, stirring, for 5
minutes.
Alternatively, sprinkle with 50 g/2 oz of the
cheese and place under a preheated hot grill until
lightly browned.
SERVES 4

ROOT VEGETABLE DAUPHINOIS

METRIC/IMPERIAL
225 g/8 oz carrots, peeled and chopped
225 g/8 oz swede, peeled and chopped
225 g/8 oz parsnip, peeled and chopped
225 g/8 oz turnip, peeled and chopped
grated nutmeg
salt
freshly ground black pepper
150 ml/¼ pint single cream
150 ml/¼ pint skimmed milk
chopped parsley, to garnish

Preheat the oven to 180°C/350°F, Gas Mark 4.
In a large, greased, shallow ovenproof dish
layer the vegetables, sprinkling each layer with
nutmeg, salt and pepper.
Mix together the cream and milk, then pour
over the vegetables. Cover the dish with foil and
cook for 1½ to 2 hours or until the vegetables are
just tender. Serve garnished with parsley.
SERVES 4

Variation
Remove from the oven 15 minutes before the end
of the cooking time, sprinkle thickly with grated
cheese and return to the oven until golden.

RAINBOW OF SEASONAL VEGETABLES

METRIC/IMPERIAL
50 g/2 oz polyunsaturated margarine
1 tablespoon chopped fresh herbs
salt
freshly ground black pepper
4 courgettes, cut in half lengthwise
2 leeks, trimmed, washed, and thickly sliced
2 large carrots, peeled and cut into thick
    matchsticks
100 g/4 oz French beans, topped and tailed
4 celery stalks, cut into thick matchsticks
small bunch watercress, washed

Mix the margarine with the herbs and season
well. Place the courgette, leek, carrot, beans and
celery in a steamer and season well.
Cover and steam over boiling water for 3 to 5
minutes. Add the watercress and steam for 1
minute. Turn on to a warmed serving dish and
dot with the herb mixture.
SERVES 4

PEA, AVOCADO AND MINT PURÉE

METRIC/IMPERIAL
450 g/1 lb shelled fresh peas or minted, frozen
  peas
few mint sprigs
1 ripe avocado, peeled and stoned
1 clove garlic, peeled and crushed
2 teaspoons lemon juice
3-4 tablespoons skimmed milk
salt
freshly ground black pepper
mint sprig, to garnish

If fresh, place the peas in boiling salted water with the mint and cook for 5 to 10 minutes or until tender. If frozen, follow the cooking instructions on the packet, and omit the mint.

Place in a blender or food processor with the avocado, garlic, lemon juice and milk; alternatively, place the ingredients in the pan and use a multi-blender. Work until smooth, adding salt and pepper to taste.

Transfer the purée to a warmed dish and serve garnished with a sprig of mint.
SERVES 4

PARSNIP AND CARROT PURÉE

METRIC/IMPERIAL
450 g/1 lb parsnips, peeled and chopped
450 g/1 lb carrots, peeled and thinly sliced
2 tablespoons skimmed milk
salt
freshly ground black pepper
grated nutmeg

Cook the parsnips and carrots separately in boiling salted water for 15 to 20 minutes or until tender. Drain thoroughly, reserving 4 tablespoons of the liquid.

Place the vegetables in a blender with the liquid and milk, or use a multi-blender in the pan. Work until almost smooth, retaining some texture. Add salt, pepper and nutmeg to taste. Spoon into a serving dish or pipe through a 12 mm/½ inch round vegetable nozzle using a forcing bag, directly on to the dish. Alternatively, pipe directly on to individual plates.

This mixture may also be used to make vegetable-stuffed marrow (use half the quantity).
SERVES 4 to 6

ORIENTAL VEGETABLES

METRIC/IMPERIAL
450 g/1 lb mixed vegetables (e.g. cauliflower,
  onions, mushrooms, leeks, fennel)
1 wine glass white wine
1 wine glass wine vinegar
1 teaspoon ground coriander
1 teaspoon ground mace
1 teaspoon dried rosemary
salt

Cut the cauliflower into florets, the peeled onions into quarters or eighths depending on size, the leeks and fennel into slices.

Place all the vegetables in a saucepan with the white wine, vinegar, spices, rosemary and salt. Add enough water to cover, bring to the boil and simmer gently for 15 to 20 minutes. The vegetables should be slightly crisp.
SERVES 4

GLOBE ARTICHOKES WITH MUSHROOM AND TOMATO STUFFING

METRIC/IMPERIAL
100 g/4 oz long-grain rice
100 g/4 oz onions, peeled and sliced
1 vegetable stock cube, crumbled
225 g/8 oz tomatoes, skinned and quartered
100 g/4 oz mushrooms, wiped and trimmed
100 g/4 oz ham, chopped
1 teaspoon chopped parsley
1 teaspoon chopped thyme
salt
freshly ground black pepper
4 globe artichokes, cooked

Place the rice in a saucepan of boiling water with the sliced onion and stock cube added. Cook for about 12 minutes until just tender.

Add the tomatoes and mushrooms and cook for a further 5 minutes. Drain. Stir in the ham, herbs and salt and pepper to taste.

Remove the chokes from the artichokes and push back the leaves to make room for the stuffing. If necessary, remove a few of the inner leaves.

Spoon the mushroom and tomato mixture into the centre of the artichokes.
SERVES 4

CUCUMBER WITH FRESH PEAS AND MINT

METRIC/IMPERIAL
1 cucumber
100 g/4 oz shelled fresh or frozen peas
1 teaspoon lemon juice
1 teaspoon chopped mint
1 teaspoon sugar
25 g/1 oz polyunsaturated margarine
salt
freshly ground black pepper
mint sprigs, to garnish

Rinse the cucumber and cut it into matchsticks. Cut a piece of foil large enough to seal the vegetables. Mix all ingredients together lightly. Pile on to the foil, season well with salt and pepper. Seal completely and cook in a steamer over boiling water for 8 minutes.

Remove from the foil and garnish with sprigs of mint. Serve at once.
SERVES 4

CHINESE STIR-FRIED VEGETABLES

METRIC/IMPERIAL
1 tablespoon polyunsaturated vegetable oil
50 g/2 oz lean bacon, derinded and chopped
1 large onion, peeled and chopped
1 clove garlic, peeled and crushed
1 tablespoon peeled and grated fresh root ginger
50 g/2 oz mushrooms, wiped and sliced
450 g/1 lb mangetout, topped and tailed
450 g/1 lb Chinese or other cabbage, shredded
100 g/4 oz bean-sprouts
50 g/2 oz whole peanuts, shelled
1 tablespoon soy sauce
5 tablespoons stock or water
salt
freshly ground black pepper

Heat the oil in a wok or large frying pan. Add the bacon, onion, garlic, ginger and mushrooms and fry briskly for 3 minutes, stirring constantly.

Add the peas and cabbage and fry for a further 2 minutes, stirring constantly.

Add the remaining ingredients and stir-fry over moderate heat for about 5 minutes until the vegetables are tender but still crisp, and most of the liquid has evaporated. Taste and adjust the seasoning and serve immediately.
SERVES 4

A TRIO OF COULIS

METRIC/IMPERIAL
Carrot coulis:
225 g/8 oz carrots, peeled and finely sliced
150 ml/¼ pint orange juice
50 g/2 oz Quark
salt
freshly ground black pepper
pinch of ground coriander
1 teaspoon lemon juice
Brussels sprout coulis:
225 g/8 oz Brussels sprouts, trimmed and sliced
150 ml/¼ pint vegetable or chicken stock
50 g/2 oz Quark
1 teaspoon lemon juice
½ teaspoon chopped mint
salt
freshly ground black pepper
Parsnip coulis:
225 g/8 oz parsnips, peeled and finely sliced
150 ml/¼ pint vegetable or chicken stock
50 g/2 oz Quark
1 teaspoon lemon juice
salt
freshly ground black pepper
pinch of freshly grated nutmeg

Cook the carrots in a steamer over the orange juice for 10 minutes. Blend with the juice in a blender, stir in the Quark and season with salt, pepper, coriander and lemon juice. Taste and adjust the seasoning, if necessary. Cover and keep warm to one side.

Cook the Brussels sprouts in a steamer over the stock for 10 minutes. Blend with the stock in a blender, and stir in the Quark, lemon juice and mint. Season with salt and pepper. Taste and adjust the seasoning, if necessary. Cover and keep warm, to one side.

Cook the parsnips in a steamer over the stock for 10 minutes. Blend with the stock in a blender, and stir in the Quark and lemon juice. Season well with salt, pepper and nutmeg. Cover and keep warm to one side.

To serve, spoon the Brussels sprout and parsnip coulis next to each other on each warmed plate. Garnish with the carrot coulis to your own design for a pretty effect.
SERVES 4

POTATO PATTIES

METRIC/IMPERIAL
450 g/1 lb cooked potato, mashed
100 g/4 oz cheese, grated
1 egg, beaten
1 tablespoon skimmed milk
25 g/1 oz finely chopped onion
salt
freshly ground black pepper
polyunsaturated vegetable oil for frying

Mix the mashed potato and grated cheese together.
Beat the egg with the skimmed milk and slowly add to the potato mixture, making sure it does not become too moist. Add the chopped onion and salt and pepper to taste. Shape into 8 little cakes.
Spray a frying pan with a little oil and fry the cakes on both sides until brown. Alternatively, place under a preheated hot grill until browned on both sides, spraying with a little oil if necessary.
SERVES 4

CHEESE-STUFFED BAKED POTATOES

METRIC/IMPERIAL
1 large potato per person
freshly chopped parsley, to garnish
Blue cheese filling:
50 g/2 oz Danish blue cheese, crumbled
4 teaspoons plain low-fat yogurt
salt
freshly ground black pepper
Cottage cheese filling:
50 g/2 oz cottage cheese
2 teaspoons tomato purée
salt
freshly ground black pepper
Camembert filling:
50 g/2 oz Camembert cheese, derinded
50 g/2 oz cottage cheese
salt
freshly ground black pepper

Choose even-sized potatoes, if you are cooking more than one.
Scrub and dry the potatoes, then prick all over with a fork. Place on a baking sheet and bake in a preheated moderately hot oven (200°C/400°F, Gas Mark 6) for 1 to 1¼ hours until tender when pierced with a knife. Serve with any one of the following fillings.

To make the blue cheese filling: combine the cheese with the yogurt and season with salt and pepper to taste. Cut a cross in the top of each potato and spoon on the cheese and yogurt mixture. Return to the oven for 2 minutes to heat through.
To make the cottage cheese filling: mix the cottage cheese and tomato purée and season with salt and pepper to taste. Cut the potato in half, scoop out the flesh and combine with the cheese mixture. Spoon back into the potato shells and return to the oven for 2 minutes to heat through.
To make the Camembert filling: mash the Camembert with the cottage cheese and season with salt and pepper to taste. Cut the potato in half, scoop out the flesh and combine with the cheese mixture. Spoon back into the potato shells. Place under a heated grill for 2 minutes to heat through.
Garnish with chopped parsley and serve at once as a light lunch or supper dish with a green salad or mixed vegetables.
Each filling serves 1

POTATO AND AVOCADO PURÉE

METRIC/IMPERIAL
450 g/1 lb potatoes, peeled and cut in chunks
mint sprig
piece of blade mace
1 ripe avocado, halved, stoned and peeled
finely grated rind of ½ lemon
salt
freshly ground black pepper

Put the potatoes into a pan with the mint and blade of mace; add cold water to cover and bring to the boil. Lower the heat and simmer gently until the potatoes are just tender. Drain thoroughly, discarding the mint and mace.
Put the cooked potatoes into a blender or food processor. Add the avocado flesh, lemon rind and salt and pepper to taste; blend until smooth.
Heat the purée through gently in either a heavy-bottomed pan or a double boiler.
SERVES 4

POTATO CAKE

METRIC/IMPERIAL
450 g/1 lb potatoes, grated
1 onion, peeled and chopped
2 tablespoons chopped parsley
1 egg, beaten
salt
freshly ground black pepper
2 tablespoons olive oil

Place the potatoes in a bowl with the onion, parsley, egg and salt and pepper to taste. Mix thoroughly.

Heat the oil in a 20 to 23 cm/8 to 9 inch heavy frying pan. Add the potato mixture and pat lightly into a cake. Fry gently for 5 to 7 minutes until the underside is crisp and brown.

Slide on to a plate then invert back into the pan and fry the other side for 5 to 7 minutes until crisp and brown. Cut into wedges and serve immediately while still hot.
SERVES 4

POTATO AND LEEK LAYER

METRIC/IMPERIAL
450 g/1 lb potatoes, peeled and thinly sliced
225 g/8 oz leeks, trimmed and thinly sliced
¼ teaspoon grated nutmeg
salt
freshly ground black pepper
300 ml/½ pint skimmed milk

Heat the oven to moderately hot (190°C/375°F, Gas Mark 5).

Arrange the potatoes and leeks in layers in a 1.2 litre/2 pint casserole. Sprinkle the layers with nutmeg, salt and pepper and finish with a layer of potatoes with a few leeks in the centre. Pour over the milk, cover and bake for 1 hour.

Uncover and cook for a further 30 minutes until the potatoes are browned and tender, and most of the milk has been absorbed. Serve hot.
SERVES 4

BAKED POTATO AND ONION LAYER

METRIC/IMPERIAL
4 medium potatoes, peeled and finely sliced
4 medium onions, peeled and finely sliced
salt
freshly ground black pepper
1 clove garlic, peeled and crushed
1-2 teaspoons chopped fresh sage or
½-1 teaspoon dried sage
about 175 ml/6 fl oz skimmed milk

Arrange the potato and onion slices in alternate layers in a shallow ovenproof dish, sprinkling salt, pepper, garlic and sage between each layer.

Pour over the skimmed milk – it should come about two-thirds of the way up the sides. Cover and bake in a preheated moderately hot oven (200°C/400°F, Gas Mark 6) for about 50 minutes or until the potatoes are cooked.

Uncover to allow the top to brown, then cook for a further 10 minutes. If the dish becomes too dry during cooking add a little more milk, but the finished dish should have absorbed all the milk.
SERVES 4

BACON-STUFFED POTATOES

METRIC/IMPERIAL
4 large potatoes, well scrubbed
25 g/1 oz polyunsaturated margarine
75 g/3 oz bacon, derinded, chopped and grilled
2 tablespoons skimmed milk
25 g/1 oz walnuts, chopped
50 g/2 oz Cheddar cheese, grated
1 tablespoon chopped parsley
salt
freshly ground black pepper
parsley sprigs, to garnish

Prick the potatoes with a fork and bake in a preheated moderately hot oven (200°C/400°F, Gas Mark 6) for 1 to 1½ hours.

When cooked, cut off the tops of the potatoes lengthwise and scoop out the centres, taking care to keep the skins intact. Mash the potato in a bowl, and add the margarine, bacon, milk, nuts, cheese, parsley, salt and pepper. Fill the potato shells with the mixture and bake in a preheated moderately hot oven (190°C/375°F, Gas Mark 5) for 15 minutes. Garnish with sprigs of parsley.
SERVES 4

CABBAGE BRAISED WITH APPLE AND YOGURT

METRIC/IMPERIAL
450 g/1 lb cabbage, shredded
1 onion, peeled and grated
1 cooking apple, peeled, cored and grated
salt
freshly ground white pepper
150 ml/¼ pint plain low-fat yogurt
pinch of grated nutmeg

Put half the cabbage in a baking dish. Sprinkle with half the onion and apple and salt and pepper to taste. Spoon over half the yogurt.

Add the remaining cabbage, then top with the remaining apple and onion and sprinkle with salt and pepper to taste. Spoon over the remaining yogurt and sprinkle with the nutmeg.

Bake in a preheated moderately hot oven (190°C/375°F, Gas Mark 5) for about 20 minutes or until the cabbage is just tender. Serve hot.
SERVES 4

STUFFED CABBAGE LEAVES

METRIC/IMPERIAL
8 large cabbage leaves
salt
1 tablespoon polyunsaturated vegetable oil
1 onion, peeled and chopped
1 cooking apple, peeled, cored and chopped
1 clove garlic, peeled and crushed
225 g/8 oz minced lean pork or veal
50 g/2 oz fresh wholemeal breadcrumbs
finely grated rind and juice of ½ lemon
1 tablespoon chopped sage
1 tablespoon chopped parsley
freshly ground black pepper
4 tomatoes, cut into wedges

Blanch the cabbage leaves in boiling salted water for 2 minutes or until soft enough to roll up. Drain thoroughly and set aside.

Heat the oil in a pan. Add the onion, apple and garlic and fry gently for 5 minutes, stirring occasionally. Add the pork or veal and fry for a further 5 minutes, stirring constantly to break up the meat. Remove from the heat and stir in the breadcrumbs, lemon rind and juice, herbs and salt and pepper to taste.

Divide the stuffing mixture equally between the cabbage leaves, then roll up, from the stalk end, folding in the edges to enclose the stuffing completely.

Put the stuffed cabbage in a shallow baking dish and surround with the tomato wedges.

Cover and bake in a preheated moderate oven (180°C/350°F, Gas Mark 4) for 20 to 30 minutes until the cabbage is tender. Serve hot.
SERVES 4

BAKED WHITE CABBAGE AND APPLES

METRIC/IMPERIAL
1 small white cabbage, finely shredded
3 large Granny Smith apples, peeled and grated
150 ml/¼ pint grapefruit juice
150 ml/¼ pint plain low-fat yogurt
salt
freshly ground black pepper

Place the cabbage and apple in layers in a baking dish. Pour over the grapefruit juice, cover and place in a preheated moderately hot oven (200°C/400°F, Gas Mark 6) for about 30 minutes.

Season the yogurt with salt and pepper. Uncover the baking dish, pour in the yogurt and stir well. Reduce the oven temperature to moderate (180°C/350°F, Gas Mark 4) and continue cooking for 10 to 15 minutes.
SERVES 4 to 6

DANISH RED CABBAGE

METRIC/IMPERIAL
1 tablespoon polyunsaturated vegetable oil
1 medium red cabbage, trimmed and finely shredded
1 large onion, peeled and finely sliced
1 large cooking apple, skinned, cored and sliced
1 tablespoon caraway seeds
2 tablespoons wine vinegar
salt
freshly ground black pepper
2 tablespoons vegetable stock
chopped parsley, to garnish

Heat the oil in a large pan. Add the cabbage, onion, apple, caraway seeds, vinegar, salt, pepper and stock. Stir well and cover with a lid.

Allow to cook gently for 40 to 45 minutes, stirring or shaking from time to time. Garnish decoratively with parsley.
SERVES 4

SPICED RED CABBAGE

METRIC/IMPERIAL
1 red cabbage, trimmed and sliced
1 large cooking apple, peeled, cored and thickly sliced
1 onion, peeled and sliced
300 ml/½ pint wine vinegar
1 teaspoon mixed spice

Place the cabbage in a flameproof casserole and arrange the apple and onion slices on top.
Add the vinegar and sprinkle over the mixed spice. Add just enough water to cover the cabbage completely.
Bring to the boil, cover and simmer for about 30 minutes. Serve hot.
SERVES 4

CHINESE CABBAGE AND MUSHROOMS

METRIC/IMPERIAL
8 dried Chinese mushrooms
450 g/1 lb Chinese cabbage leaves
1 tablespoon polyunsaturated vegetable oil
1 × 2.5 cm/1 inch piece root ginger, shredded
1 clove garlic, peeled and sliced
3 chillies, deseeded and sliced
1 green pepper, cored, deseeded and sliced
1 tablespoon wine vinegar
1 tablespoon light soy sauce
1 teaspoon sesame seed oil

Soak the mushrooms in warm water for 15 minutes. Squeeze dry and remove the hard stalks. Tear the cabbage leaves into pieces.
Heat the oil in a wok or deep frying pan, add the ginger, garlic and chillies and stir-fry for 1 minute. Stir in the green pepper, mushroom caps and cabbage and cook for 1 minute. Add the vinegar and soy sauce and mix well.
Pile into a warmed serving dish and sprinkle over the sesame seed oil. Serve immediately.
SERVES 4 to 6

LEEKS AU GRATIN

METRIC/IMPERIAL
8 medium leeks, trimmed
salt
25 g/1 oz polyunsaturated margarine
25 g/1 oz plain wholemeal flour
150 ml/¼ pint skimmed milk
pinch of grated nutmeg
175 g/6 oz cheese, grated
freshly ground black pepper
50 g/2 oz fresh breadcrumbs

Remove most of the top green leaves from the leeks. Wash thoroughly under running water, then drain. Place the leeks in a saucepan of boiling salted water and cook for 15 to 20 minutes until tender, depending on thickness.
Drain, reserving the cooking liquid, and put the leeks into a flameproof serving dish. Keep hot.
Melt the margarine in a saucepan and stir in the flour. Cook for 2 minutes, stirring. Gradually add the milk and enough leek cooking liquid to make a medium thick sauce. Add the nutmeg and 100 g/4 oz of the cheese and stir until melted. Add salt and pepper to taste. Pour the cheese sauce over the leeks in the dish.
Mix the remaining cheese with the breadcrumbs and sprinkle over the top. Place under a preheated hot grill for a few minutes until the top is golden brown.
SERVES 4

LEEKS NIÇOISE

METRIC/IMPERIAL
6 leeks, trimmed and cleaned
1 × 200 g/7 oz can tomatoes, chopped
1 teaspoon chopped basil
1 clove garlic, peeled and crushed
salt
freshly ground black pepper
chopped parsley, to garnish

Put the leeks in a deep pan. Add the tomatoes with their juice, the chopped basil and the garlic. Season to taste with salt and pepper. Bring to the boil, lower the heat and cover. Simmer for about 20 minutes, or until the leeks are tender, stirring occasionally.
Sprinkle over the chopped parsley and serve immediately while hot.
SERVES 4

BROCCOLI AU GRATIN

METRIC/IMPERIAL
1 medium onion, peeled and sliced
1 green pepper, cored, deseeded and sliced
1 kg/2 lb broccoli
2 tablespoons cornflour
600 ml/1 pint skimmed milk
100 g/4 oz Cheddar cheese, grated
pinch of grated nutmeg
salt
freshly ground black pepper

Place the onion, pepper and broccoli in a saucepan of boiling water. Cover and cook for about 15 minutes until tender.
Mix the cornflour with the skimmed milk. Pour into a saucepan and heat gently, stirring. Add 50 g/2 oz of the cheese and, when thickened, add the nutmeg and salt and pepper to taste.
Transfer the drained broccoli and pepper mixture to a heated gratin dish and pour over the sauce. Sprinkle with the remaining cheese and place under a hot grill until the cheese melts.
SERVES 6

BROCCOLI CASSEROLE

METRIC/IMPERIAL
750 ml/1¼ pints vegetable stock
450 g/1 lb broccoli, divided into florets
pinch of grated nutmeg
1 tablespoon chopped herbs (chives, parsley or thyme)
3 eggs
1 tablespoon skimmed milk
1 tablespoon grated Parmesan cheese

Grease an ovenproof casserole. Preheat the oven to moderately hot (200°C/400°F, Gas Mark 6).
Bring the stock to the boil in a large pan, add the broccoli and nutmeg. Bring back to the boil, lower the heat, cover and cook gently for 10 minutes. Drain and place in the dish. Sprinkle with the chopped herbs.
Beat the eggs with the milk and Parmesan cheese and pour over the cauliflower. Place the casserole in the oven and cook for about 20 minutes or until the egg custard has set.
SERVES 4

BROCCOLI AND ALMONDS

METRIC/IMPERIAL
450 g/1 lb broccoli spears
salt
2 tablespoons olive oil
1 onion, peeled and sliced
1 clove garlic, peeled and crushed
50 g/2 oz blanched almonds
5 tomatoes, skinned and chopped
freshly ground black pepper
1 tablespoon chopped parsley

Cook the broccoli spears in boiling salted water for about 15 minutes until just tender.
Heat the oil in a pan and sauté the onion, garlic and almonds until the onion is soft and the almonds are beginning to brown. Stir in the tomatoes and heat through. Season with salt and pepper to taste.
Drain the broccoli and place in a heated serving dish. Spoon the sauce over the broccoli and sprinkle with chopped parsley. Serve hot.
SERVES 4

Variation
This recipe may also be prepared using young French breans in place of the broccoli. Top and tail the beans and cook in boiling salted water until just tender but still firm to the bite. Continue as described above.

CALABRESE LYONNAISE

METRIC/IMPERIAL
150 ml/¼ pint chicken stock
1 clove garlic, peeled and crushed
1 large onion, peeled and finely chopped
salt
450 g/1 lb calabrese, sliced

Pour the stock into a large saucepan and add the garlic, onion and salt to taste. Bring to the boil. Add the calabrese, reduce the heat, cover and simmer for 10 to 15 minutes, until tender.
Transfer the calabrese to a heated serving dish with a slotted spoon.
Boil the cooking liquid rapidly to reduce to about half its volume. Adjust the seasoning, if necessary, and pour over the calabrese to serve.
SERVES 4

FRENCH-STYLE MANGETOUT

METRIC/IMPERIAL

15 g/½ oz polyunsaturated margarine
1 bunch (about 8) spring onions, trimmed and
cut into 5 cm/2 inch lengths
500 g/1¼ lb mangetout, topped and tailed
300 ml/½ pint vegetable stock
1 bouquet garni
salt
1 tablespoon cornflour
2 tablespoons water
1 firm lettuce, trimmed and cut into 8 wedges
4 tablespoons low-fat soft cheese
1 tablespoon green peppercorns, drained

Melt the margarine in a pan, add the spring onions
and cook for 2 minutes without browning. Add
the mangetout, stock and bouquet garni. Season
with salt, bring to the boil, then lower the heat
and simmer for 10 to 12 minutes until the vegetables are just tender.

Discard the bouquet garni. Blend the cornflour
with the water and stir into the vegetables. Bring
to the boil, stirring constantly. Lower the heat and
simmer for 2 minutes, then add the lettuce and
soft cheese. Heat through gently for 1 to 2
minutes, then add the peppercorns. Taste and
adjust seasoning. Serve at once.
SERVES 4

BRUSSELS SPROUTS WITH CARAWAY SEEDS

METRIC/IMPERIAL

750 g/1½ lb Brussels sprouts
chicken stock
15 g/½ oz polyunsaturated margarine
½ teaspoon salt
freshly ground black pepper
2 teaspoons caraway seeds

Wash the Brussels sprouts, trim off the tough
outer leaves and cut a small cross in the bottom of
each. Pour chicken stock to a depth of 2.5 cm/
1 inch in a saucepan. Bring the stock to the boil
and add the sprouts.

Return to the boil and simmer, uncovered, for 5
minutes. Cover and cook for 6 to 10 minutes
longer, or until just tender. Drain, if necessary.
Add the remaining ingredients, toss lightly and
serve at once.
SERVES 6

BRUSSELS SPROUTS WITH CHESTNUTS

METRIC/IMPERIAL

1 kg/2 lb Brussels sprouts, trimmed
225 g/8 oz chestnuts
salt
2 teaspoons polyunsaturated vegetable oil
grated rind and juice of ½ lemon

Cut a small cross in the base of each Brussels
sprout stalk so they cook evenly.

Snip the tops of the chestnuts with a pair of scissors. Put them into a saucepan, cover with cold
water and bring to the boil. Boil for 3 minutes,
then remove the chestnuts one at a time. Allow
to cool a little and peel off both the outer and inner
skins.

Cook the sprouts in boiling, salted water for
15 minutes, adding the peeled chestnuts for the
last 5 minutes of cooking time. Drain well. Heat
the oil in the same pan. Add the lemon rind and
juice, return the sprouts and chestnuts to the pan
and toss well in the oil before serving.
SERVES 6

SPICED CAULIFLOWER

METRIC/IMPERIAL

2 tablespoons polyunsaturated vegetable oil
1 teaspoon ground ginger
2 teaspoons ground coriander
1 teaspoon ground turmeric
1 cauliflower, broken into florets
2 carrots, peeled and thinly sliced
1 onion, peeled and sliced
2 celery stalks, sliced
120 ml/4 fl oz stock
salt
freshly ground black pepper
150 ml/¼ pint plain low-fat yogurt
Garnish:
2 teaspoons chopped coriander
2 teaspoons chopped parsley

Heat the oil in a pan, add the spices and fry gently
for 1 minute. Add the vegetables and cook gently
for a further 3 minutes, stirring occasionally. Add
the stock, and salt and pepper to taste.

Cover and simmer for 10 minutes until the
vegetables are just tender. Stir in the yogurt,
sprinkle with the coriander and parsley, and serve
immediately while hot.
SERVES 4

MEXICAN-STYLE CAULIFLOWER

METRIC/IMPERIAL
1 medium cauliflower
3 tomatoes, skinned, deseeded and chopped
2 tablespoons chopped parsley
pinch of dried cloves
¼ teaspoon ground cinnamon
1 tablespoon capers
2 tablespoons chopped olives
3 tablespoons grated cheese
2 tablespoons fine breadcrumbs
1 tablespoon olive oil

Trim the cauliflower and divide into florets. Cook the florets, covered, in a small amount of boiling salted water until just tender. Drain.

Mix the tomatoes, parsley, cloves, cinnamon, capers and olives and heat gently to make a sauce. Pour a little of the sauce into an ovenproof serving dish, add the cauliflower and cover with the remaining sauce.

Sprinkle with the cheese, breadcrumbs and oil and bake until brown in a preheated hot oven (220°C/425°F, Gas Mark 7) for about 20 minutes.
SERVES 6

CAULIFLOWER WITH TARRAGON TOMATO SAUCE

METRIC/IMPERIAL
1 tablespoon olive oil
2 shallots, peeled and finely chopped
2 cloves garlic, peeled and crushed
2 × 400 g/14 oz cans chopped tomatoes in natural juice
15 g/½ oz fructose
2 tablespoons tarragon vinegar
1 tablespoon chopped tarragon
salt
freshly ground black pepper
1 large cauliflower
chopped tarragon, to garnish

Heat the oil in a pan, fry the shallot and garlic for 2 minutes. Stir in the tomatoes, fructose, vinegar and tarragon. Season with salt and black pepper. Bring to the boil and simmer for 2 minutes.

Wash the cauliflower and cut into quarters. Place in a suitable bowl, and season with salt and pepper. Pour over the sauce. Cover with foil or greaseproof paper and tie down. Place in a

steamer or covered saucepan half-filled with boiling water and steam for 25 minutes. Check the liquid level frequently and add more boiling water if necessary.

Remove the greaseproof paper or foil, transfer to a serving dish (if wished), and serve sprinkled with chopped fresh tarragon.
SERVES 4 to 6

GINGERED CARROTS

METRIC/IMPERIAL
450 g/1 lb carrots, peeled and thinly sliced
about 300 ml/½ pint orange juice
about 300 ml/½ pint chicken stock
1 teaspoon ground ginger
½ teaspoon ground mace
salt
freshly ground black pepper

Place the carrots in a saucepan and cover with the orange juice and stock. Add the spices and salt and pepper, bring to the boil and simmer gently for about 20 minutes until tender.

Drain off any excess liquid, then turn into a heated serving dish.
SERVES 4

SPICED CARROT AND YOGURT PURÉE

METRIC/IMPERIAL
750 g/1½ lb carrots, scraped and sliced
salt
250 ml/8 fl oz plain low-fat yogurt
pinch of mace
freshly ground black pepper

Place the carrots in a saucepan of boiling salted water and simmer for about 15 minutes until they are tender.

Drain, reserving the cooking liquid. Blend the carrots to a purée in a liquidizer with the yogurt, or rub through a sieve. Add a little carrot cooking liquid, if necessary.

Return the mixture to the rinsed-out pan and stir in the mace and salt and pepper to taste. Reheat carefully and serve.
SERVES 6

CARROT SOUFFLÉ

METRIC/IMPERIAL
450 g/1 lb carrots, peeled and chopped
1 onion, peeled and chopped
450 ml/¾ pint water
salt
freshly ground white pepper
25 g/1 oz polyunsaturated margarine
1 tablespoon flour
150 ml/¼ pint skimmed milk
100 g/4 oz lean cooked ham, diced
4 eggs, separated

Put the carrots in a pan with the onion, water and salt. Bring to the boil, then lower the heat, cover and simmer for about 20 minutes or until the carrots are soft. Drain, then mash or work to a purée in a blender. Add salt and pepper to taste.

Melt the margarine in a pan. Add the flour and cook for 1 to 2 minutes, stirring constantly. Remove from the heat, and gradually stir in the milk, beating well after each addition. Return to the heat and simmer until the sauce is thick and smooth, stirring constantly.

Stir the sauce into the carrot purée with the ham. Beat in the egg yolks. Beat the egg whites until stiff, then fold gently into the carrot mixture. Pour into a well-greased 1.5 litre/2½ pint soufflé dish.

Bake at once in a preheated moderate oven (180°C/350°F, Gas Mark 4) for 45 minutes until well risen and set. Serve immediately.
SERVES 4

BAKED ONIONS

METRIC/IMPERIAL
4 large onions, peeled and halved
75 g/3 oz wholemeal breadcrumbs
4 dessertspoons crunchy peanut butter

Scoop out the centres of the onions and chop finely. Mix with the breadcrumbs and then combine with the peanut butter.

Spoon the mixture into the onion cavities. Reform the onions and wrap in foil. Cook in a preheated moderately hot oven (200°C/400°F, Gas Mark 6) for about 1 hour until tender.
SERVES 4

STUFFED PEPPERS WITH BROWN RICE

METRIC/IMPERIAL
175 g/6 oz brown rice
300 ml/½ pint water
salt
4 tomatoes, skinned and chopped
1 onion, peeled and grated
50 g/2 oz pine nuts
25 g/1 oz seedless raisins
100 g/4 oz Cheddar cheese, grated
2 tablespoons chopped parsley
pinch of ground cinnamon
freshly ground black pepper
4 green peppers, cored and deseeded, tops reserved
5 tablespoons stock or water

Cook the rice in the boiling salted water for 30 minutes or until the rice is tender and all the water has been absorbed. Remove from the heat and gently fold in all of the tomatoes, onion, pine nuts and raisins.

Fold in most of the cheese, reserving a little for the topping, then fold in the parsley, cinnamon and salt and pepper to taste.

Stand the peppers upright in a baking dish, cutting a small slice off the bottoms if necessary. Divide the filling equally between the peppers, sprinkle the top with the reserved cheese and then replace the lids.

Pour the stock or water into the dish and cover with foil. Bake in a preheated moderately hot oven (190°C/375°F, Gas Mark 5) for 30 to 40 minutes until the peppers are tender. Serve hot or cold according to taste.
SERVES 4

PEPPER POTS

METRIC/IMPERIAL
4 yellow, green or red peppers
salt
freshly ground black pepper
1 tablespoon olive oil
50 g/2 oz smoked bacon, derinded and diced
4 spring onions, trimmed and sliced
175 g/6 oz shelled broad beans
100 g/4 oz broccoli florets, roughly chopped
100 g/4 oz cottage cheese
7 g/¼ oz fresh horseradish, grated (use ½ tablespoon horseradish sauce if necessary)
1 tablespoon chopped parsley

Slice the tops off the peppers, deseed, and rinse under cold water. Season the insides of the peppers with salt and pepper. Heat the oil in a pan. Gently fry the bacon and spring onions for 3 minutes. Stir in the beans and broccoli and cook for 2 minutes. Stir in the cottage cheese, horseradish and parsley. Season with salt and pepper.

Spoon the mixture into the pepper shells and place in a steamer. Cover with a tight-fitting lid and steam over boiling water for 10 minutes.

Serve the pepper pots whole on warmed plates or slice open to show the creamy filling.
SERVES 4

STUFFED PEPPERS WITH APPLE AND WALNUTS

METRIC/IMPERIAL
4 even-sized peppers
175 g/6 oz lean bacon, derinded and chopped
1 onion, peeled and chopped
100 g/4 oz wholemeal breadcrumbs
1 medium cooking apple, peeled, cored and chopped
25 g/1 oz walnuts, chopped
1 teaspoon mixed dried herbs
salt
freshly ground black pepper
1 egg, beaten
1 tablespoon polyunsaturated vegetable oil
2-3 tablespoons water

Cut off the stalk end of each pepper and reserve. Carefully remove the core and all the seeds without breaking the sides. Stand the peppers in a deep dish. Cover with boiling water and leave for 5 minutes while preparing the filling.

Fry the bacon over a medium heat and as soon as the fat starts to run, add the onion and cook until softened. Remove the pan from the heat and stir in the breadcrumbs, apple, walnuts, herbs, salt and pepper. Mix in enough of the beaten egg to make a firm, moist mixture.

Drain the peppers well and stand them in a deep, well-greased dish. Spoon in the filling, replace the reserved stalk ends and brush with the oil. Add the water to the dish, cover with foil or a lid and cook in a preheated moderately hot oven (190°C/375°F, Gas Mark 5) for about 35 minutes or until the peppers are tender.
SERVES 4

SPINACH FRIED WITH GARLIC

METRIC/IMPERIAL
2 tablespoons polyunsaturated vegetable oil
1 large onion, peeled and chopped
1 large clove garlic, peeled and crushed
100 g/4 oz lean bacon, derinded and chopped (optional)
450 g/1 lb spinach leaves
1 tablespoon lemon juice
salt
freshly ground black pepper

Heat the oil in a large pan. Add the onion, garlic and bacon (if using), and fry gently for 5 minutes, stirring frequently.

Wash the spinach thoroughly, then add to the pan with only the water clinging to the leaves. Add the lemon juice and salt and pepper to taste. Fry gently for 3 to 5 minutes until the spinach is just tender but still bright green, stirring constantly. Check the seasoning and serve at once.
SERVES 4

TOMATOES WITH YOGURT AND BASIL

METRIC/IMPERIAL
450 g/1 lb tomatoes, skinned and coarsely chopped
15 g/½ oz polyunsaturated margarine
salt
freshly ground black pepper
300 ml/½ pint plain low-fat yogurt, at room temperature
2 tablespoons chopped basil
25 g/1 oz pine kernels

Drain away any excess juice from the tomatoes by leaving them on a sloping board for 10 minutes.

Melt the margarine in a shallow pan and cook the tomatoes gently for a few minutes, until just softened without becoming mushy. Remove the pan from the heat. Add salt and pepper to taste.

Beat the yogurt until smooth, and stir into the tomatoes. Stir in the chopped basil, pour into a shallow serving dish and scatter the pine kernels over the top.

Serve immediately, or keep warm for a little, but do not attempt to reheat after you have added the yogurt. This is a dish that should be served warm rather than hot.
SERVES 4

177

BAKED STUFFED TOMATOES

METRIC/IMPERIAL
4 large tomatoes
1 small onion, peeled and grated
1 tablespoon chopped parsley
175 g/6 oz low-fat soft cheese
100 g/4 oz lean cooked ham, chopped
salt
freshly ground black pepper
2 tablespoons water

Cut the tops off the tomatoes and reserve for lids. Scoop out the insides of the tomatoes, then work the pulp through a sieve to remove the pips. Put the tomato pulp in a bowl. Add the onion, parsley, soft cheese and ham and mix well. Add salt and pepper to taste.

Spoon the mixture into the hollowed-out tomatoes and place the lids on top. Stand the tomatoes in a baking dish then pour in the water. Bake in a preheated hot oven (220°C/425°F, Gas Mark 7) for 15 minutes. Serve hot or cold.
SERVES 4

CHICORY IN MUSTARD SAUCE

METRIC/IMPERIAL
salt
150 ml/¼ pint water
juice of 1 lemon
4 heads of chicory, trimmed
1 tablespoon polyunsaturated vegetable oil
scant 1 tablespoon plain wholemeal flour
150 ml/¼ pint vegetable stock
scant 2 tablespoons made mild mustard
1 tablespoon chopped dill

Salt the water, add the lemon juice and bring to the boil. Add the chicory heads, lower the heat and cook for about 10 minutes. Drain, reserving the cooking liquid.

Heat the oil in a small pan, stir in the flour and cook until golden. Gradually add the reserved cooking liquid and the stock, stirring constantly. Add the mustard and bring to the boil, stirring constantly. Add the par-cooked chicory and cook for a further 10 minutes over a very low heat until just tender.

Transfer to a warmed serving dish and sprinkle with the chopped dill. Serve immediately.
SERVES 4

CHICORY WITH FRESH PARMESAN

METRIC/IMPERIAL
4 heads of chicory, cut in half lengthwise
1 teaspoon lemon juice
15 g/½ oz polyunsaturated margarine
2 onions, peeled and finely sliced
1 large clove garlic, peeled and crushed
4 tomatoes, skinned and deseeded
salt
freshly ground black pepper
100 g/4 oz spinach, stalks discarded
50 g/2 oz Parmesan cheese, freshly grated

Remove the core from each piece of chicory. Brush with 1 teaspoon of lemon juice. Heat the margarine in a pan and fry the onion, garlic and tomatoes for 3 minutes. Season well with salt and pepper to taste.

Lay a piece of wet greaseproof paper in a steamer; arrange the spinach in an even layer on the top. Top with chicory and spoon on the tomato and onion. Cover with a tight-fitting lid and steam for 8 minutes.

Transfer to a warmed serving dish, sprinkle with Parmesan and serve at once.
SERVES 4

MUSHROOM TERRINE

METRIC/IMPERIAL
350 g/12 oz mushrooms, wiped and chopped
175 g/6 oz minced lean ham
350 g/12 oz minced lean pork
75 g/3 oz minced onion
40 g/1½ oz wholemeal breadcrumbs
2 tomatoes, skinned and chopped
1 tablespoon chopped parsley
1 teaspoon chopped thyme
1 large egg
salt
freshly ground black pepper

Place all the ingredients in a bowl and mix together thoroughly.

Turn into an earthenware terrine, cover with foil, and bake in a moderately hot oven (190°C/375°F, Gas Mark 5) for 1 to 1½ hours. Serve with crusty wholemeal bread.
SERVES 8

BRAZIL MUSHROOM CASSEROLE

METRIC/IMPERIAL
450 g/1 lb button mushrooms
4 tomatoes, sliced
4 spring onions, trimmed and chopped
1 tablespoon chopped oregano or marjoram
1 tablespoon chopped basil
1 teaspoon rosemary leaves
salt
freshly ground black pepper
4 tablespoons dry white wine or stock
100 g/4 oz Brazil nuts, coarsely ground
50 g/2 oz fresh wholemeal breadcrumbs

Wipe the mushrooms and cut the larger ones into halves or quarters, leaving the small ones whole. Arrange the mushroom, tomatoes and spring onions in layers in a casserole dish, sprinkling each layer with the herbs and salt and pepper to taste. Pour on the wine or stock.

Mix the nuts and breadcrumbs together and sprinkle over the top of the casserole. Bake in a preheated moderately hot oven (190°C/375°F, Gas Mark 5) for 20 to 30 minutes until the mushrooms are tender and the topping is browned. Serve hot.
SERVES 4

STUFFED MUSHROOMS

METRIC/IMPERIAL
3-4 tablespoons olive oil
8 flat mushrooms (about 6 cm/2½ inch diameter), trimmed and stalks cut level with caps
350 g/12 oz tomatoes, skinned and finely chopped
1 clove garlic, peeled and crushed
1 bunch spring onions, trimmed and thinly sliced
3 tablespoons snipped chives
salt
freshly ground black pepper
1½ teaspoons lemon juice

Preheat the oven to moderate (180°C/350°, Gas Mark 4). Oil a baking sheet and lay the mushrooms on it, stalk side uppermost. Brush a little olive oil over each one and bake in the oven for 20 minutes. Remove the mushrooms from the oven and leave to cool.

Pile the tomatoes, garlic and spring onions together on a chopping board and chop until re-

duced to a purée. Put into a bowl, stir in the chives, and season with salt and pepper. Add 1 tablespoon of the olive oil and the lemon juice. Pile a little of the mixture on top of each of the cooled mushroom caps.
SERVES 4

ARTICHOKES WITH TOMATOES

METRIC/IMPERIAL
1 kg/2 lb Jerusalem artichokes, peeled
salt
3 tablespoons olive oil
4 tomatoes, skinned and chopped
1 teaspoon chopped marjoram
freshly ground black pepper

Simmer the artichokes in boiling salted water for 20 minutes until almost cooked. Drain and cut into even-sized pieces.

Heat the oil in a pan, add the tomatoes, marjoram, artichokes, and salt and pepper to taste. Cover and simmer for 5 to 10 minutes. Transfer to a warmed dish. Serve immediately.
SERVES 4 to 6

ARTICHOKE PURÉE

METRIC/IMPERIAL
450 g/1 lb Jerusalem artichokes, peeled and thickly sliced
salt
1 teaspoon wine vinegar
1 tablespoon skimmed milk powder
freshly ground black pepper
pinch of grated nutmeg

Place the artichokes in a saucepan of boiling salted water with the vinegar added. Simmer for about 20 minutes until tender. Drain, reserving the cooking liquid, and allow to cool slightly.

Work the artichokes to a purée in a blender with 1 tablespoon of the cooking liquid. Add a little more liquid if necessary. Alternatively, rub them through a sieve.

Add the skimmed milk powder, salt and pepper to taste and nutmeg. Blend again until smooth. Return to the saucepan and dry off the purée slightly, stirring continuously.

Spoon smooth mounds of purée on to hot plates and serve with grilled steaks or lamb chops.
SERVES 4

179

HONEY-GLAZED PARSNIPS

METRIC/IMPERIAL
8 baby parsnips, peeled and trimmed
1 tablespoon clear honey, warmed
3 tablespoons toasted sesame seeds
salt
freshly ground black pepper
450 ml/¾ pint vegetable stock or water

Brush the parsnips with the honey. Coat them evenly in toasted sesame seeds and season well with salt and pepper.

Place in a steamer and cover with a tight-fitting lid. Steam over the boiling stock or water for 20 minutes or until tender. Keep hot, or serve immediately.

SERVES 4

BAKED BEETROOT WITH YOGURT

METRIC/IMPERIAL
4 medium beetroots, cooked, skinned and grated
salt
freshly ground black pepper
1 teaspoon dry mustard
300 ml/½ pint low-fat yogurt

Mix the grated beetroot with salt, pepper, mustard and half the yogurt. Place in a wide, shallow dish and pour the rest of the yogurt on top.

Bake in a preheated moderately hot oven (200°C/400°F, Gas Mark 6) for about 10 minutes or until the mixture is heated through. (Do not let the yogurt reach boiling point as it will curdle.) Serve hot or cold.

SERVES 4 to 6

BEETROOT SOUFFLÉ

METRIC/IMPERIAL
450 g/1 lb cooked beetroots, skinned and diced
1 teaspoon dry mustard
175 ml/6 fl oz orange juice
3 tablespoons cornflour
4 eggs, separated

Place the beetroot in a blender with the mustard and half the orange juice and liquidize to a purée.

Mix the remaining orange juice with the corn-flour and heat gently until the mixture thickens. Add to the blender and liquidize until smooth.

Beat the egg yolks, one by one, into the mixture. Whisk the egg whites until very stiff and fold into the mixture. Put into a soufflé dish and bake in a preheated hot oven (220°C/425°F, Gas Mark 7) for 20 to 25 minutes until risen. Serve immediately while hot.

SERVES 4

SWEETCORN WITH TOMATO SAUCE

METRIC/IMPERIAL
450 g/1 lb frozen or canned sweetcorn kernels
Sauce:
50 g/2 oz polyunsaturated margarine
450 g/1 lb tomatoes, skinned and finely chopped, or 1 × 400 g/14 oz can tomatoes
4 cloves garlic, peeled and crushed
1 tablespoon paprika
½ teaspoon brown sugar
salt
freshly ground black pepper
dash of vinegar
4–6 tablespoons water

Heat the margarine in a saucepan and sauté the tomatoes and garlic for 2 minutes, breakin; the tomatoes down with a wooden spoon. Add the paprika, sugar, salt and pepper to taste, and the vinegar. Cook over a very low heat for about 15 minutes or until the mixture is reduced to a pulp.

Meanwhile, cook the frozen sweetcorn in a little water until tender. If using canned sweetcorn, heat through. Drain the sweetcorn and transfer to a serving dish.

Add just enough water to the tomato mixture to make a thick sauce. Spoon the tomato sauce over the sweetcorn and serve hot.

SERVES 4

CORN AND BUTTER BEAN CASSEROLE

METRIC/IMPERIAL
1 × 300 g/11 oz can sweetcorn kernels
1 × 425 g/15 oz can butter beans, drained
1 tablespoon cornflour
scant 600 ml/1 pint skimmed milk
½ teaspoon caraway seeds
salt
freshly ground black pepper

Drain the sweetcorn, reserving the liquid. Place the sweetcorn and butter beans in a saucepan.

Mix the cornflour and skimmed milk together and heat gently. Add the liquid from the can of sweetcorn and stir until the mixture thickens. Add the caraway seeds and salt and pepper to taste.

Pour the sauce over the vegetables, cover and cook for about 15 minutes, then turn into a heated serving dish.

SERVES 4

COURGETTES LYONNAISE

METRIC/IMPERIAL
1 clove garlic, peeled and crushed
100 g/4 oz onion, peeled and chopped
150 ml/¼ pint chicken or vegetable stock
salt
450 g/1 lb courgettes, sliced
freshly ground black pepper

Stir the garlic and onion into the stock. Add salt and bring to the boil.

Add the courgettes, cover and simmer for 10 to 15 minutes until tender. Taste and adjust the seasoning. Serve hot or cold.

SERVES 4

COURGETTE MEDLEY

METRIC/IMPERIAL
1 large onion, peeled and sliced
1 clove garlic, peeled and crushed
2 tablespoons olive oil
large pinch of salt
freshly ground black pepper
3 tablespoons chopped parsley
1 teaspoon chopped thyme or sage
450 g/1 lb French beans
450 g/1 lb courgettes
4 large tomatoes, quartered
4 tablespoons water

Sauté the onion and garlic in the oil in a frying pan. Season with salt and pepper to taste and add the herbs. Cut the beans into lengths, and the courgettes into chunks. Add the beans, courgettes, tomatoes and water to the pan and simmer, covered, for 10 minutes or until just tender. Serve at once.

SERVES 4

COURGETTES PROVENÇAL

METRIC/IMPERIAL
450 g/1 lb courgettes, sliced
4 tomatoes, sliced
1 small onion, peeled and grated
2 tablespoons chopped parsley
1 tablespoon thyme leaves
salt
freshly ground black pepper
5 tablespoons stock

Arrange the courgettes and tomatoes in layers in a baking dish or casserole, sprinkling each layer with the onion, half of the parsley, the thyme and salt and pepper to taste. Pour in the stock.

Cover and bake in a preheated moderate oven (180°C/350°F, Gas Mark 4) for 30 to 40 minutes until the courgettes are tender but not soft.

Alternatively, put all the ingredients, except half the parsley, in a large saucepan. Cover and cook gently for 10 minutes until just tender, stirring occasionally.

Taste and adjust the seasoning. Sprinkle with the remaining parsley and serve hot or cold.

SERVES 4

COURGETTES À LA GRECQUE

METRIC/IMPERIAL
2 tablespoons sunflower oil
1 onion, peeled and sliced
1-2 cloves garlic, peeled and crushed
750 g/1½ lb courgettes, peeled and sliced
1 tablespoon wine vinegar
2 tablespoons tomato purée
6 tablespoons water
1-2 teaspoons brown sugar
1 teaspoon dried thyme
salt
freshly ground black pepper

Heat the oil and sauté the onion for 3 minutes. Add the garlic and courgettes and cook for 5 minutes with the lid on; toss occasionally.

Add the vinegar, tomato purée, water, sugar, thyme, salt and pepper. Stir, bring to the boil, cover and simmer for 15 minutes. Transfer to a serving dish and serve hot or cold.

SERVES 4

BAKED COURGETTE SOUFFLÉ

METRIC/IMPERIAL
2 tablespoons polyunsaturated vegetable oil
750 g/1½ lb courgettes, grated
50 g/2 oz polyunsaturated margarine
50 g/2 oz wholemeal flour
250 ml/8 fl oz skimmed milk
3 eggs, separated
salt
freshly ground black pepper
Tomato sauce:
25 g/1 oz polyunsaturated margarine
450 g/1 lb tomatoes, skinned and chopped
1 tablespoon chopped parsley
1 tablespoon snipped chives

Heat the oil in a large pan, add the courgettes and cook gently for 10 minutes, stirring occasionally.

Melt the margarine in another pan, remove from the heat and stir in the flour. Add the milk and mix well. Return to the heat and slowly bring to the boil, stirring; simmer for 3 minutes. Cool slightly, then add the egg yolks, courgettes, and salt and pepper to taste.

Whisk the egg whites until stiff and carefully fold into the mixture. Turn into a greased 1.2 litre/2 pint ovenproof dish and place in a roasting tin containing 2.5 cm/1 inch water. Cook in a pre-heated moderately hot oven (190°C/375°F, Gas Mark 5) for 55 minutes to 1 hour.

Meanwhile, make the tomato sauce. Melt the margarine in a pan and add the tomatoes, herbs, and salt and pepper to taste. Cook gently for 5 to 10 minutes, stirring occasionally. Sieve, or work in an electric blender until smooth; strain.

Serve the soufflé immediately, with the tomato sauce handed separately.
SERVES 4 to 6

FENNEL WITH CORIANDER

METRIC/IMPERIAL
2 tablespoons polyunsaturated vegetable oil
2 tomatoes, skinned and chopped
6 coriander seeds
1 bay leaf
thyme sprig
salt
freshly ground black pepper
3–4 fennel bulbs, trimmed and quartered
juice of ½ lemon

Put the oil, tomatoes, coriander seeds, bay leaf and thyme into a saucepan. Add 2 tablespoons water and season with salt and pepper. Bring to the boil and simmer for 3 to 4 minutes.

Toss the fennel in lemon juice and add to the pan. Cook gently until the fennel is tender but not too soft. Using a slotted spoon, transfer the fennel to a serving dish.

Cook the sauce quickly over a high heat until it starts to thicken. Pour it over the fennel and allow to cool before serving.
SERVES 4

AVOCADO POPOVERS

METRIC/IMPERIAL
8 lettuce leaves
1 large avocado, stoned, peeled and cut into strips
juice of 1 lemon
2 slices lean smoked ham, cut into strips
bunch of spring onions, trimmed and finely sliced
salt
freshly ground black pepper
pared rind of ¼ lemon, cut into thin strips and blanched, to garnish
Lemon sauce:
3 egg yolks
3 tablespoons lemon juice
salt
freshly ground black pepper
100 g/4 oz polyunsaturated margarine, melted

Steam the lettuce leaves over boiling water for 15 to 20 seconds. Refresh in ice-cold water.

Mix the avocado, lemon juice, ham and spring onion in a bowl. Season with salt and pepper. Divide the avocado mixture between each lettuce leaf and wrap tightly. Lay side by side in a steamer. Cover with a tight-fitting lid and steam over boiling water for 5 minutes.

Meanwhile, make the sauce. Place the egg yolks and lemon juice in a blender or food processor. Season well with salt and pepper and blend for a few seconds. With the machine running, gradually add the melted margarine until the sauce is thick and light. Taste and adjust the seasoning.

Flood the base of 4 individual plates with the lemon sauce. Top with the hot avocado popovers and garnish with the thin strips of blanched lemon rind. Serve immediately.
SERVES 4

VEGETABLE-STUFFED MARROW

METRIC/IMPERIAL
1 medium marrow, peeled
salt
freshly ground black pepper or pinch of curry
powder
450 g/1 lb parsnip and carrot purée

Cut the marrow in half lengthwise and scoop out the seeds. Add salt and pepper or curry powder to the parsnip and carrot purée and spoon into the marrow cavities. Reform the marrow and wrap in foil.

Cook in a preheated moderately hot oven (200°C/400°F, Gas Mark 6) for 30 to 45 minutes until tender. Unwrap the foil and cut the marrow into slices for serving.
SERVES 4

STUFFED MARROW WITH TOMATO SAUCE

METRIC/IMPERIAL
15 g/½ oz polyunsaturated margarine
1 small onion, peeled and chopped
2 rashers lean bacon, derinded
15 g/½ oz wholemeal flour
1 × 400 g/14 oz can tomatoes
150 ml/¼ pint cold water
1 teaspoon horseradish sauce
pinch of nutmeg
bay leaf
salt
freshly ground black pepper
1 medium marrow, cut in half lengthwise, seeds
removed
Stuffing:
1 tablespoon polyunsaturated vegetable oil
1 large onion, peeled and chopped
225 g/8 oz cooked pork, trimmed of fat and
minced
100 g/4 oz wholemeal breadcrumbs
1 clove garlic, peeled and crushed (optional)
1 teaspoon dried basil
1 tablespoon grated lemon rind
1 tablespoon lemon juice
salt
freshly ground black pepper

To make the sauce, melt the margarine, add the onion and bacon and fry gently for 1 minute. Stir in the flour, then, off the heat, blend in the tomatoes and their juice with the water. Stirring all the time, bring the sauce to the boil, then mix in the horseradish sauce, nutmeg, bay leaf, salt and pepper. Simmer, uncovered, for 15 minutes. Rub the sauce through a sieve or liquidize in a blender. Taste and adjust the seasoning.

Place the marrow in a pan of boiling salted water and cook gently for 5 minutes. Drain well and arrange in a lightly greased ovenproof dish.

To make the stuffing, heat the oil in a pan. Add the onion and fry gently until golden brown. Stir in the pork, breadcrumbs, garlic, basil, lemon rind and juice and plenty of salt and pepper. Bind the ingredients together with 4 tablespoons of the tomato sauce, then divide the filling between the marrow halves, packing it well down. Bake in a preheated moderately hot oven (200°C/400°F, Gas Mark 6), uncovered, for 20 to 25 minutes. Heat the remaining tomato sauce and serve it in a separate bowl.
SERVES 6

STUFFED MARROW RINGS

METRIC/IMPERIAL
1 × 1 kg/2 lb marrow, cut crosswise into 5 cm/
2 inch thick rings, seeds removed
1 tablespoon polyunsaturated vegetable oil
1 onion, peeled and chopped
100 g/4 oz mushrooms, wiped and chopped
100 g/4 oz cooked lean ham, diced
25 g/1 oz fresh wholemeal breadcrumbs
1 tablespoon chopped parsley
1 tablespoon chopped marjoram or oregano
salt
freshly ground black pepper

Put the marrow in a lightly greased baking dish. Set aside.

Heat the oil in a pan. Add the onion and fry gently for 3 minutes, stirring occasionally. Add the mushrooms and fry for a further 3 minutes. Remove from the heat, add the remaining ingredients and mix well.

Spoon the stuffing mixture into the centre of the marrow rings, then cover the dish with foil. Bake in a preheated moderate oven (180°C/350°F, Gas Mark 4) for 20 to 30 minutes until the marrow is just tender. Serve hot.
SERVES 4

TURKISH AUBERGINES

METRIC/IMPERIAL
2 large aubergines
salt
ground mace
2 teaspoons olive oil
shredded rind of 1 orange, to garnish
Dressing:
300 ml/½ pint plain low-fat yogurt
2 teaspoons olive oil
2 teaspoons fresh unsweetened orange juice
pinch of ground mace
salt
freshly ground black pepper

Preheat the oven to 200°C/400°F, Gas Mark 6.

Halve the aubergines lengthwise and sprinkle with a little salt and mace.

Cut 4 pieces of foil each large enough to contain an aubergine half. Lightly brush each aubergine half with oil and wrap in the foil. Bake in the oven for 20 to 30 minutes, or until tender.

Meanwhile, to make the dressing, mix together the yogurt, olive oil, orange juice, mace and salt and pepper.

Unwrap the aubergines and place on a serving dish. Pour the dressing over the hot aubergine halves, sprinkle with orange rind as a garnish and serve immediately.
SERVES 4

VEGETARIAN STUFFED AUBERGINES

METRIC/IMPERIAL
3 large aubergines, stalks removed
1 large onion, peeled and chopped
salt
100 g/4 oz tomatoes, skinned, deseeded and chopped
2 tablespoons chopped parsley
50 g/2 oz mushrooms, trimmed and chopped
1 teaspoon oregano
freshly ground black pepper
polyunsaturated vegetable oil for brushing

Preheat the oven to moderate (180°C/350°F, Gas Mark 4).

Cut the aubergines in half lengthwise. Scoop out some of the flesh and chop it finely.

Boil the onion in a very little salted water for 3 to 4 minutes, then drain well and add to the chopped aubergine flesh, together with the toma-toes, parsley, mushrooms, oregano and salt and pepper. Mix well and fill each aubergine half with the mixture.

Brush the top of each with oil and bake in the oven for 45 minutes to 1 hour. Serve hot or cold.
SERVES 4

STEAMED STUFFED AUBERGINES

METRIC/IMPERIAL
1 tablespoon polyunsaturated vegetable oil
2 cloves garlic, peeled and crushed
1 × 2.5 cm/1 inch piece root ginger, peeled and finely chopped
4 spring onions, chopped
2 red or green chillies, deseeded and chopped
225 g/8 oz minced lean pork
2 tablespoons soy sauce
2 tablespoons dry sherry
4 medium aubergines
50 g/2 oz frozen peeled prawns, thawed
Garnish:
spring onion flowers, made by shredding spring onions almost completely and immersing in iced water

Heat the oil in a wok or deep frying pan, add the garlic, ginger and spring onions and stir-fry for 1 minute. Increase the heat, add the chillies and pork and cook for 2 minutes. Stir in the soy sauce and sherry and cook for 10 minutes.

Meanwhile, cut the aubergines in half length-wise, carefully scoop out the flesh and chop finely. Reserve the shells. Add the flesh to the pan and cook for 10 minutes. Stir in the prawns and cook for 1 minute.

Bring a large pan of water to the boil, add the aubergine shells and cook for 1 minute; remove from the pan and drain well. Spoon the stuffing mixture into the shells and place in an ovenproof dish. Cover with a lid or foil, place in a steamer and steam vigorously for 25 to 30 minutes.

Arrange on a warmed serving dish, garnish with spring onion flowers and serve immediately.
SERVES 4 to 6

JUNE PEAS

METRIC/IMPERIAL
1 kg/2 lb shelled fresh peas
bunch of spring onions, trimmed and sliced
8 Cos lettuce leaves, washed and shredded
2-3 mint sprigs
1 tablespoon chopped parsley
pinch of caster sugar
25 g/1 oz polyunsaturated margarine
1 clove garlic, peeled and crushed
salt
freshly ground black pepper

Place a piece of wet greaseproof paper on the base of a steamer compartment. Top with peas, spring onions, lettuce, mint, parsley, sugar, margarine and garlic. Season well with salt and pepper.

Cover with a tight-fitting lid and steam over boiling water for 1 hour. Check the liquid level frequently and add more water if necessary.

After 1 hour, check that the peas are tender; if they are, serve at once.
SERVES 4

CELERY WITH ORANGE AND NUTS

METRIC/IMPERIAL
1 celery head, trimmed and cut into 5 cm/2 inch
lengths, leaves reserved
finely grated rind of ½ orange
juice of 1 orange
1 orange, peel and pith removed and divided
into segments
25 g/1 oz sultanas
25 g/1 oz walnuts
salt
freshly ground black pepper

Put the celery and leaves in a baking dish. Add the orange rind, juice and segments, then sprinkle with the sultanas, the walnuts and salt and pepper to taste.

Cover and bake in a preheated moderate oven (180°C/350°F, Gas Mark 4) for 30 to 40 minutes until the celery is just tender.

Alternatively, put all the ingredients in a large saucepan. Cover and cook gently for 15 to 20 minutes until just tender, stirring occasionally. If necessary, add a little water towards the end of cooking to moisten it.

Taste and adjust the seasoning. Serve hot
SERVES 4

BEANS WITH CHEESE AND HERBS

METRIC/IMPERIAL
450 g/1 lb French beans
25 g/1 oz polyunsaturated margarine
1 tablespoon polyunsaturated vegetable oil
2 tablespoons chopped parsley or 1 teaspoon
chopped sage
1 clove garlic, peeled and crushed
salt
freshly ground pepper
good pinch of grated nutmeg
2 tablespoons freshly grated Parmesan cheese

Top and tail the beans. Leave whole if young, or cut in diagonal slices if larger. Cook in boiling salted water until just tender, then drain.

Heat the margarine and oil in a saucepan, stir in 1 tablespoon of the chopped parsley or ½ teaspoon of the sage, and the garlic. Cook for 1 minute, stirring, then add the beans and season to taste with salt, pepper and nutmeg. Stir for another minute over a gentle heat until the beans are piping hot, then add the Parmesan and lightly stir through.

Turn into a serving dish and sprinkle with the remaining herbs. Serve with veal, pork or lamb.
SERVES 4

HARICOT BEAN PAPRIKA

METRIC/IMPERIAL
350 g/12 oz haricot beans, soaked overnight
salt
2 tablespoons polyunsaturated vegetable oil
1 large onion, peeled and sliced
1 clove garlic, peeled and crushed
1 tablespoon paprika
2 tablespoons tomato purée
50 g/2 oz canned pimiento, sliced
1 × 450 g/1 lb can tomatoes
150 ml/¼ pint water
4 tablespoons soured cream

Drain the haricot beans and cook in boiling salted water for 45 minutes or until almost tender; drain.

Meanwhile, heat the oil in a large pan and sauté the onion and garlic until soft. Stir in the paprika and cook, stirring, for 2 to 3 minutes.

Add the beans, tomato purée, pimiento, tomatoes and water. Bring to the boil, cover and simmer gently for about 10 minutes. Stir in the soured cream just before serving.
SERVES 4

SOUTHERN BAKED BEANS

METRIC/IMPERIAL
225 g/8 oz haricot beans, soaked overnight
600 ml/1 pint water
1 large onion, peeled and chopped
2 celery stalks, sliced
1 red pepper, cored, deseeded and sliced
4 tomatoes, skinned and chopped
1 tablespoon molasses or honey
1 tablespoon tomato purée
2 tablespoons vinegar
2 teaspoons Worcestershire sauce
2 teaspoons mustard powder
salt
freshly ground black pepper
100 g/4 oz salami, thickly sliced and skinned

Drain the beans, reserving the water. Make up to 600 ml/1 pint with more water.

Place the beans and liquid in a large pan, then bring to the boil. Lower the heat, cover and simmer for 1 to 1½ hours until the beans are tender, adding more water if necessary. Drain and reserve 300 ml/½ pint cooking liquid.

Put the beans in layers in a casserole with the onion, celery, red pepper and tomatoes. Mix the reserved cooking liquid with the remaining ingredients, except the salami. Pour over the beans.

Cover and bake in a preheated moderate oven (180°C/350°F, Gas Mark 4) for 1 hour. Arrange the salami on top and bake for a further 30 minutes until the beans are tender and well-flavoured.
SERVES 4 to 6

ITALIAN BAKED BEANS WITH BACON

METRIC/IMPERIAL
225 g/8 oz haricot beans, soaked overnight in 600 ml/1 pint water
1 tablespoon polyunsaturated vegetable oil
100 g/4 oz lean bacon, derinded and diced
1 onion, peeled and chopped
1 clove garlic, peeled and crushed
1 tablespoon chopped fresh or 1½ teaspoons dried sage
2 tablespoons chopped parsley
1 tablespoon lemon juice
1 tablespoon grated lemon rind
1 bay leaf
salt
freshly ground black pepper
1 tablespoon tomato purée

Put the beans and soaking water into a saucepan, bring to the boil and boil for 10 minutes.

Heat the oil in a saucepan and cook the bacon, onion and garlic for 5 minutes or until lightly browned. Add the beans with their liquid and all the remaining ingredients. Bring to the boil Transfer the mixture to a casserole, cover and bake in a preheated moderate oven (180°C/350°F, Gas Mark 4) for 2 to 3 hours or until the beans are tender and most of the liquid has been absorbed

Alternatively, cook on top of the cooker in a covered saucepan until the beans are tender. Serve hot, garnished with sage or parsley, if wished.
SERVES 4 to 6

RED BEAN BAKE

METRIC/IMPERIAL
1 can low-calorie spring vegetable soup
350 g/12 oz canned cooked red kidney beans
½ teaspoon mustard powder
2 teaspoons white wine
freshly ground black pepper
8 teaspoons dry breadcrumbs
pinch of dried thyme or marjoram

Heat the soup in a pan until hot, then mix with the beans, blending well. Stir in the mustard, wine and pepper to taste, blending well. Spoon into a flameproof casserole. Bake, uncovered, in a preheated moderate oven (160°C/325°F, Gas Mark 3) for 45 minutes. Sprinkle over the crumbs and herbs and cook under a hot grill until golden.
SERVES 4

DHAL

METRIC/IMPERIAL
225 g/8 oz red lentils
600 ml/1 pint water
1 bay leaf
salt
freshly ground black pepper
25 g/1 oz polyunsaturated margarine
1 tablespoon polyunsaturated vegetable oil
1 onion, peeled and finely chopped
1 clove garlic, peeled and crushed
½ teaspoon ground ginger or 1 teaspoon grated root ginger
½ teaspoon ground coriander
½ teaspoon ground cumin

Place the lentils in a saucepan and add the water, bay leaf, salt and pepper. Cover the pan and bring to the boil. Simmer for 15 to 30 minutes until the lentils are swollen and the water has been absorbed to give a thickish purée.

Heat the margarine and oil in a clean pan and sauté the onion, garlic and ginger (if using) for 5 minutes until lightly browned. Add the rest of the spices and cook for 1 minute. Add the cooked lentil purée and cook gently for 5 minutes. Remove the bay leaf. Serve hot with rice or as an accompaniment to curry, or cold with a salad.
SERVES 4

LENTILS IN TOMATO SAUCE

METRIC/IMPERIAL
225 g/8 oz brown or green lentils
1 × 400 g/14 oz can tomatoes, chopped
600 ml/1 pint water
1 onion, peeled and chopped
1 tablespoon chopped fresh oregano, marjoram
or basil, or 1 teaspoon dried herbs
salt
freshly ground black pepper

Put the lentils into a saucepan. Add the tomatoes with their juice. Pour over the water and add the onion and herbs. Season with salt and pepper, cover the pan and bring to the boil.

Simmer gently for 1 to 1¼ hours until the lentils are tender and most of the liquid has evaporated, but the mixture is still moist. Stir occasionally towards the end of cooking to prevent the lentils from sticking to the pan.
SERVES 4

GARDEN BEANS

METRIC/IMPERIAL
450 g/1 lb shelled broad beans
450 g/1 lb French beans, topped and tailed
salt
freshly ground black pepper
juice of ½ lemon
Herb hollandaise:
2 egg yolks
2 tablespoons lemon juice
salt
freshly ground black pepper
100 g/4 oz polyunsaturated margarine, melted
2 tablespoons chopped herbs (e.g. mint, parsley,
dill, tarragon)

Season the beans with salt and pepper. Toss in the lemon juice. Cover and cook in a steamer over boiling water for 5 to 7 minutes or until just tender.

Meanwhile, make the hollandaise sauce. Place the egg yolks and lemon juice in a blender or food processor and season well with salt and pepper. Blend for a few seconds. With the machine running, gradually add the melted margarine until the sauce is thick and light. Stir in the herbs. Taste and adjust seasoning, if necessary.

Place the beans in a heated serving dish, spoon over the sauce and serve at once.
SERVES 4

Note: During the summer months broad beans and French beans are ready for harvesting at the same time. This recipe is a perfect way of combining these two delicious vegetables in one dish.

FABONADE

METRIC/IMPERIAL
25 g/1 oz polyunsaturated margarine
1 onion, peeled and finely chopped
150 g/5 oz lean ham, diced
4 cloves garlic, peeled and crushed
1 kg/2 lb broad beans, shelled
2-3 savory sprigs
150 ml/¼ pint water
salt
freshly ground black pepper
3 egg yolks
2 tablespoons vinegar or lemon juice
chopped parsley, to garnish

Melt the margarine in a heavy pan, add the onion and ham and cook gently for a few minutes. Add the garlic, beans and savory, then the water, and salt and pepper to taste. Mix well. Bring to the boil, then lower the heat, cover and simmer for 20 to 30 minutes until the beans are tender.

Discard the savory. Mix the egg yolks and vinegar or lemon juice together, then stir slowly into the beans. Heat through, but do not allow to boil. Taste and adjust the seasoning, then transfer to a warmed serving dish and garnish with parsley. Serve immediately.
SERVES 6

BROAD BEAN AND GREEN PEA CASSEROLE

METRIC/IMPERIAL
450 g/1 lb green peas, shelled weight
450 g/1 lb broad beans, shelled weight
salt
1 tablespoon cornflour
300 ml/½ pint skimmed milk
300 ml/½ pint stock or vegetable cooking liquid (see method)
pinch of dried rosemary
freshly ground black pepper

Place the peas and beans together in a saucepan of boiling salted water and cook for about 15 minutes until tender. Drain, reserving the cooking liquid.

Mix the cornflour and skimmed milk together and heat gently, stirring, adding 300 ml/½ pint vegetable cooking liquid or stock, rosemary and salt and pepper to taste. Add the peas and beans and heat together for about 2 minutes, then turn into a heated serving dish.
SERVES 6

RED BEANS AND RICE LOUISIANA

METRIC/IMPERIAL
225 g/8 oz dried red kidney beans, soaked in water for 8 hours
25 g/1 oz polyunsaturated margarine
1 onion, peeled and finely chopped
4 celery stalks, finely chopped
3 cloves garlic, peeled and crushed
100 g/4 oz long-grain rice, well washed
ham or chicken stock
2 tablespoons chopped parsley
1 bay leaf
10 drops of Tabasco
salt
freshly ground black pepper
450 g/1 lb smoked sausage or salami, cut into bite-sized cubes
chopped parsley, to garnish

Drain the kidney beans and place in a saucepan. Add enough fresh water to cover the beans and bring to the boil. Boil for 3 minutes, reduce the heat, then cover and cook for 45 minutes. Drain and rinse.

Meanwhile, melt the margarine in a pan and gently fry the onion, celery, garlic and rice until the rice turns white and the onion is cooked. Add enough stock to bring the level of liquid about 2.5 cm/1 inch above the top of the rice. Add the beans and stir in the parsley, bay leaf and Tabasco. Season the mixture with salt and pepper.

Cover with a tight-fitting lid and cook for 30 minutes without lifting the lid of the saucepan. Add the cubes of sausage and continue to cook for 5 minutes.

Remove the bay leaf and pile the mixture on to a warmed serving dish, then sprinkle with parsley and serve at once.
SERVES 4

KIDNEY BEAN CASSEROLE

METRIC/IMPERIAL
2 × 275 g/10 oz cans red kidney beans, drained and rinsed
2 medium onions, peeled and sliced
2 rashers bacon, fat removed, derinded and chopped
about 300 ml/½ pint chicken stock
salt
freshly ground black pepper

Place the kidney beans, onions and bacon in a saucepan.

Pour over just enough stock to cover and add salt and pepper. Simmer gently for about 10 minutes or until the onions are tender. Turn into a heated serving dish.
SERVES 6

BARBECUE BUTTER BEANS

METRIC/IMPERIAL
1 tablespoon polyunsaturated vegetable oil
1 onion, peeled and chopped
1 clove garlic, peeled and crushed
2 tomatoes, skinned
pinch of sugar
pinch of dry mustard
pinch of chilli powder
1 tablespoon tomato purée
1 × 275 g/10 oz can butter beans, drained

Heat the oil in a saucepan, add the onion and garlic and cook until softened. Add the remaining ingredients, except the beans, and simmer for 10 minutes. Stir in the beans and heat thoroughly.
SERVES 4

BEAN CURD FRY

METRIC/IMPERIAL
4 cakes bean curd
4 tablespoons polyunsaturated vegetable oil
1 clove garlic, peeled and sliced
2 small leeks, sliced diagonally
2 celery stalks, sliced diagonally
100 g/4 oz button mushrooms, wiped and sliced
100 g/4 oz lean pork, shredded
4 dried chillies, crushed
1 tablespoon chilli paste
1 tablespoon dry sherry

Cut each bean curd into 3 thin slices, then cut each slice into 2 triangles.

Heat half the oil in a wok or deep frying pan, add the garlic, leeks and celery and fry quickly for 1 minute. Stir in the mushrooms and pork and cook for 2 minutes. Remove and keep warm.

Heat the remaining oil in the pan, add the bean curd and fry for 2 minutes; drain on kitchen paper.

Return the vegetables, pork and bean curd to the pan, stir in the dried chillies, chilli paste and sherry and cook for 1 minute.

Transfer to a warmed serving dish, discard the dried chillies and serve immediately.
SERVES 4 to 6

EASTERN MOOLI

METRIC/IMPERIAL
1 tablespoon polyunsaturated vegetable oil
1 onion, peeled and sliced
2 tablespoons chopped mint
1 teaspoon ground turmeric
¼ teaspoon chilli powder
450 g/1 lb mooli (white radish), peeled and cut into 2.5 cm/1 inch pieces
salt
3 tablespoons hot water
1 teaspoon garam masala
1 tablespoon lemon juice

Heat the oil in a frying pan. Add the onion and fry gently until beginning to soften. Add the mint, turmeric and chilli powder. Season with salt, then stir in the mooli until it is well coated. Add the water, cover and simmer for 20 minutes, shaking the frying pan occasionally.

Sprinkle with the garam masala and lemon juice. Replace the lid and cook for a further 10 minutes or until the mooli is tender.
SERVES 4 to 6

DRY-COOKED BAMBOO SHOOTS

METRIC/IMPERIAL
2 tablespoons dried shrimps (optional)
2 tablespoons polyunsaturated vegetable oil
1 × 450 g/1 lb can bamboo shoots, drained
1 × 2.5 cm/1 inch piece root ginger, peeled and finely chopped
50 g/2 oz Szechuan pickled vegetables, chopped
2 teaspoons caster sugar
pinch of salt
150 ml/¼ pint chicken stock
2 red peppers, cored, deseeded and sliced
1 tablespoon sesame seed oil

If using the dried shrimps, soak them in warm water for 15 minutes then drain.

Heat the oil in a wok or deep frying pan, add the bamboo shoots and stir-fry for 2 minutes until pale brown around the edges. Remove from the pan and drain on kitchen paper.

Add the ginger, shrimps (if using), and Szechuan pickles to the pan and cook for 1 minute. Stir in the sugar, salt and stock and bring to the boil. Return the bamboo shoots to the pan. Add the red peppers, mixing well, and cook for 2 minutes.

Transfer to a warmed serving dish and sprinkle over the sesame seed oil. Serve immediately.
SERVES 4 to 6

MEAT

BEEF AND HORSERADISH

METRIC/IMPERIAL
500 g/1¼ lb lean minced beef
300 ml/½ pint beef stock
2 tablespoons grated horseradish
salt
freshly ground black pepper

Put the beef and stock in a saucepan and bring to the boil. Cover and simmer gently for 1½ hours. Check occasionally that the beef is not getting too dry; add a little water if necessary. Leave to cool, then remove the fat.

Stir in the horseradish, bring to the boil and simmer for about 20 minutes. Taste and adjust the seasoning. Serve immediately.
SERVES 4

BEEF WITH HORSERADISH AND BASIL

METRIC/IMPERIAL
450 g/1 lb extra-lean minced beef
1 egg white
2 teaspoons freshly grated horseradish or horseradish sauce
1 tablespoon chopped basil
2 shallots, peeled and very finely chopped
2 teaspoons cornflour
salt
freshly ground black pepper
basil sprigs, to garnish
Tomato sauce:
1 × 400 g/14 oz can chopped tomatoes
2 cloves garlic, peeled and crushed
1 tablespoon chopped basil
150 ml/¼ pint beef stock

Mix the beef in a blender or food processor for a few seconds. Slowly add the egg white, horseradish and basil. Mix for a few seconds until they are fully incorporated into the meat. Add the shallots and cornflour. Season with salt and pepper according to taste.

Dust your hands with cornflour and form the mixture into 3.5 cm/1½ inch balls – about the size of a golf ball. Place all the ingredients for the tomato sauce in a saucepan and bring to the boil. Put the meatballs in a steamer. Cover with a tight-fitting lid and steam over the sauce for 10 minutes. Divide the meatballs between 4 warmed serving plates and keep warm. Work the tomato sauce in a blender or food processor until smooth. Taste and adjust the seasoning if necessary. Pour the sauce over the meatballs and garnish decoratively with sprigs of basil.
SERVES 4

CHINESE SMOKED MEATBALLS

METRIC/IMPERIAL
4 dried Chinese mushrooms
1 small can water chestnuts, drained, rinsed and finely chopped
450 g/1 lb lean minced beef
2 tablespoons soy sauce
2 tablespoons cornflour
1 tablespoon finely chopped spring onion
1 tablespoon finely chopped root ginger
1 medium carrot, peeled and grated
1 tablespoon rice wine or dry sherry
1 teaspoon sesame oil
For smoking:
2 tablespoons brown sugar
2 tablespoons black tea leaves
2 tablespoons fennel seeds
To serve:
2 teaspoons sesame oil, mixed with
2 tablespoons soy sauce
2 spring onions, finely chopped

Soak the mushrooms in hot water to cover for 15 minutes or until soft. Drain, remove the stems and chop the caps finely. Place them with the chestnuts in a large bowl, add the remaining ingredients and mix well by hand until the mixture is firm. Shape into walnut-sized balls and arrange in one layer in a steamer compartment. Cover and

190

steam over boiling water for 15 minutes.

To smoke the meatballs, you need an old frying pan, wok or other metal container, lined with aluminium foil. Combine the brown sugar, tea leaves and fennel seeds and place in the bottom. Set over high heat and when the mixture starts to smoke, put a rack containing the meatballs over the smoke. Cover tightly with a lid or aluminium foil and leave for another 5 minutes, then turn the heat off and leave the meatballs for a further 10 minutes, still covered.

To serve, brush the meatballs with a little of the sesame-soy mixture and sprinkle with the spring onions. Serve the remaining sesame-soy mixture separately, for dipping.

SERVES 4

MEXICAN HAMBURGERS

METRIC/IMPERIAL
450 g/1 lb lean minced beef
1 onion, peeled and finely grated (optional)
1 egg, lightly beaten
salt
freshly ground black pepper
2 teaspoons Worcestershire sauce
Sauce:
2 teaspoons polyunsaturated vegetable oil
2 medium onions, peeled and minced
2 garlic cloves, peeled and minced
2 small green peppers, cored, deseeded and sliced in rings
50 g/2 oz mushrooms, chopped
1 × 400 g/14 oz can tomatoes
2 teaspoons dried marjoram or oregano
dash of hot chilli sauce

Mix the beef with the onion, if used. Mix in the egg, salt and pepper to taste and the Worcestershire sauce. Divide into 4 equal pieces and shape into hamburgers about 2 cm/¾ inch thick.

To make the sauce, heat the oil in a frying pan. Add the onions and garlic and fry until they are golden. Add the pepper rings and continue cooking for 15 minutes. Stir in the mushrooms, tomatoes with their can juice and the marjoram or oregano. Season to taste with the chilli sauce, salt and pepper. Cover and cook for a further 10 minutes.

Meanwhile place the hamburgers on the rack of a grill pan. Cook under a preheated hot grill until rare or medium, to your taste. Arrange the hamburgers on a hot serving dish and pour the sauce over them. Serve with a crisp green salad.

SERVES 4

CHILLI CON CARNE

METRIC/IMPERIAL
450 g/1 lb lean minced beef
50 g/2 oz onion, peeled and sliced
1 clove garlic, peeled and crushed
1-3 teaspoons chilli powder
2 tablespoons tomato purée
300 ml/½ pint water
2 × 225 g/8 oz cans red kidney beans, drained
salt
freshly ground black pepper

Put the beef, onion, garlic, chilli powder, tomato purée and water in a casserole and bring to the boil. Cover and simmer gently for 1¼ hours, skimming the fat off occasionally.

Add the red kidney beans, salt and pepper and simmer for a further 10 minutes. Skim off the fat with a spoon. Serve at once with brown rice.

SERVES 4

SHEPHERD'S SQUARES

METRIC/IMPERIAL
2 slices brown bread, crumbed
salt
freshly ground black pepper
1 tablespoon made mustard
5 tablespoons skimmed milk
450 g/1 lb lean minced beef
350 g/12 oz potatoes, peeled, boiled, drained and mashed with 25 g/1 oz polyunsaturated margarine and a little skimmed milk
2 eggs, beaten
1 small onion, peeled and chopped
1 tablespoon chopped parsley
25 g/1 oz polyunsaturated margarine
50 g/2 oz Cheddar cheese, grated
½ teaspoon paprika

Combine the breadcrumbs, salt, pepper, mustard and milk and leave to stand until the breadcrumbs have softened. Mix in the meat. Spread the mixture into an 18 × 28 cm/7 × 11 inch baking tin.

Mix together the mashed potato, eggs, onion, parsley and seasoning. Spread evenly over the meat mixture and bake in a preheated moderate oven (180°C/350°F, Gas Mark 4) for 35 minutes. Melt the margarine and brush over the potato. Sprinkle with the cheese and paprika and return the tin to the oven for a further 10 minutes. Cut into squares to serve.

SERVES 4

TARRAGON MEATBALLS WITH MUSHROOM SAUCE

METRIC/IMPERIAL
450 g/1 lb minced steak or lean beef
1 onion, peeled and grated
75 g/3 oz fresh wholemeal breadcrumbs
1 egg
1 teaspoon dried tarragon
salt
freshly ground black pepper
1-2 tablespoons polyunsaturated vegetable oil
tarragon sprigs and tomato wedges, to garnish
Sauce:
175 g/6 oz mushrooms, finely chopped
300 ml/½ pint beef or vegetable stock
3 teaspoons cornflour
3 tablespoons skimmed milk
1½ tablespoons tomato purée
1½ teaspoons lemon juice
1-2 teaspoons brown sugar
salt
freshly ground black pepper

To make the meatballs, place the minced meat, onion, breadcrumbs, egg, tarragon, salt and pepper in a bowl and mix well. Shape into 12 balls.

Heat the oil in a large pan and gently fry the meatballs, turning to brown evenly. Remove the meatballs with a slotted spoon and drain on kitchen paper.

To make the sauce, add the mushrooms to the pan and cook gently until softened, then add the stock. Blend the cornflour with the milk and add the tomato purée, lemon juice, sugar, salt and pepper. Add to the pan and heat, stirring, until mixture comes to the boil. Cover and simmer for 5 minutes. Carefully place the meatballs in the sauce, cover and simmer for 20 to 30 minutes.

Transfer to a warmed serving dish, spoon the sauce over and garnish with tomato wedges and tarragon sprigs.

SERVES 4

BEEF AND TOMATO CASSEROLE

METRIC/IMPERIAL
750 g/1½ lb stewing steak, trimmed of fat and cut into bite-sized pieces
4 celery stalks, chopped
4 carrots, scraped and sliced
4 tomatoes, skinned and chopped
250 ml/8 fl oz tomato juice
1 teaspoon dry mustard
salt
freshly ground black pepper
2 beef stock cubes, crumbled

Put the steak in a casserole dish. Add the remaining ingredients and mix well.

Cover and cook in a preheated cool oven (140°C/275°F, Gas Mark 1) for about 2½ hours or until the beef is tender.

Check occasionally that the casserole is not getting too dry, adding a little water if necessary. Serve immediately while hot.

SERVES 4

BEEF AND PRUNE CASSEROLE

METRIC/IMPERIAL
2 tablespoons polyunsaturated vegetable oil
1 onion, peeled and chopped
450 g/1 lb stewing steak, trimmed of fat and cut into cubes
1 tablespoon flour
1 tablespoon tomato purée
¼ teaspoon mixed herbs
1 × 425 g/15 oz can tomatoes
300 ml/½ pint beef stock
225 g/8 oz prunes, soaked in water overnight
1 × 400 g/14 oz can cannellini beans
salt
freshly ground black pepper
1 tablespoon chopped parsley, to garnish

Heat the oil in a saucepan and sauté the onion until soft. Add the meat and brown it evenly. Stir in the flour then add the tomato purée, mixed herbs and tomatoes with their juice, and the stock.

Bring to the boil, stirring constantly. Add the prunes, cover and simmer gently for about 1½ hours. Add the drained beans and adjust seasoning to taste. Cook for a further 30 minutes. Sprinkle with parsley before serving.

SERVES 4

CURRIED BEEF CASSEROLE

METRIC/IMPERIAL
2 onions, peeled
4 carrots, scraped
450 g/1 lb stewing steak, trimmed of fat and
cubed
2 celery stalks, chopped
1 tablespoon chopped fresh parsley
600 ml/1 pint beef stock
½ teaspoon mild curry powder
salt
freshly ground black pepper

Halve 1 of the onions and 2 of the carrots and chop the remainder.

Place all the ingredients in a large flameproof casserole and bring to the boil. Reduce the heat, cover and simmer gently on top of the cooker for 2 hours or until the beef is tender. From time to time, skim off any fat that rises to the surface.

Remove from the heat and leave the casserole to cool, then skim off the fat. Lift out the onion and carrot halves and purée in a blender or food processor. Stir the purée back into the dish. Reheat gently, adjust the seasoning to taste and serve hot.
SERVES 4

SPRING BEEF CASSEROLE

METRIC/IMPERIAL
750 g/1½ lb chuck steak, trimmed of fat and cut
into cubes
300 ml/½ pint dry red wine
1 clove garlic, peeled and crushed
2 cloves
1 bay leaf
1 teaspoon salt
¼ teaspoon freshly ground black pepper
1 lean bacon rasher, derinded and diced
2 celery stalks, chopped
3 parsley sprigs
150 ml/¼ pint beef stock
6 small pickling onions, peeled
4 carrots, peeled and sliced
12 button mushrooms, wiped
100 g/4 oz peas
chopped parsley, to garnish

Put the beef in a shallow dish. Mix together the wine, garlic, cloves, bay leaf, salt and pepper and pour over the beef. Leave to marinate for 2 hours, stirring frequently.

Put the bacon in a heavy pan and heat gently until the fat begins to run. Drain the meat, reserving the marinade. Add the meat to the bacon and fry briskly until browned on all sides.

Transfer the beef and bacon to a casserole. Pour in the reserved marinade, then add the celery, parsley sprigs and stock. Cover and cook in a preheated moderate oven (160°C/325°F, Gas Mark 3) for 1 hour.

Add the onions and carrots. Cover and continue cooking for 30 minutes or until the beef is tender. Add the mushrooms and peas and cook for a further 30 minutes. Remove the bay leaf and parsley sprigs. Taste and adjust the seasoning, if necessary, then sprinkle with the chopped parsley and serve hot.
SERVES 4

FARMHOUSE BEEF AND SWEETCORN STEW

METRIC/IMPERIAL
15 g/½ oz polyunsaturated margarine
450 g/1 lb stewing steak, trimmed of fat and
cubed
2 large onions, peeled and chopped
1 carrot, peeled and chopped
600 ml/1 pint stock
salt
freshly ground black pepper
1 teaspoon ground paprika
1 × 350 g/12 oz can sweetcorn
1 × 65 g/2½ oz can tomato purée
150 ml/¼ pint plain low-fat yogurt

Melt the margarine in a flameproof casserole, add the meat and brown on all sides. Add the onions and carrot and cook for about 5 minutes. Gradually add the stock, blending well. Season with salt and pepper to taste and the paprika. Cover and cook in a preheated moderate oven (160°C/325°F, Gas Mark 3) for 1 to 1¼ hours or until the beef is tender.

Add the sweetcorn with the can juice, mixing well. Cover and cook for a further 30 minutes, stirring occasionally. Add the tomato purée, blending well. Reheat gently on top of the cooker but do not allow to boil. Add the yogurt and serve immediately.
SERVES 4

MUSTARD BEEF CASSEROLE

METRIC/IMPERIAL
750 g/1½ lb lean braising steak, trimmed and cubed
1 tablespoon plain wholemeal flour
salt
freshly ground black pepper
2 tablespoons polyunsaturated vegetable oil
1 large onion, peeled and sliced
4 carrots, peeled and sliced
300 ml/½ pint beer
4 tablespoons beef stock
3 teaspoons wholegrain mustard
1 teaspoon polyunsaturated margarine
½ stick brown French bread, sliced
chopped parsley, to garnish

Preheat the oven to 180°C/350°F, Gas Mark 4. Toss the meat in seasoned flour. Heat the oil in a flameproof casserole and sauté the onion. Add the meat and cook until browned.

Stir in the carrots, then the beer and stock. Add 2 teaspoons mustard and seasoning. Bring to the boil, cover and cook in the oven for 1½ hours.

Meanwhile, blend the remaining mustard with the margarine and spread over the slices of French bread. Place on top of the casserole, mustard side up. Return to the oven, uncovered, for 20 minutes until piping hot. Serve the casserole sprinkled with chopped parsley.
SERVES 4

GINGERED BEEF WITH TURNIP

METRIC/IMPERIAL
1.25 kg/2½ lb stewing steak, trimmed of fat, in two pieces
3 slices root ginger
1 teaspoon black peppercorns
120 ml/4 fl oz soy sauce
2 tablespoons dry sherry
1 kg/2 lb turnips, peeled and cut into 1 cm/½ inch thick slices
2 teaspoons cornflour, blended with 2 tablespoons water
chopped parsley, to garnish

Put the meat into a saucepan with the ginger, peppercorns, soy sauce and sherry. Add enough water just to cover the meat and bring to the boil. Cover and simmer for 1 hour or until tender.

Meanwhile, parboil the turnips for 2 minutes, then drain well.

Remove the beef from the pan and cut into 1 cm/½ inch thick slices. Put the slices of beef into a deep, heatproof bowl and arrange the turnips on top. Pour the liquid from the pan over the turnips and cook in a steamer for 30 minutes. Drain the liquid from the bowl into a saucepan, discarding the ginger. Arrange the beef and turnips in a warmed serving dish and keep hot.

Add the blended cornflour to the pan and simmer, stirring constantly, until thickened. Pour over the beef and turnips and serve at once, garnished with chopped parsley.
SERVES 8

OLD ENGLISH MEAT LOAF

METRIC/IMPERIAL
450 g/1 lb lean stewing steak or topside of beef, finely minced
350 g/12 oz lean bacon, derinded and finely minced
100 g/4 oz lamb's liver, finely minced
1 onion, peeled and finely chopped
50 g/2 oz fresh brown breadcrumbs
2 eggs, beaten
2 tablespoons chopped parsley
small pinch of dried thyme
2 teaspoons chopped basil
salt
freshly ground black pepper

Grease a 1.2 litre/2 pint pudding basin. Mix all of the ingredients together in a large mixing bowl. Season very well with salt and pepper. Pile the mixture into the pudding basin. Cover with foil or greaseproof paper and tie down with string.

Gently cook in a steamer or covered sauccpan half-filled with boiling water, for 2 hours. Check the liquid level frequently and add more boiling water if necessary.

Cool the loaf in the pudding basin, pressing it down with weights. Slice the meat loaf and serve hot or cold.
SERVES 4 to 6

Note: It is important to buy lean stewing beef or topside for this recipe, and mince it yourself, because ready minced beef is usually too fatty and coarse

PROVENÇAL BEEF STEW

METRIC/IMPERIAL
3 tablespoons olive oil
2 medium onions, peeled and sliced
175 g/6 oz piece unsmoked lean bacon, derinded
and cut into 1 cm/½ inch cubes
1.5 kg/3 lb piece boneless braising steak,
trimmed of fat
1 tablespoon plain unbleached white flour
salt
freshly ground black pepper
4 large tomatoes, skinned and quartered
2 carrots, peeled and sliced
2 cloves garlic, peeled and crushed
2 thinly pared strips orange rind, 1 bay leaf, a
sprig thyme, 2 sprigs parsley, tied together for
bouquet garni
150 ml/¼ pint red wine
50 g/2 oz small black olives, rinsed (optional)

Heat the oil in a flameproof casserole into which
the meat fits fairly closely. Add the onions and
sauté gently for 5 minutes, then add the cubed
bacon and cook gently until the fat begins to run.
Meanwhile, wipe the meat with damp kitchen
paper towels and dust lightly with flour, well seasoned with salt and pepper. Increase the heat a
little, put the meat into the pan and cook until
lightly browned on each side.

Add the tomatoes, carrots, garlic, bouquet
garni, salt and pepper. Pour in the wine. Bring to
the boil, allow to simmer for a few minutes, then
cover the pan tightly and transfer to a preheated
cool oven (150°C/300°F, Gas Mark 2) and cook for
about 4 hours or until the meat is tender when
pierced with a skewer.

Turn the meat halfway through cooking and
add the olives, if using, 30 minutes before the end.
To serve, remove the trussing strings and arrange
the meat on a hot serving dish, and either leave
whole or slice as much as required. Skim off any
fat from the gravy, remove the solid ingredients
with a slotted spoon and arrange them around the
meat. Remove and discard the bouquet garni. Reduce the gravy by boiling briskly for a few
minutes, then taste and adjust the seasoning and
pour it over the meat.

Serve with creamed potatoes and a green vegetable or follow with a green salad.
SERVES 8

FAMILY POT ROAST

METRIC/IMPERIAL
2 tablespoons olive oil
1.5 kg/3 lb topside or silverside of beef, rolled
and tied
salt
freshly ground black pepper
900 ml/1½ pints beef stock
150 ml/¼ pint red wine
2 onions, peeled and quartered
8 small carrots, scrubbed
8 small turnips, peeled
1 small swede, peeled and cubed
1 teaspoon chopped fresh thyme or ¼ teaspoon
dried thyme
4 cloves garlic, peeled and crushed
450 g/1 lb cap mushrooms, wiped

Heat the oil in a heavy-based pan. Season the beef
with salt and pepper and fry until golden brown
on all sides. Remove from the pan and put to one
side. Pour the stock and wine into the same pan.
Bring to the boil, scraping the sediment from the
base of the pan. Pour into a clean saucepan and
bring to the boil.

Arrange the vegetables, thyme and garlic in a
steamer compartment and season to taste. Place
the joint of beef on top. Cover the steamer with a
tight-fitting lid and steam over the boiling stock
for 1 hour 45 minutes. Check the liquid level frequently and add more boiling stock if necessary.
Add the mushrooms, and continue cooking the
beef for a further 20 minutes. Serve the meat on a
warmed dish surrounded by the vegetables. Remove the pan from the heat and skim off all fat
from the surface of the stock, then boil to reduce
until syrupy and serve separately.
SERVES 4

Note: Pot roasting is one of the oldest methods of
cooking. Choose a joint of beef that has little fat,
such as topside or silverside, which require slow
gentle cooking.

RED-COOKED BEEF WITH BROCCOLI

METRIC/IMPERIAL
1 kg/2 lb lean stewing steak
1 × 2.5 cm/1 inch piece root ginger, peeled and
finely chopped
2 cloves garlic, peeled and crushed
6 tablespoons soy sauce
3 tablespoons dry sherry
50 g/2 oz sugar crystals
1 teaspoon 5-spice powder
600 ml/1 pint beef stock
450 g/1 lb broccoli
Garnish:
radish flower, made by cutting V shapes out of
the top of a trimmed radish
shredded spring onions

Cut the meat into 2.5 cm/1 inch cubes and place in
a saucepan. Add the ginger, garlic, soy sauce and
sherry. Sprinkle over the sugar and 5-spice
powder.
Pour in the stock and bring to the boil, then
cover and simmer for 1 to 1½ hours, until the meat
is tender.
Divide the broccoli into florets and add to the
pan. Boil vigorously, uncovered, until the broccoli is just cooked and the stock reduced and
thickened.
Arrange the meat and broccoli on a warmed
serving dish and garnish with a radish flower and
shredded spring onions. Serve immediately.
SERVES 4 to 6

CATALAN BEEF STEW

METRIC/IMPERIAL
1 kg/2 lb topside of beef
polyunsaturated vegetable oil for frying
4 rashers lean bacon, derinded and chopped
1 medium onion, peeled and sliced
2 carrots, peeled and sliced
50 g/2 oz mushrooms, sliced
1 clove garlic, peeled and crushed
pinch each dried parsley, dried thyme and dried
rosemary
grated nutmeg
1 bay leaf
1 × 210 g/7½ oz can tomatoes
1 teaspoon black treacle
300 ml/½ pint cider
salt
freshly ground black pepper

Brown the meat on all sides in the oil in a frying
pan, then drain on kitchen paper towels. Lightly
fry the bacon, onion and carrots in the same pan,
drain and transfer to an ovenproof pot or casserole. Add the mushrooms, garlic, herbs and
nutmeg, and place the meat on top.
Mix together the tomatoes, treacle, cider and
salt and pepper to taste and pour over the joint.
Cook in a hot oven (220°C/425°F, Gas Mark 7) for
10 minutes and then turn the oven down to moderate (160°C/325°F, Gas Mark 3) and cook for a
further 1½ to 2 hours or until the meat is tender.
Lift the meat on to a warmed serving dish; leave
whole or cut into thick slices. Quickly sieve the
sauce or blend in a blender or food processor. Reheat in a separate pan, adjusting consistency and
seasoning if necessary.
SERVES 4 to 6

SILVERSIDE WITH MUSTARD AND HERB DUMPLINGS

METRIC/IMPERIAL
1.25 kg/2½ lb silverside of beef
2 carrots, peeled and diced
2 celery stalks, diced
2 onions, peeled and sliced
4 leeks, trimmed, washed and sliced
2 cloves garlic, peeled and crushed
salt
freshly ground black pepper
600 ml/1 pint boiling beef stock
sprigs of parsley, sage, marjoram and thyme, to
garnish
Dumplings (optional):
50 g/2 oz self-raising flour
50 g/2 oz fresh white breadcrumbs
1 teaspoon mustard powder
40 g/1½ oz shredded suet
2 tablespoons chopped fresh herbs
salt
freshly ground black pepper
1 egg, beaten
2 teaspoons prepared mustard

Place the meat on the vegetables in a steamer.
Season well with salt and pepper. Cover with a
tight-fitting lid and steam over the stock for 2
hours. Check the liquid level frequently and add
more boiling stock if necessary.
Meanwhile, mix together all the ingredients
for the dumplings, except the egg and prepared

mustard, in a mixing bowl. Blend in the beaten egg. Lightly flour your hands and shape the mixture into balls the size of walnuts. Make a hole in each by pushing a finger into it. Put a small amount of mustard in each hole and squeeze the dough to seal it in tightly. Drop the dumplings into the stock and continue to steam the beef as before for 8 minutes. Turn the dumplings over and cook for a further 8 minutes.

To serve, arrange the joint and vegetables on a large serving dish surrounded with dumplings and keep warm.

Reduce the stock until rich and syrupy and pour over the meat. Garnish with sprigs of parsley, sage, marjoram and thyme.
SERVES 4

PEPPERED TENDERLOIN WITH MUSTARD AND SPINACH

METRIC/IMPERIAL
50 g/2 oz black peppercorns
1.75 kg/4 lb beef tenderloin, trimmed
3 teaspoons Dijon mustard
2 tablespoons polyunsaturated vegetable oil
300 ml/½ pint beef stock
300 ml/½ pint red wine
2 tablespoons brandy
225 g/8 oz spinach, washed and large stalks discarded

Place the peppercorns in a plastic bag or tea towel. Crush with a mallet or rolling pin.

Spread the tenderloin with 2 teaspoons of the mustard and cover all sides with the crushed peppercorns. Heat the oil until very hot in a heavy-based pan. Fry the peppered beef to seal all of the edges. (Ventilate the kitchen well as the peppercorns can make your eyes sting.) Remove from the pan and set aside. Pour the beef stock, red wine and brandy into the frying pan. Bring to the boil, scraping the sediment from the base of the pan. Pour into a saucepan and stir in the remaining mustard. Bring to the boil.

Cut a piece of foil large enough to seal the meat completely. Arrange the spinach on the foil and place the meat on top. Fold up the edges and seal completely. Put the parcel in a steamer. Cover with a tight-fitting lid and steam over the stock mixture for 30 minutes.

Remove the meat parcel and leave to one side while finishing the sauce. Reduce the stock by boiling rapidly until syrupy.

Slice the beef and arrange with the spinach on 4 individual plates. Spoon over the sauce and serve immediately while hot.
SERVES 4

RAW BEEF WITH MUSTARD AND GHERKINS

METRIC/IMPERIAL
3 tablespoons plain low-fat yogurt
2 teaspoons coarse-grain mustard
1 tablespoon snipped chives
1 clove garlic, peeled and crushed
1 tablespoon dry sherry
salt
freshly ground black pepper
450 g/1 lb fillet of beef, in one piece
2 tablespoons olive oil
2 tablespoons minced gherkin
2 spring onions, cut into thin strips
Garnish:
thin slices of cucumber
fresh basil sprigs
gherkin fans

Mix the yogurt with the mustard, chives, garlic, sherry, and salt and pepper to taste.

Using a very sharp knife, cut the beef into paper-thin slices (it is easier to slice if it has been well chilled first). Arrange them overlapping on 4 dinner plates. Trickle a little olive oil over each portion; add a little gherkin and thin strips of spring onion to each portion.

Garnish each one with 3 slices of cucumber topped with a little of the prepared sauce, a sprig of fresh basil and a gherkin fan.
SERVES 4

BEEF STROGANOFF

METRIC/IMPERIAL
150 ml/¼ pint plain low-fat yogurt
1 teaspoon Dijon mustard
salt
freshly ground black pepper
450 g/1 lb beef fillet or sirloin steak, trimmed
2 large onions, peeled and chopped
about 150 ml/¼ pint beef stock
3 dessertspoons dry sherry
100 g/4 oz mushrooms, sliced

Mix the yogurt, mustard, salt and pepper together and set aside. Cut the steak carefully into wafer thin strips.

Put the onions in a saucepan with just enough stock to cover the bottom of the pan. Add the sherry and cook gently for about 10 minutes until softened, adding more stock if necessary. When the onions are transparent, add the beef and mushrooms and turn up the heat.

Cook for 1 minute, stirring rapidly. (If the beef is not cut wafer thin, the cooking time will be longer – about 3 to 5 minutes.) Remove from the heat and stir in the yogurt mixture. Serve immediately while piping hot.
SERVES 4

HERB-STUFFED SIRLOIN

METRIC/IMPERIAL
750 g/1½ lb sirloin steak, in one piece, trimmed of fat
2 slices bread
50 g/2 oz grated Parmesan cheese
2 teaspoons chopped fresh mixed herbs or
1 teaspoon dried mixed herbs
50 g/2 oz onion, peeled and finely chopped
salt
freshly ground black pepper
1 tablespoon Worcestershire sauce

Beat the steak into a thin strip using a meat mallet or rolling pin.

Dip the bread slices into cold water, squeeze and break into small pieces. Mix the bread with the Parmesan cheese, herbs, onion and salt and pepper to taste.

Sprinkle the steak with Worcestershire sauce and salt. Spoon the stuffing on to the steak and spread evenly. Roll up the steak and tie firmly with string at intervals. Place on a piece of foil large enough to enclose it and wrap like a parcel.

Cook in a preheated moderately hot oven (190°C/375°F, Gas Mark 5) for about 1 hour. Remove the string before serving, sliced crosswise. This may be eaten hot or cold.
SERVES 4

SIRLOIN STEAKS WITH TOMATO-GARLIC SAUCE

METRIC/IMPERIAL
4 sirloin steaks, trimmed
2 teaspoons polyunsaturated margarine
Tomato-garlic sauce:
750 g/1½ lb tomatoes, skinned and chopped
3 cloves garlic, peeled and crushed
1 tablespoon chopped fresh basil or 1 teaspoon dried basil
salt
freshly ground black pepper
basil sprigs, to garnish

Preheat the grill to high.

Beat the steaks with a meat mallet or rolling pin until fairly thin, then spread with the margarine. Place the steaks on the grill rack and grill for 8 to 10 minutes, or until cooked to your liking, turning them once.

Meanwhile, make the sauce: place the tomatoes, garlic, basil and salt and pepper in a saucepan and simmer gently for about 10 minutes, until the tomatoes are soft.

Transfer the steaks to a heated serving dish and pour over the sauce. Serve immediately, garnished with sprigs of basil.
SERVES 4

STEAK AU POIVRE

METRIC/IMPERIAL
4 sirloin steaks, each about 100 g/4 oz, trimmed
4 tablespoons black peppercorns, crushed
2 teaspoons polyunsaturated margarine, melted
Sauce:
2 × 150 g/5 oz cartons plain low-fat yogurt
2 tablespoons brandy
salt
freshly ground black pepper
watercress sprigs, to garnish

Preheat the grill to high.

Coat the steaks with the crushed peppercorns, pressing them in well.

Brush the steaks with the margarine and place

on the grill rack. Grill, turning several times, until cooked to your liking. Transfer to a heated serving dish and keep hot.

To make the sauce, place the yogurt in a saucepan and stir in the brandy and salt and pepper to taste. Heat gently without allowing to boil, then pour over the steaks. Garnish with watercress sprigs and serve immediately.
SERVES 4

SZECHUAN HOT SHREDDED BEEF

METRIC/IMPERIAL
450 g/1 lb rump or frying steak
2 tablespoons cornflour
salt
3 tablespoons polyunsaturated vegetable oil
4 spring onions, chopped
2 celery stalks, sliced diagonally
4 carrots, peeled and sliced diagonally
2 tablespoons soy sauce
1 tablespoon hoisin sauce
3 teaspoons chilli sauce
2 tablespoons dry sherry
Garnish:
carrot flowers, made by making V cuts along the length of a trimmed, peeled carrot and then cutting into slices
celery leaves

Cut the steak into 5 cm/2 inch long thin slices. Toss the steak in the cornflour and season with salt to taste.

Heat the oil in a wok or deep frying pan, add the spring onions and fry for 1 minute. Add the meat slices and cook for 4 minutes, stirring, until the meat is lightly browned. Add the celery and carrots and cook for 2 minutes. Stir in the soy, hoisin and chilli sauces and the sherry, bring to the boil and cook for 1 minute.

Arrange on a warmed serving dish, garnish decoratively with carrot flowers and celery leaves and serve immediately.
SERVES 4 to 6

MEXICAN BEEF KEBABS

METRIC/IMPERIAL
4 tablespoons polyunsaturated vegetable oil
1 small onion, peeled and chopped
4 tablespoons red wine vinegar
½ teaspoon salt
½ teaspoon oregano
½ teaspoon ground cumin
½ teaspoon ground cloves
½ teaspoon ground cinnamon
1 clove garlic, peeled and crushed
800 g/1¾ lb rump steak, trimmed of fat and cut into 2.5 cm/1 inch cubes
freshly ground black pepper
225 g/8 oz button mushrooms, wiped

Heat 2 tablespoons of the oil in a saucepan. Add the onion and sauté until golden brown. Stir in the vinegar, salt, oregano, spices and garlic. Cover and simmer for 15 to 20 minutes, then allow to cool. Lay the meat cubes in a dish, brush with the remaining oil and sprinkle with pepper. When the basting sauce has cooled, pour over the steak and leave in the refrigerator for 2 to 4 hours.

Thread the steak cubes on to skewers alternately with the mushrooms. Brush with the marinade and cook under a hot grill, for 12 to 15 minutes for rare steak, 20 minutes for well done. Turn and baste frequently with the marinade.
SERVES 6 to 8

GINGERED BEEF

METRIC/IMPERIAL
750 g/1½ lb rump, boneless sirloin or good blade steak, trimmed of fat and cut
4 cm/1½ inches thick
120 ml/4 fl oz soy sauce
2 tablespoons polyunsaturated vegetable oil
3 tablespoons honey
1 clove garlic, peeled and crushed
1 tablespoon grated root ginger

Slice the meat across the grain into 5 mm/¼ inch strips and place in a bowl. Mix the remaining ingredients and pour over, turning to coat evenly. Marinate for 1 hour, turning the meat frequently.

Remove the meat strips from the marinade and thread on to skewers, concertina or 'snake' fashion. Cook under a very hot grill for about 3 minutes, turning once and brushing with the marinade. The meat should be rare on the inside.
SERVES 4 to 6

QUICK-FRIED BEEF IN OYSTER SAUCE

METRIC/IMPERIAL
4 carrots, peeled
2 celery stalks
2 tablespoons polyunsaturated vegetable oil
4 spring onions, chopped
2 cloves garlic, peeled and sliced
350 g/12 oz rump or sirloin steak, trimmed of fat
salt
100 g/4 oz bean-sprouts
1 tablespoon soy sauce
2 tablespoons dry sherry
3 tablespoons oyster sauce
Garnish:
carrot flower, made by making V cuts along the length of a trimmed, peeled carrot and then cutting into slices
celery leaves

Slice the carrots and celery stalks diagonally.

Heat the oil in a wok or frying pan, add the spring onions and garlic and fry quickly for about 30 seconds. Add the carrots and celery and stir-fry for 1 minute.

Cut the steak into thin slices and sprinkle with salt. Add to the pan and fry until browned on all sides. Stir in the bean-sprouts, soy sauce, sherry and oyster sauce and cook for 2 minutes.

Spoon the mixture on to a serving dish and garnish with the carrot flower and celery leaves.

SERVES 4 to 6

FRIED STEAK WITH CHILLI

METRIC/IMPERIAL
500 g/1¼ lb rump steak or topside of beef, trimmed of fat
2 teaspoons ground coriander
2 tablespoons tamarind water (see page 82)
1 teaspoon brown sugar
salt
freshly ground black pepper
8 red chillies, deseeded and chopped
4 shallots, peeled and chopped
2 cloves garlic, peeled and chopped
6 tablespoons polyunsaturated vegetable oil
1 teaspoon lemon juice

Slice the meat thinly across the grain, then cut the slices into 5 cm/2 inch squares. Arrange in a single layer on a plate and sprinkle with the coriander, tamarind water, sugar, and salt and pepper to taste. Press each piece with your hands so that the spices are thoroughly absorbed into the meat, then spread the slices out on the plate again. Leave to stand for 2 to 3 hours.

Put the chillies, shallots and garlic in a mortar and pound until broken, but not reduced to a paste. Heat the oil in a heavy frying pan. Add the meat and fry until evenly browned and cooked through. Remove from the pan with a slotted spoon and keep hot.

Add the pounded mixture to the oil remaining in the pan and sauté for 2 to 3 minutes, stirring constantly. Return the meat to the pan and stir to coat with the spice mixture. Add the lemon juice and salt to taste and stir well. Serve hot.

SERVES 4

BEEF OLIVES

METRIC/IMPERIAL
750 g/1½ lb rump steak, trimmed of fat
2 tablespoons corn oil
1 onion, peeled and chopped
2 cloves garlic, peeled and crushed
50 g/2 oz mushrooms, chopped
1 tablespoon chopped parsley
1 teaspoon chopped thyme
1 large slice wholemeal bread, crusts removed
salt
freshly ground black pepper
300 ml/½ pint beef stock
parsley sprigs, to garnish

Cut the beef into 4 thin slices. Place between sheets of greaseproof paper and beat to flatten. Trim each slice.

Heat 1 tablespoon oil in a saucepan and sauté the onion and garlic until softened. Add the mushrooms and herbs and fry, stirring, for 2 minutes.

Place the bread in an electric blender and grind coarsely. Remove the vegetable mixture from the heat and stir in the breadcrumbs. Add salt and pepper to taste and mix well.

Divide the stuffing between the beef slices and spread evenly. Roll up and secure with string. Heat the remaining oil in a flameproof casserole and fry the beef rolls until evenly browned.

Pour in the stock and wine. Cover and cook in a preheated moderate oven (160°C/325°F, Gas Mark 3) for 1½ hours. Serve hot, garnished with sprigs of parsley.

SERVES 4

BOEUF EN DAUBE

METRIC/IMPERIAL
4 × 100 g/4 oz rump steaks, trimmed of fat
2-3 lean bacon rashers, derinded and chopped
1 wine glass red wine
1 teaspoon chopped fresh mixed herbs or
½ teaspoon dried mixed herbs
2 carrots, scraped and chopped
2 tomatoes, peeled and chopped
salt
freshly ground black pepper
50 g/2 oz onions, peeled and sliced
strip of orange peel
300 ml/½ pint beef stock

Place the steaks under a preheated hot grill and cook for 1 minute on each side. Transfer to a casserole and add all the remaining ingredients. Place in a preheated very hot oven (240°C/475°F, Gas Mark 9) for 15 minutes. By this time the casserole should be boiling.

Reduce the oven temperature to 160°C/325°F, Gas Mark 3, cover and cook for 1 hour. Remove from the oven and leave to cool. Remove all the fat from the top of the casserole.

Replace in a preheated moderate oven (180°C/350°F, Gas Mark 4) for 1 hour, adding more stock if necessary. Serve immediately.
SERVES 4

FRENCH-STYLE LAMB

METRIC/IMPERIAL
450 g/1 lb lean boned leg of lamb
2 tablespoons polyunsaturated vegetable oil
1 large onion, peeled and sliced
1 clove garlic, peeled and crushed
1 × 450 g/1 lb can tomatoes
1 tablespoon tomato purée
150 ml/¼ pint dry white wine
1 rosemary sprig
1 thyme sprig
1 bay leaf
salt
freshly ground black pepper
100 g/4 oz mushrooms, sliced
1 green pepper, cored, deseeded and sliced
chopped parsley, to garnish

Trim any excess fat from the lamb and cut into 2.5 cm/1 inch cubes. Heat the oil in a flameproof casserole or heavy-based pan. Add the onion and garlic and sauté until golden.

Add the lamb cubes and cook, stirring frequently, for 5 minutes or until evenly browned. Stir in the tomatoes and their juice, tomato purée and wine. Add the rosemary, thyme, bay leaf and salt and pepper to taste. Stir well, then cover and simmer for 45 minutes.

Add the sliced mushrooms and green pepper to the casserole. Check the seasoning, cover and continue simmering for a further 20 minutes.

Discard the herbs. Sprinkle with chopped parsley and serve with brown rice.
SERVES 4

LAMB AND BARLEY STEW

METRIC/IMPERIAL
1 tablespoon polyunsaturated vegetable oil
750 g/1½-1¾ lb boned shoulder of lamb,
trimmed and cut into 5 cm/2 inch cubes
25 g/1 oz pearl barley, soaked for 2 hours in
cold water
50 g/2 oz unsoaked dried apricots
few parsley stalks
25 g/1 oz sultanas
1 onion, peeled and sliced
1 garlic clove, peeled and crushed
450 ml/¾ pint stock
1 tablespoon lemon juice
salt
freshly ground black pepper
chopped parsley, to garnish

Heat the oil in a frying pan, add the lamb in batches and fry until browned on all sides. Transfer to a flameproof casserole with a slotted spoon. Drain the pearl barley and add to the casserole, with the apricots, parsley stalks and sultanas.

Add the onion and garlic to the frying pan and fry gently for 5 minutes without browning. Stir in the stock, lemon juice and salt and pepper to taste and bring to the boil, then pour over the lamb.

Place the casserole over a moderate heat and bring to the boil. Lower the heat, then cover the casserole and simmer for 1 hour or until the lamb is tender, stirring occasionally.
SERVES 4

LAMB BIRYANI

METRIC/IMPERIAL
1.25 kg/2½ lb shoulder of lamb, trimmed of fat
50 g/2 oz polyunsaturated margarine
4 whole cardamom pods
2 cloves
1 small cinnamon stick
2 cloves garlic, peeled and crushed
15 g/½ oz fresh root ginger, peeled and grated
1 large onion, peeled and roughly chopped
20 cashew nuts, toasted
20 almonds, toasted
1 tablespoon sultanas
salt
freshly ground black pepper
225 g/8 oz basmati rice
450 ml/¾ pint water
1 teaspoon saffron threads, or 2 drops yellow food colouring
2 tablespoons warm skimmed milk
Garnish:
2 hard-boiled eggs, sliced
2 tomatoes, sliced

Take the lamb off the bone and cut into bite-sized pieces. Reserve the bones. Heat the margarine in a pan. Fry the lamb to brown on all sides. Remove from the pan and put to one side. Fry the cardamoms, cloves and cinnamon stick in the same pan for 2 minutes, being careful not to burn them. Add the garlic, ginger and onion and continue to cook for 5 minutes. Stir in half the quantity of nuts and all of the sultanas. Return the meat to the pan. Season very well with salt and black pepper.

Lay a piece of wet greaseproof paper in the base of a steamer compartment, and arrange the meat mixture on top. Wash the rice and put in a saucepan with the lamb bones and the water. Bring to the boil, cover the steamer and steam the meat over the rice for 12 to 15 minutes. Meanwhile, mix the saffron or food colouring with the milk.

Remove the bones from the rice. Season very well with salt and pepper. Place the rice on top of the meat, piling it up in the shape of a hill. Make a deep hole in the centre with the long handle of a wooden spoon. Dribble the saffron milk over the sides of the hill. Cover again and steam over boiling water for 1 hour. Check the liquid level frequently and add more boiling water if necessary.

To serve, transfer the rice mixture to a warmed serving dish, remove the cinnamon stick and mix gently. Garnish with sliced egg and tomatoes, and the remaining cashew nuts and almonds.
SERVES 4

YOGURT LAMB KEBABS

METRIC/IMPERIAL
750 g/1½ lb lamb fillet pieces
1 clove garlic, peeled and crushed
salt
freshly ground black pepper
150 ml/¼ pint plain low-fat yogurt
8 small onions, peeled
4 small tomatoes
1 large green pepper, cored, deseeded and sliced
8 button mushrooms, wiped
4 bay leaves
rosemary or parsley sprigs, to garnish

Put the lamb pieces in a dish. Stir the garlic and salt and pepper into the yogurt, pour over the lamb and leave to marinate for several hours or overnight.

Drain the lamb and thread on to 4 skewers, alternating with the onions, tomatoes, pepper, mushrooms and bay leaves. Put the skewers on a wire tray over a roasting tin and cook in a pre-heated moderately hot oven (190°C/375°F, Gas Mark 5) for about 30 minutes.

Garnish with the rosemary or parsley sprigs. If liked, serve with plain boiled rice and the remaining yogurt marinade.
SERVES 4

MARROW STUFFED WITH LAMB

METRIC/IMPERIAL
750 g/1½ lb lamb fillet pieces or steak, trimmed and finely chopped
120 ml/4 fl oz chicken stock
25 g/1 oz onion, peeled and chopped
2 teaspoons chopped fresh rosemary or
1 teaspoon dried rosemary
250 ml/8 fl oz tomato juice
salt
freshly ground black pepper
100 g/4 oz long-grain rice
1 medium-sized marrow, skinned, cut lengthwise and deseeded

Put the lamb, stock, chopped onion and rosemary in a saucepan and bring to the boil. Add the tomato juice, salt and pepper and simmer for 15 to 20 minutes until the mixture thickens.

Remove from the heat and leave to marinate overnight. Carefully remove all the fat.

Put the rice in a saucepan of boiling salted water

and cook for about 12 minutes or until just tender. Drain the rice, mix with the lamb and spoon into the marrow halves. Wrap the stuffed marrow in foil and bake in a preheated moderately hot oven (200°C/400°F, Gas Mark 6) for 1 to 1¼ hours. Serve immediately.
SERVES 4

NORTH COUNTRY LAMB

METRIC/IMPERIAL
225 g/8 oz dried haricot beans, soaked overnight
2 tablespoons polyunsaturated vegetable oil
1 kg/2 lb boned leg of lamb
1 large onion, peeled and sliced
1 small swede, peeled and cubed
1 large turnip, peeled and cubed
2 cloves garlic, peeled and crushed
1 parsnip, peeled and cubed
salt
freshly ground black pepper
150 ml/¼ pint lamb or beef stock
½ teaspoon fresh or ¼ teaspoon dried rosemary
1 teaspoon chopped mint
1 tablespoon redcurrant jelly
Garnish:
rosemary sprigs
mint sprigs

Drain the haricot beans and boil in clean water for 20 minutes. Drain well. Heat the oil in a heavy-based pan and fry the lamb until brown on all sides. Transfer to a large pudding basin. Fry the vegetables in the same pan for 5 minutes and spoon over the lamb. Stir in the drained beans. Season very well with salt and pepper.

Pour the stock into the frying pan, stir in the rosemary, mint and redcurrant jelly. Bring to the boil, scraping the sediment from the base of the pan. Pour over the lamb. Cover with foil and tie down with string. Cook in a steamer or covered saucepan half-filled with boiling water for 1½ hours. Check the liquid level frequently and add more boiling water if necessary.

Arrange the meat and vegetables on a warmed serving dish and keep warm. Boil any remaining stock until rich and syrupy, tasting and adjusting seasoning as necessary. Pour over the meat and garnish with sprigs of rosemary and mint.
SERVES 4

CHILLI BEANS WITH LAMB

METRIC/IMPERIAL
100 g/4 oz each dried pinto beans, dried red kidney beans, black beans and white haricot beans
300 ml/½ pint vegetable stock
250 ml/8 fl oz dry red wine
1 kg/2¼ lb ripe tomatoes
1 large onion
1 clove garlic
2 tablespoons polyunsaturated vegetable oil
750 g/1½ lb minced lean lamb
1 tablespoon dried oregano
hot chilli powder
salt
2 tablespoons chopped parsley

Rinse the beans in cold water. Cover with the vegetable stock and soak for 12 hours.

The following day add the red wine, bring to the boil and boil hard for 5 minutes. Reduce the heat and cook the beans gently for about 30 minutes.

Meanwhile, blanch the tomatoes in boiling water for 30 seconds, rinse in cold water and peel. Dice the tomatoes, removing the seeds.

Peel and finely chop the onion and garlic. Heat the oil in a saucepan. Cook the minced lamb over a moderate to high heat, stirring continuously, until it is grey in colour and of crumbly texture. Add the onion and garlic and fry until transparent. Add the tomatoes and cook until they form a juice.

Add the beans and their cooking liquid and stir in well. Season with the oregano and a generous pinch of chilli powder. Bring to the boil, then cover the pan and cook over a low heat for about 1½ hours until the beans are tender but not mushy. Stir frequently as it cooks, adding a little more stock from time to time if necessary.

Season to taste with salt and chilli powder and serve sprinkled with parsley.
SERVES 6

PAPRIKA AND ORANGE LAMB KEBABS

METRIC/IMPERIAL
500 g/1¼ lb lamb fillet, trimmed and cut into
2.5 cm/1 inch cubes
1 large red pepper, cored, deseeded and cut into
2.5 cm/1 inch pieces
Marinade:
1 tablespoon olive oil
2 tablespoons tomato purée
1 teaspoon paprika
2 tablespoons red wine
1 small onion, peeled and grated
grated rind and juice of 1 small orange
2 teaspoons honey
3 drops Tabasco
salt
freshly ground black pepper
Garnish:
4 sprigs of rosemary
4 orange slices

Place the lamb cubes in a shallow dish. Combine the marinade ingredients in a bowl and mix well. Pour over the lamb and stir. Cover and refrigerate for 6 to 8 hours or overnight.
Preheat the oven to 190°C/375°F, Gas Mark 5.
Arrange the lamb on 4 kebab skewers with the pepper pieces. Place on a rack over a dish or tin and spoon the remaining marinade over the kebabs. Place rosemary sprigs below the kebabs and cook in the oven for 20 to 30 minutes, or under a preheated medium hot grill for 15 to 20 minutes, turning once. Transfer to a heated serving dish and garnish the kebabs with rosemary sprigs and orange slices. Serve with brown rice and a fresh green salad.
SERVES 4

WHITE LAMB CASSEROLE

METRIC/IMPERIAL
2 medium onions, peeled and thinly sliced
1 tablespoon olive oil
1 clove garlic, peeled and crushed
450 g/1 lb lean lamb, cut in small cubes
1 × 450 g/1 lb can chick peas, rinsed and drained
300 ml/½ pint chicken stock
1 teaspoon saffron strands, soaked in
2 tablespoons boiling water
salt
freshly ground black pepper
2 tablespoons plain low-fat yogurt

Sauté the onions gently in the oil in a non-stick pan for 3 minutes; add the garlic and lamb and cook until the meat is evenly browned on all sides.
Transfer the lamb and onions to a casserole and add half the drained chick peas. Put the remaining chick peas into a blender or food processor with the chicken stock, strained saffron liquid, and salt and pepper to taste; blend until smooth.
Pour the blended sauce into the casserole. Cover and cook in a preheated moderate oven (180°C/350°F, Gas Mark 4) for about 1 hour, or until the lamb is tender (the total cooking time will depend on the cut of lamb used). Swirl the yogurt over the top and serve immediately.
SERVES 4

Variation
Red kidney beans can be used in place of chick peas, but they will change the colour of the dish. Use canned beans, or well-cooked dried ones.

RED-COOKED LAMB

METRIC/IMPERIAL
1.5 kg/2-3 lb boned shoulder of lamb, cubed
salt
freshly ground black pepper
2 tablespoons polyunsaturated vegetable oil
1 onion, peeled and chopped
1 clove garlic, peeled and crushed
3 tablespoons soy sauce
4 tablespoons dry sherry
2 teaspoons sugar
120 ml/¼ pint brown stock
2 slices root ginger
2 bay leaves
2 teaspoons cornflour
1 small red pepper, cored, deseeded and cut into strips

Season the meat well. Heat the oil in a frying pan, brown the meat and sauté the onion and garlic until transparent. Drain and transfer to an oven-proof dish or casserole. Mix together the soy sauce, sherry, sugar and stock. Pour over the meat and mix well. Add the ginger and bay leaves. Cook in a preheated moderate oven (180°C/350°F, Gas Mark 4) for 1½ to 2 hours, or until the meat is tender. About 30 minutes before serving, stir in the cornflour, blended with 2 tablespoons cold water. Just before serving, remove the ginger and bay leaves from the casserole, and sprinkle with red pepper. Serve with plain boiled rice.
SERVES 4 to 6

LAMB AND VEGETABLE CASSEROLE

METRIC/IMPERIAL

750 g/1½ lb boned leg or shoulder of lamb,
trimmed of fat and cut into cubes
2 onions, peeled and chopped
1 clove garlic, peeled and crushed
2 carrots, peeled and sliced
2 green peppers, cored, deseeded and chopped
300 ml/½ pint tomato juice
salt
freshly ground black pepper
2 potatoes, peeled and diced
225 g/8 oz French beans, diced

Take a piece of fat from the lamb and rub over the base of a heavy pan. Add the lamb and cook gently until the meat is browned on all sides.

Add the onions and garlic and continue cooking gently for 5 minutes, stirring occasionally. Add the carrots, peppers, tomato juice and salt and pepper to taste, then cover and simmer for 1 hour.

Add the potatoes and beans to the pan, cover and continue simmering for 30 minutes. Taste and adjust the seasoning, then serve hot with a seasonal green vegetable.

SERVES 4

MARINATED LAMB SKEWERS

METRIC/IMPERIAL

750 g/1½ lb boneless lamb, trimmed of fat and
cut into 2.5 cm/1 inch cubes
8 button onions, peeled
8 button mushrooms, wiped and trimmed
4 small tomatoes
1 large green pepper, cored, deseeded and cut
into 2.5 cm/1 inch pieces
4 bay leaves, to garnish
Marinade:
1 clove garlic, peeled and crushed
salt
freshly ground black pepper
juice of 2 large lemons
2 tablespoons tomato purée
½ teaspoon Tabasco

Place the lamb cubes in a shallow dish. Combine the marinade ingredients and pour over the lamb. Stir to mix, cover and store in the refrigerator for at least 3 hours, stirring from time to time.

Remove the lamb from the marinade, dry the pieces well, then thread on to 4 greased kebab skewers, alternating with the onions, mushrooms, tomatoes and pepper. Preheat the grill to moderate.

Place the skewers on the grill rack and grill for about 15 minutes, turning frequently and basting with the marinade, until the lamb is cooked but still slightly pink inside. Transfer the skewers to a heated serving dish, garnish with bay leaves and serve immediately.

SERVES 4

ITALIAN LAMB STEW

METRIC/IMPERIAL

1 kg/2 lb boneless lamb, cut from leg or
shoulder
2 tablespoons polyunsaturated vegetable oil
225 g/8 oz lean bacon, derinded and diced
1 onion, peeled and sliced
2 cloves garlic, peeled and crushed
salt
freshly ground black pepper
1 teaspoon chopped fresh marjoram or
½ teaspoon dried marjoram
1 teaspoon chopped fresh rosemary or
¼ teaspoon dried rosemary
120 ml/4 fl oz red wine
2 tablespoons tomato purée

Trim excess fat from the meat and cut into bite-sized squares. Heat the oil in a large heavy frying pan. Add the bacon, onion and garlic and sauté until golden. Remove with a slotted spoon and set aside. Add half the meat and brown on all sides, then remove from the pan and repeat with the remaining meat.

Return the meat to the pan and season with salt, pepper, marjoram and rosemary. Stir in the red wine and cook gently until the wine reduces to half its original quantity. Add the bacon mixture, tomato purée and enough water to cover the meat. Cover and simmer slowly for about 1½ hours or until tender. Serve with flat ribbon noodles or brown rice and a crisp green salad.

SERVES 4 to 6

LAMB REINE CLAUDE

METRIC/IMPERIAL
450 g/1 lb Reine Claude plums, or greengages, halved and stoned
150 ml/¼ pint chicken stock
3 tablespoons Crème de Cassis
450 g/1 lb lamb fillet, cut in small medallions
2 tablespoons olive oil
salt
freshly ground black pepper

Put the plums or greengages into a pan with the chicken stock and simmer gently for 5 minutes. Cool slightly, then put into a blender or food processor with the liquid and the Crème de Cassis; blend to a smooth purée.

Cook the lamb medallions in the olive oil until evenly browned on all sides; add the plum and Cassis purée to the medallions and season to taste with salt and pepper.

Cover and simmer for about 15 to 20 minutes until the lamb is quite tender. Serve immediately.
SERVES 4

LAMB KEBABS WITH BARBECUE SAUCE

METRIC/IMPERIAL
450 g/1 lb lean lamb, trimmed and cut into 4 cm/1½ inch cubes
8 small tomatoes, washed
12 small mushrooms, wiped and trimmed
5 tablespoons lemon juice
3 tablespoons soy sauce
4 teaspoons Worcestershire sauce
1 garlic clove, peeled and crushed
40 g/1½ oz polyunsaturated margarine
To finish:
½ small cabbage, washed and shredded
4 carrots, grated
2 small apples, unpeeled, washed and diced

Thread the meat, tomatoes and mushrooms alternately on to 4 skewers. Put the lemon juice, soy sauce, Worcestershire sauce, garlic and margarine into a small pan and heat to melt the fat. Marinate the skewered kebabs in the mixture for 2 hours.

Cook the kebabs on a barbecue or under a preheated hot grill for 10 to 15 minutes or until the meat is tender, turning and basting with the remaining sauce. Serve on a bed of shredded cabbage, carrot and apple.
SERVES 4

GREEK LAMB WITH YOGURT DRESSING

METRIC/IMPERIAL
1 kg/2 lb lamb, cut from the leg in bite-sized cubes
3 tablespoons dry sherry
2 cloves garlic, peeled and finely chopped
2 shallots, peeled and finely chopped
2 tablespoons olive oil
salt
freshly ground black pepper
1 green pepper, deseeded and cut into bite-sized pieces
8 cherry tomatoes
2 courgettes, thickly sliced
4 small onions, peeled and cut in halves or quarters (depending on size)
3 teaspoons chopped fresh mint
4 teaspoons chopped chives
150 ml/¼ pint lamb or beef stock
150 ml/¼ pint plain low-fat yogurt

Trim any fat from the lamb and place in a shallow dish. Mix together the sherry, garlic, shallots and half of the oil in a bowl. Season well with salt and pepper and spoon over the lamb. Stir the lamb so that it is thoroughly coated. Cover with cling film and leave to marinate for 12 to 24 hours.

Carefully remove the lamb from the marinade and dry on absorbent kitchen paper reserving the marinade for the dressing. Heat the remaining oil in a heavy-based pan. Fry the lamb cubes over high heat until brown on all sides. Stir in the pepper, tomatoes, courgette and onion, and season well with salt and pepper.

Cut a piece of foil large enough to seal the food completely. Spoon on the food, and sprinkle with half of the mint and chives. Pour the stock into the frying pan, and bring to the boil scraping the sediment from the base of the pan. Boil to reduce until syrupy. Pour over the meat. Fold up the edges and squeeze to seal the food. Place in the steamer, cover with a tight-fitting lid and steam over boiling water for 25 to 30 minutes. Check the liquid level frequently and add more boiling water, if necessary.

Meanwhile, bring the marinade to the boil in a pan. Stir in the remaining herbs. Taste and adjust the seasoning if necessary. Leave to cool, then stir in the yogurt.

Remove the foil, and transfer the contents to a warmed serving plate. Spoon the dressing over the meat or serve separately.
SERVES 4

EASTERN LAMB

METRIC/IMPERIAL

100 g/4 oz onion, peeled and chopped
1 clove garlic, peeled and crushed
120 ml/4 fl oz tomato juice
750 g/1½ lb lamb fillet pieces (or lamb steak, cut into pieces)
½ teaspoon ground mace
½ teaspoon ground coriander
1 teaspoon chopped fresh rosemary or
½ teaspoon dried rosemary
120 ml/4 fl oz chicken stock
1 tablespoon lemon juice
salt
freshly ground black pepper

Put the onion and crushed garlic in a saucepan with the tomato juice. Bring to the boil, then simmer until the onion is softened. Add the lamb pieces and stir in the spices and rosemary. Add the stock, lemon juice, salt and pepper and bring to the boil.

Transfer all the ingredients to a casserole dish. Cover and cook in a preheated moderate oven (160°C/325°F, Gas Mark 3) for about 30 minutes until tender. (The cooking time depends on the size of the lamb pieces.) Skim off any fat with a spoon or fat whisk, or leave until cold and remove the fat, then reheat.

SERVES 4

LEG OF LAMB WITH HERBS

METRIC/IMPERIAL

1 teaspoon polyunsaturated vegetable oil
1 small onion, peeled and chopped
2 leeks, trimmed, washed and finely sliced
100 g/4 oz salsify, peeled and chopped
2 large cloves garlic, peeled and crushed
1 × 1 kg/2 lb lean leg of lamb, boned
150 ml/¼ pint lamb or beef stock
1½ tablespoons redcurrant jelly
rosemary sprigs
mint sprigs
salt
freshly ground black pepper
rosemary or mint sprigs, to garnish

Heat the oil in a heavy-based pan, fry the onion, leek, salsify and garlic for 3 minutes. Cut a piece of foil large enough to seal the meat and vegetables completely. Spoon the vegetables into the centre of the foil. Fry the meat over a high heat to brown on all sides. Place on top of the vegetables. Pour the stock into the frying pan and bring to the boil scraping all sediment from the base of the pan. Fold the edges of the foil up around the meat. Pour in the stock. Add the redcurrant jelly, rosemary and mint, season with salt and pepper, seal completely. Place in a steamer, cover with a tight-fitting lid and steam over boiling water for 1 hour. Check the liquid every 15 minutes and add more boiling water, if necessary.

Remove the lamb and leave to stand for 10 minutes. Meanwhile, pour the vegetables and stock into a saucepan and boil to reduce until syrupy. Taste and adjust the seasoning if necessary. Slice the lamb into 1 cm/½ inch slices; arrange on a warmed serving dish and pour the sauce over the lamb. Garnish with sprigs of rosemary or mint.

SERVES 4

HONEY-GINGER LAMB

METRIC/IMPERIAL

1 boned shoulder of lamb, trimmed of fat and rolled
175 g/6 oz warmed honey
2 tablespoons lemon juice
1 tablespoon soy sauce
¼ teaspoon ground cloves
1 teaspoon ground ginger
stock or vegetable water for gravy

Weigh the meat to calculate the required cooking time. Lamb should be roasted for 25 minutes per 450 g/1 lb, plus 25 minutes extra. Roast the meat in a preheated hot oven (220°C/425°F, Gas Mark 7) for the first 20 minutes.

Meanwhile, mix the warmed honey, lemon juice, soy sauce, cloves and ginger, then baste the meat with the mixture. Turn the oven down to moderate (180°C/350°F, Gas Mark 4) and roast the meat for the remaining required time, basting and turning it frequently. Place the meat on a serving dish. Skim the pan juices and add stock or vegetable water to make a gravy.

SERVES 4 to 6

207

SHOULDER OF LAMB STUFFED WITH APRICOTS

METRIC/IMPERIAL
175 g/6 oz dried apricots
25 g/1 oz onion, peeled and chopped
2 teaspoons chopped fresh rosemary or
1 teaspoon dried rosemary
75 g/3 oz wholemeal breadcrumbs
1 egg, beaten
salt
freshly ground black pepper
1 × 1.5 kg/3 lb shoulder of lamb, boned and trimmed

Soak the apricots overnight. Drain and reserve the soaking liquid. Roughly chop the apricots and mix with the onion, rosemary and breadcrumbs. Stir in the beaten egg to bind the mixture. Add a little apricot soaking liquid, if necessary, and salt and pepper to taste.

Spoon the stuffing into the lamb bone cavity and sew up the edges, using a trussing needle and string, to enclose the stuffing completely. Roast in a preheated moderately hot oven (200°C/400°F, Gas Mark 6) for 1½ hours or until tender. Serve immediately with seasonal vegetables.
SERVES 6

LAMB EN PAPILLOTE

METRIC/IMPERIAL
150 ml/¼ pint lamb stock
2 tablespoons red wine
8 lamb cutlets, trimmed of fat
salt
freshly ground black pepper
1 tablespoon olive oil
1 onion, peeled and finely chopped
175 g/6 oz fresh runner beans, topped, tailed and cut into bite-sized pieces
175 g/6 oz shelled broad beans
100 g/4 oz shelled fresh or frozen peas
4 teaspoons mint sauce
2 teaspoons redcurrant jelly
small sprigs of rosemary
2 cloves of garlic, peeled and finely chopped

Boil the stock and red wine until syrupy. Season the cutlets of lamb with salt and pepper. Heat the oil in a heavy-based pan, and fry the cutlets until golden brown on all sides. Remove them from the pan and set aside. Fry the onion in the same pan until cooked but not brown. Pour in the stock and

bring to the boil, scraping any sediment from the base of the pan. Keep to one side. Cook the vegetables in a steamer for 3 minutes then plunge them in cold water.

Cut 4 × 35 cm/14 inch square pieces of foil. Arrange 2 lamb cutlets and a quarter of the vegetables on each piece of foil. Divide the mint sauce, redcurrant jelly, the sprigs of rosemary and garlic between each portion. Fold up the sides but leave open. Spoon on the stock and onions and season well with salt and pepper. Seal the parcels completely and place in the steamer. Cover with a tight-fitting lid and steam over boiling water for 15 minutes. Allow your guests to open the parcels themselves at the table.
SERVES 4

LAMB CUTLETS WITH PROVENÇAL SAUCE

METRIC/IMPERIAL
4 tablespoons wholemeal breadcrumbs
1 teaspoon salt
½ teaspoon pepper
8 lamb cutlets, trimmed of fat
1 egg, beaten
polyunsaturated vegetable oil for shallow frying
Provençal sauce:
2 tablespoons olive oil
1 onion, peeled and sliced
1 red and 1 green pepper, cored, seeded and sliced
4 tomatoes, skinned
1 clove garlic, peeled and crushed
1 teaspoon tomato purée
1 teaspoon chopped thyme
salt
freshly ground black pepper
Garnish:
chopped parsley
chopped basil (optional)

Mix the breadcrumbs with the salt and pepper. Brush the cutlets with the egg and roll in the breadcrumbs, pressing them on well with a palette knife.

To make the sauce: heat the oil in a pan, add the onion and peppers and fry until softened. Cut the tomatoes into 8 and add to the pan. Add the remaining ingredients, with salt and pepper to taste. Cover and simmer for 7 to 8 minutes.

Pour the oil into a frying pan and place over moderate heat. When the oil is hot, add the chops and fry for 4 to 5 minutes on each side until tender and golden brown; drain on kitchen paper. Alternatively, grill the chops under a medium heat.

Arrange the cutlets along one side of a warmed serving dish and spoon the sauce on the other side. Sprinkle with the parsley and basil (if using), and serve with brown rice.

SERVES 4

LAMB WITH PIQUANT SAUCE

METRIC/IMPERIAL
8 lamb cutlets or 4 lamb chops, trimmed of fat
2 beef stock cubes
8 tablespoons Worcestershire sauce
2 teaspoons chopped fresh rosemary or
1 teaspoon dried rosemary
1 teaspoon ground coriander
120 ml/4 fl oz water
salt
freshly ground black pepper

Put the cutlets or chops in a flameproof dish. Crumble the stock cubes into the Worcestershire sauce and stir in the rosemary and coriander. Pour over the lamb and leave to marinate for at least 3 hours, turning frequently.

Remove the lamb from the marinade and cook under a hot grill for 10 minutes or until the lamb is cooked to your taste. Turn the meat frequently, spooning over the marinade to prevent burning.

Put the rest of the marinade in a saucepan with the water, salt and pepper, and bring to the boil. Arrange the lamb cutlets on a heated serving dish and pour the sauce over. Serve immediately.

SERVES 4

LEMON CHOPS

METRIC/IMPERIAL
4 lamb chops, trimmed of fat
2 tablespoons corn oil
grated rind of 1 lemon
2 tablespoons lemon juice
2 teaspoons Muscovado sugar
1 teaspoon ground ginger
salt
freshly ground black pepper
parsley sprigs, to garnish

Put the chops into a shallow dish. Mix together the oil, lemon rind and juice, sugar and ginger and pour over the chops. Cover and leave to marinate

in a cool place for 3 hours, turning the chops over occasionally.

Transfer the chops to a grill rack and brush with the marinade. Cook under a preheated grill for 15 minutes, turning the chops 2 or 3 times and basting them frequently.

Garnish with parsley sprigs and serve immediately accompanied by brown rice and a crisp green salad or vegetables.

SERVES 4

DOLMADES

METRIC/IMPERIAL
12 vine, cabbage or spinach leaves
1 tablespoon olive oil
1 onion, peeled and finely chopped
4 tablespoons long-grain rice
salt
freshly ground black pepper
pinch of allspice
pinch of crushed rosemary
juice of 1 lemon
100 g/4 oz mushrooms, wiped and sliced
300 ml/½ pint chicken stock
100 g/4 oz lean minced lamb
2 tablespoons chopped parsley
25 g/1 oz pine nuts
1 teaspoon chopped mint
lemon wedges, to garnish (optional)

Cook the leaves in a steamer for 30 seconds over boiling water. Lay out flat and dry on absorbent kitchen paper. If using canned vine leaves, just unravel them carefully without breaking. Heat the oil and fry the onion and rice until lightly coloured. Season well with salt and pepper.

Stir in the allspice, rosemary, lemon juice, mushroom and just enough stock to bring the liquid 2.5 cm/1 inch above the top of the rice. Cover with a tight-fitting lid and cook gently for 12 minutes without lifting the lid. Leave to cool.

Stir in the lamb, parsley, nuts and mint. Season once more with salt and pepper. Spoon about 2 teaspoons of the mixture on to each leaf and wrap up tightly. Pack the dolmades in layers in the steamer. Cover and steam over the remaining stock for 1 hour. Check the liquid level frequently and add more boiling stock or water if necessary.

Arrange the dolmades on a warmed serving dish. Serve with a bowl of chilled yogurt.

SERVES 4

STEAMED LANCASHIRE HOT POT

METRIC/IMPERIAL
2 joints best end neck of lamb, cut into cutlets
and trimmed of fat
salt
freshly ground black pepper
1 kg/2 lb potatoes, peeled and thickly sliced
3 lambs' kidneys, skinned, cored and quartered
4 small carrots, peeled and quartered
2 onions, peeled and sliced
225 g/8 oz cap mushrooms, wiped
½ teaspoon chopped thyme
2 tablespoons chopped parsley
300 ml/½ pint beef or chicken stock
chopped parsley, to garnish

Season the cutlets with salt and pepper. Place a layer of potatoes in the base of a large suitable bowl and season. Arrange the cutlets and kidney on top. Add the carrot, onion and mushrooms. Season to taste, then sprinkle with the chopped thyme and parsley.

Finish with a neat layer of potatoes. Pour in the stock. Cover the bowl with foil and tie down with string. Place in a steamer or covered saucepan half filled with boiling water and steam for 2 hours. Check the liquid level frequently and add more boiling water if necessary.

Remove the foil and sprinkle the hot pot with chopped parsley. Serve at once.
SERVES 4

POTATO CHOPS

METRIC/IMPERIAL
1 × 450 g/16 oz can baked beans
450 g/1 lb potatoes, peeled and sliced
salt
freshly ground black pepper
4 lamb leg bone steaks, trimmed of fat
25 g/1 oz polyunsaturated margarine, melted
1 tablespoon chopped fresh rosemary

Place the baked beans in the bottom of a greased ovenproof dish. Arrange the potato slices on top of the beans and sprinkle with salt and pepper. Place the lamb on top and sprinkle with more salt and pepper.

Mix together the margarine and rosemary and spoon over the meat and potatoes. Cover the dish and cook in a preheated moderate oven (180°C/350°F, Gas Mark 4) for 30 minutes.

Uncover the dish, increase the oven temperature to hot (220°C/425°F, Gas Mark 7) and cook for a further 15 minutes or until the meat and potatoes are tender. Serve with a green salad.
SERVES 4

SESAME LAMB BALLS

METRIC/IMPERIAL
125 g/4½ oz fresh spinach
100 g/4 oz feta cheese
500 g/1¼ lb minced lean lamb
½ bunch parsley, finely chopped
1 onion, peeled and finely chopped
2 cloves garlic, peeled and finely chopped
4 tablespoons sesame seeds
1 egg
herb salt
freshly ground black pepper
about 125 ml/4 fl oz sunflower oil

Pick over the spinach, remove any tough stalks and wash well. Shake dry and finely chop. Crush the cheese with a fork until smooth.

Mix the minced lamb with the spinach, parsley, onion, garlic, cheese, sesame seeds and egg. Season to taste with herb salt and pepper. Using wet hands, shape the mixture into walnut-sized balls.

Heat the oil a little at a time in a frying pan and fry the meat balls in batches over a moderate heat for about 8 minutes. Drain well on kitchen paper. Serve the balls very hot with a salad.
SERVES 6

LAMB NOISETTE

METRIC/IMPERIAL
1 × 100 g/4 oz lamb noisette, trimmed of fat
1 clove garlic, peeled and thinly sliced
few rosemary sprigs
½ teaspoon French mustard with herbs
salt
freshly ground black pepper
juice of ½ lemon

Make small incisions all over the lamb and insert the slices of garlic and a few sprigs of rosemary. Spread the mustard on both sides of the meat, season with a little salt and pepper, and sprinkle over the lemon juice. Leave to marinate for about 30 minutes. Preheat the grill and cook the lamb for 4 to 6 minutes each side or as preferred.
SERVES 1

LAMB IN MINT JELLY

METRIC/IMPERIAL
450 g/1 lb lean cooked lamb, thinly sliced
1 packet aspic jelly powder, to set 600 ml/1 pint
    liquid
salt
freshly ground white pepper
2 tablespoons dry sherry
2 tablespoons chopped mint

Arrange the lamb slices on a flat serving dish.
Make up the aspic according to packet directions.
Leave in a cool place until the liquid is thick and
syrupy. Add salt and pepper to taste and stir in the
sherry and mint.

Spoon over the lamb slices very carefully so
that the meat is evenly covered. Chill in the refrigerator for 2 hours until set. Serve with salad.
SERVES 4

MINCED LAMB WITH THYME FLOWERS

METRIC/IMPERIAL
450 g/1 lb minced lean lamb
1 egg white
1 tablespoon redcurrant jelly
½ teaspoon fresh thyme flowers (if available)
    and leaves from sprigs of thyme
2 cloves garlic, peeled and crushed
4 spring onions, trimmed and finely chopped
1 teaspoon cornflour
salt
freshly ground black pepper
300 ml/½ pint lamb or beef stock
sprigs of thyme
8 baby carrots, scraped
8 baby turnips, peeled
50 g/2 oz mangetout, topped and tailed
8 radishes, tailed
sprigs of flowering thyme or flat-leaf parsley, to
    garnish

Blend the lamb in a blender or food processor for a
few seconds. Slowly add the egg white, redcurrant jelly and thyme flowers and leaves. Process
for a few more seconds until they are fully incorporated into the meat. Mix in the garlic, spring
onion and cornflour; season well with salt and
pepper. Dust your hands with cornflour and form
the mixture into 3.5 cm/1½ inch balls. Bring the
stock to the boil in a saucepan. Place the meatballs, thyme sprigs and vegetables in a steamer.

Cover with a tight-fitting lid and steam over the
boiling stock for 10 minutes.

Arrange the food on 4 warmed plates and keep
warm. Boil the stock to reduce until syrupy. Pour
over the meatballs and vegetables. Garnish with
flowering thyme or flat-leaf parsley.
SERVES 4

MOUSSAKA

METRIC/IMPERIAL
2 large aubergines, diced
salt
freshly ground black pepper
2 tablespoons olive oil
2 large onions, peeled and finely chopped
2 cloves garlic, peeled and crushed
750 g/1½ lb cooked lean lamb, minced
750 g/1½ lb tomatoes, peeled, deseeded and
    chopped
pinch of dried thyme
pinch of dried rosemary
20 g/¾ oz polyunsaturated margarine
20 g/¾ oz plain flour
½ teaspoon mustard powder
250 ml/8 fl oz skimmed milk, infused with
    onion, mace, parsley stalks and peppercorns
1 egg, separated
4-6 tablespoons grated Parmesan cheese

Place the aubergines in a colander and sprinkle
with plenty of salt. Leave to one side for 30
minutes. Rinse under cold water to remove the
salt and bitter juices. Dry on kitchen paper.

Heat the oil in a pan. Fry the aubergine, onion
and garlic until cooked, but not brown. Stir in the
minced cooked lamb, tomatoes, thyme, rosemary, and salt and pepper to taste. Spoon into a
suitable container.

Melt the margarine in a clean pan. Stir in the
flour and mustard, cook for 2 minutes. Add the
milk and bring to the boil, stirring constantly
until thickened. Remove from the heat, whisk in
the egg yolk. Season well with salt and pepper.
Whisk the egg white to a stiff peak and fold into
the sauce with the Parmesan. Pour over the meat.
Cover with foil and tie down with string. Place in
a steamer or covered saucepan half-filled with
boiling water and steam gently for 15 to 20
minutes.

Heat the grill. Remove the foil and place the
bowl under the grill until the surface is golden
brown all over. Serve at once.
SERVES 4

LAMB CHOPS WITH ROSEMARY BUTTER

METRIC/IMPERIAL
4 lamb chops, trimmed of fat
25 g/1 oz butter (see method)
25 ml/1 fl oz water
2 teaspoons chopped fresh rosemary or
1 teaspoon dried rosemary
salt
freshly ground black pepper
watercress sprigs, to garnish

Put the lamb chops under a preheated hot grill and cook for about 15 minutes, turning frequently.

Place the butter and water in a blender and liquidize until combined. (It is best to blend the butter and water together in larger quantities and use as required. The mixture, which has half the calories of butter, keeps in a container in the refrigerator for up to a week.)

Put into a small bowl and mix in the rosemary, salt and pepper. Arrange the chops on a heated serving dish and top each with a knob of the rosemary-flavoured butter. Garnish the dish with small sprigs of watercress.
SERVES 4

PORK AND CABBAGE CASSEROLE

METRIC/IMPERIAL
1 bouquet garni
120 g/4½ oz peeled chestnuts
750 g/1½-1¾ lb boned pork shoulder, trimmed of fat
1 large potato, peeled and quartered
2 medium onions, peeled and quartered
4 medium carrots, scraped
1 tablespoon tomato purée
2 tablespoons white wine vinegar
600 ml/1 pint vegetable stock
salt
freshly ground black pepper
2 bay leaves
225 g/8 oz red cabbage, thinly sliced

Put all the ingredients, except the red cabbage, into a large flameproof casserole. Bring to the boil, lower the heat, cover and simmer for about 1½ hours or until the pork has become tender.

Add the cabbage, increase the heat and cook for a further 5 minutes.
SERVES 4

BRAISED LEG OF PORK

METRIC/IMPERIAL
1 × 1.5-1.75 kg/3-4 lb leg of pork
salt
6 spring onions, each cut into 3 pieces
1 × 5 cm/2 inch piece root ginger, peeled and chopped
150 ml/¼ pint soy sauce
6 tablespoons dry sherry
50 g/2 oz soft brown sugar
Garnish:
radish flowers, made by cutting V shapes out of the top of trimmed radishes
spring onions

Rub the pork with salt; do not score the skin. Put the spring onions and ginger in a large pan, pour over the soy sauce and sherry, then stir in the sugar. Put the pork in the pan, turning to coat with the soy sauce mixture. Bring to the boil, cover and simmer for 2 to 2½ hours, until very tender, turning occasionally.

Remove the pork from the pan and keep hot. Boil the sauce until well reduced and thickened; pour into a sauce bowl. Carve the meat into thick slices, arrange on a serving dish and garnish with radish flowers and spring onions. Serve hot or cold, with the sauce.
SERVES 6 to 8

WINTER PORK AND BEAN HOT POT

METRIC/IMPERIAL
2 tablespoons polyunsaturated vegetable oil
1 large onion, peeled and chopped
450 g/1 lb pork, trimmed and cubed
225 g/8 oz carrots, peeled and thickly sliced
250 ml/8 fl oz chicken stock
1 × 450 g/16 oz can baked beans
Worcestershire sauce
salt
freshly ground black pepper

Heat the oil in a saucepan and sauté the onion until soft. Add the pork and brown well. Stir in the sliced carrots and chicken stock. Bring to the boil, reduce the heat, cover, and simmer for 1 hour.

Stir in the baked beans and adjust the seasoning to taste with Worcestershire sauce, salt and pepper. Heat for a further 5 minutes and serve sprinkled with parsley, if wished.
SERVES 4

PORK VINDALOO

METRIC/IMPERIAL
½ teaspoon cardamom seeds
½ teaspoon ground cloves
½ teaspoon ground ginger
1 tablespoon ground coriander
2 teaspoons ground turmeric
4 teaspoons ground chilli
1 teaspoon ground cumin
1 teaspoon salt
½ teaspoon freshly ground black pepper
200 ml/⅓ pint vinegar
450 g/1 lb boned pork, cut into 4 cm/1½ inch cubes
50 g/2 oz polyunsaturated margarine
5 cloves garlic, peeled and sliced

Mix the spices and seasonings to a thick paste with a little of the vinegar, then rub into the pork. Melt the margarine in a heavy frying pan, add the garlic and sauté for 1 to 2 minutes, stirring frequently. Add the pork to the pan and cover with the remaining vinegar. Bring to the boil, then lower the heat, cover and simmer for about 1 hour or until the meat is tender. Serve hot.
SERVES 4

BRAISED PORK WITH PUMPKIN

METRIC/IMPERIAL
350 g/12 oz lean pork
4 tablespoons soy sauce
3 tablespoons dry sherry
450 g/1 lb pumpkin
4 spring onions
2 tablespoons polyunsaturated vegetable oil
1 × 2.5 cm/1 inch piece root ginger, peeled and shredded
2 cloves garlic, peeled and sliced
Garnish:
carrot flowers, made by making V-shaped cuts along the length of a trimmed carrot and then cutting into slices
spring onion slices
coriander leaves

Cut the pork into 1 cm/½ inch slices. Put the soy sauce and sherry in a bowl and add the pork. Mix well and leave to marinate for 20 minutes.
Cut the pumpkin into 2.5 cm/1 inch cubes. Slice each spring onion into 3 pieces. Heat the oil in a wok or frying pan, add the pumpkin and fry quickly until browned. Add the spring onions, ginger and garlic and cook for 1 minute. Add the pork and marinade and cook for 12 to 15 minutes, until the pork and pumpkin are tender.
Spoon the mixture on to a warmed serving dish, garnish with carrot flowers, spring onion slices and coriander. Serve immediately.
SERVES 4 to 6

PORK CHOP SUEY

METRIC/IMPERIAL
2 tablespoons soy sauce
1 tablespoon dry sherry
2 teaspoons cornflour
225 g/8 oz pork fillet (or chicken meat), cut into 2.5 cm/1 inch slices
100 g/4 oz fresh bean-sprouts, rinsed and thoroughly dried
1 tablespoon polyunsaturated vegetable oil
2 spring onions, cut into 2.5 cm/1 inch lengths
1 slice ginger root, peeled and finely chopped
1 small green pepper, cored, deseeded and cut into 1 cm/½ inch pieces
2-3 tomatoes, cut into 1 cm/½ inch pieces
a few cauliflower or broccoli florets, cut into 1 cm/½ inch pieces
1-2 carrots, peeled and cut into 1 cm/½ inch pieces
50 g/2 oz French beans, cut into 1 cm/½ inch pieces
1 teaspoon salt
stock or water, if necessary

Mix together the soy sauce, sherry and cornflour, and stir in the meat until each slice is coated with the mixture.
Heat about half the oil in a wok or frying pan and stir-fry the meat slices for about 1 minute, stirring constantly, then remove with a perforated spoon and put them on one side.
Heat the remaining oil, add the spring onions and ginger root, followed by the remaining vegetables and the salt. Stir for about 1 minute and add the meat. Blend everything well and moisten with a little stock or water if necessary. Serve with boiled rice.
SERVES 4

213

SPANISH PORK WITH PINEAPPLE

METRIC/IMPERIAL
50 g/2 oz polyunsaturated margarine
1.5 kg/3 lb lean boneless pork, cut into
3.5 cm/1½ inch cubes
1 tablespoon sugar
3 tablespoons unbleached white flour
salt
freshly ground black pepper
2 onions, peeled and chopped
450-750 ml/¾-1¼ pints beef stock
1 teaspoon coriander seeds, soaked in 2
tablespoons warm water
1 clove garlic, peeled and chopped
1 teaspoon crushed chilli chipotle (or other chilli
pepper)
2 tomatoes, skinned, seeded and coarsely
chopped
225 g/8 oz fresh pineapple, peeled, cored and
coarsely chopped
2 medium yams or sweet potatoes, peeled and
diced

Heat the margarine in a heavy frying pan and sauté the pork, turning frequently, until browned on all sides. Using a slotted spoon, transfer to a large flameproof casserole. Sprinkle with sugar and cook, stirring constantly, over a very low heat for 3 to 5 minutes, or until the sugar dissolves completely. Add the flour, salt and pepper to taste and cook, stirring, for 5 minutes. Remove from the heat. Add the onions to the fat remaining in the frying pan and sauté until transparent and soft, but not brown. Add the stock, stirring well to scrape any sediment from the bottom of the pan, and bring to the boil. Lower the heat.

Strain the liquor from the coriander seeds and mix the liquor with the garlic and crushed chilli, then add to the pan. Add the tomatoes and cook for 5 minutes, stirring to blend. Pour over the pork cubes and bring to the boil. Cover and bake in a preheated moderate oven (180°C/350°F, Gas Mark 4) for 1½ to 2 hours or until tender.

Using a slotted spoon, remove the meat and set aside. Strain the gravy into a large container and skim off excess fat. Return the meat to the casserole and add the gravy with the remaining ingredients. Return to the oven for 20 to 25 minutes, until the fruit and vegetables are tender.
SERVES 6

GRECIAN PORK

METRIC/IMPERIAL
2 tablespoons polyunsaturated vegetable oil
750 g/1½ lb pork fillet or boneless pork chops,
trimmed and cut into strips
1 clove garlic, peeled and crushed
1 teaspoon coriander seeds, crushed
225 g/8 oz frozen spinach, thawed
1 teaspoon plain wholemeal flour
1 teaspoon unbleached plain white flour
1 × 150 g/5 oz carton plain low-fat yogurt
salt
freshly ground black pepper
grated nutmeg
Garnish:
tomato slices
flat-leaf parsley

Heat the oil in a pan and fry the pork for 5 minutes, stirring to brown evenly. Add the garlic and coriander and cook for a further 10 minutes.

Add the spinach, stir and cook for 5 minutes. Blend together the flours and yogurt, then add to the pan. Heat, stirring, until the mixture comes to the boil. Add salt, black pepper and a pinch of grated nutmeg to taste.

Cover the pan and simmer for 10 minutes. Garnish with tomato slices and flat-leaf parsley and serve immediately in a warmed dish.
SERVES 4

HUNGARIAN PORK

METRIC/IMPERIAL
25 g/1 oz polyunsaturated margarine
750 g/1½ lb boned leg of pork, trimmed of fat
and cubed
1 large onion, peeled and chopped
1 clove garlic, peeled and finely chopped
1 tablespoon paprika
½ teaspoon caraway seeds
½ teaspoon cayenne
salt
freshly ground black pepper
large pinch of dried thyme
large pinch of dried marjoram
100 g/4 oz button mushrooms
2 red peppers, cored, deseeded and sliced
150 ml/¼ pint chicken stock
2 teaspoons cornflour, blended with
2 tablespoons cold water
150 ml/¼ pint soured cream or yogurt
chopped parsley, to garnish

Heat the margarine in a heavy frying pan and lightly brown the meat, onion and garlic. Stir in all the seasonings and herbs. Place the mushrooms and red peppers in the bottom of a casserole and add the meat mixture and stock. Cook in a pre-heated moderate oven (180°C/350°F, Gas Mark 4) for about 1½ hours or until the meat is tender.

Half an hour before serving, stir in the blended cornflour. Just before serving, pour in the soured cream or yogurt and garnish with parsley.
SERVES 4 to 6

MARINATED PORK FILLETS WITH FRESH GARDEN HERBS

METRIC/IMPERIAL
8 × 150 g/5 oz pork fillets
salt
freshly ground black pepper
300 ml/½ pint red wine
juice of 1 lemon
3 tablespoons chopped fresh mixed herbs (e.g. sage, oregano, marjoram, thyme, parsley)
1 kg/2 lb leeks, trimmed, washed and finely sliced
100 g/4 oz Gruyère cheese, grated
1 tablespoon polyunsaturated vegetable oil
300 ml/½ pint pork or chicken stock
1 tablespoon apple sauce
Garnish:
2 tablespoons chopped fresh herbs (e.g. parsley, sage, oregano, marjoram, thyme)
red- and green-skinned apple slices (optional)

Beat each pork fillet flat between 2 sheets of wet greaseproof paper, using a mallet or rolling pin. Season both sides well. Lay the fillets in a dish with the red wine, lemon juice and 1 tablespoon of the herbs. Marinate for up to 2 hours.

Lay a piece of wet greaseproof paper in a steamer and spread the sliced leeks on top.

Remove the fillets from the marinade. Sprinkle the cheese evenly over each fillet, then roll up. Heat the oil in a heavy-based pan and fry the pork rolls to brown on all sides. Lay, side by side, on top of the leeks and sprinkle with the remaining herbs. Bring the stock, remainder of the marinade, and the apple sauce to the boil in the pan in which the pork rolls were browned, scraping the sediment from the base of the pan. Pour into a saucepan, place the steamer on top and cover with a tight-fitting lid. Steam over the stock mixture

for 20 minutes. Arrange the pork rolls and leeks on 4 warmed plates; keep hot. Boil the sauce to reduce until syrupy. Taste and adjust the seasoning, if necessary.

Pour over the meat rolls, sprinkle with mixed herbs and garnish with apple slices, if liked.
SERVES 6 to 8

PORK WITH ORANGE

METRIC/IMPERIAL
4 × 100 g/4 oz pork fillets, trimmed of fat
300 ml/½ pint unsweetened orange juice
12-20 juniper berries
salt
freshly ground black pepper

Place the fillets in a dish and pour the orange juice over. Crush the juniper berries with the back of a spoon and add to the orange juice with the salt and pepper. Cover and leave to marinate for 5 hours.

Remove the fillets and place under a preheated hot grill. Cook for 10 to 15 minutes, turning frequently and spooning over some of the orange marinade to prevent burning.

Strain the remaining orange marinade and pour into a saucepan. Bring to the boil and boil briskly to reduce slightly. Arrange the pork on a heated serving dish and pour the orange sauce over.
SERVES 4

PORK NORMANDY

METRIC/IMPERIAL
1 large cooking apple, cored and cut into chunks
4 × 175 g/6 oz pork chops, trimmed of fat
100 g/4 oz onions, peeled and sliced
1 tablespoon chopped fresh sage or 1 teaspoon dried sage
salt
freshly ground black pepper
250 ml/8 fl oz unsweetened apple juice

Put the apple pieces on the bottom of a casserole dish. Arrange the pork chops on top and sprinkle over the sliced onion, sage and salt and pepper. Pour over the apple juice.

Cook in a preheated hot oven (220°C/425°F, Gas Mark 7) for 15 minutes.

Lower the temperature to 160°C/325°F, Gas Mark 3, for about 1 hour or until the chops are tender. Serve immediately.
SERVES 4

PORK TENDERLOIN WITH GRAPEFRUIT SAUCE

METRIC/IMPERIAL
450 g/1 lb pork loin, trimmed and cut in 6 mm/¼ inch thick medallions
3 spring onions, trimmed and minced
finely grated rind and juice of ½ grapefruit
1 teaspoon light brown sugar
salt
freshly ground black pepper
2 tablespoons chopped parsley
2 tablespoons olive oil
150 ml/¼ pint unsweetened apricot purée
150 ml/¼ pint chicken stock
peeled segments from 2 grapefruit

Marinate the pork medallions with the spring onions, grapefruit rind and juice, brown sugar, salt and pepper to taste, and the parsley. Cover and chill for 3 to 4 hours.

Drain the pork medallions, reserving the marinade. Sauté the medallions briskly in the oil until sealed on all sides.

Mix the apricot purée with the stock and marinade and pour over the pork; cover and simmer for about 7 minutes until the pork is tender.

Stir in the grapefruit segments and heat through.
SERVES 4

ITALIAN PORK CHOPS WITH FENNEL

METRIC/IMPERIAL
2 large bulbs fennel, trimmed and chopped
3 juniper berries, crushed
4 large pork chops, trimmed of fat
salt
freshly ground black pepper
2 tablespoons olive oil

Mix the fennel and juniper berries together and put a layer of this mixture in the base of a flat flameproof dish. Lay the pork chops on top, season with salt and pepper to taste and sprinkle with the remaining fennel mixture. Spoon over the oil, cover and refrigerate for at least 4 hours, basting occasionally.

Heat the grill, uncover the dish and place the chops in the dish under the grill. Cook the chops for 12 to 15 minutes each side, turning them over frequently, until cooked through.
SERVES 4

PORK AND PRUNE CASSEROLE

METRIC/IMPERIAL
20 stoned prunes, soaked overnight
4 × 175 g/6 oz pork chops, trimmed of fat
1 chicken stock cube, crumbled
salt
freshly ground black pepper
1 teaspoon dry mustard
1 tablespoon wine vinegar

Put a layer of prunes on the bottom of a casserole dish. Arrange the pork chops on top. Add the remaining ingredients and enough of the prunes' soaking liquid to cover.

Place in a preheated hot oven (220°C/425°F, Gas Mark 7) for 15 minutes. Lower the temperature to 160°C/325°F, Gas Mark 3, for about 1 hour until the chops are tender.
SERVES 4

PORK CHOPS IN ORANGE SAUCE

METRIC/IMPERIAL
4 pork chops, trimmed of fat
salt
freshly ground black pepper
2 teaspoons dried sage
25 g/1 oz polyunsaturated margarine
1 garlic clove, peeled and crushed
15 g/½ oz cornflour
300 ml/½ pint chicken stock
6 tablespoons orange juice
2 fresh oranges, peeled, pith removed and segmented
watercress, to garnish

Season the chops with salt and pepper and sprinkle sage over each one. Heat the margarine in a pan and fry the garlic for 1 minute, then brown the chops on both sides. Remove and leave on one side. Stir the cornflour into the remaining fat in the pan and cook for a few minutes. Gradually add the stock and orange juice and bring to the boil. Return the chops to the pan, reduce the heat, add the segments from 1 of the oranges, cover and cook for about 40 minutes. Adjust the seasoning

Place the chops on a serving plate with the orange segments. Pour the sauce over and serve garnished with segments from the remaining orange and the watercress.
SERVES 4

CÔTES DE PORC AUX LENTILLES

METRIC/IMPERIAL
450 g/1 lb green lentils, soaked for 1 hour in
    cold water
1 bay leaf
2 onions, peeled
1 whole clove
salt
freshly ground black pepper
6 pork chops, trimmed of fat
4 sage leaves, trimmed
6 small low-fat sausages
15 g/½ oz polyunsaturated margarine
2 carrots, scraped and diced
about 600 ml/1 pint chicken stock

Rinse the lentils under cold running water and
pick them over carefully to remove any grit or
discoloured lentils. Place in a large pan with the
bay leaf and 1 onion stuck with the clove. Cover
with water, bring to the boil and simmer for 1
hour. Add salt and pepper to taste halfway
through the cooking time.

Meanwhile, sprinkle the chops with the sage
and salt and pepper to taste. Grill the chops for 10
minutes until browned on all sides. Prick the
sausage skins with a fork and grill.

Melt the margarine in a flameproof casserole.
Chop the remaining onion and put in the casserole
with the carrots and fry over a brisk heat for 10
minutes until lightly coloured, stirring constantly.

Drain the lentils, then add to the casserole with
the chops. Cover with the stock and bring to the
boil. Lower the heat, cover and cook gently for
1 hour or until the chops are tender.

Taste and adjust the seasoning. Remove the
chops and sausages from the casserole and arrange
around the edge of a warmed serving platter. Pile
the lentils in the centre. Serve immediately.
SERVES 6

SINGAPORE SPARE-RIBS

METRIC/IMPERIAL
1 medium onion, peeled and chopped
1 clove garlic, peeled and chopped
3 tablespoons wine vinegar
1 tablespoon soy sauce
1 teaspoon sesame oil
¼ teaspoon aniseed
450 ml/¾ pint water
1.5 kg/3 lb pork spare-ribs
1 medium mango, peeled and diced
1 small pineapple, peeled, cored and cut into
    2.5 cm/1 inch fingers

Combine the onion, garlic, vinegar, soy sauce,
oil, spice and water in a large pan, then add the
spare-ribs. Bring to the boil, lower the heat, cover
and simmer for 1 hour or until the spare-ribs are
tender, turning them after 30 minutes.

Remove the pork from the pan and cut into
separate ribs. Boil the liquid in the pan until reduced to one-third of its original volume. Taste
for seasoning. Add the fruit and simmer for 2-3
minutes, then pour over the ribs.
SERVES 4

STUFFED BREAST OF VEAL

METRIC/IMPERIAL
1 kg/2 lb breast of veal, boned
4 eggs, beaten
salt
freshly ground black pepper
4 slices lean ham
1-2 teaspoons chopped fresh tarragon or
½-1 teaspoon dried tarragon

Unroll the veal and flatten out, if necessary. Remove as much fat as possible.

Season the eggs with salt and pepper. Pour into
a non-stick omelette or small frying pan, or ordinary pan using a little oil, and make an omelette.
Place the open omelette on the veal; trim the sides
and put the pieces on top.

Lay the slices of ham over the omelette, again
trimming to fit the veal. Sprinkle with the tarragon. Roll up the veal and tie at intervals with
string. Place in a roasting tin and roast in a preheated moderately hot oven (200°C/400°F, Gas
Mark 6) for about 1½ hours, basting and turning
frequently. Serve hot or cold.
SERVES 6 to 8

ROAST VEAL WITH ORANGE

METRIC/IMPERIAL
1 × 1.75 kg/4 lb leg of veal
2 cloves garlic, peeled and quartered lengthwise
salt
freshly ground black pepper
rosemary sprig
300 ml/½ pint water
finely grated rind of 1 orange
juice of 2 oranges
1 orange, peeled and sliced, to garnish

Make 8 small slits in the surface of the veal with a sharp, pointed knife. Insert garlic into the slits. Put the meat in a roasting tin, sprinkle with salt and pepper then place the rosemary on top.

Pour the water around the meat, then roast in a preheated hot oven (220°C/425°F, Gas Mark 7) for 15 minutes. Lower the heat to moderate (180°C/350°F, Gas Mark 4) and continue roasting for 1¼ hours.

Sprinkle the orange rind over the meat, then stir orange juice into the cooking juices. Continue cooking for 30 minutes, basting once.

To serve the veal, carve into slices and arrange on a warmed serving dish. Taste and adjust the seasoning of the gravy, then pour a little gravy over the veal and garnish with orange slices. Serve the remaining gravy in a sauceboat. The meat can also be served cold with a selection of salads.
SERVES 4

VEAL OLIVES

METRIC/IMPERIAL
2 × 100 g/4 oz veal escalopes, beaten flat
1 teaspoon polyunsaturated vegetable oil
1 celery stalk, sliced
2 teaspoons tomato purée
150 ml/¼ pint light stock
Marinade:
2 teaspoons lemon juice
grated rind of ½ lemon
freshly ground black pepper
2 tablespoons dry white wine
Stuffing:
1 small onion, peeled and chopped
2 lean bacon rashers, grilled and chopped
25 g/1 oz wholemeal breadcrumbs
2 teaspoons mixed dried herbs
beaten egg

Place the escalopes in a flat dish, mix the marinade ingredients, pour over the veal and leave to marinate for several hours.

To make the stuffing, place all the dry ingredients in a bowl, season with salt and pepper to taste and mix with just enough egg to bind. Divide between the escalopes and roll them into olive shapes. Tie securely with string.

Heat the oil in a heavy-based saucepan and brown the olives on all sides. Add the marinade and remaining ingredients. Bring to the boil, cover and simmer gently for about 30 to 35 minutes or until tender. Remove the veal olives, cut off the string, and transfer to a warmed serving dish. Boil the sauce until reduced by half. Strain and pour over the veal.
SERVES 2

VEAL PURSES

METRIC/IMPERIAL
4 × 150 g/5 oz veal escalopes, cut into strips, trimmed of fat
2 teaspoons cornflour
juice of 1 lemon
6 tablespoons white wine
1 tablespoon polyunsaturated vegetable oil
450 ml/¾ pint veal stock
50 g/2 oz mangetout
75 g/3 oz salsify, peeled and cut into strips
4 spring onions, trimmed and finely chopped
1 carrot, peeled and cut into strips
salt
freshly ground black pepper
Pancakes:
100 g/4 oz plain unbleached white flour, sifted
pinch of salt
1 egg, beaten
150 ml/¼ pint skimmed milk
150 ml/¼ pint water

Place the veal in a shallow dish, mix the cornflour with the lemon juice to a smooth cream. Add the white wine and pour over the veal. Leave to marinate for 1 to 2 hours.

Meanwhile, make the pancakes. Place all the pancake ingredients in a blender, blend for 10 seconds until the mixture looks smooth and creamy. Refrigerate for 30 minutes. Prepare the pancake pan by heating well and wiping out with oil. Pour in about 1 tablespoon of batter and swirl about the pan until evenly spread across the bottom. Place over high heat for 30 seconds to 1 minute. Turn the pancake over by using a palette knife. Cook until brown. Make all the pancakes, turning them out on to a plate.

Place 150 ml/¼ pint of the veal stock and all the marinade in a pan, having put the veal strips to one side. Bring to the boil and reduce until thick and syrupy, stirring constantly. Blanch the vegetables for 10 seconds in boiling water. Mix the veal strips, the sauce and three-quarters of the vegetables together. Season well with salt and pepper.

Wrap up equal amounts of the mixture in 12 pancakes. Arrange side by side in a steamer. Bring the remaining stock to the boil. Cover the food with a tight-fitting lid and steam over the stock for 10 minutes.

Arrange 3 purses on each plate and keep warm. Reduce the stock by boiling rapidly until syrupy and serve separately. Garnish the purses with the remaining vegetables. Eat at once.
SERVES 4

Note: Pancakes freeze well, if separated with pieces of greaseproof paper, and so can be made in advance. Different vegetable combinations can be used according to season.

MEDITERRANEAN-STYLE VEAL CHOPS
METRIC/IMPERIAL
25 g/1 oz polyunsaturated margarine
1 tablespoon polyunsaturated vegetable oil
4 veal chops, trimmed
salt
freshly ground black pepper
350 g/12 oz mushrooms, wiped and sliced
2 large green or red peppers, cored, deseeded and sliced
350 g/12 oz tomatoes, skinned and sliced
1 tablespoon chopped basil
300 ml/½ pint chicken stock or water
lemon wedges, to garnish

Melt the margarine and oil together in a frying pan and fry the chops quickly until browned on both sides. Season and remove from pan. Fry the prepared mushrooms and peppers until soft, add the tomatoes, seasoning, basil and stock or water. Boil for 3 minutes. Return chops to the pan and simmer, uncovered, for about 30 minutes. The sauce should be very thick. Arrange the chops on a heated dish with the sauce and garnish with lemon wedges.
SERVES 4

LOIN OF VEAL WITH ROSEMARY
METRIC/IMPERIAL
1 × 2.5 kg/5 lb loin of veal, boned and trimmed
salt
freshly ground black pepper
2 tablespoons crumbled fresh rosemary or
1 tablespoon dried rosemary
75 g/3 oz polyunsaturated margarine, softened
250 ml/8 fl oz dry white wine

Season the veal generously with salt and pepper, then rub on both sides with the rosemary and margarine. Roll up and tie into a neat shape with thin white string.

Place in a roasting tin, pour over the wine, and roast in a preheated moderate oven (180°C/350°F, Gas Mark 4), allowing 30 minutes per 450 g/1 lb or until cooked to your liking. Baste with the pan juices every 20 minutes. Remove the string and serve cut in slices with the juices poured over.
SERVES 6

ITALIAN VEAL
METRIC/IMPERIAL
10 anchovy fillets
12 capers
salt
freshly ground black pepper
8 thin slices fillet of veal

Pound the anchovies and capers together with salt and pepper, using a pestle and mortar or the back of a wooden spoon.

Put 4 veal fillets on pieces of foil large enough to enclose them. Spread with the anchovy and caper mixture. Lay a second veal fillet on top. Wrap the fillets in the foil. Cook in a preheated hot oven (220°C/425°F, Gas Mark 7) for 20 minutes or until the veal is tender. Serve with a tomato and onion salad as an accompaniment.
SERVES 4

219

VEAL WITH GARLIC AND TOMATOES

METRIC/IMPERIAL
4 × 175 g/6 oz pieces fillet of veal
2 tomatoes, skinned and chopped
2 cloves garlic, peeled and crushed
1 celery stalk, finely chopped
salt
freshly ground black pepper

Put the veal fillets on pieces of foil large enough to enclose them. Mix together the tomatoes, garlic and celery, and spoon over the veal. Season with salt and pepper and then wrap the fillets in the foil.

Cook in a preheated hot oven (220°C/425°F, Gas Mark 7) for about 20 minutes or until the veal is tender. Serve immediately with a salad or seasonal vegetables.
SERVES 4

VEAL AND ORANGE CASSEROLE

METRIC/IMPERIAL
1 tablespoon polyunsaturated vegetable oil
1 medium onion, peeled and finely chopped
2 tablespoons finely grated orange rind
3-4 fresh sage leaves, finely chopped
275 g/10 oz lean boneless veal, cut into 2.5 cm/1 inch cubes
wholemeal flour
salt
freshly ground black pepper
150 ml/¼ pint chicken stock
150 ml/¼ pint dry vermouth
3 tablespoons orange juice
Garnish:
chopped sage (optional)
grated orange rind (optional)

Heat the oil in a heavy saucepan or flameproof casserole. Add the onion and fry gently for 3 minutes. Add the orange rind and sage leaves and cook gently for 1 minute.

Dust the cubed veal in flour, season with salt and pepper, and add to the onion mixture. Fry steadily until the veal is sealed on all sides. Gradually stir in the stock, vermouth and orange juice. Cover and simmer gently for about 1 hour or until the veal is tender. Taste and adjust the seasoning before serving. Garnish with more chopped fresh sage or grated orange rind.
SERVES 2

VEAL PAPRIKA

METRIC/IMPERIAL
4 × 175 g/6 oz pieces fillet of veal
1 tablespoon lemon juice
4 tablespoons tomato purée
3 teaspoons paprika
300 ml/½ pint plain low-fat yogurt
salt
freshly ground black pepper

Put the veal fillets on the rack of a grill pan. Cook under a fairly hot grill for about 5 minutes on each side (depending on the thickness of the fillets), spooning over lemon juice to prevent burning.

Mix together the tomato purée, paprika and remaining lemon juice and heat gently. Remove from the heat and stir in the yogurt and salt and pepper to taste.

Put the fillets of veal on to a heated serving plate and pour the sauce over.
SERVES 4

VEAL AND COURGETTE CASSEROLE

METRIC/IMPERIAL
450 g/1 lb courgettes, thinly sliced
salt
450 g/1 lb lean veal, sliced or cubed
freshly ground black pepper
pinch of ground nutmeg
2 tablespoons stock
50 g/2 oz Parmesan cheese, grated

Sprinkle the courgette slices with salt and leave to drain for 1 to 2 hours. Place a layer of courgettes in a casserole dish, cover with a layer of veal. Repeat the layers until all the veal and courgettes have been used, ending with courgettes.

Add salt, pepper, nutmeg and stock. Sprinkle with the Parmesan cheese.

Cook in a preheated moderately hot oven (200°C/400°F, Gas Mark 6) for about 40 minutes or until the veal is tender.
SERVES 4

BLANQUETTE OF VEAL

METRIC/IMPERIAL
2 tablespoons polyunsaturated margarine
750 g/1½ lb pie veal, cubed
2 onions, peeled and sliced
300 ml/½ pint chicken stock
3 tablespoons lemon juice
salt
freshly ground black pepper
1 tablespoon chopped parsley
2 egg yolks
Garnish:
1 tablespoon finely chopped parsley
lemon slices

Melt the margarine in a flameproof casserole, add the veal and fry for 2 to 3 minutes, stirring, without allowing the veal to brown. Add the onions and fry for a further 2 minutes, stirring.

Add the stock, 1 tablespoon of lemon juice, seasoning and parsley. Bring to the boil, then simmer, covered, for 35 minutes, or until cooked through. Transfer the veal and onions to a heated serving dish.

Strain the cooking liquid and return to the rinsed-out pan. Beat together the egg yolks and remaining lemon juice and mix in a little of the hot cooking liquid. Add this to the pan and heat gently, stirring constantly, until the sauce thickens. Spoon the sauce over the veal and garnish with the parsley and lemon.
SERVES 4

LEMON AND TARRAGON VEAL

METRIC/IMPERIAL
1 kg/2 lb pie veal, cut into bite-sized pieces
1 wine glass white wine
1 wine glass lemon juice
2 teaspoons chopped fresh tarragon or
1 teaspoon dried tarragon
salt
freshly ground black pepper
about 150 ml/¼ pint chicken stock

Put the veal in a casserole dish with all the other ingredients except the stock. Pour in just enough stock to cover the veal.

Cover and cook in a preheated cool oven (150°C/300°F, Gas Mark 2) for about 2 hours or until the veal is tender.
SERVES 6

VEAL WITH PINEAPPLE

METRIC/IMPERIAL
750 g/1½ lb lean pie veal, trimmed and cubed
300 ml/½ pint chicken stock
salt
freshly ground black pepper
175 ml/6 fl oz orange juice
½ medium pineapple, peeled and cut into chunks

Place the veal in a saucepan with the stock and bring to the boil. Add salt and pepper, cover and simmer for about 30 minutes. Leave to cool, then skim off all the fat.

Transfer to a casserole dish and add the orange juice and pineapple. Cover and cook in a preheated moderately hot oven (200°C/400°F, Gas Mark 6) for 1 hour or until tender.
SERVES 6

VITELLO TONNATO

METRIC/IMPERIAL
350 g/12 oz lean roast veal, trimmed of fat
1 × 200 g/7 oz can tuna fish, drained
2-3 anchovy fillets, drained
1 tablespoon sherry
1 tablespoon reduced-calorie mayonnaise
salt
freshly ground black pepper
1 tablespoon chopped capers, to garnish
(optional)

Slice the roast veal thinly. Place the tuna fish, anchovies, sherry, mayonnaise, salt and pepper in a blender and liquidize until smooth. Pour over the veal and chill slightly.

Alternatively, liquidize the ingredients until they are combined but still a thick consistency. Place a spoonful in the centre of each veal slice and roll up. Chill slightly.

Scatter the chopped capers over the dish, if using, before serving.
SERVES 4

Note: The best way to roast veal for this dish is to place the meat on a rack over a roasting dish half-filled with water. Roast in a preheated moderately hot oven (200°C/400°F, Gas Mark 6) for 20 minutes per 450 g/1 lb, plus 20 minutes. Baste with water frequently.

MINCED VEAL WITH GREEN PEPPERCORNS

METRIC/IMPERIAL
1 tablespoon olive oil
1 small onion, peeled and finely chopped
¼ red pepper, peeled, deseeded and diced
2 cloves garlic, peeled and crushed
275 g/10 oz lean pie veal, minced
75 g/3 oz shelled broad beans, finely chopped
50 g/2 oz fresh or frozen sweetcorn
1 tablespoon chopped parsley
1 teaspoon well-rinsed green peppercorns
salt
freshly ground black pepper
8 large Chinese lettuce leaves
Sauce:
300 ml/½ pint boiling veal or chicken stock
2 tablespoons white wine vinegar with green
peppercorns
1 teaspoon well-rinsed green peppercorns
1 teaspoon honey

Heat the oil in a pan. Gently fry the onion, diced red pepper and garlic until cooked but not brown. Stir in the veal, broad beans, sweetcorn, parsley and peppercorns. Season well with salt and pepper. Fry for 4 minutes, stirring well. Cook the Chinese leaves in a steamer over the boiling stock for 20 seconds or until just limp.

Divide the mixture between the 8 leaves and wrap up tightly. Lay side by side in the steamer. Season the outside of the leaves with salt and pepper. Cover with a tight-fitting lid and steam over the stock for 10 minutes. Arrange 2 lettuce parcels on each plate. Keep warm.

Reduce the veal or chicken stock until rich and syrupy. Stir in the vinegar, green peppercorns and honey. Taste and adjust seasoning if necessary. Pour over the parcels and serve.
SERVES 4

BACON AND NUT RING

METRIC/IMPERIAL
2 tablespoons polyunsaturated vegetable oil
1 onion, peeled and chopped
1 clove garlic, peeled and crushed
100 g/4 oz lean bacon, derinded and chopped
2 celery stalks, chopped
1 tablespoon wholemeal flour
175 ml/6 fl oz tomato juice
100 g/4 oz wholemeal breadcrumbs
100 g/4 oz hazelnuts, coarsely ground
1 tablespoon rolled oats
1 tablespoon chopped parsley
1 egg, beaten
salt
freshly ground black pepper
watercress, to garnish

Heat the oil in a pan, add the onion, garlic, bacon and celery and fry for 4 minutes until softened. Mix in the flour, then add the tomato juice, stirring until the mixture thickens. Add the remaining ingredients, seasoning with ½ teaspoon salt and pepper to taste. Mix thoroughly.

Press the mixture into a greased 19 cm/7½ inch ring mould and cover with foil. Cook in a preheated moderate oven (180°C/350°F, Gas Mark 4) for 1 hour. Turn out on to a warmed serving dish, garnish with watercress and serve hot with tomato sauce. Alternatively, serve cold with salad.
SERVES 4

CATALAN BROAD BEAN CASSEROLE

METRIC/IMPERIAL
100 g/4 oz polyunsaturated margarine
225 g/8 oz lean bacon, derinded and diced
225 g/8 oz butifarra or garlic sausage, sliced
1 onion, peeled and chopped
2 cloves garlic, peeled and chopped
2 tomatoes, skinned and chopped
bouquet garni (mint, thyme and parsley)
few leaves summer savory
1 teaspoon ground cinnamon
2 cloves
2 kg/4½ lb broad beans, shelled
150 ml/¼ pint sweet red wine
150 ml/¼ pint ham or chicken stock
freshly ground black pepper
salt

Heat the margarine in a large flameproof casserole or heavy saucepan and fry the bacon and sausage until lightly coloured. Remove with a slotted spoon and reserve.

Sauté the onion, garlic and tomatoes in the fat remaining in the pan until soft. Add the bouquet garni, summer savory and spices. Stir in the beans, bacon and sausage, then pour the wine and stock into the casserole. Season with pepper, and salt if necessary. Cover and cook over a low heat for about 30 minutes. Remove the bouquet garni. Serve piping hot, as a main dish.
SERVES 4

CHICORY AND HAM IN YOGURT SAUCE

METRIC/IMPERIAL
2 heads chicory
4 thin slices lean cooked ham
150 ml/¼ pint plain low-fat yogurt
4 tablespoons skimmed milk
1 egg yolk
salt
freshly ground black pepper
2 teaspoons grated Parmesan cheese
chopped parsley, to garnish

Put the chicory in a bowl and cover with boiling water. Leave to stand for 3 minutes, then drain very thoroughly.

Split each head in half lengthwise to make 4 pieces, then roll a slice of ham around each piece. Place side by side in a shallow baking dish.

Put the yogurt, milk and egg yolk in a bowl and whisk with a fork until well mixed. Add salt and pepper to taste. Pour the sauce over the ham, then sprinkle with the cheese. Bake in a preheated moderate oven (180°C/350°F, Gas Mark 4) for 25 minutes. Serve hot, garnished with parsley.
SERVES 4

HAM AU GRATIN

METRIC/IMPERIAL
8 slices cooked lean ham
2 tablespoons dry white wine
250 ml/8 fl oz béchamel sauce (see page 343)
1 teaspoon French mustard
2 tablespoons grated Parmesan cheese
1 tablespoon dry wholemeal breadcrumbs

Place the ham in a buttered ovenproof dish, over-lapping slices. Moisten with white wine. Season the béchamel sauce with mustard and 1 tablespoon of the cheese and spoon over the ham. Mix the re-maining cheese and crumbs together and scatter over the top. Bake in a preheated moderate oven (180°C/350°F, Gas Mark 4) for 30 minutes.
SERVES 4

HAM AND PINEAPPLE KEBABS

METRIC/IMPERIAL
50 g/2 oz fresh coconut
175 g/6 oz brown rice
350 ml/12 fl oz water
salt
Kebabs:
½ large or 1 small pineapple, peeled and cut into 2 cm/¾ inch cubes
450 g/1 lb cooked ham, cut in 1 thick slice and diced
1 tablespoon polyunsaturated vegetable oil
¼ teaspoon ground ginger
Sauce:
300 ml/½ pint plain low-fat yogurt
1-2 teaspoons curry powder

Rub the coconut against the coarse side of a grater, put into a saucepan and heat very gently until lightly browned. Add the rice, water and a pinch of salt to the coconut in the saucepan. Bring the water to the boil. Stir briskly with a fork, cover the pan, lower the heat and simmer for 30 to 45 minutes.

Meanwhile, thread the pineapple and ham on to metal skewers. Blend the oil and ginger; brush over the pineapple and ham. Cook the kebabs under a preheated grill for 2 to 3 minutes.

To make the sauce, blend the yogurt and curry paste. Spoon into a sauceboat.

Serve the coconut rice on a heated dish, and place the kebabs on top.
SERVES 4

BROAD BEAN AND HAM FLAN

METRIC/IMPERIAL
wholemeal pastry made with 225 g/8 oz wholemeal flour (see page 334)
40 g/1½ oz polyunsaturated margarine
25 g/1 oz plain unbleached white flour
1 × 275 g/10 oz can broad beans
skimmed milk
2 tablespoons chopped parsley
225 g/8 oz cooked lean ham, chopped
salt
freshly ground black pepper

Roll out the pastry and line a 20 cm/8 inch flan case. Prick well with a fork and bake blind in a preheated moderately hot oven (200°C/400°F,

Gas Mark 6) for 20 to 25 minutes until lightly browned.

For the filling, melt the margarine in a saucepan, add the flour and cook, for 1 minute, stirring. Drain the beans and add enough milk to the liquor from the can to give 300 ml/½ pint. Gradually add this mixture to the flour, stirring well. Bring to the boil, and cook for 2 minutes. Remove from the heat. Add the beans, parsley, chopped ham and seasoning to taste. Pile into the warm flan case and serve immediately with a salad.

SERVES 4 to 6

HONEY ROAST HAM

METRIC/IMPERIAL

1 × 1 kg/2 lb oven-ready gammon joint, soaked in cold water overnight
12 cloves
2 tablespoons Demerara sugar
1 tablespoon clear honey
3 tablespoons orange juice
orange slices, to garnish
Sauce:
2 tablespoons redcurrant jelly
rind of ½ orange, finely shredded
3 tablespoons orange juice
2 tablespoons lemon juice
150 ml/¼ pint chicken stock

Drain the gammon and place in a large saucepan, then pour in fresh cold water to cover. Bring to the boil, skim off the scum that rises to the surface, reduce the heat and simmer for 30 minutes.

Heat the oven to 180°C/350°F, Gas Mark 4.

Remove the gammon from the pan and lay it on a board. Carefully strip off the skin.

Score the fat surface diagonally with a sharp knife and stud with the cloves. Place the gammon in a baking tin. Blend the sugar, honey and orange juice and pour over the gammon. Roast in the oven for 30 minutes, then increase the oven temperature to 220°C/425°F, Gas Mark 7 and roast for a further 15 minutes. Transfer the gammon to a heated serving platter.

Meanwhile, to make the sauce, melt the redcurrant jelly in a small saucepan and add the orange rind and juice, lemon juice and stock. Heat through gently.

Serve the gammon carved into slices and garnished with the orange slices, with the sauce served separately in a heated sauceboat.

SERVES 4

GAMMON AND BROAD BEANS

METRIC/IMPERIAL

225 g/8 oz shelled broad beans
salt
25 g/1 oz polyunsaturated margarine
25 g/1 oz plain unbleached white flour
350 g/12 oz cooked gammon, cut into bite-sized pieces
freshly ground black pepper
½ teaspoon grated nutmeg

Cook the beans in boiling salted water for about 15 minutes. Drain and reserve the cooking liquid.

Melt the margarine in a saucepan and add the flour. Cook gently for 2 minutes.

Stir in about 300 ml/½ pint of the beans' cooking liquid and cook for a few minutes until thickened. Add the gammon and heat gently until warmed through, stirring frequently.

Add more of the beans' cooking liquid if the mixture is too thick. Taste and adjust the seasoning if necessary.

Add the beans and transfer to a heated serving dish. Sprinkle with the nutmeg.

SERVES 4

GAMMON WITH APPLE

METRIC/IMPERIAL

750 g/1½ lb potatoes, peeled and thickly sliced
750 g/1½ lb gammon, soaked and cut into bite-sized pieces, rind and fat removed
1 large onion, peeled and sliced
1 clove garlic, peeled and crushed
2 turnips, peeled and quartered
2 carrots, peeled and thickly sliced
3 small cooking apples, peeled and thickly sliced
salt
freshly ground black pepper
½ teaspoon chopped fresh or ¼ teaspoon dried sage
¼ teaspoon chopped fresh or pinch of dried thyme
300 ml/½ pint chicken stock
thyme sprigs, to garnish

Layer the potatoes, gammon, onion, garlic, turnip, carrot and apple in a bowl, seasoning with salt, pepper, sage and thyme as you go.

Pour over enough stock to just cover the filling. Cover the bowl with foil or greaseproof paper and tie down. Place in a steamer or covered saucepan half-filled with boiling water and steam for 1½ hours. Check the liquid level frequently and add more boiling water if necessary.

Remove the foil. Pour the cooking liquid carefully into a pan, leaving the meat and vegetables in the bowl. Keep the food warm to one side. Boil the sauce to reduce to half of the original volume. Taste and adjust seasoning if necessary. Pour the sauce over the food and garnish with thyme.
SERVES 4

SAUSAGE HOT POT

METRIC/IMPERIAL
450 g/1 lb low-fat chipolata sausages
1 large onion, peeled and chopped
450 g/1 lb tomatoes, skinned and chopped
2 carrots, peeled and chopped
600 ml/1 pint beef stock
50 g/2 oz sweetcorn kernels

Cook the sausages under a preheated hot grill for 10 minutes so that the fat is drained off. Place in a casserole together with the remaining ingredients. Cover and cook in a moderately hot oven (190°C/375°F, Gas Mark 5) for 40 minutes.
SERVES 4

SAUSAGE AND BEAN CASSEROLE

METRIC/IMPERIAL
450 g/1 lb low-fat pork sausages
100 g/4 oz lean bacon, derinded and chopped
1 large onion, peeled and chopped
2 celery stalks, sliced
1 green pepper, cored, deseeded and chopped
2 tablespoons plain unbleached white flour
500 ml/¾ pint chicken stock
2 × 425 g/15 oz can kidney beans
4 carrots, peeled and sliced
1 bay leaf
salt
freshly ground black pepper

Cook the sausages and bacon in a large saucepan over low heat until the fat begins to run then increase the heat and cook until golden. Remove with a slotted spoon and reserve.

Add the onion, celery and green pepper to the fat in the saucepan and cook until the onions are translucent. Stir in the flour then gradually add the hot stock.

Bring to the boil, stirring constantly. Add kidney beans, carrots, bay leaf, fried bacon and sausage, salt and pepper Cover the pan and simmer gently for about 30 minutes. Serve with brown rice and a green salad.
SERVES 4 to 6

CHICK PEAS WITH TOMATOES AND SAUSAGES

METRIC/IMPERIAL
275 g/10 oz chick peas, soaked overnight
225 g/8 oz low-fat pork sausages
150 g/5 oz lean bacon, derinded and diced
1 large onion, peeled and finely chopped
2 cloves garlic, peeled and chopped
1 large green pepper, cored, deseeded and diced
4 large ripe tomatoes, skinned, deseeded and chopped
grated nutmeg or cinnamon
¼ teaspoon dried thyme
salt
freshly ground black pepper

Drain the chick peas, place in a saucepan and add fresh cold water to cover. Simmer, covered, for about 1 hour. Prick the sausages and brown in a frying pan. Remove and cut into 2.5 cm/1 inch pieces. Set aside.

Blanch the bacon in boiling water for 1 minute, then drain. Brown the bacon, onion, garlic and green pepper in the frying pan, stirring. Add the tomatoes, spice, thyme, salt and pepper. Cover and cook over low heat for 10 minutes. Fold in the sausage pieces.

Drain the chick peas, reserving 500 ml/18 fl oz liquid. Turn into a lightly greased ovenproof baking dish and cover with the tomato and sausage mixture. Moisten with the reserved liquid. Cover and bake in a preheated moderately hot oven (190°C/375°F, Gas Mark 5) for about 1½ hours, stirring from time to time. Serve in wide soup plates.
SERVES 4 to 6

SAUSAGE BRAN BURGERS

METRIC/IMPERIAL
1 egg, beaten
4 tablespoons skimmed milk
50 g/2 oz All Bran breakfast cereal
450 g/1 lb pork or beef low-fat sausage meat
salt
freshly ground black pepper

Mix together the egg, milk and cereal and allow to stand until the milk has been absorbed. Mix this with the sausage meat and seasoning. Divide the mixture into 8 and shape into burgers. At this stage the burgers may be covered and refrigerated overnight.

Place the burgers on a baking sheet and bake in a moderately hot oven (200°C/400°F, Gas Mark 6) for about 30 minutes or until cooked through.
SERVES 4

PEACHY SAUSAGES

METRIC/IMPERIAL
1 kg/2 lb thick low-fat sausages
1 tablespoon polyunsaturated vegetable oil
1 tablespoon vinegar
120 ml/4 fl oz peach juice
4 tablespoons tomato sauce
1 tablespoon brown sugar
1 tablespoon grated onion
½ teaspoon Worcestershire sauce
¼ teaspoon salt
2 teaspoons chopped fresh oregano or
½ teaspoon dried oregano
dash of Tabasco or chilli sauce
summer savory, to garnish (optional)

Prick the sausages in several places, place in a frying pan with water to cover and simmer for 5 minutes, then drain. Parboiled in this way, the sausages will cook through without scorching or bursting.

Place the remaining ingredients in a saucepan and simmer for 5 minutes, stirring now and again. Pour over the sausages and allow to stand for 30 minutes.

Cook the sausages under the grill until crisp and brown on all sides, brushing frequently with the glaze. Spoon the remaining glaze over the sausages and garnish with summer savory, if available. Serve with plain boiled potatoes and green beans.
SERVES 6 to 8

BLACK BEAN CASSEROLE

METRIC/IMPERIAL
350 g/12 oz black beans, soaked overnight
2 tablespoons olive oil
2 onions, peeled and sliced
2 celery stalks, sliced
2 carrots, sliced
2 cloves garlic, peeled and crushed
450 g/1 lb frankfurter sausages, thickly sliced
1 tablespoon tomato purée
1 bay leaf
450 g/1 lb tomatoes, skinned and chopped
salt
freshly ground black pepper
1 tablespoon chopped parsley, to garnish

Drain the beans, place in a pan and cover with cold water. Bring to the boil and simmer gently for 1 hour. Drain the beans and reserve 450 ml/¾ pint of the liquid.

Heat the oil in a flameproof casserole, add the onions and fry for 5 to 10 minutes until transparent. Add the celery, carrots and garlic and fry for 3 to 4 minutes.

Add the remaining ingredients, with the beans, reserved liquid, and salt and pepper to taste. Cover and cook in a preheated moderate oven (180°C/350°F, Gas Mark 4) for 1 to 1½ hours until the beans are soft. Sprinkle with the parsley and serve immediately.
SERVES 4

RABBIT WITH GREEN OLIVES

METRIC/IMPERIAL
1 tablespoon olive oil
100 g/4 oz lean bacon, derinded and diced
2 onions, peeled and thickly sliced
2 celery stalks, thickly sliced
1 rabbit, jointed
1 tablespoon unbleached white flour
500 ml/18 fl oz hot chicken stock
1 bay leaf
1 rosemary sprig
salt
freshly ground black pepper
8 green olives, stoned
1 tablespoon capers (optional)

Put the oil, bacon, onions and celery into a large flameproof casserole and heat gently, stirring occasionally, until the fat runs from the bacon.

Add the rabbit pieces and fry gently, turning, until lightly browned on all sides. This will take about 10 minutes.

Sprinkle in the flour and stir for 1 minute. Stir in the hot stock, bay leaf, rosemary, and salt and pepper to taste. Bring to the boil, then cover tightly, reduce the heat and simmer for 45 minutes to 1½ hours or until the rabbit is tender.

Add the olives and capers (if using), and simmer for a further 10 minutes. Discard the bay leaf before serving.

SERVES 4

RABBIT WITH ROSEMARY AND MUSTARD

METRIC/IMPERIAL
1 medium onion, peeled and minced
2 tablespoons olive oil
4 rabbit portions
300 ml/½ pint chicken stock
150 ml/¼ pint dry white wine
2 teaspoons coarse-grain mustard
1 tablespoon chopped rosemary
salt
freshly ground black pepper
3 tablespoons fromage blanc
2 egg yolks
rosemary sprigs, to garnish

Sauté the onion gently in the olive oil for 3 minutes; add the rabbit portions and brown evenly on all sides. Add the chicken stock, white wine, mustard, rosemary, and salt and pepper to taste; cover and simmer for 45 minutes until the rabbit is just tender. Remove the rabbit portions to a serving dish and keep warm.

Boil the cooking liquid rapidly until reduced by half; beat the fromage blanc with the egg yolks and beat into the cooking liquid over a gentle heat, without boiling. Spoon the prepared sauce over the rabbit and garnish with sprigs of fresh rosemary before serving.

SERVES 4

Variation
Chicken portions may be used in place of the rabbit portions, if preferred.

BOBOTIE

METRIC/IMPERIAL
1 slice of white bread
300 ml/½ pint skimmed milk
1 onion, peeled and finely chopped
2 cloves garlic, peeled and crushed
2 celery stalks, roughly chopped
4 carrots, peeled, sliced and cooked
25 g/1 oz polyunsaturated margarine
3 teaspoons curry powder
1 tablespoon mango chutney
juice of 1 lemon
750 g/1½ lb cooked meat (e.g. lamb, beef, chicken), minced
salt
freshly ground black pepper
Topping:
2 eggs
12 blanched almonds, toasted
chopped parsley, to garnish

Soak the bread in the milk. Grease a pudding basin with a little margarine. Gently fry the onion, garlic, celery and carrot in the margarine until cooked but not brown. Stir in the curry powder, chutney, lemon juice and meat. Season well with salt and pepper. Spoon into the pudding basin. Squeeze the milk from the bread, reserving the milk, and fork the bread into the meat mixture.

Mix the eggs with the reserved milk. Season well with salt and pepper. Pour the topping over the meat. Arrange the blanched almond halves over the top. Cover with a piece of foil or greaseproof paper and tie down. Place in a steamer or covered saucepan half-filled with simmering water and steam gently for 40 minutes or until the custard is set.

Serve sprinkled with chopped parsley.

SERVES 4

Note: This famous South African recipe is the perfect rechauffé dish. Fish can be used instead of meat and any leftover ingredients you like – just follow the outline of the recipe above.

BACON-TOPPED LIVER

METRIC/IMPERIAL
350 g/12 oz lambs' or pig's liver, cut into 8 thick
slices
salt
freshly ground black pepper
1 × 425 g/15 oz can tomatoes
6 tablespoons wholemeal breadcrumbs, mixed
with dried parsley and dried thyme
2 tablespoons water
6 rashers lean bacon, derinded and halved
15 g/½ oz polyunsaturated margarine
chopped parsley, to garnish

Put half the liver in a casserole or ovenproof dish
and season well with salt and pepper. Cover with
the tomatoes, reserving a little of the juice, then
sprinkle with half of the breadcrumb mixture.
Cover with the remaining liver, pour over the reserved tomato juice and the water. Add salt and
pepper to taste. Lay the pieces of bacon on top.
Sprinkle with the remaining breadcrumb mixture
and dot with the margarine.
Cover and cook in a preheated moderately hot
oven (190°C/375°F, Gas Mark 5) for 30 minutes.
Remove the lid and return to the oven for a further
20 to 30 minutes or until the liver is tender. Garnish with parsley before serving.
SERVES 4

BAKED LIVER IN YOGURT SAUCE

METRIC/IMPERIAL
25 g/1 oz polyunsaturated margarine
450 g/1 lb lambs' liver, thinly sliced
300 ml/½ pint plain low-fat yogurt
2 teaspoons chopped mixed herbs
salt
freshly ground white pepper
pinch of paprika, to garnish

Melt the margarine in a flameproof casserole. Add
the liver and fry gently until browned on both
sides. Drain off any excess fat.
Mix the yogurt with the herbs and salt and pepper to taste, then pour over the liver and bring to
the boil.
Cover the casserole, transfer to a preheated
moderate oven (160°C/325°F, Gas Mark 3) and
cook for 25 minutes. Taste and adjust the seasoning, then sprinkle with paprika and serve hot.
SERVES 4

BRAISED LIVER

METRIC/IMPERIAL
450 g/1 lb chicken livers or lambs' liver, cut into
pieces
1 large cooking apple, cored and cut into chunks
50 g/2 oz onion, peeled and sliced
350 ml/12 fl oz tomato juice
2 teaspoons Worcestershire sauce
salt
freshly ground black pepper

Put the liver in a casserole dish. Add the apple and
sliced onion. Pour in the tomato juice, Worcestershire sauce and add salt and pepper.
Cover and cook in a preheated moderate oven
(180°C/350°F, Gas Mark 4) for about 30 minutes.
Serve immediately while piping hot with potatoes
and seasonal vegetables.
SERVES 4

LIVER WITH HERBS

METRIC/IMPERIAL
2 tablespoons wholemeal flour
salt
freshly ground black pepper
450 g/1 lb lambs' liver, sliced
2 tablespoons polyunsaturated vegetable oil
2 onions, peeled and chopped
150 ml/¼ pint red wine
150 ml/¼ pint stock
2 tablespoons tomato purée
1 teaspoon chopped thyme
2 tomatoes, skinned, deseeded and sliced
1 tablespoon chopped parsley, to garnish

Season the flour with salt and pepper and use to
coat the liver. Heat the oil in a pan, add the liver
and fry gently for 2 minutes on each side. Remove
from the pan and keep hot.
Add the onions to the pan and fry gently until
softened. Stir in the wine, stock, tomato purée,
and salt and pepper to taste. Bring to the boil. Return the liver to the pan, cover and simmer for 15
minutes. Add the tomatoes and cook for a further
5 minutes or until the liver is tender.
Arrange the liver on a warmed serving dish.
Pour the sauce over the liver. Sprinkle with
parsley and serve immediately.
SERVES 4

LIVER KEBABS

METRIC/IMPERIAL
450 g/1 lb lambs' liver, cut into bite-sized pieces
4 onions, peeled and quartered
4 tomatoes, quartered
100 g/4 oz mushrooms
8 bay leaves
salt
freshly ground black pepper
lemon juice

Thread the liver pieces, onion, tomato, mushrooms and bay leaves alternately on to 4 skewers. Sprinkle with salt and pepper.

Cook under a preheated hot grill for about 20 minutes, turning occasionally and spooning over the lemon juice to prevent burning.
SERVES 4

LIVER PROVENÇAL

METRIC/IMPERIAL
350 g/12 oz lambs' liver, cut into strips
1 tablespoon plain wholemeal flour
salt
freshly ground black pepper
1½ tablespoons polyunsaturated vegetable oil
1 small onion, peeled and finely sliced
½ green pepper, cored, deseeded and cut into strips
50 g/2 oz mushrooms, sliced
1 clove garlic, peeled and crushed
1 × 198 g/7½ oz can tomatoes
1 teaspoon fresh marjoram, or ½ teaspoon dried oregano
150 ml/¼ pint chicken or vegetable stock
1 bay leaf
watercress sprigs, to garnish

Coat the liver with the flour seasoned with salt and pepper. Heat the oil in a pan, add the liver strips and seal, turning once. Remove from the pan and set aside in a covered dish.

In the same pan, cook the onion and green pepper slices for 2 minutes, adding a little extra oil if necessary. Add the mushrooms, garlic, tomatoes, marjoram, stock and bay leaf. Simmer gently for 10 to 15 minutes until the vegetables have softened. Add the liver and continue cooking for a further 4 to 5 minutes.

Transfer to a hot serving dish and garnish with watercress sprigs.
SERVES 4

LAMBS' LIVER WITH BABY ONIONS AND CHIVE SAUCE

METRIC/IMPERIAL
450 g/1 lb lambs' liver, trimmed and cut into strips
salt
freshly ground black pepper
juice of ½ lemon
2 tablespoons sherry
½ teaspoon honey
16 button onions, peeled
3 tablespoons snipped chives
150 ml/¼ pint beef stock
50 g/2 oz polyunsaturated margarine, cut into walnut-sized pieces
Garnish:
50 g/2 oz lean smoked bacon, derinded, grilled and diced
1 tablespoon snipped chives

Season the strips of liver with salt and pepper. Lay in a dish with the lemon juice, sherry, honey, onions and 1 tablespoon of the chives. Marinate for up to 2 hours. Cut a piece of foil or greaseproof paper large enough to seal all of the ingredients in a large parcel.

Spoon the food on to the foil. Fold up the edges, pour in all of the marinade and seal completely. Place in a steamer. Bring the stock and remaining chives to the boil in a saucepan. Cover the steamer with a tight-fitting lid and steam over the stock for 10 minutes. Remove the foil packet and pour the juices from the meat into the hot stock in the saucepan. Keep the food warm to one side while you finish the chive-flavoured sauce.

Boil the stock until syrupy, then reduce the heat. Whisk in the margarine, nut by nut, until the sauce is creamy. Turn off the heat. Arrange the liver and onions on 4 warmed plates. Pour over the sauce and garnish with bacon dice and chives. Serve at once.
SERVES 4

MEDITERRANEAN LIVER

METRIC/IMPERIAL

450 g/1 lb lambs' liver, washed, trimmed and thinly sliced
1 onion, peeled and finely sliced
1 green pepper, cored, deseeded and sliced
1 red pepper, cored, deseeded and sliced
1 garlic clove, peeled and crushed
1 × 400 g/14 oz can tomatoes
salt
freshly ground black pepper
1 tablespoon chopped parsley, to garnish

Layer the liver in a shallow casserole with the onion, green and red peppers and the garlic. Pour over the canned tomatoes with the juice and season to taste with salt and pepper. Cover and cook in a preheated moderate oven (180°C/350°F, Gas Mark 4) for 1 hour. Remove, adjust seasoning and sprinkle with the finely chopped parsley.
SERVES 4

LIVER AND ONIONS

METRIC/IMPERIAL

4 tablespoons olive oil
350 g/12 oz onions, peeled and thinly sliced
1 tablespoon fresh sage or ¼ teaspoon dried sage
salt
freshly ground black pepper
400–450 g/14 oz–1 lb calves' or lambs' liver, very thinly sliced and veins removed
1 tablespoon wine vinegar
1 tablespoon water
2 tablespoons chopped chives or parsley, to garnish

Heat 2 tablespoons of the oil in a large, heavy-based frying pan. When hot, put in the onions and cook over a low heat, stirring frequently, for 15 to 20 minutes, until the onions are soft and golden. Stir in the sage and a little salt and pepper, then spread the mixture over the base of a hot serving dish. Keep hot.

While the onions are cooking, pat each slice of liver dry with kitchen paper and cut into pieces roughly 4 cm/1½ inches square. Using kitchen paper towels, wipe clean the pan in which the onions were cooked. Pour the remaining oil into the pan and, when sizzling hot, put in the pieces of liver and fry briskly, turning frequently, for 2 to 3 minutes, until the liver changes colour on the outside but is still juicy inside. Add salt and pepper

and pile the liver on top of the onions. Add the vinegar and water to the pan, boil for a few seconds, stirring and scraping up the juices from the base of the pan, and pour over the liver. Sprinkle with chives or parsley.
SERVES 4

LIVER CHILLI

METRIC/IMPERIAL

100 g/4 oz red kidney beans, soaked overnight
2 tablespoons polyunsaturated vegetable oil
1 onion, peeled and sliced
50 g/2 oz mushrooms, wiped and finely chopped
350 g/12 oz lambs' liver, trimmed and finely chopped
1 clove garlic, peeled and crushed
½–1 teaspoon chilli powder
2 teaspoons plain wholemeal flour
1 × 400 g/14 oz can tomatoes
salt
freshly ground black pepper
1 teaspoon cumin seeds
parsley, to garnish

Drain the beans, rinse and cover with cold water. Bring to the boil and boil rapidly for 10 minutes, reduce heat and simmer for 35 to 45 minutes until tender. (You can add 1 teaspoon oil with the water to prevent it boiling over.) Drain and rinse.

Heat the oil in a pan and sauté the onion for 5 minutes. Add the mushrooms and cook for 1 minute. Add the liver and garlic and cook, stirring, for 5 minutes.

Stir in the chilli powder and flour and cook for 1 minute. Add the tomatoes with their juice, salt, pepper and cumin. Bring to the boil, add the beans, cover and simmer for 20 minutes. Transfer to a warmed serving dish and garnish with parsley. Serve immediately.
SERVES 4

CALVES' LIVER FLORENTINE

METRIC/IMPERIAL
750 g/1½ lb fresh spinach, cooked and
thoroughly drained
freshly ground nutmeg
salt
freshly ground black pepper
450 g/1 lb calves' liver, cut in thin slices
15 g/½ oz polyunsaturated margarine
2 tablespoons olive oil
1 tablespoon chopped sage
1 clove garlic, peeled and crushed
150 ml/¼ pint plain low-fat yogurt
1 egg yolk
50 g/2 oz Edam or Gouda cheese, grated

Season the spinach with nutmeg, salt and pepper;
spoon into a lightly greased heatproof dish. Sauté
the slices of liver gently in the margarine and oil,
along with the sage and garlic, until sealed on all
sides. Spoon the liver and its juices over the
spinach.

Beat the yogurt with the egg yolk and spoon
evenly over the liver and spinach; sprinkle with
the cheese. Place under a preheated grill until the
sauce is lightly golden and bubbling. Serve immediately while piping hot.
SERVES 4

CALVES' LIVER SPIKED WITH MUSTARD AND SAGE

METRIC/IMPERIAL
350 g/12 oz calves' liver, trimmed
175-225 g/6-8 oz fresh white or brown
breadcrumbs
1 egg white
4 teaspoons Dijon mustard
1 teaspoon chopped sage
2 shallots, peeled and very finely chopped
5 teaspoons cornflour
salt
freshly ground black pepper
15 g/½ oz polyunsaturated margarine
2 cloves garlic, peeled and crushed
450 g/1 lb mushrooms, wiped and finely
chopped
300 ml/½ pint veal or beef stock
100 g/4 oz polyunsaturated margarine, cut into
walnut-sized pieces (optional)
sage sprigs, to garnish

Mix the liver with enough breadcrumbs in a blender or food processor to form a smooth paste.
Add the egg white, 2 teaspoons of the mustard
and ½ teaspoon of the sage. Mix them for a few
seconds until they are thoroughly incorporated
into the meat. Mix in the shallots and the cornflour. Season well with salt and pepper.

Dust your hands with cornflour and form the
mixture into 3.5 cm/1½ inch balls – about the size
of a golf ball. Heat the margarine in a pan, fry the
garlic and chopped mushrooms for 2 minutes.

Bring the stock to the boil in a saucepan. Lay a
piece of wet greaseproof paper in a steamer.
Spread the chopped mushrooms on top. Arrange
the liver balls on the mushrooms, cover with a
tight-fitting lid and steam over the stock for 6
minutes.

Arrange the meatballs on 4 warmed serving
plates and keep warm.

Stir the mushrooms and any meat juices into
the stock. Add the remaining mustard and sage.
Boil rapidly to reduce until syrupy. Whisk in the
margarine, bit by bit, until the sauce is creamy.

Pour over the meatballs, garnish with sprigs of
sage and serve at once with brown rice and a fresh
green salad.
SERVES 4

KIDNEY AND MUSHROOM CASSEROLE

METRIC/IMPERIAL
450 g/1 lb lambs' kidneys, skinned and cored
100 g/4 oz onions, peeled and sliced
300 ml/½ pint beef stock
120 ml/4 fl oz sherry
salt
freshly ground black pepper
225 g/8 oz mushrooms, stalks removed, sliced if
large

Slice or halve the kidneys. Place under a preheated
hot grill and cook for 1 minute on each side.

Transfer to a casserole dish and add the onions,
stock, sherry, salt and pepper. Stir in the mushrooms. Cover and cook in a preheated moderately
hot oven (200°C/400°F, Gas Mark 6) for about 40
minutes or until the kidneys are tender. Serve
with plain boiled rice.
SERVES 4

DEVILLED KIDNEYS ON TOAST

METRIC/IMPERIAL
2 tablespoons finely chopped mushrooms
juice of 1 lemon
1 tablespoon Worcestershire sauce
150 ml/¼ pint water
1 teaspoon mustard powder
salt
freshly ground black pepper
8 lambs' kidneys, skinned, cores removed and split in half lengthwise
4 slices wholemeal bread
chopped parsley, to garnish

Mix together the mushrooms, lemon juice, Worcestershire sauce, water, mustard and salt and pepper to taste.

Grill the kidneys under medium heat for 3 minutes on the cut sides. Pour the devilled mixture into the grill pan, then turn the kidneys and grill the other sides for 2 minutes. Baste and turn the kidneys, then grill for a further 2 minutes.

Meanwhile, toast the bread lightly on both sides. Arrange on warmed individual serving plates, then place 2 kidneys on each slice of toast. Pour the sauce over the kidneys, garnish with chopped parsley and serve immediately.
SERVES 4

CURRIED KIDNEYS

METRIC/IMPERIAL
450 g/1 lb lambs' kidneys, skinned, cored and diced
100 g/4 oz onions, peeled and chopped
2 cloves garlic, peeled and crushed
250 ml/8 fl oz tomato juice
1 tablespoon curry powder
1 tablespoon lime or lemon juice
salt
freshly ground black pepper
beef stock (if necessary)

Put all the ingredients except the beef stock in a non-stick saucepan. Bring to the boil, cover and simmer for about 30 minutes.

Check occasionally that the kidney mixture is not getting too dry, add a little beef stock if necessary. Serve with rice and a vegetable curry.
SERVES 4

MARINATED KIDNEYS

METRIC/IMPERIAL
12 lambs' kidneys, skinned, cored and halved
1 small onion, peeled and thinly sliced
1 clove garlic, peeled and crushed
salt
freshly ground black pepper
150 ml/¼ pint red wine
1 teaspoon chopped fresh thyme
1 teaspoon Dijon mustard
2 tablespoons olive oil

Put the kidneys into a shallow dish; add the onion, garlic, salt and pepper to taste, red wine, thyme and mustard. Cover and chill for 3 to 4 hours.

Lift the kidneys out of their marinade and thread flat on to 4 kebab skewers. Brush the kidneys with the olive oil and grill for 3 minutes; turn the skewers over, brush once again, and grill for a further 3 minutes.

Heat the marinade until boiling. Arrange the kebabs on a serving dish, spoon over the hot marinade and serve immediately.
SERVES 4

KIDNEY AND BACON KEBABS

METRIC/IMPERIAL
12 rashers lean bacon, derinded
2 green peppers, cored and deseeded
12 lambs' kidneys, skinned and cored
6 small onions, peeled and quartered
2 tablespoons olive oil
1 tablespoon thyme leaves
Pilaff:
2 tablespoons olive oil
1 onion, peeled and chopped
1 red pepper, cored, deseeded and chopped
1 clove garlic, peeled and crushed
225 g/8 oz brown rice
600 ml/1 pint stock
1 bay leaf
salt
freshly ground black pepper
50 g/2 oz raisins
2 tablespoons soy sauce
2 tablespoons chopped parsley

First, prepare the pilaff. Heat the oil in a pan, add the onion and cook until softened. Add the pepper, garlic and rice and cook for a further 2 minutes, stirring. Add the stock, bay leaf, and salt and pepper to taste. Bring to the boil, stirring occasionally, cover and simmer for 35 minutes. Add the raisins and cook for a further 5 to 10 minutes until the stock is absorbed.

Cut the bacon rashers in half and roll up. Cut the peppers into 24 pieces and halve the kidneys. Thread the kidney, bacon, onion and pepper alternately on to 8 skewers. Mix the oil and thyme with ½ teaspoon salt and ¼ teaspoon pepper; brush over the kebabs. Cook under a preheated hot grill for 8 to 10 minutes, turning and basting with the oil mixture frequently.

Stir the soy sauce and parsley into the pilaff. Arrange the kebabs on top of the rice to serve.
SERVES 4

KIDNEYS WITH HOT PEPPER SAUCE

METRIC/IMPERIAL
450 g/1 lb lambs' kidneys, skinned, trimmed of fat and cored
juice of 1 orange
juice of 1 lemon
salt
freshly ground black pepper
2 red peppers, cored and deseeded
2 green or red chillies, deseeded and finely chopped
150 ml/¼ pint veal stock
1 tablespoon tomato purée
100 g/4 oz lean smoked bacon, derinded and cut into strips

Cut the kidneys into bite-sized pieces. Lay in a dish with the orange and lemon juice, salt and pepper. Marinate for 2 hours.

Roughly chop one and a half peppers and cut the remaining half pepper into fine strips for the garnish. Place the roughly chopped red pepper pieces, chilli, stock, tomato purée and three-quarters of the bacon strips into a saucepan. Stir in all of the marinade. Bring to the boil. Arrange the kidneys on a piece of wet greaseproof paper in a steamer. Cover with a tight-fitting lid and steam over the pepper mixture for 7 minutes. Grill the remaining bacon strips for garnish.

Arrange the kidneys on 4 warmed plates and keep warm. Work the pepper mixture in a blender or food processor until smooth. Taste and adjust seasoning if necessary. Spoon the sauce over the kidneys, decorate with the reserved thin strips of red pepper and cooked bacon. Serve at once.
SERVES 4

COUNTRY GRILL

METRIC/IMPERIAL
3 tablespoons polyunsaturated vegetable oil
4 slices lambs' liver
4 lambs' kidneys, skinned, cored and split lengthwise
salt
freshly ground black pepper
4 tomatoes, halved
8 large mushrooms, wiped

Remove the rack from the grill pan, then line the pan with foil and brush with a little of the oil. Put the liver in the centre of the pan, then arrange the kidneys around the liver. Brush with a little oil.

Grill under medium heat for 3 minutes until the liver and kidneys change colour then turn them over carefully and sprinkle with salt and pepper. Arrange the tomatoes around the kidneys, cut sides uppermost. Put the mushrooms in the pan, caps uppermost. Sprinkle both the tomatoes and mushrooms lightly with salt and pepper and brush with oil. Return the pan to the grill for a further 5 minutes.
SERVES 4

BAKED TONGUE

METRIC/IMPERIAL
1 × 1.75 kg/4 lb pickled ox tongue
3 onions, peeled and sliced
2 cloves
1 bay leaf
1 × 450 g/1 lb can tomatoes
freshly ground black pepper

Put the tongue in a large pan, then add enough cold water just to cover. Bring to the boil, then drain off the water. Cover with fresh cold water and bring to the boil again. Lower the heat, cover and simmer for 2 hours. Drain well and reserve 300 ml/½ pint cooking liquid.

Discard the skin, fat and bones and place the tongue in a casserole. Add the remaining ingredients and the reserved cooking liquid. Bake in a preheated moderate oven (180°C/350°F, Gas Mark 4) for 1 hour, basting twice.

Carve the tongue across the grain in thick slices and arrange on a flat serving dish. Remove the cloves and bay leaf from the casserole, taste and adjust the seasoning of the sauce, then pour over the tongue and serve hot.
SERVES 4

OX TONGUE

METRIC/IMPERIAL
1 × 1.5-1.6 kg/3-3½ lb ox tongue
salt
freshly ground black pepper
2 tablespoons chopped herbs (e.g. thyme,
parsley, chervil, sage)
1 large carrot, peeled and cut into matchsticks
1 large onion, peeled and sliced
2 small turnips, peeled and sliced
2 celery stalks, sliced
900 ml/1½ pints beef stock
15 g/½ oz gelatine (if serving cold)

Soak the tongue in cold water for 2 hours. Drain and season it with salt and pepper. Sprinkle with chopped herbs. Arrange the vegetables in a steamer compartment and top with the tongue. Cover with a tight-fitting lid and steam over the stock for 3 hours. Check the liquid level frequently and add more boiling stock if necessary.

When cooked, lift the tongue on to a board, remove the bones at the root and the skin. Discard the vegetables. Serve hot with mustard sauce.

To serve cold, curl the cooked tongue into a large round cake tin or soufflé dish. Make the stock up to 600 ml/1 pint using water or additional stock. Dissolve the gelatine in the stock, and pour over the tongue. Cover with foil and place a heavy weight on the meat.

Refrigerate overnight. To serve, turn out, and carve thin round slices. Serve with salads.

SERVES 4

GRILLED SWEETBREADS

METRIC/IMPERIAL
2 pairs sweetbreads
1 tablespoon vinegar
600 ml/1 pint water
1 teaspoon salt
40 g/1½ oz polyunsaturated margarine, melted
25 g/1 oz wholemeal breadcrumbs
lemon wedges, to garnish

Wash the sweetbreads, put them in a bowl and cover with cold water. Leave to stand for 20 minutes, then drain off the water.

Put the sweetbreads in a pan with the vinegar, water and salt. Bring to the boil, then lower the heat, cover and simmer for 20 minutes.

Drain thoroughly, then transfer to a bowl. Cover with cold water and leave to stand again for 20 minutes. Drain the sweetbreads thoroughly, then pat dry with kitchen paper towels. Remove the membranes and split the sweetbreads in half lengthwise.

Brush the grill pan with a little of the margarine. Brush the sweetbreads with a little more of the margarine, then roll in the breadcrumbs.

Place the sweetbreads in the pan and coat with the remaining margarine. Grill under high heat for 3 minutes on each side. Serve immediately garnished with lemon wedges.

SERVES 4

CALVES' SWEETBREADS WITH SPINACH AND COURGETTES

METRIC/IMPERIAL
500 g/1¼ lb calves' sweetbreads
450 g/1 lb courgettes, cut into matchsticks
salt
freshly ground black pepper
1 tablespoon olive oil
2 shallots, peeled and finely chopped
75 g/3 oz lean smoked bacon, derinded and diced
300 ml/½ pint veal or beef stock
½ tablespoon red wine vinegar
450 g/1 lb spinach, washed, and large stalks discarded
flat-leaf parsley sprigs, to garnish (optional)

Cover and soak the sweetbreads for several hours, changing the water frequently. Place the courgette matchsticks in a colander, sprinkle with salt and leave for 30 minutes. Heat the oil in a pan, and fry the shallots and bacon until golden brown. Blanch the sweetbreads in boiling water for 5 to 10 minutes. Refresh in cold water and remove the skin with a small knife. Rinse the courgette matchsticks under cold water to remove all of the salt.

Bring the veal stock and vinegar to the boil in a saucepan. Arrange the spinach, courgette, shallot, bacon and sweetbreads in a steamer on top. Season well. Cover with a tight-fitting lid and steam over the stock for 20 to 25 minutes. Remove and slice the sweetbreads, then arrange the food on 4 individual plates and keep warm. Boil the stock to reduce until syrupy. Pour over the sweetbreads, and garnish with parsley sprigs if liked.

SERVES 4

OXTAIL AND KIDNEY CASSEROLE

METRIC/IMPERIAL
25 g/1 oz polyunsaturated margarine
1 oxtail, trimmed of excess fat and cut into pieces
100 g/4 oz ox kidney, skinned, cored and chopped
1 large onion, peeled and sliced
450 g/1 lb carrots, peeled and sliced
1 large potato, peeled and grated
1 clove garlic, peeled and crushed
2 teaspoons paprika
1 teaspoon caraway seeds
1 tablespoon tomato purée
salt
freshly ground black pepper
600 ml/1 pint beef stock

Melt the margarine in a heavy pan. Add the oxtail and fry briskly until browned on all sides. Lower the heat, add the kidney, onion, carrots, potato and garlic and cook gently until the vegetables are lightly coloured, stirring frequently.

Drain off any excess fat, then stir in the remaining ingredients. Bring to the boil, then lower the heat, cover and simmer for 3½ hours or until the oxtail is tender. Taste and adjust the seasoning.

Serve hot with plain boiled potatoes, brown rice or wholewheat bread.
SERVES 4

SWEETBREADS IN LEMON SAUCE

METRIC/IMPERIAL
500 g/1¼ lb lambs' sweetbreads
1 tablespoon lemon juice
salt
freshly ground black pepper
1 large red pepper, cored, deseeded and thinly sliced
25 g/1 oz polyunsaturated margarine
15 g/½ oz plain flour
1 tablespoon dried skimmed milk powder

Soak the sweetbreads in cold water for 1 hour. Discard the water. Put the sweetbreads in a saucepan and add water to cover. Bring to the boil, then drain. Put the sweetbreads back in the pan, add fresh water and poach gently for about 10 minutes, skimming as necessary. Add the lemon juice and salt and pepper. Cover the saucepan

tightly and simmer for 30 minutes or until the sweetbreads are tender. Blanch the red pepper strips in boiling water for 1 minute.

Drain the sweetbreads, reserving the cooking liquid. Allow them to cool slightly then remove the membranes. Set aside and keep warm.

Melt the margarine in a saucepan and stir in the flour. Cook for 2 minutes. Stir in the sweetbreads' cooking liquid, red pepper and skimmed milk powder. Add salt and pepper to taste and cook for a few minutes. Pour the sauce over the sweetbreads and serve.
SERVES 4

STEAMED OXTAIL CASSEROLE

METRIC/IMPERIAL
2 tablespoons polyunsaturated vegetable oil
salt
freshly ground black pepper
15 g/¼ oz plain flour
1 medium oxtail, jointed
2 medium onions, peeled and sliced
4 carrots, peeled and thinly sliced
2 leeks, trimmed, washed and sliced
2 cloves garlic, peeled and crushed
2 large turnips, peeled and roughly chopped
pinch of dried thyme
2 bay leaves
pinch of dried sage
small pinch of ground cloves
450 ml/¾ pint beef stock
2 tablespoons chopped parsley, to garnish

Heat the oil in a heavy-based pan. Season the flour and dip in the oxtail, then fry over high heat until golden brown on all sides. Transfer to a pudding basin. Fry the vegetables for 5 minutes. Spoon over the meat. Stir in the herbs and cloves. Season well with salt and pepper.

Pour the stock into the frying pan. Bring to the boil, scraping the sediment from the base of the pan. Pour over the meat and vegetables. Cover with a piece of foil or greaseproof paper and tie down with string. Place in a steamer or covered saucepan, half-filled with boiling water, and steam for 3½ hours. Check the liquid level frequently and add more boiling water when necessary.

Arrange the oxtail on a warmed serving dish and keep warm. Blend the vegetables and stock in a blender or food processor. Spoon over the meat, sprinkle with chopped parsley and serve at once.
SERVES 4

'LOVE-IN-DISGUISE'

METRIC/IMPERIAL
4 small lambs' hearts
50 g/2 oz low-fat pork sausage meat
50 g/2 oz lean smoked bacon, derinded
½ teaspoon chopped fresh or ¼ teaspoon dried
sage
1 tablespoon chopped parsley
½ onion, peeled and finely chopped
1 clove garlic, peeled and crushed
2 teaspoons tomato purée
1 egg yolk, beaten
25 g/1 oz fresh white breadcrumbs
salt
freshly ground black pepper
15 g/½ oz plain flour
1 tablespoon olive oil
450 ml/¾ pint beef or lamb stock
sage sprigs, to garnish

Soak the hearts in slightly salted water for 1 hour changing the water every 15 minutes. Cut away the lobes and white membrane and remove any blood from the cavity. Dry the hearts on absorbent kitchen paper.

Place the sausage meat, bacon, sage, parsley, onion, garlic, tomato purée, egg and breadcrumbs in a blender or food processor. Blend until the ingredients are finely minced. Season well with salt and pepper. Fill each heart with the stuffing, fold over the flap at the top and secure with a skewer. Season the flour with salt and pepper and dip in the stuffed hearts. Heat the oil in a heavy-based pan and fry them until golden brown on all sides. Transfer to a pudding basin.

Pour the stock into the frying pan. Bring to the boil, scraping the sediment from the base of the pan. Pour over the hearts. Cover with foil or greaseproof paper and tie down well with string. Gently cook in a steamer or covered saucepan, half filled with water, for 2 to 2½ hours. Check the liquid level frequently and add more boiling water if necessary.

Remove the paper and arrange the hearts on a warmed serving dish and keep warm. Tip the stock into a clean pan and boil rapidly to reduce until rich and syrupy. Pour over the hearts and garnish with sprigs of sage.
SERVES 4

CALVES' BRAINS WITH BLACK BUTTER

METRIC/IMPERIAL
4 calves' brains (or lambs' brains)
juice of 1 lemon
300 ml/½ pint court bouillon
salt
freshly ground black pepper
75 g/3 oz polyunsaturated margarine
1 tablespoon capers
1 shallot, peeled and finely chopped
½ tablespoon white wine vinegar
1 tablespoon chopped parsley, to garnish

Soak the brains in water with the lemon juice for 2 to 3 hours. Drain them. Bring the court bouillon to the boil in a saucepan. Arrange the brains in a steamer. Cover with a tight-fitting lid, and steam over the bouillon for 15 minutes. Cut the brains into slices, removing any membranes. Lay on a heated serving dish, season with salt and pepper, and keep them warm.

Heat the margarine in a pan until brown but not burnt. Stir in the capers, shallot and vinegar. Bring to the boil and pour over the brains. Sprinkle with parsley and serve immediately.
SERVES 4

OXTAIL WITH GRAPES

METRIC/IMPERIAL
2 medium to large oxtails, cut into 5 cm/2 inch
pieces
4 rashers lean bacon, derinded and chopped
2 large onions, peeled and chopped
2 cloves garlic, peeled and crushed
4 large carrots, peeled and sliced
2 bay leaves
1 parsley sprig
1 thyme sprig
salt
freshly ground black pepper
750 g/1½ lb seedless white grapes

Remove the excess fat from the oxtail pieces. Place in a pan, cover with cold water and bring to the boil. Simmer for 10 minutes. Drain and dry well on paper towels.

Fry the bacon in a large flameproof casserole over a gentle heat until the fat runs. Add the onions, garlic and carrots and fry gently, stirring a few times, for about 10 minutes. Add the oxtail pieces, bay leaves, parsley and thyme sprigs, salt and pepper, and cook for a further 20 minutes over gentle heat.

Remove the stalks from the grapes and crush them lightly in a bowl. Add to the casserole, cover with a sheet of foil, then the lid, and transfer to a preheated cool oven (150°C/300°F, Gas Mark 2). Cook for 3 to 3½ hours or until the meat is very tender and comes away easily from the bones. Remove from the oven and leave to cool, then refrigerate.

The next day, remove all the fat that has risen to the top. Take all the meat off the bones. Remove the carrots and place the meat and carrots in a clean saucepan. Remove the herbs and place the remaining contents of the casserole in a blender or food processor. Blend at high speed for about 30 seconds, or push through a sieve. Pour over the meat and carrots and reheat gently on top of the stove. Taste and adjust the seasoning. Spoon into a heated serving dish, garnish with extra grapes, if liked, and serve with wholemeal bread.

SERVES 8

BRAISED OXTAIL

METRIC/IMPERIAL
3 tablespoons polyunsaturated vegetable oil
1 large oxtail, jointed
2 large onions, peeled and quartered
2 large carrots, peeled and quartered
2 celery stalks, cut into 5 cm/2 inch lengths
1 tablespoon unbleached white flour
600 ml/1 pint beef stock
1 bouquet garni
salt
freshly ground black pepper
finely chopped parsley, to garnish

Heat the oil in a flameproof casserole and brown the oxtail joints all over. Remove the oxtail.

Add the onions, carrots and celery to the casserole and brown lightly over medium heat. Sprinkle the flour over and stir well, then remove from the heat and pour on the beef stock. Heat gently and stir until boiling and thick. Return the oxtail to the casserole with the bouquet garni and season with salt and pepper.

Cover the casserole and cook in a preheated moderate oven (180°C/350°F, Gas Mark 4) for 1½ to 2 hours or until the meat is very tender and comes away from the bone easily. Skim off the fat from the surface, discard the bouquet garni and serve very hot, sprinkled with chopped parsley.

SERVES 4

Note: Cook oxtail a day ahead if you have time and refrigerate overnight to improve the flavour and make the fat easier to remove.

SWEETBREADS WITH POULETTE SAUCE

METRIC/IMPERIAL
450 g/1 lb calves' sweetbreads
1 onion, peeled and sliced
1 carrot, peeled and sliced
1 bouquet garni
veal or chicken stock
40 g/1½ oz polyunsaturated margarine
2 tablespoons unbleached white flour
1 egg yolk
5 tablespoons single cream
squeeze of lemon juice
1 tablespoon finely chopped parsley
salt
freshly ground black pepper

Cover and soak the sweetbreads for several hours, changing the water frequently. Then blanch the sweetbreads in boiling water for 5 to 10 minutes. Refresh in cold water and remove the skin with a small knife.

Place the sweetbreads in a saucepan with the onion, carrot, bouquet garni and stock just to cover. Bring to the boil and simmer for about 45 minutes. Strain off 350 to 500 ml/12 to 18 fl oz stock and reserve. Slice the sweetbreads thickly and keep warm.

Melt the margarine in a clean pan, stir in the flour and cook for a few seconds, then pour on the reserved stock and bring to the boil, stirring constantly. Cook until the sauce has a coating consistency. Beat the egg yolk with the cream, add to the sauce and reheat without boiling. Add the lemon juice, parsley, and salt and pepper to taste. Serve the sweetbreads with the sauce.

SERVES 4

POULTRY

HERBED CHICKEN

METRIC/IMPERIAL
1 × 1.75 kg/4 lb roasting chicken
1 tablespoon polyunsaturated vegetable oil
3 tablespoons lemon juice
salt
freshly ground black pepper
1 × 450 g/1 lb can tomatoes
1 teaspoon chopped marjoram
1 teaspoon chopped parsley
1 teaspoon snipped chives
1 teaspoon chopped thyme

Put the chicken in a roasting tin, brush with oil and lemon juice, then sprinkle with salt and pepper.

Roast in a preheated moderately hot oven (190°C/375°F, Gas Mark 5) for 45 minutes.

Mix together the tomatoes, herbs, and salt and pepper to taste, then pour over the chicken. Reduce the oven temperature to moderate (180°C/350°F, Gas Mark 4) and continue roasting for 45 minutes, basting the chicken frequently with the tomato mixture. Serve hot with seasonal vegetables or a salad as an accompaniment.

SERVES 4 to 6

CITRUS CHICKEN

METRIC/IMPERIAL
1 × 1.5 kg/3 lb chicken
2 small turnips, peeled
2 carrots, peeled
grated rind of 1 lemon
100 g/4 oz onion, peeled and chopped
salt
freshly ground black pepper
2 tablespoons lemon juice
1 large wine glass wine vinegar
1 tablespoon cornflour
orange slices, to garnish

Place the chicken in a large saucepan with the turnips, carrots, lemon rind, chopped onion, salt and pepper. Cover with water and bring to the boil.

Cover and simmer for about 2 hours, skimming the water occasionally.

When the bird is cooked, remove from the pan. Spoon 300 ml/½ pint stock into a saucepan with the lemon juice and wine vinegar. Simmer for 4 minutes.

Blend the cornflour with a little of the remaining stock. Add to the mixture and cook for 3 minutes until fairly thick and almost transparent.

Carve the chicken into slices and place on a heated serving dish. Pour over the lemon and vinegar sauce and leave to cool. Garnish with the orange slices.

If liked, serve with the vegetables cooked with the chicken or with a green salad.

SERVES 4

CHICKEN WITH HONEY

METRIC/IMPERIAL
3 tablespoons clear honey
1 teaspoon dry mustard
1 teaspoon salt
½ teaspoon pepper
2 teaspoons soy sauce
1 × 1.5 kg/3 lb oven-ready chicken
150 ml/¼ pint chicken stock
150 ml/¼ pint white wine
100 g/4 oz green grapes, halved and deseeded
150 g/5 oz plain low-fat yogurt

Place the honey, mustard, salt, pepper and soy sauce in a small basin and mix well. Spread the mixture over the chicken, place in a roasting tin and pour in the stock.

Roast in a preheated moderately hot oven (200°C/400°F, Gas Mark 6) for 1 to 1¼ hours, basting occasionally. Carve and arrange on a warmed serving dish; keep hot.

Pour the wine into the roasting tin and stir to mix in the juices. Bring to the boil, add the grapes and check the seasoning. Stir in the yogurt. Pour over the chicken to serve.

SERVES 4

CHICKEN WITH PRUNE AND APPLE STUFFING

METRIC/IMPERIAL
1 × 1.5 kg/3 lb chicken
Stuffing:
175 g/6 oz fresh wholemeal breadcrumbs
12 prunes, soaked overnight and chopped
2 large apples, cored and cut into chunks
grated rind and juice of 1 lemon
1 egg, beaten
skimmed milk, if necessary
salt
freshly ground black pepper

For the stuffing, mix together the breadcrumbs, prunes, apple and lemon rind. Add the beaten egg and lemon juice to bind. If necessary, stir in a little milk. Add salt and pepper to taste. Spoon the stuffing into the body cavity of the bird.

Place the chicken in a roasting tin half-filled with water and roast for about 1½ hours in a preheated moderately hot oven (200°C/400°F, Gas Mark 6). Baste frequently.
SERVES 4

CHICKEN WITH GARLIC AND ROOT VEGETABLES

METRIC/IMPERIAL
1 × 1.75 kg/4 lb oven-ready roasting chicken with giblets
1 small onion, peeled and roughly chopped
1 teaspoon olive oil
2 bay leaves
6 peppercorns
300 ml/½ pint dry white wine
600 ml/1 pint water
1 tablespoon vegetable peelings
grated rind and juice of 1 lemon
tarragon and chervil sprigs
salt
freshly ground black pepper
20 cloves garlic, *not* peeled
8 baby carrots
4 small parsnips, peeled
8 baby leeks, trimmed
2 tablespoons chopped herbs (e.g. tarragon, chervil, parsley), to garnish

Fry the giblets and onion in the oil until golden brown. Add the bay leaves, peppercorns, wine, water and vegetable peelings. Bring to the boil and simmer for 20 minutes, in order to make a stock. Meanwhile, wipe the chicken, pour on the lemon juice, sprinkle inside and outside with the lemon rind and herbs. Season very well with salt and pepper.

Strain the stock into the base of a steamer. Bring to the boil. Arrange the chicken on the unpeeled garlic cloves in the steamer. Cover with a tight-fitting lid and steam for 45 minutes. Check the liquid level frequently and add more boiling stock or water if necessary.

Season the vegetables with salt and pepper and place in the steamer with the chicken, cover and continue to cook for 15 minutes.

Push the garlic cloves through a sieve into the stock. Discard the skins, stir well, taste and adjust the seasoning if necessary. If the stock is already the thickness of single cream then pour over the chicken. If not, boil to reduce until it is the right thickness. Sprinkle the bird with herbs and serve at once while piping hot.
SERVES 4

CHICKEN IN A BRICK

METRIC/IMPERIAL
1 × 1.5 kg/3 lb roasting chicken
1 teaspoon sea salt
2 teaspoons dried marjoram
thinly pared rind of ½ lemon
1 clove garlic, peeled and cut into slivers
freshly ground black pepper
2 tablespoons lemon juice
fresh rosemary sprigs, to garnish

Prepare the chicken brick according to the manufacturer's instructions. Place the lemon rind, salt and half the marjoram inside the chicken.

Make small incisions in the chicken skin and insert a garlic sliver into each. Rub the remaining marjoram and pepper over the chicken and sprinkle with half the lemon juice.

Place the chicken in the prepared brick, cover and place it in a cold oven. Set the oven to 220°C/425°F, Gas Mark 7, and cook for 1 hour, then uncover and cook for a further 30 minutes. Transfer the chicken to a heated serving dish and keep warm.

Skim the fat from the juices in the brick and pour the juices into a small saucepan. Add the remaining lemon juice and bring to the boil. Adjust the seasoning to taste. Carve the chicken and serve garnished with rosemary sprigs, with the sauce served separately in a heated sauceboat.
SERVES 4

BRAISED SPRING CHICKEN

METRIC/IMPERIAL
4-6 large flat mushrooms, wiped
2 teaspoons chopped fresh thyme or 1 teaspoon
dried thyme
4 slices lean ham, trimmed of fat
2 spring chickens, prepared
salt
freshly ground black pepper
1 wine glass white wine

Cut off the mushroom stalks, place the mushrooms in the bottom of a large casserole and sprinkle over the thyme. Lay the slices of ham over the mushrooms. Place the spring chickens on top. Add salt, pepper and the white wine.

Cover and cook in a preheated moderately hot oven (200°C/400°F, Gas Mark 6) for about 1 hour. Uncover and continue cooking for 5 minutes.

Cut each spring chicken in half and serve on a bed of mushrooms and ham.
SERVES 4

BOILED CHICKEN WITH TARRAGON RICE

METRIC/IMPERIAL
1 × 1.5 kg/3 lb boiling chicken
1 large carrot, peeled
1 small turnip, peeled
1 large onion, peeled
1 bouquet garni
salt
freshly ground black pepper
Tarragon rice:
100 g/4 oz long-grain rice
salt
1 red pepper, cored, deseeded and sliced
1 tablespoon tarragon vinegar
1 tablespoon olive oil
freshly ground black pepper
1 dessertspoon chopped fresh tarragon or
1 teaspoon dried tarragon

Put the boiling fowl in a large saucepan with the whole carrot, turnip and onion. Add the bouquet garni, salt and pepper. Cover with water and bring to the boil. Cover and simmer for about 2 hours (depending on the age of the bird), skimming the water occasionally.

Put the rice in a saucepan of boiling salted water and simmer for 12 to 15 minutes or until cooked

but still slightly firm. Blanch the pepper in boiling water for 1 minute. Drain the rice and add the red pepper to it.

Stir in the tarragon vinegar, olive oil and salt and pepper to taste. Spoon into a heated serving dish and sprinkle with the chopped tarragon.

Remove the bird from the pan, take off the skin and carve the meat. Serve the chicken with the tarragon rice. Also delicious served cold.
SERVES 4

BOILED CHICKEN AND PASTA

METRIC/IMPERIAL
25 g/1 oz polyunsaturated margarine
2 onions, peeled and chopped
2 cloves garlic, peeled and crushed
3 celery stalks, chopped
1.75 kg/4 lb boiling chicken with giblets
salt
freshly ground black pepper
1 bay leaf
1 tablespoon dried oregano
175-225 g/6-8 oz wholemeal pasta
2 tablespoons Parmesan cheese
tomato wedges, to garnish

Melt the margarine in a saucepan. Add the onions, garlic and celery and cook until softened. Add the chicken with its giblets, cover with water and bring to the boil. Skim well, season with salt and pepper to taste and add the bay leaf. Simmer gently for 2 to 2½ hours or until cooked.

Remove the chicken from the pan and allow to cool slightly, then remove the skin. Take the meat from the bones and dice it.

Strain the cooking stock into another saucepan and add the oregano and pasta. Cook until tender. Strain the stock back into the first saucepan, and reheat the chicken in this. Drain the hot chicken and pile on to a warmed serving dish. Surround with the pasta and sprinkle over the Parmesan. Garnish with tomato wedges.
SERVES 4

CURRIED CHICKEN WITH CORIANDER

METRIC/IMPERIAL
1 onion, peeled and halved
1 carrot, scraped and coarsely chopped
1 celery stalk, coarsely chopped
1.5 kg/3 lb roasting chicken
1 bay leaf
3 parsley sprigs
3 lovage sprigs
1 teaspoon sea salt
6 black peppercorns
Sauce:
3 tablespoons desiccated coconut
25 g/1 oz polyunsaturated margarine
1 large onion, peeled and finely chopped
2 cloves garlic, peeled and crushed
1 tablespoon mild curry powder
¼ teaspoon ground turmeric
¼ teaspoon ground cumin seed
¼ teaspoon ground coriander
pinch of ground chilli
3 tablespoons lemon juice
1 tablespoon wholemeal flour
4 tablespoons plain low-fat yogurt
2 tablespoons chopped almonds
2 tablespoons chopped coriander or
3 tablespoons chopped basil

Put the vegetables in a saucepan with the chicken, bay leaf, parsley, lovage, salt and peppercorns. Pour in enough cold water just to cover the chicken and poach for 1 hour. Lift out the chicken when it is tender. When the chicken is cool enough to handle, remove all the skin and bones and cut the meat into neat small pieces. Set aside.

Strain the liquid in which the chicken was cooked, discarding the vegetables and herbs. Taste the stock: if it is too weak, reduce it by fast boiling until it has a good flavour. Measure off 600 ml/1 pint.

To make the sauce, pour 300 ml/½ pint of the stock over the desiccated coconut in a bowl and leave for 15 minutes to form a coconut 'milk'. Melt the margarine in a large saucepan and cook the onion gently until pale golden, adding the garlic halfway through. Sprinkle on the curry powder and spices, stirring all the time. Pour on the remaining stock and stir until blended. Simmer gently for 15 minutes, then add the lemon juice. Pour the coconut 'milk' through a sieve into the curry sauce, pushing lightly with the back of a wooden spoon to extract all the liquid. Stir the flour into the yogurt to make a smooth paste and

add it to the curry sauce, continuing to stir until all is blended.

Add the chicken pieces to the sauce. Reheat, stirring, and finally add the almonds and the coriander (or basil). Stand, covered, for 5 minutes before serving. This dish should be accompanied by plain boiled rice.
SERVES 4

GALANTINE OF CHICKEN WITH LEMON SAGE STUFFING

METRIC/IMPERIAL
225 g/8 oz sausage meat
100 g/4 oz lean cooked ham, finely chopped
1 large onion, peeled and finely chopped
8 sage leaves, finely chopped or 1 teaspoon rubbed sage
grated rind and juice of 1½ lemons
1 egg, beaten
salt
freshly ground black pepper
1 × 1.75 kg/4 lb chicken, boned and wiped
600 ml/1 pint boiling chicken stock
Garnish:
lemon slices
fresh sage leaves

Place the sausage meat, ham, onion, sage, the lemon rind and juice, and the egg in a bowl and mix thoroughly. Season well with salt and pepper. Lay the chicken on a board, skin side down. Season all over with salt and pepper. With a knife, spread the stuffing mixture on the chicken to within 1 cm/½ inch of the edges. Draw the sides of the chicken over the stuffing to reshape and sew neatly together with fine string. Place the chicken in a steamer.

Cover with a tight-fitting lid and steam over the chicken stock for about 1½ hours. (Time permitting, you can always steam the chicken over the ingredients for the stock. Remember you will have to increase the time for reducing the liquid to make the glaze.) Check the liquid level frequently and add more boiling stock if necessary. When cooked, press the chicken parcel between 2 plates with a heavy weight on top. Leave until cold. Remove the sewing thread.

Meanwhile, strain the stock and boil rapidly to reduce. Allow to cool.

Arrange the garnish on top of the galantine and glaze with the reduced stock. Serve cold.
SERVES 6

LEMON CHICKEN

METRIC/IMPERIAL

1 × 1.5 kg/3 lb oven-ready chicken with giblets
salt
1 medium onion, peeled
1 small bay leaf
1 lemon
1 carrot, peeled and quartered
2 celery stalks, chopped
1 tablespoon fresh marjoram or 1 teaspoon dried marjoram
4 black peppercorns
600 ml/1 pint water
Sauce:
450 ml/¾ pint hot stock (strained from the chicken)
40 g/1½ oz polyunsaturated margarine
40 g/1½ oz plain unbleached white flour
1 egg yolk
4 tablespoons single cream
juice of ½ lemon
parsley sprigs, to garnish

Sprinkle the body cavity of the chicken with salt and insert the onion and the bay leaf. Cut the lemon in half, rub one cut surface over the chicken and reserve the other half for garnishing. Place the bird in a deep pan with a tight-fitting lid. Add the washed giblets, a thin strip of lemon rind, the carrot, celery, marjoram, peppercorns, 1 teaspoon salt and the water. Bring to the boil, cover the pan with a tight-fitting lid and simmer gently for about 1 hour, or until the chicken is tender and the juices run clear when the thickest part of the thigh is pierced with a metal skewer.

Strain the stock from the chicken, leaving the bird in the pan to keep warm. Melt the margarine in a small saucepan, remove from the heat, stir in the flour and cook gently, stirring, for 2 minutes. Gradually add the hot stock, stirring briskly until smoothly blended. Return the pan to the heat and cook, stirring continuously, until the sauce boils, then simmer gently for 5 to 10 minutes until it has thickened.

Mix the egg yolk with the cream, stir in 2 tablespoons of the hot sauce, then pour into the sauce and stir over low heat for 1 minute, but do not boil. Add lemon juice to taste and adjust the seasoning. To serve, carve the chicken into joints, arrange on a serving dish and spoon over the sauce. Garnish with the reserved lemon half cut into wedges and sprigs of parsley and serve with plain boiled rice as an accompaniment.

SERVES 4 to 6

MILD SPICY CHICKEN IN A BRICK

METRIC/IMPERIAL

1 clove garlic, peeled and halved
1 onion
1 clove garlic, peeled and crushed
1 teaspoon ground ginger
3 teaspoons coriander seeds, crushed
2 teaspoons paprika
150 ml/¼ pint plain low-fat yogurt
1 tablespoon white wine or vermouth
salt
freshly ground black pepper
1 × 1.5 kg/3 lb roasting chicken
mint sprigs, to garnish

Wipe the chicken brick with the cut garlic clove. Grate half the onion and place in a bowl with the crushed garlic, ginger, coriander, paprika, yogurt, wine, salt and pepper. Mix well. Wash and dry the chicken and place the remaining half of onion inside. Slash the flesh thoroughly all over and place the chicken in the brick. Pour the yogurt mixture over and cover. Leave to marinate for 3 to 4 hours.

Place the brick in a cold oven and set to 240°C/475°F, Gas Mark 9. Cook for 1½ hours. Remove the chicken from the brick and cut into 8 pieces. Arrange the pieces on a serving dish, garnish decoratively with mint sprigs and serve with some of the juices from the brick.

SERVES 4

POACHED CHICKEN WITH AVOCADO

METRIC/IMPERIAL

1 × 1.5 kg/3 lb roasting chicken
finely grated rind and juice of 2 limes
2 tarragon sprigs or ½ teaspoon dried tarragon
450 ml/¾ pint hot chicken stock
salt
freshly ground black pepper
Garnish:
1 ripe avocado, peeled and sliced
¼ head of curly endive
lime slices

Place the lime rind and juice, the tarragon, stock and seasoning in a flameproof casserole. Add the chicken, breast side down, cover and simmer for 1 to 1¼ hours, turning the chicken halfway through cooking. To test the chicken is cooked, pierce the leg with a knife; the juices should run clear. Cut the chicken into quarters, remove the skin and discard. Keep the chicken warm. Boil the liquid on top of the cooker until reduced by half.

Arrange the avocado and endive on a serving dish and lay the chicken on top. Spoon over some of the sauce and serve the rest separately. Garnish with lime slices.

SERVES 4

STEAMED CHICKEN CARIBBEAN

METRIC/IMPERIAL
1 × 1.75 kg/4 lb oven-ready chicken, giblets removed
salt
freshly ground black pepper
juice of 1 lemon
1 tablespoon polyunsaturated vegetable oil
1 onion, peeled and finely sliced
3 cloves garlic, peeled
15 g/½ oz fresh root ginger, peeled and grated
2 chillies, deseeded and finely chopped
3 tomatoes, skinned, deseeded and chopped
750 g/1½ lb sweet potato, peeled and cubed
750 g/1½ lb pumpkin, peeled and cubed
2 plantains, roughly sliced
600 ml/1 pint chicken stock
1 cinnamon stick
Garnish:
lemon slices
flat-leaf parsley sprigs

Season the chicken with salt, pepper and lemon juice. Heat the oil in a heavy-based pan. Fry the chicken over high heat to brown on all sides. Remove and put to one side. Fry the onion, garlic, ginger, chilli and tomato until cooked but not brown. Stir in the sweet potato, pumpkin and plantain. Season well with salt and pepper.

Spoon the vegetables and spices into a steamer. Place the chicken on top. Bring the stock to the boil and stir in the cinnamon stick. Cover the chicken mixture with a tight-fitting lid and steam over the boiling stock for 1½ hours. Check the liquid level frequently and add more boiling stock if necessary.

Remove the cinnamon stick. Transfer the chicken to a hot serving plate and keep warm. Blend the vegetables and the stock in a blender or food processor. Spoon over the chicken. Garnish with slices of lemon and parsley sprigs. Serve at once while piping hot.

SERVES 4

SPRING CHICKENS WITH FRESH PARSLEY SAUCE

METRIC/IMPERIAL
2 × 1 kg/2 lb spring chickens, or
1 × 1.75 kg/4 lb chicken, giblets reserved
salt
freshly ground black pepper
1 shallot, peeled and finely sliced
2 small carrots, peeled and roughly chopped
1 leek, trimmed, washed and sliced
6 peppercorns
1 bay leaf
300 ml/½ pint white wine
2 parsley sprigs
1.2 litres/2 pints water
Parsley sauce:
25 g/1 oz polyunsaturated margarine
25 g/1 oz plain unbleached white flour
300 ml/½ pint skimmed milk
4 tablespoons chopped parsley

Wipe the chickens and season well with salt and pepper. Put the giblets in a saucepan with the vegetables, peppercorns, bay leaf, wine and parsley. Add the water and bring to the boil. Put the chickens in a steamer, cover with a tight-fitting lid and steam gently over the giblet stock for 1½ hours. Check the liquid level frequently and add more boiling water if necessary.

When the chickens are cooked, remove the skin and keep warm. Strain the stock into a clean pan and discard the giblets and vegetables. Bring to the boil and remove any scum from the surface.

Melt the margarine in a separate saucepan over a gentle heat, add the flour and cook for 2 minutes, stirring constantly. Remove from the heat and add 300 ml/½ pint of the stock and the milk. Bring to the boil and stir well until smooth and thickened. Add the parsley and taste to check the seasoning. Adjust if necessary. Either spoon the sauce over the chickens or serve separately.

SERVES 4

QUEEN'S CORONATION CHICKEN

METRIC/IMPERIAL
1 × 1.75 kg/4 lb chicken, giblets removed
1 teaspoon lemon juice
salt
freshly ground black pepper
600 ml/1 pint boiling chicken stock
300 ml/½ pint reduced-calorie mayonnaise
2 teaspoons apricot jam, sieved
½ teaspoon tomato purée
2 teaspoons curry powder
2 tablespoons Quark
skimmed milk
watercress sprigs, to garnish

Wipe the chicken and season with lemon juice, salt and pepper. Place in a steamer. Cover with a tight-fitting lid and steam over the stock for 1½ hours. Check the liquid level frequently and add more boiling stock or water if necessary. Let the chicken get cold.

Meanwhile, make the sauce. Mix together all the remaining ingredients and stir in enough milk to make a smooth coating consistency.

Remove the meat from the chicken bones and, when cold, mix with the sauce, reserving a small quantity of the sauce.

Pile the chicken into the middle of a serving dish and coat with the remaining sauce. Garnish with watercress and serve with wild rice salad.
SERVES 4 to 6

SPRING CHICKENS WITH MUSHROOM STUFFING

METRIC/IMPERIAL
2 spring chickens or 4 poussins
polyunsaturated margarine
Stuffing:
225 g/8 oz mushrooms, wiped and chopped
100 g/4 oz onions, peeled and finely chopped
1 tablespoon tomato purée
50 g/2 oz fresh breadcrumbs
1 teaspoon chopped parsley
salt
freshly ground black pepper
1 egg, beaten, to bind

Mix the stuffing ingredients together and bind together with the beaten egg. Spoon the stuffing into the body cavities of the chickens or poussins. Place a little margarine on each bird and wrap completely in foil. Roast in a preheated moderately hot oven (200°C/400°F, Gas Mark 6) until the chickens are tender, about 1 hour for the spring chickens or 40 minutes for the poussins.

Unfold the top of the foil 10 minutes before the end of the cooking time to allow the spring chickens or poussins to brown.
SERVES 4

TARRAGON CHICKEN EN COCOTTE

METRIC/IMPERIAL
1 × 1.75 kg/4 lb oven-ready chicken
salt
freshly ground black pepper
50 g/2 oz polyunsaturated margarine
8 fresh tarragon sprigs or 1 teaspoon dried tarragon
1 tablespoon polyunsaturated vegetable oil
1 onion, peeled and sliced
1 carrot, peeled and sliced
1 celery stalk, sliced
450 ml/¾ pint chicken stock
1 tablespoon cornflour
2 tablespoons medium sherry
2 tablespoons chopped tarragon or parsley
tarragon sprig, to garnish

Rinse the chicken under running cold water, drain and pat dry with kitchen paper towels. Season the body cavity with salt and pepper and insert 15 g/½ oz of the margarine and half the tarragon. Truss the bird if necessary. Heat the oil and remaining margarine in a flameproof casserole. Place the chicken breast-down in the dish and adjust the heat so that the chicken browns in 3 to 5 minutes but the fat is not hot enough to discolour. Turn the chicken at intervals to brown the sides and then the back; this gentle browning process takes a total of 10 to 15 minutes.

Lift the chicken on to a plate. Add the onion, carrot and celery to the pan and sauté gently for 5 minutes. Sprinkle with a little salt and pepper and add the rest of the tarragon. Replace the bird on top of the vegetables and cover with aluminium foil and a lid. Transfer to a preheated moderate oven (180°C/350°F, Gas Mark 4) and cook for 1 hour 20 minutes. Pierce the thickest part of the thigh with a metal skewer and if the juices run clear the bird is cooked.

Place the chicken on a hot serving dish, discard any trussing strings and keep hot. Add the stock to the pan and boil for a few minutes, stirring to free any sediment from the base of the pan. Skim off any surface fat. Stir in the cornflour blended with the sherry and bring to the boil. Stir until the sauce thickens slightly. Adjust the seasoning, strain the sauce into a hot sauceboat and stir in the chopped herbs. Immediately before serving, garnish the breast of the bird with a sprig of tarragon and spoon over a little of the sauce.

SERVES 4 to 6

CHICKEN HOT POT

METRIC/IMPERIAL
2 tablespoons olive oil
1 × 1.75 kg/4 lb chicken, jointed into 8 pieces
salt
freshly ground black pepper
juice of 1 lemon
225 g/8 oz Jerusalem artichokes, peeled and halved
225 g/8 oz Brussels sprouts, trimmed
225 g/8 oz carrots, peeled and cut into bite-sized pieces
225 g/8 oz swede, peeled and cut into bite-sized pieces
100 g/4 oz small turnips, peeled and quartered
100 g/4 oz parsnips, peeled and cut into bite-sized pieces
300 ml/½ pint chicken stock
300 ml/½ pint red wine
50 ml/2 fl oz port
large bunch of herbs (e.g. thyme, parsley, tarragon)
sprigs of herbs (e.g. thyme, parsley, tarragon), to garnish

Heat the oil in a heavy-based pan. Season the chicken with salt, pepper and lemon juice. Fry the chicken on both sides until golden brown. Place in a heatproof mixing bowl that will fit inside your largest saucepan or steamer.
Fry the vegetables for 2 minutes until golden brown. Spoon them over the chicken. Pour the stock, wine and port into the frying pan. Bring to the boil, scraping the sediment from the base of the pan. Pour over the chicken. Add the herbs. Season well with salt and pepper. Cover the bowl with foil or greaseproof paper and tie down with string.
Place in a saucepan of boiling water with a tight-fitting lid, or in a steamer, and steam for 1½ hours. Check the liquid level frequently and add more boiling water if necessary.
Remove the foil or paper. Pour the liquid from the chicken into a small saucepan. Arrange the meat and vegetables in a warmed serving dish and keep warm. Boil the stock to reduce to a syrupy consistency. Spoon over the meat and garnish with sprigs of herbs.

SERVES 4

SLIMMER'S COQ-AU-VIN

METRIC/IMPERIAL
4 chicken pieces
4 tablespoons brandy
225 g/8 oz button onions, peeled
900 ml/1½ pints chicken stock
225 g/8 oz button mushrooms, wiped and trimmed
chopped parsley, to garnish
Marinade:
1 clove garlic, peeled and crushed
150 ml/¼ pint red wine vinegar
150 ml/¼ pint red wine
1 tablespoon Worcestershire sauce
salt
freshly ground black pepper

Combine all the marinade ingredients.
Place the chicken in a large shallow bowl and pour over the marinade. Set aside in a cool place for at least 3 hours.
Preheat the oven to 220°C/425°F, Gas Mark 7 and heat the grill to high. Remove the chicken from the marinade and brown briefly under the grill. Transfer the pieces to a casserole.
Pour the brandy over the chicken and ignite. When the flames die down, add the onions and stock. Cover and cook in the oven for 50 minutes.
Add the mushrooms and cook for a further 10 minutes, or until the chicken is tender and the juices run clear when it is pierced in the thickest part. Meanwhile, pour the marinade into a saucepan and boil rapidly, uncovered, until reduced in volume by half. Stir into the casserole and garnish with the chopped parsley. Serve immediately.

SERVES 4

CHICKEN AND OLIVE BAKE

METRIC/IMPERIAL

4 chicken pieces
5 tablespoons cider vinegar
4 tomatoes, skinned and chopped
2 green peppers, cored, deseeded and chopped
2 onions, peeled and chopped
1 small clove garlic, peeled and crushed
1 teaspoon chopped marjoram
salt
freshly ground black pepper
1 tablespoon olive oil
2 tablespoons tomato purée
75 g/3 oz stuffed olives
chopped thyme, to garnish

Put the chicken in a shallow dish. Mix together the vinegar, tomatoes, peppers, onions, garlic, marjoram and salt and pepper to taste. Pour over the chicken. Leave to marinate for 2 hours, turning the chicken once.

Heat the oil in a deep frying pan. Drain the chicken, reserving the marinade. Add the chicken to the pan and fry until browned on all sides. Stir in the reserved marinade with the tomato purée and the olives. Cover and simmer over low heat for 1 hour. Taste and adjust the seasoning, sprinkle with thyme and serve hot.

SERVES 4

SESAME CHICKEN WITH RICE

METRIC/IMPERIAL

50 g/2 oz unbleached white flour
1 tablespoon sesame seeds
¾ teaspoon ground ginger
salt
freshly ground black pepper
1 × 1.5 kg/3 lb oven-ready chicken, jointed, or 4 chicken quarters
50 g/2 oz polyunsaturated margarine
1 tablespoon polyunsaturated vegetable oil
300 ml/½ pint stock
4 tablespoons dry white wine
175 g/6 oz long-grain rice
½ teaspoon ground coriander
pinch of chilli powder
chopped parsley, to garnish

Mix together the flour, sesame seeds, two-thirds of the ginger, and salt and pepper to taste. Coat the chicken pieces with the mixture and fry till golden in the margarine and oil in a frying pan. Drain on kitchen paper towels and place in a casserole.

Blend the remaining flour mixture with the fat left in the pan, add the stock and wine, bring to the boil and cook to thicken. Pour over the chicken and cook in a preheated cool oven (150°C/300°F, Gas Mark 3) for 1½ to 2 hours.

Put the rice in a saucepan with 600 ml/1 pint cold water and 1 teaspoon salt. Bring to the boil, stir, then simmer, covered, for 10 to 12 minutes until tender. Drain the rice and rinse with boiling water. Mix with the remaining ginger and seasonings. Pile on a serving dish, arrange the chicken on top and garnish with parsley.

SERVES 4

PEANUT SPICED CHICKEN

METRIC/IMPERIAL

2 tablespoons polyunsaturated vegetable oil
1 onion, peeled and sliced
1½ teaspoons ground coriander
½ teaspoon cumin seeds
½ teaspoon ground ginger
½ teaspoon ground cinnamon
1-2 cloves garlic, peeled and crushed
4 chicken pieces, skin removed
3 tablespoons peanut butter
1 tablespoon plain wholemeal flour
300 ml/½ pint chicken or vegetable stock
salt
freshly ground black pepper
50 g/2 oz salted peanuts, crushed
flat-leaf parsley or crushed peanuts, to garnish

Preheat the oven to 180°C/350°F, Gas Mark 4. Heat the oil in a flameproof casserole and sauté the onion for 5 minutes. Add the spices to the casserole and cook for 1 minute.

Add the garlic and chicken and cook until the chicken has browned all over. Stir in the peanut butter and flour, then gradually add the stock. Bring to the boil, stirring, then add salt and pepper to taste.

Add the peanuts, cover and cook in the oven for 1 hour, adding extra stock if the dish becomes a little dry. Serve hot garnished with flat-leaf parsley or a few crushed peanuts.

SERVES 4

WEST INDIAN CHICKEN

METRIC/IMPERIAL
4 × 175 g/6 oz chicken pieces
1 teaspoon curry powder, or to taste
1 teaspoon ground ginger
1 × 225 g/8 oz can pineapple chunks
1 green pepper, cored, deseeded and chopped
salt
freshly ground black pepper

Skin the chicken portions and score the flesh with a sharp knife. Mix the curry powder and ginger together and rub into the chicken flesh. Place the chicken in a shallow dish and pour over the pineapple juice from the can. Marinate for 2 hours.

Put the chicken under a hot grill and cook for about 20 minutes until tender, turning frequently and using the marinade to baste and prevent the chicken burning.

Put the pineapple chunks, remaining marinade and chopped pepper into a blender and liquidize until smooth. Pour the purée into a pan and heat through. Taste and adjust the seasoning.

Place the grilled chicken joints on a heated serving dish and pour the sauce over or serve it separately. Serve with a green salad.
SERVES 4

NEW WAVE COQ AU VIN

METRIC/IMPERIAL
1 × 1.5 kg/3 lb chicken, jointed into 8 pieces
15 g/½ oz plain flour
salt
freshly ground black pepper
2 tablespoons olive oil
150 g/5 oz lean bacon, derinded and diced
2 cloves garlic, peeled and finely chopped
12 button onions, peeled
12 button mushrooms, wiped and trimmed
2 tablespoons brandy
150 ml/¼ pint red wine
300 ml/½ pint chicken stock
¼ teaspoon chopped thyme
Garnish:
2 tablespoons chopped parsley
triangular bread croûtons

Dust the chicken pieces with the flour and season well with salt and pepper. Heat the oil in a heavy-based pan and fry the joints over a high heat until golden brown on all sides. Remove from the pan. Fry the bacon, garlic and onions for 2 minutes.

Add the mushrooms and continue cooking for 2 minutes. Return the chicken to the pan. Turn off the heat.

Warm the brandy in a spoon, set light to it and pour flaming over the chicken. As soon as the flames subside, pour in the wine and stock. Bring to the boil, scraping any sediment from the base of the pan. Pour the contents of the pan into a suitable dish. Season well with salt, pepper and the thyme. Cover with foil and tie down with string.

Place in a steamer or covered saucepan half-filled with boiling water, and steam for 45 minutes. Remove the pudding basin and then the foil. Pour the cooking liquid into an empty saucepan and bring to the boil. Boil the liquid to reduce until syrupy. Spoon over the chicken and sprinkle with parsley. Arrange the croûtons on top.
SERVES 4

Note: Steaming the chicken may seem an unusual method, but the results are always succulent and tender.

CHICKEN FROM PROVENCE

METRIC/IMPERIAL
1 clove garlic, peeled and crushed
4 × 175 g/6 oz chicken pieces, skinned
lemon juice
Sauce:
100 g/4 oz button mushrooms, wiped
25 g/1 oz chopped onion
120 ml/4 fl oz unsweetened apple juice
120 ml/4 fl oz wine vinegar
120 ml/4 fl oz tomato juice
salt
freshly ground black pepper
1 teaspoon cornflour (optional)

Rub the crushed garlic over the chicken flesh. Put the chicken under a preheated hot grill and cook for about 25 minutes, turning frequently and using the lemon juice for basting.

Meanwhile, put all the sauce ingredients in a saucepan, except the cornflour, and simmer, uncovered, for 25 minutes. Add salt and pepper according to taste.

For a thicker sauce, mix the cornflour with 2 teaspoons cold water. Stir into the sauce and simmer for another 3 minutes.

Place the chicken portions on a heated serving dish, pour the sauce over and serve.
SERVES 4

MUSHROOM CHICKEN CASSEROLE

METRIC/IMPERIAL
4 × 175 g/6 oz chicken pieces
175 g/6 oz mushrooms, wiped and trimmed
25 g/1 oz chopped onion
250 ml/8 fl oz chicken stock
salt
freshly ground black pepper

Skin the chicken and place in a casserole with the mushrooms, whole if small or sliced if large.
Add the chopped onion, stock and salt and pepper. Cover and cook in a preheated hot oven (220°C/425°F, Gas Mark 7) for 35 to 40 minutes or until the chicken is tender (when pierced with a sharp knife the juices run clear). Serve immediately while piping hot.
SERVES 4

CHICKEN AND VEGETABLE CASSEROLE

METRIC/IMPERIAL
1 medium onion, peeled and roughly chopped
3-4 celery stalks, roughly chopped
4 carrots, peeled and roughly chopped
4 turnips, peeled and roughly chopped
1 small swede, peeled and roughly chopped
4 × 225 g/8 oz chicken pieces, skinned
1 bay leaf
1 bouquet garni
300 ml/½ pint chicken stock
salt
freshly ground black pepper

Place half of the vegetables in a casserole. Put the chicken pieces on top and cover with the remaining vegetables. Add the bay leaf, bouquet garni, stock, salt and pepper. If using a flameproof casserole, bring to the boil on top of the cooker and skim off any scum.
Cover and cook in a preheated moderate oven (180°C/350°F, Gas Mark 4) for about 1½ hours. Skim off any fat and serve.
Alternatively, leave overnight and carefully remove all the fat from the surface, then reheat in a moderate oven for about 30 minutes.
SERVES 4

CHICKEN AND ORANGE CASSEROLE

METRIC/IMPERIAL
2 medium onions, peeled and quartered
2 celery stalks, sliced
4 chicken pieces, skinned
1 tablespoon chopped herbs
3 tablespoons grated orange rind
5 tablespoons orange juice
150 ml/¼ pint chicken stock
salt
freshly ground black pepper
Garnish:
1 orange, thinly sliced
watercress

Blanch the onions and celery in boiling water for 2 minutes. Put the chicken, celery and onion into a casserole, sprinkle over the herbs, orange rind and juice, and add the stock. Add salt and pepper to taste. Cover tightly and cook in a preheated moderate oven (180°C/350°F, Gas Mark 4) for about 1 hour, until the chicken is tender. Serve garnished with orange slices and watercress.
SERVES 4

CARIBBEAN CHICKEN WITH PINEAPPLE

METRIC/IMPERIAL
4 × 175 g/6 oz chicken pieces
1 large red pepper, cored, deseeded and chopped
1 teaspoon curry powder
250 ml/8 fl oz chicken stock
salt
freshly ground black pepper
4 fresh or canned pineapple rings
1 banana
1 orange, peeled and sliced, to garnish

Put the chicken portions in a casserole with the chopped pepper and curry powder. Pour over the stock and add salt and pepper. Cover and cook in a preheated hot oven (220°C/425°F, Gas Mark 7) for 50 minutes.
Chop the pineapple rings and banana and add to the casserole. Cook for a further 10 minutes or until the chicken is tender. Garnish the casserole with the orange slices.
SERVES 4

CHICKEN AND VEGETABLE FRICASSÉE

METRIC/IMPERIAL
4 chicken pieces
3 onions, peeled and finely chopped
1 clove garlic, peeled and crushed
2 celery stalks, thinly sliced
2 carrots, peeled and thinly sliced
1 bay leaf
150 ml/¼ pint chicken stock
1 teaspoon chopped thyme
1 teaspoon paprika
salt
freshly ground black pepper
chopped parsley, to garnish

Take a piece of fat from the chicken and rub over the base of a heavy pan. Put in the chicken and cook gently over very low heat until golden on all sides. Add the onions and garlic and continue cooking gently for 3 minutes, meanwhile stirring occasionally.

Add the remaining ingredients, except the parsley, then cover and cook over low heat for 1¼ hours or until the chicken is tender. Taste and adjust the seasoning. Sprinkle with parsley and serve immediately while hot.
SERVES 4

CHICKEN AND BEAN CASSEROLE

METRIC/IMPERIAL
2 tablespoons polyunsaturated vegetable oil
4 chicken pieces, skinned
450 g/1 lb small new potatoes, scrubbed
1 onion, peeled and chopped
2 carrots, peeled and sliced
225 g/8 oz tomatoes, skinned and chopped
100 g/4 oz mushrooms, wiped and sliced
2 tablespoons tomato purée
50 g/2 oz cornflour
600 ml/1 pint chicken stock
4 tablespoons sherry
1 × 284 g/10 oz can haricot beans
salt
freshly ground pepper
chopped parsley, to garnish

Heat the oil in a large saucepan and cook the chicken until brown all over. Remove with a slotted spoon and place in a casserole with the potatoes. Add the onion and carrots to the pan and

sauté for 5 minutes, then add the tomatoes and mushrooms and cook for a further 2 minutes.
Blend together the tomato purée and cornflour and add to the vegetables. Blend in the stock and bring to the boil, stirring, then add the sherry, haricot beans and salt and pepper to taste.
Pour over the chicken and potatoes, cover and cook in a preheated moderate oven (180°C/350°F, Gas Mark 4) for 1 hour or until the chicken and potatoes are tender. Add a little more stock or water if the casserole is becoming too dry. Serve garnished with parsley.
SERVES 4

CHICKEN MUSSALAM

METRIC/IMPERIAL
1.5 kg/3 lb chicken, skinned and cut into 8 pieces
175 ml/6 fl oz plain low-fat yogurt
1 large onion, peeled and chopped
3 cloves garlic, peeled and sliced
3 green chillies
1 teaspoon ground coriander
175 g/6 oz polyunsaturated margarine
2.5 cm/1 inch piece cinnamon stick
10 whole cardamoms
10 whole cloves
1 teaspoon ground ginger
salt
freshly ground black pepper
½ teaspoon saffron, soaked in 1 tablespoon boiling water for 30 minutes

Make 3 deep cuts in each piece of chicken with a sharp knife. Work the yogurt, onion, garlic, chillies and coriander in a blender or food processor, then pour over the chicken. Cover, place in the refrigerator and leave to marinate overnight.
Drain the chicken, reserving the marinade. Melt the margarine in a flameproof casserole, add the chicken and fry for about 15 minutes until browned on all sides. Add the spices and seasonings, except the saffron, and fry for a further 3 minutes, stirring constantly. Add the saffron with its liquid, then add the reserved marinade. Cover the casserole and cook in a preheated moderately hot oven (190°C/375°F, Gas Mark 5) for about 30 minutes or until the chicken is tender and the sauce is very thick. Serve hot.
SERVES 4

CHICKEN PAPRIKA

METRIC/IMPERIAL
4 chicken pieces
1 teaspoon salt
2 teaspoons paprika
150 ml/¼ pint chicken stock
1 onion, peeled and finely chopped
150 ml/¼ pint plain low-fat yogurt
freshly ground black pepper
2 tablespoons finely chopped parsley, to garnish

Sprinkle the chicken portions with the salt and paprika. Put in a grill pan, without the rack, and cook under a preheated grill for 5 minutes on each side, or until well browned. (Do not put too near the heat or they will scorch before browning.)

Remove and place in a lidded casserole with the chicken stock and the onion. Cover and simmer over a moderate heat for 30 to 40 minutes or until tender, adding more stock if necessary. Lift out the chicken portions, place on a warmed serving dish and keep hot.

If there is excess liquid, reduce to 150 ml/¼ pint. Stir in the yogurt and adjust the seasoning. Heat slowly, stirring well, but do not allow to boil. Pour over the chicken and sprinkle with chopped parsley.
SERVES 4

CHICKEN DOPIAZZA

METRIC/IMPERIAL
3 onions, peeled and thinly sliced
2 tablespoons polyunsaturated vegetable oil
¼ teaspoon garlic powder
1 tablespoon coriander seeds
1 tablespoon ground cumin
½ teaspoon ground turmeric
1 teaspoon ground ginger
½-1 teaspoon chilli powder
350 g/12 oz fresh tomatoes, halved
350 g/12 oz small new potatoes, washed
freshly ground black pepper
750 g/1½-1¾ lb chicken meat, cut into
2.5 cm/1 inch cubes
salt

Fry the onions in the oil in a large pan until they are golden brown. Mix the garlic powder with the spices and a little pepper. Add the spice mixture to the pan with the chicken meat. Fry, stirring all the time, for about 1 minute.

Pour in sufficient water to cover the chicken and add salt to taste. Bring to the boil, cover and simmer for 45 minutes or until the chicken is nearly cooked. Add water during cooking, if necessary, to ensure the mixture does not become dry. Then add the tomatoes and potatoes and continue to simmer until the vegetables are cooked.
SERVES 4

SPICED CHICKEN DRUMSTICKS

METRIC/IMPERIAL
8 chicken drumsticks
Coating:
1 egg
1 tablespoon water
4 tablespoons rolled oats
grated rind of 1 orange
1 teaspoon curry powder
1 tablespoon plain flour
50 g/2 oz polyunsaturated margarine, melted

Beat the egg with the water. Crush the oats with a rolling pin and mix with the orange rind and curry powder. Coat each drumstick with flour, then egg. Finally pat the oats firmly on to the drumsticks, coating them evenly.

Arrange the drumsticks in a roasting tin, pour the melted margarine over them and bake in a preheated moderate oven (180°C/350°F, Gas Mark 4) for 20 minutes. Increase the oven temperature to hot (220°C/425°F, Gas Mark 7) and cook the drumsticks for a further 15 minutes or until crisp and golden. Serve with jacket potatoes or brown rice and green salad.
SERVES 4

CHICKEN AND TARRAGON LOAF

METRIC/IMPERIAL
350 g/12 oz minced lean chicken
175 g/6 oz minced lean ham
1 small onion, peeled and finely minced
1½ tablespoons chopped tarragon
50 g/2 oz soft wholemeal breadcrumbs
1 egg, beaten
salt
freshly ground black pepper
3 tablespoons dry vermouth

Grease and line a loaf tin with non-stick silicone or greased waxed paper. Mix the chicken with the ham, onion, tarragon, breadcrumbs, beaten egg, salt and pepper to taste, and the dry vermouth. Press the mixture into the prepared tin.

Stand the tin in a large roasting tin and add hot water to come halfway up the side of the loaf tin; cover the loaf tin with a piece of greased foil. Cook in a preheated oven at 180°C/350°F, Gas Mark 4 for 1¼ hours.

Allow to cool in the tin for a few minutes; unmould carefully on to a warm serving dish. Serve hot, cut in slices, with tomato sauce. This loaf may also be served cold: press it down lightly with a weight and allow it to cool in the tin.
SERVES 4

CHICKEN WITH ASPARAGUS

METRIC/IMPERIAL
4 chicken breasts
450 g/1 lb asparagus
salt
Sauce:
25 g/1 oz polyunsaturated margarine
1 clove garlic, peeled
1 dessertspoon cornflour
about 300 ml/½ pint skimmed milk
about 300 ml/½ pint chicken stock
1 bay leaf
2 tablespoons sherry
25 g/1 oz grated Parmesan cheese

Place the chicken breasts under a preheated hot grill and cook for about 15 minutes until tender.

Meanwhile, cook the asparagus in boiling salted water for about 12 minutes until just tender. Arrange the asparagus on a heated serving dish and place the chicken breasts on top. Keep hot.

To make the sauce, melt the margarine in a saucepan and add the garlic. Cook gently for a few seconds then stir in the cornflour. Cook for 2 minutes, stirring. Remove the garlic.

Add enough skimmed milk and chicken stock to make a thin sauce. Add the bay leaf and cook for a few minutes, stirring, until the sauce thickens. Add the sherry and remove the bay leaf.

Pour over the chicken breasts and asparagus. Sprinkle on the Parmesan cheese and place under a preheated hot grill until lightly browned.
SERVES 4

Variation
Turkey breasts can be prepared in the same way, and broccoli used instead of the asparagus.

CHICKEN IN LETTUCE

METRIC/IMPERIAL
600 ml/1 pint chicken stock
300 ml/½ pint dry cider
8 large Cos lettuce leaves, washed
4 chicken breasts, skinned
50 g/2 oz polyunsaturated margarine, softened
2 cloves garlic, peeled and crushed
salt
freshly ground black pepper
2 large carrots, peeled and cut into matchsticks
2 celery stalks, cut into matchsticks
50 g/2 oz smoked ham, cut into strips
juice of 1 lemon
100 g/4 oz polyunsaturated margarine
fennel, to garnish

Bring the chicken stock and cider to the boil in the base of a steamer. Place the lettuce leaves in a steamer container and steam over the stock and cider for 20 seconds or until just limp. Dry on absorbent kitchen paper.

With a knife, spread the chicken breasts with the softened margarine and garlic and season both sides well with salt and pepper. Lay down the lettuce leaves in pairs, overlapping slightly. Lay each chicken breast at the stalk end of the leaves. Divide three-quarters of the vegetables and all of the ham into 4 portions and spoon on top of each chicken breast.

Blanch the remaining vegetables, drain them, and put to one side for the garnish. Squeeze the lemon juice over the chicken, fold the leaves over the mixture and lay the chicken parcels in a steaming compartment. Cover and steam for 20 minutes. Check the liquid level frequently and add more boiling cider if necessary.

When cooked, remove the chicken parcels and keep warm. Reduce the stock until syrupy by boiling rapidly. Lower the heat and whisk in the margarine, bit by bit, until you have a smooth, creamy sauce. Check the seasoning.

Flood 4 individual plates with cider sauce, then lay the chicken parcels on top. Sprinkle with the remaining vegetables and garnish with fennel.
SERVES 4

BARBECUE BEANS AND CHICKEN

METRIC/IMPERIAL
4 chicken legs, washed and dried
salt
2 teaspoons paprika
1 tablespoon wholemeal flour
2 tablespoons polyunsaturated vegetable oil
1 × 425 g/15 oz can red kidney beans, drained
40 g/1½ oz polyunsaturated margarine
1 onion, peeled and chopped
1 tablespoon vinegar
½ teaspoon chilli powder
3 tablespoons tomato purée
85 ml/3 fl oz plain low-fat yogurt

Season the chicken legs with salt and 1 teaspoon of the paprika and coat with the flour. Heat the oil in a frying pan and fry the chicken quickly until golden brown. Transfer to a medium casserole. Add the kidney beans.

Melt the margarine in a small pan, add the onion and cook for 5 minutes. Add the vinegar, chilli powder and remaining paprika. Mix the tomato purée with the yogurt and add to the pan, stirring well to combine. Bring to the boil, then pour the sauce over the chicken and beans. Cook in a preheated moderately hot oven (200°C/400°F, Gas Mark 6) for about 20 minutes.
SERVES 4

DICED CHICKEN WITH CHILLIES

METRIC/IMPERIAL
2 tablespoons polyunsaturated vegetable oil
1 clove garlic, peeled and sliced
350 g/12 oz boned chicken breast, diced
1 red pepper, cored, deseeded and diced
2 green chillies, deseeded and sliced
50 g/2 oz bean-sprouts
2 tablespoons soy sauce
2 tablespoons chilli sauce
coriander leaves, to garnish

Heat the oil in a wok or frying pan, add the garlic and fry for 1 minute. Add the chicken and stir-fry for 1 minute. Add the pepper and chillies and cook for a further minute. Stir in the bean-sprouts, soy sauce and chilli sauce and cook for 2 minutes.

Turn into a warmed serving dish, garnish with coriander and serve immediately.
SERVES 4

SUPRÊME OF CHICKEN ON A WARM SALAD OF CHICORY

METRIC/IMPERIAL
4 chicken breasts, skinned, wingbone cleaned
but all other bones removed
salt
freshly ground black pepper
4 tablespoons walnut oil
juice of 1 lemon
tarragon sprigs
50 g/2 oz walnuts, finely chopped
3 red or small white onions, peeled and sliced
head of oak leaf lettuce
head of chicory
Dressing:
4 tablespoons walnut oil
2 tablespoons tarragon vinegar
1 teaspoon prepared mustard
1 tablespoon chopped walnuts
salt
freshly ground black pepper
Garnish:
chopped walnuts
tarragon sprigs

Season the chicken breasts with salt and pepper. Lay them in a shallow dish with the oil, lemon juice, tarragon, walnuts and onions. Leave to marinate for 2 hours.

Cut 4 × 35 cm/14 inch square sheets of foil. Place a chicken breast on each and spoon on equal amounts of marinade. Fold up the edges of the foil to seal the parcels completely. Cook in a steamer over boiling water for 15 minutes.

Meanwhile, wash and dry the lettuce, wash the chicory and separate it into leaves; shake the dressing ingredients together in a screw-topped jar, and arrange the salad leaves on 4 plates. Pour the contents of a parcel on each plate and spoon on the extra dressing. Garnish with walnuts and tarragon sprigs before serving.
SERVES 4

SPICED CHICKEN

METRIC/IMPERIAL
¼ teaspoon ground coriander
½ teaspoon chilli powder
½ teaspoon garam masala
pinch of salt
2 tablespoons lemon juice
4 boneless chicken breasts, about 100 g/4 oz
each, skinned
polyunsaturated vegetable oil
Sauce:
300 ml/½ pint plain low-fat yogurt
½ teaspoon ground ginger
1 teaspoon curry powder
1 tablespoon cayenne pepper
1 clove garlic, peeled and crushed
1 bay leaf
1 tablespoon tomato purée
1 tablespoon grated lemon rind
Garnish:
parsley sprigs
lemon slices

Combine the coriander, chilli powder, garam masala, salt and lemon juice. Prick the chicken breasts all over with a fork and rub in the spice and lemon mixture. Leave to marinate for 4 to 5 hours.

Drain the chicken breasts and fry them in oil over a moderate heat until they are brown all over and cooked through. Transfer to a serving dish and keep warm.

Meanwhile, mix together all the ingredients for the sauce and warm over a gentle heat, stirring constantly. Remove the bay leaf and pour the sauce over the fried chicken breasts. Garnish with parsley and lemon slices.
SERVES 4

BRAISED CHICKEN WITH PEPPERS AND CORN

METRIC/IMPERIAL
1 tablespoon polyunsaturated vegetable oil
3 spring onions, chopped
1 × 5 cm/2 inch piece root ginger, peeled and shredded
450 g/1 lb boned chicken breast, shredded
2 tablespoons light soy sauce
2 tablespoons dry sherry
2 green peppers, cored, deseeded and sliced
1 × 425 g/15 oz can baby corn or sweetcorn, drained

Heat the oil in a wok or frying pan, add the spring onions and ginger and fry for 1 minute. Add the chicken and brown lightly. Pour in the soy sauce and sherry and cook for a further 1 minute. Stir in the peppers and corn and stir-fry for 2 minutes.

Pile the mixture on to a warmed serving dish and serve immediately.
SERVES 4 to 6

ARROZ CON POLLO

METRIC/IMPERIAL
4 boneless chicken breasts
juice of ½ lemon
salt
freshly ground black pepper
1 tablespoon olive oil
1 onion, peeled and finely chopped
2 cloves garlic, peeled and crushed
2 red peppers, cored, deseeded and diced
300 g/10 oz long-grain rice, well washed
1 × 400 g/14 oz can chopped tomatoes
generous pinch of saffron
2 tablespoons chopped parsley
10 black olives, stoned and halved
1 teaspoon capers
300 ml/½ pint chicken stock
100 g/4 oz frozen peas, defrosted
Garnish:
8 black olives, stoned
flat-leaf parsley sprigs

Season the chicken breasts with lemon juice, salt and pepper. Heat the oil in a heavy-based pan and fry the chicken until golden brown on all sides. Transfer to a pudding basin. Fry the onion, garlic, pepper and rice in the same pan until the rice has turned white. Stir in the remaining ingredients. Season well with salt and pepper and pour over the chicken breasts.

Cover with foil or greaseproof paper and tie down with string. Place in a steamer or covered saucepan half-filled with boiling water and steam for 40 minutes. Check the liquid level frequently and add more boiling water if necessary.

Remove the foil and spoon the cooked chicken and rice on to a warmed serving plate. Garnish with olives and flat-leaf parsley. Serve at once.
SERVES 4

Note: This is Spain's traditional chicken dish and, like most Spanish recipes, it contains saffron which gives the dish its yellow colour. If unavailable, turmeric may be used instead.

CHICKEN IN FOIL

METRIC/IMPERIAL
1 tablespoon soy sauce
1 tablespoon dry sherry
1 tablespoon sesame seed oil
450 g/1 lb boned chicken breast, cut into 16
equal pieces
4 spring onions, each cut into 4 pieces
1 × 5 cm/2 inch piece root ginger, peeled and
shredded
1 celery stalk, shredded

Mix the soy sauce, sherry and sesame seed oil together. Add the chicken and toss well to coat, then leave to marinate for 15 to 20 minutes.

Cut out 16 pieces of foil large enough to enclose the pieces of chicken generously. Brush the foil with oil, place a piece of chicken in the centre and top with a piece of spring onion, some ginger and celery. Fold the foil over to enclose the chicken and seal the edges well. Place in a steamer and steam for 10 to 12 minutes. Serve hot in the foil.
SERVES 4 to 6

CHICKEN PINWHEELS

METRIC/IMPERIAL
4 boneless chicken breasts
salt
freshly ground black pepper
leaves from sprig of thyme
2 tablespoons snipped chives
juice of 1 lemon
2 cloves garlic, peeled and crushed
100 g/4 oz chicken livers, trimmed and washed
polyunsaturated margarine
Stilton sauce:
175 g/6 oz blue Brie, rind removed
300 ml/½ pint Quark
150 ml/¼ pint soured cream
1½ tablespoons red wine vinegar
½ yellow pepper, cored, deseeded and very
finely chopped
½ red pepper, cored, deseeded and very finely
chopped
salt
freshly ground black peper
Garnish:
snipped chives
coriander sprigs

Place each chicken breast between 2 pieces of greaseproof paper Beat to flatten slightly with a

rolling pin. Season the breasts with salt and pepper. Sprinkle each with thyme leaves, chives, lemon juice and garlic. Spread about 25 g/1 oz of chicken livers on each breast, leaving a gap of about 1 cm/½ inch around the perimeter of the chicken breast. Roll up and spread the outsides with a little margarine, then wrap the breasts tightly in foil. Steam over boiling water for 40 minutes. Leave until completely cold.

To make the sauce, blend the blue Brie, Quark, soured cream and vinegar in a food processor or blender. Stir in half of the chopped peppers and season well with salt and pepper. Unwrap the chicken rolls and add any chicken juices to the sauce, stirring well.

Pour the sauce on to 4 individual plates. Slice the chicken rolls and arrange on the sauce. Sprinkle on the remaining peppers. Garnish with chives and coriander sprigs.
SERVES 4

CHICKEN ROLLS WITH ORANGE AND NUT STUFFING

METRIC/IMPERIAL
4 boneless chicken breasts, skinned
finely grated rind of 1 orange
4 tablespoons soft wholemeal
breadcrumbs
1 small onion, peeled and minced
salt
freshly ground black pepper
1 tablespoon chopped rosemary
2 tablespoons chopped walnuts
1 egg, beaten
150 ml/¼ pint chicken stock
150 ml/¼ pint fresh orange juice
Garnish:
rosemary sprigs
peeled orange segments

Place the chicken breasts between dampened sheets of waxed paper and beat with a meat mallet or a rolling pin. Press the chicken breasts out flat and trim off any uneven edges.

Mix the orange rind with the breadcrumbs, onion, salt and pepper to taste, rosemary and walnuts, and bind together with the beaten egg. Spread the stuffing mixture evenly over each chicken breast; roll up securely and tie with strong cotton or fine twine.

Put the chicken rolls into a shallow pan and add

the chicken stock and orange juice; cover, bring to the boil, lower the heat and simmer for 25 to 30 minutes, until the chicken is just tender.

Remove the chicken rolls and keep warm on a serving dish. Boil the cooking liquid until reduced by half. Spoon the cooking liquid over the chicken rolls and garnish with rosemary sprigs and orange segments.

SERVES 4

CHICKEN TANDOORI

METRIC/IMPERIAL
4 chicken breasts, skinned (about 175 g/6 oz each)
1 clove garlic, peeled and crushed
1 tablespoon tandoori powder
300 ml/½ pint plain low-fat yogurt
onion slices, to garnish

Make incisions in the chicken flesh and rub with the garlic. Place the chicken in a large shallow bowl. Mix the tandoori powder with the yogurt and pour over the chicken. Cover and store in the refrigerator to marinate for 3 hours.

Heat the grill to moderate. Remove the chicken from the marinade and place on the grill rack. Grill for about 20 minutes or until the chicken is cooked through, turning frequently and basting with the marinade.

Transfer the chicken to a heated serving dish, garnish with onion slices and serve immediately.

SERVES 4

CHICKEN WITH CASHEW NUTS

METRIC/IMPERIAL
3 tablespoons dry sherry
1 egg white
1 teaspoon cornflour
2 boned chicken breasts, cut into small pieces
2 tablespoons polyunsaturated vegetable oil
2 spring onions, chopped
1 green pepper, cored, deseeded and diced
100 g/4 oz canned bamboo shoots, drained and shredded
1 tablespoon soy sauce
100 g/4 oz unsalted cashew nuts

Mix 2 tablespoons of the sherry, the egg white and cornflour together. Add the chicken and toss well until evenly coated.

Heat the oil in a wok or frying pan, add the spring onions and stir-fry for 30 seconds. Add the chicken and cook for 3 minutes. Add the remaining ingredients and cook for 2 minutes.

Pile into a warmed serving dish and serve immediately.

SERVES 4

CHICKEN WITH CUCUMBER IN SESAME SAUCE

METRIC/IMPERIAL
8 chicken fillets (boned, skinless breasts)
2 spring onions
2 slices root ginger, peeled
750 ml/1¼ pints water
2 small cucumbers
Sesame sauce:
1 teaspoon finely chopped spring onion
2 tablespoons sesame paste or crunchy peanut butter
1 tablespoon light soy sauce
¼ teaspoon dry mustard
3 tablespoons water
1 teaspoon salt
1 teaspoon chilli oil (or 1 teaspoon peanut oil with a dash of Tabasco)
Garnish:
spring onion tassels (see method)
salad burnet

Place the chicken fillets in a saucepan with the spring onions, ginger and water. Bring to the boil, reduce the heat, cover the pan and simmer gently for 6 minutes. Allow to cool in the stock, then remove and cut into matchstick strips.

Peel the cucumbers, leaving a few strips of green skin for colour, then halve them and scoop out the seeds with a teaspoon. Cut the cucumber into strips the same size as the chicken. Cover the chicken and cucumber with plastic wrap and refrigerate until needed.

Place all the ingredients for the sesame sauce in a small bowl and mix well to combine. Arrange the chicken on one side of a dish, and the cucumber next to it. Garnish with spring onion tassels and salad burnet. (To prepare the spring onions, trim the ends and finely shred the green ends. Leave in iced water for 1 hour to allow them to open.) Just before serving, spoon a little sauce over the chicken and cucumber.

SERVES 4

CHICKEN WITH PEPPERS

METRIC/IMPERIAL
350 g/12 oz cooked chicken meat
1 large green pepper, cored, deseeded and sliced
1 large red pepper, cored, deseeded and sliced
1 medium avocado, peeled, stoned and chopped
2 tablespoons reduced-calorie mayonnaise

Cut the chicken meat into bite-sized pieces.
Blanch the peppers in boiling water for 1 minute.
Mix the pepper, avocado and chicken together
then stir in the mayonnaise. Serve with a green
salad as an accompaniment.
SERVES 2 to 3

CHICKEN TOASTIES

METRIC/IMPERIAL
100 g/4 oz cold cooked chicken, diced
100 g/4 oz cooked sweetcorn
6 tablespoons plain low-fat yogurt
8 slices wholemeal bread
25 g/1 oz polyunsaturated margarine

Combine the chicken, sweetcorn and yogurt.
Spread the bread with the margarine and trim to
fit a sandwich toaster. Place the bread 'sunnyside
down' in the toaster and spoon some of the filling
into the centre. Place another slice of bread
'sunnyside up' on top and cook according to the
toaster manufacturer's instructions.
SERVES 2 to 6

CHICKEN BAKE WITH YOGURT TOPPING

METRIC/IMPERIAL
15 g/½ oz polyunsaturated margarine
1 small onion, peeled and finely chopped
2 celery stalks, finely chopped
100 g/4 oz button mushrooms
350 g/12 oz cooked chicken, finely chopped
1 tablespoon chopped parsley
salt
freshly ground white pepper
Topping:
300 ml/½ pint plain low-fat yogurt
2 egg yolks
1 teaspoon prepared mustard

Melt the margarine in a pan. Add the onion, celery and mushrooms and fry gently for 5 minutes,
stirring frequently. Add the chicken, parsley and
salt and pepper to taste. Transfer the mixture to a
casserole and press down firmly.
To make the topping: put the yogurt in a bowl
with the egg yolks, mustard and salt and pepper to
taste. Mix and then pour over the chicken.
Bake in a preheated moderately hot oven
(190°C/375°F, Gas Mark 5) for 25 minutes. Serve
immediately while hot.
SERVES 4

CHICKEN AND MUSHROOM PIE

METRIC/IMPERIAL
Pastry:
225 g/8 oz wholemeal flour
pinch of salt
100 g/4 oz polyunsaturated margarine
2-3 tablespoons water
beaten egg, to glaze
Filling:
2 tablespoons polyunsaturated vegetable oil
1 onion, peeled and chopped
1 clove garlic, peeled and crushed
100 g/4 oz mushrooms, wiped and sliced
1 tablespoon wholemeal flour
300 ml/½ pint chicken stock
450 g/1 lb cooked chicken, diced
1 tablespoon chopped parsley
salt
freshly ground black pepper

Make the pastry as for Basic wholemeal pastry
(see page 334); chill for 15 minutes.
Meanwhile, heat the oil in a pan, add the onion
and fry until softened. Add the garlic and mushrooms and cook for 2 minutes. Remove from the
heat and stir in the flour; add the stock and stir
until blended. Return to the heat and bring to the
boil, stirring until thickened. Add the remaining
ingredients, with salt and pepper to taste. Mix
well, then transfer to a 1.2 litre/2 pint pie dish.
Roll out the pastry to a shape about
5 cm/2 inches larger than the dish. Cut off a narrow strip all round and place on the dampened
edge of the dish. Moisten the strip, then cover
with the pastry, pressing the edges firmly.
Trim and flute the edges, decorate with pastry
leaves made from the trimmings, and make a hole
in the centre. Brush with beaten egg and bake in a
preheated moderately hot oven (200°C/400°F,
Gas Mark 6) for 30 minutes until golden.
SERVES 4

CHICKEN AND HAM MOULD

METRIC/IMPERIAL
1 tablespoon powdered gelatine
3 tablespoons water
2 × 425 g/15 oz cans chicken soup
1 teaspoon Worcestershire sauce
salt
freshly ground black pepper
1 × 185 g/6½ oz can pimientos, drained and chopped
50 g/2 oz lean ham, cubed
100 g/4 oz cooked chicken, chopped
1 × 10 cm/4 inch piece of cucumber, cut into 5 mm/¼ inch cubes
Garnish:
pimiento strips
cucumber slices

Sprinkle the gelatine over the water in a heatproof bowl, then place over a pan of gently simmering water. Stir until dissolved. Mix together the soup, Worcestershire sauce and gelatine mixture. Season to taste with salt and pepper.

Add the pimientos, ham, chicken and cucumber. Mix well and pour into a 1.2 litre/2 pint mould. Leave to set, before turning out on to a serving platter. Garnish with strips of pimiento and cucumber slices.
SERVES 4

FRUIT AND NUT CHICKEN

METRIC/IMPERIAL
2 tablespoons polyunsaturated vegetable oil
2 large leeks or 1 onion, peeled and sliced
1 green pepper, cored, deseeded and sliced
1 tablespoon plain wholemeal flour
grated rind of 1 orange
4 tablespoons unsweetened orange juice
300 ml/½ pint chicken or vegetable stock
100 g/4 oz no-soak dried apricots, quartered
150 ml/¼ pint white wine and water mixed
350 g/12 oz cooked chicken, roughly chopped
50 g/2 oz walnuts, chopped
grated nutmeg
salt
freshly ground black pepper
orange slices, to garnish

Heat the oil in a pan and sauté the leeks or onion for 5 minutes until soft, then add the pepper and

cook for 1 minute. Stir in the flour and the orange rind and cook for a further 1 minute.
Gradually stir in the orange juice and stock. Add the apricots with the white wine and water, the chicken and the walnuts. Add grated nutmeg and salt and pepper to taste.
Bring to the boil, cover and simmer for 15 to 20 minutes. Transfer to a warmed serving dish and garnish with orange slices. Serve with brown risotto rice and a green salad.
SERVES 4

Note: Use leftover roast chicken for this recipe or poach a whole bird in a chicken stock with 1 onion, 1 carrot and 2 bay leaves. The stock makes an ideal base for a soup.

CHICKEN AND BEAN BAKE

METRIC/IMPERIAL
50 g/2 oz polyunsaturated margarine
50 g/2 oz unbleached white flour
600 ml/1 pint skimmed milk
225 g/8 oz cooked chicken, chopped
1 × 450 g/16 oz can baked beans
100 g/4 oz pasta shells, cooked
100 g/4 oz Cheddar cheese, grated
2 large tomatoes, sliced
2 tablespoons flaked almonds

Melt the margarine in a large saucepan and add the flour. Cook for 2 minutes, then remove from heat and gradually stir in the milk. Bring to the boil, stirring constantly. Add the chicken, beans and pasta and two-thirds of the cheese. Turn into a well-greased 1 litre/1¾ pint ovenproof dish and top with tomato slices.
Sprinkle with the remaining cheese and almonds and place under a preheated grill until the cheese has melted and golden. Alternatively, the dish may be left in a cool place until required and then reheated in a preheated moderate oven (180°C/350°F, Gas Mark 4) for 45 minutes.
SERVES 3 to 4

CHICKEN LIVER SKEWERS

METRIC/IMPERIAL
16 mushrooms
4 lean bacon rashers, derinded
225 g/8 oz chicken livers
salt
freshly ground black pepper
few drops of Tabasco
1 tablespoon polyunsaturated vegetable oil

Wipe the mushrooms but do not wash or peel them. Cut each bacon slice into 3 pieces. Cut each chicken liver in half.

Take 4 kebab skewers, thread 1 mushroom on each. Alternate bacon, chicken livers and mushrooms on each skewer, finishing with a mushroom. Sprinkle with salt, pepper and Tabasco, then brush with oil.

Grill under medium heat for 6 minutes, turning the skewers frequently until the bacon and livers are completely cooked. Serve hot with salad.
SERVES 4

POUSSINS WITH ORANGE

METRIC/IMPERIAL
4 poussins
2 oranges, quartered
2 teaspoons chopped fresh tarragon or
1 teaspoon dried tarragon
salt
freshly ground black pepper
25 g/1 oz polyunsaturated margarine
orange slices, to garnish

Preheat the oven to 180°C/350°F, Gas Mark 4.

Cut 4 pieces of foil large enough to contain a poussin. Place a poussin on each piece of foil. Squeeze 2 orange quarters over each bird. Then place the 2 orange quarters and half the tarragon in the body cavity of each poussin. Rub the poussins with the peel of the squeezed orange quarters, a little salt and plenty of freshly ground black pepper.

Rub the birds all over with the margarine and sprinkle with the remaining tarragon. Wrap each poussin in the foil, to make parcels. Place the parcels in a roasting tin and roast in the oven for 25 minutes. Open the foil and turn the birds over, then rewrap in the foil and return to the oven for a further 5 minutes.

Remove from the oven, open the foil and turn the poussins breast-side up. Return to the oven for

a further 10 minutes with the foil open, to allow the poussins to brown.

Transfer the poussins to a heated serving dish and serve immediately with the juice poured over, garnished with orange slices.
SERVES 4

POUSSINS WITH SPICY HOT SAUCE

METRIC/IMPERIAL
2 tablespoons walnut oil or olive oil
4 × 350 g/12 oz poussins
salt
freshly ground black pepper
juice of 1 lemon
2 bunches of spring onions, trimmed and finely chopped
2 chillies, deseeded and finely chopped
pinch of cayenne
300 ml/½ pint chicken stock
large bunch of watercress, washed and large stalks removed
50 g/2 oz Quark
watercress sprigs, to garnish

Heat the oil in a heavy-based pan. Season the birds with salt, pepper and lemon juice. Fry over a high heat until golden brown on all sides. Remove from the pan and set aside. Fry the spring onions and chilli in the same pan with the cayenne and a little salt for 3 minutes. Lay a piece of wet greaseproof paper in a steamer compartment. Spread the spring onion mixture on top. Arrange the poussins in the spring onions.

Pour the chicken stock into the frying pan. Bring to the boil, scraping the sediment from the base of the pan. Pour into the saucepan. Cover the poussins with a tight-fitting lid and steam over the stock for 20 minutes. Add three-quarters of the watercress and continue to cook for 10 minutes. Check the liquid level frequently and add more stock or boiling water if necessary.

Remove the poussins to one side and keep warm. Add the spring onion and chilli mixture and the remaining watercress to the stock. Work in a blender until smooth, then add the Quark. Taste and adjust the seasoning if necessary.

Flood 4 warmed plates with the watercress sauce. Top with the poussins and garnish with watercress sprigs.
SERVES 4

POUSSINS WITH TARRAGON

METRIC/IMPERIAL
4 poussins
2 lemons
1 dessertspoon chopped fresh tarragon or
1 teaspoon dried tarragon
salt
freshly ground black pepper
polyunsaturated margarine

Place the poussins on pieces of foil large enough to cover them. Cut the lemons in half and squeeze a lemon half over each poussin. Cut the halves into quarters and put 2 quarters into the body cavity of each bird.

Sprinkle each poussin with the tarragon and salt and pepper. Place a little margarine on each bird and wrap firmly in the foil. Cook in a preheated moderate oven (180°C/350°F, Gas Mark 4) for 25 minutes.

Open the foil and turn the birds over. After 5 minutes, turn the birds back, breast side up. Leave the foil open and cook for a further 10 minutes to brown the poussins.

Transfer the poussins to a heated serving dish and pour the cooking liquid over them. They can be served hot or cold. When served cold the tarragon mixture turns to jelly.
SERVES 4

POUSSINS WITH OLIVES

METRIC/IMPERIAL
4 poussins
1 orange, cut in chunks
2 cloves garlic, peeled and split in half
12 parsley sprigs
3 celery stalks, chopped
2 medium carrots, peeled and sliced
100 g/4 oz green olives, stoned
salt
freshly ground black pepper
750 ml/1¼ pints chicken stock

Ease the cavity of each poussin open: tuck a few orange chunks, half a garlic clove and a few sprigs of parsley into each one. Secure the opening with a wooden cocktail stick.

Put the prepared poussins into a large casserole; add the celery, carrots, half the green olives, salt and pepper to taste, and the stock. Cover the casserole and cook in a preheated moderate oven

(180°C/350°F, Gas Mark 4) for about 1 hour, or until the birds are tender.

Lift the poussins on to a warm serving dish, remove the cocktail sticks and keep warm. Place the cooking juices, vegetables and olives in a food processor or blender and blend until smooth. Add the remaining olives and heat through gently.

Spoon the olive sauce over the poussins and serve immediately.
SERVES 4

POUSSINS WITH SCOTTISH EGG SAUCE

METRIC/IMPERIAL
4 × 350 g/12 oz poussins
salt
freshly ground white pepper
2 teaspoons lemon juice
1 tablespoon snipped chives
600 ml/1 pint boiling chicken stock
snipped chives, to garnish
Egg sauce:
300 ml/½ pint skimmed milk
1 bay leaf
4 white peppercorns
2 tablespoons snipped chives
25 g/1 oz polyunsaturated margarine
25 g/1 oz plain unbleached white flour
2 hard-boiled eggs, finely chopped
salt
freshly ground white pepper

Wipe the poussins, season well with salt, pepper and lemon juice. Sprinkle with chives and place in a steamer. Cover with a tight-fitting lid and steam over the chicken stock for 45 minutes.

Meanwhile, heat the milk, bay leaf, white peppercorns and chives over a low heat for a few minutes. Cover and leave to one side to infuse for 15 minutes; then strain. When the poussins are cooked transfer to a warmed serving dish and keep warm. Melt the margarine over low heat, stir in the flour and cook for 3 minutes.

Mix the strained milk and remaining stock in a measuring jug and add water, if necessary, to make the amount up to 600ml/1pint. Lower the heat and add the liquid to the margarine and flour. Bring to the boil and simmer for 3 minutes, stirring continuously until the sauce thickens. Stir in the chopped hard-boiled eggs. Season well.

Spoon the sauce over the poussins and garnish with chives, or serve separately in a sauceboat.
SERVES 4

POUSSINS WITH HERB SAUCE

METRIC/IMPERIAL
2 tablespoons polyunsaturated vegetable oil
4 × 400 g/14 oz poussins
grated rind and juice of 1 lemon
2 tablespoons chicken stock
salt
freshly ground black pepper
2 tablespoons chopped mixed herbs (e.g.
parsley, chives, thyme, marjoram)
150 ml/¼ pint plain low-fat yogurt
watercress, to garnish

Heat the oil in a large pan, add the poussins and brown lightly all over. Add the lemon rind and juice, stock, and salt and pepper to taste.

Cover and simmer for 20 to 25 minutes until tender. Place the poussins on a warmed serving dish and keep hot.

Add the herbs and yogurt to the pan and heat gently. Taste and adjust the seasoning. Pour the sauce around the poussins and garnish with watercress to serve.
SERVES 4

LEMON-SCENTED POUSSINS

METRIC/IMPERIAL
4 × 350 g/12 oz poussins
grated rind and juice of 1 lemon
150 ml/¼ pint dry white wine
sprigs of thyme, marjoram and oregano for the
marinade
salt
freshly ground black pepper
2 tablespoons olive oil
½ red cabbage, cut into julienne strips
½ white cabbage, cut into julienne strips
4 tablespoons chopped thyme, marjoram and
oregano
600 ml/1 pint chicken stock
lemon grass sprig
sprigs or chopped mixed herbs, to garnish

Place the poussins in a dish with the lemon rind and juice, white wine and herbs. Season well with salt and pepper. Marinate for up to 2 hours. Remove from the marinade and dry well. Heat the oil in a heavy-based pan. Fry the poussins over high heat until golden brown on all sides.

Spread the red and white cabbage over the base of a steamer compartment. Top with the 4 poussins. Season well with salt and pepper. Spoon over the chopped fresh herbs. Pour the remaining marinade into the saucepan with the chicken stock and lemon grass. Cover with a tight-fitting lid and steam over the stock for 40 to 45 minutes. Check the liquid level frequently and add more boiling stock or water if necessary.

Arrange each poussin on a bed of mixed cabbage and keep warm. Remove the lemon grass and reduce the stock. Pour over the poussins, garnish with sprigs of herbs and serve immediately.
SERVES 4

DEVILLED TURKEY

METRIC/IMPERIAL
350 g/12 oz cubed turkey meat
2 tablespoons Worcestershire sauce
2 tablespoons lemon juice
1 teaspoon dry mustard
1 teaspoon Tabasco
25 g/1 oz polyunsaturated margarine
1 tablespoon plain unbleached white flour
300 ml/½ pint skimmed milk
1 red pepper, cored, deseeded and cut into strips
salt
freshly ground black pepper
chopped parsley, to garnish

Place the turkey pieces in a shallow dish. Mix together the Worcestershire sauce, lemon juice, mustard and Tabasco, add the turkey and leave to marinate overnight.

Place the turkey and marinade in a saucepan and simmer for about 25 minutes until tender. (Cooking time depends on the size of the turkey pieces.)

Meanwhile, melt the margarine in a saucepan and stir in the flour. Cook for 2 minutes, stirring. Remove from the heat and stir in the milk. When blended, return to the heat, bring to the boil and simmer the sauce gently for 2 minutes, stirring continuously.

Add the turkey pieces, marinade mixture and red pepper. Season and cook for a further 5 minutes, stirring gently. Place in a heated serving dish and sprinkle with parsley before serving.
SERVES 2 to 3

CURRIED TURKEY

METRIC/IMPERIAL
100 g/4 oz onions, peeled and sliced
1 tablespoon sunflower oil
1 tablespoon curry powder
350 g/12 oz turkey pieces
450 ml/¾ pint chicken stock
1 tablespoon lime juice
½ tablespoon cornflour (optional)

Gently fry the onion in the oil for 5 minutes. Stir in the curry powder and cook for a few minutes. Add the turkey pieces and cook until browned. Stir in the chicken stock and lime juice and simmer for about 30 minutes until the turkey is tender. Skim off any fat.

If necessary, thicken with the cornflour mixed with a little of the liquid. Serve with plain boiled rice as an accompaniment.
SERVES 2 to 3

TURKEY KEBABS WITH FRESH ONION MARMALADE

METRIC/IMPERIAL
1 kg/2 lb boneless turkey, cut into bite-sized pieces
4 red onions, peeled and quartered
2 tablespoons light soy sauce
2 tablespoons dry sherry
15 g/½ oz fresh root ginger, peeled and finely chopped
2 cloves garlic, peeled and crushed
450 ml/¾ pint chicken stock
750 g/1½ lb onions, peeled and finely sliced
salt
freshly ground black pepper
2 tablespoons red wine vinegar
2 tablespoons clear honey
Garnish:
¼ yellow pepper, cored, deseeded and finely chopped
¼ green pepper, cored, deseeded and finely chopped
coriander sprigs

Thread the turkey and red onion quarters on to 4 kebab skewers. Lay in a shallow dish with the soy sauce, sherry, ginger and garlic. Leave to marinate for 2 hours, turning occasionally. Pour the marinade and stock into the base of a steamer. Stir

in the onions and bring to the boil. Lay a piece of wet greaseproof paper in the top compartment. Arrange the kebabs on top. Season well with salt and pepper. Cover with a tight-fitting lid and steam over the stock for 15 to 20 minutes. Check the liquid level frequently, and add more boiling stock or water if necessary.

Remove the kebabs to one side and keep warm. Stir the vinegar and honey into the onion mixture. Boil to reduce until syrupy. Taste and adjust the seasoning if necessary.

Arrange the kebabs on warmed plates. Spoon over the sauce and garnish with chopped peppers and coriander leaves.
SERVES 4

TURKEY FRICASSÉE ON ANGEL HAIR PASTA

METRIC/IMPERIAL
1 kg/2 lb boneless turkey pieces, skinned
1 tablespoon olive oil
2 cloves garlic, peeled and crushed
2 leeks, trimmed, washed and finely sliced
225 g/8 oz cap mushrooms, wiped and trimmed
1 × 400 g/14 oz can chopped tomatoes
50 ml/2 fl oz red wine vinegar
50 ml/2 fl oz red wine
2 tablespoons chopped basil
salt
freshly ground black pepper
450 g/1 lb angel hair pasta (see page 114)
1 tablespoon olive oil
basil leaves, to garnish

Cut the turkey into bite-sized pieces. Heat the oil in a pan. Fry the turkey until golden brown on all sides. Transfer to a pudding basin. Gently fry the garlic and leeks in the same pan until cooked but not brown. Add the mushrooms, tomatoes, vinegar, wine and 1 tablespoon of the basil. Season very well with salt and pepper. Bring to the boil and pour the sauce over the turkey. Cover with foil and place in a steamer or a saucepan half-filled with boiling water. Cover with a tight-fitting lid and steam for 20 minutes.

Two minutes before serving the fricassée, put the pasta and oil into the boiling water. Be careful not to overcook the pasta. Drain well, season and stir in the remaining chopped basil. Divide the pasta between 4 warmed plates. Spoon on the turkey and sauce. Garnish with basil leaves and serve at once while piping hot.
SERVES 4

TURKEY NUT LOAF

METRIC/IMPERIAL
1 medium onion, peeled and finely chopped
100 g/4 oz shelled walnuts, chopped
750 g/1½ lb raw turkey meat, minced
175 g/6 oz wholemeal breadcrumbs
1 tablespoon Worcestershire sauce
½ teaspoon chopped fresh mixed herbs or
 ¼ teaspoon dried mixed herbs
1 tablespoon chopped parsley
1 egg
salt
freshly ground black pepper
Garnish:
1 × 425 g/15 oz can unsweetened apricot halves,
 drained
stuffed olives, sliced
lettuce leaves

Blend all the ingredients together with plenty
of salt and pepper. Spoon the mixture into a
well-greased 1kg/2lb loaf tin and cover with
greased foil. Bake in a preheated moderate oven
(180°C/350°F, Gas Mark 4) for 1½ hours. Cool in
the tin for 30 minutes, then turn out and allow to
become quite cold.

Arrange some of the apricot halves over the top
of the loaf. Any left over can be added to a salad to
serve with the loaf. Place the olives on the top
edges of the loaf. Garnish with lettuce.
SERVES 8

TURKEY WITH BROCCOLI

METRIC/IMPERIAL
4 turkey breasts, skinned
450 g/1 lb broccoli
Sauce:
25 g/1 oz polyunsaturated margarine
1 clove garlic, peeled
1 tablespoon cornflour
about 300 ml/½ pint skimmed milk
about 300 ml/½ pint chicken stock
1 bay leaf
2 tablespoons dry sherry
2 tablespoons grated Parmesan cheese
pinch of paprika

Preheat the grill to high.

Place the turkey breasts on the grill rack and
grill for about 15 minutes, turning once, until
cooked through.

Meanwhile, steam the broccoli for about 12
minutes, until tender. Arrange the broccoli on a
heated serving dish and place the turkey breasts on
top. Keep hot.

To make the sauce, melt the margarine in a
saucepan and add the garlic. Cook gently for a few
seconds, then stir in the cornflour and cook for a
further 2 minutes, stirring. Remove from the
heat, discard the garlic clove and stir in enough
skimmed milk and chicken stock to make a thin
sauce. Add the bay leaf and cook for 2 to 3
minutes, stirring, until the sauce thickens. Discard the bay leaf and stir in the sherry.

Pour the sauce over the turkey and broccoli.
Sprinkle over the Parmesan cheese and place
under a hot grill until lightly browned. Sprinkle
with a little paprika and serve immediately.
SERVES 4

TURKEY MORNAY

METRIC/IMPERIAL
225 g/8 oz turkey breasts
lemon juice for basting
25 g/1 oz polyunsaturated margarine
1 tablespoon plain unbleached white flour
300 ml/½ pint skimmed milk
50 g/2 oz Cheddar cheese, grated
salt
freshly ground black pepper

Place the turkey breasts on the grid of a grill pan
and spoon over a little lemon juice. Put under a
hot grill for 20 minutes, turning occasionally. If
necessary, spoon over more lemon juice.

Meanwhile, melt the margarine in a saucepan
and stir in the flour. Cook for 2 minutes, stirring.

Remove from the heat and stir in the milk.
When blended, return to the heat, bring to the boil
and simmer gently for 2 minutes, stirring continuously. Add the grated cheese and salt and pepper and stir until the cheese has melted.

Cut the cooked turkey breasts into small portions and place on a heated serving dish. Pour the
sauce over and serve with a salad.
SERVES 2

TURKEY AND PROSCIUTTO KEBABS

METRIC/IMPERIAL
450 g/1 lb turkey fillet, cut in 3.5 cm/1½ inch
cubes
grated rind of 1 lemon
1 small onion, peeled and finely chopped
1 clove garlic, peeled and crushed
1 teaspoon pesto sauce
3 tablespoons olive oil
2 teaspoons chopped fresh basil or 1 teaspoon
dried basil
salt
freshly ground black pepper
100 g/4 oz prosciutto, cut in long strips
8 small button mushrooms, wiped and trimmed
8 small bay leaves
8 lemon wedges
shredded lettuce

Put the turkey fillet into a shallow dish. Mix the lemon rind with the onion, garlic, pesto sauce, olive oil, basil and salt and pepper to taste. Stir the marinade into the turkey; cover and chill for 3 to 4 hours.

Drain the turkey, reserving the marinade. Wrap each piece of turkey in a strip of prosciutto. Thread the turkey and ham rolls on to kebab skewers, alternating with the mushrooms, bay leaves and wedges of lemon.

Brush the threaded skewers with the marinade; grill for 4 to 5 minutes. Turn the kebab skewers, brush once again with the marinade, and grill for a further 4 to 5 minutes. Serve piping hot on a bed of shredded lettuce.
SERVES 4

GINGERED TURKEY

METRIC/IMPERIAL
225 g/8 oz dried apricots
1-2 teaspoons ground ginger
4 × 100 g/4 oz turkey fillets

Place the apricots in a bowl. Just cover with water and add the ground ginger. Leave the apricots to stand overnight.

Place the turkey fillets on the grid of a grill pan and spoon over a little of the apricot soaking liquid. Put under a hot grill for about 10 minutes, turning once. If necessary, spoon over more apricot liquid.

Meanwhile, simmer the apricots in the rest of the soaking liquid for about 10 minutes. Pour the cooked apricots into a blender and liquidize them until smooth.

Place the cooked turkey fillets on a heated serving dish and pour the apricot sauce over. Serve with green beans.
SERVES 4

TURKEY PORTUGAISE

METRIC/IMPERIAL
4 × 100 g/4 oz turkey fillets
1 clove garlic, peeled and crushed
2 tomatoes, roughly chopped
1 carrot, peeled and very thinly sliced
25 g/1 oz chopped onion
salt
freshly ground black pepper
watercress sprigs, to garnish

Place each turkey fillet on a piece of foil large enough to cover it. Spread a little crushed garlic on each one. Divide the tomato, carrot and onion between the fillets. Sprinkle over salt and pepper.

Wrap the fillets completely in foil and cook in a preheated hot oven (220°C/425°F, Gas Mark 7) for about 20 minutes until tender.

Serve in the packages with a tomato or green salad and garnished with watercress.
SERVES 4

TURKEY MILANESE

METRIC/IMPERIAL
350 g/12 oz cooked turkey meat
100 g/4 oz pasta
salt
1 × 225 g/8 oz can artichoke hearts, drained
2 teaspoons chopped fresh oregano or
1 teaspoon dried oregano
freshly ground black pepper

Cut the turkey into bite-sized pieces.

Put the pasta in a saucepan of boiling salted water and cook for about 10 minutes until just cooked but still firm. Drain and return to the saucepan.

Add the turkey, drained artichoke hearts and herbs to the pan and place over a gentle heat, stirring, until thoroughly heated through. Taste and adjust the seasoning, if necessary, then transfer to a heated serving dish.
SERVES 4

ORANGE-STUFFED TURKEY OLIVES

METRIC/IMPERIAL
4 turkey escalopes
polyunsaturated vegetable oil for frying
Stuffing:
50 g/2 oz fresh wholemeal breadcrumbs
1 tablespoon grated orange rind
8 stuffed olives, sliced
40 g/1½ oz cooked lean ham, chopped
salt
freshly ground black pepper
25 g/1 oz polyunsaturated margarine
1 small onion, peeled and finely chopped
Sauce:
15 g/½ oz polyunsaturated margarine
1 onion, peeled and chopped
1 clove garlic, peeled and crushed
2 teaspoons wholemeal flour
3 tablespoons orange juice
150 ml/¼ pint water or stock
1 × 275 g/10 oz can sweetcorn, mashed
Garnish:
stuffed olive slices
orange slices
parsley sprigs

Place the turkey escalopes between 2 pieces of greaseproof paper and beat until thin.

To make the stuffing, mix together the breadcrumbs, orange rind, olives, ham and salt and pepper to taste. Melt the margarine in a pan and cook the onion for 5 minutes. Stir into the stuffing to bind it together.

Divide the stuffing between the escalopes and roll up, securing with cocktail sticks. Heat the oil in a pan and fry the turkey olives gently for 10 to 15 minutes, turning occasionally, until almost cooked through. Remove with a slotted spoon and place in a shallow ovenproof dish. Cook in a preheated moderate oven (180°C/350°F, Gas Mark 4) for 15 minutes.

To make the sauce, heat the margarine in a pan, add the onion and garlic and cook gently for 5 minutes. Stir in the flour and cook for 1 minute. Gradually blend in the orange juice and water or stock. Stir in the corn and add salt and pepper to taste. Heat through gently and pour over the turkey olives. Return to the oven for 15 minutes. Serve hot, garnished with olives, orange slices and sprigs of parsley.
SERVES 4

TURKEY-STUFFED AUBERGINES

METRIC/IMPERIAL
2 large aubergines
lemon juice
salt
100 g/4 oz macaroni, cooked
350 g/12 oz cooked turkey meat, cut into chunks
about 300 ml/½ pint tomato juice
1 teaspoon ground coriander
freshly ground black pepper

Cut each aubergine in half and sprinkle with lemon juice and salt. Leave to drain for at least 30 minutes.

Place each half on a piece of foil large enough to completely enclose it. Wrap the aubergine halves and cook in a preheated moderately hot oven (200°C/400°F, Gas Mark 6) for about 30 minutes.

Meanwhile, gently heat the macaroni and turkey meat in the tomato juice, coriander and salt and pepper. When the aubergines are tender, unwrap and carefully scoop out the flesh. Mix with the macaroni and turkey pieces and pile back into the aubergine shells.
SERVES 4

SOY-BRAISED DUCK

METRIC/IMPERIAL
1 × 1.5-1.75 kg/3-4 lb oven-ready duck
2 × 5 cm/2 inch pieces root ginger
1 large onion
1 teaspoon salt
6 tablespoons soy sauce
3 tablespoons malt vinegar
1 tablespoon polyunsaturated vegetable oil
4 spring onions, each cut into 3 pieces
150 ml/¼ pint chicken stock
1 × 225 g/8 oz can pineapple slices, halved
3 tablespoons dry sherry
1 tablespoon cornflour, blended with
2 tablespoons water
Garnish:
pineapple slices
shredded spring onions

Prick the skin of the duck all over. Peel and finely chop the ginger and onion. Mix with the salt and rub inside the duck. Put in a large bowl and add the soy sauce and vinegar. Leave for 1 hour, basting occasionally.

Transfer to a roasting tin. Cook in a preheated hot oven (220°C/425°F, Gas Mark 7) for 30 minutes.

Heat the oil in a pan, add the spring onions and fry until lightly browned. Remove and set aside.

Remove the duck from the oven and pour off any excess fat. Lower the oven temperature to 190°C/375°F, Gas Mark 5. Sprinkle the duck with the spring onions, remaining marinade and stock. Cover with foil. Return to the oven for 1 hour, basting occasionally.

Place the duck on a board, joint it and chop into 16 pieces. Reassemble on a warmed serving dish; keep hot.

Put the pineapple and juice in a pan. Stir in the sherry, blended cornflour and duck juices. Cook for 2 minutes and serve in a sauce bowl. Garnish the duck with the pineapple slices and shredded spring onions to serve.

SERVES 4 to 6

DUCK WITH ALMONDS

METRIC/IMPERIAL
450 g/1 lb duck meat, cut into bite-sized pieces
2 slices root ginger, shredded
salt
3 tablespoons polyunsaturated vegetable oil
2 spring onions, cut in 1 cm/½ inch pieces
pinch of sugar
2½ tablespoons soy sauce
5 tablespoons green peas
5 tablespoons toasted almonds
2 teaspoons cornflour
3 tablespoons stock
2 tablespoons dry sherry

Rub the duck with the ginger, salt and 1 table-spoon of the oil. Leave for 30 minutes.

Heat the remaining oil in a pan over high heat. Add the duck and spring onions and stir-fry for 1½ minutes. Add the sugar and soy sauce, and stir-fry for 30 seconds. Add the peas and almonds. Stir-fry for a further 1 minute. Dissolve the corn-flour in the stock and sherry. Add to the pan, stir-ring until the sauce thickens. Simmer for a final 30 seconds. Serve hot with braised celery and rice.

SERVES 3

GINGERED DUCK BREASTS

METRIC/IMPERIAL
3 oranges
4 duck breasts, skinned
15 g/½ oz root ginger, peeled and finely chopped
2 tablespoons sherry
1 tablespoon red wine vinegar
salt
freshly ground black pepper
450 ml/¾ pint chicken or duck stock
100 g/4 oz polyunsaturated margarine (optional)
flat-leaf parsley, to garnish

Pare the rind of one of the oranges and cut into needle shreds; blanch for 20 seconds and set to one side. Lay the duck breasts in a dish with the juice of 2 oranges, the ginger, sherry, vinegar and half of the prepared needle shreds. Season well with salt and pepper. Marinate for up to 2 hours.

Peel the remaining orange, removing all of the pith, and cut into segments, retaining the juice. Bring the stock and all of the marinade to the boil in a saucepan, stirring in the segments and juice.

Lay a piece of wet greaseproof paper in a steamer compartment and arrange the duck breasts on top. Cover with a tight-fitting lid and steam over the stock for 20 minutes. Check the liquid level frequently and add more boiling stock or water if necessary. Remove the duck and keep warm while you finish the sauce.

Work the stock in a blender and rub through a sieve. Reduce by boiling rapidly until rich and syrupy. Lower the heat, whisk in the margarine, bit by bit (if using), until you have a rich creamy sauce. Taste and adjust the seasoning.

Arrange the duck on warmed plates and pour over the sauce. Garnish with the remaining needle shreds and parsley.

SERVES 4

Note: Duck with orange is a popular and success-ful combination of flavours. The addition of ginger will both intrigue and delight your guests. Use wild duck if you can, but domestic will do perfectly well.

STEAMED DUCK LIVERS

METRIC/IMPERIAL

450 g/1 lb duck livers, washed and trimmed
50 ml/2 fl oz skimmed milk
300 ml/½ pint chicken stock
3 spring onions, trimmed and sliced
1 carrot, peeled and finely diced
salt
freshly ground black pepper
1 tablespoon honey
2 teaspoons red wine vinegar
small head of radicchio, washed
1 bunch watercress, trimmed
Garnish:
50 g/2 oz smoked ham, cut into strips (optional)
finely chopped spring onion tops (optional)

Soak the livers in the milk for 30 minutes. Discard the milk, rinse the livers and pat dry. Bring the stock to the boil in a saucepan. Lay a sheet of wet greaseproof paper in a steamer. Place the livers, spring onion and carrot on top. Season well.

Steam over the stock for 5 minutes. Remove the liver and vegetables, set aside and keep warm. Add the honey and vinegar to the stock. Boil to reduce until syrupy.

Arrange the radicchio and watercress on 4 plates, then spoon on the liver and vegetables. Pour on the sauce, sprinkle with strips of ham and spring onion tops, if liked, and serve at once.
SERVES 4

TIMBALES OF DUCK

METRIC/IMPERIAL

3 slices of fresh brown bread, crusts removed, and made into crumbs
150 ml/¼ pint skimmed milk
225 g/8 oz cooked duck trimmings, roughly chopped
2 tablespoons sherry
1 small onion, peeled and quartered
1 tablespoon parsley sprigs
salt
freshly ground black pepper
grated nutmeg
ground cloves
3 egg whites
watercress sprigs, to garnish

Place the breadcrumbs in a small pan, add the milk and cook very gently until most of the milk has been absorbed.

Mix together the duck, sherry, onion and parsley. Add the bread mixture, and salt and pepper, nutmeg and cloves to taste. Work in a blender or food processor until smooth. Adjust the seasoning and place the mixture in a large bowl.

Whisk the egg whites until stiff but not dry and fold into the meat mixture. Divide between 4 buttered individual moulds, leaving room for the mixture to rise. Stand in a baking tin half-filled with hot water. Bake in a preheated moderate oven (180°C/350°F, Gas Mark 4) for 30 minutes. Allow to stand for a few minutes before unmoulding on to a heated serving dish. Garnish with watercress.
SERVES 4

WILD DUCK WITH CRACKED PEPPER AND APPLES

METRIC/IMPERIAL

4 Granny Smith apples, peeled and cored
juice of 1 lemon
1 tablespoon whole black peppercorns
600 ml/1 pint red wine
2 tablespoons Calvados
2 shallots, peeled and finely chopped
4 wild duck breasts, wiped
salt
1 tablespoon olive oil
150 ml/¼ pint chicken or game stock
50 ml/2 fl oz single cream

Brush the apples with the lemon juice. Crush the peppercorns in a tea towel with a mallet or rolling pin. Put the apples, peppercorns, wine, Calvados, shallots and duck breasts in a shallow dish. Marinate for 2 hours, turning frequently.

Remove the duck breasts and apples from the marinade and reserve the liquid. Dry the duck on absorbent kitchen paper and sprinkle with a little salt. Heat the oil in a heavy-based pan and fry the meat until golden brown on all sides. Lay the duck in a steamer with the apples. Bring the remaining marinade, stock and cream to the boil. Steam the duck over the stock mixture for 10 to 12 minutes.

Slice the apples. Arrange the duck and apples on a warmed serving dish and keep hot. Reduce the peppered stock by boiling until syrupy. Taste and adjust the seasoning, if necessary, and spoon the sauce over the duck.
SERVES 4

DUCK COOKED WITH YAMS

METRIC/IMPERIAL
1 × 1.5 kg/3-3½ lb duck, washed and dried
salt
1 teaspoon freshly ground white pepper
1 tablespoon hoisin sauce
3 tablespoons Chinese rice wine or dry sherry
3 spring onions, finely chopped
6 slices root ginger, peeled
450 g/1 lb small yams, washed, peeled and cut
into 2.5 cm/1 inch chunks

Rub the dry duck with salt and pepper and leave for 2 hours.

Place the duck on a rack in an ovenproof dish and put in a preheated moderately hot oven (200°C/400°F, Gas Mark 6). Roast for 15 minutes on each side until the oil starts to seep out of the duck and both sides are lightly browned.

Pour off the oil, then brush the duck all over with the hoisin sauce and also brush inside the body cavity. Place the wine, spring onions, ginger slices and yams in the body cavity. Cover the dish completely with foil and turn down the oven to moderate (180°C/350°F, Gas Mark 4). Roast for 1 hour.

After 1 hour, baste the duck with the pan juices, reseal the foil and cook for another hour. The duck should now be ready. Test by inserting a skewer into the leg: if the juices run clear, the duck is cooked.

SERVES 4

DUCK ON SKEWERS

METRIC/IMPERIAL
4 duck breasts, boned and skinned
Marinade:
2 tablespoons brown sugar
salt
4 tablespoons soy sauce
1 tablespoon sesame seed oil
1 cm/½ inch piece fresh root ginger, peeled and finely chopped
1 teaspoon sesame seeds

Cut the duck breasts into 32 small pieces. In a large bowl, mix together the ingredients for the marinade, then stir in the duck. Cover and leave to marinate for 3 to 4 hours in a cool place, or overnight in the refrigerator. Spoon the marinade over the duck several times so that the pieces become evenly coated. Remove the duck with a perforated spoon and thread onto 8 bamboo skewers or 4 large metal skewers.

Place on the grid of a moderately hot barbecue and cook the small skewers for 8 to 10 minutes, the larger ones for 10 to 12 minutes. Turn the skewers several times during cooking and baste with the remaining marinade. Serve the barbecued duck hot or cold, either on or off the skewers, with brown rice and salad.

SERVES 4

Note: Filleted duck breasts, which are available at large supermarkets, are meaty and tender, and convenient to use for kebabs and barbecues. This recipe makes either 8 small or 4 large skewers. If cooking on the larger, metal skewers, remove the pieces of duck after cooking and skewer one or two pieces on to wooden cocktail sticks to serve.

DUCK WITH MUSHROOMS AND BAMBOO SHOOTS

METRIC/IMPERIAL
1 × 1.75 kg/4 lb duck, cut into serving pieces
5 tablespoons soy sauce
4 tablespoons polyunsaturated vegetable oil
3 spring onions
4 slices root ginger
3 whole star anise
1 teaspoon black peppercorns
2 teaspoons dry sherry
4 dried Chinese mushrooms, soaked for 20 minutes, drained and stemmed
100 g/4 oz canned bamboo shoots, drained and sliced
2 tablespoons cornflour
2-3 spring onions, to garnish

Rub the duck pieces with a little of the soy sauce. Heat the oil in a pan and add the duck pieces. Fry, turning, until golden brown on all sides. Transfer to a saucepan and add the spring onions, ginger, star anise, peppercorns, dry sherry, the remaining soy sauce and sufficient water to cover. Bring to the boil, then reduce the heat and cover. Simmer for 1½ to 2 hours or until the duck is tender, adding the mushrooms and bamboo shoots 20 minutes before the end of the cooking time.

Mix the cornflour to a smooth paste with 2 tablespoons water and add to the pan. Stir until the liquid has thickened. Serve hot, garnished with spring onions.

SERVES 4

VEGETARIAN & WHOLEFOOD

PISSALADIÈRE

METRIC/IMPERIAL
175 g/6 oz plain wholemeal flour
½ teaspoon ground cinnamon
salt
75 g/3 oz polyunsaturated margarine
1 egg yolk
Filling:
3 tablespoons olive oil
450 g/1 lb onions, peeled and thinly sliced
2 cloves garlic, peeled and crushed
450 g/1 lb tomatoes, skinned and chopped
1 bouquet garni
2 tablespoons tomato purée
freshly ground black pepper
50 g/2 oz stoned black olives

Sift the flour, cinnamon and a pinch of salt together into a bowl. Add the margarine and rub it in until the mixture resembles breadcrumbs. Mix in the egg yolk, adding a little cold water, if necessary, to make a fairly firm dough. Knead the dough for a few seconds on a floured surface until smooth. Roll it out and use to line a 20 cm/8 inch flan ring. Leave in a cool place for 15 minutes.
Preheat the oven to moderately hot (200°C/400°F, Gas Mark 6).
To make the filling, heat the oil in a frying pan, add the onions and garlic and fry gently for about 10 minutes. Stir in the tomatoes, bouquet garni and tomato purée. Season with salt and pepper and bring the mixture to the boil. Lower the heat and simmer, uncovered, for about 40 minutes, then remove the bouquet garni.
Line the flan ring with greaseproof paper, weigh down with baking beans and bake blind for 15 minutes. Remove the paper and beans.
Spoon the tomato mixture into the flan case. Arrange the olives on top and return to the oven for a further 20 minutes, brushing the olives with a little extra oil if they become dry.
SERVES 4 to 6

PAN HAGGERTY

METRIC/IMPERIAL
2 tablespoons polyunsaturated vegetable oil
450 g/1 lb potatoes, peeled and thinly sliced
salt
freshly ground black pepper
75 g/3 oz mature Cheddar cheese, grated
225 g/8 oz onions, peeled and thinly sliced

Heat the oil in a heavy-based non-stick frying pan about 20 cm/8 inches in diameter. Remove the pan from the heat, and arrange half the potatoes overlapping in the bottom of the pan. Sprinkle with a little salt and pepper, then cover with the cheese. Add a layer of onions, more salt and pepper, then make a final layer of potatoes.
Cover the pan and cook over a medium heat for 20 minutes or until the potatoes on the bottom are brown. Invert the mixture on to a plate, then slip it back into the pan to brown the other side and complete the cooking, about 20 minutes. Serve the pan haggerty with a tomato salad, if liked.
SERVES 4

MUSHROOM AND PEPPER PIZZA

METRIC/IMPERIAL
225 g/8 oz wholemeal pizza dough (page 334)
2 tablespoons polyunsaturated vegetable oil
225 g/8 oz onions, peeled and sliced
1 red pepper
1 green pepper
1 clove garlic, peeled and crushed
100 g/4 oz mushrooms, trimmed and sliced
salt
freshly ground black pepper
50 g/2 oz Cheddar cheese, grated

Grease a large baking sheet and preheat the oven to hot (220°C/425°F, Gas Mark 7). On a lightly floured surface, roll out the pastry to a 20 cm/8 inch diameter circle and carefully transfer to the baking sheet.

Heat the oil in a frying pan, add the onions and fry gently until softened.

Cut 2 or 3 rings from each pepper, then core and seed the remainder and chop the flesh roughly. Add the chopped peppers to the onion with the garlic and mushrooms and cook for a further 5 minutes.

Spread the mixture over the pastry base. Cover with the cheese, garnish with the pepper rings and cook in the oven for 12 minutes or until the base is cooked.

SERVES 4

WHOLEMEAL VEGETABLE SAMOSAS

METRIC/IMPERIAL
3 carrots, scraped and diced
4 medium potatoes, peeled and diced
½ teaspoon salt
½ teaspoon ground cumin
½ teaspoon ground coriander
½ teaspoon ground turmeric
½ teaspoon chilli powder
about 120 ml/4 fl oz boiling water
5-6 spinach leaves, finely chopped
Pastry:
350 g/12 oz self-raising wholemeal flour
½ teaspoon salt
75 g/3 oz polyunsaturated margarine
about 200 ml/⅓ pint cold water
a little milk

Put the carrots and potatoes into a saucepan with the salt, spices and boiling water. Cover tightly and simmer for 10 minutes. Shake the pan occasionally to prevent the vegetables sticking. Add the spinach leaves and simmer for a further 5 minutes, adding a little more boiling water if necessary.

Meanwhile make the pastry. Sift the flour and salt into a large mixing bowl, tipping in any bran left in the sieve. Rub in the margarine until the mixture resembles fine crumbs. Stir in enough water to make a soft dough, then shape the dough into a ball and divide into 3 portions.

Put one-third of the dough on to a floured board and roll out into a rectangle about 18 × 23 cm/7 × 9 inches. Spread one-third of the vegetable mixture along the length of the rectangle. Bring the long edges together, moistening each

edge with a little milk to make them stick. Dust with a little flour and cut into the rectangle to make 3 squares. Repeat with the remaining dough and vegetable mixture.

Place the samosas on a greased and floured baking sheet. Cook in a preheated moderately hot oven (200°C/400°F, Gas Mark 6) for 25 minutes. Serve hot with an accompanying salad.
SERVES 4

MEXICAN PANCAKE MEDLEY

METRIC/IMPERIAL
8 basic wholemeal pancakes (see page 151)
watercress sprigs, to garnish
Filling:
15 g/½ oz polyunsaturated margarine
2 celery stalks, trimmed and chopped
2 tablespoons plain wholemeal flour
150 ml/¼ pint skimmed milk
1 × 350 g/12 oz can sweetcorn kernels, drained
2 tomatoes, skinned and chopped
50 g/2 oz shelled walnuts, chopped
1 tablespoon snipped chives
salt
freshly ground black pepper
50 g/2 oz Cheddar cheese, grated

Make the pancakes and keep them warm.

To make the filling, melt the margarine in a saucepan, add the celery and fry gently for 5 minutes. Add the flour and cook, stirring, until thickened. Add the remaining ingredients, except the cheese, and season with salt and pepper. Stir over low heat until the mixture is thoroughly heated through. Remove from the heat and stir in the cheese.

Divide the mixture between the pancakes and roll up. Arrange the pancakes in a warm shallow serving dish, garnish with sprigs of watercress and serve immediately.
SERVES 4

FRESH VEGETABLE MOUNTAIN

METRIC/IMPERIAL

Parsnip layer:
225 g/8 oz parsnips, peeled and roughly chopped
16 flat-leaf parsley leaves
1 large egg
50 ml/2 fl oz half-fat cream
generous pinch of grated nutmeg
salt
freshly ground black pepper
Carrot layer:
225 g/8 oz carrots, peeled and roughly chopped
1 large egg
50 ml/2 fl oz half-fat cream
generous pinch of ground coriander
Spinach layer:
1 large egg
50 ml/2 fl oz half-fat cream
450 g/1 lb chopped frozen spinach, defrosted and drained thoroughly
generous pinch of grated nutmeg

Lightly oil a 1.2 litre/2 pint pudding basin. Drain inverted on absorbent kitchen paper. Cook the parsnips and carrots in separate compartments of a steamer until soft, about 25 minutes.

Arrange the parsley leaves on the base of the pudding basin. Work the parsnips in a blender or food processor with one lot of egg and cream until smooth. Season with nutmeg, salt and pepper. Blend the carrots with egg and cream, seasoning with coriander, salt and pepper. Beat the remaining egg and cream into the spinach until smooth and creamy; season with nutmeg, salt and pepper.

Spoon the parsnip mixture into the base of the pudding basin. Top with a layer of carrot and finish with a smooth layer of spinach. Cover with foil or greaseproof paper and tie down with string. Place in a steamer or covered saucepan half-filled with boiling water and steam for 1 hour or until the mousse is firm to the touch.

Run a knife around the sides of the mousse and turn out on to a plate. Serve hot or cold.
SERVES 4

Note: This layered vegetable mousse is not too difficult to prepare and is stunning to look at. Use half the quantity of the ingredients in the recipe to serve as a first course with herb vinaigrette, or use all the recipe as a vegetarian main course with baked potatoes, topped with chives and yogurt.

COURGETTE AND TOMATO PIE

METRIC/IMPERIAL
3 tablespoons olive oil
2 onions, peeled and sliced
750 g/1½ lb courgettes, sliced
2 cloves garlic, peeled and crushed
6 tomatoes, skinned and chopped
1 tablespoon tomato purée
salt
freshly ground black pepper
Topping:
750 g/1½ lb potatoes, boiled and mashed
4 spring onions, finely chopped
4 tablespoons skimmed milk

Heat the oil in a pan, add the onions and courgettes and fry for 10 minutes, stirring occasionally. Add the garlic, tomatoes, tomato purée and salt and pepper to taste. Cover and simmer for 5 minutes, then turn into a 1.5 litre/2½ pint ovenproof dish.

Beat the potatoes with the spring onions, oil, milk, and salt and pepper to taste. Spoon over the courgette mixture to cover. Cook in a preheated moderately hot oven (200°C/400°F, Gas Mark 6) for 30 to 40 minutes until the potato topping is golden. Serve immediately.
SERVES 4

WATERCRESS AND SPRING ONION QUICHE

METRIC/IMPERIAL
wholemeal shortcrust pastry made with
75 g/3 oz plain wholemeal flour and 2 oz mashed potato (see page 334)
Filling:
15 g/½ oz polyunsaturated margarine
8 large spring onions, trimmed and chopped
1 large bunch watercress, trimmed and roughly chopped
3 eggs
150 ml/¼ pint skimmed milk
1 teaspoon French mustard
pinch of dried mixed herbs
50 g/2 oz mature Cheddar cheese, grated
salt
cayenne pepper
Garnish:
few watercress sprigs
few spring onions, trimmed and sliced

Roll out the pastry and use to line a 20 cm/8 inch flan ring about 2.5 cm/1 inch deep, placed on a baking sheet. Chill for 30 minutes.

To make the filling, melt the margarine in a pan, add the spring onions and fry gently for 3 minutes without browning. Stir in the watercress and cook for 1 minute until just soft, then remove from the heat and leave to cool.

Meanwhile, preheat the oven to moderately hot (200°C/400°F, Gas Mark 6).

Beat the eggs, milk, mustard and herbs together in a bowl. Stir in the cheese, then season to taste with salt and cayenne pepper.

Prick the base and sides of the dough. Line with foil and weigh down with baking beans. Bake blind for 10 minutes, then remove the foil and beans and return to the oven for a further 5 minutes. Spoon the spring onions and watercress over the base, pour over the egg and milk mixture and bake in the oven for 25 minutes, until the filling is well risen and golden brown. Leave to cool. Serve garnished with sprigs of watercress and spring onions.
SERVES 4

WHOLEMEAL VEGETABLE PASTIES

METRIC/IMPERIAL
100 g/4 oz plain wholemeal flour
100 g/4 oz plain white flour
salt
100 g/4 oz polyunsaturated margarine
2-3 tablespoons water
Filling:
100 g/4 oz shelled broad beans
225 g/8 oz turnips, peeled and diced
225 g/8 oz carrots, scraped and grated
2 tablespoons snipped chives
2 tablespoons curd cheese
2 tablespoons plain low-fat yogurt
salt
freshly ground black pepper
beaten egg, to glaze

Sift the flours and a pinch of salt together into a bowl. Rub in the fat until the mixture resembles breadcrumbs. Stir in sufficient water to make a fairly stiff dough. Turn the dough on to a floured surface and knead until smooth. Wrap in grease-proof paper and chill in the refrigerator for about 30 minutes.

To make the filling, cook the beans and turnips in boiling salted water for 10 minutes or until just tender. Drain well, then stir in the carrots, chives, curd cheese and yogurt. Season with salt and pepper and leave on one side to cool.

Meanwhile, preheat the oven to moderately hot (200°C/400°F, Gas Mark 6).

On a floured surface, roll out the dough to a 3 mm/⅛ inch thickness and cut out four 15 cm/6 inch circles, using a saucer as a guide. Divide the filling between the pastry rounds. Moisten the edges, then lift them up over the filling to enclose it completely and form the shape of a Cornish pasty. Seal the edges, scallop them and brush all over with the beaten egg. Make a small air vent in the top of each pasty, then cook in the oven for 25 to 30 minutes or until golden brown. Serve warm or cold.
SERVES 4

SPINACH SOUFFLÉ

METRIC/IMPERIAL
15 g/½ oz polyunsaturated margarine
1 clove garlic, peeled
1 small onion, peeled and finely chopped
400 g/14 oz fresh leaf spinach, trimmed and finely chopped
salt
grated nutmeg
3 eggs, separated
2 tablespoons skimmed milk
1 tablespoon grated Parmesan cheese
1 teaspoon lemon juice

Grease a 1.2 litre/2 pint soufflé dish and preheat the oven to moderately hot (200°C/400°F, Gas Mark 6).

Melt the margarine in a flameproof casserole, add the garlic and fry until golden brown. Remove the garlic with a slotted spoon. Add the onion to the casserole and cook until softened. Add the spinach and season with salt and nutmeg to taste.

Cook for 2 to 3 minutes, then remove from the heat. Beat the egg yolks with the milk and stir into the spinach mixture with cheese. Whisk the egg whites and lemon juice until stiff, then fold into the spinach mixture with a metal spoon.

Spoon into the soufflé dish and cook in the oven for about 30 minutes until golden, well risen and just firm to the touch. Serve immediately.
SERVES 4

LEEK PIE

METRIC/IMPERIAL
Pastry:
175 g/6 oz wholemeal flour
pinch each of salt and pepper
75 g/3 oz polyunsaturated margarine
75 g/3 oz mature Cheddar cheese, finely grated
2 tablespoons cold water
beaten egg or milk, to glaze
Filling:
1 tablespoon polyunsaturated margarine
750 g/1½ lb leeks, trimmed and sliced into
1 cm/½ inch rounds
25 g/1 oz flour
300 ml/½ pint vegetable stock (or milk and
water mixed)
finely grated rind and juice of ½ lemon
¼ teaspoon grated nutmeg
50 g/2 oz shelled hazelnuts
50 g/2 oz seedless raisins
salt
freshly ground black pepper

To make the pastry dough, put the flour and salt and pepper in a bowl, then add the margarine in pieces. Rub into the flour until the mixture resembles fine breadcrumbs, then stir in the cheese. Add the water and mix to a firm dough. Wrap in greaseproof paper and chill for 30 minutes.

To make the filling, melt the margarine in a pan. Add the leeks and fry gently for 5 minutes, stirring constantly until soft but not brown.

Stir in the flour and cook for 1 to 2 minutes, then gradually stir in the stock or milk and water. Bring to the boil, then lower the heat and simmer until the sauce is thick and smooth, stirring constantly. Add the remaining filling ingredients, simmer for 2 minutes, then transfer to a 1 litre/1¾ pint pie dish. Leave to cool.

Meanwhile, roll out the pastry dough on a lightly floured surface until 2.5 cm/1 inch larger than the circumference of the pie. Cut a 1 cm/½ inch strip from the edge, then press it on to the moistened rim of the dish. Moisten the strip, then cover the dish with the remaining pastry dough, pressing the edges firmly to seal. Trim and flute the edges and decorate the top of the pie with the trimmings.

Brush with beaten egg or milk. Bake in a pre-heated moderately hot oven (200°C/400°F, Gas Mark 6) for 30 minutes until the pastry is crisp and golden brown. Serve hot or cold.
SERVES 4

MOZZARELLA AND PEPPER PIZZA

METRIC/IMPERIAL
Pizza dough:
100 g/4 oz self-raising flour
100 g/4 oz plain wholemeal flour
1 teaspoon baking powder
50 g/2 oz polyunsaturated margarine
150 ml/¼ pint skimmed milk
Topping:
2 tablespoons tomato chutney
2 tablespoons tomato purée
1 teaspoon Worcestershire sauce
1 tablespoon polyunsaturated vegetable oil
1 large onion, peeled and finely sliced
3 large tomatoes, sliced
1 teaspoon dried mixed herbs
175 g/6 oz Mozzarella cheese, thinly sliced
1 green pepper, cored, deseeded and cut into
rings
6 stuffed green olives, sliced

Preheat the oven to 200°C/400°F, Gas Mark 6.

To make the base, place the flours and baking powder in a bowl. Rub in the margarine until the mixture resembles fine breadcrumbs. Add the milk and mix to make a firm dough. Turn on to a floured surface and knead until smooth. Roll out to a circle approximately 28 cm/11 inches in diameter and place on a greased baking tray. Pinch the edge of the dough to make a rim.

Mix together the tomato chutney, tomato purée and Worcestershire sauce, then spread over the pizza base. Heat the oil in a pan and sauté the onion for 5 minutes. Remove with a slotted spoon and place on the pizza. Arrange the tomato slices on top and sprinkle with the herbs. Top with the cheese slices, green pepper rings and olives and cook in the oven for 20 to 25 minutes. Serve hot with coleslaw or salad.
SERVES 4 to 6

VINE-LEAF PARCELS

METRIC/IMPERIAL
2 × 225 g/8 oz canned or bottled vine leaves,
drained
salt
½ teaspoon ground turmeric
175 g/6 oz long-grain brown rice, well washed
1 tablespoon polyunsaturated vegetable oil
1 small onion, peeled and finely chopped
100 g/4 oz dried apricots, finely chopped

50 g/2 oz sultanas
pinch of ground cinnamon
pinch of ground allspice
1 tablespoon chopped mint
1 teaspoon lemon juice
300 ml/½ pint orange juice
150 ml/¼ pint water

Unroll the vine leaves carefully and put them into a bowl of water to remove the preserving liquid. Pat them dry on absorbent kitchen paper. You will need about 30 leaves; reserve the remainder.

Bring a large saucepan of salted water to the boil and stir in the turmeric. Add the rice and simmer for 30 minutes or until the rice is just tender. Drain thoroughly and turn into a bowl.

Heat the oil in a small frying pan. Add the onion to the rice with the apricots, sultanas, spices, mint and lemon juice. Mix well together.

Take one vine leaf at a time. Place it flat on the work surface and put a heaped teaspoon of the rice mixture in the centre. Fold the base of the leaf over the filling, then fold over first one side, then the other. Fold over the top to make a neat parcel. Continue making parcels until you have used up all the filling.

Line a large frying pan with leftover vine leaves. Arrange the parcels, seam sides down, in a single layer in the pan. Cover the layer with more leaves, then make a second layer of parcels and cover them with leaves.

Pour on the orange juice and water and cover the pan. Cook gently over a low heat for 1 hour, adding a little boiling water from time to time, if necessary.

To serve warm, allow the parcels to cool slightly in the pan, then arrange uncooked vine leaves on a flat serving dish and carefully transfer the parcels to the dish. Serve immediately.

To serve cold, allow the parcels to cool completely in the pan, then arrange on top of uncooked vine leaves on a serving dish as above. Cover and chill.

SERVES 4

COURGETTE AND TOMATO GOUGÈRE

METRIC/IMPERIAL
350 g/12 oz courgettes, trimmed and sliced
salt
2 tablespoons polyunsaturated vegetable oil
2 medium onions, peeled and chopped
1 green pepper, cored, deseeded and sliced
225 g/8 oz tomatoes, skinned and quartered
1 teaspoon dried oregano
freshly ground black pepper
2 teaspoons grated Parmesan cheese
Choux paste:
65 g/2½ oz plain wholemeal flour
pinch of salt
50 g/2 oz polyunsaturated margarine
150 ml/¼ pint water
2 eggs, beaten

Put the courgette slices into a colander and sprinkle with salt, then leave them for 15 minutes to remove some of the moisture.

Preheat the oven to moderately hot (200°C/400°F, Gas Mark 6). Heat the oil in a large non-stick frying pan, add the onions and cook slowly for 5 minutes. Stir in the green pepper. Rinse and drain the courgettes and add them to the pan. Cook for a further 5 minutes, stirring occasionally. Add the tomatoes, oregano and salt and pepper to taste. Cook for about 10 minutes until beginning to soften. Leave on one side.

To make the choux paste, sift the flour and salt together on to a sheet of paper, returning the bran retained in the sieve to the flour. Melt the margarine in a saucepan, add the water and bring to the boil. When bubbling, remove the pan from the heat and immediately add the flour all at once. Beat the mixture until it is smooth and leaves the sides of the pan clean. Allow to cool slightly, then gradually add the eggs, beating well between each addition.

Spoon the mixture around the edge of a shallow 1.2 litre/2 pint ovenproof dish. Turn the vegetable mixture into the centre and sprinkle over the Parmesan cheese. Cook in the oven for 30 to 35 minutes until the choux paste is golden brown and well risen.

Serve the gougère immediately, accompanied by a fresh green salad.

SERVES 2 to 3

VEGETARIAN BURGERS

METRIC/IMPERIAL
225 g/8 oz butter beans or other pulse, soaked
overnight
1 tablespoon polyunsaturated vegetable oil
1 onion, peeled and finely chopped
2 carrots, peeled and grated
150 g/5 oz rolled oats
1 teaspoon vegetable extract
2 teaspoons dried mixed herbs
salt
freshly ground black pepper
flour for shaping
Sauce:
3 tablespoons tomato ketchup
1 tablespoon tomato purée
1 teaspoon made mustard
1 teaspoon wine vinegar
1 teaspoon brown sugar
150 ml/¼ pint water
salt
freshly ground black pepper

Drain the beans and rinse, then place in a pan and cover with cold water. Bring to the boil. Cook rapidly for 10 minutes, then reduce the heat and simmer for 30 minutes or until the beans are soft. (You can add 1 teaspoon oil to help prevent the water boiling over.)

Transfer the beans with a little of the cooking liquid to a blender or food processor and blend to make a purée.

Preheat the oven to moderately hot (190°C/375°F, Gas Mark 5).

Heat the oil and sauté the onion for 3 minutes. Add the carrot and cook for 2 minutes.

In a bowl mix together the bean purée, onion, carrot, oats, vegetable extract, herbs and salt and pepper. Using a little flour, shape into 8 burgers. Place on a greased baking tray and cook in the oven for 20 to 25 minutes.

To make the sauce, place all the ingredients in a pan and cook for 10 minutes.
SERVES 4

AUBERGINE PIE

METRIC/IMPERIAL
1 kg/2 lb aubergines
salt
100 ml/4 fl oz olive oil
1 onion, peeled and chopped
1 clove garlic, peeled and crushed

450 g/1 lb tomatoes, skinned and chopped
150 ml/¼ pint plain low-fat yogurt
100 g/4 oz cottage cheese
freshly ground black pepper
25 g/1 oz grated Parmesan cheese

Slice the aubergines, sprinkle with salt and leave in a colander for 1 hour. Drain and pat dry with kitchen paper.

Heat 2 tablespoons of the oil in a pan, add the onion and fry until softened. Add the garlic and chopped tomatoes and simmer, uncovered, for 5 to 7 minutes.

Mix the yogurt and cottage cheese together, adding salt and pepper to taste.

Heat the remaining oil in a frying pan and cook the aubergines on both sides until golden. Drain on kitchen paper. Arrange a third of the aubergines in an ovenproof dish. Cover with half the tomato mixture, then top with half the yogurt mixture. Repeat the layers, finishing with a layer of aubergines. Sprinkle with the Parmesan and cook in a preheated moderate oven (180°C/350°F, Gas Mark 4) for 35 to 40 minutes.
SERVES 4

GNOCCHI WITH TOMATO SAUCE

METRIC/IMPERIAL
225 g/8 oz potato, boiled and mashed
1 egg
15 g/½ oz flour
salt
freshly ground black pepper
20 g/¾ oz Edam cheese, grated, to serve
Tomato sauce:
1 tablespoon polyunsaturated vegetable oil
50 g/2 oz onion, peeled and chopped
1 × 225 g/8 oz can tomatoes
freshly chopped basil or parsley

Place the mashed potato in a bowl, add the egg, flour and seasoning and mix well. Mould into small walnut-sized balls and place in a sieve. Lower into a saucepan of boiling water and cook until the gnocchi rise to surface. Drain and keep warm.

Heat the oil in a saucepan and fry the onion gently until soft. Add the tomatoes with their juice, and salt and pepper to taste. Simmer until the liquid has reduced, then stir in the herbs. Pour the sauce over and sprinkle with cheese.
SERVES 1

LAYERED VEGETABLE TERRINE

METRIC/IMPERIAL
Spinach layer:
15 g/½ oz powdered gelatine
2 tablespoons water
350 g/12 oz cooked spinach, thoroughly drained
2 tablespoons lemon juice
225 g/8 oz curd cheese
salt
freshly ground black pepper
Carrot layer:
350 g/12 oz carrots, peeled and thinly sliced
100 ml/3½ fl oz fresh orange juice
pinch of grated nutmeg
salt
freshly ground black pepper
15 g/½ oz powdered gelatine
2 tablespoons water
225 g/8 oz curd cheese
Cucumber layer:
15 g/½ oz powdered gelatine
2 tablespoons water
1 medium cucumber, peeled and diced
pinch of ground mace
225 g/8 oz curd cheese

To make the spinach layer, sprinkle the gelatine over the water in a small heatproof bowl. Leave for a few minutes until spongy, then place the bowl in a pan of hot water and stir over gentle heat until dissolved.

Place the spinach, lemon juice, curd cheese, gelatine and seasoning in a blender and process until smooth. Pour into the base of a 1kg/2lb loaf tin. Chill in the refrigerator.

To make the carrot layer, place the carrots, orange juice, nutmeg and salt and pepper in a saucepan and bring to the boil. Reduce the heat and simmer for 20 minutes, stirring occasionally.

Remove the carrots with a slotted spoon and process in a blender until smooth. Dissolve the gelatine in the water. Add the curd cheese and gelatine to the carrot purée in the blender and process again until smooth. Spoon evenly over the spinach layer and return to the refrigerator.

To make the cucumber layer, dissolve the gelatine in the water. Place the cucumber, mace, curd cheese and gelatine in a blender and process until smooth.

Spoon evenly over the carrot layer and chill for about 3 hours, until set. Unmould the terrine on to a serving plate and serve chilled.
SERVES 6 to 8

SPINACH LOAF ON YELLOW PEPPERS

METRIC/IMPERIAL
25 g/1 oz polyunsaturated margarine
2 cloves garlic, peeled and crushed
225 g/8 oz leeks, trimmed, washed and finely chopped
salt
freshly ground black pepper
275 g/10 oz spinach, tough stalks discarded
50 g/2 oz fresh white breadcrumbs
2 eggs
1 egg yolk
pinch of grated nutmeg
350 ml/12 fl oz skimmed milk
chervil sprigs, to garnish
Sauce:
2 yellow peppers, cored, deseeded and roughly chopped
juice of ½ lemon
1 shallot, peeled and finely chopped
150 ml/¼ pint vegetable stock

Melt the margarine in a pan and fry the garlic and leek until soft but not brown. Season with salt and pepper. Cook the spinach leaves in a steamer until just limp, about 10 seconds. Remove 15 of the best leaves and dry on absorbent kitchen paper. Squeeze all water from the remaining spinach between 2 plates, and chop the spinach finely.

Grease or oil a 450g/1lb loaf tin and line with the spinach leaves. Stir the chopped spinach into the leeks. Remove from heat and add the breadcrumbs, eggs, egg yolk and nutmeg; season well with salt and pepper.

Heat the milk to just below boiling point and stir it into the vegetable mixture. Spoon into the prepared loaf tin. Cover with greased foil or greaseproof paper and tie down. Cover with a tight-fitting lid and cook in a steamer over water that is barely boiling for 50 to 60 minutes. If the mixture gets too hot the eggs will curdle.

Meanwhile, make the sauce. Put the yellow peppers, lemon juice, shallot and stock in a pan, bring to the boil and simmer for 10 minutes. Work in a blender or food processor, then sieve. Taste, and adjust the seasoning if necessary. Flood the serving dish with yellow sauce. Ease the sides of the loaf tin with a sharp knife and turn out on to the sauce. Garnish with sprigs of chervil.
SERVES 4

HUNGARIAN-STYLE VEGETABLES

METRIC/IMPERIAL
1 tablespoon polyunsaturated vegetable oil
1 onion, peeled and sliced
1 tablespoon paprika
½ teaspoon ground cinnamon
2 tablespoons tomato purée
2 × 400 g/14 oz cans tomatoes
1.5 kg/3 lb mixed vegetables, diced
(e.g. potatoes, carrots, cauliflower, celery,
leeks, courgettes)
150 ml/¼ pint water
½ teaspoon caraway seeds
salt
freshly ground black pepper
4 hard-boiled eggs, quartered
4 tablespoons plain low-fat yogurt
flat-leaf parsley sprigs, to garnish

Heat the oil and sauté the onion for 5 minutes.
Add the paprika and cinnamon and cook for 1
minute, then stir in the tomato purée and the
tomatoes with their juice.

Add the vegetables, water, caraway seeds and
salt and pepper to taste. Bring to the boil, cover
and simmer for 30 to 45 minutes. Add the eggs
and heat through. Put in a warmed serving dish
and spoon the yogurt over the top. Garnish with
flat-leaf parsley.
SERVES 6

POTATO AND TOMATO PIE

METRIC/IMPERIAL
25 g/1 oz polyunsaturated margarine
25 g/1 oz plain wholemeal flour
300 ml/½ pint skimmed milk
100 g/4 oz Cheddar cheese, grated
450 g/1 lb potatoes, peeled, boiled and thinly
sliced
2 onions, peeled and sliced
450 g/1 lb tomatoes, skinned and sliced
salt
freshly ground black pepper
pinch of dried basil

Melt the margarine in a saucepan, stir in the flour
and gradually add the milk. Bring to the boil, stirring continuously, and cook the sauce for 2 to 3
minutes. Add 50 g/2 oz of the grated Cheddar
cheese and stir until melted.

Grease a shallow, ovenproof dish and arrange
the potatoes in layers with the onions, tomatoes
and cheese sauce, seasoning with salt, pepper and
basil between each layer. Finish with a layer of
potato, sprinkle with the remaining cheese and
bake in a preheated moderate oven (180°C/350°F,
Gas Mark 4) for 45 minutes.
SERVES 4

COURGETTE ROULADE

METRIC/IMPERIAL
25 g/1 oz polyunsaturated margarine
450 g/1 lb courgettes, grated
4 eggs, separated
1 teaspoon chopped savory
1 tablespoon chopped parsley
salt
freshly ground black pepper
2 tablespoons Parmesan cheese
Filling:
2 tablespoons polyunsaturated vegetable oil
1 onion, peeled and chopped
175 g/6 oz mushrooms, wiped and sliced
1 tablespoon wholemeal flour
120 ml/4 fl oz skimmed milk

Melt the margarine in a pan, add the courgettes
and fry for 7 to 8 minutes, stirring frequently,
until coloured.

Place in a bowl with the egg yolks, herbs, and
salt and pepper to taste, and mix well. Whisk the
egg whites until fairly stiff, fold 2 tablespoons into
the courgette mixture to lighten it, then carefully
fold in the rest.

Turn the mixture into a lined and greased 30 ×
20 cm/12 × 8 inch Swiss roll tin and spread evenly.
Cook in a preheated moderately hot oven
(200°C/400°F, Gas Mark 6) for 10 to 15 minutes,
until risen and firm.

Meanwhile, prepare the filling. Heat the oil in a
pan, add the onion and fry until softened. Add the
mushrooms and fry for 3 minutes. Stir in the
flour, then gradually stir in the milk. Add salt and
pepper to taste and simmer for 3 minutes.

Sprinkle the Parmesan cheese on a sheet of
greaseproof paper. Turn the roulade out on to the
paper and peel off the lining paper. Spread with
the mushroom filling and roll up like a Swiss roll.
Serve immediately.
SERVES 4

CARROT AND ALMOND LOAF WITH TOMATO SAUCE

METRIC/IMPERIAL

100 g/4 oz flaked almonds
15 g/½ oz polyunsaturated margarine
1 medium onion, peeled and sliced
2 cloves garlic, peeled and chopped
275 g/10 oz fresh wholemeal breadcrumbs
225 g/8 oz carrots, peeled and grated
2 eggs, beaten
juice of 1 lemon
1 tablespoon chopped parsley
1 teaspoon grated nutmeg
salt
freshly ground black pepper

Sauce:

1 tablespoon polyunsaturated vegetable oil
1 medium onion, peeled and sliced
1 clove garlic, peeled and chopped
1 × 400 g/14 oz can tomatoes
2 tablespoons tomato purée
1 tablespoon chopped fresh basil or
1½ teaspoons dried basil
salt
freshly ground black pepper

Grease a 450 g/1 lb loaf tin and preheat the oven to moderately hot (200°C/400°F, Gas Mark 6).

Put the almonds into a pan and dry-fry for a few minutes, shaking the pan frequently. Remove from the pan.

Melt the margarine in the pan and fry the onion and garlic for 5 minutes until soft.

In a large bowl, combine the breadcrumbs, carrots and toasted almonds. Add the onion and garlic and stir well. Add the beaten eggs, lemon juice, parsley and nutmeg. Season with salt and pepper and mix thoroughly. Add a little water if more liquid is required, then spoon the mixture into the loaf tin and bake in the oven for 45 minutes or until a sharp knife inserted in the centre of the loaf comes out clean.

Towards the end of the cooking time, prepare the tomato sauce. Heat the oil in a frying pan and gently fry the onion and garlic for about 5 minutes until soft. Add the tomatoes, tomato purée and basil. Season with salt and pepper, stir well and simmer gently until the carrot loaf is cooked. Ease the sides of the loaf away from the tin with a sharp knife and turn out.

Serve immediately with broccoli, green beans or courgettes, or a fresh green salad.

SERVES 8

SAVOURY SPINACH CHEESECAKE

METRIC/IMPERIAL

75 g/3 oz plain wholemeal flour
25 g/1 oz medium oatmeal
50 g/2 oz polyunsaturated margarine
1-2 tablespoons water

Filling:

1 tablespoon polyunsaturated vegetable oil
1 onion, peeled and finely chopped
1 clove garlic, peeled and crushed
225 g/8 oz frozen spinach, thawed and well drained
1 teaspoon dried basil
225 g/8 oz low-fat soft cheese
2 eggs, separated
75 g/3 oz Gruyère or mature Cheddar cheese, grated
2 tablespoons plain low-fat yogurt
salt
freshly ground black pepper

Topping:

25 g/1 oz Parmesan cheese
2 tablespoons wholemeal breadcrumbs

Garnish:

rings of green pepper
few flat-leaf parsley sprigs

Preheat the oven to moderately hot (190°C/375°F, Gas Mark 5).

To make the base, mix the flour and oatmeal in a bowl. Rub in the fat until the mixture resembles fine breadcrumbs. Add the water and mix to a firm dough. Turn on to a floured surface, knead until smooth and roll out to line the bottom of a 20 cm/8 inch loose-bottomed cake tin. Prick with a fork and bake blind for 15 minutes. Remove from the oven and reduce the oven temperature to 160°C/325°F, Gas Mark 3.

To make the filling, heat the oil in a pan and sauté the onion and garlic for 5 minutes. Add the spinach and basil and cook for 2 minutes.

Beat together the soft cheese and egg yolks, then add the cheese, yogurt, salt and pepper and spinach mixture. Beat the egg whites until stiff and fold into the mixture. Spoon over the base and return to the oven for 45 minutes.

Mix the Parmesan cheese and breadcrumbs together and sprinkle over the cheesecake. Cook for a further 15 minutes. Allow to cool in the tin before transferring to a serving plate. Garnish with the green pepper rings and sprigs of flat-leaf parsley. Serve warm or cold.

SERVES 4 to 6

GRILLED AUBERGINE

METRIC/IMPERIAL
1 tablespoon wine vinegar
2 tablespoons polyunsaturated vegetable oil
1 teaspoon sesame seed oil
salt
freshly ground black pepper
1 aubergine, about 450g/1lb, cut into
5mm/¼inch thick slices
3 teaspoons sesame seeds

Beat the vinegar, oils, salt and pepper together.
Brush the aubergine slices on both sides with this
mixture and put in a large fireproof dish. Allow to
marinate for up to 2 hours, if possible.
Place under a grill and cook until brown. Turn
over and coat with more of the marinade, sprinkle
with sesame seeds and continue grilling until the
seeds turn a golden brown. Serve with warm
wholemeal pitta bread and a mixed salad.
SERVES 4

DEEP DISH VEGETABLE PIE

METRIC/IMPERIAL
175 g/6 oz basic wholemeal pastry (see page 334)
Filling:
15 g/½ oz polyunsaturated margarine
1 teaspoon cumin seeds, crushed
1 teaspoon coriander seeds, crushed
450 g/1 lb small carrots, scraped and quartered
lengthways
225 g/8 oz small potatoes, scraped and diced
1 medium cauliflower, trimmed and cut into
florets
225 g/8 oz small white turnips, peeled and diced
225 g/8 oz courgettes, trimmed and sliced
225 g/8 oz shelled broad beans
225 g/8 oz young French beans, trimmed and
cut in half
300 ml/½ pint water
beaten egg, to glaze
Sauce:
40 g/1½ oz polyunsaturated margarine
1 medium onion, peeled and chopped
2 cloves garlic, peeled and crushed
1 tablespoon medium curry powder
1½ tablespoons plain wholemeal flour
300 ml/½ pint skimmed milk
salt
freshly ground black pepper
2 tablespoons chopped parsley

To make the filling, heat the margarine in a large
pan and fry the cumin seeds until they begin to
pop. Add the vegetables and fry until lightly
browned. Stir in the water and bring to the boil,
then cover and simmer until the vegetables are
just tender. Drain the vegetables, reserving the
liquid.
To make the sauce, melt the margarine in a
saucepan, add the onion and garlic and fry over a
moderate heat for 3 minutes, stirring occasionally. Stir in the curry powder and cook for 1
minute. Stir in the flour and cook for a further 1
minute. Add 120ml/4floz of the vegetable cooking water and stir. Add the milk and stir until the
sauce thickens. Season to taste with salt and pepper. Stir the vegetables and parsley into the sauce
and mix well.
Place a pie funnel in the centre of a 2 litre/3½
pint deep pie dish. Spoon the vegetables and sauce
into the dish and leave to cool. Preheat the oven to
200°C/400°F, Gas Mark 6.
Roll out the pastry on a lightly floured board.
Cut a strip of dough to fit the rim of the dish.
Dampen the rim and press on the pastry strip.
Cover the dish with the remaining dough and
press to the strip on the rim. Trim the edges and
flute them. Brush the pastry with beaten egg. Reroll the pastry trimmings and cut out leaf shapes.
Arrange them on the pie and brush them with
beaten egg. Stand the dish on a baking sheet. Bake
in the oven for 20 to 25 minutes or until the top is
golden brown.
SERVES 4

CABBAGE FLAN

METRIC/IMPERIAL
750 g/1½ lb cabbage (spring, summer, primo or
Savoy), trimmed
salt
2 eggs, beaten
150 ml/¼ pint plain low-fat yogurt
50 g/2 oz Cheddar cheese, grated
freshly ground black pepper
large pinch of grated nutmeg

Preheat the oven to moderately hot (190°C/
375°F, Gas Mark 5). Grease a 20cm/8inch
diameter flan dish.
Remove the outside leaves of the cabbage and
shred the heart finely. Place the large leaves in a
pan of boiling, salted water with the shredded
cabbage on top and cook for 5 minutes. Drain
well, then separate the large leaves from the

shredded cabbage and remove the thick parts of the stems. Line the base and sides of the prepared flan dish with 6 to 8 of the outside leaves, pressing them firmly into place.

Mix together the eggs, shredded cabbage, yogurt and cheese and season with salt and pepper. Pour the filling into the lined dish and sprinkle the nutmeg over the surface.

Cook in the oven for 25 to 30 minutes or until the filling is set. The leaves around the edge may need to be brushed with a little oil during the cooking time so that they do not dry out.

SERVES 4 to 6

SPINACH AND MUSHROOM ROULADE

METRIC/IMPERIAL
225 g/8 oz frozen spinach or 450 g/1 lb fresh
  spinach
4 eggs, separated
salt
freshly ground black pepper
25 g/1 oz Parmesan cheese
Filling:
15 g/½ oz polyunsaturated margarine
175 g/6 oz mushrooms, trimmed and sliced
1 tablespoon plain wholemeal flour
150 ml/¼ pint skimmed milk
pinch of grated nutmeg
salt
freshly ground black pepper

Line a 30 × 20 cm/12 × 8 inch Swiss roll tin with greaseproof paper and oil lightly. Preheat the oven to 200°C/400°F, Gas Mark 6.

Cook the spinach with a little water until softened. Drain well, chop if fresh, and place in a large bowl. Add the egg yolks and beat them well into the spinach. Season with salt and pepper.

Whisk the egg whites until just holding their shape. Using a metal spoon, quickly fold into the spinach. Turn the mixture into the tin, sprinkle with Parmesan and bake for 10 minutes.

To make the filling, heat the margarine in a saucepan and fry the mushrooms until soft. Stir in the flour and cook for 1 minute. Gradually stir in the milk and cook until thickened. Stir in the nutmeg, salt and pepper to taste.

Remove the roulade from the oven and turn out on to a sheet of greaseproof paper. Spread the mushroom filling over the surface and gently roll the roulade up. Serve immediately.

SERVES 4

VEGETABLE KEBABS WITH PILAFF

METRIC/IMPERIAL
Pilaff:
2 tablespoons polyunsaturated vegetable oil
1 large onion, peeled and chopped
2 celery stalks, sliced
225 g/8 oz brown rice
600 ml/1 pint vegetable stock
50 g/2 oz seedless raisins
50 g/2 oz dried apricots, roughly chopped
50 g/2 oz walnuts, roughly chopped
1 cinnamon stick
1 bay leaf
salt
freshly ground black pepper
Kebabs:
225 g/8 oz courgettes, sliced
8 small tomatoes
1 large onion, cut into wedges with skin
8 button mushrooms, wiped
1 green pepper, cored, deseeded and cut into
  8 pieces
1 tablespoon polyunsaturated vegetable oil
1 tablespoon lemon juice
1 tablespoon thyme leaves

To make the pilaff, heat the oil in a pan, add the onion and celery, and fry gently for 5 minutes until golden brown. Add the rice and cook for 1 minute, stirring constantly. Pour on the stock, then add the raisins, apricots and walnuts.

Bring to the boil, stirring occasionally, then add the cinnamon, bay leaf and salt and pepper to taste. Lower the heat, cover the pan and simmer for 30 minutes or until the rice is tender and all the stock has been absorbed.

To make the kebabs, blanch the courgettes in boiling water for 1 minute, then drain. Thread the vegetables on to 4 large kebab skewers, alternating the different ingredients.

Mix together the oil, lemon juice, thyme and salt and pepper to taste, then brush over the vegetables. Cook on a barbecue or under the grill for 5 to 10 minutes until cooked through, turning and basting from time to time.

Spoon the pilaff into a warmed shallow serving dish and arrange the vegetable kebabs on top. Serve immediately.

SERVES 4

CLIVEDEN LOAF

METRIC/IMPERIAL
225 g/8 oz mushrooms, wiped and chopped
175 g/6 oz onions, peeled and chopped
25 g/1 oz polyunsaturated margarine
1 teaspoon mixed dried sweet herbs
75 g/3 oz Cheddar cheese, grated
1 egg
100 g/4 oz wholemeal breadcrumbs, toasted
15 g/½ oz polyunsaturated margarine for topping

Fry the mushrooms and onions in the margarine until they appear translucent. Remove from the heat and add the mixed herbs and grated cheese. Mix together and bind with the egg.

Line the base and sides of a well-greased 450g/1lb loaf tin with the toasted breadcrumbs. Spoon in the mushroom mixture, cover the top with the remaining breadcrumbs and dot with margarine.

Bake in a preheated moderately hot oven (200°C/400°F, Gas Mark 6) for 40 minutes. Turn out and serve hot. Alternatively, wrap in foil, refrigerate and serve with a salad.
SERVES 4 to 6

FRENCH BEAN AND TOMATO CASSEROLE

METRIC/IMPERIAL
2 tablespoons sesame seeds
750 g/1½ lb French beans, topped and tailed
225 g/8 oz courgettes, trimmed and sliced
salt
15 g/½ oz polyunsaturated margarine
2 onions, peeled and sliced
1-2 cloves garlic, peeled and sliced
500 g/1¼ lb tomatoes, skinned, deseeded and chopped
2 spring onions, trimmed and chopped
freshly ground black pepper
225 g/8 oz Mozzarella cheese, thinly sliced
few sprigs of fresh herbs, to garnish

Dry-fry the sesame seeds for about 1 minute until they are lightly browned, shaking the pan frequently. Set aside.

Blanch the beans and courgettes in boiling, salted water for 3 minutes. Drain.

Melt the margarine in a pan, add the onions and garlic and fry gently for 5 minutes until soft. Stir in the tomatoes, bring to the boil and cook, un-covered, for 15 minutes until thickened. Stir in the spring onions and season with salt and pepper, then add the drained beans and courgettes.

Lightly grease an ovenproof dish and preheat the oven to moderate (180°C/350°F, Gas Mark 4).

Spoon a layer of bean and tomato mixture into the bottom of the dish. Cover with a layer of cheese, then another layer of bean and tomato mixture. Continue with these layers until all the ingredients are used up, finishing with a layer of cheese slices.

Bake for 30 to 35 minutes. Sprinkle over the sesame seeds, return to the oven and bake for a further 5 minutes. Serve hot, garnished with sprigs of fresh herbs.
SERVES 6

VEGETABLE PÂTÉ

METRIC/IMPERIAL
450 g/1 lb courgettes, grated
1 tablespoon coarse salt
15 g/½ oz polyunsaturated margarine
1 small onion, peeled and grated or finely chopped
3 cloves garlic, peeled and crushed
2 eggs
150 ml/¼ pint skimmed milk
½ tablespoon herb mustard
2 tablespoons chopped mixed fresh herbs (e.g. chervil, chives, mint, parsley)
freshly ground black pepper
large pinch of cayenne pepper
225 g/8 oz fresh spinach, rinsed and drained
Garnish:
1 medium tomato
few snipped chives
8 tablespoons shredded white cabbage
2 large carrots, scrubbed and grated

Put the courgettes into a colander and sprinkle them with the coarse salt. Leave to drain for 30 minutes. Rinse the courgettes under cold running water, then drain again.

Meanwhile, line a well-greased 1kg/2lb loaf tin with non-stick silicone paper and preheat the oven to moderate (180°C/350°F, Gas Mark 4).

Melt the margarine in a non-stick frying pan, add the onion and garlic and fry over a moderate heat for 3 minutes, stirring occasionally. Add the courgettes, stir well and cook gently for 10 minutes, stirring once or twice. Remove the pan from the heat and leave to cool.

Beat the eggs and milk together. Stir in the

cooled vegetables, the mustard and herbs and season to taste with pepper and cayenne – it should not be too bland.

Pour the mixture into the prepared tin and cover the tin with foil. Stand the tin in a roasting tin and pour in about 4cm/1½inches of cold water. Cook in the oven for 30 minutes. Leave the pâté to cool in the tin.

Strip the stalks from the spinach leaves. Place the spinach in a large saucepan of boiling salted water, cover and cook for 2 minutes. Drain the leaves, and pat dry.

Turn the pâté out on to a dish and peel off the lining paper. Arrange the drained spinach leaves in an attractive pattern on top of the pâté.

Skin the tomato and cut in half. Remove the seeds and cut the tomato flesh into neat slices. Decorate the pâté with the tomato and chives and arrange the cabbage and carrot around it. This pâté is also excellent for picnics and packed lunches. Transport it in a rigid, lidded container and use a separate container for the garnish.
SERVES 6 to 8

PROVENÇAL TARTLETS WITH HERBS

METRIC/IMPERIAL
225 g/8 oz rich wholemeal pastry (see page 334)
175 g/6 oz courgettes, thinly sliced
salt
1 tablespoon olive oil
1 onion, peeled and chopped
1 clove garlic, peeled and crushed
1 red pepper, cored, deseeded and sliced
4 tomatoes, skinned and chopped
1 tablespoon chopped marjoram
1 tablespoon chopped basil
freshly ground black pepper
1 egg
75 ml/3 fl oz single cream
50 g/2 oz Gruyère cheese, grated

Roll out the pastry on a lightly floured surface and use to line 6 × 11cm/4½ inch individual flan tins. Prick the base of each and chill for 20 minutes.

Meanwhile, put the courgette slices in a colander and sprinkle with salt. Leave for 15 minutes to remove some of the moisture, then rinse well, drain and pat dry with kitchen paper.

Cover the pastry cases with foil and fill with baking beans or rice. Bake in a preheated moderately hot oven (200°C/400°F, Gas Mark 6) for 10 minutes. Remove the foil and beans or rice.

Heat the oil in a pan, add the onion and fry until softened. Add the garlic, remaining vegetables, herbs, and salt and pepper to taste. Cover and simmer for 15 minutes, then spoon into the pastry cases.

Beat the egg, cream and cheese together, seasoning with a little salt and pepper, and pour over the filling. Lower the oven temperature to 190°C/375°F, Gas Mark 5, and cook the tartlets for 15 to 20 minutes, until set.
MAKES 6

UNDERGROUND HOT POT

METRIC/IMPERIAL
450 g/1 lb potatoes, peeled and thinly sliced
225 g/8 oz onions, peeled and sliced
225 g/8 oz carrots, peeled and sliced
225 g/8 oz parsnips, peeled and sliced
225 g/8 oz Jerusalem artichokes, peeled and sliced
2 celery stalks, sliced
100 g/4 oz whole peanuts, shelled
100 g/4 oz mature Cheddar cheese, grated
2 tablespoons rosemary leaves
salt
freshly ground black pepper
300 ml/½ pint vegetable stock

Put half the potato slices in the bottom of a 1.75 litre/3 pint casserole dish.

Arrange the remaining vegetables in the dish in layers, sprinkling each layer with the nuts, cheese, rosemary and salt and pepper to taste. Reserve a little cheese for the topping.

Finish with a layer of potatoes arranged neatly in circles on top, then pour on the stock and sprinkle with the reserved cheese. Bake in a preheated moderately hot oven (190°C/375°F, Gas Mark 5) for 1½ hours until the top is browned and the vegetables are tender when pierced with a skewer. Serve hot.
SERVES 4 to 6

Note: Other root vegetables such as turnips, swedes or celeriac may be used. Whole peanuts are usually obtainable but, if not, substitute salted peanuts and do not use extra salt in the recipe.

VEGETABLE GOUGÈRE

METRIC/IMPERIAL
Sauce:
2 teaspoons olive oil
1 onion, peeled and chopped
100 g/4 oz celery, chopped
1 green pepper, cored, deseeded and chopped
1 small cauliflower, cut into small florets
1 clove garlic, peeled and crushed
1 × 400 g/14 oz can tomatoes
salt
freshly ground black pepper
2 bay leaves
Choux paste:
150 ml/¼ pint water
50 g/2 oz polyunsaturated margarine
65 g/2½ oz plain wholemeal flour
salt
freshly ground black pepper
2 eggs, beaten
Topping:
50 g/2 oz Cheddar cheese, grated
25 g/1 oz fresh wholemeal breadcrumbs
20 g/¾ oz walnuts, chopped

To make the sauce, heat the oil in a pan and sauté the onion, celery and pepper for 3 minutes. Add the cauliflower and garlic and cook for a further 3 minutes. Stir in the tomatoes with their juice, salt and pepper and the bay leaves. Bring to the boil, cover and simmer for 20 to 25 minutes.

Meanwhile, preheat the oven to moderately hot (200°C/400°F, Gas Mark 6).

To make the choux paste, place the water and margarine in a pan and bring to the boil. Remove from the heat and quickly add all the flour, beating well with a wooden spoon until the mixture leaves the sides of the pan clean. Cool slightly. Add a little salt and pepper to the eggs, then gradually beat into the flour mixture, blending well. Spoon the choux pastry around the edge of a greased, ovenproof, 23 cm/9 inch flan dish. Remove the bay leaves from the vegetable sauce and spoon into the centre of the pastry.

For the topping, mix together the cheese, breadcrumbs and walnuts then spoon over the vegetables. Cook in the oven for 30 to 40 minutes until well risen and bubbling.
SERVES 4

SPINACH TIMBALE

METRIC/IMPERIAL
4 eggs
300 ml/½ pint skimmed milk
225 g/8 oz frozen, chopped spinach, thawed
50 g/2 oz fresh wholemeal breadcrumbs
50 g/2 oz Cheddar cheese, grated
¼ teaspoon grated nutmeg
salt
freshly ground black pepper
fresh tomato sauce, to serve (see page 341)

Grease a 1.5 litre/2½ pint ovenproof ring mould and preheat the oven to moderate (180°C/350°F, Gas Mark 4).

Beat the eggs and the milk together in a bowl. Stir in the spinach, breadcrumbs, cheese and nutmeg. Season with salt and pepper and pour into the prepared dish. Bake in the oven for about 1 hour (exact time depends on the depth of the dish) until the custard is set and slightly risen. Test with a skewer, which should come out clean. Serve immediately with fresh tomato sauce.

Alternatively, allow the timbale to cool in the dish and serve cold.
SERVES 4

VEGETABLE LOAF

METRIC/IMPERIAL
100 g/4 oz mushrooms, wiped and trimmed
4 stuffed green olives, sliced
25 g/1 oz polyunsaturated margarine
1 large onion, peeled and chopped
100 g/4 oz brown rice, cooked
100 g/4 oz peas, cooked
1 tablespoon tomato purée
1 tablespoon soy sauce
½ teaspoon ground allspice
2 eggs, beaten
2 hard-boiled eggs
Garnish:
sliced tomatoes
shredded lettuce

Preheat the oven to hot (220°C/425°F, Gas Mark 7) and grease a 450 g/1 lb loaf tin. Line the base with greaseproof paper and brush it with oil.

Thinly slice 2 of the mushrooms and arrange them in a line down the centre of the tin. Place a row of sliced stuffed olives on either side.

Melt the margarine in a saucepan. Chop the rest of the mushrooms and add to the pan with the onion, then fry gently until beginning to soften. Remove from the heat and stir in the rice, peas, tomato purée, soy sauce, allspice and beaten eggs. Spoon half the mixture into the loaf tin. Arrange the hard-boiled eggs lengthways in the tin and spoon the rest of the mixture on top, pressing it well down.

Put a piece of greased greaseproof paper on top of the mixture and cook in the oven for 35 to 40 minutes or until firm to the touch. Leave to cool in the tin, then carefully turn it on to a serving plate and garnish with lettuce and tomatoes.
SERVES 4

PIZZA WITH DRIED HERBS

METRIC/IMPERIAL
Dough:
1 teaspoon dried yeast
150 ml/¼ pint lukewarm water
pinch of sugar
225 g/8 oz plain wholemeal flour
½ teaspoon salt
Topping:
300 ml/½ pint thick tomato sauce (see page 340)
1 teaspoon dried oregano
½ teaspoon dried thyme
75-100 g/3-4 oz Mozzarella cheese, coarsely grated
1 tablespoon freshly grated Parmesan cheese

To make the dough, put the yeast in a cup with 2 tablespoons of the warm water and a pinch of sugar. Leave in a warm place for 10 minutes until the liquid is frothy.

Sift the flour with the salt into a large bowl. Stir in the bran remaining in the sieve. Make a depression in the centre of the flour and pour in the yeast liquid and the remaining warm water. Beat with a wooden spoon until it all clings together, adding more water if required, then turn out on to a floured surface and knead for 5 minutes.

Put the dough back into a clean bowl, lightly oiled, and cover it with cling film. Stand the bowl in a warm place for 1 to 1½ hours until the dough has roughly doubled in volume. When the dough has risen sufficiently, knock it back and turn out on to a floured board. Knead again briefly for 2 to 3 minutes and divide into two.

Preheat the oven to hot (220°C/425°F, Gas Mark 7).

Roll each piece of dough out fairly thinly. Pick up each one and pull it gently between the hands to make a large thin round, roughly 25 cm/10 inches across. Lay the 2 circles of dough on oiled baking sheets and cover each one with 150 ml/¼ pint of the thick tomato sauce, spreading it evenly almost up to the edge. Sprinkle over each one ½ teaspoon dried oregano and ¼ teaspoon dried thyme. Scatter half the Mozzarella over each pizza and sprinkle the grated Parmesan on top. Bake for about 12 minutes in the oven or until the edges are browned and the centre lightly coloured.
SERVES 4

VEGETABLE STRUDEL

METRIC/IMPERIAL
2 tablespoons polyunsaturated vegetable oil
1 small onion, peeled and chopped
1 clove garlic, peeled and crushed
1 celery stalk, sliced
100 g/4 oz button mushrooms, wiped and sliced
2 tablespoons plain wholemeal flour
150 ml/¼ pint vegetable stock
1 tablespoon tomato purée
225 g/8 oz tomatoes, skinned and chopped
1 small cauliflower, cooked and roughly chopped
1 tablespoon chopped parsley
¼ teaspoon dried basil
salt
freshly ground black pepper
1 × 375 g/13 oz packet puff pastry, thawed
1 egg, beaten

Heat the oil in a frying pan and sauté the onion, garlic and celery until soft. Add the mushrooms and cook for 1 minute. Add the flour, then gradually stir in the stock and tomato purée. Bring to the boil, stirring.

Remove from the heat, and add the tomatoes, cauliflower and herbs. Season with salt and pepper to taste, then leave to cool.

Roll out the pastry to a 36 cm/14 inch square. Spread the cooked vegetable filling over the pastry, leaving a 2.5 cm/1 inch border around the edge. Brush this border with beaten egg. Fold the pastry in half and press the edges together to seal. Brush the pastry with beaten egg and roll up like a Swiss roll.

Carefully place on a baking tray. Brush with beaten egg to glaze and make several slits along the top of the strudel. Bake in a preheated moderately hot oven (200°C/400°F, Gas Mark 6) for 30 minutes. Cut into slices to serve.
SERVES 4

AUBERGINE CASSEROLE

METRIC/IMPERIAL
450 g/1 lb aubergine, cut into 1 cm/½ inch thick
slices
600 ml/1 pint vegetable stock
2 teaspoons polyunsaturated vegetable oil
100 g/4 oz onions, peeled and finely chopped
2 cloves garlic, peeled and chopped
2 × 400 g/14 oz cans tomatoes
¼ teaspoon dried oregano
¼ teaspoon dried basil
salt
freshly ground black pepper
175 g/6 oz Mozzarella cheese, sliced

Place the aubergine slices in a large pan and cover
with the vegetable stock. Bring to the boil, simmer for 10 minutes and drain.

Heat the oil in a heavy-based frying pan and
cook the onions and garlic in it until lightly
coloured. Add the tomatoes, herbs and seasoning
and cook, stirring occasionally, for about 30
minutes.

Preheat the oven to moderate (180°C/350°F,
Gas Mark 4).

Place alternate layers of aubergine, tomato
sauce and cheese in a large casserole, finishing
with a layer of Mozzarella. Bake in the oven for 30
minutes. Serve with a curly endive salad.
SERVES 4

TOMATO TART

METRIC/IMPERIAL
175 g/6 oz wholemeal cheese pastry
(see page 335)
750 g/1½ lb tomatoes
1 onion, peeled and chopped
1 clove garlic, peeled and chopped
4 sprigs fresh thyme
salt
freshly ground black pepper

Roll out the pastry dough on a lightly floured surface and use to line a 20 cm/8 inch flan dish or flan
ring placed on a baking sheet. Prick the base
lightly with a fork, cover with foil, then weigh
down with baking beans or rice.

Bake in a preheated moderately hot oven
(200°C/400°F, Gas Mark 6) for 15 minutes. Remove the beans or rice and the foil, return the flan
case to the oven and bake for a further 5 minutes.
Meanwhile, make the filling. Skin 450 g/1 lb of

the tomatoes, then chop them roughly. Put the
tomatoes in a pan with the onion, garlic, thyme
and salt and pepper to taste. Cover and simmer
gently until the tomatoes are reduced to a pulp.
Discard the thyme sprigs.

Spread the tomato mixture in the flan case. Slice
the remaining tomatoes and arrange them, overlapping, around the edge of the tart. Return to the
oven and bake for a further 15 minutes. Serve hot
or cold.
SERVES 4 to 6

SPINACH AND PEANUT GALETTE

METRIC/IMPERIAL
polyunsaturated vegetable oil for shallow frying
wholemeal pancake batter (see page 292)
Filling:
1 tablespoon polyunsaturated vegetable oil
1 small onion, peeled and sliced
225 g/8 oz button mushrooms, wiped and sliced
450 g/1 lb frozen spinach, cooked and drained
salt
freshly ground black pepper
Sauce:
25 g/1 oz polyunsaturated margarine
50 g/2 oz shelled peanuts
2 tablespoons plain wholemeal flour
300 ml/½ pint vegetable stock

Heat a little oil in a 15 cm/6 inch frying pan. Pour
in enough batter to coat the bottom of the pan
thinly. Cook until set and golden brown underneath, then turn the pancake and cook the other
side. Repeat with the remaining batter to make 8
pancakes.

To prepare the filling, heat the oil in a pan and
sauté the onion and mushrooms until soft. Stir in
the spinach and season with salt and pepper to
taste. Spread each pancake with a little of the
spinach filling and pile the pancakes on top of one
another in a straight-sided ovenproof dish.

To make the sauce, heat the margarine in a pan
and fry the peanuts until golden brown. Stir in the
flour and cook for 1 minute. Add the stock gradually, stirring constantly. Cook, stirring, until
thickened.

Pour the sauce over the galette and cook in a
preheated moderately hot oven (200°C/400°F,
Gas Mark 6) for 30 minutes. Serve hot.
SERVES 4 to 6

STIR-FRIED VEGETABLES WITH CAMEMBERT

METRIC/IMPERIAL
2 tablespoons polyunsaturated vegetable oil
5 cm/2 inch piece fresh root ginger, peeled and chopped
1 onion, peeled and sliced
3 carrots, scraped and sliced
225 g/8 oz white cabbage, shredded
1 clove garlic, peeled and crushed
1 red pepper, cored, deseeded and sliced
3 heads of chicory, sliced
3 tablespoons soy sauce
2 tablespoons sherry
225 g/8 oz bean-sprouts
175 g/6 oz Camembert cheese, cubed
50 g/2 oz unsalted peanuts

Heat the oil in a large wok or frying pan and stir-fry the ginger, onion and carrots for 5 minutes. Add the cabbage and garlic and stir-fry for 5 minutes. Add the red pepper and chicory and stir-fry for 3 minutes.
Stir in the soy sauce and sherry, cover and cook for 5 minutes, adding the bean-sprouts 1 minute before the end of the cooking time. Stir in the cheese and nuts, heat through and serve.
SERVES 4

VEGETABLE PIE WITH HERB PASTRY

METRIC/IMPERIAL
25 g/1 oz polyunsaturated margarine
175 g/6 oz onions, peeled and sliced
175 g/6 oz carrots, scraped and chopped
225 g/8 oz new potatoes, scrubbed and sliced
225 g/8 oz broad beans, shelled
225 g/8 oz fresh peas, shelled
100 g/4 oz mushrooms, wiped and sliced
225 g/8 oz tomatoes, sliced
1 teaspoon yeast extract
just under 300 ml/½ pint lukewarm water
Herb pastry:
225 g/8 oz plain wholemeal flour
2 teaspoons baking powder
pinch of salt
100 g/4 oz polyunsaturated margarine
2 teaspoons dried mixed herbs
cold water

Melt the margarine in a saucepan, add the onions, carrots and potatoes and gently fry for about 7 minutes, then turn into a large pie dish. Place the beans, peas and mushrooms on top, then arrange the slices of tomato over all. Set aside.
To make the pastry, sift the flour, baking powder and salt together into a mixing bowl, add the margarine and rub in until evenly distributed. Mix in the herbs, then bind the ingredients together with enough cold water to make a soft but not sticky dough. Knead the dough lightly until smooth. Preheat the oven to moderately hot (190°C/375°F, Gas Mark 5).
Dissolve the yeast extract in the water and pour sufficient into the dish to come within 2.5 cm/1 inch of the rim. Roll out the pastry, cut a strip to fit the rim of the pie dish and dampen it. Roll out the remaining pastry to cover the pie and press on to the strip to seal. Cut a hole in the top, then leave in a cool place for 15 minutes. Cook in the oven for 30 minutes, then reduce the temperature to 160°C/325°F, Gas Mark 3, and cook for a further 30 minutes until the pastry is golden.
SERVES 4

TOMATO AND OLIVE PIZZA

METRIC/IMPERIAL
225 g/8 oz wholemeal pizza dough (see page 334)
Topping:
1 tablespoon polyunsaturated vegetable oil
275 g/10 oz onions, peeled and chopped
350 g/12 oz tomatoes, skinned and chopped
½ teaspoon oregano
1 tablespoon tomato purée
50 g/2 oz Cheddar cheese, grated
salt
freshly ground black pepper
15 black olives, halved and stoned

On a lightly floured surface, roll out the dough to a 20 cm/8 inch diameter circle and carefully transfer it to a large greased baking sheet. Preheat the oven to hot (220°C/425°F, Gas Mark 7).
To make the topping, heat the oil in a non-stick frying pan, add the onions and gently fry for about 5 minutes until soft. Stir in the tomatoes and oregano and cook rapidly for 10 minutes or until thick. Season and add the tomato purée.
Spread the mixture over the pizza base to within 1 cm/½ inch of the edges. Sprinkle over the cheese, then arrange the black olive halves on top. Cook in the oven for 12 minutes until the base is cooked and the cheese golden brown.
SERVES 4 to 6

MIXED VEGETABLE TERRINE

METRIC/IMPERIAL
450 g/1 lb fresh spinach, trimmed or 225 g/8 oz frozen spinach
4 tomatoes, thinly sliced
350 g/12 oz potatoes, peeled and coarsely grated
100 g/4 oz mushrooms, trimmed and finely chopped
1 onion, peeled and grated
50 g/2 oz Cheddar cheese, grated
2 tablespoons mixed fresh herbs, finely chopped
2 eggs
2 tablespoons skimmed milk
salt
freshly ground black pepper

Cook the fresh spinach with a minimum of water until soft. Cook frozen spinach as instructed on the packet. Drain thoroughly, chop and set aside.
Preheat the oven to moderate (180°C/350°F, Gas Mark 4). Grease the base and sides of a 900ml/1½ pint soufflé dish and cover with the tomato slices, retaining a few.
Mix together the spinach, potatoes, mushrooms, onion, cheese and herbs, then beat in the eggs and milk. Season with salt and pepper. Turn the mixture into the prepared dish and arrange the remaining tomato slices on top. Cover with foil or a lid and cook in the oven for 1½ hours. Leave the terrine to cool overnight, then turn out and serve in wedges.
SERVES 4

BUTTER BEAN, HERB AND TOMATO SOUFFLÉ

METRIC/IMPERIAL
100 g/4 oz butter beans
600 ml/1 pint water
150 ml/¼ pint semi-skimmed milk
1 large onion, peeled and grated
4 tomatoes, skinned and chopped
1 tablespoon chopped parsley
1 tablespoon chopped thyme
1 teaspoon chopped sage
salt
freshly ground black pepper
4 eggs, separated

Put the beans in a large bowl, cover with the water, then leave to soak overnight. Alternatively, pour over boiling water and soak for several hours. Transfer the beans and water to a pan, then bring to the boil. Lower the heat, cover and simmer for about 1½ hours until the beans are soft, adding more water if necessary.
Drain the beans, return to the rinsed-out pan and mash well. Add the milk and onion, bring to the boil, stirring constantly, and simmer for 1 minute. Remove the pan from the heat, then stir in the tomatoes, herbs and salt and pepper to taste. Stir in the egg yolks and leave to cool slightly.
Beat the egg whites until just stiff, then fold into the bean sauce. Pour the mixture into a 1.5 litre/2½ pint soufflé dish. Bake in a preheated moderate oven (180°C/350°F, Gas Mark 4) for 1 hour until the soufflé has risen and is lightly browned on top. Serve immediately.
SERVES 4 to 6

TANDOORI CUTLETS

METRIC/IMPERIAL
225 g/8 oz black-eye beans, soaked overnight
2 cloves garlic, peeled and crushed
1 tablespoon soy sauce
2 teaspoons tandoori spice mixture
2 tablespoons chopped coriander
8 spring onions, chopped
2 carrots, peeled and grated
salt
freshly ground black pepper
polyunsaturated vegetable oil for shallow frying
Coating:
1 teaspoon tandoori spice mixture
50 g/2 oz wholemeal breadcrumbs

Drain the beans, place in a pan and cover with cold water. Bring to the boil, boil rapidly for 10 minutes, then cover and simmer for 20 to 25 minutes, until tender. Drain well, then mash.
Add the remaining ingredients, with salt and pepper to taste, and mix well. Shape in 8 ovals and flatten to about 1 cm/½ inch thick. Mix the tandoori spice mixture with the breadcrumbs and use to coat the cutlets completely. Fry in hot shallow oil for 4 minutes on each side. Serve hot.
SERVES 4

LENTIL STEW

METRIC/IMPERIAL
3 tablespoons polyunsaturated vegetable oil
2 onions, peeled and chopped
1 clove garlic, peeled and crushed
4 carrots, peeled and sliced
4 celery stalks, sliced
450 g/1 lb tomatoes
1 bay leaf
300 ml/½ pint tomato juice
900 ml/1½ pints water
300 g/11 oz red lentils
2 tablespoons chopped parsley
salt
freshly ground black pepper
chopped parsley, to garnish

Heat the oil in a large pan, add the onions, garlic, carrots and celery and fry for 10 minutes.

Skin the tomatoes and cut into quarters. Add to the pan with the remaining ingredients, seasoning with salt and pepper to taste. Cover and simmer for 50 minutes to 1 hour, stirring occasionally, until the lentils are tender.

Sprinkle with chopped parsley. Serve with crusty wholemeal bread.
SERVES 4

LENTIL RISSOLES

METRIC/IMPERIAL
2 tablespoons polyunsaturated vegetable oil
1 onion, peeled and chopped
2 celery stalks, chopped
2 carrots, peeled and chopped
225 g/8 oz red lentils
600 ml/1 pint water
1 teaspoon ground coriander
salt
freshly ground black pepper
2 tablespoons chopped parsley
175 g/6 oz wholemeal breadcrumbs
2 tablespoons wholemeal flour
1 egg, beaten
polyunsaturated vegetable oil for shallow frying
parsley sprigs, to garnish
Yogurt sauce:
300 ml/½ pint plain low-fat yogurt
1 tablespoon chopped parsley
1 clove garlic, peeled and crushed

Heat the oil in a pan, add the onion, celery and carrots and fry until softened. Add the lentils,

water, coriander, and salt and pepper to taste. Bring to the boil, cover and simmer for 50 minutes to 1 hour, stirring occasionally. Mix in the parsley and one-third of the breadcrumbs. Turn on to a plate to cool.

Using floured hands, shape the mixture into rissoles and coat with the flour. Dip into the beaten egg and coat with the remaining breadcrumbs.

Pour the oil into a frying pan to a depth of 5 mm/¼ inch and place over moderate heat. When hot, add the rissoles and fry until crisp and golden brown, turning once or twice. Drain well.

To make the sauce, mix the yogurt, chopped parsley and garlic together. Serve the rissoles hot, garnished with sprigs of parsley and accompanied by the sauce.
SERVES 4

MEDITERRANEAN LENTIL STEW

METRIC/IMPERIAL
2 tablespoons polyunsaturated vegetable oil
2 onions, peeled and chopped
1 clove garlic, peeled and crushed
2 celery stalks, sliced
4 small courgettes, sliced
4 tomatoes, skinned and quartered
900 ml/1½ pints water or vegetable stock
¼ teaspoon ground coriander
salt
freshly ground black pepper
225 g/8 oz brown lentils
2 tablespoons chopped parsley

Heat the oil in a large pan. Add the onions, garlic, celery and courgettes and fry gently for 10 minutes until lightly browned, stirring the mixture frequently.

Add the tomatoes, water or stock, coriander and salt and pepper to taste. Bring to the boil. Add the lentils, then cover and simmer for 1 to 1½ hours until the lentils are tender.

Alternatively, transfer the ingredients to a casserole, cover and bake in a preheated moderate oven (180°C/350°F, Gas Mark 4) for 1½ hours to 2 hours. Sprinkle with the parsley and serve hot.
SERVES 4

Note: Lentils do not need soaking before cooking, and mixed with vegetables they make a delicious stew in which most of the liquid has been absorbed to give a moist sauce.

LENTIL PATTIES

METRIC/IMPERIAL
2 tablespoons polyunsaturated vegetable oil
1 clove garlic, peeled and crushed
1 onion, peeled and finely chopped
1 celery stalk, chopped
1 carrot, peeled and chopped
225 g/8 oz brown lentils
450 ml/¾ pint water
salt
freshly ground black pepper
4 tablespoons plain wholemeal flour
½ teaspoon ground ginger
½ teaspoon ground cumin
1 teaspoon curry powder
1 tablespoon mango chutney, chopped
polyunsaturated vegetable oil for shallow frying
Dressing:
150 ml/¼ pint plain low-fat yogurt
1 clove garlic, peeled and crushed
1 tablespoon chopped parsley

Heat the oil in a large pan. Add the garlic, onion, celery and carrot and sauté until the vegetables begin to soften.

Add the lentils, water, salt and pepper. Bring to the boil, then lower the heat, cover and simmer for about 1 hour until the lentils are soft and all the liquid is absorbed.

Add 2 tablespoons flour, the spices and chutney to the pan and mix well. Continue to cook gently for 2 to 3 minutes, stirring constantly. Adjust the seasoning, if necessary. Turn the mixture on to a plate and leave until cool enough to handle.

Divide the mixture into 18 equal pieces and form each one into a patty, about 1 cm/½ inch thick. Coat with the remaining flour. Heat a little oil in a frying pan and fry the lentil patties, a few at a time, until crisp and golden brown, turning them once.

Mix together the yogurt, garlic and parsley for the dressing. Serve the patties on a bed of rice, topped with the yogurt dressing.
SERVES 6

LENTIL AND NUT LOAF

METRIC/IMPERIAL
225 g/8 oz red, green or brown lentils
1 onion, peeled and finely sliced
1 carrot, peeled and finely sliced
1 × 400 g/14 oz can tomatoes
200 ml/⅓ pint vegetable stock
100 g/4 oz fresh breadcrumbs
100 g/4 oz chopped nuts
2 eggs, beaten
1 teaspoon curry powder
½ teaspoon cumin seeds
salt
freshly ground black pepper
Sauce:
15 g/½ oz polyunsaturated margarine
15 g/½ oz plain unbleached white flour
300 ml/½ pint skimmed milk
4 tablespoons chopped parsley
1 teaspoon lemon juice
finely grated rind of ½ lemon
freshly ground black pepper
Garnish:
cherry tomatoes
flat-leaf parsley

Wash the lentils and drain well. Place in a pan with the onion, carrot, tomatoes with their juice, and the stock. Bring to the boil, cover and simmer for 30 minutes or until the lentils are soft, adding more liquid if too dry. Cool slightly.

Preheat the oven to moderate (180°C/350°F, Gas Mark 4).

Stir in the breadcrumbs, nuts, eggs, curry powder, cumin, salt and pepper. Mix well and spoon into a greased 1 kg/2 lb loaf tin. Cook in the oven for 1 hour.

To make the sauce, melt the margarine in a saucepan and stir in the flour to make a smooth paste. Gradually incorporate the milk. Stirring on a low heat, bring to the boil. The sauce should thicken, so beat well to ensure it is smooth and glossy. Add the parsley, lemon juice and rind and freshly ground black pepper.

Leave the loaf in the tin for 5 minutes, then turn on to a warmed serving plate. Garnish with cherry tomatoes and flat-leaf parsley and serve hot with the sauce, accompanied by jacket potatoes and courgettes à la Grecque. Alternatively, the loaf may be served cold without the sauce.
SERVES 6

SOYA BEAN MOUSSAKA

METRIC/IMPERIAL
225 g/8 oz soya beans, soaked overnight in cold
water
600 ml/1 pint water
3-4 tablespoons polyunsaturated vegetable oil
2 onions, peeled and chopped
2 celery stalks, trimmed and sliced
1 large carrot, scraped and sliced
100 g/4 oz mushrooms, trimmed and sliced
4 tomatoes, skinned and chopped
1 tablespoon tomato purée
1 teaspoon dried marjoram
salt
freshly ground black pepper
1 bay leaf
750 g/1½ lb aubergines, thinly sliced
chopped parsley, to garnish
Sauce:
25 g/1 oz polyunsaturated margarine
25 g/1 oz plain wholemeal flour
300 ml/½ pint skimmed milk
50 g/2 oz Cheddar cheese, grated
1 egg, beaten
½ teaspoon made mustard

Drain the beans, reserving the water. Make up to
1.2 litres/2 pints with more water. Put the beans
and liquid into a large pan, then bring to the boil.
Skim, then lower the heat, cover and simmer for
about 2 hours until the beans are just tender. Drain
and reserve 300 ml/½ pint cooking liquid.

Heat 1 tablespoon of the oil in a large pan. Add
the onions, celery and carrot and fry gently for 5
minutes. Add the mushrooms and fry for a
further 2 minutes. Stir in the reserved cooking
liquid together with the tomatoes, tomato purée,
marjoram and salt and pepper to taste. Bring to
the boil, stirring constantly. Add the beans and
bay leaf, cover and simmer for 1 hour or until the
beans are tender and most of the liquid has been
absorbed to give a moist mixture. Remove and
discard the bay leaf.

Meanwhile, put the aubergine slices in a colander, sprinkling the layers with salt. Leave for
about 1 hour to allow the water to drain off and remove the bitterness. Rinse under cold running
water to remove the salt, then pat dry.

Preheat the oven to moderate (180°C/350°F,
Gas Mark 4).

Place the aubergine slices in a single layer in the
grill pan. Brush lightly with oil and grill for about
5 minutes until lightly browned, turning once.
Repeat with any remaining aubergine.

Place one-third of the aubergines in a 1.75
litre/3 pint ovenproof dish. Cover with half the
bean mixture, then another third of the aubergines. Spread the remaining bean mixture on top,
then finish with a layer of aubergines.

To make the sauce, melt the margarine in a pan,
add the flour and cook for 1 to 2 minutes, stirring
constantly. Remove from the heat and stir in the
milk gradually. Return to the heat and bring to the
boil, stirring constantly. Simmer for 2 minutes
until thick, then stir in half the cheese and the
beaten egg. Add the mustard and salt and pepper
to taste.

Pour the cheese sauce over the top of the moussaka, then sprinkle with the remaining cheese.
Bake in the preheated oven for 30 minutes until
the topping is browned. Garnish the moussaka
with chopped parsley and serve hot.
SERVES 6

CHICK PEA CURRY

METRIC/IMPERIAL
450 g/1 lb chick peas, soaked overnight
3 tablespoons polyunsaturated vegetable oil
2 onions, peeled and chopped
1 teaspoon chilli powder
2 teaspoons ground cumin
1 teaspoon ground coriander
2 teaspoons chopped root ginger
6 cardamoms, split and seeds removed
2 cloves garlic, peeled and crushed
450 g/1 lb tomatoes, skinned and chopped
2 tablespoons tomato purée
salt
freshly ground black pepper
1 tablespoon chopped coriander or parsley, to
garnish

Drain the chick peas, place in a pan and cover with
cold water. Bring to the boil and simmer for 2
hours. Drain and reserve the liquid.

Heat the oil in a large pan, add the onions and
fry until softened. Add the spices and garlic and
cook for a further 2 minutes. Add the tomatoes,
tomato purée, chick peas, 300 ml/½ pint of the reserved liquid, and salt and pepper to taste.

Cover and simmer gently for 1 hour or until the
peas are tender. Sprinkle with the coriander or
parsley. Serve immediately.
SERVES 6

VEGETARIAN CHICK PEA HOT POT

METRIC/IMPERIAL
225 g/8 oz chick peas, soaked overnight
1 medium aubergine
salt
3 tablespoons polyunsaturated vegetable oil
1 onion, peeled and finely sliced
1-2 cloves garlic, peeled and crushed
2-3 teaspoons garam masala
600 ml/1 pint tomato juice
1 teaspoon yeast extract
50 g/2 oz unsalted peanuts
¼ teaspoon sugar
freshly ground black pepper
1 tablespoon chopped parsley, to garnish

Drain the chick peas and rinse; then place in a pan and cover with cold water and bring to the boil. (You can add 1 teaspoon of the oil with the water, if you like – it helps to prevent it boiling over.) Cook rapidly for 10 minutes, then reduce the heat and simmer for 40 minutes or until the chick peas are soft. Drain and leave aside.

Slice the aubergine and place in a colander. Sprinkle with some salt and leave for 30 minutes; then rinse, drain and dry on kitchen paper.

Heat the oil in a large pan and sauté the onion for 5 minutes. Add the aubergine and garlic and cook for 2 minutes. Stir in the garam masala and cook for 2 minutes. Add the chick peas, tomato juice, yeast extract, peanuts, sugar, salt and pepper. Mix well and bring to the boil. Cover and simmer for 45 minutes.

Check the seasoning then transfer to a warmed serving dish and sprinkle with the chopped parsley. Serve with a mixed salad.
SERVES 4

PEANUT AND MUSHROOM ROAST

METRIC/IMPERIAL
3 tablespoons polyunsaturated vegetable oil
1 onion, peeled and chopped
2 celery stalks, chopped
2 cloves garlic, peeled and crushed
225 g/8 oz peanut kernels, ground
100 g/4 oz wholemeal breadcrumbs
225 g/8 oz potato, peeled, boiled and mashed
1 egg, beaten
1 tablespoon soy sauce
1 tablespoon tomato purée

2 tablespoons chopped parsley
salt
freshly ground black pepper
225 g/8 oz mushrooms, sliced
coriander leaves, to garnish

Heat 1 tablespoon of the oil in a pan, add the onion, celery and garlic and fry until softened.

Mix the peanuts and breadcrumbs together in a bowl. Add the fried vegetables, potato, egg, soy sauce, tomato purée, parsley, and salt and pepper to taste, and mix thoroughly.

Heat the remaining oil in a pan, add the mushrooms and fry for 2 minutes, stirring.

Grease a 1 kg/2 lb loaf tin and press in half the nut mixture. Cover with the mushrooms, then press the remaining nut mixture on top.

Cover with foil and bake in a preheated moderate oven (180°C/350°F, Gas Mark 4) for about 1 hour. Leave in the tin for 5 minutes, then turn out. Garnish with coriander and serve at once.
SERVES 4 to 6

NUT AND VEGETABLE LOAF

METRIC/IMPERIAL
15 g/½ oz polyunsaturated margarine
1 small onion, peeled and chopped
1 small carrot, scraped and chopped
1 celery stalk, trimmed and chopped
2 teaspoons tomato purée
225 g/8 oz tomatoes, skinned and chopped
2 eggs
1 teaspoon dried thyme
salt
freshly ground black pepper
100 g/4 oz nuts, chopped or minced
Garnish:
onion rings
chopped parsley

Grease a 450 g/1 lb loaf tin and preheat the oven to hot (220°C/425°F, Gas Mark 7).

Melt the margarine and gently fry the onion, carrot and celery until soft, then add the tomato purée and tomatoes and cook for 5 minutes.

Put the eggs into a bowl with the thyme. Season with salt and pepper and beat well. Stir in the nuts and then the vegetable mixture and transfer to the loaf tin. Bake in the oven for 25 to 30 minutes. Turn out and garnish with onion rings and parsley.
SERVES 4

HERB AND NUT ROAST

METRIC/IMPERIAL
100 g/4 oz hazelnuts
100 g/4 oz wholemeal bread, cubed
100 g/4 oz polyunsaturated margarine
450 g/1 lb onions, peeled and chopped
1 tablespoon yeast extract
100 g/4 oz unsalted cashews or peanuts
2 tablespoons chopped parsley
2 tablespoons chopped mixed herbs
salt
freshly ground black pepper

Put the hazelnuts in a blender, reserving about 12 whole ones. Add the bread and grind coarsely.

Melt the margarine in a large pan, add the onions and fry gently for 10 minutes until soft. Stir in the yeast extract.

Remove from the heat, then stir in the ground nuts and bread, cashews or peanuts, herbs, and salt and pepper to taste.

Press the mixture into a 900 ml/1½ pint pie dish or casserole. Press the reserved nuts into the top. Bake in a preheated moderate oven (180°C/350°F, Gas Mark 4) for 40 minutes until lightly browned on top. Serve hot.
SERVES 4 to 6

BRAZIL NUT LOAF

METRIC/IMPERIAL
225 g/8 oz shelled Brazil nuts
100 g/4 oz wholemeal bread, cubed, with crusts
1 tablespoon polyunsaturated vegetable oil
100 g/4 oz lean bacon, derinded and chopped (optional)
2 onions, peeled and chopped
1 clove garlic, peeled and crushed
1 tablespoon chopped parsley
1 tablespoon chopped thyme
salt
freshly ground black pepper
1 egg
1 teaspoon Worcestershire sauce

Put the nuts and bread in a blender and grind coarsely.

Heat the oil in a pan, add the bacon (if using), onions and garlic and fry gently for 4 to 5 minutes until soft. Remove the pan from the heat, then add the ground nuts and bread, chopped parsley and thyme, and salt and pepper to taste. Mix well. Beat the egg with the Worcestershire sauce, then

add to the nut mixture and bind thoroughly. Press the mixture into a lightly greased 450 g/ 1 lb loaf tin and level the surface. Bake in a preheated moderately hot oven (190°C/375°F, Gas Mark 5) for 40 minutes until the top is crisp and lightly browned.

Turn the loaf out on to a serving dish and serve hot. Alternatively, leave to cool in the tin, then turn out and serve cold with sliced tomatoes.
SERVES 4 to 6

WALNUT AND CHEESE BURGERS

METRIC/IMPERIAL
175 g/6 oz shelled walnuts
50 g/2 oz wholemeal bread, cubed
100 g/4 oz Cheddar cheese, grated
1 onion, peeled and grated
salt
freshly ground black pepper
1 egg
1 tablespoon tomato purée
polyunsaturated vegetable oil for shallow frying
Garnish:
tomato slices
watercress sprigs

Put the nuts in a blender, reserving 50 g/2 oz for the coating. Add the bread and grind coarsely. Transfer to a bowl, add the cheese, onion, and salt and pepper to taste, and stir well. Beat the egg with the tomato purée. Add to the nut mixture and stir until well combined.

Divide the mixture into 4 on a lightly floured surface. Shape into burgers, about 8 cm/3½ inches in diameter and 1 cm/½ inch thick. Chop the reserved walnuts and press into both sides of the burgers.

Heat a little oil in a frying pan, add the burgers and fry for about 5 minutes until browned on both sides, turning once. Alternatively, place the burgers on a lightly greased baking sheet and bake in a preheated moderately hot oven (200°C/400°F, Gas Mark 6) for 20 minutes until browned.

Serve hot or cold, garnished with tomatoes and watercress.
SERVES 4

BEAN AND PEANUT LOAF

METRIC/IMPERIAL
1 × 225 g/8 oz packet sage and onion stuffing mix
250 ml/8 fl oz boiling water
1 × 450 g/16 oz can baked beans
salt
freshly ground black pepper
1 egg, beaten
2 tablespoons single cream
75 g/3 oz peanuts, chopped
Topping:
1 tomato, sliced
parsley sprigs

Grease and line the bottom of a 1 kg/2 lb loaf tin.
Mix the stuffing mix with the boiling water, then stir in the baked beans, salt, pepper, egg, cream and nuts. Spoon the mixture into the loaf tin and level the top. Cover with greased foil and bake in a preheated moderately hot oven (190°C/375°F, Gas Mark 5) for 45 minutes.
Carefully turn out the loaf on to a serving dish and serve hot or cold, topped with tomato slices and parsley.
SERVES 6

Variation
If liked, add 100 g/4 oz grated Cheddar cheese.

BASIC WHOLEMEAL PANCAKES

METRIC/IMPERIAL
100 g/4 oz plain wholemeal flour
1 egg
300 ml/½ pint semi-skimmed milk
salt
freshly ground black pepper
sunflower oil for frying

Sift the flour into a bowl and make a well in the centre, add the egg and half the milk and beat until smooth. Beat in the remaining milk.
Heat a little oil in a 15 cm/6 inch heavy-based frying pan, running it around the base and sides of the pan until hot. Pour off any surplus. Pour in just enough batter to thinly coat the base of the pan. Cook for 1 to 2 minutes until golden brown, then turn and cook the other side. Transfer the pancake to a plate and keep warm. Repeat with the remaining batter.
MAKES 8

LEEK AND POTATO RAMEKINS

METRIC/IMPERIAL
175 g/6 oz potato, roughly chopped
100 g/4 oz potato, diced
2 eggs
8 tablespoons single cream
2 tablespoons skimmed milk
100 g/4 oz leeks, thinly sliced, blanched and drained
freshly grated nutmeg

Boil the chopped potatoes, then drain and mash. Mix with the diced potato, eggs, cream and skimmed milk. Stir in the leeks, nutmeg and seasoning. Grease 4 ramekin dishes and spoon in the mixture. Bake in a preheated moderate oven (180°C/350°F, Gas Mark 5) for 20 to 25 minutes until golden brown.
SERVES 4

LEEK AND THYME QUICHE

METRIC/IMPERIAL
50 g/2 oz plain white flour
50 g/2 oz wholemeal flour
pinch of salt
pinch of cayenne pepper
50 g/2 oz polyunsaturated margarine
ice-cold water
Filling:
200 g/7 oz leeks, trimmed and thinly sliced
3 eggs
150 ml/¼ pint skimmed milk
50 g/2 oz Cheddar cheese, finely grated
salt
cayenne pepper
2 teaspoons chopped thyme

Place the flours in a bowl with the salt and cayenne. Rub the margarine into the flour until the mixture resembles fine breadcrumbs. Stir in 2 teaspoons of cold water at a time until the dough is firm.
Lightly knead the pastry on a floured board. Roll out and use to line 4 individual tins, 7.5cm/3 inches in diameter. Chill for 20 minutes while making the filling.
Blanch the leeks in boiling salted water for 2 minutes, then drain and dry on kitchen paper towels. Mix the eggs, milk, cheese, salt, cayenne and thyme together. Divide the leeks into 4

portions and arrange in the bottom of the pastry cases. Spoon over the egg mixture.

Bake in a preheated moderately hot oven (200°C/400°F, Gas Mark 6) for 20 to 25 minutes or until set and golden brown. Serve hot or cold.
SERVES 4

RATATOUILLE PIES

METRIC/IMPERIAL
50 g/2 oz wholemeal flour
50 g/2 oz plain white flour
pinch of salt
ice-cold water
Filling:
15 g/½ oz polyunsaturated margarine
1 medium onion, thinly sliced
1 small aubergine, diced
1 courgette, thinly sliced
2 tomatoes, skinned, deseeded and chopped
½ green pepper, deseeded and chopped
1 tablespoon tomato purée
salt
freshly ground black pepper
2 teaspoons coriander seeds

Place the flours in a bowl and mix together with the salt. Add 2 teaspoons cold water at a time to give a firm dough. Knead lightly. Roll out and use to line 4 × 7.5 cm/3 inch individual flan tins. Prick the bottoms and chill for 30 minutes.

Melt the margarine in a saucepan, add the onion and aubergine and cook gently for 10 minutes. Stir in the courgette, tomatoes, pepper and tomato purée. Add seasoning and the coriander seeds. Bring to the boil, cover and simmer for 2 minutes.

Line the pastry cases with foil or greaseproof paper and beans and bake in a preheated moderately hot oven (200°C/400°F, Gas Mark 6) for 12 to 15 minutes until golden brown. Remove the foil or paper and cook for a further 2 to 3 minutes. Spoon in the filling and serve hot or cold.
SERVES 4

VEGETABLE CURRY

METRIC/IMPERIAL
1 tablespoon polyunsaturated vegetable oil
2 teaspoons ground coriander
1½ teaspoons ground cumin
½ teaspoon turmeric
½ teaspoon ground ginger
2 large cloves garlic, peeled and thinly sliced

100 g/4 oz carrots, peeled and sliced diagonally
4 spring onions, chopped
2 celery stalks, sliced diagonally
2 leeks, washed and sliced
3 courgettes, sliced
1 small cauliflower, broken into florets
300 ml/½ pint stock
150 ml/¼ pint plain low-fat yogurt
25 g/1 oz cashew nuts

Heat the oil in a saucepan, add the spices and cook for 5 minutes without browning. Add the garlic, carrots, spring onions and celery. Cook for 2 minutes, then add the leeks, courgettes and cauliflower. Pour over the stock, bring to the boil, and simmer gently for 8 to 10 minutes. Stir in the yogurt and heat gently, without boiling. Sprinkle with cashew nuts and serve at once.
SERVES 4

LAYERED VEGETABLE MOULD

METRIC/IMPERIAL
225 g/8 oz fresh asparagus, trimmed
175 g/6 oz carrots, peeled and thinly sliced
175 g/6 oz small turnips, peeled and thinly sliced
4-6 canned artichoke hearts, sliced
175 g/6 oz courgettes, thinly sliced
100 g/4 oz French beans, halved
2 teaspoons agar powder dissolved in 600 ml/1 pint vegetable stock
2 tablespoons dry sherry
1 tablespoon chopped parsley
1 tablespoon chopped basil

Blanch and drain all the fresh vegetables. Mix the liquid agar with the sherry and fresh herbs. Spoon a thin layer over the base of a 1 kg/2 lb loaf tin or terrine and chill until set. Spoon each of the selection of vegetables in the agar liquid, then arrange in layers in the terrine, pouring a thin layer of agar over each time. Set each layer in the refrigerator. Continue layering until all the vegetables and agar liquid are used, finishing with the agar. Chill well.

To turn out, quickly dip the terrine in a bowl of boiling water, then invert onto a serving dish. Garnish with parsley and basil, if desired.
SERVES 4

DESSERTS

SPICED CRANBERRY AND APPLE PIE

METRIC/IMPERIAL
Pastry:
175 g/6 oz plain wholemeal flour
50 g/2 oz light soft brown sugar
1 tablespoon ground mixed spice
100 g/4 oz polyunsaturated margarine
50 g/2 oz chopped nuts
1 egg, beaten
Filling:
450 g/1 lb cooking apples, peeled, cored and
sliced
finely grated rind and juice of 1 orange
225 g/8 oz cranberries
50 g/2 oz fructose

To make the pastry dough, put the flour, sugar
and spice into a bowl and mix well. Add the margarine in pieces and rub into the flour until the
mixture resembles breadcrumbs.

Stir in the nuts, then 2 tablespoons of beaten
egg and mix to a firm dough. Turn out on to a
lightly floured surface and knead lightly, then
cover and chill until required.

To make the filling, put all the ingredients in a
bowl and mix well. Spoon into a 900 ml/1½ pint
pie dish.

Roll out the dough on the lightly floured surface to a shape 2.5 cm/1 inch larger than the circumference of the pie dish. Cut a 1 cm/½ inch strip
of dough from around the edge and press it on to
the moistened rim of the pie dish. Moisten the
strip, then place the large piece of dough on top.
Press firmly to seal, then trim and flute the edge.
Decorate the top of the pie with the trimmings
and make a slit in the centre. Brush with the remaining beaten egg.

Bake in a preheated moderately hot oven
(200°C/400°F, Gas Mark 6) for 30 to 40 minutes
until the pastry is crisp and brown. Serve hot.
SERVES 4 to 6.

RHUBARB CRUMBLE

METRIC/IMPERIAL
450 g/1 lb rhubarb, wiped clean and cut into
2.5 cm/1 inch chunks
1 tablespoon fructose
juice of 1 orange
Crumble:
100 g/4 oz plain wholemeal flour
50 g/2 oz polyunsaturated margarine
50 g/2 oz light soft brown sugar
finely grated rind of 1 orange

Preheat the oven to moderately hot (200°C/400°F,
Gas Mark 6). Put the rhubarb into a 900 ml/
1½ pint ovenproof pie dish. Sprinkle over the
fructose, then pour over the orange juice.

To make the crumble, put the flour in a bowl,
then rub in the margarine. Stir in the brown sugar
and grated orange rind, then spoon on top of the
rhubarb to cover it completely.

Bake in the oven for 30 minutes or until the
crumble is crisp and brown. Serve hot.
SERVES 4

WHOLEWHEAT CRÊPES

METRIC/IMPERIAL
100 g/4 oz self-raising wholemeal flour
1 egg, beaten
300 ml/½ pint skimmed milk
4 tablespoons clear honey
50 g/2 oz seedless raisins
pinch of grated nutmeg
polyunsaturated vegetable oil for frying

Put the flour in a bowl and make a well in the
centre. Pour in the egg and milk and beat well to
give a smooth batter.

Mix the honey, raisins and nutmeg in a separate
bowl.

Heat a little oil in a 20 cm/8 inch frying pan.
When the oil is hot, quickly pour in enough batter
to coat the bottom of the pan thinly, tilting the
pan to spread the batter evenly. Cook until the top

of the batter is set and the underside is golden brown. Turn and cook the other side.

Slide on to a warm plate, cover and keep warm by standing the plate over a pan of hot water. Continue until all the batter has been used up, making 8 crêpes in all.

Spread each crêpe with a spoonful of the honey mixture, then fold to form wedge-shaped parcels. Serve immediately.

SERVES 4

PLUM AND ORANGE COBBLER

METRIC/IMPERIAL

Filling:
450 g/1 lb Victoria plums
juice of 2 oranges
1 orange, peel and pith removed and divided into segments
3 tablespoons honey

Scones:
225 g/8 oz plain wholemeal flour
1 teaspoon ground mixed spice
2 teaspoons baking powder
½ teaspoon salt
25 g/1 oz polyunsaturated margarine
25 g/1 oz light soft brown sugar
finely grated rind of 1 orange
150 ml/¼ pint plain low-fat yogurt or skimmed milk
skimmed milk or beaten egg, to glaze

To make the filling, place the plums in a baking dish. Add the orange juice and segments and spoon over the honey.

To make the scones, put the flour, spice, baking powder and salt in a bowl and stir well. Rub in the margarine, then stir in the sugar and orange rind. Add the yogurt or milk and mix to a soft dough.

Turn the dough out on to a lightly floured surface and roll out to about 1 cm/½ inch thickness. Cut out 8 to 10 rounds with a 4 cm/1½ inch biscuit cutter, then arrange them, overlapping, around the edge of the dish. Brush with a little milk or beaten egg.

Bake in a preheated hot oven (220°C/425°F, Gas Mark 7) for about 15 minutes until the scones are risen and brown and the plums are just tender when pierced with a skewer. Serve hot.

SERVES 4

BLACK PEAR PUDDING

METRIC/IMPERIAL
4 pears, peeled, cored and sliced
100 g/4 oz blackberries
finely grated rind and juice of 1 lemon
75 g/3 oz soft brown sugar
50 g/2 oz polyunsaturated margarine
1 large egg, beaten
100 g/4 oz plain wholemeal flour
1 teaspoon ground cinnamon
2 teaspoons baking powder
1 tablespoon skimmed milk

Put the pears and blackberries in a 900 ml/1½ pint pie dish. Sprinkle over the lemon rind and juice and 2 tablespoons sugar.

Cream the margarine and remaining sugar together until pale and fluffy. Beat in the egg with a little of the flour and the cinnamon.

Fold in the remaining flour, the baking powder and milk to give a soft dropping consistency, then spread the mixture over the fruit and level the surface. Bake in a preheated moderate oven (180°C/350°F, Gas Mark 4) for 45 minutes until the topping is risen and brown. Serve hot.

SERVES 4

HARLEQUIN SOUFFLÉ

METRIC/IMPERIAL
175 g/6 oz mixed dried fruit
450 ml/¾ pint water
finely grated rind and juice of 1 lemon
25 g/1 oz soft brown sugar
4 egg whites

Put the dried fruit in a bowl, pour over the water and lemon rind and juice and leave to soak overnight. Alternatively, pour over boiling water and soak for a few hours.

Transfer to a pan and bring to the boil. Lower the heat, cover and simmer for 30 minutes or until the fruit is tender. Drain and reserve the liquid.

Remove any stones from the fruit. Make up the liquid to 150 ml/¼ pint with water, if necessary, then work the fruit and liquid to a smooth purée in a blender. Stir in the sugar and leave to cool.

Beat the egg whites until just stiff, then fold into the purée. Pour into a 1.5 litre/2½ pint soufflé dish. Bake in a preheated moderately hot oven (200°C/400°F, Gas Mark 6) for 20 minutes until risen and lightly browned. Serve immediately.

SERVES 4

SULTANA CHEESECAKE

METRIC/IMPERIAL
75 g/3 oz strudel paste (see page 335)
2 teaspoons polyunsaturated vegetable oil
Filling:
175 g/6 oz curd or sieved cottage cheese
1 egg, separated
1 teaspoon lemon juice
25 g/1 oz fructose
1½ tablespoons plain unbleached white flour
2 tablespoons plain low-fat yogurt
50 g/2 oz sultanas

Preheat the oven to moderate (160°C/325°F, Gas Mark 3).
Cut three 25 cm/10 inch squares of strudel paste. Brush each lightly with oil. Press evenly over the bottom and sides of an oiled, fluted 18-20 cm/7-8 inch round flan dish. Turn over the surplus paste into the flan dish to make a neat edge and brush well with the remaining oil.
Soften the cheese in a large mixing bowl. Beat in the egg yolk, lemon juice, fructose, flour and yogurt. Fold in the sultanas. Whisk the egg white until stiff. Fold lightly but thoroughly into the cheese mixture. Spoon the mixture into the prepared tin and smooth the surface.
Bake in the oven for 30 to 40 minutes or until firm but still spongy to the touch. Serve at once.
SERVES 6

FRUIT SEMOLINA SOUFFLÉ

METRIC/IMPERIAL
450 g/1 lb fresh fruit (rhubarb, gooseberries, apples)
2 tablespoons soft brown sugar
600 ml/1 pint skimmed milk
5 tablespoons wholemeal or white semolina
1 egg, separated
grated nutmeg

Wash and chop the fruit, then place in a pan with a tablespoon of sugar. Cover and simmer for 10 minutes or until the fruit is soft. Spoon into a greased 1.2 litre/2 pint ovenproof dish.
Heat the milk until just coming to the boil. Sprinkle over the semolina and remaining sugar. Cook, stirring, until it thickens, then continue to cook for 1 minute. Stir in the egg yolk and allow to cool slightly.

Whisk the egg white until stiff and fold into the semolina. Spoon on top of the fruit and sprinkle with the nutmeg. Bake in a preheated moderate oven (180°C/350°F, Gas Mark 4) for 20 minutes until risen and golden.
SERVES 4

WHOLEMEAL FRUIT QUICHE

METRIC/IMPERIAL
Filling:
50 g/2 oz prunes, stoned
grated rind of 1 orange
1 × 300 g/11 oz can mandarins in natural juice
2 eggs, beaten
150 ml/¼ pint plain low-fat yogurt
15 g/½ oz light soft brown sugar
Pastry:
100 g/4 oz plain wholemeal flour
50 g/2 oz polyunsaturated margarine
1 tablespoon water

Wash and chop the prunes and place in a bowl with the orange rind and the juice drained from the mandarins. Leave to soak for a few hours.
To make the pastry, place the flour in a bowl and rub in the fat until the mixture resembles fine breadcrumbs. Add the water and mix to a stiff dough. Turn on to a floured surface and knead until smooth. Roll out to line an 18 cm/7 inch flan dish. Line with foil and baking beans and bake in a preheated moderately hot oven (190°C/375°F, Gas Mark 5) for 10 minutes. Remove the foil and beans and return to the oven for 5 minutes. Remove from the oven and cool.
Drain the prunes and place in the pastry case with the mandarins, reserving a few pieces for decoration.
Beat the eggs, yogurt and sugar and pour over the fruit. Bake for 30 to 40 minutes until the pastry is crisp and the filling set. Serve decorated with the remaining mandarins.
SERVES 4 to 6

CRUNCHY FRUIT COMPOTE

METRIC/IMPERIAL
225 g/8 oz mixed dried fruit (apricots, peaches, prunes, etc)
150 ml/¼ pint water
1 tablespoon honey
juice of ½ lemon
40 g/1½ oz polyunsaturated margarine
2 tablespoons Demerara sugar
75 g/3 oz muesli
low-fat plain yogurt, to serve

Place the dried fruits in a bowl with enough water to cover and leave to soak overnight. The next day, drain the fruit well, then place in a saucepan with the 150 ml/¼ pint water, the honey and lemon juice. Bring to the boil, cover and cook gently until the fruits are tender, about 20 minutes.

Transfer to an ovenproof dish. Melt the margarine in a small saucepan and stir in the sugar and muesli. Sprinkle this mixture over the fruit and place under a preheated hot grill until golden. Serve warm with plain yogurt.
SERVES 2

BLACKBERRY AND ORANGE STUFFED APPLES

METRIC/IMPERIAL
4 large cooking apples
225 g/8 oz blackberries
finely grated rind and juice of 1 large orange
4 tablespoons light soft brown sugar
1 tablespoon chopped mint

Remove the cores from the apples, making a large hole for the stuffing. Make a shallow cut through the skin around the centre of each apple to prevent the skins bursting.

To make the stuffing, mix the blackberries with the orange rind, sugar and mint. Place the apples in a baking dish and divide the stuffing equally between the apples, pressing it well down into the centres. Spoon any remaining stuffing around the apples, then spoon over the orange juice.

Bake in a preheated moderate oven (180°C/350°F, Gas Mark 4) for 45 minutes or until the apples are tender. Serve hot.
SERVES 4

FIGGY APPLES

METRIC/IMPERIAL
4 large cooking apples
1 tablespoon clear honey
75 g/3 oz dried figs, chopped
1 tablespoon lemon juice
4 tablespoons apple juice

Remove the cores from the apples, making a large hole for the stuffing. Make a shallow cut round the middle of each apple.

Place the honey, figs and lemon juice in a small pan and heat gently, stirring, until well blended. Use to fill the apple cavities, pressing down firmly.

Place the stuffed apples in an ovenproof dish and pour over the apple juice. Bake in a preheated moderate oven (180°C/350°F, Gas Mark 4) for 45 to 55 minutes until soft. Serve hot with plain low-fat yogurt.
SERVES 4

BAKED GRAPEFRUIT SOUFFLÉ

METRIC/IMPERIAL
finely grated rind of 2 large grapefruit.
25 g/1 oz polyunsaturated margarine
25 g/1 oz plain unbleached white flour
juice of 1 large grapefruit
1 grapefruit, peel and pith removed and divided into segments
25 g/1 oz fructose
4 egg yolks
5 egg whites

Put the grapefruit rind and margarine in a pan and heat gently until the margarine has melted. Stir in the flour, then the grapefruit juice. Bring to the boil, stirring constantly to give a thick smooth sauce.

Add the grapefruit segments and simmer for 1 minute. Stir in the fructose, then remove from the heat and leave to cool slightly.

Beat the egg yolks into the grapefruit sauce. Beat the egg whites until stiff, then fold gently into the grapefruit mixture.

Pour at once into a lightly greased 1.5 litre/2½ pint soufflé dish. Bake in a preheated moderate oven (180°C/350°F, Gas Mark 4) for 45 minutes until the soufflé is well risen, set and a light golden brown. Serve immediately.
SERVES 4

DRIED FRUIT SALAD

METRIC/IMPERIAL
175 g/6 oz dried apricots
100 g/4 oz dried prunes
100 g/4 oz dried figs
100 g/4 oz dried apples
600 ml/1 pint apple juice
2 tablespoons Calvados or brandy
25 g/1 oz walnuts, coarsely chopped

Place the dried fruits in a bowl with the apple juice and leave to soak overnight.

Transfer to a saucepan and simmer for 10 to 15 minutes. Turn into a glass bowl, pour over the Calvados or brandy and sprinkle with the walnuts. Serve hot with plain low-fat yogurt.
SERVES 6

Note: This fruit salad can be made in advance and served cold. Alternatively, serve hot or cold with sesame snaps (page 333) instead of walnuts.

CHERRY CUSTARD PUDDING

METRIC/IMPERIAL
350 g/12 oz cherries, stoned
50 g/2 oz polyunsaturated margarine
25 g/1 oz fructose
finely grated rind and juice of 1 large lemon
2 eggs, separated
300 ml/½ pint skimmed milk
50 g/2 oz self-raising flour
½ teaspoon ground cinnamon

Put the cherries in a baking dish.

Cream together the margarine, fructose and lemon rind until pale and fluffy. Beat in the egg yolks, a little at a time, then stir in the milk, lemon juice, flour and cinnamon to give a loose, curd-like mixture.

Beat the egg whites until just stiff, then fold into the mixture and spoon on top of the cherries.

Place the dish in a roasting tin, then pour in enough hot water to come halfway up the sides of the tin. Bake in a preheated moderate oven (180°C/350F, Gas Mark 4) for 40 to 45 minutes until the top is set, firm and golden. Serve hot.
SERVES 4

HOT FRUIT COMPOTE

METRIC/IMPERIAL
175 g/6 oz dried apricots
450 ml/¾ pint dry cider
3 tablespoons clear honey
150 ml/¼ pint water
1 cinnamon stick
2 cloves
50 g/2 oz seedless raisins
1 large grapefruit, peel and pith removed and divided into segments
2 bananas, peeled and cut into chunks

Soak the apricots in the cider for 2 to 3 hours.

Place the apricots, cider, honey, water, cinnamon and cloves in a large pan. Bring to the boil, then lower the heat, cover and simmer gently for 15 to 25 minutes, until the apricots are just soft. Add the raisins and continue to simmer for a further 5 minutes.

Discard the cinnamon stick and cloves. Add the grapefruit segments and banana chunks to the pan and heat through gently. Serve warm, with yogurt if liked.
SERVES 4

GOOSEBERRY AND ALMOND CRUMBLE

METRIC/IMPERIAL
450 g/1 lb gooseberries, topped and tailed
1 tablespoon fructose
finely grated rind and juice of 1 orange
Crumble:
100 g/4 oz plain wholemeal flour or rolled oats
50 g/2 oz polyunsaturated margarine
50 g/2 oz light soft brown sugar
50 g/2 oz blanched almonds, flaked or chopped

Put the gooseberries in a 900 ml/1½ pint pie dish. Sprinkle over the fructose, then pour over the orange juice, reserving the rind for the crumble.

To make the crumble, put the flour or oats in a bowl, then rub in the margarine. Stir in the brown sugar, almonds and reserved orange rind, then spoon on top of the gooseberries to cover them completely.

Bake in a preheated moderately hot oven (200°C/400°F, Gas Mark 6) for 30 minutes until the crumble is crisp and browned on top. Serve hot with plain yogurt.
SERVES 4

HOT BERRY SNOW

METRIC/IMPERIAL
450 g/1 lb mixed red berries (strawberries,
raspberries, red currants), hulled and stalks
removed
1 tablespoon honey
150 ml/¼ pint plain low-fat yogurt
2 eggs, separated
1 tablespoon plain flour
25 g/1 oz ground almonds
2 tablespoons light soft brown sugar

Wash the fruit and place in a baking dish. Spoon
over the honey.
Put the yogurt in a bowl and beat in the egg
yolks, flour and almonds. Beat the egg whites
until stiff, then fold into the yogurt mixture.
Spoon over the fruit and sprinkle with the sugar.
Bake in a preheated moderately hot oven
(200°C/400°F, Gas Mark 6) for 15 to 20 minutes
until the topping is risen and golden brown.
SERVES 4

BLACKBERRY AND APPLE COBBLER

METRIC/IMPERIAL
750 g/1½ lb cooking apples, peeled, cored and
sliced
1 tablespoon fructose
4 tablespoons water
225 g/8 oz blackberries, cleaned
Topping:
225 g/8 oz wholemeal flour
2 teaspoons baking powder
pinch of salt
25 g/1 oz polyunsaturated margarine
1 tablespoon fructose
150 ml/¼ pint skimmed milk
skimmed milk, to glaze

Preheat the oven to hot (220°C/425°F, Gas Mark
7) and place a shelf near the top.
Put the apples into a saucepan with the fructose
and water. Poach until softened, then add the
blackberries and cook for a further 3 minutes.
Pour the cooked fruit into a 1.2 litre/2 pint ovenproof pie dish.
To make the topping, put the flour, baking
powder and salt into a bowl and rub in the fat,
until the mixture resembles fine breadcrumbs.
Stir in the fructose and enough milk to bind the
mixture together. (It should not be wet.)

Turn the dough on to a lightly floured board
and roll out to a thickness of 1 cm/½ inch. Cut out
rounds with a 4 cm/1½ inch fluted cutter. Arrange
the scone rounds, overlapping, around the edge of
the pie dish and glaze with a little milk.
Bake in the oven for 10 to 15 minutes until the
topping is golden brown.
SERVES 4

DANISH BLACKCURRANT PUDDING

METRIC/IMPERIAL
350 g/12 oz blackcurrants, washed and stalks
removed
1 dessert apple, peeled and diced
25-50 g/1-2 oz light soft brown sugar
Topping:
50 g/2 oz polyunsaturated margarine
75 g/3 oz fresh wholemeal breadcrumbs
50 g/2 oz rolled oats
25 g/1 oz light soft brown sugar
½ teaspoon ground cinnamon

Place the fruit in a greased 750 ml/1¼ pint ovenproof dish. Sprinkle the sugar over and mix well.
To make the topping, melt the margarine in a
pan and add the remaining ingredients. Cook,
stirring, over a medium heat until the mixture
becomes toasted and crisp (about 6 to 8 minutes).
Spoon over the fruit and bake in a preheated moderate oven (180°C/350°F, Gas Mark 4) for 25
minutes. Serve hot with plain low-fat yogurt.
SERVES 4

ROSY PEARS

METRIC/IMPERIAL
4 large firm pears, peeled
250 ml/8 fl oz orange juice
120 ml/4 fl oz red wine
20-30 cardamom seeds, crushed
light soft brown sugar

Preheat the oven to moderately hot (200°C/400°F,
Gas Mark 6).
Place the pears in an ovenproof dish and pour
on the orange juice and red wine with the cardamom seeds. Bake in the oven for about 30
minutes, or until tender. Taste the juice for sweetness and, if desired, add a little sugar. Serve hot or
chilled with the strained sauce.
SERVES 4

DATE AND APPLE PANCAKES

METRIC/IMPERIAL

wholemeal pancake batter made with 100 g/4 oz wholemeal flour (see page 292)

Filling:

25 g/1 oz polyunsaturated margarine
450 g/1 lb dessert apples, peeled, cored and sliced
25 g/1 oz Muscovado sugar
½ teaspoon ground mixed spice
75 g/3 oz dates, stoned and chopped

To finish:

2 tablespoons clear honey
25 g/1 oz flaked almonds, roasted

Brush a small non-stick frying pan with a little oil. Pour in a little batter and tilt the pan to coat it evenly. Cook until the underside is brown, then turn over and cook for 10 seconds. Transfer to a plate and keep warm. Continue cooking pancakes in this way until all the batter is used up.

To make the filling, melt the margarine in a pan and add the apples, sugar, mixed spice and dates. Cook gently, stirring frequently, for 10 to 15 minutes until the apples are tender.

Place a little of the filling on each pancake, roll up and arrange in an ovenproof dish. Warm the honey and spoon over the pancakes to glaze. Bake in a preheated moderate oven (180°C/350°F, Gas Mark 4) for 15 to 20 minutes until heated through. Sprinkle with the almonds before serving.

SERVES 4

FRENCH ORANGE FLANS

METRIC/IMPERIAL

Pastry:

175 g/6 oz plain wholemeal flour
50 g/2 oz light soft brown sugar
1 tablespoon ground mixed spice
100 g/4 oz polyunsaturated margarine
2 tablespoons beaten egg

Topping:

2 small, thin-skinned oranges, thinly sliced
2 tablespoons clear honey

Filling:

1 egg, beaten
50 g/2 oz ground almonds
2 teaspoons fructose

To make the pastry dough, put the flour, sugar and spice in a bowl and mix well. Add the marga-

rine in pieces and rub into the flour until the mixture resembles breadcrumbs. Add the beaten egg and mix to a firm dough. Turn out on to a lightly floured surface and knead lightly. Cover and chill in the refrigerator until required.

To make the topping, put the orange slices in a pan and simmer for about 30 minutes until the peel is tender. Drain.

Divide the dough into 4 pieces. Roll out on a lightly floured surface and use to line individual flan rings, about 10 cm/4 inches in diameter. Alternatively, roll out 4 × 10 cm/4 inch circles and place on a baking sheet. Line the dough with foil, then fill with baking beans or rice. Bake in a preheated moderately hot oven (200°C/400°F, Gas Mark 6) for 15 minutes, then remove the beans or rice and foil.

To make the filling, put the egg, almonds and fructose in a bowl and beat well to mix. Spread in the bottom of the flan cases, then arrange the orange slices on top, overlapping each other Spoon over the honey. Bake the flans in a moderate oven (180°C/350°F, Gas Mark 4) for 20 minutes. Serve hot or cold.

SERVES 4

APPLE STRUDEL

METRIC/IMPERIAL

Dough:

75 g/3 oz strudel paste, sufficient to make 2 × 25 cm/10 inch squares (see page 335)

Filling:

275 g/10 oz cooking apples, peeled, cored and coarsely grated
25 g/1 oz raisins
25 g/1 oz currants
1 tablespoon fructose
¼ teaspoon ground cinnamon
2 teaspoons finely grated lemon rind
1 teaspoon polyunsaturated vegetable oil

Warm a rolling pin, and flour a large clean tea towel. Roll the dough on the towel according to the instructions on page 335, then leave it to rest for 15 minutes, covered with a damp cloth.

Mix all the filling ingredients together and spread on the dough to within 2.5 cm/1 inch of the edges. Brush the edges with a little water. Lift the 2 corners of the tea towel nearest to you and roll the dough away from you. Pinch the edges of the strudel to seal. Place the dough on a greased baking sheet and form into a horseshoe.

Brush all over with the oil. Bake in a preheated

moderately hot oven (200°C/400°F, Gas Mark 6) for about 20 minutes, then reduce the temperature to 180°C/350°F, Gas Mark 4 for a further 30 minutes. Serve warm or cold, cut into slices, with plain low-fat yogurt, if liked.
SERVES 4

WALNUT PIE

METRIC/IMPERIAL
Pastry:
175 g/6 oz plain wholemeal flour
100 g/4 oz polyunsaturated margarine
50 g/2 oz light soft brown sugar
1 tablespoon ground mixed spice
2 tablespoons beaten egg
Filling:
2 eggs, separated
100 g/4 oz light soft brown sugar
100 g/4 oz walnut halves, chopped
finely grated rind and juice of 1 lemon
few walnut halves, to decorate

To make the pastry dough, put the flour in a bowl, then rub in the margarine until the mixture resembles breadcrumbs. Stir in the sugar and spice, then the egg. Mix to a firm dough.

Turn the dough out on to a lightly floured surface, then roll out and use to a line a 20 cm/8 inch flan dish or flan ring placed on a baking sheet. Line the dough with foil, then fill with baking beans or rice. Bake in a preheated moderately hot oven (200°C/400°F, Gas Mark 6) for 15 minutes, then remove the foil and beans or rice.

Meanwhile, make the filling: beat the egg yolks and sugar together until light and creamy. Stir in the walnuts and lemon rind and juice. Beat the egg whites until just stiff, then fold into the walnut mixture.

Pour the filling into the flan case. Bake in a preheated moderate oven (180°C/350°F, Gas Mark 4) for 30 minutes until lightly browned and risen. Decorate the pie with walnut halves and serve hot or cold.
SERVES 6

PEARS IN CASSIS

METRIC/IMPERIAL
300 ml/½ pint medium or sweet white wine
100 g/4 oz blackcurrants, washed and stalks removed
4 tablespoons honey
1 cinnamon stick
2 strips lemon rind
4-6 pears
1 teaspoon arrowroot

Pour the wine into a pan, then add the blackcurrants, honey, cinnamon and lemon rind. Heat gently until the honey has dissolved, then bring to the boil. Boil for 1 minute.

Peel the pears, leaving the stalks attached. Put the pears in the pan, covering them as much as possible in the wine mixture. Cover the pan and cook gently for about 20 minutes until the pears are tender, turning occasionally. Lift the pears carefully out of the pan and transfer to a serving bowl. Discard the cinnamon stick and lemon rind.

Blend the arrowroot with a little cold water, then pour into the wine mixture. Bring to the boil, then lower the heat and simmer for 1 minute until the sauce thickens, stirring constantly. Pour over the pears. Serve hot or cold.
SERVES 4 to 6

SPICED FRUIT COMPOTE

METRIC/IMPERIAL
450 g/1 lb mixed dried fruit (apples, apricots, figs, peaches, pears, prunes, sultanas, etc)
300 ml/½ pint orange juice
300 ml/½ pint water
1 cinnamon stick
2 cloves
50 g/2 oz blanched slivered almonds
plain low-fat yogurt, to serve (optional)

Put the dried fruit in a bowl and pour over the orange juice and water. Add the spices and leave to soak overnight. Alternatively, pour over boiling juice and water and soak for a few hours.

Transfer to a pan and bring to the boil. Lower the heat, cover and simmer for about 20 minutes or until the fruit is tender, adding more water if the syrup becomes absorbed. Remove the spices.

Sprinkle with the slivered almonds and serve warm or cold with low-fat yogurt, if liked.
SERVES 4 to 6

LEMON FLUMMERY

METRIC/IMPERIAL
300 ml/½ pint water
25 g/1 oz polyunsaturated margarine
grated rind and juice of 1 lemon
25 g/1 oz plain unbleached white flour
25 g/1 oz fructose
1 egg, separated

Place the water, margarine and lemon rind in a saucepan and bring to the boil, stirring to melt the fat. Mix the flour and fructose in a bowl. Gradually stir in the hot liquid. Add a little of this mixture to the egg yolk and mix well, then stir into the remaining mixture. Return to the saucepan and cook gently for 5 minutes, stirring.

Pour the mixture into a bowl and stir in the lemon juice. Beat the egg white until stiff and fold into the mixture. Serve hot or cold with fruit.

SERVES 4

STUFFED PEACHES

METRIC/IMPERIAL
4 large peaches
juice of 2 oranges
2 tablespoons red currant jelly
1 cinnamon stick
2 cloves
½ teaspoon whole allspice
Filling:
1 egg, lightly beaten
50 g/2 oz ground almonds
1 tablespoon finely chopped preserved ginger
1 tablespoon light soft brown sugar

Cut the peaches in half and remove the stones. Scoop out and reserve some of the flesh from the centre of each peach half to allow room for the filling.

To make the filling, put the egg in a bowl with the almonds, ginger, sugar and reserved peach flesh. Mix well, then spoon into the peach halves. Place the peaches in a baking dish.

Put the orange juice, red currant jelly and spices in a small pan. Heat gently until the jelly has dissolved, then bring to the boil. Pour over the peaches.

Bake in a preheated moderate oven (180°C/350°F, Gas Mark 4) for about 20 minutes until the peaches are tender when pierced with a skewer. Serve hot or cold.

SERVES 4

RHUBARB, ORANGE AND GINGER FOOL

METRIC/IMPERIAL
450 g/1 lb rhubarb, trimmed and chopped
finely grated rind and juice of 1 orange
4 tablespoons light soft brown sugar
150 ml/¼ pint skimmed milk
1 egg, lightly beaten
1 tablespoon cornflour
2 teaspoons fructose
¼ teaspoon vanilla essence
150 ml/¼ pint plain low-fat yogurt
1 tablespoon finely chopped preserved ginger
few orange slices, to decorate

Put the rhubarb in a pan with the orange rind and juice and the brown sugar. Cover and simmer gently for 10 to 15 minutes until tender. Mash the rhubarb to a pulp by beating vigorously with a wooden spoon, or work to a purée in an electric blender. Leave to cool.

Heat the milk to just below boiling point. Put the egg in a bowl with the cornflour, fructose and vanilla essence. Beat lightly, then gradually stir in the hot milk. Pour the mixture back into the pan and bring to the boil slowly, stirring constantly. Cook, stirring, until the custard thickens.

Leave to cool, stirring occasionally to prevent a skin from forming, then whisk in the yogurt. Stir the custard into the rhubarb purée with the chopped ginger.

Spoon into a large serving bowl or individual dishes or glasses. Chill in the refrigerator, then decorate with orange slices before serving. Serve chilled.

SERVES 4

STRAWBERRY AND ORANGE SOUFFLÉ

METRIC/IMPERIAL
450 g/1 lb strawberries, hulled
4 eggs, separated
65 g/2½ oz fructose
finely grated rind and juice of 1 large orange
15 g/½ oz gelatine
150 ml/¼ pint plain low-fat yogurt
25 g/1 oz flaked almonds, toasted and chopped
1 orange, peeled and segmented, to decorate

Mash the strawberries or work to a purée in an electric blender, reserving a few whole ones for decoration.

Put the egg yolks in a bowl with the fructose, orange rind and half the juice. Stand the bowl over a pan of gently simmering water and whisk until the mixture is thick and pale. Remove from the heat and continue whisking until cool.

Pour the remaining orange juice into a small cup and sprinkle the gelatine on top. Stand the cup in a pan of hot water and stir until the gelatine has dissolved.

Stir the strawberry purée into the egg mixture with the yogurt and mix well. Stir in the dissolved gelatine. Leave in a cool place until thick and just beginning to set. Beat the egg whites until just stiff and fold into the mixture.

Tie a double-thickness of greaseproof paper around a 900 ml/1½ pint soufflé dish so that it stands 5 cm/2 inches above the rim of the dish. Pour in the soufflé mixture. Chill in the refrigerator for at least 2 hours before serving.

Remove the paper collar carefully and press the chopped nuts around the side. Decorate the top with the reserved strawberries and the orange segments.
SERVES 4 to 6

Note: This soufflé has a strong natural flavour as no cream is used to mask the fresh flavour of the strawberries and orange. The yogurt also adds to the tangy, refreshing taste.

MINTED APPLE SNOW

METRIC/IMPERIAL
1 kg/2 lb cooking apples, peeled, cored and sliced
finely grated rind and juice of 1 orange
3 tablespoons honey
4 large mint sprigs
2 large egg whites

Put the apples in a pan, then add the orange rind and juice and the honey. Add the mint, reserving the top leaves for decoration. Cover and cook gently for about 15 minutes until the apples are cooked to a pulp, stirring occasionally.

Discard the mint, then beat the pulp vigorously with a wooden spoon until smooth. Alternatively, rub through a sieve or work to a purée in an electric blender. Leave to cool.

Beat the egg whites until stiff, then fold into the apple purée. Spoon into a serving bowl or individual dishes or glasses. Decorate with the reserved mint leaves. Serve chilled.
SERVES 4

RED CURRANT SNOW WITH MINT

METRIC/IMPERIAL
2 egg whites
300 ml/½ pint plain low-fat yogurt
1 tablespoon fructose
450 g/1 lb red currants, stalks removed
2 tablespoons chopped mint

Beat the egg whites until they form stiff peaks. Beat the yogurt until it is smooth. Mix the egg whites with the yogurt, folding them together lightly with a metal spoon. Stir in the fructose and fold in the red currants. Stir in the chopped mint and serve soon after making.
SERVES 4

RASPBERRY CHANTILLY

METRIC/IMPERIAL
450 g/1 lb raspberries
2 tablespoons Grand Marnier or other liqueur
2 egg whites
150 ml/¼ pint plain low-fat yogurt
grated rind of ½ lemon
2 teaspoons fructose
25 g/1 oz flaked almonds, toasted

Put the raspberries in 4 glasses and spoon over the liqueur. Just before serving, beat the egg whites until stiff. Fold in the yogurt carefully with the lemon rind and fructose. Spoon over the raspberries and sprinkle with the almonds.
SERVES 4

ORANGE AND PRUNE CRUNCH

METRIC/IMPERIAL
175 ml/6 fl oz plain low-fat yogurt
¼ teaspoon ground ginger
2 large oranges
75 g/3 oz cooked prunes, stoned and chopped
50 g/2 oz muesli
honey, to serve

Combine the yogurt and the ginger. Remove the skin, pith and membrane from the oranges and slice finely. Mix the orange slices with the yogurt, chopped prunes and muesli. Spoon into individual dishes and serve with honey to sweeten.
SERVES 4

LAYERED SUMMER PUDDING

METRIC/IMPERIAL
750 g/1½ lb soft fruits (e.g. raspberries,
blackcurrants, red currants, strawberries),
hulled and stems removed, with a few reserved
to decorate
25 g/1 oz light soft brown sugar
5 tablespoons water
1 tablespoon sherry
6 slices wholemeal bread, crusts removed
1 teaspoon powdered gelatine
2 tablespoons soft fruits, to decorate

Place the fruit in a pan with the sugar and water.
Simmer gently for 15 minutes until the fruit is
soft. Stir in the sherry and allow to cool. Strain off
some of the juice and reserve about two-thirds.

In a 1.2 litre/2 pint glass dish or flat-bottomed
mould, layer the fruit and bread. Dissolve the
gelatine in the reserved juice according to the
packet instructions. Spoon the mixed juice and
gelatine over the top layer of bread. Cover with
foil and chill in the refrigerator overnight.

Remove the foil, and then carefully turn out the
pudding on to a dish. Arrange the reserved fruits,
chopped and whole, on top of the pudding.
SERVES 4 to 6

ALMOND AND STRAWBERRY MALAKOFF

METRIC/IMPERIAL
18 sponge fingers
finely grated rind and juice of 2 oranges
2 tablespoons sherry
Filling:
100 g/4 oz polyunsaturated margarine
100 g/4 oz light soft brown sugar
225 g/8 oz curd cheese
175 g/6 oz ground almonds
350 g/12 oz strawberries

Line the bottom of a 15 × 7 cm/6 × 3 inch round
cake tin with greased greaseproof paper or non-
stick parchment. Trim one end off the sponge
fingers so they fit the depth of the tin; reserve the
trimmings.

Mix the orange juice with the sherry. Dip in the
sponge fingers, one at a time, for a few seconds to
soften slightly, then arrange them, rounded end
down, around the edge of the tin. Reserve any remaining juice for the filling.

To make the filling, beat together the margarine and sugar until light and creamy. Add the
cheese, ground almonds, orange rind and reserved juice and beat well. Set aside about one-
third of the strawberries; slice the remainder.

Spread one-third of the almond mixture in the
bottom of the tin. Cover with half the sliced
strawberries and sponge trimmings. Spread
another third of the almond mixture on top, then
the remaining sliced strawberries and sponge
trimmings. Finish with the remaining almond
mixture and level the surface. Cover with a small
plate or saucer, place a weight on top, then chill in
the refrigerator for at least 4 hours until firm.

To serve, invert the malakoff on to a serving
plate and decorate the top with the reserved
strawberries.
SERVES 6

HAZELNUT AND RASPBERRY TORTE

METRIC/IMPERIAL
Torte:
4 eggs, separated
100 g/4 oz light soft brown sugar
100 g/4 oz shelled hazelnuts, coarsely ground
Filling:
450 g/1 lb cooking apples, peeled, cored and
sliced
finely grated rind and juice of ½ lemon
225 g/8 oz raspberries
50 g/2 oz light soft brown sugar
Decoration:
150 ml/¼ pint plain low-fat yogurt
few whole hazelnuts

To make the torte, beat the egg yolks and sugar
together until thick and creamy. Beat the egg
whites until just stiff. Fold the ground hazelnuts
and egg whites carefully into the egg yolk and
sugar mixture.

Line the bottoms of 2 greased 23 cm/9 inch
sandwich tins with greased greaseproof paper or
non-stick parchment. Divide the mixture equally
between the tins and level the surface.

Bake the torte in a preheated moderate oven
(180°C/350°F, Gas Mark 4) for 30 minutes until
risen and firm to touch. Leave in the tins until
cold; do not turn out on to a wire rack or the cakes
will stick.

To make the filling, put the apples in a pan with
the lemon rind and juice, raspberries and sugar.
Cook for 10 to 15 minutes until pulpy, stirring

occasionally. Remove from the heat and beat until smooth, or rub through a sieve for a smoother texture. Leave to cool.

Meanwhile, place a sieve over a bowl and line with a piece of muslin. Pour in the yogurt and leave to drain for about 3 hours until most of the liquid has drained through, leaving the yogurt with a smooth, creamy consistency in the sieve.

To assemble the torte, lift the cakes carefully out of the tins and peel off the paper. Place one cake on a serving plate and spread with the filling mixture. Cover with the other cake, then pipe the creamy yogurt in rosettes on the top. Decorate with whole hazelnuts.

SERVES 6 to 8

GRAPE JELLY

METRIC/IMPERIAL
15 g/½ oz powdered gelatine
3 tablespoons cold water
150 ml/¼ pint boiling water
450 ml/¾ pint grape juice
225 g/8 oz seedless white grapes, washed and peeled
350 g/12 oz cottage cheese
120 ml/4 fl oz skimmed milk
mint leaves, to decorate

Sprinkle the gelatine over the cold water in a heat-proof bowl and leave for a few minutes until spongy. Place the bowl in a saucepan of hot water and stir until the gelatine is dissolved.

Remove from the heat and stir in the boiling water and grape juice.

Allow to cool slightly, then pour the mixture into 6 tall glasses.

Reserve a few grapes for decoration and divide the remainder equally among the glasses. Tilt the glasses and leave in a cool place to set at an angle.

Process the cottage cheese in a blender until smooth, or press through a fine sieve. Stir in the milk. Top each of the glasses with a portion of the cheese mixture and decorate with the reserved grapes and mint leaves. Chill.

SERVES 6

BRAMBLE MOUSSE

METRIC/IMPERIAL
450 g/1 lb blackberries, washed and stalks removed
225 g/8 oz cooking apples, peeled, cored and sliced
finely grated rind and juice of 1 orange or lemon
4 tablespoons light soft brown sugar
15 g/½ oz powdered gelatine
2 tablespoons water
150 ml/¼ pint plain low-fat yogurt
2 egg whites

Put the blackberries in a pan, reserving a few for decoration. Add the apples, orange or lemon rind and juice and the sugar. Cover and heat gently for 10 to 15 minutes until the fruit is soft, stirring occasionally. Rub through a sieve into a bowl.

Sprinkle the gelatine over the water in a small cup and leave until spongy. Stand the cup in a pan of hot water and stir until the gelatine has dissolved. Stir the gelatine into the fruit purée with the yogurt and mix well. Leave in a cool place until thick and just beginning to set.

Beat the egg whites until just stiff, then fold into the mousse. Transfer to a large serving bowl or individual dishes or glasses. Chill in the refrigerator until set, then decorate with the reserved blackberries. Serve chilled.

SERVES 4 to 6

SUNSHINE FRUIT SALAD

METRIC/IMPERIAL
juice of 2 large oranges
juice of 1 lemon
2 tablespoons Cointreau, Grand Marnier or other liqueur (optional)
225 g/8 oz strawberries, hulled and halved
2 large peaches
2 large bananas
2 passion fruit or pomegranates

Put the orange and lemon juices in a serving bowl, then stir in the liqueur (if using). Add the strawberries.

Cut the peaches in half, remove the stones, then slice the flesh. Peel and slice the bananas. Cut the passion fruit or pomegranates in half, then scoop out the flesh with the seeds. Add the prepared fruit to the strawberries and fold gently to coat with the juice. Serve chilled.

SERVES 4

FIGS IN SHERRIED YOGURT

METRIC/IMPERIAL
12 fresh figs
3 tablespoons chopped shelled pistachios
6 dried apricots, finely chopped
pinch of mixed spice
1 teaspoon grated orange rind
75 ml/3 fl oz plain low-fat yogurt
1 tablespoon medium-dry sherry
Decoration:
split pistachios
thin strips of orange peel

Make a criss-cross cut in the top of each fresh fig, and open each one out slightly. Mix the pistachios, apricots, spice and orange rind together; press some of this mixture gently into the centre of each fig.

Mix the yogurt with the sherry and put a spoonful on to 4 dessert plates; carefully arrange three stuffed figs on each plate. Scatter the split pistachios over the top and arrange the strips of orange peel at the edge of each plate.
SERVES 4

TRADITIONAL SUMMER PUDDING

METRIC/IMPERIAL
750 g/1½ lb mixed berry fruit (e.g. loganberries, blackcurrants, red currants, blackberries, strawberries, raspberries), hulled and stalks removed
150 ml/¼ pint water
25 g/1 oz fructose
8 slices slightly stale wholemeal bread, crusts removed
150 ml/¼ pint plain low-fat yogurt, to decorate

Put the fruit and water into a heavy pan with the fructose and cook gently for 10 minutes. If using strawberries or raspberries, add them after the rest of the fruit has been cooked. Strain the fruit, reserving the cooking juice.

Cut a circle from one of the slices of bread to line the base of a 900 ml/1½ pint pudding basin. Cut sufficient wedges of bread to line the sides of the basin, reserving any scraps to fill gaps in the bread lining.

Dip each piece of this bread into the reserved juice and line the basin. Fill with half the fruit, place another layer of bread on top, then spoon in the rest of the fruit and top with another layer of bread. Spoon over any remaining fruit juice. Put a plate that just fits inside the basin's rim on the pudding and put several heavy weights on top. Chill overnight.

Place a sieve over a bowl and line with muslin. Pour in the yogurt and leave to drain for about 3 hours until most of the liquid has drained through, leaving the yogurt in the sieve with a smooth, creamy consistency.

To serve, turn the pudding on to a dish and spoon or pipe yogurt on top to decorate.
SERVES 6

WATERMELON WITH HONEY

METRIC/IMPERIAL
1 small watermelon
2 tablespoons clear honey
juice of ½ lemon
2 tablespoons sherry
25 g/1 oz flaked almonds, roasted

Scoop the flesh out of the watermelon, discarding the seeds, and cut into cubes.

Mix together the honey, lemon juice and sherry, then fold in the melon. Chill for 1 hour.

Spoon into glasses and sprinkle with the almonds to serve.
SERVES 4

POLYNESIAN PAWPAW SALAD

METRIC/IMPERIAL
1 pawpaw
juice of ½ lime
1 pink-fleshed grapefuit
lime slices, to decorate

Cut the pawpaw into quarters and remove the seeds. Peel and slice into a glass bowl. Pour over the lime juice.

Peel the grapefruit, removing all pith, and cut into segments. Add to the bowl and chill until required.

Decorate with lime slices to serve.
SERVES 4

APRICOT JELLY

METRIC/IMPERIAL
225 g/8 oz dried apricots, soaked overnight
juice of ½ lemon
1-2 tablespoons clear honey
15 g/½ oz powdered gelatine
3 tablespoons water

Place the apricots in a pan with the liquid in which they were soaked, adding more water, if necessary, to cover. Simmer for 20 to 30 minutes until tender.

Place the apricots and liquid in a blender with the lemon juice and honey and blend until smooth. Add water to make up to 750 ml/1¼ pints, if necessary.

Sprinkle the gelatine over the water in a small heatproof bowl and leave until spongy. Place the bowl in a pan of hot water and stir until dissolved. Stir into the apricot mixture.

Pour into a 900 ml/1½ pint ring mould and chill until set. Dip the mould quickly into hot water to loosen and turn out on to a serving dish.
SERVES 4 to 6

LIME AND MANGO PARFAIT

METRIC/IMPERIAL
475 ml/¾ pint fresh mango purée
finely grated rind of 2 limes
juice of 1 lime
2 tablespoons light soft brown sugar
50 ml/2 fl oz Quark
2 tablespoons powdered gelatine
3 tablespoons water
2 egg whites
twists of lime peel, to decorate

Mix the mango purée with the lime rind and juice, brown sugar and Quark.

Put the gelatine and water into a small bowl and set aside for 1 minute; stand the bowl in a pan of hot water and leave until the gelatine has dissolved, about 3 minutes.

Stir the dissolved gelatine into the mango mixture and leave on one side until it starts to thicken.

Beat the egg whites until stiff but not dry; fold lightly but thoroughly into the semi-set mango mixture. Spoon into tall glasses and decorate with twists of lime peel. Chill in the refrigerator for 1 hour before serving.
SERVES 4 to 6

ORANGE SNOW EGGS

METRIC/IMPERIAL
3 eggs, separated
300 ml/½ pint plain low-fat yogurt
75 g/3 oz light soft brown sugar
finely grated rind of 1 orange
about 300 ml/½ pint skimmed milk
peeled segments of 2 oranges

Beat the egg yolks with the yogurt, half the sugar and the orange rind; pour into a shallow ovenproof dish. Stand the dish in a roasting tin and add hot water to come halfway up the sides. Bake in a preheated moderate oven (160°C/325°F, Gas Mark 3) for about 20 to 25 minutes, until just set. Remove from the oven and let cool.

Heat the skimmed milk gently in a frying pan. Beat the egg whites until stiff but not dry, and then beat in the remaining brown sugar. Slide spoonfuls of the meringue mixture into the simmering milk; poach gently for 3 to 4 minutes, turning the meringues once. Drain briefly on paper towels.

Arrange the orange segments on top of the cooled custard and then arrange the cooked meringues on the top. Serve this dessert within 1 hour of finishing.
SERVES 4

PRUNE MOUSSE

METRIC/IMPERIAL
225 g/8 oz dried prunes, stoned
50 g/2 oz Muscovado sugar
300 ml/½ pint plain low-fat yogurt
1 teaspoon lemon juice
15 g/½ oz powdered gelatine
3 tablespoons water
150 ml/¼ pint whipping cream, whipped
25 g/1 oz chopped walnuts, to decorate

Cover the prunes with water, bring to the boil and simmer for 20 minutes until soft. Sieve, or work in an electric blender with a little of the cooking liquid until smooth; leave to cool. Stir in the sugar, yogurt and lemon juice.

Sprinkle the gelatine over the water in a small heatproof bowl and leave until spongy. Place the bowl in a pan of hot water and stir until dissolved. Cool slightly, then fold into the prune mixture with the cream. Pour into ramekins and chill until set. Decorate with the walnuts to serve.
SERVES 6

GINGERED PEAR AND YOGURT MOUSSE

METRIC/IMPERIAL
1 kg/2 lb pears, peeled, cored and chopped
finely grated rind and juice of 1 lemon
¼ teaspoon ground ginger
3-4 pieces preserved ginger in syrup
2 eggs, separated
300 ml/½ pint plain low-fat yogurt
15 g/½ oz powdered gelatine
2 tablespoons water

Put the pears in a pan with the lemon rind and juice, ginger and 2 tablespoons syrup from the preserved ginger. Cover and cook gently for 10 to 15 minutes until the pears are tender, stirring occasionally. Take out the preserved ginger; chop one of the pieces, slice the remainder and set aside.

Put the pears and juice, egg yolks and yogurt in a blender and blend to a smooth purée. Alternatively, rub the pears and juice through a sieve, then beat in the egg yolk and yogurt.

Sprinkle the gelatine over the water in a small cup and leave until spongy. Stand the cup in a pan of hot water and stir until the gelatine has dissolved. Stir into the pear purée, with the chopped ginger. Leave in a cool place until thick and just beginning to set.

Beat the egg whites until stiff, then fold into the mixture. Spoon into 6 individual glasses or dishes and chill in the refrigerator until set. Decorate with slices of preserved ginger. Serve chilled.
SERVES 6

COMPOTE OF PEARS

METRIC/IMPERIAL
4 large Williams pears, peeled, cored and quartered
2 tablespoons light soft brown sugar
½ tablespoon chopped sweet Cicely

Pour a little cold water into a large, heavy-based saucepan to just cover the bottom and lay the pears in it. Add the sugar and bring to the boil, then lower the heat, cover the pan and simmer gently until the pears are tender when pierced with a skewer.

Carefully transfer the pears to a serving dish. Stir the sweet Cicely into the syrup, pour over the pears and set aside to cool for 1 to 2 hours. Serve with yogurt.
SERVES 4

STRAWBERRY CHEESECAKE

METRIC/IMPERIAL
50 g/2 oz polyunsaturated margarine, melted
100 g/4 oz digestive biscuits, crushed
25 g/1 oz Muscovado sugar
350 g/12 oz curd cheese
4 tablespoons clear honey
150 ml/¼ pint plain low-fat yogurt
grated rind and juice of 1 lemon
15 g/½ oz powdered gelatine
3 tablespoons water
3 egg whites
225 g/8 oz strawberries, to decorate

Combine the melted margarine, biscuit crumbs and sugar. Press the mixture over the base of a 20 cm/8 inch loose-bottomed cake tin and place in the refrigerator for 20 minutes until firm.

Place the cheese in a bowl and mix in the honey, yogurt, lemon rind and juice. Beat until smooth. Sprinkle the gelatine over the water in a small heatproof bowl and leave until spongy. Place the bowl in a pan of hot water and stir until dissolved. Stir into the cheese mixture.

Whisk the egg whites until stiff, then fold lightly into the cheese mixture. Spoon over the biscuit base and chill for 2 to 3 hours until set.

Remove the cheesecake from the tin and arrange the strawberries on top.
SERVES 6 to 8

RASPBERRY AND HAZELNUT CRUNCH

METRIC/IMPERIAL
75 g/3 oz polyunsaturated margarine
100 g/4 oz wholemeal breadcrumbs
75 g/3 oz Muscovado sugar
50 g/2 oz hazelnuts, chopped and roasted
350 g/12 oz raspberries

Melt the margarine in a frying pan, add the breadcrumbs and cook until golden. Cool, then stir in the sugar and hazelnuts.

Set aside 4 raspberries for decoration. Divide half the remainder between individual glass dishes and cover with half the crumbs; repeat the layers.

Top with the reserved raspberries and serve chilled, with plain low-fat yogurt.
SERVES 4

ORANGE AND LEMON MOUSSE

METRIC/IMPERIAL
4 large eggs, separated
100 g/4 oz light soft brown sugar
finely grated rind and juice of 2 lemons
finely grated rind and juice of 2 oranges
15 g/½ oz powdered gelatine
150 ml/¼ pint plain low-fat yogurt

Put the egg yolks and sugar in a bowl. Add the lemon rind and juice, orange rind and half of the orange juice.

Pour the remaining orange juice into a small cup and sprinkle on the gelatine. Stand the cup in a pan of hot water and stir until the gelatine has dissolved.

Stand the bowl with the egg yolk mixture over a pan of gently simmering water and whisk until the mixture is thick and pale. Remove from the heat and continue whisking until cool.

Stir the yogurt into the mixture with the dissolved gelatine. Leave in a cool place until thick and just beginning to set.

Beat the egg whites until just stiff, then fold into the mousse. Pour into a serving bowl and chill in the refrigerator for at least 2 hours before serving. Serve chilled.

Alternatively, pour into a 900 ml/1½ pint soufflé dish tied with a collar of greaseproof paper so that the mousse will set above the rim of the dish. Remove the collar carefully before serving.
SERVES 4 to 6

APRICOT WHIP

METRIC/IMPERIAL
225 g/8 oz dried apricots, soaked overnight
275 g/10 oz plain low-fat yogurt
2 egg whites
2 tablespoons Muscovado sugar
1 tablespoon flaked almonds, toasted

Place the apricots in a pan with the water in which they were soaked. Bring to the boil and simmer for 20 minutes until soft. Sieve, or work in a blender with a little of the cooking liquid until smooth. Leave to cool, then stir in the yogurt.

Whisk the egg whites until stiff, then whisk in the sugar a little at a time. Fold into the apricot mixture and spoon into glasses. Sprinkle with the almonds and chill until required.
SERVES 6

HONEY MINT FRUIT

METRIC/IMPERIAL
8 dried apricots, chopped
2 dessert pears, peeled, cored and chopped
2 bananas, peeled and thickly sliced
2 red dessert apples, cored and sliced
2 pineapple rings, chopped
2 teaspoons lemon juice
2 tablespoons dry cider
2 tablespoons clear honey
12 mint leaves, finely chopped or ½ teaspoon dried mint

Preheat the oven to moderate (180°C/350°F, Gas Mark 4). Place all the fruit in a 1.2 litre/2 pint heat-proof dish.

Mix together the lemon juice, cider and honey, then pour over the fruit. Stir in the mint and mix well. Cover and cook in the oven for 20 to 25 minutes. Chill slightly then serve.
SERVES 4

FRESH FRUIT SALAD

METRIC/IMPERIAL
2 tablespoons clear honey
120 ml/4 fl oz water
thinly pared rind and juice of 1 lemon
1 red dessert apple, quartered and cored
1 pear, quartered and cored
1 banana
1 small pineapple
2 oranges
100 g/4 oz black grapes, halved and deseeded
100 g/4 oz strawberries, sliced

Place the honey, water and lemon rind in a small pan. Bring to the boil, simmer for 2 minutes, then strain and leave to cool. Stir in the lemon juice.

Slice the apple, pear and banana into a bowl, pour over the lemon syrup and stir to coat the fruit completely.

Peel the pineapple with a sharp knife and cut the flesh into sections, discarding the central core.

Peel the oranges, removing all pith, and divide into segments. Add to the bowl with the pineapple, grapes and strawberries and mix well.

Turn into a glass dish and chill until required.
SERVES 4 to 6

RHUBARB AND RASPBERRY LAYER

METRIC/IMPERIAL
450 g/1 lb fresh rhubarb
225 g/8 oz fresh or frozen raspberries
50-75 g/2-3 oz light soft brown sugar
225 g/8 oz low-fat soft cheese
150 ml/¼ pint plain or raspberry low-fat yogurt
fresh raspberries or toasted almonds, to decorate

Wash and chop the rhubarb and place in a pan with the raspberries and sugar. Simmer for 10 to 15 minutes until soft.

Blend the cheese with the yogurt. In 4 individual glass dishes layer the fruit and yogurt mixture. Chill in the refrigerator and decorate the pudding with raspberries or with toasted almonds before serving.

SERVES 4

PRUNE AND ORANGE RING

METRIC/IMPERIAL
225 g/8 oz prunes
finely grated rind of 1 orange
juice of 2 large oranges
15 g/½ oz powdered gelatine
juice of 1 lemon
2 egg whites
2 oranges, peel and pith removed and sliced, to serve

Put the prunes and orange rind in a bowl. Make the orange juice up to 300 ml/½ pint with water, then pour over the prunes. Leave to soak overnight. Alternatively, pour over boiling juice and water and soak for a few hours.

Transfer to a pan and bring to the boil. Lower the heat, cover and simmer for 20 minutes until the prunes are tender, then drain, reserving the cooking juice.

Measure the juice and make up to 300 ml/½ pint with water. Remove the stones from the prunes. Put the prune flesh and juice in a blender and work to a smooth purée.

Sprinkle the gelatine over the lemon juice in a small cup and leave until spongy. Stand the cup in a pan of hot water and stir until the gelatine has dissolved. Stir into the prune purée.

Beat the egg whites until just stiff, then fold into the mixture. Pour into a 900 ml/1½ pint ring mould or serving bowl and chill in the refrigerator until set.

To serve, dip the mould in hot water for a few seconds, then invert on to a serving plate. Fill the centre of the ring with the orange slices.

SERVES 4 to 6

RHUBARB COMPOTE

METRIC/IMPERIAL
750 g/1½ lb rhubarb, cut into 2.5 cm/1 inch pieces
3 tablespoons fructose
Decoration:
young angelica leaves
1 teaspoon chopped crystallized angelica

Pour a little cold water into a large, heavy-based saucepan to just cover the bottom. Add the rhubarb and fructose. Bring to the boil, then lower the heat, cover the pan and simmer gently until the rhubarb is tender, stirring once or twice.

Spoon the rhubarb into individual glasses and cool for 1 to 2 hours.

Decorate with angelica leaves and crystallized angelica just before serving at room temperature.
SERVES 4

STRAWBERRY CRÈME CARAMEL

METRIC/IMPERIAL
600 ml/1 pint skimmed milk
4 eggs, beaten
225 g/8 oz strawberries, hulled and halved
50 g/2 oz Demerara sugar for topping

Preheat the oven to moderate (160°C/325°F, Gas Mark 3).

Warm the milk in a saucepan over a low heat. Mix the beaten eggs with the warmed milk and pour into a 1.2 litre/2 pint soufflé dish. Add the strawberries, cover the dish with foil and place in a small roasting tin, half filled with water.

Bake in the oven for 1¼ hours or until set. Allow to cool completely.

Sprinkle the surface with Demerara sugar and place under a hot grill until the sugar has caramelized. Serve immediately.
SERVES 4

BAKED YOGURT CUSTARD

METRIC/IMPERIAL
300 ml/½ pint plain low-fat yogurt
few drops of natural vanilla essence
2 eggs, beaten
150 ml/¼ pint skimmed milk
¼ teaspoon grated nutmeg

Put the yogurt and vanilla into a bowl and mix well. Add the eggs and milk and beat well to an even colour.

Pour into an ovenproof dish and sprinkle with the nutmeg. Stand the dish in a roasting pan and pour in enough water to come 2.5 cm/1 inch up the sides of the pan. Bake in a preheated moderate oven (160°C/325°F, Gas Mark 3) for 40 minutes.

Serve hot or cold with fresh or stewed fruit.
SERVES 4

RASPBERRY JELLY

METRIC/IMPERIAL
450 g/1 lb raspberries, fresh or frozen
25 g/1 oz fructose
1½ packets gelatine (¾ oz)
2 ripe peaches

Put the raspberries in a pan with the fructose. (If using frozen raspberries, thaw first.) Heat slowly until the juice runs, then increase the heat until it boils. Cook for 10 minutes, watching to see that the berries don't stick. Push through a coarse sieve or fine food mill, pressing through everything except the seeds. Measure the juice and make up to 500 ml/18 fl oz with water. Soak the gelatine in a cup in 4 tablespoons water for 10 minutes, then stand in a small pan of very hot water and stir until dissolved. Mix the gelatine with the juice, strain again, and cool.

Chill 6 small moulds in the freezer. Oval *oeuf en gelée* moulds are ideal. Peel the peaches and remove the stones; cut them into small slices.

Pour a thin layer of liquid jelly into each mould and chill again until set. Arrange a layer of sliced peaches over the jelly, then add more liquid jelly to come level. Chill again and, when the second layer has set, fill up the moulds with the remaining sliced peaches and liquid jelly. Chill in the refrigerator until completely set. Unmould on to small flat plates and serve with yogurt folded into a little whipped low-fat cream.
SERVES 4

PEACH AND RASPBERRY CHEESECAKE

METRIC/IMPERIAL
Biscuit base:
75 g/3 oz polyunsaturated margarine
175 g/6 oz digestive biscuits, crushed
1 tablespoon Demerara sugar
Filling:
350 g/12 oz cottage cheese, sieved
150 ml/¼ pint plain low-fat yogurt
25 g/1 oz fructose
finely grated rind and juice of 1 lemon
15 g/½ oz powdered gelatine
2 tablespoons water
2 egg whites
Topping:
2 large peaches
225 g/8 oz raspberries

To make the base, melt the margarine in a pan, then stir in the biscuits and sugar. Spoon the mixture into a lightly greased 18 to 20 cm/7 to 8 inch loose-bottomed cake tin, spread evenly and press down firmly with the back of a spoon. Chill in the refrigerator.

Meanwhile, make the filling. Put the cottage cheese in a bowl with the yogurt, fructose, lemon rind and juice, reserving 1 tablespoon of lemon juice for the topping. Beat well.

Sprinkle the gelatine over the water in a small cup and leave until spongy. Stand the cup in a pan of hot water and stir until the gelatine has dissolved. Fold into the cheese mixture.

Beat the egg whites until stiff, then fold into the cheese mixture. Pour on top of the biscuit base and level the surface. Chill in the refrigerator until the cheesecake is set.

To serve, run a knife around the edge of the cheesecake, then remove from the tin. Cut the peaches in half, remove the stones, then slice the flesh. Brush the cut surfaces with the reserved lemon juice. Arrange the peach slices on top of the cheesecake with the raspberries. Serve chilled.
SERVES 6 to 8

Note: If you do not have a loose-bottomed cake tin, make this cheesecake in an ordinary cake tin and turn it out on to a serving plate so that the crust is on top rather than underneath.

FRUIT PICTURES

METRIC/IMPERIAL
300 ml/½ pint plain low-fat yogurt
2 tablespoons Cointreau (optional)
2 tablespoons fresh raspberry purée, strained
2 passion fruit, halved
2 kiwi fruit, peeled and thinly sliced
4 whole strawberries, hulled, sliced and fanned
2 fresh figs, sliced
10 black grapes, halved and deseeded
2 nectarines, halved, stoned and sliced
1 large orange, peeled and segmented
12 fresh raspberries or blackcurrants
fresh mint leaves, to decorate

Mix the yogurt with the Cointreau (if using) and spoon on to 4 dessert plates.

Put a small spoonful of the raspberry purée into the centre of the yogurt on each plate; using the tip of a small knife, drag the purée through the yogurt. Spoon a little of the passion fruit pulp into the centre of each plate.

Arrange the prepared fruits decoratively in sections, around the purée. Serve immediately, decorated with mint leaves.

SERVES 4

APRICOT TART

METRIC/IMPERIAL
Pastry:
100 g/4 oz wholemeal flour
75 g/3 oz polyunsaturated margarine
75 g/3 oz ground almonds
25 g/1 oz fructose
1 egg yolk, mixed with 2 teaspoons cold water
4 drops of almond essence
Filling:
300 ml/½ pint skimmed milk
2 eggs
2 tablespoons cornflour
1 tablespoon fructose
150 ml/¼ pint plain low-fat yogurt
1 tablespoon sherry
450 g/1 lb apricots
4 tablespoons apricot jam
2 tablespoons orange juice
25 g/1 oz shelled almonds

To make the pastry dough, put the flour in a bowl. Add the margarine and rub into the flour until the mixture resembles breadcrumbs. Stir in the almonds and fructose, then the egg yolk mix-ture and almond essence. Mix to a firm dough.

Turn on to a lightly floured surface, roll out and use to line a 20 cm/8 inch flan dish or flan ring placed on a baking sheet. Line the dough with foil, then fill with baking beans or rice. Bake in a pre-heated moderately hot oven (200°C/400°F, Gas Mark 6) for 15 minutes, then remove the beans or rice and foil and bake for a further 5 to 10 minutes until the bottom of the pastry is crisp. Remove from the oven and leave to cool.

To make the filling, heat the milk to just below boiling point. Put the eggs in a bowl with the cornflour and fructose. Beat lightly, then gradu-ally stir in the hot milk. Return to the pan and bring to the boil, stirring constantly. Simmer for 2 minutes until the custard is thick and smooth.

Leave to cool, stirring occasionally to prevent a skin forming. Whisk in the yogurt and sherry, then spoon into the flan case and level the surface.

Cut the apricots in half and remove the stones. Put the jam and orange juice in a pan and heat gently until the jam has melted. Add the apricots to the pan, cut side down, and simmer for 5 to 10 minutes until tender. Arrange the apricots and almonds on top. Pour over the syrup from the pan, then leave to cool and set. Serve cold.

SERVES 4 to 6

APPLE AND SULTANA SORBET

METRIC/IMPERIAL
600ml/1 pint apple juice
25 g/1 oz fructose
50 g/2 oz sultanas
2 egg whites

Put the apple juice and fructose into a heavy-based saucepan. Heat gently until the sugar has dis-solved. Increase the heat and cook rapidly until the temperature registers 110 to 112°C/230 to 234°F on a sugar thermometer, or a little of the syrup forms a fine, thin thread when falling from a teaspoon on to a dish. Stir in the sultanas and allow to cool.

Pour the mixture into a freezer container and, stirring occasionally, freeze for about 1½ hours until mushy. Beat the egg whites until they form soft peaks and fold into the mixture. Cover, seal and freeze.

To serve, allow the sorbet to soften slightly at room temperature for 10 to 15 minutes, or in the refrigerator for 20 minutes.

SERVES 4 to 6

BLACKCURRANT AND ORANGE ICE CREAM

METRIC/IMPERIAL
225 g/8 oz blackcurrants, washed and stalks removed
finely grated rind and juice of 1 orange
6-8 mint leaves
4 tablespoons soft brown sugar
300 ml/½ pint plain low-fat yogurt
2 eggs, separated
4-6 small mint sprigs, to decorate

Put the blackcurrants in a blender, reserving a few for decoration. Add the orange rind and juice, the mint leaves, sugar, yogurt and egg yolks. Blend until smooth.

Transfer the purée to a bowl, then place in the freezer, or freezing compartment of the refrigerator; freeze until half frozen and beginning to thicken.

Beat the egg whites until stiff, then fold into the ice cream. Freeze until half frozen, then beat again to prevent large ice crystals forming, then freeze until firm.

To serve, allow the ice cream to soften slightly at room temperature for about 10 minutes, or in the refrigerator for 20 minutes. Spoon into individual dishes or glasses, then decorate with the reserved blackcurrants and the mint sprigs.
SERVES 4 to 6

CHERRY SORBET

METRIC/IMPERIAL
1 × 425 g/15 oz can red cherries
water
100 g/4 oz fructose
2 tablespoons cherry brandy
2 egg whites

Drain the cherries and make the juice up to 600 ml/1 pint with water. Put the liquid and fructose into a heavy-based saucepan. Heat gently until the fructose has dissolved. Increase the heat and cook rapidly until the temperature registers 110 to 112°C/230 to 234°F on a sugar thermometer, or a little of the syrup forms a fine, thin thread when falling from a teaspoon on to a dish. Allow to cool.

Stone the cherries and work in a blender or sieve them to a purée. Stir the purée into the cold syrup and add the cherry brandy.

Pour the mixture into a freezer container and,

stirring occasionally, freeze for about 1½ hours until mushy. Beat the egg whites until they form soft peaks and fold into the cherry mixture. Cover, seal and freeze.

To serve, allow the sorbet to soften slightly at room temperature for 10 to 15 minutes, or in the refrigerator for 20 minutes.
SERVES 4 to 6

GERANIUM LEAF SORBET

METRIC/IMPERIAL
12 scented geranium leaves
50 g/2 oz fructose
300 ml/½ pint water
juice of 1 large lemon
1 egg white
4 tiny geranium leaves, to decorate

Wash the geranium leaves and shake them dry. Put the fructose and water in a pan and boil until the fructose has dissolved. Put the leaves in the pan, cover it and turn off the heat. Leave for 20 minutes, then taste. If the flavour is too weak, bring the liquid to the boil once more, turn off the heat, cover the pan and leave it for a further 10 minutes.

When the flavour is satisfactory, strain the syrup into a rigid container, add the lemon juice and leave to cool. Freeze until semi-frozen, about 45 minutes to 1 hour, then fold in the stiffly beaten egg white. Continue to freeze until a firm mush, about 1 hour.

Allow the sorbet to soften slightly at room temperature for 10 to 15 minutes, or in the refrigerator for 20 minutes before serving in 4 glasses, each one decorated with a tiny geranium leaf.
SERVES 4

Note: There are two scented geraniums, the nutmeg-scented *Pelargonium* × *fragrans* and the peppermint-scented *Pelargonium tomentosum*.

COFFEE SORBET

METRIC/IMPERIAL
600 ml/1 pint hot water
4 tablespoons skimmed milk powder
4 teaspoons instant coffee powder
2 or 3 drops of vanilla essence
sugar or fructose to taste
2 egg whites

Place the water in a bowl and stir in the skimmed milk powder, instant coffee, vanilla essence and sugar or fructose to taste. Stir well to mix.

Pour into a shallow rigid container and place in the freezer or freezing compartment of the refrigerator for 1 to 1½ hours or until the edges are frozen. Whisk the egg whites until stiff. Beat the sorbet well, fold the egg whites into it and return to the freezer or freezing compartment for 1 hour, then beat again.

Return the sorbet to the freezer or freezing compartment and freeze for a further 1 hour. Transfer to the refrigerator for 10 minutes before serving in chilled individual glasses.
SERVES 4

KIWI FRUIT SORBET

METRIC/IMPERIAL
600 ml/1 pint water
2 tablespoons lemon juice
50 g/2 oz fructose
8 kiwi fruit, peeled
2 egg whites

Put the water, lemon juice and fructose into a heavy-based saucepan. Heat gently until the fructose has dissolved. Increase the heat and cook rapidly until the temperature registers 110 to 112°C/230 to 234°F on a sugar thermometer, or a little of the syrup forms a fine, thin thread when falling from a teaspoon. Allow to cool.

Blend or rub the kiwi fruit through a nylon sieve, using a wooden spoon. Stir the purée into the sugar syrup.

Pour the mixture into a freezer container and, stirring occasionally, freeze for about 1½ hours until mushy. Beat the egg whites to form soft peaks. Fold into the mixture and freeze. Beat once after 1 hour, then cover, seal and freeze.

To serve, allow the sorbet to soften slightly at room temperature for 10 to 15 minutes, or in the refrigerator for 20 minutes.
SERVES 4 to 6

GOOSEBERRY AND MINT SORBET

METRIC/IMPERIAL
450 g/1 lb fresh, frozen or bottled gooseberries
2 tablespoons soft brown sugar
1 tablespoon clear honey
8 large mint sprigs or ½ teaspoon dried mint
150 ml/¼ pint plain low-fat yogurt
1 egg white
mint sprigs, to decorate

Place the gooseberries in a pan with 1 tablespoon sugar, the honey and mint. Cover and simmer for 10 to 15 minutes until soft, then allow to cool. Work the fruit in a blender or briefly in a food processor to make a purée. Rub through a sieve to remove the pips.

Blend the purée with the yogurt. Whisk the egg white until stiff, then gradually whisk in the remaining sugar. Fold into the fruit, then spoon the mixture into a rigid freezerproof container. Cover and freeze for 3 hours.

Place in the refrigerator for 20 minutes before serving. Scoop into glass bowls and decorate with mint sprigs.
SERVES 4

Variation
Other fruits can be used; try apples with mint or apricots stewed with cinnamon.

CRUNCHY HAZELNUT ICE

METRIC/IMPERIAL
75 g/3 oz wholemeal breadcrumbs
50 g/2 oz hazelnuts, ground
175 g/6 oz Muscovado sugar
3 egg whites
300 ml/½ pint plain low-fat yogurt

Mix together the breadcrumbs, hazelnuts and 50 g/2 oz of the sugar. Spread on a baking sheet. Place under a preheated hot grill for about 2 minutes until golden brown, stirring occasionally. Leave to cool.

Whisk the egg whites until stiff, then gradually whisk in the remaining sugar. Fold in the yogurt and breadcrumb mixture. Turn into a freezer-proof container. Cover, seal and freeze.

Transfer to the refrigerator 20 minutes before serving to soften. Scoop into chilled glasses.
SERVES 6 to 8

314

PINEAPPLE SORBET

METRIC/IMPERIAL
1 × 1.5 kg/3 lb pineapple
finely grated rind and juice of 1 large orange
sugar or fructose to taste
2 egg whites

Cut the pineapple in half lengthwise, leaving the green leaves attached. Scoop out the pineapple flesh and discard the central core. Reserve the pineapple shells for serving.

Work the pineapple flesh to a purée with the orange rind and juice in a blender. Add sugar or fructose to taste. Transfer the purée to a bowl, then place in the freezer, or freezing compartment of the refrigerator; freeze until half frozen and beginning to thicken.

Beat the egg whites until stiff. Beat the sorbet well to break down the ice crystals, then fold in the beaten egg whites. Spoon the mixture into the pineapple shells and return to the freezer or freezing compartment. If there is too much sorbet to fill the shells, freeze in a separate container.

To serve, allow the sorbet to soften slightly at room temperature for 10 to 15 minutes, or in the refrigerator for 20 minutes.
SERVES 6 to 8

MUESLI ICE CREAM

METRIC/IMPERIAL
50 g/2 oz fructose
300 ml/½ pint water
100 g/4 oz muesli
300 ml/½ pint plain low-fat yogurt
150 ml/¼ pint low-fat whipping cream

Put the fructose and water into a heavy-based saucepan and heat gently until the fructose has dissolved. Increase the heat and cook rapidly until the temperature registers 110 to 112°C/230 to 234°F on a sugar thermometer, or a little of the syrup forms a fine, thin thread when falling from a teaspoon on to a dish. Allow to cool.

Stir the muesli into the yogurt, then stir in the syrup. Beat the cream until it forms soft peaks and fold into the mixture. Pour into a freezer container and freeze. Beat the mixture twice, at hourly intervals. Cover, seal and freeze.

To serve, allow the ice cream to soften slightly at room temperature for about 10 minutes, or in the refrigerator for 20 minutes.
SERVES 6

BAKED CITRUS CHEESECAKE

METRIC/IMPERIAL
225 g/8 oz cottage cheese
finely grated rind of 1 orange
75 g/3 oz light brown sugar
3 eggs, beaten
50 ml/2 fl oz plain low-fat yogurt or Quark
2 tablespoons plain unbleached white flour
Decoration:
3 tablespoons plain low-fat yogurt or Quark
grated orange rind

Grease and line a 20 cm/8 inch loose-bottomed cake tin with greased greaseproof paper.

Beat the cottage cheese with the orange rind, sugar, eggs, yogurt or Quark and flour; spread the mixture evenly in the prepared tin.

Baked in a preheated moderate oven (180°C/350°F, Gas Mark 4) for 40 minutes, until just firm and set to the touch. Let the cheesecake cool in its pan.

Invert the cooled cheesecake on to a flat serving plate. Spread the yogurt or Quark evenly over the top and sprinkle with orange rind.
SERVES 6

Variation
Use other citrus fruits in place of oranges; try lemons, limes or grapefruit.

CHEESE AND YOGURT CREAMS

METRIC/IMPERIAL
225 g/8 oz low-fat soft cheese
150 ml/¼ pint plain low-fat yogurt
2 tablespoons clear honey
1 egg white
225 g/8 oz strawberries, hulled

Place the cheese, yogurt and honey in a bowl and mix well. Whisk the egg white until fairly stiff then fold into the cheese mixture.

Line 6 heart-shaped moulds with muslin, spoon in the cheese mixture and smooth the tops. Place on a plate and leave to drain in the refrigerator for 3 to 4 hours. Turn out on to individual dishes and surround with strawberries.

Alternatively, spoon the cheese mixture into ramekin dishes, arrange the strawberries on top and chill until required.
SERVES 6

CHESTNUT WHIP

METRIC/IMPERIAL
450 g/1 lb chestnuts
600 ml/1 pint water
200 ml/⅓ pint skimmed milk
¼ teaspoon vanilla essence
finely grated rind and juice of 1 small orange
2 tablespoons rum
100 g/4 oz soft brown sugar
2 egg whites
orange twists, to decorate

Put the chestnuts in a pan and cover with the water. Bring to the boil, then lower the heat and simmer for 10 minutes. Drain and leave until cool enough to handle.

Peel off the skins with a sharp knife, then return the chestnuts to the pan and add the milk and vanilla essence. Cover and cook gently for about 15 minutes until the chestnuts are soft and have absorbed the milk, stirring occasionally.

Rub through a sieve to give a thick, dry purée, then stir in the orange rind and juice, rum and sugar. Beat the egg whites until just stiff, then fold into the chestnut mixture.

Spoon into a serving bowl or 6 individual dishes or glasses. Chill for at least 1 hour before serving, then decorate with orange twists.
SERVES 6

OATMEAL AND YOGURT CREAM

METRIC/IMPERIAL
40 g/1½ oz blanched almonds, finely chopped
40 g/1½ oz medium oatmeal
25 g/1 oz Muscovado sugar
grated rind and juice of ½ lemon
150 ml/¼ pint plain low-fat yogurt
150 ml/¼ pint low-fat whipping cream, whipped
1 tablespoon flaked almonds, roasted

Mix together the chopped almonds and oatmeal. Spread on a baking sheet and place under a pre-heated hot grill for about 2 minutes, stirring frequently to brown evenly. Leave to cool.

Mix the sugar with the lemon rind and juice. Stir into the yogurt with the almond mixture, then fold in the cream.

Spoon into individual glass dishes and chill until required. Decorate with almonds to serve.
SERVES 4

SLIMMER'S COEUR À LA CRÈME

METRIC/IMPERIAL
2 teaspoons powdered gelatine
2 tablespoons water
350 g/12 oz cottage cheese, sieved
150 ml/¼ pint plain low-fat yogurt
juice of ½ lemon
salt
freshly ground black pepper

Sprinkle the gelatine over the water in a small heatproof bowl and leave until spongy. Place the bowl in a pan of hot water and stir well until the gelatine becomes syrupy. Remove from the heat and cool for 2 minutes.

Put the cottage cheese, yogurt and lemon juice in a bowl and mix well. Add the gelatine and salt and pepper to taste; mix thoroughly.

Spoon the mixture into 4 individual ramekins, then chill in the refrigerator for 4 hours. Turn out and serve with fresh fruit in season.
SERVES 4

FLAPJACK GINGER CHEESECAKE

METRIC/IMPERIAL
Base:
75 g/3 oz polyunsaturated margarine
50 g/2 oz soft brown sugar
1 tablespoon golden syrup
150 g/5 oz porridge oats
½ teaspoon ground ginger
Filling:
350 g/12 oz low-fat soft cheese
2 tablespoons plain low-fat yogurt
2 eggs, separated
3-4 pieces stem ginger, chopped and
2 tablespoons syrup from the jar
Decoration:
65 ml/2½ fl oz Quark
stem ginger pieces

Preheat the oven to moderately hot (200°C/400°F, Gas Mark 6).

Place the margarine, sugar and syrup in a pan and heat until melted. Stir in the oats and ginger, then mix well. Press into the base of a greased 20 cm/8 inch loose-bottomed cake tin. Bake in the oven for 10 minutes, remove and allow to cool. Reduce the oven temperature to 160°C/325°F, Gas Mark 3.

To make the filling, blend together the cheese, yogurt and egg yolks. Stir in the ginger and syrup, then mix well. Whisk the egg whites until stiff and fold into the mixture. Spoon over the flapjack base and bake in the oven for 45 minutes to 1 hour or until the topping is set and golden.

Remove from the oven and leave to cool in the tin. Transfer to a serving plate and chill before serving. Decorate with Quark and ginger pieces.
SERVES 6 to 8

YOGURT AND ORANGE JELLY

METRIC/IMPERIAL
15 g/½ oz powdered gelatine
1 tablespoon water
300 ml/½ pint orange juice
150 ml/¼ pint plain low-fat yogurt

Sprinkle the gelatine over the water in a small heatproof bowl and leave until spongy. Place the bowl in a pan of hot water and stir well until the gelatine becomes syrupy. Remove from the heat and cool for 2 minutes.

Put the orange juice and yogurt in a separate bowl, pour in the gelatine, then mix thoroughly.

Pour into a chilled 600 ml/1 pint mould. Leave to set, then chill in the refrigerator for 2 hours before serving.
SERVES 4

FROSTED ALMOND CREAMS

METRIC/IMPERIAL
2 eggs, separated
50 g/2 oz soft brown sugar
50 g/2 oz chopped almonds, toasted
300 ml/½ pint plain low-fat yogurt
2 tablespoons orange liqueur
25 g/1 oz toasted slivered almonds, to decorate

Beat the egg yolks and sugar together until thick and creamy. Stir in the chopped almonds, yogurt and liqueur. Beat the egg whites until just stiff, then fold into the almond mixture. Pour into 6 individual ramekin dishes and freeze until firm.

To serve, remove from the freezer and leave to soften slightly at room temperature for 15 minutes, or in the refrigerator for 30 minutes. Sprinkle with slivered almonds before serving.
SERVES 6

HAZELNUT SHORTCAKE

METRIC/IMPERIAL
Hazelnut pastry:
75 g/3 oz polyunsaturated margarine
50 g/2 oz Muscovado sugar
100 g/4 oz wholemeal flour
75 g/3 oz hazelnuts, ground and roasted
egg white for brushing
1 tablespoon chopped hazelnuts
Filling:
450 g/1 lb dessert apples, peeled, cored and sliced
2 tablespoons apple juice
50 g/2 oz raisins
50 g/2 oz sultanas
1 teaspoon ground mixed spice

Beat the margarine and sugar together until soft. Stir in the flour and ground hazelnuts and mix to a firm dough. Turn on to a floured surface and knead lightly until smooth. Divide in half and roll each piece into a 20 cm/8 inch round on a baking sheet. Brush one round with egg white and sprinkle with the chopped nuts.

Bake both rounds in a preheated moderately hot oven (190°C/375°F, Gas Mark 5) for 10 to 15 minutes. Cut the nut-covered round into 8 sections while still warm. Cool on a wire rack.

Place the apples and juice in a pan, cover and cook gently for 15 minutes, stirring occasionally. Add the remaining ingredients and leave to cool.

Spread over the hazelnut round and arrange the cut triangles on top. Serve with plain yogurt.
SERVES 8

SLICED PEACHES WITH YOGURT CREAM

METRIC/IMPERIAL
4 large peaches or 6 apricots
65 ml/2½ fl oz plain low-fat yogurt
2 tablespoons whipping cream, whipped
1 egg white, beaten
½ tablespoon vanilla sugar

Remove the stones from the peaches, skin them and slice. (Stone and slice apricots, if using.) Divide the slices between 6 glass bowls. Beat the yogurt until smooth, then fold in the whipped cream and the beaten egg white. Finally, fold in the vanilla sugar. Put a spoonful on the sliced fruit in each of the bowls.
SERVES 6

BAKING

BASIC BROWN BREAD

METRIC/IMPERIAL
15 g/½ oz dried yeast
2 tablespoons light soft brown sugar
900 ml/1½ pints water heated to 50°C/110°F
1 tablespoon salt
1.5 kg/3 lb wholemeal flour
25 g/1 oz polyunsaturated margarine
1 egg, beaten with a pinch of salt
cracked wheat or bran for sprinkling

Put the dried yeast into a small bowl with 1 teaspoon of the sugar and whisk in 300 ml/½ pint of the water. Leave in a warm place for 10 to 15 minutes, until the surface is frothy.

Add the salt and the remaining sugar to the rest of the water. Either of the following two methods may be used for mixing the dough:
1 Put the flour into a large bowl and rub in the margarine. Pour in both the salted water and the yeast liquid. Quickly work the flour and liquid together to a dough with the fingertips. If the mixture seems dry, add a little more water. Knead the dough for 5 minutes until smooth, pulling the outside dough into the centre.
2 Using an electric mixer, put the flour into the mixer bowl with the margarine, salt water and yeast liquid. Mix on a slow speed, using the dough hook attachment, until the liquid is absorbed. Continue mixing for 2 minutes.

Put the kneaded dough into a greased bowl and cover with a damp cloth. Leave to rise in a warm place for about 1 to 1½ hours. The dough should double in size.

Turn out the risen dough on a floured working surface and knead lightly, using as little flour as possible. The dough is now ready for shaping.

Loaves: Warm and grease a 1 kg/2 lb loaf tin. Halve the dough and keep one half warm. Knead the other portion into a smooth ball and punch into a shape to fit the prepared loaf tin.

Warm and grease 2 × 450 g/1 lb loaf tins. Halve the remaining dough and shape to fit the two tins. Brush the loaves with the beaten egg mixture.

Sprinkle with a little cracked wheat or bran.
Cover with polythene bags and leave to rise in a warm place for 20 minutes until the dough reaches the top of the tins.

Meanwhile, preheat the oven to hot (230°C/450°F, Gas Mark 8).

Bake the loaves in the oven for 20 minutes, then reduce the temperature to moderately hot (200°C/400°F, Gas Mark 6) for a further 20 minutes for the large loaf, and 10 minutes for the smaller loaves. Tip the loaves out of their tins and tap them on the bottom – the loaves should sound hollow if they are cooked. Cool on a wire tray.

Rolls: Grease baking sheets. Divide the dough into 50 g/2 oz portions; this amount will make about 40 rolls. Roll under a cupped hand on a lightly floured surface until round and smooth. Arrange on the prepared baking sheets and brush with a little beaten egg mixture. They can be sprinkled with sesame, poppy or caraway seeds, or bran. Cover with polythene bags and leave in a warm place to rise for 10 to 15 minutes. Meanwhile, preheat the oven to hot (230°C/450°F, Gas Mark 8). Bake the rolls for 10 to 15 minutes.
MAKES one 1 kg/2 lb loaf and two 450 g/1 lb loaves or about 40 rolls

WHOLEMEAL BREAD

METRIC/IMPERIAL
1.5 kg/3 lb plain wholemeal flour
50 g/2 oz fine oatmeal
1 tablespoon salt
25 g/1 oz fresh yeast
900 ml/1½ pints warm water
2 tablespoons malt extract
2 tablespoons polyunsaturated vegetable oil
2 tablespoons rolled oats

Mix the flour, oatmeal and salt together in a bowl.
Mix the yeast with a little of the water and leave until frothy. Add to the flour and oatmeal with the remaining water, malt extract and oil and mix to a smooth dough.

318

Turn on to a floured surface and knead for 8 to 10 minutes until smooth and elastic. Place in a clean bowl, cover with a damp cloth and leave to rise in a warm place for about 1 to 1½ hours, until doubled in size.

Turn on to a floured surface, knead for a few minutes, then divide into 4 pieces. Shape and place in greased 450 g/1 lb loaf tins. Brush with water and sprinkle with the oats.

Cover with polythene bags and leave to rise in a warm place for about 30 minutes, until the dough just reaches the top of the tins. Bake in a preheated hot oven (220°C/425°F, Gas Mark 7) for 15 minutes.

Lower the temperature to 190°C/375°F, Gas Mark 5, and bake for a further 20 to 25 minutes. Tip the loaves out of their tins and tap them on the bottom – the loaves should sound hollow if they are cooked. Cool on a wire tray.

MAKES four 450 g/1 lb loaves

RYE BREAD

METRIC/IMPERIAL
25 g/1 oz dried yeast
2 tablespoons black treacle
900 ml/1½ pints water
1 tablespoon salt
1 kg/2 lb wholemeal flour
450 g/1 lb rye flour
25 g/1 oz polyunsaturated margarine
1 egg, beaten with a pinch of salt
cracked wheat or bran for sprinkling

Put the yeast into a small bowl with the black treacle, then follow the same method as for basic brown bread, using the mixed wholemeal and rye flours in place of the wholemeal flour. Allow the dough to rise for 1 to 1½ hours and then knead lightly.

Preheat the oven to hot (230°C/450°F, Gas Mark 8). Grease 2 baking sheets.

Halve the risen dough and shape each portion into a long, oval loaf. Place the shaped loaves on the prepared baking sheets, brush the surface with the beaten egg mixture and sprinkle with cracked wheat or bran.

Make several diagonal cuts in the surface of the loaves with a sharp knife. These cuts allow the loaves to rise or 'bloom' well, hence the name 'bloomer'. Bake for 20 minutes, then reduce the temperature to moderately hot (200°C/400°F, Gas Mark 6) for a further 20 minutes.

MAKES 2 loaves

Note: Fresh yeast may be used in place of dried – 25 g/1 oz fresh yeast is equivalent to 15 g/½ oz dried yeast. If using fresh yeast, dissolve it in the liquid – no sugar is needed. Make sure when dissolving yeast that the liquid is heated to 50°C/110°F; if it is too cool, the dough will not rise properly.

BRAN BREAD

METRIC/IMPERIAL
500 g/1¼ lb wholemeal bread flour
100 g/4 oz bran
15 g/½ oz sea salt
25 g/1 oz Muscovado sugar
25 g/1 oz fresh yeast
450 g/¾ pint lukewarm water
1 tablespoon corn oil
Topping:
2 tablespoons cold water
pinch of salt
2 tablespoons rolled oats

Put the flour, bran, salt and sugar in a warm bowl and mix well. Blend the yeast with a little of the water and leave until frothy. Then add to the dry ingredients with the oil and the remaining water. Mix to a firm dough.

Turn out on to a lightly floured surface and knead for 5 minutes until smooth. Shape the dough into a ball and place in a greased polythene bag. Tie loosely and leave in a warm place for about 1 to 1½ hours until doubled in size.

Remove the dough and knead again on the floured surface for 5 minutes, then divide in half. Shape each piece of dough and place in greased, warmed 450 g/1 lb loaf tins, tucking in the corners lightly but firmly. Cover with greased polythene and leave in a warm place for about 30 minutes until the dough rises to the tops of the tins.

Mix the cold water and salt together, then brush over the tops of the loaves and sprinkle with the oats. Bake in a preheated hot oven (230°C/450°F, Gas Mark 8) for 35 minutes until well-risen and crisp. Turn the loaves out on to a wire rack and leave to cool.

MAKES two 450 g/1 lb loaves

GRANARY STICK

METRIC/IMPERIAL
225 g/8 oz granary flour
225 g/8 oz plain wholemeal flour
1 teaspoon salt
15 g/½ oz fresh yeast
300 ml/½ pint warm water
1 tablespoon malt extract
1 tablespoon polyunsaturated vegetable oil
cracked wheat for sprinkling

Mix the flours and salt in a bowl.
Cream the yeast with a little of the water and leave until frothy. Add to the flour with the remaining water, malt extract and oil; mix to a soft dough.
Turn on to a floured surface and knead for 5 minutes until smooth and elastic. Place in a clean bowl, cover with a damp cloth and leave to rise in a warm place for 1 to 1½ hours until the dough is doubled in size.
Turn on to a floured surface and knead for a few minutes. Shape into a long stick and place on a greased baking sheet. Make slits slantwise along the length of the stick. Brush with water and sprinkle with cracked wheat. Cover and leave to rise in a warm place for about 30 minutes until almost doubled in size.
Bake in a preheated hot oven (220°C/425°F, Gas Mark 7) for 25 to 30 minutes or until it sounds hollow when tapped. Cool on a wire rack.
MAKES 1 granary stick

HERBED BREAD ROUND

METRIC/IMPERIAL
225 g/8 oz plain unbleached white flour
225 g/8 oz plain wholemeal flour
½ teaspoon salt
1 teaspoon bicarbonate of soda
25 g/1 oz polyunsaturated margarine
2 large onions, peeled and grated
3 celery stalks, sliced
1 teaspoon dried mixed herbs
2 tablespoons chopped parsley
250 ml/8 fl oz buttermilk or plain low-fat yogurt
a little milk to glaze

Combine the flours, salt and soda in a large mixing bowl. Rub in the margarine, then stir in the onion, celery and herbs. Mix well. Add enough of the buttermilk or yogurt to give a soft dough.

Turn out on to a floured surface and knead lightly.
Shape into a 22 cm/9 inch round and place on a floured baking sheet. Score the top into 8 segments and brush with milk. Bake in a preheated moderately hot oven (200°C/400°F, Gas Mark 6) for 30 to 35 minutes or until well risen and golden. Serve warm with soups, salads or cheese.
SERVES 8

SPICY APPLE, DATE AND SESAME LOAF

METRIC/IMPERIAL
350 g/12 oz self-raising wholemeal flour
¼ teaspoon fine salt
¼ teaspoon grated nutmeg
1 teaspoon ground mixed spice, or ¼ teaspoon ground allspice, ¼ teaspoon ground mace, ¼ teaspoon ground cardamom and ¼ teaspoon ground ginger
1 teaspoon ground cinnamon
grated rind of ½ lemon
50 g/2 oz Muscovado sugar
2 eggs, beaten
150 ml/¼ pint plain low-fat yogurt
1 large cooking apple, peeled, cored and grated
225 g/8 oz stoned dates, chopped
50 g/2 oz sesame seeds

Preheat the oven to moderate (160°C/325°F, Gas Mark 3). Grease and lightly flour a 1 kg/2 lb loaf tin.
Sift the flour, salt and spices into a large bowl, tipping in any bran left in the sieve. Stir in the lemon rind and sugar and make a well in the centre. Pour in the eggs and yogurt and gradually mix the dry ingredients into the liquid. Stir in apple, dates and 25 g/1 oz of the sesame seeds.
Shape the mixture into a loaf and put into the prepared loaf tin. Press the mixture down in the corners and smooth the top with the back of a spoon. Scatter over the rest of the sesame seeds and press them into the top of the loaf.
Bake in the oven for 1½ to 1¾ hours until well risen and lightly browned. Allow the loaf to cool in the tin for 5 to 10 minutes before turning it out on to a wire tray to cool completely. Store for at least 1 day before serving.
MAKES one 1 kg/2 lb loaf

Variation
For 100 g/4 oz of the dates, substitute 100 g/4 oz chopped walnuts or 100 g/4 oz chopped glacé cherries.

FRUIT MALT LOAF

METRIC/IMPERIAL

225 g/8 oz plain wholemeal flour
¼ teaspoon sea salt
100 g/4 oz sultanas
25 g/1 oz polyunsaturated margarine
50 g/2 oz malt extract
25 g/1 oz black treacle
25 g/1 oz fresh yeast
65 ml/2½ fl oz lukewarm water
1 tablespoon clear honey, to glaze

Put the flour, salt and sultanas in a warm bowl and mix well. Put the margarine, malt extract and black treacle in a pan and heat gently until the margarine has melted. Leave to cool for 5 minutes.

Blend the yeast with the water and leave until frothy. Then add to the dry ingredients with the melted mixture. Mix to a soft dough.

Turn out on to a lightly floured surface and knead for 5 minutes until smooth. Place the dough in a warmed, greased bowl. Cover and leave in a warm place for about 1 hour until doubled in size.

Turn out on to the floured surface and knead again for 5 minutes. Fold the dough into 3, then place in a greased, warmed 450 g/1 lb loaf tin. Cover with a clean damp cloth and leave in a warm place for about 20 minutes until the dough rises to the top of the tin.

Bake in a preheated moderately hot oven (200°C/400°F, Gas Mark 6) for 45 minutes. Turn out on to a wire rack, brush with honey, then leave to cool.

MAKES one 450 g/1 lb loaf

SAVOURY CHEESE AND WALNUT LOAF

METRIC/IMPERIAL

100 g/4 oz self-raising unbleached white flour
100 g/4 oz granary flour
1 teaspoon baking powder
50 g/2 oz polyunsaturated margarine
100 g/4 oz Cheddar cheese, grated
2 eggs, beaten
150 ml/¼ pint skimmed milk
2 teaspoons wholegrain mustard
75 g/3 oz walnuts, chopped

Preheat the oven to moderately hot (190°C/375°F, Gas Mark 5). Place the flours in a bowl with the

baking powder. Rub in the margarine until the mixture resembles fine breadcrumbs, then stir in the grated cheese.

Beat together the eggs, milk and mustard and stir into the flour with the walnuts. Mix to a stiff dough.

Spoon into a greased 450 g/1 lb loaf tin and bake in the oven for 45 to 50 minutes or until firm and risen. Cool on a wire rack.

MAKES one 450 g/1 lb loaf

Note: If you don't have any self-raising flour, use plain flour and increase the quantity of baking powder to 2 teaspoons.

FARMHOUSE BREAD

METRIC/IMPERIAL

1.5 kg/3 lb plain wholemeal flour
25 g/1 oz sea salt
25 g/1 oz Muscovado sugar
25 g/1 oz fresh yeast
900 ml/1½ pints lukewarm water
1 tablespoon polyunsaturated vegetable oil
beaten egg, to glaze

Put the flour, salt and sugar in a warm bowl and mix well. Blend the yeast with a little of the water and leave until frothy. Then stir into the remaining water and add to the dry ingredients with the oil. Mix to a soft dough.

Turn out on to a lightly floured surface and knead for 5 minutes until smooth. Place the dough in a warm, greased bowl. Cover with a damp cloth and leave in a warm place for about 1 to 1½ hours until doubled in size.

Turn out on to the floured surface and knead again for 5 minutes, then divide the dough into 4 pieces. Fold each piece into 3, then place in greased, warmed 450 g/1 lb loaf tins. Cover with a damp cloth and leave in a warm place for about 30 minutes until the dough rises to the tops of the tins.

Brush the dough with beaten egg, then bake in a pre-heated hot oven (230°C/450°F, Gas Mark 8) for 40 minutes. Turn out on to a wire rack and leave to cool.

MAKES four 450 g/1 lb loaves

SWEDISH FLAT BREAD

METRIC/IMPERIAL
225 g/8 oz stoneground wholemeal flour
225 g/8 oz rye or barley flour
1 teaspoon salt
250-350 ml/8-12 fl oz lukewarm water

Blend the flours together with the salt. Mix in sufficient water to bind into a dough – the quantity will depend on the types of flour used. Beat until the dough leaves the sides of the bowl, then turn on to a floured board and knead thoroughly.

Heat a griddle or frying pan over a moderate heat and grease it. Divide the dough into 4 and roll out one quarter into a round as thin as possible. Using a plate about 20 cm/8 inches wide, trim the edges into a neat circle. Prick all over to prevent the dough bubbling during cooking.

Transfer to the griddle or frying pan and cook over a moderate heat for about 15 minutes or until slightly coloured, then turn and cook the other side. Repeat with the rest of the dough, working up the trimmings for re-rolling and baking. Cool on a wire tray.

MAKES 4 crispbreads

OATMEAL PLAIT

METRIC/IMPERIAL
2 teaspoons light soft brown sugar
150 ml/¼ pint lukewarm skimmed milk
150 ml/¼ pint lukewarm water
1½ teaspoons dried yeast
400 g/14 oz strong plain unbleached white flour
1 teaspoon salt
25 g/1 oz polyunsaturated margarine
100 g/4 oz fine or medium oatmeal
skimmed milk or water, to glaze
coarse oatmeal for sprinkling

To make the dough, dissolve 1 teaspoon of the sugar in the milk and water and blend the yeast into it. Leave in a warm place for 10 to 15 minutes, until the surface is frothy.

Sift the flour, salt and the remaining sugar into a bowl, rub in the margarine, then mix in the oatmeal. Add the yeast liquid and mix to form a fairly soft dough. Turn out on to a floured surface and knead for 10 minutes or until smooth and no longer sticky (or for 3 to 4 minutes in an electric mixer fitted with a dough hook). Shape the dough into a ball, place in an oiled polythene bag and tie loosely. Leave to rise in a warm place for about

1 to 1½ hours, until it has doubled in size. Grease a baking sheet. Remove the dough from the bag, knock back and knead for about 2 minutes or until smooth. Divide into 3 equal pieces. Roll into 3 sausage shapes, all the same length and about 4 cm/1½ inches in diameter.

Lay the lengths close to each other and, beginning in the middle, plait towards you. Pinch the ends together to secure them. Turn the plait round and complete, again securing the ends.

Place on the baking sheet, brush with milk or water and sprinkle with coarse oatmeal. Cover with a sheet of oiled polythene and leave to rise in a warm place until doubled in size. Preheat the oven to hot (230°C/450°F, Gas Mark 8). When the dough has doubled, bake in the oven for 25 to 35 minutes or until well risen and lightly browned and it sounds hollow when the base is tapped. Cool on a wire rack.

MAKES 2 smaller plaits or 1 cob loaf

CHEESE LOAF

METRIC/IMPERIAL
225 g/8 oz plain wholemeal flour
1 teaspoon sea salt
1 teaspoon mustard powder
100 g/4 oz Cheddar cheese, grated
15 g/½ oz fresh yeast
150 ml/¼ pint lukewarm water

Put the flour, salt, mustard and cheese in a warm bowl and mix well. Blend the yeast with a little of the water and leave until frothy. Then stir into the remaining water and add to the dry ingredients. Mix to a soft dough.

Turn out on to a lightly floured surface and knead for 5 minutes until smooth. Place the dough in a warm, greased bowl. Cover and leave to rise in a warm place for about 1 hour until doubled in size.

Turn out on to the floured surface and knead again for 2 minutes, then fold into 3 and place in a greased, warmed 450 g/1 lb loaf tin. Cover with a clean cloth and leave in a warm place for about 20 minutes until the dough rises to the top of the tin.

Bake in a preheated hot oven (220°C/425°F, Gas Mark 7) for 10 minutes, then reduce the heat to moderately hot (190°C/375°F, Gas Mark 5) and bake for a further 35 minutes. Turn out on to a wire rack and leave to cool.

MAKES one 450 g/1 lb loaf

WHOLEWHEAT BAPS

METRIC/IMPERIAL
675 g/1½ lb plain wholemeal flour
1 teaspoon sea salt
25 g/1 oz Muscovado sugar
25 g/1 oz fresh yeast
450 ml/¾ pint lukewarm water
1 tablespoon polyunsaturated vegetable oil

Put the flour, salt and sugar in a warm bowl and mix well. Blend the yeast with a little of the water and leave until frothy. Then stir into the remaining water and add to the dry ingredients with the oil. Mix to a soft dough. Turn out on to a lightly floured surface and knead for 5 minutes until smooth. Place the dough in a warm, greased bowl. Cover and leave in a warm place for about 1 hour until doubled in size.

Turn out on to the floured surface and knead again for 2 minutes, then divide the dough into 12 pieces and shape into round flat baps. Place the baps on greased, warmed baking sheets and sprinkle with a little wholemeal flour. Cover with a piece of oiled polythene and leave to rise in a warm place until doubled in size.

Bake in a preheated hot oven (220°C/425°F, Gas Mark 7) for 15 minutes. Remove the baps and wrap them in a clean cloth; this will keep them soft by trapping the steam as they cool.
MAKES 12

HONEY FRUIT LOAF

METRIC/IMPERIAL
75 g/3 oz polyunsaturated margarine
75 g/3 oz Muscovado sugar
1 egg, beaten
2 tablespoons honey
225 g/8 oz self-raising wholemeal flour
¼ teaspoon salt
1 teaspoon ground mixed spice
175 g/6 oz mixed dried fruit
4 tablespoons skimmed milk

Cream the margarine and sugar until light and fluffy, then beat in the egg and honey. Stir in the flour, salt and spice, then beat in the fruit and milk until thoroughly mixed.

Spoon the mixture into a greased 750 g/1½ lb loaf tin and bake in a preheated moderately hot oven (190°C/375°F, Gas Mark 5) for 45 minutes. Turn out on to a wire rack and leave to cool.
MAKES one 750 g/1½ lb loaf

LEMON BANANA TEABREAD

METRIC/IMPERIAL
50 g/2 oz bran breakfast cereal
150 ml/¼ pint skimmed milk
75 g/3 oz polyunsaturated margarine
50 g/2 oz Muscovado sugar
grated rind of 1 lemon
4 tablespoons lemon curd
2 small bananas, mashed
1 egg
150 g/5 oz plain wholemeal flour
2 teaspoons baking powder

Place the bran cereal in a bowl with the milk and leave to soak for 30 minutes. Add the margarine, sugar, lemon rind and curd, bananas and egg, and beat well.

Stir in the flour and baking powder and mix well. Spoon into a greased 450 g/1 lb loaf tin. Cook in a preheated moderate oven (180°C/350°F, Gas Mark 4) for 45 minutes to 1 hour until firm. Cool, then turn on to a wire rack.
MAKES 10 to 12 slices

APPLE AND SULTANA LOAF

METRIC/IMPERIAL
50 g/2 oz polyunsaturated margarine
50 g/2 oz dark soft brown sugar
1 egg, beaten
100 g/4 oz plain wholemeal flour
100 g/4 oz fresh wholemeal breadcrumbs
1½ teaspoons baking powder
¼ teaspoon ground cinnamon
½ teaspoon ground mixed spice
½ teaspoon grated nutmeg
100 g/4 oz sultanas
450 g/1 lb dessert apples, peeled, cored and sliced
2 tablespoons apple juice

Preheat the oven to moderate (180°C/350°F, Gas Mark 4).

In a bowl, cream together the margarine and sugar until fluffy. Gradually beat in the egg. Fold in the flour, breadcrumbs, baking powder and spices. Stir in the sultanas, apple slices and juice.

Press into a greased 450 g/1 lb loaf tin. Bake in the oven for 1 hour or until firm and slightly risen. Cool on a wire rack.
MAKES one 450 g/1 lb loaf

HERB AND ONION BREAD

METRIC/IMPERIAL
750 g/1½ lb plain wholemeal flour
2 teaspoons salt
15 g/½ oz fresh yeast
450 ml/¾ pint lukewarm water
1 large onion, peeled and minced
1 tablespoon each chopped parsley, thyme and
sage
1 tablespoon polyunsaturated vegetable oil
1 tablespoon sesame seeds

Mix the flour and salt together in a bowl. Cream the yeast with a little of the water and leave until frothy. Add to the flour with the remaining water, the onion, herbs and oil and mix to a dough.

Turn on to a floured surface and knead for 8 to 10 minutes until smooth and elastic. Place in a clean bowl, cover with a damp cloth and leave to rise in a warm place for about 1½ hours, until doubled in size.

Turn on to a floured surface and knead for a few minutes. Form into a fairly wide roll and place on a greased baking sheet. Brush with water and sprinkle with the sesame seeds.

Cover and leave to rise in a warm place for about 30 minutes, until almost doubled in size. Bake in a preheated hot oven (220°C/425°F, Gas Mark 7) for 15 minutes. Lower the temperature to 190°C/375°F, Gas Mark 5, and bake for a further 20 to 25 minutes, until the bread sounds hollow when tapped. Turn on to a wire rack to cool.
MAKES 1 loaf

HONEY CAKE

METRIC/IMPERIAL
100 g/4 oz polyunsaturated margarine
50 g/2 oz Muscovado sugar
3 tablespoons honey
2 eggs, lightly beaten
225 g/8 oz plain wholemeal flour
1 teaspoon baking powder
1 teaspoon ground cinnamon
about 120 ml/4 fl oz skimmed milk
25 g/1 oz flaked almonds

Cream the margarine and sugar until light and fluffy, then beat in the honey. Add the eggs a little at a time, adding a little of the flour after each addition.

Mix the remaining flour with the baking powder and cinnamon, then beat into the creamed mixture with enough milk to make a soft dropping consistency.

Sprinkle the almonds over the base of a greased 18 cm/7 inch square cake tin. Spoon in the mixture.

Bake in a preheated moderate oven (180°C/ 350°F, Gas Mark 4) for 1 hour. Turn out on to a wire rack and leave to cool.
MAKES one 18 cm/7 inch square cake

CARROT AND APPLE CAKE

METRIC/IMPERIAL
100 g/4 oz dark soft brown sugar
2 eggs
150 ml/¼ pint polyunsaturated vegetable oil
75 g/3 oz self-raising unbleached white flour
100 g/4 oz plain wholemeal flour
2 teaspoons baking powder
½ teaspoon bicarbonate of soda
1 teaspoon mixed spice
½ teaspoon ground ginger
½ teaspoon grated nutmeg
175 g/6 oz carrots, grated
1 dessert apple, peeled, cored and grated
50 g/2 oz sultanas
2 tablespoons apple juice

Preheat the oven to moderate (180°C/350°F, Gas Mark 4).

Beat together the sugar and eggs until creamy and frothy. Gradually beat in the oil.

Mix together the flours, baking powder, bicarbonate of soda and the spices. Stir into the egg mixture with the carrot, apple and sultanas. Add apple juice to give the mixture the consistency of a thick batter.

Pour into a greased and base-lined 18 cm/7 inch square cake tin. Bake in the oven for 50 minutes to 1 hour or until firm and risen. Cool on a wire rack. Cut into slices or squares, to serve.
MAKES 16 to 20 pieces

Variation
For contrasting colour and flavour, make a soft topping for the cake. Beat together 75 g/3 oz low-fat soft cheese and 100 ml/3½ fl oz plain yogurt until smooth. Drizzle over the top of the cake.

MALTED CHOCOLATE CAKE

METRIC/IMPERIAL
175 g/6 oz dark soft brown sugar
2 eggs
120 ml/4 fl oz corn oil
120 ml/4 fl oz skimmed milk
2 tablespoons malt extract
175 g/6 oz plain wholemeal flour
25 g/1 oz cocoa powder
2 teaspoons baking powder
100 g/4 oz curd cheese
75 g/3 oz plain chocolate

Place the sugar, eggs, oil, milk and malt extract in a bowl and mix thoroughly. Add the flour, sift in the cocoa and baking powder and beat until smooth.

Divide the mixture between 2 lined and greased 18 cm/7 inch sandwich tins and smooth with a palette knife. Bake in a preheated moderate oven (160°C/325°F, Gas Mark 3) for 25 to 30 minutes until the cakes spring back when lightly pressed. Turn on to a wire rack to cool.

Beat the cheese in a bowl until smooth. Melt the chocolate in a basin over a pan of hot water, add to the cheese and beat thoroughly.

Use half the mixture to sandwich the cakes together. Spread the remainder over the top of the cake and mark a swirl pattern, using a palette knife.

MAKES one 18 cm/7 inch cake

COUNTRY FRUIT CAKE

METRIC/IMPERIAL
250 g/9 oz self-raising wholemeal flour
½ teaspoon ground mixed spice
½ teaspoon ground bicarbonate of soda
75 g/3 oz polyunsaturated margarine
50 g/2 oz fructose
100 g/4 oz raisins
100 g/4 oz sultanas
25 g/1 oz peeled and grated apple
25 g/1 oz mixed peel
1 egg, beaten
175 ml/6 fl oz skimmed milk
5 sugar cubes

Grease and line a 15 cm/6 inch round cake tin, or a 22 × 11 × 6 cm/8½ × 4½ × 2½ inch loaf tin, and pre-heat the oven to moderate (180°C/350°F, Gas Mark 4).

Sift the flour, spice and bicarbonate of soda together into a large bowl. Return the bran remaining in the sieve to the flour. Rub in the margarine. Stir in the fructose, dried fruit, grated apple and mixed peel. Pour in the beaten egg and mix well. Stir in the milk to give the mixture a soft dropping consistency.

Spoon the mixture into the prepared cake tin. Roughly crush the sugar cubes with the end of a rolling pin and scatter them over the cake. Bake in the centre of the oven for about 1 to 1¼ hours until golden brown. Cool slightly before turning out on to a wire tray.

MAKES one 15 cm/6 inch round cake

BANANA CRUNCH CAKE

METRIC/IMPERIAL
100 g/4 oz polyunsaturated margarine
150 g/5 oz Demerara sugar
225 g/8 oz mashed banana
2 eggs, beaten
1 teaspoon natural vanilla essence
100 g/4 oz oat flour, made by grinding rolled oats in a food processor or blender
100 g/4 oz plain wholemeal flour
1 teaspoon salt
1 teaspoon bicarbonate of soda
50 g/2 oz walnuts, chopped
Topping:
50 g/2 oz rolled oats
50 g/2 oz Demerara sugar
25 g/1 oz polyunsaturated margarine, melted
2 tablespoons chopped walnuts
½ teaspoon ground cinnamon

First make the topping by combining all the ingredients. Mix well and reserve.

Beat together the margarine and sugar until light and fluffy. Blend in the mashed banana, eggs and vanilla. Combine the dry ingredients, then fold into the beaten mixture. Finally fold in chopped nuts. Pour the mixture into a greased 20 cm/8 inch square baking tin and sprinkle the crunch topping evenly over the top.

Bake in a preheated moderate oven (180°C/350°F, Gas Mark 4) for about 1 hour or until the cake is golden and a skewer when inserted in the centre of the cake comes out clean. Leave the cake to cool in the tin.

MAKES one 1 kg/2 lb cake

MUESLI CAKE

METRIC/IMPERIAL
175 g/6 oz muesli
100 g/4 oz molasses sugar
175 g/6 oz sultanas
2 tablespoons malt extract
250 ml/8 fl oz apple juice
2 cooking apples, peeled, cored and grated
175 g/6 oz plain wholemeal flour
3 teaspoons baking powder
8 walnut halves

Place the muesli, sugar, sultanas, malt extract and apple juice in a mixing bowl and leave to soak for 30 minutes. Add the grated apple and wholemeal flour, sift in the baking powder and mix together thoroughly.

Turn into a lined and greased 18 cm/7 inch round cake tin and arrange the walnuts around the edge. Bake in a preheated moderate oven (180°C/350°F, Gas Mark 4) for 1½ to 1¾ hours, or until a skewer inserted into the centre comes out clean. Leave in the tin for a few minutes, then turn on to a wire rack to cool.
MAKES one 18 cm/7 inch cake

PARKIN

METRIC/IMPERIAL
100 g/4 oz plain wholemeal flour
350 g/12 oz medium oatmeal
1 teaspoon ground ginger
100 g/4 oz polyunsaturated margarine
100 g/4 oz honey
100 g/4 oz black treacle
4 tablespoons skimmed milk
½ teaspoon bicarbonate of soda

Put the flour, rolled oats and ginger in a bowl and mix well. Put the margarine, honey and black treacle in a pan and heat gently until the margarine has melted. Add to the dry ingredients and mix thoroughly.

Heat the milk until lukewarm, stir in the soda, then add to the flour mixture and beat well. Pour the mixture into a greased 28 × 18 cm/11 × 7 inch cake tin.

Bake in a preheated moderate oven (160°C/325°F, Gas Mark 3) for 1½ hours. Leave to cool in the tin for 10 minutes, then turn out on to a wire rack and leave to cool completely. Store in an airtight tin for 3 to 4 days before cutting.
MAKES one 28 × 18 cm/11 × 7 inch cake

GINGER HONEY CAKE

METRIC/IMPERIAL
75 g/3 oz polyunsaturated margarine
50 g/2 oz Muscovado sugar
2 tablespoons honey
1 egg, beaten with 1 egg yolk
175 g/6 oz self-raising wholemeal flour
pinch of salt
1 teaspoon ground ginger
1 teaspoon ground cinnamon
about 6 tablespoons skimmed milk

Cream the margarine and sugar until light and fluffy, then beat in the honey. Add the egg mixture a little at a time, adding a little of the flour after each addition.

Mix the remaining flour with the salt, ginger and cinnamon, then beat into the creamed mixture with enough milk to make a soft dropping consistency. Spoon the mixture into a greased 18 cm/7 inch round cake tin lined with greased greaseproof paper or non-stick parchment.

Bake in a preheated moderate oven (180°C/350°F, Gas Mark 4) for 50 minutes. Turn out on to a wire rack, carefully remove the paper and leave to cool.
MAKES one 18 cm/7 inch round cake

ORANGE, CARROT AND NUT CAKE

METRIC/IMPERIAL
100 g/4 oz polyunsaturated margarine
75 g/3 oz fructose
1 teaspoon ground cinnamon
1 teaspoon grated orange rind
2 eggs, lightly beaten
75 g/3 oz carrot, peeled and finely grated
50 g/2 oz shelled walnuts, finely chopped
1 tablespoon orange juice
225 g/8 oz self-raising wholemeal flour
1 teaspoon baking powder

Preheat the oven to moderate (180°C/350°F, Gas Mark 4). Grease and line a 20 cm/8 inch cake tin with greaseproof paper and grease the paper.

Cream the margarine and fructose together in a bowl until pale and fluffy. Beat in the ground cinnamon and orange rind. Gradually add the eggs, beating well after each addition. Stir in the grated carrot, chopped nuts and orange juice. Mix the flour and baking powder together and fold into the creamed mixture.

Turn into the prepared cake tin and smooth the top. Bake in the oven for 45 to 55 minutes, or until the centre of the cake springs back when lightly pressed with a fingertip. Turn out on a wire tray to cool.

MAKES one 20 cm/8 inch cake

Note: This cake improves in flavour if kept for at least one day before cutting.

OATCAKES

METRIC/IMPERIAL
100 g/4 oz medium oatmeal
½ teaspoon salt
pinch of bicarbonate of soda
2 teaspoons polyunsaturated vegetable oil
about 50 ml/2 fl oz hot water

Mix the oatmeal, salt and bicarbonate of soda in a bowl. Make a well in the centre, pour in the oil and add enough water to make a stiff dough which can be squeezed into a ball.

Sprinkle the board and your hands with oatmeal and knead the mixture until there are no cracks. Flatten the ball and roll it out into a round just under 5 mm/¼ inch thick. Invert a plate on top and trim off the ragged edges. (Work up the trimmings and roll out and add them to the next batch of dough.)

Cut the round 'bannock' across into 4 triangles, called 'farls'. With a palette knife lift them on to a warmed and greased griddle or thick-based frying pan and cook over a moderate heat for 20 minutes or until the farls curl at the corners. Turn and cook the other side for 5 minutes or finish under a preheated moderate grill.

Store the oatcakes in an airtight tin and toast under a moderate grill or in the oven before serving.

If you prefer very thin oatcakes, make a slightly softer dough and roll it out as thin as possible. Trim the bannock and cut it into 6 farls. The thin oatcakes will cook more quickly and need care in handling.

MAKES 4 or 6

BANANA AND WALNUT SLICES

METRIC/IMPERIAL
100 g/4 oz polyunsaturated margarine
100 g/4 oz molasses sugar
2 eggs
100 g/4 oz plain wholemeal flour
2 teaspoons baking powder
2 bananas, mashed
100 g/4 oz walnuts, chopped

Cream the margarine and sugar together until light and fluffy. Beat in the eggs, one at a time, adding a tablespoon of flour with the second egg. Fold in the remaining flour and baking powder with the bananas.

Spread the mixture evenly in a lined and greased 20 cm/8 inch square shallow tin. Sprinkle with the walnuts and bake in a preheated moderately hot oven (190°C/375°F, Gas Mark 5) for 20 to 25 minutes until the cake springs back when lightly pressed.

Leave in the tin for 2 minutes, then cut into 16 slices. Transfer to a wire rack to cool.

MAKES 16 slices

Variation
The same quantity of chopped almonds or hazelnuts may be used in place of the walnuts.

HONEY CRISPS

METRIC/IMPERIAL
100 g/4 oz polyunsaturated margarine
100 g/4 oz Demerara sugar
75 g/3 oz honey
250 g/9 oz plain wholemeal flour
½ teaspoon ground ginger
½ teaspoon ground cinnamon
¼ teaspoon bicarbonate of soda

Beat together the margarine, sugar and honey until the mixture is light and fluffy. Stir in the remaining ingredients, mixing well. (The dough will be stiff and dry.) Shape a teaspoonful of the dough into a ball and place on an ungreased baking sheet. Continue until all the mixture is used.

Bake in a preheated moderately hot oven (190°C/375°F, Gas Mark 5) for 10 to 12 minutes. Allow to cool on the baking sheet for 1 minute and then transfer to a wire cooling rack. Store in an airtight container.

MAKES about 36

WHOLEFOOD BROWNIES

METRIC/IMPERIAL
100 g/4 oz polyunsaturated margarine
75 g/3 oz Muscovado sugar
25 g/1 oz cocoa powder
6 tablespoons skimmed milk
2 eggs, beaten
90 g/3½ oz plain wholemeal flour
1 teaspoon baking powder
50 g/2 oz walnuts, chopped
50 g/2 oz sultanas

Preheat the oven to moderately hot (190°C/375°F, Gas Mark 5). Put the margarine, sugar, cocoa and milk into a saucepan and melt over a gentle heat, stirring. Remove from the heat.

Put the cocoa mixture, eggs, flour, baking powder, walnuts and sultanas into a bowl and mix thoroughly.

Pour into a greased and base-lined 18 cm/7 inch square cake tin. Cook for about 20 minutes or until firm to touch. Cool and cut into 16 squares.
MAKES 16

MUESLI FLAPJACKS

METRIC/IMPERIAL
150 g/5 oz polyunsaturated margarine
75 g/3 oz Muscovado sugar
1 tablespoon honey
225 g/8 oz muesli
50 g/2 oz hazelnuts, chopped

Heat the margarine gently in a pan until melted. Remove from the heat and stir in the sugar and honey. Then add the muesli and nuts and mix thoroughly.

Press the mixture firmly into a greased 18 cm/7 inch square cake tin. Bake in a preheated moderately hot oven (190°C/375°F, Gas Mark 5) for 25 minutes. Mark into 9 squares while still hot, then leave in the tin until almost cold. Transfer carefully to a wire rack and leave to cool completely.
MAKES 9

WALNUT SQUARES

METRIC/IMPERIAL
1 egg, beaten
225 g/8 oz Muscovado sugar
75 g/3 oz plain wholemeal flour
1 teaspoon bicarbonate of soda
¼ teaspoon salt
100 g/4 oz walnuts, finely chopped

Put the egg and sugar in a bowl and mix well. Mix the flour, soda and salt together, then stir into the egg mixture. Stir in the nuts.

Spread the mixture in a greased 20 cm/8 inch square tin. Bake in a preheated moderate oven (180°C/350°F, Gas Mark 4) for 20 minutes. Leave to cool in the tin, then cut into squares before serving.
MAKES 16

COCONUT SNOWBALLS

METRIC/IMPERIAL
100 g/4 oz rolled oats
100 g/4 oz plain wholemeal flour
75 g/3 oz ground almonds
25 g/1 oz icing sugar
100 g/4 oz polyunsaturated margarine
few drops of natural almond essence
Coating:
40 g/1½ oz desiccated coconut
1½ tablespoons icing sugar (optional)

Stir together the oats, flour and ground almonds. Sift the icing sugar into a bowl. Add the margarine and almond essence and cream together until light and fluffy. Fold in the oat mixture, mixing thoroughly. The dough will be rather sticky at this stage, so allow it to stand in the refrigerator for about 15 minutes.

Shape the mixture into 36 to 40 small balls. Spread the coconut on to a flat dish and roll the balls in the coconut until well coated. Place on an ungreased baking sheet allowing about 3 cm/1½ inches between the balls. Bake in a preheated moderate oven (180°C/350°F, Gas Mark 4) for about 15 minutes.

Cool on the baking sheet for 5 minutes, then transfer the biscuits to a wire cooling rack. When cold sift the icing sugar over the balls, if liked.
MAKES 36 to 40

WHOLEMEAL TREACLE SCONES

METRIC/IMPERIAL
100 g/4 oz plain unbleached white flour
100 g/4 oz plain wholemeal flour
25 g/1 oz caster sugar
½ teaspoon cream of tartar
½ teaspoon bicarbonate of soda
1 teaspoon ground mixed spice
50 g/2 oz polyunsaturated margarine
2 tablespoons black treacle, warmed
7 tablespoons skimmed milk

Preheat the oven to moderately hot (190°C/375°F, Gas Mark 5).
Put the dry ingredients into a bowl and stir until thoroughly mixed. Rub in the margarine, then stir in the warmed treacle and the milk.
Turn the dough out on a floured surface and knead lightly. Roll out gently until about 1 cm/½ inch thick and stamp out about 10 rounds with a 5 cm/2 inch cutter.
Place the scones on a greased and floured baking sheet and brush with remaining milk. Bake in the oven for 20 minutes. Transfer to a wire rack and serve very fresh.
MAKES 10 to 12

FRUIT SLICES

METRIC/IMPERIAL
225 g/8 oz rich wholemeal pastry (see page 334)
100 g/4 oz currants
100 g/4 oz sultanas
1 large cooking apple, peeled, cored and grated
finely grated rind of 1 orange
juice of ½ lemon
50 g/2 oz Demerara sugar
Topping:
1 egg white, lightly beaten
little Demerara sugar

Divide the pastry dough in half. Roll out one piece and use to line the base of a shallow 28 × 20 cm/ 11 × 8 inch tin.
Mix the fruit, orange rind, lemon juice and sugar together, then spread this mixture over the dough. Roll out the remaining dough and use to cover the fruit mixture. Brush with egg white and sprinkle with sugar. Bake in a preheated hot oven (220°C/425°F, Gas Mark 7) for 25 minutes. Leave to cool in the tin and cut into slices.
MAKES 16

OATMEAL CRUNCHIES

METRIC/IMPERIAL
225 g/8 oz plain wholemeal flour
75 g/3 oz medium oatmeal
75 g/3 oz bran
150 g/5 oz Muscovado sugar
½ teaspoon ground ginger
½ teaspoon ground mixed spice
100 g/4 oz polyunsaturated margarine
about 150 ml/¼ pint cold water

Put the dry ingredients in a bowl and mix well. Rub in the margarine until the mixture resembles coarse breadcrumbs, then add enough water to make a stiff dough.
Turn the dough out on to a lightly floured surface, then roll out to 1 cm/½ inch thickness. Stamp out about 48 rounds with a 6 cm/2½ inch biscuit cutter.
Place on greased baking sheets, then bake in a preheated moderate oven (180°C/350°F, Gas Mark 4) for 25 minutes. Transfer to a wire rack and leave to cool.
MAKES 48

FARMHOUSE SCONES

METRIC/IMPERIAL
225 g/8 oz plain wholemeal flour
pinch of sea salt
1 teaspoon baking powder
50 g/2 oz polyunsaturated margarine
25 g/1 oz Muscovado sugar
25 g/1 oz sultanas
1 egg
5 tablespoons skimmed milk
milk, to glaze

Put the flour, salt and baking powder in a bowl and mix well. Rub in the margarine until the mixture resembles coarse breadcrumbs, then stir in the sugar and sultanas. Beat the egg with the milk, then gradually add to the dry mixture and mix to a soft dough.
Turn out on to a lightly floured surface and roll out to 1 cm/½ inch thickness. Cut out 12 rounds with a 5 cm/2 inch biscuit cutter and place on a greased baking sheet.
Brush the tops with a little milk to glaze, then bake in a preheated moderately hot oven (200°C/ 400°F, Gas Mark 6) for 15 minutes. Transfer to a wire rack and leave to cool.
MAKES 12

NUTTY FLAPJACKS

METRIC/IMPERIAL
100 g/4 oz polyunsaturated margarine
120 ml/4 fl oz clear honey
75 g/3 oz Muscovado sugar
225 g/8 oz rolled oats
50 g/2 oz walnuts, chopped

Melt the margarine with the honey and sugar in a saucepan. Stir in the oats and walnuts and mix thoroughly. Turn into a greased 18 × 28 cm/7 × 11 inch shallow tin and smooth the top with a palette knife.

Bake in a preheated moderate oven (180°C/350°F, Gas Mark 4) for 25 to 30 minutes.

Cool in the tin for 2 minutes, then cut into fingers. Cool completely before removing from the tin.
MAKES 20

MALTED OAT FINGERS

METRIC/IMPERIAL
120 ml/4 fl oz polyunsaturated vegetable oil
3 tablespoons malt extract
50 g/2 oz Muscovado sugar
100 g/4 oz jumbo oats
100 g/4 oz rolled oats
2 tablespoons sesame seeds, toasted

Place the oil, malt extract and sugar in a saucepan and heat gently. Add the remaining ingredients and mix thoroughly. Press into a greased 20 cm/8 inch square shallow cake tin and smooth the top with a palette knife.

Bake in a preheated moderate oven (180°C/350°F, Gas Mark 4) for 30 minutes.

Cool in the tin for 2 minutes, then cut into 16 fingers. Cool completely before removing from the tin.
MAKES 16

NUTTY FRUIT CHEWS

METRIC/IMPERIAL
450 g/1 lb mixed dried fruit
100 g/4 oz chopped mixed nuts
120 ml/4 fl oz clear honey

Put the large fruit, such as dried apricots and prunes, in a bowl and pour on enough boiling water to cover. Leave to stand for 5 minutes, then

drain off the water. Put all the fruit through the fine blade of a mincer, then stir in the nuts and honey until well mixed.

Spread the mixture in a 20 cm/8 inch square tin lined with foil. Cover with more foil, then place weights on top so that the surface is evenly pressed down. Leave in a cool place for 12 hours. Cut into squares before serving.
MAKES 16

YOGURT WHOLEMEAL SCONES

METRIC/IMPERIAL
225 g/8 oz plain wholemeal flour
½ teaspoon salt
1½ teaspoons baking powder
25 g/1 oz polyunsaturated margarine
150 ml/¼ pint plain low-fat yogurt

Put the flour, salt and baking powder in a bowl and stir well to mix. Rub in the margarine, then stir in the yogurt and mix to a soft dough.

Turn out on to a lightly floured surface and knead lightly for 30 seconds. Roll out to 2 cm/¾ inch thickness, cut out 10 rounds with a 5 cm/2 inch biscuit cutter and place on a greased baking sheet.

Bake in a preheated moderately hot oven (200°C/400°F, Gas Mark 6) for 12 minutes. Transfer to a wire rack and leave to cool. Serve with honey or a low-fat cheese spread.
MAKES 10

PEANUT BUTTER DREAMS

METRIC/IMPERIAL
225 g/8 oz polyunsaturated margarine
225 g/8 oz peanut butter
175 g/6 oz Demerara sugar
2 eggs, beaten
1 teaspoon natural vanilla essence
275 g/10 oz oat flour, made by grinding rolled oats in a food processor or blender
2 teaspoons bicarbonate of soda
½ teaspoon salt
150 g/5 oz peanuts (dry roasted), chopped

Beat together the margarine, peanut butter and brown sugar until light and fluffy. Gradually beat in the egg, followed by the vanilla essence. Combine all the dry ingredients then stir into the peanut butter mixture. Fold in the nuts.

Chill the mixture for about 1 hour, then shape into 2.5 cm/1 inch balls. Place these balls well apart on an ungreased baking sheet. Flatten with the tines of a fork dipped in sugar to form a criss-cross pattern.

Bake in a preheated moderate oven (180°C/350°F, Gas Mark 4) for about 15 minutes or until the edges turn golden. Cool on a wire rack.
MAKES about 65

DATE AND HAZELNUT FINGERS

METRIC/IMPERIAL
2 eggs
175 g/6 oz Muscovado sugar
75 g/3 oz self-raising wholemeal flour
pinch of salt
50 g/2 oz bran cereal
50 g/2 oz hazelnuts, chopped
100 g/4 oz stoned dates, chopped

Put the eggs and sugar in a bowl and whisk until light and creamy. Stir in the remaining ingredients and mix thoroughly.

Spread the mixture evenly in a 28 × 18 cm/11 × 7 inch tin lined with greased greaseproof paper or non-stick parchment.

Bake in a preheated moderate oven (180°C/350°F, Gas Mark 4) for 30 minutes. Leave to cool in the tin. Cut in slices before serving.
MAKES 12

CHOCOLATE BISCUITS

METRIC/IMPERIAL
50 g/2 oz polyunsaturated margarine
100 g/4 oz plain wholemeal flour
3 tablespoons cocoa powder
25 g/1 oz fructose
1 tablespoon skimmed milk

Preheat the oven to moderately hot (190°C/375°F, Gas Mark 5).

Rub the margarine into the flour. Add the cocoa powder and fructose. Using a knife, mix all together with the milk. Knead to a smooth ball and roll out on a floured board. Cut into rounds with a 6 cm/2½ inch pastry cutter and place on a greased baking sheet.

Bake in the oven for 15 minutes and cool on a wire tray.
MAKES 14

DIGESTIVE BISCUITS

METRIC/IMPERIAL
350 g/12 oz plain wholemeal flour
2 teaspoons sea salt
150 g/5 oz polyunsaturated margarine
50 g/2 oz Muscovado sugar
1 egg, beaten with 4 tablespoons cold water

Put the flour and salt in a bowl, then rub in the margarine until the mixture resembles fine bread-crumbs. Stir in the sugar, then add the egg and water mixture and mix to a soft dough.

Turn out on to a lightly floured surface and knead lightly. Roll out to 5 mm/¼ inch thickness, then cut out 40 rounds with a 6 cm/2½ inch biscuit cutter.

Place the rounds on greased baking sheets and prick each one 4 times with a fork. Bake in a preheated moderate oven (180°C/350°F, Gas Mark 4) for 25 minutes. Transfer to a wire rack and leave to cool.
MAKES 40

SESAME AND OAT BISCUITS

METRIC/IMPERIAL
75 g/3 oz rolled oats
50 g/2 oz medium oatmeal
2 tablespoons sesame seeds, toasted
75 g/3 oz molasses sugar
120 ml/4 fl oz polyunsaturated vegetable oil
1 egg, beaten

Place the oats, oatmeal, sesame seeds, sugar and oil in a mixing bowl. Stir well and leave to stand for 1 hour. Add the egg and mix thoroughly.

Place teaspoons of the mixture well apart on a greased baking sheet and then flatten with a palette knife.

Bake in a preheated moderate oven (160°C/325°F, Gas Mark 3) for 15 to 20 minutes until golden brown. Leave to cool for 2 minutes then transfer to a wire rack to cool completely.
MAKES about 25

OATMEAL AND PEANUT BISCUITS

METRIC/IMPERIAL
50 g/2 oz polyunsaturated margarine
75 g/3 oz crunchy peanut butter
25 g/1 oz Muscovado sugar
1 large egg
75 g/3 oz self-raising flour
75 g/3 oz medium oatmeal
milk for brushing

Preheat the oven to moderately hot (190°C/375°F, Gas Mark 5).

Cream together the margarine, peanut butter and sugar. Beat in the egg, then stir in the flour and oatmeal to make a stiff dough. Turn on to a floured surface and roll out to a 5 mm/¼ inch thickness. Using a 5 cm/2 inch cutter, stamp out biscuits.

Place on a greased baking tray. Brush with milk and cook in the oven for 10 to 15 minutes. Cool on a wire rack.
MAKES 24

Note: These are good served as a snack with cheese or as part of a packed lunch or picnic.

SULTANA SPICE BISCUITS

METRIC/IMPERIAL
100 g/4 oz polyunsaturated margarine
175 g/6 oz light soft brown sugar
50 g/2 oz mashed potato, sieved
175 g/6 oz plain wholemeal flour
50 g/2 oz sultanas
1 teaspoon mixed spice
Topping:
1 tablespoon caster sugar
½ teaspoon mixed spice

Cream together the margarine and sugar until smooth and fluffy, then beat in the potato. Add the flour, sultanas and spice and mix well.

Turn on to a lightly floured surface and roll out to a 5 mm/¼ inch thickness. Using a 7 cm/3 inch cutter, cut out rounds and place them on greased baking sheets.

Bake in a preheated moderate oven (180°C/350°F, Gas Mark 4) for 15 to 20 minutes until golden brown. Mix together the sugar and spice and sprinkle over the hot biscuits. Transfer to a wire rack and allow to cool.
MAKES about 20

CHEESE CRACKERS

METRIC/IMPERIAL
225 g/8 oz Cheddar cheese, grated
50 g/2 oz Parmesan cheese
100 g/4 oz polyunsaturated margarine
3 tablespoons water
150 g/5 oz plain unbleached white flour
½ teaspoon mustard powder
pinch of salt
75 g/3 oz rolled oats

Beat together the cheeses, margarine and water until thoroughly blended. Sift together the flour, mustard and salt and fold into the cheese mixture, followed by the rolled oats.

Shape the dough into a roll about 30 cm/12 inches long. Wrap securely in foil or greaseproof paper and refrigerate for about 4 hours.

Uncover and cut the roll into 5 mm/¼ inch slices and transfer to a greased baking sheet. Flatten slightly with a fork then bake in a preheated moderately hot oven (200°C/400°F, Gas Mark 6) for 8 to 10 minutes or until the edges are light golden. Transfer to a wire rack and allow to cool.
MAKES about 60

HONEY AND NUT COOKIES

METRIC/IMPERIAL
100 g/4 oz polyunsaturated margarine
100 g/4 oz Demerara sugar
1 egg, beaten
1 tablespoon honey
225 g/8 oz self-raising unbleached white flour
pinch of salt
50 g/2 oz mixed nuts, chopped

Cream the margarine and sugar until light and fluffy, then beat in the egg and honey. Sift the flour and salt together, then beat gradually into the creamed mixture. Add the nuts and mix well.

Divide the dough into 36 pieces, about the size of walnuts, and roll each one into a ball. Place on greased baking sheets, flattening each ball with a fork dipped in cold water. Bake in a preheated moderate oven (180°C/350°F, Gas Mark 4) for 12 minutes. Transfer carefully to a wire rack and leave to cool.
MAKES 36

SESAME SNAPS

METRIC/IMPERIAL
175 g/6 oz medium oatmeal
50 g/2 oz sesame seeds, toasted
6 tablespoons clear honey
6 tablespoons polyunsaturated vegetable oil
50 g/2 oz Muscovado sugar

Place all the ingredients in a bowl and mix thoroughly. Press into a greased 20 × 30 cm/8 × 12 inch Swiss roll tin and smooth the top.

Bake in a preheated moderate oven (180°C/350°F, Gas Mark 4) for 20 to 25 minutes. Cool in the tin for 2 minutes, then cut into 24 squares. Cool completely before removing from the tin.
MAKES 24

BRAN, HAZELNUT AND OAT SLICE

METRIC/IMPERIAL
100 g/4 oz polyunsaturated margarine
100 g/4 oz Muscovado sugar
2 eggs
2 tablespoons skimmed milk
75 g/3 oz plain wholemeal flour
2 teaspoons baking powder
50 g/2 oz rolled oats
3 tablespoons bran
50 g/2 oz hazelnuts, chopped
Topping:
100 g/4 oz low-fat cream cheese
2 teaspoons sifted icing sugar
3 tablespoons orange juice

Cream the margarine with the sugar in a bowl until light and fluffy. Blend in the eggs and milk. Fold in the flour, baking powder, oats, bran and hazelnuts, blending well.

Spoon and spread evenly into a greased and lined 20 cm/8 inch square shallow cake tin. Bake in a preheated moderately hot oven (190°C/375°F, Gas Mark 5) for 20 to 25 minutes until firm and springy to the touch. Allow to cool slightly, then turn out and allow to cool on a wire rack.

To make the topping, beat the cream cheese with the icing sugar and orange juice. Swirl over the cake and cut into slices to serve.
MAKES about 16

SPICED COCONUT COOKIES

METRIC/IMPERIAL
100 g/4 oz polyunsaturated margarine
100 g/4 oz light Muscovado sugar
1 egg
100 g/4 oz self-raising wholemeal flour
pinch of salt
½ teaspoon ground cinnamon
½ teaspoon ground mixed spice
50 g/2 oz desiccated coconut

Cream the margarine with the sugar and egg in a bowl until light and fluffy. Fold in the flour, salt, cinnamon, ground mixed spice and coconut, blending well.

Place heaped teaspoonfuls of the mixture on to 2 greased baking trays, spacing them about 5 cm/2 inches apart.

Bake in a preheated moderate oven (180°C/350°F, Gas Mark 4) until crisp and golden, about 20 to 25 minutes. Allow to cool on a wire rack.
MAKES 24

APRICOT AND RAISIN SLICES

METRIC/IMPERIAL
50 g/2 oz raisins
3 tablespoons orange juice
50 g/2 oz polyunsaturated margarine
1 tablespoon honey
1 tablespoon golden syrup
225 g/8 oz digestive biscuits, crushed
½ teaspoon ground mixed spice
50 g/2 oz no-soak apricots, chopped

Place the raisins and orange juice in a bowl and leave to soak for 30 minutes.

Melt the margarine in a pan with the honey and syrup. Stir in the crushed biscuits, spice, soaked fruit and apricots, then mix well. Press into a greased 20 cm/8 inch loose-bottomed flan tin or cake tin. Allow to cool then chill before cutting into slices.
MAKES 16 to 20

WHOLEMEAL PIZZA DOUGH

METRIC/IMPERIAL
1 teaspoon light soft brown sugar
150 ml/¼ pint lukewarm water
1 teaspoon dried yeast
100 g/4 oz plain wholemeal flour
100 g/4 oz strong white flour
1 teaspoon salt
2 teaspoons polyunsaturated vegetable oil

Dissolve the sugar in the water. Sprinkle over the yeast. Leave in a warm place until frothy. Mix the flours and the salt in a bowl. Add the yeast liquid and the oil. Mix to a soft dough, then turn on to a floured surface and knead for 5 minutes. Replace in the bowl and cover with a clean cloth. Leave to rise in a warm place for 30 minutes or until doubled in size.
  Knead the risen dough briefly, then roll out and use according to the recipe.
MAKES a 20 cm/8 inch diameter pizza

BASIC WHOLEMEAL PASTRY

METRIC/IMPERIAL
225 g/8 oz plain wholemeal flour (see note)
pinch each of salt and pepper
100 g/4 oz polyunsaturated margarine
2-3 tablespoons cold water
beaten egg or milk, to glaze (optional)

Put the flour and salt and pepper in a bowl, then add the margarine. Rub into the flour until the mixture resembles fine breadcrumbs. Add the water and mix to a firm dough. Wrap in grease-proof paper and chill for 30 minutes before using. If wished, brush the pastry with egg or milk before baking.
MAKES 225 g/8 oz quantity

Note: For a 175 g/6 oz quantity, use 175 g/6 oz plain wholemeal flour, 75 g/3 oz margarine and 2 tablespoons cold water.

WHOLEMEAL AND POTATO PASTRY

METRIC/IMPERIAL
75 g/3 oz plain wholemeal flour
40 g/1½ oz polyunsaturated margarine
50 g/2 oz cold mashed potato
1 tablespoon ice-cold water

Put the flour in a bowl. Add the margarine and rub into the flour until the mixture resembles breadcrumbs. Stir in the potato and then the water. Knead to a firm dough.
  Turn on to a lightly floured surface, roll out and use according to the recipe.
MAKES sufficient to line one 20 cm/8 inch flan ring

RICH WHOLEMEAL PASTRY

METRIC/IMPERIAL
225 g/8 oz plain wholemeal flour
pinch of salt
100 g/4 oz polyunsaturated margarine
2 egg yolks
1 tablespoon cold water

Put the flour and salt in a bowl, then rub in the margarine until the mixture resembles fine bread-crumbs. Beat the egg yolks with the water, then add to the dry mixture and mix to a dough.
  As this pastry is a little difficult to handle, it is best to roll it out on a piece of foil so that it can be easily lifted.
MAKES 225 g/8 oz quantity

Note: The best flour to use for this pastry is 85 per cent wholemeal. For sweet pies and flans, 25 g/1 oz Muscovado sugar may be added to the pastry before mixing in the liquid.

WHOLEMEAL CHEESE PASTRY

METRIC/IMPERIAL
175 g/6 oz plain wholemeal flour
pinch of salt
½ teaspoon mustard powder
pinch of cayenne pepper
75 g/3 oz polyunsaturated margarine
75 g/3 oz Cheddar cheese, finely grated
2 tablespoons cold water

Mix together the flour, salt, mustard and cayenne in a large mixing bowl. Rub in the margarine until the mixture resembles breadcrumbs. Mix in the grated cheese. Add the water and, using a knife, cut the mixture until it comes together to form a dough. Use your hands to knead lightly. Chill for 30 minutes before using for pies, pasties or to line savoury flan cakes.

MAKES 175 g/6 oz quantity

STRUDEL PASTE

METRIC/IMPERIAL
225 g/8 oz plain unbleached white flour
½ teaspoon salt
1 large egg, lightly beaten
2 tablespoons polyunsaturated vegetable oil
3 tablespoons lukewarm water

Sieve together the flour and salt. Make a well in the centre and pour in the egg and oil. Add the water gradually, stirring with a fork, to make a soft sticky dough. Work the dough in the bowl until it leaves the sides clean, then turn out on to a lightly floured surface and knead for about 15 minutes or until the dough feels smooth and elastic. Form into a ball, place in a bowl and cover with a warm cloth. Leave to rest for 1 hour.

Warm the rolling pin, and flour a large clean tea towel. Place the dough on the towel and roll it out to a rectangle as thinly as possible, lifting and turning it to prevent it from sticking to the cloth. Using the backs of your hands, gently stretch the dough, working from the centre to the outside until it is paper thin – you should be able to read through the dough, but to do this takes years of practice and patience. Leave the dough to rest for 15 minutes before using.

MAKES 225 g/8 oz quantity

FLAKY PASTRY

METRIC/IMPERIAL
225 g/8 oz plain wholemeal flour
1 teaspoon salt
2 teaspoons baking powder
75 g/3 oz polyunsaturated margarine
75 g/3 oz vegetable fat
1 teaspoon lemon juice
7-8 tablespoons cold water

Sift the flour, salt and baking powder into a bowl. Work the fats together in another bowl and divide into 4. Rub one quarter of the softened fat into the flour and mix to a soft elastic dough with the water and lemon juice.

Roll out the dough to an oblong on a floured board and flake the second quarter of fat over the top two-thirds. Fold the bottom third up and the top third down and give the pastry half a turn, so that the folds are now at the sides. Seal the edges of the pastry by pressing with the rolling pin. Reroll as before, and continue until all the fat is used up. Wrap the pastry loosely in greaseproof paper and leave to rest in the refrigerator for at least 30 minutes before using.

Sprinkle a board or table with very little flour, roll out the pastry until 3 mm/⅛ inch thick, use as required and bake in a very hot oven (240°C/450°F, Gas Mark 9).

MAKES 225 g/8 oz quantity

CHAPPATIS

METRIC/IMPERIAL
225 g/8 oz plain wholemeal flour
pinch of salt
about 150 ml/¼ pint water
polyunsaturated margarine for spreading

Sift the flour and salt into a large bowl and make a hollow in the centre. Add the water gradually, working in the flour to make a firm dough. Knead well for about 15 minutes, until the dough is smooth. Cover with a damp cloth and leave to stand for about 30 minutes. The dough should be quite firm and hard.

Divide the dough into 8 portions. Roll each into a circle, about 15 cm/6 inches in diameter, sprinkling the rolling pin and work surface with flour to prevent sticking.

Cook each chappati in a very hot heavy frying pan, without fat. When the top surface shows signs of bubbling, turn the chappati over and cook for 30 to 40 seconds on the other side. Then place the chappati under a warm grill until it puffs up. Spread margarine lightly on one side, fold over and serve hot.

MAKES 8

SAUCES & DRESSINGS

FRENCH DRESSING

METRIC/IMPERIAL
175 ml/6 fl oz olive oil
4 tablespoons wine vinegar
1 teaspoon French mustard
1 clove garlic, peeled and crushed
salt
freshly ground black pepper

Put all the ingredients in a screw-topped jar, adding salt and pepper to taste. Shake well to blend before serving.
MAKES 250 ml/8 fl oz

HERB VINAIGRETTE

METRIC/IMPERIAL
175 ml/6 fl oz olive oil
2 tablespoons vinegar
2 tablespoons lemon juice
1 clove garlic, peeled and crushed
½ teaspoon mustard
2 tablespoons chopped mixed herbs (e.g. mint, parsley, chervil, chives and thyme)
salt
freshly ground black pepper

Put all the ingredients in a screw-topped jar, adding salt and pepper to taste. Shake well to blend before serving.
MAKES 250 ml/8 fl oz

WATERCRESS MAYONNAISE

METRIC/IMPERIAL
1½ tablespoons cornflour
1 teaspoon celery seed
1 teaspoon dried mustard
1 teaspoon salt
250 ml/8 fl oz skimmed milk
2 egg yolks, beaten
50 ml/2 fl oz vinegar
1 bunch watercress, washed

Mix together the cornflour, celery seed, mustard and salt in a small heavy-based saucepan. Beat in the milk, a little at a time, and cook over a low heat, stirring constantly, until the mixture thickens. Continue to cook for 2 minutes. Cool slightly, add the beaten egg yolks and cook for a further 2 to 3 minutes.

Remove from the heat and stir in the vinegar. Place in a blender or food processor with the watercress and blend. Chill before serving. The mayonnaise may be refrigerated for 2 to 3 days.
MAKES 300 ml/½ pint

TOMATO AND GARLIC DRESSING

METRIC/IMPERIAL
300 ml/½ pint tomato juice
1 tablespoon lemon juice
1 clove garlic, peeled and crushed
2 tablespoons snipped chives
2 tablespoons olive oil
salt
freshly ground black pepper

Put all the ingredients in a screw-topped jar, adding salt and pepper to taste. Shake well to blend before serving.
MAKES 300 ml/½ pint

SOY SAUCE DRESSING

METRIC/IMPERIAL
175 ml/6 fl oz olive oil
4 tablespoons soy sauce
2 tablespoons lemon juice
1 clove garlic, peeled and crushed
1 cm/½ inch piece root ginger, finely chopped
salt
freshly ground black pepper

Put all the ingredients in a screw-topped jar, adding salt and pepper to taste. Shake well to blend before serving.
MAKES 300 ml/½ pint

HONEY AND LEMON DRESSING

METRIC/IMPERIAL
4 tablespoons lemon juice
2 tablespoons clear honey
3 tablespoons olive oil
salt
freshly ground black pepper

Put all the ingredients in a screw-topped jar, adding salt and pepper to taste. Shake well to blend before serving.
MAKES 150 ml/¼ pint

GREEN HERB DRESSING

METRIC/IMPERIAL
25 g/1 oz parsley
15 g/½ oz mint
15 g/½ oz snipped chives
1 clove garlic, peeled and chopped
150 g/5 oz plain low-fat yogurt
120 ml/4 fl oz polyunsaturated vegetable oil
juice of ½ lemon
salt
freshly ground black pepper

Rinse the bunches of parsley and mint under running water and pat dry. Remove the stalks and place the leaves in a blender with the remaining ingredients, seasoning with ½ teaspoon salt and ¼ teaspoon freshly ground black pepper. Blend for 2 to 3 minutes.
  Store in an airtight container in the refrigerator. Shake well to blend before serving.
MAKES 300 ml/½ pint

GARLIC DRESSING

METRIC/IMPERIAL
175 ml/6 fl oz olive oil
4 tablespoons wine vinegar
1 teaspoon French mustard
4 cloves garlic, peeled and crushed
1 teaspoon clear honey
salt
freshly ground black pepper

Put all the ingredients in a screw-topped jar, adding salt and pepper to taste. Shake well to blend before serving.
MAKES 250 ml/8 fl oz

GINGER DRESSING

METRIC/IMPERIAL
175 ml/6 fl oz sunflower oil
4 tablespoons soy sauce
2 tablespoons lemon juice
1 clove garlic, peeled and crushed
2.4 cm/1 inch piece root ginger, peeled and finely chopped
salt
freshly ground black pepper

Put all the ingredients in a screw-topped jar, adding salt and pepper to taste. Shake well to blend before serving.
MAKES 300 ml/½ pint

LEMON YOGURT DRESSING

METRIC/IMPERIAL
150 ml/¼ pint plain low-fat yogurt
finely grated rind and juice of ½ lemon
1 tablespoon chopped parsley
1 tablespoon snipped chives
1 tablespoon chopped thyme, mint, watercress or sorrel
salt
freshly ground black pepper

Put all the ingredients in a bowl and beat well. Taste and adjust the seasoning, then pour over the salad just before serving.
MAKES 150 ml/¼ pint

CHILLI DRESSING

METRIC/IMPERIAL
175 ml/6 fl oz sunflower oil
4 tablespoons soy sauce
2 tablespoons lemon juice
1 clove garlic, peeled and crushed
1 green chilli, deseeded and finely chopped
salt
freshly ground black pepper

Put all the ingredients in a screw-topped jar, adding salt and pepper to taste. Shake well to blend.
MAKES 300 ml/½ pint

LEMON AND PARSLEY DRESSING

METRIC/IMPERIAL
175 ml/6 fl oz olive oil
4 tablespoons lemon juice
1 teaspoon clear honey
1 clove garlic, peeled and crushed
1 tablespoon chopped parsley
salt
freshly ground black pepper

Put all the ingredients in a screw-topped jar, adding salt and pepper to taste. Shake well to blend before serving.
MAKES 250 ml/8 fl oz

MINT AND HONEY DRESSING

METRIC/IMPERIAL
2 tablespoons clear honey
4 tablespoons cider vinegar
3 tablespoons olive oil
1 tablespoon chopped mint
salt
freshly ground black pepper

Put all the ingredients in a screw-topped jar, adding salt and pepper to taste. Shake well to blend before serving.
MAKES 150 ml/¼ pint

BLENDER MAYONNAISE I

METRIC/IMPERIAL
1 egg
salt
freshly ground black pepper
½ teaspoon mustard powder
4 tablespoons olive oil
2 tablespoons lemon juice

Place the egg, salt and pepper and mustard in a blender or food processor and blend on medium speed for a few seconds. Remove the centre cap from the lid and add the oil, drop by drop, with the motor still running on low speed.
Gradually add the lemon juice until the mixture is thick. Serve at once or keep for up to 1 week in a screw-topped jar in the refrigerator.
SERVES 4

BLENDER MAYONNAISE II

METRIC/IMPERIAL
1 egg
½ teaspoon salt
½ teaspoon black pepper
½ teaspoon mustard powder
2 teaspoons wine vinegar
150 ml/¼ pint olive oil
150 ml/¼ pint sunflower oil

Place the egg, seasonings and vinegar in a blender or food processor and blend on medium speed for a few seconds. Still on medium speed, add the oils through the lid, drop by drop to begin with, then in a thin stream as the mixture thickens.
Store in an airtight container in the refrigerator for up to 10 days.
MAKES about 300 ml/½ pint

YOGURT SAUCE WITH HERBS

METRIC/IMPERIAL
1 large clove garlic, peeled and crushed
pinch of salt
150 ml/¼ pint plain low-fat yogurt
freshly ground black pepper
2 teaspoons chopped tarragon
2 teaspoons chopped chervil
2 teaspoons snipped chives
2 teaspoons chopped parsley
2 teaspoons chopped fresh herbs, to garnish

Put the garlic into a bowl, add the salt and mash together with a fork, to make a paste. Gradually beat in the yogurt. Taste and adjust the seasoning, then stir in the herbs, cover and chill in the refrigerator for at least 1 hour.

Serve the yogurt sauce with grilled lamb chops, chicken pieces, fish steaks, or with baked stuffed vegetables. Sprinkle over the chopped herbs to garnish just before serving.
MAKES 150 ml/¼ pint

YOGURT DRESSING

METRIC/IMPERIAL
275 g/10 oz plain low-fat yogurt
2 tablespoons lemon juice
1 clove garlic, peeled and crushed
salt
freshly ground black pepper

Place all the ingredients in a bowl, seasoning with ½ teaspoon salt and ½ teaspoon pepper. Mix together thoroughly. Store in an airtight container in the refrigerator.
MAKES 300 ml/½ pint

GINGER YOGURT SALAD DRESSING

METRIC/IMPERIAL
150 ml/¼ pint plain low-fat yogurt
25 g/1 oz stem ginger, finely chopped
¼ teaspoon ground ginger

Put all the ingredients in a bowl and beat with a fork until well mixed. Chill for 1 hour.

Serve with a cucumber salad, citrus fruit salad or meat balls.
MAKES 150 ml/¼ pint

MUSTARD AND DILL DRESSING

METRIC/IMPERIAL
1½ teaspoons Dijon mustard
1½ teaspoons polyunsaturated vegetable oil
4 tablespoons plain low-fat yogurt
juice of ½ lemon
2 tablespoons chopped dill

Put the mustard into a bowl and stir in the oil, drop by drop. When the mustard and oil have blended together smoothly, stir in the yogurt. Add lemon juice to taste and stir in the chopped dill. If at any stage the sauce separates, purée it in a blender to emulsify.
MAKES 150 ml/¼ pint

PIQUANT TOMATO DRESSING

METRIC/IMPERIAL
6 tablespoons tomato juice
2 tablespoons lemon juice
1-2 teaspoons Worcestershire sauce
1 tablespoon chopped herbs (e.g. parsley, chives or mint)
salt
freshly ground black pepper

Put all the ingredients in a bowl and beat well. Taste and adjust the seasoning, then pour over the salad just before serving.
MAKES about 120 ml/4 fl oz

MINTED FRUIT JUICE DRESSING

METRIC/IMPERIAL
150 ml/¼ pint fresh orange or grapefruit juice
1-2 teaspoons chopped mint
salt
freshly ground black pepper

Put all the ingredients in a bowl and beat well. Taste and adjust the seasoning, then pour over the salad just before serving.
MAKES 150 ml/¼ pint

LEMON AND MUSTARD DRESSING

METRIC/IMPERIAL
juice and grated rind of 1 lemon
1 teaspoon Dijon mustard
1 teaspoon chopped parsley
1 teaspoon chopped thyme
1 teaspoon snipped chives

Mix all the ingredients together thoroughly. Store in the refrigerator for 1 week.
SERVES 2

THICK TOMATO SAUCE

METRIC/IMPERIAL
1 tablespoon polyunsaturated vegetable oil
1 medium onion, peeled and chopped
1 clove garlic, peeled and crushed
1½ × 400 g/14 oz cans Italian plum tomatoes
4 tablespoons tomato purée
salt
freshly ground black pepper
pinch of sugar
½ bay leaf
2 teaspoons chopped basil

Heat the oil in a broad pan. Cook the onion slowly until softened. Do not let the onion colour more than a pale yellow. Add the garlic towards the end. Pour in the canned tomatoes with their juice and the tomato purée. Chop roughly in the pan with the edge of a palette knife. Add the salt, pepper, sugar and bay leaf.

Simmer slowly for 1 hour with the lid off, until reduced to a thick sauce, stirring now and then. Add the chopped basil for the last few minutes of cooking only.
MAKES about 450 ml/¾ pint

MINT SAUCE

METRIC/IMPERIAL
4 tablespoons finely chopped mint
1 teaspoon sugar
2 tablespoons lemon juice
1 tablespoon white wine vinegar
4 tablespoons boiling water

Put the mint and sugar in a mortar and pound with a pestle until thoroughly blended, or process briefly in a food processor or blender.

Add the lemon juice, vinegar and finally boiling water. Stir well to mix, then set aside for 30 minutes to cool. Serve with roast lamb.
MAKES 120 ml/4 fl oz

PESTO SAUCE

METRIC/IMPERIAL
50 g/2 oz basil leaves
3 cloves garlic, peeled
25 g/1 oz pine nuts
salt
25 g/1 oz freshly grated Parmesan cheese
3 tablespoons olive oil

Put the basil, garlic, pine nuts and salt into a mortar and pound together thoroughly. Stir in the Parmesan cheese and pound until smooth and thick. Gradually add the oil, drop by drop. This should give a creamy sauce which is just a little difficult to pour.

Add 1 tablespoon or more to vegetable soups such as minestrone, and to meat sauces served with pasta.
MAKES 3 to 4 tablespoons

MAÎTRE D'HÔTEL 'BUTTER'

METRIC/IMPERIAL
100 g/4 oz polyunsaturated margarine
2-3 tablespoons finely chopped parsley
2 tablespoons lemon juice
salt
freshly ground black pepper

Cream the margarine until light and fluffy then beat in all the other ingredients.

Turn on to greaseproof paper and form into a 2.5 cm/1 inch diameter roll. Wrap the paper around the roll, overwrap in aluminium foil and chill in the refrigerator for several hours until firm. To use, cut into slices.

Variations
Herb: Add 1 to 2 tablespoons chopped fresh tarragon, mint or chives.
Orange: Omit the parsley and add ¼ teaspoon ground coriander and a large pinch of paprika.
Mustard: Add 2 tablespoons Dijon mustard.
Garlic: Add 2 tablespoons finely grated shallot and 2 cloves garlic, finely crushed.
Anchovy: Omit the salt and parsley. Add 6 to 8 canned anchovy fillets, previously drained and pounded to a paste.

FRESH TOMATO SAUCE

METRIC/IMPERIAL
1 kg/2 lb ripe tomatoes, skinned and chopped
1 onion, peeled and finely chopped
1 carrot, scraped and finely chopped
1 celery stalk, trimmed and finely chopped
1 small leek, trimmed and chopped
½ teaspoon salt
½ teaspoon dried oregano
½ teaspoon dried basil
1 tablespoon tomato purée
freshly ground black pepper

Put all the ingredients into a saucepan and bring to the boil. Stir, then cover tightly and simmer for 40 to 45 minutes.

Purée in a blender or food processor and strain into a clean pan. Boil, uncovered, for a few minutes to thicken the sauce, then taste and adjust the seasoning.

The sauce may be stored in the refrigerator or frozen.

MAKES 600 ml/1 pint

TOMATO AND MUSHROOM SAUCE

METRIC/IMPERIAL
4 teaspoons polyunsaturated vegetable oil
1 onion, peeled and chopped
1 clove garlic, peeled and crushed
1 × 400 g/14 oz can crushed tomatoes or
450 g/1 lb ripe tomatoes, skinned, deseeded and chopped
1 × 150 g/5 oz can tomato purée
4 tablespoons vegetable stock
1 tablespoon brown sugar
1 teaspoon Worcestershire sauce
½ teaspoon dried oregano
½ teaspoon dried basil
salt
freshly ground black pepper
175 g/6 oz cooked sliced mushrooms

Heat the oil in a pan. Add the onion and garlic and cook gently until softened, about 6 to 8 minutes.

Add the tomatoes, tomato purée, stock, sugar, Worcestershire sauce, oregano, basil, and salt and pepper to taste, blending well. Cook over a gentle heat until thick and pulpy, about 20 to 25 minutes.

Stir in the mushrooms and heat through to serve. Delicious served hot over cooked pasta.

MAKES 450 ml/¾ pint

DAMSON SAUCE

METRIC/IMPERIAL
2 kg/4½ lb damsons
450 g/1 lb onions, peeled and chopped
600 ml/1 pint vinegar
25 g/1 oz salt
1 tablespoon ground cinnamon
15 g/½ oz root ginger, bruised
1 tablespoon allspice berries
150 g/5 oz fructose

Wash the damsons and put into a pan with the onions, vinegar and salt, together with the cinnamon, ginger and allspice berries tied in muslin. Simmer for about 45 minutes, stirring from time to time to break up the flesh of the damsons.

Remove the bag of spices, then rub the mixture through a sieve or purée in a blender or food processor. Return to the rinsed pan, add the fructose and simmer for a further 45 minutes or until the sauce is a thick pouring consistency.

Pour into heated jars and seal while hot. Allow to mature for 1 to 2 months before using. Serve with roast meats.

MAKES about 900 ml/1½ pints

BREAD SAUCE

METRIC/IMPERIAL
1 dessertspoon chopped onion
450 ml/¾ pint skimmed milk
100 g/4 oz white breadcrumbs
2-3 bay leaves
¼ teaspoon ground coriander
salt
freshly ground black pepper

Simmer the onion in a little of the skimmed milk until soft. Add the breadcrumbs, bay leaves, coriander and salt and pepper with the rest of the milk. Stir thoroughly and simmer for a further 5 minutes, stirring constantly.

Remove the bay leaves and serve immediately.

MAKES 450 ml/¾ pint

HOT CURRY SAUCE

METRIC/IMPERIAL
1 medium marrow, peeled, sliced and deseeded
salt
2 teaspoons curry paste

Cook the marrow in boiling salted water for 10 to 15 minutes until tender. Drain and cool.

Put 225 g/8 oz cooked marrow and the curry paste into a blender and process until smooth. Pour the mixture into a saucepan and reheat thoroughly.

This sauce is very good served with hard-boiled eggs or fish.

MAKES 150 ml/¼ pint

HORSERADISH SAUCE WITH WALNUTS

METRIC/IMPERIAL
2 tablespoons freshly grated horseradish
150 ml/¼ pint soured cream
12 walnut halves, finely chopped
salt
freshly ground black pepper

Fold the freshly prepared horseradish into the soured cream with the nuts and salt and pepper to taste. Taste and add a little more horseradish, if necessary.

Serve with meats, especially beef, or fish such as mackerel.

MAKES 300 ml/½ pint

GARLIC AND HERB SAUCE

METRIC/IMPERIAL
150 ml/¼ pint plain low-fat yogurt
1 large clove garlic, crushed with a pinch of salt
salt
freshly ground black pepper
2 tablespoons chopped mixed herbs
(e.g. parsley, chives, dill, tarragon)

Gradually beat the yogurt into the crushed garlic, pounding all the time. When it has all been added, season with salt and black pepper to taste. Stir in the chopped mixed herbs and chill in the refrigerator until ready to serve.

This sauce is especially good with stuffed aubergines.

MAKES 150 ml/¼ pint

LOW-FAT GRAVY

METRIC/IMPERIAL
sediment from the pan
150 ml/¼ pint dry white or red wine
pinch of mixed dried herbs
dash of Worcestershire sauce or Tabasco
salt
freshly ground black pepper

Drain any fat from the pan, or use a special fat-removing brush to do this. Place the pan over a low heat and cook until it becomes 'sticky'. Add the wine (use red wine for red meat and white wine for pork, veal and poultry), stirring constantly. Add a little Worcestershire sauce or Tabasco and seasoning. Serve at once.

SERVES 2

Note: This recipe may be used to serve with roasted meat, or when a dry frying pan is used to cook steaks and chops.

ONION YOGURT SAUCE

METRIC/IMPERIAL
15 g/½ oz polyunsaturated margarine
1 small onion, peeled and finely chopped
¼ teaspoon paprika
¼ teaspoon ground coriander
salt
freshly ground black pepper
150 ml/¼ pint plain low-fat yogurt
1 tablespoon snipped chives (optional)

Melt the margarine in a small pan. Add the onion and cook gently until softened, about 6 to 8 minutes.

Stir in the paprika, coriander, and salt and pepper to taste, blending well.

Allow to cool slightly then stir in the yogurt and chives, if using. Mix well to blend and serve at once.

MAKES about 200 ml/7 fl oz

WHITE SAUCE

METRIC/IMPERIAL
1½ teaspoons polyunsaturated margarine
25 g/1 oz plain unbleached white flour
300 ml/½ pint skimmed milk
salt
freshly ground black pepper

Melt the margarine in a saucepan and stir in the flour. Cook, stirring, for 1 minute and then gradually add the milk. Keep on stirring all the time to prevent lumps. Bring to the boil and simmer for 2 minutes, stirring until smooth, and season to taste.
MAKES 300 ml/½ pint

WHITE BÉCHAMEL SAUCE

METRIC/IMPERIAL
1 small onion, peeled
6 cloves
6 peppercorns
1 bay leaf
1 small carrot, peeled
300 ml/½ pint skimmed milk
25 g/1 oz polyunsaturated margarine
25 g/1 oz unbleached white or wholemeal flour
salt
freshly ground black pepper

Place the onion, cloves, peppercorns, bay leaf, carrot and milk in a pan. Bring to the boil then remove from the heat, cover and leave to stand for 10 minutes. Strain into a jug.
Melt the margarine in a pan. Stir in the flour and cook for 1 minute. Remove from the heat and gradually add the strained milk, blending well. Bring to the boil and cook for 2 to 3 minutes, stirring constantly, until smooth and thickened. Season to taste with salt and pepper and use as required.
MAKES 300 ml/½ pint

Variations
Cheese or mornay sauce: Prepare and cook as above but add 50 g/2 oz grated mature Cheddar cheese to the hot sauce.
Aurore sauce: Prepare and cook as above but add 2 tablespoons tomato purée and ½ teaspoon sugar to the sauce before serving.
Parsley or herb sauce: Prepare and cook as above but add 1 to 2 tablespoons chopped fresh parsley or other herb to the sauce before serving.

CAROB SAUCE

METRIC/IMPERIAL
50 g/2 oz polyunsaturated margarine
25 g/1 oz carob powder
1 egg
½ teaspoon natural vanilla essence
2 tablespoons golden syrup

Melt the margarine in a pan. Add the carob powder, blending well.
Whisk in the egg, vanilla essence and syrup. Cook over a gentle heat, stirring constantly until the sauce thickens to a coating consistency, about 10 minutes.
Serve warm as an alternative to chocolate sauce with cooked fruit such as pears or other dessert dishes.
SERVES 4

WHIPPED CREAM TOPPING

METRIC/IMPERIAL
5 tablespoons whipping cream
5 tablespoons plain low-fat yogurt
1 egg white

Whip the cream until thick, then gradually beat in the yogurt. Beat the egg white until stiff, then fold into the cream and yogurt mixture.
SERVES 4 to 6

APPLE SAUCE

METRIC/IMPERIAL
2 tablespoons water
450 g/1 lb cooking apples, peeled and cored
25 g/1 oz fructose
15 g/½ oz polyunsaturated vegetable margarine
lemon juice

Place the water in a heavy saucepan and heat gently. Cut the apples into quarters and thinly slice into the saucepan. Cover and cook very gently for 10 to 15 minutes until the apples are reduced to a pulp.
Whisk to a purée, stir in the fructose, margarine and a few drops of lemon juice, and beat well. Serve hot or cold.
MAKES about 300 ml/½ pint

INDEX